14

EDEXCEL
AS/A LEVEL
HISTORY

ActiveBook included

endorsed for
edexcel

Paper 1&2 Student Book:

Conquest, control and resistance in the medieval world

Simon Davis | Simon Taylor | Georgina Blair |
Series editor: Rosemary Rees

ALWAYS LEARNING

PEARSON

Published by Pearson Education Limited, 80 Strand, London, WC2R 0RL.

www.pearsonschoolsandfecolleges.co.uk

Copies of official specifications for all Edexcel qualifications may be found on the website: www.edexcel.com

Text © Pearson Education Limited 2015

Designed by Elizabeth Arnoux for Pearson

Typeset and illustrated by Phoenix Photosetting, Chatham, Kent

Produced by Out of House Publishing

Original illustrations © Pearson Education Limited 2015

Cover design by Malena Wilson-Max for Pearson

Cover photo/illustration © Art Archive/Archives Nationales Paris/Kharbine-Tapabor/Coll. Jean Vigne

The rights of Georgina Blair, Simon Davis and Simon Taylor to be identified as authors of this work have been asserted by them in accordance with the Copyright, Designs and Patents Act 1988.

First published 2015

20

10 9 8 7 6 5

British Library Cataloguing in Publication Data

A catalogue record for this book is available from the British Library

ISBN 978 1 447 985280

Printed by CPI Group (UK) Ltd, Croydon CR0 4YY

Websites

Pearson Education Limited is not responsible for the content of any external internet sites. It is essential for tutors to preview each website before using it in class so as to ensure that the URL is still accurate, relevant and appropriate. We suggest that tutors bookmark useful websites and consider enabling students to access them through the school/college intranet.

A note from the publisher

In order to ensure that this resource offers high-quality support for the associated Pearson qualification, it has been through a review process by the awarding body. This process confirms that; this resource fully covers the teaching and learning content of the specification or part of a specification at which it is aimed. It also confirms that it demonstrates an appropriate balance between the development of subject skills, knowledge and understanding, in addition to preparation for assessment.

Endorsement does not cover any guidance on assessment activities or processes (e.g. practice questions or advice on how to answer assessment questions), included in the resource nor does it prescribe any particular approach to the teaching or delivery of a related course.

While the publishers have made every attempt to ensure that advice on the qualification and its assessment is accurate, the official specification and associated assessment guidance materials are the only authoritative source of information and should always be referred to for definitive guidance.

Pearson examiners have not contributed to any sections in this resource relevant to examination papers for which they have responsibility.

Examiners will not use endorsed resources as a source of material for any assessment set by Pearson.

Endorsement of a resource does not mean that the resource is required to achieve this Pearson qualification, nor does it mean that it is the only suitable material available to support the qualification, and any resource lists produced by the awarding body shall include this and other appropriate resources.

Contents

How to use this book

STRUCTURE

This book covers Route A of the Edexcel A Level and AS Level History qualifications. Route A consists of three papers which are linked by the theme 'Conquest, control and resistance in the medieval world'.

- Paper 1: The crusades, c1095–1204
- Paper 2a: Anglo-Saxon England and the Anglo-Norman kingdom, c1053–1106
- Paper 2b: England and the Angevin Empire in the reign of Henry II, 1154–89

To take Route A, you must study Paper 1, plus **one** of the two Paper 2 options. You do not need to study the other Paper 2 topic for your exam, but you might like to read it for interest – it deals with similar themes to the topics you are studying.

If you are studying for A Level History, you will also need to study a Paper 3 option and produce coursework in order to complete your qualification. All Paper 3 options are covered by other textbooks in this series.

AS LEVEL OR A LEVEL?

This book is designed to support students studying both the Edexcel AS Level and A Level qualifications. The content required for both qualifications is identical, so all the material in the papers you are studying is relevant, whichever qualification you are aiming for.

The questions you will be asked in the exam differ for the two different qualifications, so we have included separate exam questions, sample answers and advice. If you are studying for an AS Level, you should use the features and pages highlighted in blue. If you are studying for an A Level, you should use the features and pages highlighted in green.

AS Level Exam-Style Question Section A

Were castles and fortified settlements the main reason for the survival of the crusader states in the years 1100–44? Explain your answer. (20 marks)

Tip
This question draws on material from two sections in this chapter. Consider both defensive measures and the influx of settlers.

A Level Exam-Style Question Section B

How far do you agree that the defensive situation was transformed between the First and Second Crusades? (20 marks)

Tip
This question is asking you to reach a judgement on the extent of change. Make sure you are clear how the situation had changed before you begin writing.

The 'Preparing for your exams' section at the end of each paper contains sample answers of different standards, with comments on how weaker answers could be improved. Make sure you look at the right section for the exam you are planning to take.

FEATURES

Extend your knowledge

These features contain additional information that will help you gain a deeper understanding of the topic. This could be a short biography of an important person, extra background information about an event, an alternative interpretation, or even a research idea that you could follow up. Information in these boxes is not essential to your exam success, but still provides insights of value.

EXTEND YOUR KNOWLEDGE

Papal legate
A papal legate's authority came straight from the pope. They were his representatives in places he could not travel to. Adhemar, Bishop of Le Puy, was a legate for Pope Urban II on the First Crusade. He had a military background and travelled with Raymond of Toulouse, who set out in October 1096. During the campaign, he appealed for soldiers, discussed plans for the future of the eastern churches with Symeon II, patriarch of Jerusalem, and reinstated the Greek Orthodox patriarch, John IV Oxeites, after the conquest of Antioch. He died in 1098 in an epidemic. His life illustrates how a papal legate could give a crusade legitimate authority, even though the pope could not go himself.

Knowledge check activities

These activities are designed to check that you have understood the material that you have just studied. They might also ask you questions about the sources and extracts in the section to check that you have studied and analysed them thoroughly.

ACTIVITY
KNOWLEDGE CHECK

The campaigns of Saladin in Outremer, 1187–92

1 Summarise the main stages of Saladin's campaign between 1187 and 1192.

2 Identify one period when Saladin was most successful and one when he was least successful.

3 To what extent was Saladin's campaign in Outremer a success? Use three criteria to explain your answer.

Summary activities

At the end of each chapter, you will find summary activities. These are tasks designed to help you think about the key topic you have just studied as a whole. They may involve selecting and organising key information or analysing how things changed over time. You might want to keep your answers to these questions safe – they are handy for revision.

ACTIVITY
SUMMARY

Reasons to go on a crusade

1 Bullet point nine different reasons why people went on a crusade. Try to choose three religious, three political and three knightly motives for crusading.

2 Create a table with five columns:

- Important to a knight in 1095

- Important to Pope Urban II in 1095

- Important to Emperor Alexius Comnenus I in 1095

- Important to Bernard of Clairvaux in 1146

- Important to a knight in 1187

3 Choose three reasons from your list for each column and rank them in order of importance. You should not use the same reason more than once. Explain your top choice for a knight in 1095.

4 Explain whether you have changed your order for 1187 and why. Refer to religious motivation, the political background or the value system of knights in your answer.

Thinking Historically activities

These activities are found throughout the book and are designed to develop your understanding of history, especially around the key concepts of evidence, interpretations, causation and change. Each activity is designed to challenge a conceptual barrier that might be holding you back. This is linked to a map of conceptual barriers developed by experts. You can look up the map and find out which barrier each activity challenges by downloading the conceptual map from this website: www.pearsonschools.co.uk/historyprogressionapproach.

conceptual map reference

THINKING HISTORICALLY Evidence (3b)

It depends on the question

When considering the usefulness of a piece of evidence, people often think about authenticity in the case of artefacts, reliability in the case of witness statements, or methodology and structure in the case of secondary accounts. A better historical approach to the usefulness of a piece of evidence would be to think about the statements that we can make about the past based on it. Different statements can be made with different degrees of certainty, depending on the evidence.

Work in small groups and answer the following questions:

1 Look at Source 6, the photograph of a carving, on page 30.

a) Write three statements that you can reasonably make about reasons to join the Second Crusade based solely on the carving.

b) Which of the statements can be made with the greatest degree of certainty? Why is this? Which statement can be made with the smallest degree of certainty?

c) What else might you need to increase your confidence in your statements?

2 The photograph is of an artefact and Source 7 is a witness statement in the form of a contemporary song. Which is more useful to the historian studying the motivations for joining the Second Crusade?

3 Look at Extract 2.

How would the historian have gone about constructing this piece? What kinds of evidence would they have needed?

Getting the most from your online ActiveBook

This book comes with three years' access to ActiveBook* – an online, digital version of your textbook. Follow the instructions printed on the inside front cover to start using your ActiveBook.

Your ActiveBook is the perfect way to personalise your learning as you progress through your AS/A Level History course. You can:

- access your content online, anytime, anywhere

- use the inbuilt highlighting and annotation tools to personalise the content and make it really relevant to you.

Highlight tool – use this to pick out key terms or topics so you are ready and prepared for revision.

Annotations tool – use this to add your own notes, for example links to your wider reading, such as websites or other files. Or, make a note to remind yourself about work that you need to do.

*For new purchases only. If the access code has already been revealed, it may no longer be valid. If you have bought this textbook secondhand, the code may already have been used by the first owner of the book.

Introduction
AS/A Level History

WHY HISTORY MATTERS

History is about people and people are complex, fascinating, frustrating and a whole lot of other things besides. This is why history is probably the most comprehensive and certainly one of the most intriguing subjects there is. History can also be inspiring and alarming, heartening and disturbing, a story of progress and civilisation and of catastrophe and inhumanity.

History's importance goes beyond the subject's intrinsic interest and appeal. Our beliefs and actions, our cultures, institutions and ways of living, our languages and means of making sense of ourselves are all shaped by the past. If we want to fully understand ourselves now, and to understand our possible futures, we have no alternative but to think about history.

History is a discipline as well as a subject matter. Making sense of the past develops qualities of mind that are valuable to anyone who wants to seek the truth and think clearly and intelligently about the most interesting and challenging intellectual problem of all: other people. Learning history is learning a powerful way of knowing.

WHAT IS HISTORY?

History is a way of constructing knowledge about the world through research, interpretation, argument and debate.

Building historical knowledge involves identifying the traces of the past that exist in the present – in people's memories, in old documents, photographs and other remains, and in objects and artefacts ranging from bullets and lipsticks, to field systems and cities. Historians interrogate these traces and *ask questions* that transform traces into *sources of evidence* for knowledge claims about the past.

Historians aim to understand what happened in the past by *explaining why* things happened as they did. Explaining why involves trying to understand past people and their beliefs, intentions and actions. It also involves explaining the causes and evaluating the effects of large-scale changes in the past and exploring relationships between what people aimed to do, the contexts that shaped what was possible and the outcomes and consequences of actions.

Historians also aim to *understand change* in the past. People, states of affairs, ideas, movements and civilisations come into being in time, grow, develop, and ultimately decline and disappear. Historians aim to identify and compare change and continuity in the past, to measure the rate at which things change and to identify the types of change that take place. Change can be slow or sudden. It can also be understood as progressive or regressive – leading to the improvement or worsening of a situation or state of affairs. How things change and whether changes are changes for the better are two key issues that historians frequently debate.

Figure 1 Photo of partial bust of Marcus Aurelius, Louvre, Paris.

Debate is the essence of history. Historians write arguments to support their knowledge claims and historians argue with each other to test and evaluate interpretations of the past. Historical knowledge itself changes and develops. On the one hand, new sources of knowledge and new methods of research cause *historical interpretations* to change. On the other hand, the questions that historians ask change with time and new questions produce new answers. Although the past is dead and gone, the interpretation of the past has a past, present and future.

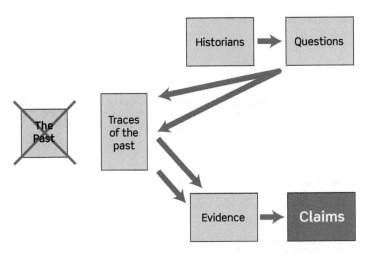

Figure 2 Constructing knowledge about the past.

THE CHALLENGES OF LEARNING HISTORY

Like all other Advanced Level subjects, A Level and AS Level history are difficult – that is why they are called 'advanced'. Your advanced level studies will build on knowledge and understanding of history that you developed at GCSE and at Key Stage 3 – ideas like 'historical sources', 'historical evidence' and 'cause', for example. You will need to do a lot of reading and writing to progress in history. Most importantly, you will need to do a lot of thinking, and thinking about your thinking. This book aims to support you in developing both your knowledge and your understanding.

History is challenging in many ways. On the one hand, it is challenging to build up the range and depth of knowledge that you need to understand the past at an advanced level. Learning about the past involves mastering new and unfamiliar concepts arising from the past itself (such as the Inquisition, Laudianism, *Volksgemeinschaft*) and building up levels of knowledge that are both detailed and well organised. This book covers the key content of the topics that you are studying for your examination and provides a number of features to help you build and organise what you know – for example, diagrams, timelines and definitions of key terms. You will need to help yourself too, of course, adding to your knowledge through further reading, building on the foundations provided by this book.

Another challenge is to develop understandings of the discipline of history. You will have to learn to think historically about evidence, cause, change and interpretations and also to write historically, in a way that develops clear and supported argument.

Historians think with evidence in ways that differ from how we often think in everyday life. In history, as Figure 2 shows, we cannot go and 'see for ourselves' because the past no longer exists. Neither can we normally rely on 'credible witnesses' to tell us 'the truth' about 'what happened'. People in the past did not write down 'the truth' for our benefit. They often had clear agendas when creating the traces that remain and, as often as not, did not themselves know 'the truth' about complex historical events.

A root of the word 'history' is the Latin word *historia*, one of whose meanings is 'enquiry' or 'finding out'. Learning history means learning to ask questions and interrogate traces, and then to reason about what the new knowledge you have gained means. This book draws on historical scholarship for its narrative and contents. It also draws on research on the nature of historical thinking and on the challenges that learning history can present for students. Throughout the book you will find 'Thinking Historically' activities designed to support the development of your thinking.

You will also find – as you would expect given the nature of history – that the book is full of questions. This book aims to help you build your understandings of the content, contexts and concepts that you will need to advance both your historical knowledge and your historical understanding, and to lay strong foundations for the future development of both.

QUOTES ABOUT HISTORY

'Historians are dangerous people. They are capable of upsetting everything. They must be directed.'

Nikita Khrushchev

'– History, Stephen said, is a nightmare from which I am trying to awake.'

James Joyce, *Ulysses*

'To be ignorant of what occurred before you were born is to remain forever a child. For what is the worth of human life, unless it is woven into the life of our ancestors by the records of history?'

Marcus Tullius Cicero

The crusades, c1095–1204

CONQUEST, CONTROL AND RESISTANCE

The crusades were born in a brutal, violent world where life expectancy was low, prospects for advancement poor and religion ever present. The crusader concept was created and formalised by the papacy in an attempt to channel aggression into a religious cause. It resulted in the conquest of a portion of the Near East and the control of the Holy Land by western Europeans. However, this control was a hotly contested issue. The pope, European nobles, kings and even emperors tried to bend the crusade and crusader states to their will, but with mixed success. They had to tackle resistance from the Islamic world, which at first was weak, but over the course of the 12th century became a serious challenge.

This was a world where crusading knights, with an entourage of thousands, fought to conquer the Holy Land; crusading nobles, with a desire for power, tried to control a new territory in the name of God; and counter-crusading Muslims fought to resist their new enemy.

Where and when were the crusades?

The time of the crusades involved a Europe that looked very different from the nation states of the present day. Italy, from which several crusades were proclaimed, was divided into a series of rival city states. Its nearest neighbour, France, had a weak king and a powerful nobility who were used to fighting. Its other neighbour, the German or western Empire, was ruled by a Holy Roman Emperor who was engaged in a dispute for control with the pope. Further afield, the remnants of the Roman Empire in Greece, Thrace and a small part of western Asia Minor, were centred upon the then famous city of Constantinople and formed the Byzantine Empire. It was these countries that first joined together to create and control the crusader states in the Near East.

This process began in 1095, with a sermon by Pope Urban II at Clermont, which heralded the start of the First Crusade and the conquest of the Near East. It was followed by a period of consolidation and control of the newly formed crusader states of Edessa, Antioch, Tripoli and Jerusalem in the early 12th century. However, as Muslim resistance grew, the Second and Third Crusades were launched. Despite these attempts, by the end of the 12th century many of the conquests of the First Crusade were lost and a Fourth Crusade was called to recover them. The Fourth Crusade failed in this goal, but rather unexpectedly conquered Constantinople instead and laid the foundations for a new empire, called Romania, in 1204.

969	The Fatimid Dynasty takes control of Egypt and parts of Syria and Palestine
1074	The pope, Gregory VII, fails to start his own holy war to help the Christians in the East and offers to lead 50,000 volunteers towards the Holy Land
1099	July 1099 – Jerusalem is captured by Godfrey of Bouillon
1119	A group of knights come together, under the leadership of Hugh of Payns, to protect pilgrims who are on their way to Jerusalem; they become known as the Knights Templar
1144	The ruler of Aleppo and Mosul, Emir Imad ad-Din Zengi, captures the city of Edessa from the Christians
1146	Nur ad-Din comes to power as ruler of Aleppo after the murder of Zengi
1153	The last important port of Jerusalem, Ascalon, is captured by the Franks with the help of pilgrims from Europe
1174	Baldwin IV, a leper, is crowned King of Jerusalem, but Raymond of Tripoli acts as regent on his behalf
1191	The Siege of Acre comes to an end and the Muslim garrison of Acre surrenders
1198	Pope Innocent III launches the Fourth Crusade with the fully developed idea of a plenary indulgence
1204	Baldwin of Flanders is crowned Emperor of Romania, the former Byzantine Empire
1291	Acre falls to the Muslim Mamluk dynasty. The Christian occupation of Outremer is over

1037	1037 - The Seljuk tribe emerges and takes control of Khorasan; they begin to take territory from the Fatimids
1071	1071 - The Battle of Manzikert. The Byzantine emperor is defeated and captured by the Seljuk Turks
1095	1095 - The First Crusade is proclaimed at the Council of Clermont by Pope Urban II
1100	1100 - Baldwin, Count of Edessa, is crowned King Baldwin I of Jerusalem and begins the consolidation of Outremer's territories
1136	1136 - The Hospitaller movement becomes militarised and is given the Castle of Beitgibelin
1145	1145 - The Second Crusade is launched by Pope Eugenius III who issues *Quantum praedecessores*
1148	1148 - The Siege of Damascus fails. The Second Crusade is over
1169	1169 - Saladin becomes the vizier of Egypt after power is usurped from the Fatimid vizier, Shawar, by Saladin's predecessor
1187	1187 - The Battle of Hattin and the capture of Jerusalem by Saladin. 1187 - The Third Crusade is announced by Pope Gregory VIII in his papal bull *Audita tremendi*
1192	1192 - Rather than launch an attack, the crusaders decide to withdraw from Jerusalem. The Third Crusade is over
1203	1203 - The crusaders attack Constantinople and force its emperor, Alexius III, to flee
1261	1261 - Constantinople is retaken by the Greeks and the Empire of Romania, formed after the Fourth Crusade, collapses

The legacy of the crusades

The challenges of control and resistance that followed the creation of Romania fall outside the scope of this book. Nevertheless, crusading did not end there. The last formal crusade was proclaimed against the English in 1588 and formed the backdrop for the Spanish Armada. Crusading leagues continued into the 17th century and the military orders of the 11th and 12th centuries were still active until the end of the 18th century. The history of the crusade is therefore one of endurance and a legacy that reaches far beyond anything Pope Urban II could have envisioned in 1095.

It even lingers in the present day and has formed part of the rhetoric of war. It was used to rally troops against Nazism during the D-Day landings, when General Eisenhower described them as a 'great crusade'. More recently, the term was employed by President Bush when he declared a 'crusade' against terror in response to the attacks of 9/11. It is therefore tempting to believe that there is great continuity between the past and the present. While it is true the word 'crusade' has endured, what it meant to the peoples of the 11th century was very different from what it means to those of the 21st. The following chapters will attempt to explain that world and to understand it on its own terms, with its own geography, its own leaders and its own 'crusades'.

1.1

Reasons for the crusades, 1095–1192

KEY QUESTIONS

- How did religious belief motivate people to go on a crusade?
- How did the changing political situation lead to the call for crusaders?
- What inspired knights to go on a crusade?

INTRODUCTION

The moment Urban II was elected pope in 1088 his fight for survival began. His enemies were extremely powerful. One, the German Emperor, had appointed a rival pope called Clement III and put his military might behind him. Urban II spent 10 years in a war of both words and actions against this **antipope**. It was during this fight, which aimed to secure control of Rome, that Urban II chose a new path for the **papacy**. His predecessors had been used to fighting; they had been driven out of Rome before. However, Urban II no longer planned to stay on the defensive. In 1095, he created a brand new type of war: a crusade. It was time for medieval Europe to stop the fight against the pope and begin a fight in his name.

Urban II's First Crusade was proclaimed in 1095 at the Council of Clermont. He wanted the Christians of western Europe to recapture Jerusalem from the Turks. The result was that around 60,000 people set off overland from France and Italy towards the **Holy Land**. Their success set in motion the crusades of the 12th century, which aimed to defend the newly conquered land. In 1147, the Second Crusade began in response to the capture of Edessa and, in 1189, the Third Crusade was launched after the Muslim recapture of Jerusalem. These later crusades drew on the support of the most powerful figures in the West, including the king of France and the emperor of Germany. They also relied on leaders who achieved near legendary status as a result, such as King Richard I of England.

This chapter will focus on what motivated these leaders, and the recruits who joined up by the thousands, to become crusaders. It will consider how religious belief drove people to give up several years of their life in order to fight for Jerusalem: a belief that convinced participants they were doing God's work and would receive the gift of eternal life in Heaven as a reward. It will explore how political motivations led pope after pope to launch crusades, partly in order to extend their own grip on power, but chiefly to respond to the very real threats the Christian empires of Europe faced. Finally, it will examine how the top recruits, from the knightly class, were encouraged to become crusaders. This group were influenced both by the noble expectations of their class to go out and fight for a worthwhile cause and through the more worldly temptation of power and wealth.

1074 – The pope, Gregory VII, fails to start off his own holy war to help the Christians in the East and offers to lead 50,000 volunteers towards the Holy Land

1095 – The Byzantine emperor, Alexius Comnenus I, appeals to the church council at Piacenza for help to force the Turks out of Asia Minor and free Jerusalem

27 November 1095 – The First Crusade is proclaimed at the Council of Clermont by Pope Urban II

1070	1075	1080	1085	1090	1095	1100	1105	1110	1115	1120	1125	1130

August 1071 – After the Battle of Manzikert, Alp Arslan, a Muslim ruler, captures the Byzantine emperor, Romanus IV Diogenes, and has control of much of Asia Minor

1094 – Pope Urban II finally takes control of the Lateran Palace in Rome from the German emperor's papal candidate, Clement III

1119 – The nobility of Antioch are killed at the Battle of the Field of Blood, prompting Pope Calixtus II to encourage a crusade

1119 – A group of knights come together, under the leadership of Hugh of Payns, to protect pilgrims who are on their way to Jerusalem

THE WORLD OF THE CRUSADER

In order to understand why people were willing to go on a crusade in 1095, and throughout the 12th century, it is important to appreciate the world the crusader lived in.

Church and belief

In the 11th-century Christian Europe of the crusader, the vast majority of people were Catholics and, at least nominally, followed the religious instruction of the pope. Those people who did not agree, or held different beliefs, such as the Jewish communities across Europe, were considered infidels or heretics. The fundamental feature of people's faith was an obsession with the afterlife, which included heaven, hell and a middle place, which was later termed 'purgatory'. Most Christians wanted to avoid hell, minimise their time in **purgatory** and get to heaven. This prompted them, among other things, to join religious orders as monks or nuns, make donations to the church and go on **pilgrimages**.

The growth of these ideas from the tenth century onwards meant the Church had a newfound power to influence laymen. This was in part thanks to the **Cluniac** reform movement that had begun in 909 and had reached its apogee under the leadership of Abbot Hugh of Cluny between 1049 and 1109. The monastery at Cluny, and its dependent houses, encouraged nobles to think about how they could atone for their sins. They stressed the importance of good works, encouraged gifts to monasteries and actively promoted the Jerusalem pilgrimage. The motive behind their actions was to minimise lay interference in the Church. This meant they tried to influence the behaviour of nobles and were one of the earliest groups to sponsor the **Peace Movement** in France. They hoped that by bringing about a better order in French society it would encourage nobles and their vassals to perform good works.

The effect of their work was to revitalise the Church, as the influence of the monastery at Cluny spread from Burgundy across Europe into Germany, Spain and Italy. It ensured the following points.

- There was a constant flow of pilgrims to holy sites, especially Jerusalem. In 1064, for example, between 7,000 and 12,000 German pilgrims travelled to Jerusalem. This was an extraordinary event, but pilgrims continued to make their way there right up until the First Crusade.

- Christian control of Jerusalem became an issue again. It had been under Muslim control since 638, but the increasing flow of pilgrims promoted the belief that this situation should change.

- People were more receptive to the idea of a holy war in order to achieve remission of their sins. For instance, the abbots of Cluny encouraged campaigns against the Saracens in Spain in the early 11th century. This laid the groundwork for the ideas Pope Urban II used to proclaim a holy war to capture Jerusalem.

Everyday life

Most people also lived in a small world, with a limited life expectancy, little chance of social advancement and the ever-present risk of famine and disease. The Europe of the crusader was largely a feudal society, which meant those who farmed the land were tied to a warrior lord and had to perform services for the land they lived on. They had little contact with the rest of their

KEY TERMS

Purgatory
A middle place between heaven and hell where medieval Catholics believed they underwent spiritual correction for their sins until they were pure enough to enter heaven. It was not fully defined until the 13th century.

Pilgrimage
A journey with a religious purpose. Pilgrimages were considered a form of penance and often went to destinations associated with a saint or the life of Christ.

Cluniac
A monastery or religious community associated with the Abbey of Cluny in Burgundy. Cluny emphasised spiritual purity and freedom from secular control.

Peace Movement
An attempt, enforced through councils of the Church, to limit violence in Europe. The movement began in the late tenth century.

1144 – The ruler of Aleppo and Mosul, Emir Imad ad-Din Zengi, captures the city of Edessa from the Christians

October 1187 – Jerusalem falls to Saladin's army and the Franks are forced out of the city

29 October 1187 – The Third Crusade is announced by Pope Gregory VIII in his papal bull, *Audita tremendi*

| 1135 | 1140 | 1145 | 1150 | 1155 | 1160 | 1165 | 1170 | 1175 | 1180 | 1185 | 1190 | 1195 |

1 December 1145 – The Second Crusade is launched by Pope Eugenius III who issues *Quantum praedecessore*

August 1198 – Pope Innocent III launches the Fourth Crusade with the fully developed idea of a plenary indulgence

country, let alone the world. This was because literacy was confined to churchmen and the nobility, so information spread slowly. Even the most urgent news only travelled at the speed of a horse's gallop. Ordinary people received it through travelling players, travelling merchants and wandering preachers, nobles through **troubadours** and religious communities from travellers. It is their accounts, recorded in chronicles, which provide a window into the crusader's world, but which the majority would never have read.

Despite these constraints on the people of 11th-century Europe, the century that preceded the First Crusade was one of considerable change for them. The population had grown to 36 million by 1000 and increased by 20 percent over the next 100 years. Alongside this the economy improved, as trading flourished and land that had been left fallow was cultivated once more. This meant that by 1095 the Europe of the crusader had more people, more money and more resources available than it had enjoyed since the contraction and decline that marked the early medieval period.

Rulers

Another feature of the medieval world is that power and authority lay with a few key individuals, who had either inherited their positions or been elected by a few equally powerful figures. The pope was, for most of the crusading period, based in Rome and was head of the Latin Catholic Church. His chief rival was the **patriarch** of the Greek Orthodox Church based in Constantinople. In the secular world, emperors ruled over huge areas such as the Byzantine Empire and the Holy Roman Empire (covering much of modern-day Germany). However, the borders of these empires were not static. The Byzantine Empire, for example, had controlled many of the important cities along the pilgrim route to the Holy Land in the 11th century. These included key locations like Nicaea, Tarsus and Antioch, but Byzantine control of these, as well as much of Asia Minor, was lost to the Turks as the century progressed. In addition to emperors, there were also kings who ruled over smaller kingdoms such as England and parts of France.

The situation in Italian states differed somewhat from that in northern Europe because they were dominated by powerful cities, such as Pisa, Genoa and Venice. These maritime cities had increased their control of Mediterranean shipping in the 11th century. In the western Mediterranean, Pisa and Genoa had begun to drive out Muslims from their trade routes. For example, they sacked the Muslim-controlled port of Mahdia in Africa in 1087. Meanwhile, in the eastern Mediterranean, Venice had also worked hard to secure trade from the West with Constantinople. The actions of these cities on the Mediterranean Sea, coupled with the trouble that rulers like the Byzantine emperor faced, helped to create an atmosphere of expansionism that clashed with the growing Muslim threat from the East.

Warfare

During the 11th century, the Byzantine Empire, a bastion of Christianity in the East, faced an external onslaught from the Seljuk Turks that intensified as the century progressed. However, the external threat to western Europe, from the Vikings, had ended by around 1000. Instead, the most frequent examples of warfare were small-scale conflicts between rival nobles over disputed land. For example, Raymond of Toulouse fought over the Rouergue for 13 years with Robert, count of Auvergne. This type of fighting helped to train up the knights of western Europe to fight as organised units under a lord.

Knights were also helped by developments in technology, which made them into formidable warriors. The key changes were the following.

- The adoption of the stirrup and high saddle helped to ensure security on horseback.

- Horses were shod, which allowed them to cover rough terrain. This meant knights were a more mobile and adaptable force.

- They were heavily armoured. Most knights wore a hauberk (chain mail coat) with a coif (cap) and carried a kite-shaped wooden shield. This protected them, if not their horses, from arrows and glancing blows from a sword.

The effect of these changes was that knights were now a powerful fighting force. They were mobile, used to fighting in units alongside their lord and they had some protection from archer attacks. This was one of the reasons, alongside the skilled use of infantry and feigned retreat, that William of Normandy was successful at the Battle of Hastings in 1066. It was a success that demonstrated the military potential western Europe possessed by the late 11th century.

Why was a crusade possible?

In summary, crusaders lived in a world that was undergoing immense change. It is in this context that crusading motivations should be considered, because:

- the Cluniac revolution in the Church meant people were open to new opportunities to make up for their sinfulness

- the rise in pilgrimages to Jerusalem strengthened the desire to claim it for Christendom

- the Byzantine Empire had protected Christianity in the East and helped to assure pilgrim access to the Holy Land, but its position was now under threat

- the population had begun to rise in western Europe and this had massive implications for both its society and its economy

- the growing command of the Mediterranean by powerful Italian cities contributed to the confidence of western Europe that it could expand beyond its borders

- the military potential of the heavily armoured knight gave western Europe a newfound power with which it could achieve this expansion.

HOW DID RELIGIOUS BELIEF MOTIVATE PEOPLE TO GO ON A CRUSADE?

The concept of 'just war'

Breaking the Ten Commandments

Pope Urban II asked 11th century knights to kill Muslims in order to recapture Jerusalem, the place of Christ's crucifixion and resurrection. In effect he had asked them to break one of the Ten Commandments, 'You shall not kill'. The Commandments were a series of religious rules revealed by God to Moses and recorded in the Bible. To a knight, breaking one of them was not a very attractive prospect, because it would mean that he would be condemned to hell for eternity. Urban needed to think of a way to convince the knights it would be acceptable to kill. He turned to the Countess Mathilda of Tuscany for help to provide content for his sermons designed to promote the crusade.

The theory of a just war

Mathilda helped Urban to apply the theory of a just war to the First Crusade, because she gathered together a series of **canonists**, such as Anselm II of Lucca, to develop the idea of **penitential warfare**. This was a religious excuse for taking part in a war, which was created by Augustine of Hippo in c400 AD. He argued that it would be acceptable to kill if you had a good reason, good intentions and an official leader. The theory was applied to the First Crusade in the following ways.

- A good reason: the Holy Land was Christ's legacy to the Christian Church. It had also been a part of the Roman Empire. Christians had every right to reclaim it.

- Good intentions: the crusaders would be like pilgrims because they were going on the journey out of love for Christ.

- An official leader: the First Crusade was proclaimed by the pope, who was considered to be God's representative on Earth.

KEY TERMS

Canonist
A person who studies church law and is an expert in it.

Penitential warfare
A war fought as a penance, or punishment, to make up for sins committed. A crusade is an early example of this type of war.

These arguments were used to persuade knights it would be acceptable to break the Ten Commandments, just this once, and go on a crusade. In order to convince later crusaders, monks created compilations of religious arguments for popes and preachers to use. For example, the 12th-century canon lawyer Gratian wrote the *Concordia discordantium canonum*, which provided a question and answer guide to the just war theory. These ideas were developed further from 1140 to 1190, but ultimately they all had the same goal in mind. They reassured people that they could go on a crusade without sacrificing their souls.

ACTIVITY
KNOWLEDGE CHECK

Medieval world view

1 Re-read the section on the crusader's world view. Construct a table that identifies the key religious, political and social differences between the medieval and modern worlds.

2 Which of the following statements do you think was the most significant difference? Choose the one you believe made a crusade possible. Explain your choice.

- Religious – the majority of people in western Europe were Christian and members of the Catholic Church.

- Political – society was feudal, which meant most people were tied to a lord and their land.

- Social – there was very little contact between different communities, countries or faiths.

3 In light of your answer to (b), explain the significance of the just war theory to a potential crusader.

The impact of the papal reform movement

The justification for going on a crusade was a sound one, but it was not enough to get knights to leave their land and families behind. The pope could not offer them money; in fact, he was asking them to spend several times their annual incomes to go. Instead, the first crusade pope, Urban II, offered something money could not buy. This was called an indulgence, which was a sort of 'get out of jail free card' that could be used to escape hell itself. The indulgence came in two varieties.

What was an indulgence?

Urban offered 'version one' of the crusade indulgence. This was called *remissio peccatorum*, which translates as 'remission of all sins'. The deal was that going on a crusade to free the Holy Land from the infidel would be such a difficult journey that it would be enough for God to forgive someone for all their sins. It was marketed like an extreme pilgrimage and would ensure that no matter how bad they had been in life, they would still go to heaven.

EXTEND YOUR KNOWLEDGE

Primary source materials
The sources that have been used in this textbook are translations from contemporary historical sources. Sometimes there are a number of different translations of the same primary source, which can present subtly different interpretations. This is because a translator has to make a number of choices about the source's original meaning in order to convey it effectively in modern English. The details of the translations that have been used in this textbook are given in the Acknowledgements, which you may wish to explore further.

SOURCE

From a letter written by Pope Urban II to the people of Bologna in 1096. It is a description of the *remissio peccatorum*, the crusade indulgence. Note the different features of the just war theory that are contained within it.

...if any men among you go there not because they desire earthly profit but only for the salvation of their souls and the liberation of the Church, we, acting as much on our own authority as on that of all archbishops and bishops in the Gauls, through the mercy of almighty God and the prayers of the Catholic Church, relieve them of all penance imposed for their sins, of which they have made a genuine and full confession.

KEY TERM

Penance
This is the punishment a sinner undertakes for the sin they have committed. Pilgrimage was considered a form of penance, as were a range of charitable works.

This was a golden ticket to many knights, because they were part of what was believed to be an incredibly sinful society. For example, the world they lived in was so bad that rather than violence being illegal in day-to-day life, it was only banned on certain days of the week. Spilling blood was part of their culture; it was unavoidable and it was a massive problem. This was because priests were busy telling people that they would be punished in the afterlife for their behaviour. However, they could not tell them precisely how much **penance**, or good work, they had to do to make up for their crimes.

The crusade indulgence could therefore achieve two ends. A knight could carry on doing what they were best at – committing acts of violence – and they could sleep sound in the knowledge that they had done enough to make up for all their earlier sins. The icing on the cake was provided by the

Gregorian Reform Movement. This had popularised the idea of copying the life of Christ, which was called *imitatio Christi* and was seen as the best way to guarantee meeting the entry qualifications for heaven. The crusade offered the perfect chance to copy Christ's life because it reduced knights to a simple lifestyle without castles, fine food and other home comforts.

The plenary indulgence

However, for those who were still not convinced by the *remissio peccatorum*, in the 12th century the papacy created a new type of indulgence. This was called the plenary indulgence. The offer was simple: if a person promised to go on a crusade, they were let off all the penalties for the sins they had committed so far. This new idea was needed because religious beliefs were slowly changing. People were being told they could never do enough to make up for their sins. The 'version two' indulgence was therefore better because:

- it was a gift, so there was no question of whether you had earned it or not
- the Catholic Church had a proper theory to back it up called the **Treasury of the Church**.

This version of the indulgence was first used in 1145 by Pope Eugenius III. It was preached by Bernard of Clairvaux when recruiting for the Second Crusade and it became the norm for a crusade indulgence in 1198.

The aim of freeing Jerusalem

Jerusalem was the chosen destination for the First Crusade, because it was a city of immense religious significance to medieval Christians. It had been the backdrop to the last days of Christ's life and two locations were considered especially important:

- Calvary: the hill where Christ was crucified
- the Holy Sepulchre: the cave tomb from where Christ was said to have come back to life (been resurrected).

These sites made Jerusalem a traditional place of pilgrimage for many Christians. This was established by Empress Helena, the mother of the Roman emperor Constantine the Great, who went on the first pilgrimage there in the early 4th century. By the 11th century, this tradition was ingrained in Christian culture and many pilgrims made the journey. For example, in the 1060s, 7,000 German pilgrims set off on a journey to the Holy Land. The idea of the crusade could therefore build on the history of the Jerusalem pilgrimage.

What was new in the 1090s?

The Muslims had held Jerusalem since 638 and had allowed Christian pilgrims access to it ever since. However, the situation had begun to change by the 1090s due to the rise of the Seljuk Turks in Asia Minor and in the Holy Land itself. The effect of their incursions made it more difficult for pilgrims to reach Jerusalem, because the route was less secure from raids, had fewer cities under Byzantine control along it and the tolls that were charged were often extortionate. Nothing drastic had changed by 1095, but the prospect of maintaining access to Jerusalem by western pilgrims looked increasingly bleak as the 11th century drew to a close.

What threats did Jerusalem face?

The unique feature the crusading concept added was that the sacred nature of Jerusalem was now under threat because of its occupation by Muslims. This is a central theme in two of the four chronicle accounts of Urban's sermon at the Council of Clermont in 1095. A third account referred directly to Jerusalem, but explored its importance to crusaders in a different way. The following are three of these chroniclers.

- Baudri of Dol: he claimed Urban focused on the idea that the sacred nature of Jerusalem had been polluted by the presence of Muslims.
- Robert of Reims: he wrote that Urban thought Jerusalem was a very attractive, wealthy and spiritual location for pilgrims. He again emphasised the theme of pollution.
- Guibert of Nogent: he suggested that Urban explored the role Jerusalem played in the story of **Christ's Passion** rather than on the direct threat to it.

The First Crusade was thus launched with the stated religious goal to free Jerusalem's holy places from the perceived polluting influence of Islam and to restore it as a destination for Christian pilgrims.

The needs of Jerusalem also played an important role in the Second and Third Crusades. It was only when a threat to Jerusalem was highlighted that a significant number of participants were attracted to the call for a crusade. For example, the Second Crusade was a response to the capture of Edessa from the Christians by the Emir Imad ad-Din Zengi. Edessa was 450 miles away from Jerusalem. However, the preacher Bernard of Clairvaux chose the theme of Jerusalem under threat for his recruitment letters because he appreciated its propaganda value. Similarly, the demand for a Third Crusade in 1187 was a direct response to the capture of Jerusalem by Saladin (see pages 103–26), after which Christians were forced to leave the city.

SOURCE 2

From a letter written around 1146 by Bernard of Clairvaux addressed to the English. In this letter Bernard attempts to convince the English to participate in the Second Crusade, because he did not have time to travel to preach there in person. There are frequent references to Jerusalem in this appeal, despite the distance of the threat from Jerusalem.

Now is the acceptable time, now is the day of abundant salvation. The earth is shaken because the Lord of heaven is losing his land, the land in which he appeared to men, in which he lived amongst men for more than thirty years; the land made glorious by his miracles, holy by his blood; the land in which the flowers of his resurrection first blossomed. And now, for our sins, the enemy of the cross has begun to list his sacrilegious head there, and to devastate with the sword that blessed land, that land of promise. Alas, if there should be none to withstand him, he will soon invade the very city of the living God, overturn the arsenal of our redemption, and defile the holy places adorned by the blood of the Immaculate Lamb [Jesus]. They have cast their greedy eyes especially on the holy sanctuaries of our Christian religion, and they long particularly to violate that couch on which, for our sakes, the Lord of our life fell asleep in death.

THINKING HISTORICALLY — Change (4b&c)

The bird's-eye view

Development	Medium-term consequences	Long-term consequences
Augustine of Hippo develops the theory of the just war in *The City of God* written about AD 400.	Pope Urban II applies the criteria for a just war in his proclamation of the First Crusade in 1095.	Some political leaders still feel a need to provide moral justifications for declaring war and often draw on the ideas of a just war to do so.

Imagine you are looking at the whole of history using a zoomed-out interactive map like Google Maps. You have a general view of the sweep of developments and their consequences but you cannot see much detail. If you zoom in to the time of when Augustine of Hippo developed the theory, you can see the event in detail but will know nothing of its consequences in the medium or long term. If you zoom in to look at the medium- or long-term consequences, you will know about them in detail but will know very little about the event that caused them. For example, Pope Urban II drew on the ideas of Augustine of Hippo when he proclaimed the First Crusade, but the circumstances that caused the theory of the just war to be developed are not explicit in his speech.

Look at the table above and answer the following questions:

1 What were the immediate consequences of the development?

2 In what ways are the medium-term consequences different from the long-term consequences?

Work in groups of three.

Each student takes the role of the teacher for one of the above (the development, medium-term consequences or long-term consequences) and gives a short presentation to the other two. They may comment and ask questions. After each presentation, the other two group members write a 100-word paragraph showing how the presentation links to their own.

Answer the following questions individually:

3 What happens to the detail when you zoom out to look at the whole sweep of history?

4 What are the advantages and disadvantages of zooming in to look at a specific time in detail?

How could you use the map in order to get a good understanding of history as a whole?

Papal support for the crusades

Pope Urban II brought together the theory behind a crusade, the granting of a reward for it and the appeal on behalf of Jerusalem. In effect, his leadership turned a normal war into a religious crusade. He launched the First Crusade in a sermon to the Council of Clermont in November 1095. He then continued on a preaching tour that covered over 2,000 miles. The effect of this tour, similar to a celebrity visiting a local city today, would have been electric. Through his inspirational sermons, along with the visual power of the cross-granting ceremony, the idea of a crusade became a physical reality.

EXTEND YOUR KNOWLEDGE

Papal legates

A papal legate's authority came straight from the pope. They were his representatives in places he could not travel to. Adhemar, Bishop of Le Puy, was a legate for Pope Urban II on the First Crusade. He had a military background and travelled with Raymond of Toulouse, who set out in October 1096. During the campaign, he appealed for soldiers, discussed plans for the future of the eastern churches with Symeon II, patriarch of Jerusalem, and reinstated the Greek Orthodox patriarch, John IV Oxeites, after the conquest of Antioch. He died in 1098 in an epidemic. Adhemar's life illustrates how a papal legate could give a crusade legitimate authority, even though the pope could not go himself.

How did popes help to improve a crusade's chances of success?

Despite their central role in launching them, popes could not go on crusades themselves. However, they could help to ensure their success. Notable examples of this from the 11th and 12th centuries are the following.

- Issuing threats: Pope Paschal II threatened to **excommunicate** any First Crusaders who had abandoned the cause or did not set off in the first place.

- Writing crusade general letters: these were letters, also known as crusade bulls, which started a crusade. The first pope to do this was Calixtus II in the early 1120s. However, the letters did not have much effect on recruitment until Eugenius III wrote *Quantum praedecessores* in 1145.

- Developing propaganda: Pope Urban II came up with the idea of the ceremony of granting the cross. This provided a powerful visual symbol for the crusade. Pope Alexander III developed this and ensured his written message spread throughout western **Christendom**, as he instructed his crusade bull, *Cor nostrum*, to be published in all churches in 1181.

- Getting financial support: early on popes set out the rules of borrowing money to fund a crusade. References to this can be found in the papal letters *Quantum praedecessores* and *Audita tremendi*. Later popes tried to get directly involved in the provision of funds. For example, Pope Clement III asked the clergy of Canterbury and Genoa to provide financial support in 1188.

KEY TERMS

Excommunicate
To ban from church services. To a medieval Christian this was a serious punishment as it risked condemnation to hell.

Christendom
The name for the universal state of the Christian Church. It could be used to refer to either the Latin or Greek Orthodox Church in medieval times.

The influence of preachers

The final ingredient left in order to launch a crusade was to advertise the pope's religious message. In an age before mass pamphleteering, television advertising and social media, it fell to preachers to spread the crusading message. These preachers were usually influential figures who would go on a countrywide tour, visit important towns, villages and cities, and arrange for locals to become crusaders. For example, Archbishop Baldwin of Canterbury went on a preaching tour in Wales in 1188 and, according to his chronicler, enlisted 3,000 crusaders.

EXTEND YOUR KNOWLEDGE

Henry of Albano (a.k.a. Henry of Marcy) (1140-89)

Henry was another example of a crusade preacher who promoted the Third Crusade. His surviving work illustrates how preachers explored the theme of morality and crusading. He had a monastic background and had, at the height of his career, been Abbot of Clairvaux between 1176 and 1177. In 1188, he set out on a crusade preaching tour in France and Germany, but he also tried to reform the churches he visited. He wrote a tract called *De peregrinante*, which shows that he saw a crusade as a test from God. He saw it as a fight between good and evil, with the Muslim leader Saladin in the role of the devil. His preaching stressed the moral obligation of Christians to fight this perceived evil.

How did preachers recruit crusaders?

The recruitment process tended to follow an established pattern. When a preacher arrived in a town, people from the surrounding areas would gather in a large open space and prepare to listen to their message. There would usually be several religious features to the preacher's talk, such as a mass and a homily. The main part of the ceremony would involve a public *Invitatio*, or appeal to take the cross, and then men would come forward to get a cloth cross to pin or sew into their clothes. This was the crusader's vow and they were to wear the cross until the vow had been fulfilled.

Over time, preachers developed a range of techniques in order to get the maximum number of knightly recruits. These included the following.

- Choosing the right day: Pope Urban II established the tradition of trying to arrive in a town or city at a holy time. For example, Urban arrived at St Gilles on the same day as the feast of its patron, St Giles.

- Gathering in an outdoor location: this would ensure there was maximum space for an audience. These sites were carefully arranged. For instance, in the 1190s, preachers began to stand in front of big canvas paintings, which depicted the Muslim threat, and people flocked around them like the audience at a music festival.

- Maximising the quality of the audience: the ideal audience was one that consisted of wealthy knights and noblemen. The best example of this was when Bernard of Clairvaux preached at Vézelay in 1146, as he had the king of France and most of his nobility in the audience.

- Creating a pious mood: in order to encourage people to take the cross, they were made to feel more pious. During Urban II's visit to Angers in 1096, he ordained a feast and said that anyone who attended would earn an indulgence for one-seventh of their sins.

- Encouraging participation: miracles were used to make the audience feel energised and want to take the crusade vow. For example, during a preaching tour of Germany by Bernard of Clairvaux, 235 cripples were reported to have been restored to health.

Improvements to the selection of preachers

The process of recruitment for a crusade became more sophisticated as time went on. In the beginning, when Pope Urban II went on his preaching tour in 1095–96, there was little control over other preachers. This meant that popular evangelisers, like Peter the Hermit, would recruit the type of participants the pope did not want: the poor, the elderly and women. This led future crusade popes to specify who would preach on their behalf. For example, in 1146, Pope Eugenius III ordered a number of preachers at the Council of Reims. This level of control was increased by the use of papal legates, or local representatives of the pope, to preach the crusade. The first example of this is in 1173–74, but the idea was not fully utilised until the Fourth Crusade.

Key preacher: Bernard of Clairvaux

An example of one of the best-known preachers ordered by Pope Eugenius III at Reims is Bernard of Clairvaux. He was a powerful and influential figure who had been Eugenius's teacher and did an immense amount of work to promote the Second Crusade. He was authorised to go on a preaching tour of both Flanders and Germany, he wrote letters to churchmen and nobles across Europe and he influenced some of the most important crusaders of his time. His most notable recruits in 1146 were the king of France, Louis VII, and the king of Germany, Conrad III. It was through work like this that preachers such as Bernard turned a religiously motivated appeal into an army of knights, led by powerful secular rulers, ready to crusade.

SOURCE 3 A mid 12th century carving of the French crusader Hugues I, Count de Vaudemont, and his wife.

ACTIVITY
KNOWLEDGE CHECK

Papal support for a crusade

1 Re-read Source 1 on page 14. How does Urban apply the features of the just war to the situation in 1095? Use the following prompts to help answer the question:

- a just cause

- the authority of a prince

- right intention.

2 Between the First and the Third Crusades, the papacy made a number of changes to the recruitment process. Explain how one of these changes would have improved recruitment.

A Level Exam-Style Question Section B

To what extent was papal involvement responsible for the level of crusading recruitment between 1095 and 1146? (20 marks)

Tip
The outcome you are trying to explain changes over the time period and was not always high. Try to consider a variety of factors to account for this, such as population growth.

HOW DID THE CHANGING POLITICAL SITUATION LEAD TO THE CALL FOR CRUSADERS?

Threats to the Byzantine Empire

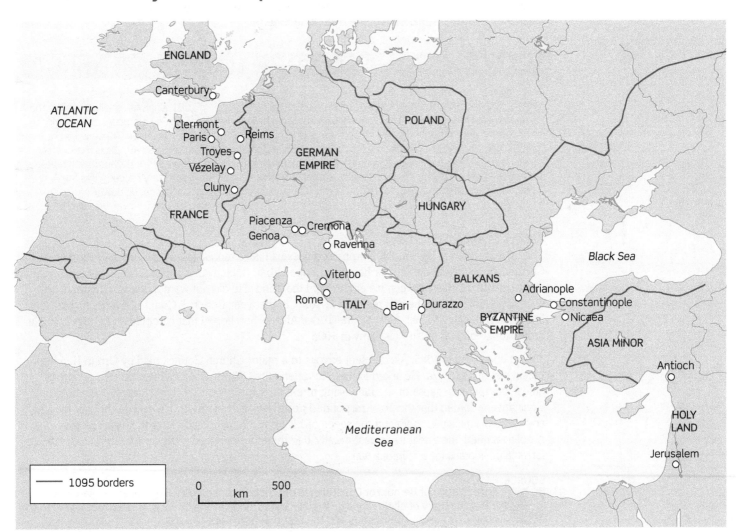

Figure 1.1 The political landscape of 11th-century Europe and the near East.

The Byzantine Empire in the 1090s

In 1095, the Byzantine Empire needed help. It was the eastern half of the Roman Empire, which had survived the collapse of the Roman Empire in the West, and in the 11th century controlled Greece, Bulgaria, Macedonia and Asia Minor. It had a magnificent capital called Constantinople and was ruled over by the Emperor Alexius I Comnenus from 1081. It was also the centre of the Greek Orthodox Christian Church, which had split from the Latin Church in the West in 1054. However, by the 1090s, their relationship had begun to improve.

This was fortunate for the Byzantines, because they faced a threat they could not deal with on their own. The Seljuk Turks had gradually taken control of Asia Minor from them. In 1078, the Seljuks took Nicaea, a mere 100 kilometres from Constantinople. In 1084, the powerful city of Antioch was taken from Philaretus, a former Byzantine general. By 1090, the whole of Asia Minor was under the control of one Seljuk Turk, Suleyman. If nothing was done to stop him, the Byzantine Empire would fall to a Muslim invasion.

Alexius I was not a weak ruler and tried to tackle the threat himself. His main strategy was a diplomatic one. In the 1090s, he began to negotiate an agreement with Abu'l-Kasim over Nicaea. However, this failed when Abu'l-Kasim was murdered and was replaced by Kilij Arslan who refused to negotiate. This state of affairs was worsened by the increased seaborne threat from Muslim pirate attacks, such as in 1094 when the islands in the Aegean were raided, and the potential threat of invasion faced from another nomadic Turkish tribe, the Cumans. This eventually took place in 1095 when they attacked Adrianople in the Byzantine Empire.

EXTEND YOUR KNOWLEDGE

Alexius I Comnenus (1057–1118)
Alexius was the ruler of the Byzantine Empire. He had come to power in 1081 when he rebelled against the previous emperor and seized the throne. He protected his own position by placing members of his family in important government roles. He faced threats on a number of fronts during his reign. These were not just from the Turks. For example, the Normans, including Bohemond of Taranto, had attacked the western Balkans in 1081-83. He also suffered financial problems, such as the debasement of Byzantine coinage, due to the cost of funding mercenaries to protect the empire. A chance for military success, like the First Crusade, would therefore help to defend his borders and maintain his hold on domestic power.

Alexius I's appeal to Urban II

The increased threat level in 1095 prompted Alexius I, as a representative of Greek Orthodox Christianity, to appeal directly for help from Pope Urban II. He wanted Nicaea back under his control and to create a buffer between his empire and the Turks. He did not want a crusade. Instead, he wanted the sort of help he had received in 1090. In that year, Robert I, Count of Flanders, had sent 500 western knights to help fight off the Turks. Alexius had hoped that he could encourage a similar professional force to bolster his army in 1095.

To that end, in early 1095, Alexius sent envoys to a major Church Council held by Urban II in the Italian city of Piacenza. He asked for help to defend the Church, not as a reaction to any recent defeat, but rather because of the increasing threat the Muslims posed. The chronicler Bernold of Constance recorded that the pope responded positively to this request. He asked others at the council to promise their help and the seeds of his appeal for a crusade later that year were sown. A political need, the threat to an eastern ally, had therefore provided a trigger for Urban to begin to formulate his plans for a religious war.

SOURCE

A translation of Bernold of Constance's description of the Council of Piacenza, March 1095. It is a summary of all the appeals and decisions made at the Council. This extract refers to the appeal by Alexius I Comnenus and the reaction from Pope Urban II.

Likewise a legation came to this synod from the Constantinopolitan emperor, who humbly implored the lord pope and all the faithful of Christ that they offer help to him against the pagans for the defence of the holy church which they already had almost annihilated in these parts, occupying those regions up to the walls of the city of Constantinople. The lord pope induced many men to offer this help, so that they promised indeed by oath that they will journey there with God's help and, to the best of their ability, will provide help to the same emperor.

Urban's political problems and ambitions for the papacy

It is of great significance that Alexius I chose to approach Pope Urban II in 1095. He could have asked for help from Henry IV, Emperor of Germany, or Philip I, King of France, or even William Rufus, King of England. However, the fact Alexius chose Urban shows that he was not seen purely as the spiritual head of the Catholic Church. He was also a political leader, with a hierarchy of bishops beneath him, and with power and influence over the whole of western Christendom. Eleventh-century popes were a part of the real world and, like other 11th-century rulers, they struggled for control. Alexius's request gave Urban a valuable opportunity to make a show of strength at a vital moment in his own struggle for control.

What challenges did Urban face to his political power from the German Empire?

When Urban was elected pope in 1088 he was in a very weak position because of the threat he faced from Henry IV of Germany. In 1076, a serious argument had broken out between the previous pope, Gregory VII, and the emperor. This was called the **Investiture** Controversy and led to Henry IV driving Gregory out of Rome and his appointment of a rival antipope called Clement III. In Urban's early years as pope, he had to fight to regain control from his imperial rival, who controlled Rome and had support from the German Empire, Denmark, Poland and Hungary. It took time, considerable military support from powerful rulers like Mathilda of Tuscany and a rebellion against Henry IV, but Urban gradually regained the papal territories.

The year 1095 was an important one in Urban's fight against the antipope, because he finally had the upper hand. In 1089, he had retaken Ravenna and by 1094 he had recovered control of the Lateran Palace in Rome. At the same time, Henry IV's position had grown weaker. His son had begun a rebellion against him in 1093 and, by 1095, had submitted to Urban's authority at Cremona. Henry had also been publicly humiliated as his second wife, Praxedis, accused him of sexual depravity. Urban used this as a chance to undermine Henry's position, as he allowed Praxedis to separate from her husband. With Henry in a weakened position, this was the perfect time for Urban to make a show of strength and to consolidate his power in western Christendom.

Problems in France

Urban needed to show that he was in charge of the Church, he enforced its rules and he appointed its officials. This was at the forefront of Urban's mind, not just because of Henry IV's challenge to his power, but also because of recent events in France. Here, King Philip I had gone against Church law in a rather dramatic fashion. King Philip had abandoned his queen to marry Bertrada of Montfort, who was already married to Count Fulk of Anjou. This was a blatant act of adultery and clearly against Church law. He had also imprisoned Ivo, Bishop of Chartres, for his opposition to the marriage. These events left Urban with little choice but to confirm Philip's excommunication at the Council of Clermont in 1095. This meant that two rulers were now in opposition to Urban. The chance to call a crusade was therefore a fantastic opportunity, because if it worked and thousands flocked to his cause, it would show both Henry IV and Philip I that Urban's power could not easily be challenged.

EXTRACT 1 From Jonathan Riley-Smith, *What Were the Crusades?* published in 2009.

> It [preaching the First Crusade] was an important move in the Investiture Controversy for, when he called on the army of Christ to recover Christian land, Urban was, consciously or unconsciously, assuming for himself the imperial function of directing the defence of the Christian Republic at a time when he did not recognize Henry as emperor. Gregory VII had deposed a king; Urban II took over the prime duty of a **temporal ruler**. With these actions the popes began to take a special place for themselves at the summit of both jurisdictions.
>
> Although it took some time for political thinkers and canon lawyers to catch up with the ideas expressed in the deposition of Henry IV and the preaching of the First Crusade, these foreshadowed what is known as the Papal Monarchy. By the early thirteenth century the pope claimed to be Christ's vicar, a special representative unlike any other earthly ruler, the ordinary judge of all things with a plenitude of power, standing in an intermediate position between God and the two hierarchies of ecclesiastical and temporal ministers.

KEY TERM

Investiture
The ceremony at which a bishop was invested with his new role. In the 11th century, this was performed by kings and emperors, contrary to Church law.

KEY TERM

Temporal ruler
A person with power over the business of the real political world rather than the spiritual world: for example, a king or a prince.

THREATS AND THE FIRST CRUSADE

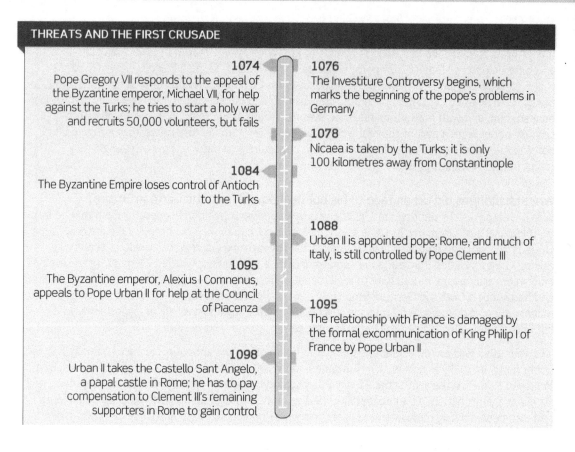

1074
Pope Gregory VII responds to the appeal of the Byzantine emperor, Michael VII, for help against the Turks; he tries to start a holy war and recruits 50,000 volunteers, but fails

1076
The Investiture Controversy begins, which marks the beginning of the pope's problems in Germany

1078
Nicaea is taken by the Turks; it is only 100 kilometres away from Constantinople

1084
The Byzantine Empire loses control of Antioch to the Turks

1088
Urban II is appointed pope; Rome, and much of Italy, is still controlled by Pope Clement III

1095
The Byzantine emperor, Alexius I Comnenus, appeals to Pope Urban II for help at the Council of Piacenza

1095
The relationship with France is damaged by the formal excommunication of King Philip I of France by Pope Urban II

1098
Urban II takes the Castello Sant Angelo, a papal castle in Rome; he has to pay compensation to Clement III's remaining supporters in Rome to gain control

Building a papal kingdom

The First Crusade not only gave Urban II a means to consolidate his power, it also gave him the opportunity to extend it. He wanted this because popes had begun to see themselves as a type of monarch and one of the aims of a monarch was to increase their kingdom. Evidence of this belief can be found from as early as 1059 when a papal coronation was first reported. There was also much written about the pope's secular power during the Gregorian Reform Movement. *Dictatus pape*, to take one example, said that a pope had the power to depose emperors if it was necessary. It was with this mindset that Urban, a reformist himself, looked to expand his control.

Urban's position both within and beyond the frontiers of western Christendom was fairly weak. The bishops of Europe, including those from France and England, took little notice of him, and abroad the situation was worse, because Rome was only one of five patriarchates. His most powerful counterpart was the patriarch of the Greek Church of Byzantium, which had split with Rome in 1054 due to arguments over **liturgy**. This meant that there was an entire Christian empire over which the pope had no formal power.

ACTIVITY
WRITING

Words to describe change over time
Use the words in the box to complete the sentences below so that they best describe the nature of the changes that led up to the First Crusade.

> progress, transform, reversed, gradually, regressed, transmute, matured

The Byzantine Empire had been a powerful force in Asia Minor until 1078 when its fortunes were _____. By 1095, the power of the Turks had _____, as they now controlled much of Asia Minor. At the same, papal power had been under threat from the German Empire. Urban _____ restored the power of the papacy between 1088 and 1098. As a result, the power of Emperor Henry IV over the pope _____ to its former state. However, the pope wanted to _____ the power of the papacy through a crusade. His aim was to _____ religious power into political power. The First Crusade helped to make _____ towards this goal.

Attempts to unify the Church

The crusade was therefore a perfect opportunity to restore good relations with the Byzantine emperor, Alexius I, and use this as a launch pad to open talks over unification. Urban's aim, or at least hope, was to bring the Greek and Latin churches under his control. There is evidence of this in both words and deeds:

- according to Fulcher of Chartres, Urban emphasised the ties between Christians in the East and West in his sermon at Clermont

- the Church Council in 1098 at Bari considered the issue of union between the churches

- when the papal legate, Adhemar, arrived with the first crusaders in Antioch, he restored control of the Church to the Greek patriarch rather than a Latin bishop.

However, despite Urban's grand plans, he failed in his attempt to unify the Greek and Latin churches. These plans were largely ruined by Bohemond of Taranto who refused to honour agreements with Alexius I over Antioch, which led to a failed crusade in 1107 against the Byzantines (see page 33). The effect of this failure was to limit the political ambitions of the papacy for the rest of the 12th century. The papal kingdom had grown into **Outremer**, but it was to extend no further in the East. The drive to expand was gone and both the Second and Third Crusades were launched as reactionary campaigns by the papacy. This explains why Pope Gregory VIII asked for the Third Crusade, but he left the organisation and leadership to Emperor Frederick Barbarossa of Germany.

Violence and growing disorder in Europe

The problem of violence in France

French society in the early 11th century had experienced a serious violence problem caused by its warrior classes. They were a class trained and prepared for war, but they lacked a clear purpose for their violence as the external threats to Europe from Viking incursions had ended by around 1000. Nevertheless, it was still essential for these men to have military training because there were wars of expansion, such as the conquests of Sicily and England by the Normans. There were also internal conflicts in France caused by the fragmentation of French society and the weakness of the French king. This meant much of the country was divided up among **castellans**, who used violence towards men, women and churchmen to assert their authority.

However, their actions clashed with the growing confidence of the Church to challenge their violence. In the absence of a strong government or a powerful leader, the Church began to scrutinise the behaviour of French knights. The Cluniac reformers promoted the idea that violence on a day-to-day basis, especially towards churchmen, was not acceptable. There was an increased aspiration to greater order in society and the situation began to improve. Initially, the Church put in place two measures to curb violent behaviour.

- Peace of God: These were orders for **ecclesiastical** protection for certain people, such as women and churchmen, and their property. They were issued by reforming Church councils from the late tenth century.

- Truce of God: This was the second stage in the Peace Movement. It was an order to stop all violence on certain days of the week and certain times of the year. The first was issued in 1027 and it was policed by oath-takers.

These elements of the Peace Movement did have a significant impact on both actions and attitudes. The problem of endemic violence began to decline after the 1020s and knights started to search for new ways to behave piously.

How might a crusade help?

The crusade was one such opportunity for the warrior classes because it could provide a holy purpose for their violence. Both Fulcher of Chartres and Baldric of Dol, in their accounts of Urban's sermon at Clermont, report that the pope said the crusade would stop the infighting between Christians. It was perhaps even another stage in the Peace Movement and was, in Urban's mind at least, a motivation to call a crusade. He hoped it would appeal to knights influenced by the Peace Movement and direct their violence outside western Europe.

KEY TERMS

Outremer
The name for the crusader states in the Holy Land. It included the counties of Edessa, Tripoli, the principality of Antioch and the kingdom of Jerusalem.

Castellan
A knight who rules over a castle. The term is most commonly applied to French knights whose castles dotted the countryside of France.

Ecclesiastical
All things related to the Church or its members.

Challenges to Europe in 1095

Use the information above on the threats faced by Europe in 1095 and the desire for change.

1 Create a spider diagram to show the challenges faced in Europe in 1095. This should include:

- threats to the Byzantine Empire

- threats to the pope from the German emperor and French king

- the disunity between the Latin and Greek churches

- the level of violence in Europe.

2 How would a crusade help to tackle these challenges? Add this into another layer in your spider diagram.

Defence of the crusader states

The need for defence

The crusades of the 12th century were chiefly caused by a significant loss or threat to the Latin states of Outremer. The earliest example of the need for defence comes from 1119. In this year, at the Battle of the Field of Blood, Roger of Antioch and many of his nobles were killed. This left Antioch in a weak position and prompted a fleet to leave Venice in August 1122. A year later, Pope Calixtus II confirmed at a church council that this was a crusade, which was to last until 1125, and that knights would receive an indulgence.

EXTEND YOUR KNOWLEDGE

Definition of a crusade
The numbering of the crusades of the 11th and 12th centuries is a construction of historians rather than contemporaries. They have only numbered crusades that attracted large numbers, involved contingents from different countries and intended to go to the Holy Land. However, there were a lot of minor ventures in the 12th century that received papal authorisation and had similar privileges granted to their participants (for examples, see page 80).

The threat from Zengi and the Second Crusade

However, the crusades in the 1120s and 1130s were not very popular. In fact, it was not until the governor of Mosul and Aleppo, the Emir Imad ad-Din Zengi, began to capture entire sections of Outremer, that the Second Crusade of 1145 was called. This did not happen straight away, as Zengi began his campaigns, which were focused around Antioch, in 1135. He captured significant fortresses, such as Cerep in 1135, and castles, such as Rafaniyah in 1137. However, his most noteworthy victory, and the one that was to prompt a call for defenders, occurred in 1144 when he captured Edessa in December and left around 15,000 dead.

The capture of Edessa showed the need for defence had now reached a crisis point. Bishop Hugh of Jeble, along with his supporters, travelled to visit the pope at Viterbo. They reached his court by November 1145 and this prompted Pope Eugenius III to proclaim the Second Crusade in *Quantum praedecessores*. In Eugenius's surviving letters, the loss of Edessa, the damage to its relics, the murder of its archbishop and the capture of its surrounding castles were explicitly referred to. He made it clear to the people of Europe that if they wanted to keep Outremer they must answer the call for defence.

EXTRACT 2 From Jonathan Phillips, *The Second Crusade: Extending the Frontiers of Christendom*, published in 2007.

Asides from reasons of family tradition, kin-association and patronage, the primary motives for many of the crusaders were, as Bernard and Eugenius so powerfully reminded them, to receive remission of their sins and to free or protect the holy places...

...Many expressed conventional religious sentiments: Hartnid of Riegersberg and Hartmann of Uberach took the cross for the salvation of their souls. Other[s] expressed a tie with the importance of the holy sites; to 'worship in the place that Christ walked' was crucial to Goswin of Randerath, while ... Raymond and William of La Baume wanted to go to Jerusalem 'for the remittance of our sins and desiring to renounce all our wicked ways.

THINKING HISTORICALLY   Evidence (3b)

It depends on the question

When considering the usefulness of a piece of evidence, people often think about authenticity in the case of artefacts, reliability in the case of witness statements or methodology and structure in the case of secondary accounts. A better historical approach to the usefulness of a piece of evidence would be to think about the statements that we can make about the past based on it. Different statements can be made with different degrees of certainty, depending on the evidence.

Work in small groups and answer the following questions:

1 Look at Source 6, the photograph of a carving, on page 30.

   a) Write three statements that you can reasonably make about reasons to join the Second Crusade based solely on the carving.

   b) Which of the statements can be made with the greatest degree of certainty? Why is this? Which statement can be made with the smallest degree of certainty?

   c) What else might you need to increase your confidence in your statements?

2 The photograph is of an artefact and Source 7 (on page 31) is a witness statement in the form of a contemporary song. Which is more useful to the historian studying the motivations for joining the Second Crusade?

3 Look at Extract 2.

How would the historian have gone about constructing this piece? What kinds of evidence would they have needed?

KEY TERMS

Vizier
The main governor of a country who ran it on a day-to-day basis. The vizier was chosen by a caliph, a Muslim leader who was head of a ruling dynasty, but had considerably more power than a caliph.

Franks
The name used to refer to crusaders. It was used due to the fact that many of the First Crusaders had connections with various French duchies, such as Normandy.

True Cross
A famous relic. This was believed to be the cross that Jesus was crucified upon and was taken by the Franks during the First Crusade.

Bezant
A gold coin used by Greeks. It was a standard unit of currency throughout the Mediterranean world.

The threat from Saladin and the Third Crusade

The next time a call for a crusade was to meet with such an overwhelming reaction again was in the 1180s. By this time, a new threat had appeared in the Latin East. Saladin, the **vizier** and later sultan of Egypt, began his invasion attempts in 1170. However, it was his 1187 campaign, itself a reaction to a Christian attack on a large Muslim caravan, which was to frighten crusaders into action. In July, the army of the **Franks** was defeated near the hills of Hattin, King Guy of Jerusalem was captured and the relic of the **True Cross** was captured. Pope Urban III reportedly died of shock and by October Jerusalem had fallen to Saladin. The Franks were forced to leave the city after payment of a ransom of 30,000 **bezants**.

SOURCE

5 From the Chronicle of Matthew Paris, written in the 13th century. It shows the Battle of Hattin in 1187 and depicts an image of Saladin taking the Relic of the True Cross from the Christians. It is unlikely the relic would have been taken in this way, but it shows how central the symbolism of the Holy Land was in the call for the Third Crusade.

The Christians had been left with limited control in Tyre, Tripoli and Antioch, which they would lose if no action was taken. The initial losses led Pope Gregory VIII to call for the defence of the settlements in Outremer in *Audita tremendi*. It was first issued on 27 October 1187, after reports of the imminent fall of Jerusalem were received from men such as the Patriarch Eraclius. It was reissued by Pope Celestine III three months later, after the loss of Jerusalem was confirmed, and prompted a big reaction. For example, in September 1189, 12,000 Frisians and Danes left to provide help. The Third Crusade was therefore launched as another holy war in reaction to a significant loss.

Limitations: the failed crusades

The Second and Third Crusades evidently had their origins in the need for defence. However, this need did not always trigger a crusade. Between 1157 and 1184, popes tried to launch crusades seven times but were largely unsuccessful. For example, in 1165, Pope Alexander III called for a crusade in reaction to the capture of Bohemond III by Nur ad-Din and the increased Muslim threat to Antioch. The only response this prompted was King Henry II of England's call for a tax to fund a crusade. Another failed attempt occurred in 1169, when the papal bull, *Inter omnia*, was issued. The fact that no crusade resulted from this call for protection from attacks by Nur ad-Din to Christian territory shows defence alone was not enough to prompt a crusade.

ACTIVITY
KNOWLEDGE CHECK

The need for defence

1 Rank the events in the 'Threats to the crusader states' timeline below from those that caused a major reaction in the West to those that caused a minor reaction. Use a scale of 1 to 10, where 1 = minor, 10 = major.

2 What links can you identify between the events that caused the biggest reaction in the West?

AS Level Exam-Style Question Section B

To what extent did the political reasons for launching a crusade change in the years 1095–1146? (20 marks)

Tip

The focus of this question is on the extent of change to the political reasons for launching a crusade. Try to establish criteria for measuring these.

THREATS TO THE CRUSADER STATES

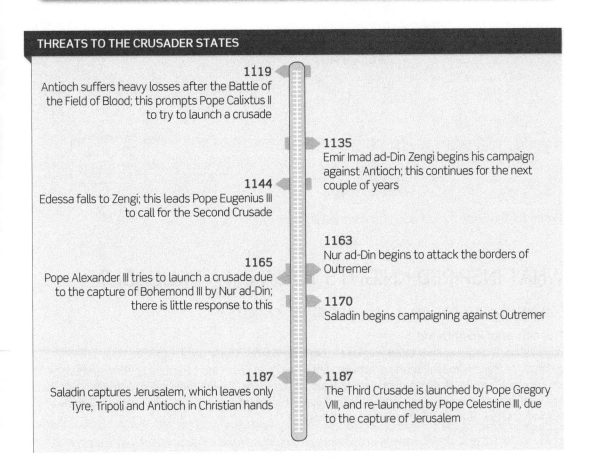

1119
Antioch suffers heavy losses after the Battle of the Field of Blood; this prompts Pope Calixtus II to try to launch a crusade

1135
Emir Imad ad-Din Zengi begins his campaign against Antioch; this continues for the next couple of years

1144
Edessa falls to Zengi; this leads Pope Eugenius III to call for the Second Crusade

1163
Nur ad-Din begins to attack the borders of Outremer

1165
Pope Alexander III tries to launch a crusade due to the capture of Bohemond III by Nur ad-Din; there is little response to this

1170
Saladin begins campaigning against Outremer

1187
Saladin captures Jerusalem, which leaves only Tyre, Tripoli and Antioch in Christian hands

1187
The Third Crusade is launched by Pope Gregory VIII, and re-launched by Pope Celestine III, due to the capture of Jerusalem

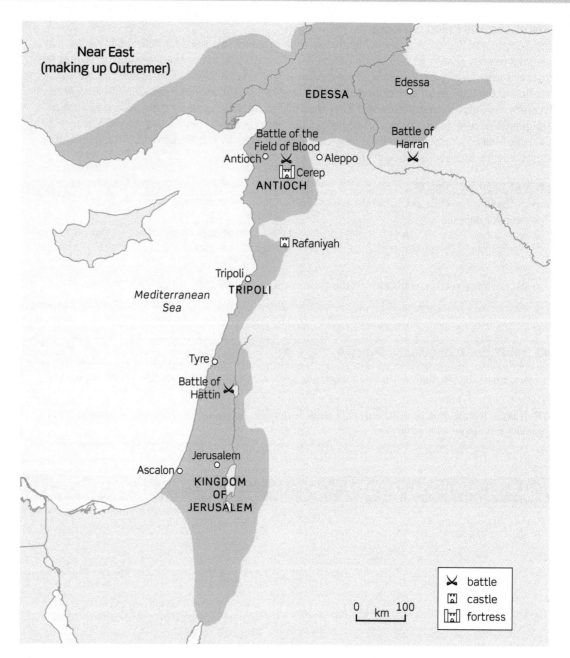

Figure 1.2 Threats to the crusader states in the 12th century.

WHAT INSPIRED KNIGHTS TO GO ON A CRUSADE?

Motivations for an 11th-century knight

The nature of knighthood

Pope Urban II desperately wanted knights to join his crusade. These were a specific group of warriors, or *milite*, who fought on horseback with a heavy lance. In the 11th century, they were not yet the chivalrous warrior elite they were to become (see page 31), but their military strength had the lethal offensive potential of modern-day tanks against the right target. They gave western Europe a newfound sense of power for the following reasons.

- They made use of developments in technology: their horses were equipped with stirrups, a high saddle and were shod. This gave them a secure position from which to fight and to charge, as well as the ability to travel across rough terrain.

THINKING HISTORICALLY Cause and consequence (5a)

Connections

Causes never simply come one after another. They are often present simultaneously and have an effect on one another. Sometimes new causes develop and interact with existing ones.

Causes of the First Crusade

Desire to free Jerusalem	Political ambitions of the pope	The theory of the just war	Threats to the Byzantine Empire	Urban's problems in Germany and France	Alexius I's appeal for help

Work in groups to produce a diagram of causes and the links between them.

1 On an A3 piece of paper, write all the causes of the First Crusade. Write these in boxes, the size of which will reflect how long they were a relevant factor. For example, if you argue that the 'desire to free Jerusalem' had been an important factor since the fall of the Roman Empire, then this will be quite a big box, whereas 'Alexius I's appeal for help' would be a lot smaller. Spread these boxes over the page.

2 Then make links between all the causes. Draw lines between the boxes and annotate them to explain how the causes are connected and in what ways each affected and altered the other. For example, between 'Political ambitions of the pope' and 'Urban's problems in Germany and France' you could write something like, 'Without the challenges that Germany and France created for Urban II, the pope would not have needed to create an opportunity to assert his political power'.

Answer the following questions:

3 How do the causes differ in their nature? (Think in terms of events, developments, beliefs, states of affairs, etc.)

4 How do the causes differ in the roles they played in causing the First Crusade? (Think about whether each cause created the right conditions, was a trigger for events or acted in some other way.)

5 Write a 200-word paragraph explaining how important it is to recognise the relationships between causes. Give examples from your diagram. Try to include connective phrases such as; 'This created conditions conducive to...', 'This triggered an immediate reaction...', 'This made the development of that situation more/less likely'.

- They were well armed: by the late 11th century, the use of the **couched lance cavalry charge** had begun to develop. However, knights also made use of traditional weapons, like swords, in hand-to-hand combat.

- They were heavily armoured: knights wore a hauberk, a coif and carried a kite-shaped wooden shield. These defences became heavier and more complex during the course of the 12th century.

These important developments were also helped by their experience of warfare. There had been several significant campaigns in the 11th century, such as Robert Guiscard's attack on the Byzantine Empire between 1081 and 1085. This, alongside other smaller-scale conflicts, provided knights and their lords with military experience, which helped to improve their tactics. For example, they realised that all-out battles were best avoided and that it was better to isolate an enemy's stronghold, raid the territory that surrounded them and gradually starve them out. The strength of small units of knights could therefore be put to good use in raiding.

They also had advantages over the enemies they faced. The Seljuk Turks used light cavalry forces that were mobile and used a bow and arrow. One of their preferred tactics was to attack a column of crusaders, while on a march, by showering them with arrows. The knight's armour would usually protect them from this, although their horses did not always survive. The Seljuk Turks were also at a disadvantage in hand-to-hand combat because of their lighter defences, such as their small, round shields.

In contrast, the light infantry of Fatimid Egypt was a mixture of fighters from different groups, such as Arabs and Berbers. They did not use mounted archers and, although some Arabs fought on horseback, they were not as mobile as the Turks. Their preference was hand-to-hand combat. This

KEY TERM

Couched lance cavalry charge
This was a form of attack used by a group of knights. The lance was clasped under the arm and they raced on horseback towards the enemy with lethal force.

made them an easier target for the heavily armoured and well-trained knights of western Europe, as they were more used to this type of warfare.

However, the knights of western Europe were not invincible and they did have weaknesses in comparison with their enemy. These included the following.

- They were often few in number.

- They were slower than the Seljuk Turks.

- They had varying levels of support crew with them who were not all combatants and would require feeding.

- They had limited value in siege warfare, as they could take part in raids, but feeding their horses was a challenge over the course of a siege that could last many months.

The appeal of a crusade to an 11th-century knight

In order to motivate knights to join the First Crusade, Urban pushed the message of crusading as a pilgrimage opportunity for them. This has been discussed above (see page 15) and can be found in several versions of the sermon at Clermont. His core message was that crusading would mean they were fighting the barbarians in the Holy Land rather than their brothers at home. He hoped his message would appeal to knights who already had strong connections with religious communities, such as Viscount Gascon IV of Béarn, who offered gifts to the Cluniacs at Ste-Foi in 1091. This tactic met with reasonable success and it is estimated that of the 60,000 who set out in 1096, 10 percent were knights.

SOURCE
6 A knight in a 12th-century relief carving. It shows all the characteristic features of an early 12th century knight, as well as the new technique of the couched lance charge used by knights during battle.

Other motivations in 1095

There were three other motivating forces that encouraged nobles and knights to go on a crusade in the 1090s. These were lordship ties, family connections and links to Cluny. The enthusiasm of a lord for a crusade would encourage those around him, as well as the knights who were tied to him, to join in. For example, Stephen of Blois inspired the nobility in the Chartrain to join him on crusade in 1096. Family also played an important role. The first crusader, Bohemond of Taranto, had 15 captains, eight of whom were close relatives. The final motivation for knights was that some had a pre-existing link to the Cluniac Order, which was at the heart of the papal reform movement and helped them to truly appreciate the religious reason for a crusade.

The development of chivalric values

In the 12th century, the concept of chivalry changed what it meant to be a knight. Chivalric values were no longer just a partial influence in the decision to go on a crusade. Nor were they just a reason why popes might think of knights as attractive recruits. Instead, they turned crusading into a duty. The old values, which included knights on foot and horseback, were:

- a focus on winning wars

- the need to behave courageously in battle

- development of personal strength.

These changed to new values that made knighthood an exclusively aristocratic position. These included:

- codes of behaviour, such as manners and courtesy

- a sense of loyalty to their house and commitment to their overlord

- development of skills, especially the use of the couched lance in a cavalry charge.

Chivalric values and crusade recruitment

Knights were indoctrinated with these values through court poetry. These poems would be read out, or more frequently sung, by troubadours. They expressed the ideals, obligations and expectations for knightly behaviour. For example, one song from around 1146 explored how crusading was a feudal duty owed to God by a knight. Another song emphasised the obligation knights had to use their carefully acquired skills. It argued that they owed it to Christ to use their training to fight in his name. Knightly culture was therefore slowly catching up with the message of crusade preachers that they were a new type of knight with a just cause.

SOURCE

7

From a *Troubadour Song* by an anonymous author, 1146–47. This was written in Old French and would have been sung to gather support for the Second Crusade. It tries to appeal to knightly classes in a number of different ways.

Knights, you are in very good hands now that God has called for your help against the Turks and the Almoravids who have done Him such dishonour. They have wrongfully snatched his fiefs; our sorrow at this should indeed be great since it was there that God was first offered service and acknowledged as Lord.

Anyone who now goes with Louis need have no fear of Hell, for his soul will be in Paradise with the angels of Our Lord.

Edessa is taken, as you know, and the Christians are sorely afflicted because of it: the churches are burnt and abandoned, God is no longer sacrificed there. Knights, make your decisions, you who are esteemed for your skill in arms; make a gift of your bodies to Him who was placed on the cross for you.

...God has organised a **tourney** between Heaven and Hell, and so He is asking all His friends who are willing to support His cause not to fail him.

At the end of the 12th century, crusading in the East had become a fundamental part of chivalric culture. It had, for example, become common for knights to undertake temporary service in the East as soldiers, rather than exclusively as crusaders. However, the most significant change occurred during the Third Crusade. During this crusade, Richard I, along with most of the knights of England, went to the East together. This mass noble participation in a crusade, along with the inspirational character of Richard I, helped to cement the idea that chivalry and crusading went hand in hand.

KEY TERM

Tourney
A medieval jousting tournament. These were condemned by the Church as they often ended in fatalities.

A Level Exam-Style Question Section B

How accurate is it to say that chivalric values were fundamental to the recruitment of knights in the years 1144–92? (20 marks)

Tip
This question is asking you to make a judgement on the importance of chivalric values, but do not forget to counter this with other motivations such as the desire for an indulgence.

ACTIVITY
KNOWLEDGE CHECK

Chivalric values
Pick one feature of the *Troubadour Song* (Source 7) and explain how it would appeal to the new chivalric values of knights in the 12th century.

Protecting Christianity and pilgrims

Why were knights needed in 12th-century Outremer?

After the First Crusade, knights went to Outremer in order to protect and support pilgrims. These pilgrims faced many dangers on their journey. Daniel of Kiev, to take one example, went on a pilgrimage between 1106 and 1107. He described how Muslims used Ascalon as a base from which to attack pilgrims. These reached a crescendo in 1120 when Muslim raids from Tyre and Ascalon killed 300 and captured 60 of the 700 pilgrims journeying to Outremer. The Muslim threat to pilgrims continued throughout the 12th century and was, for instance, referred to in King Amalric's letter to the archbishop of Reims in 1169.

The military orders

The ever-present Muslim threat inspired a group of knights to join together to provide an escort for pilgrims. In 1120, Hugh of Payns and Geoffrey of St Omer, along with a number of other knights, officially founded the **Templar** movement. Their group received formal approval by the Church at the Council of Troyes in 1129 and from then on provided a motivation for some knights to go East. They now had the opportunity to dedicate their lives to military service in Outremer like the spiritual service of monks in western Europe.

However, the popularity of this career option for knights should not be overstated. At its height there were only around 500 knights in the Templars, because the **brother knights** who joined had to take monastic vows. These were vows of poverty, chastity and obedience, but allowed for violent action in protection of Christianity. These men were praised by Bernard of Clairvaux in his *De laude novae militae* (*In Praise of the New Knighthood*) and were seen as role models for other knights for the huge commitment they had made. In spite of Bernard's praise, it was precisely because of this level of commitment that only a relatively small number of crusading knights were ever motivated to join.

The same was true of the **Hospitaller** movement. This order had its origins in the 1070s and had the stated aim of the provision of support for pilgrims. It became an independent order in 1113 and at its height had between 300 and 500 members. The main responsibility of the Hospitallers was to run the Order of St John's Hospital in Jerusalem, which in 1185 had beds for 2,000 sick or poor pilgrims. The order therefore played an important role in crusading society. However, the Hospitallers, like the Templars, also began to provide a defensive military role and started to attract knights to their order.

The Hospitallers were militarised at some point in the 1130s. This is evident because in 1136 King Fulk of Jerusalem donated the Castle of Beit Jibrin to the order and, by 1144, they had a big estate in northern Tripoli to defend. This parallels the growth of the Templars, which from 1127 could afford to maintain a small company of knights from its own financial resources. These 12th-century orders therefore helped to turn crusading, for a few knights, from a temporary venture into a permanent vocation.

Settlement in the crusader states and the acquisition of wealth

The opportunity to gain land and wealth was used as a recruitment device for the First Crusade. In Robert of Reims's version of Urban's sermon at Clermont he compares the western world with the Holy Land. He describes the West as overcrowded, with limited opportunities to make money and suffering from frequent famines. In comparison, he says, the East is a rich and fertile land. This sermon makes explicit what some knights must have been thinking: that there would be more than just spiritual rewards for a crusader.

SOURCE

From Robert of Reims's chronicle account of Urban II's sermon at Clermont in 1095. He explores a number of themes according to Robert, but most notably the pollution of holy places by Muslims and the wealth of the Holy Land. This extract focuses on the theme of wealth.

Oh most strong soldiers and the offspring of unvanquished parents, do not show yourselves to be weaker than your for[e]bears but remember their strength! ...for this land you inhabit is everywhere shut in by the sea, is surrounded by ranges of mountains and is overcrowded by your numbers; it does not overflow with copious wealth and scarcely furnishes food for its own farmers alone. This is why you devour and fight one another, make war and even kill one another as you exchange blows. Stop these hatreds among yourselves, silence the quarrels, still the wars and let all dissensions be settled. Take the road to the Holy Sepulchre, rescue that land from a dreadful race and rule over it yourselves, for the land that, as scripture says, floweth with milk and honey was given by God as a possession to the children of Israel.

This is supported by the talk of **booty** in chronicle accounts of the crusades. For example, in the First Crusade, after Jerusalem had been captured, the crusaders began a massacre of its inhabitants and plundered any valuables they could find. Only after this was complete did they travel to the Holy Sepulchre to finish their crusading journey. This illustrates that looting was a part of the mental world of a crusader and that it went alongside religious motives rather than in place of them.

The theme of opportunity is also explored in Urban's sermon. It is evident that some knights saw a crusade as an opportunity to escape their *mouvances*. This was the term to describe the world many European knights lived in. This was a world in which they were dependent upon the patronage of someone wealthier than them and had to compete against other knights for influence with their patron. This is true of first crusaders like Tancred, who lived in the shadow of his uncle, Bohemond of Taranto. The crusade was their chance to make something of their lives.

In search of power: the First Crusade

Only a few leading knights went to grab land and power in the Holy Land. There is little evidence that the rest of the crusading army went with this intention. The knights who went with this aim were:

- Bohemond of Taranto: he had control of the Norman-ruled lands in southern Italy, but he wanted to be a prince

- Baldwin of Boulogne: he had very limited inheritance opportunities back home in France; this was his chance to create a kingdom for himself

- Tancred of Hauteville: he was Bohemond's nephew and so had even fewer inheritance opportunities than his uncle

- Raymond of Toulouse: he went on crusade with his third wife, Elvira, which suggests that he planned to claim, and settle in, his own territory in the Holy Land.

ACTIVITY
KNOWLEDGE CHECK

Power and wealth

Research the motivations of one of the other First Crusaders, such as Stephen of Blois or Robert of Normandy.

In what way were their circumstances and motivations different from Bohemond, Baldwin, Tancred and Raymond?

Bohemond of Taranto

Bohemond of Taranto went on the First Crusade because he wanted to be a prince. He was a Norman from southern Italy who had tried to invade the Byzantine Empire in the 1080s. His ambition for power was evident in his behaviour during the crusade. He had taken an oath to the Byzantine Emperor, Alexius Comnenus, to hand over the city of Antioch when it was taken. However, he refused to do this and declared himself Prince of Antioch, a position he held from 1098 to 1111. In addition, in 1106–07, he travelled back to the West to raise another crusade, which failed in its attempt to attack the Byzantines. Despite the fact he failed, his choice to keep on fighting reveals that power was an important motive for some crusaders.

EXTEND YOUR KNOWLEDGE

Crusade of 1107
This crusade, launched by Bohemond of Taranto, reveals how a knight could be driven by territorial aims that were thinly disguised by religious justifications. After the defeat of the Franks at the Battle of Harran in 1104, the Turks managed to prevent the Franks from making any further military progress. It also gave the Byzantine Empire a chance to regain some important settlements. In 1105, this prompted Bohemond to travel to southern Italy and seek the support of Pope Paschal II. Bohemond had a number of arguments, but his chief point was that Alexius I had prevented pilgrims from travelling to Outremer. Pope Paschal II therefore gave his assent to a crusade and a papal legate, Bruno of Segni, was appointed. The crusade was formalised at a council at Poitiers in 1106. Bohemond's army assembled in October 1107, in Bari, southern Italy, and began to attack the Byzantine port of Durazzo. Alexius was able to wait it out, with a force of around 60,000 men, and Bohemond had to surrender due to supply problems. He submitted to the Treaty of Devol in 1108, which made Bohemond a vassal of Alexius I and restored a Greek patriarch in Antioch. Bohemond had been motivated by a desire to expand his principality but instead lost a considerable amount of power.

How many stayed behind?

Other than the infamous ambitions of men like Bohemond of Taranto and Raymond of Toulouse, there is little evidence that knights were motivated by the prospect of settlement in the Holy Land. During the final stage of the First Crusade, of the 1,200 knights who did battle at Ascalon around 200–300 settled there. There are also accounts of a reasonable number at Edessa and perhaps 3,000 in Antioch. In total, for the whole of the 12th century, there is evidence of about 200 new settlements. This suggests that most crusaders saw it as a temporary stage in their lives, not as a permanent opportunity to 'make it' in the East.

The cost of crusading

The reason there is such limited evidence for greed as a motivation for crusaders after, and to a lesser extent before, the First Crusade, was primarily cost. Many crusaders returned from Outremer in 1099 in a state of poverty. The booty they had taken during the campaign was used to fund the journey home, or was simply too heavy to carry back. This sent the very strong message to future crusaders that they would not return from the East with fabulous riches.

In fact, the knights who planned to set out on a crusade had to gather together around five to six times their annual income in order to fund it. This is why, as the 12th century wore on, popes and kings became more involved in the fundraising process. For example, Louis VII of France asked for financial help in 1146 to fund the Second Crusade, and King Henry II introduced the Saladin Tithe in 1188 to pay for the Third Crusade. Instead of wealth being a motivating factor to join a crusade, it was actually a serious barrier to potential crusader knights.

AS Level Exam-Style Question Section B

Were religious ideals the main motive for the Second and Third Crusades? Explain your answer. (20 marks)

Tip
You are being asked to balance religious motives against other factors. Do not forget to refer to political motives.

SOURCE

9 A 15th-century image of the looting of Jerusalem by the first crusaders in 1099. Notice the impracticalities of transporting this loot back to the West and the lack of horses with which to do so.

ACTIVITY
SUMMARY

Reasons to go on a crusade

1 Bullet point nine different reasons why people went on a crusade. Try to choose three religious, three political and three knightly motives for crusading.

2 Create a table with five columns:

- Important to a knight in 1095

- Important to Pope Urban II in 1095

- Important to Emperor Alexius Comnenus I in 1095

- Important to Bernard of Clairvaux in 1146

- Important to a knight in 1187

3 Choose three reasons from your list for each column and rank them in order of importance. You should not use the same reason more than once. Explain your top choice for a knight in 1095.

4 Explain whether you have changed your order for 1187 and why. Refer to religious motivation, the political background or the value system of knights in your answer.

WIDER READING

Flori, J. 'Ideology and motivations in the First Crusade', in Nicholson, H. (ed.) *Palgrave Advances in the Crusade*, Palgrave Macmillan (2005), pp. 15–36

Richard, J. *The Crusades, c.1071–c.1291*, Cambridge University Press (1999)

Riley, N. and Byrom, J. *The Crusades (Enquiring History)*, Hodder Education (2013)

Riley-Smith, J. *The Crusades: A History*, Bloomsbury (2014)

Tyerman, C. *The Crusades: A Very Short Introduction*, Oxford University Press (2005)

1.2 Leadership of the crusades, 1095–1192

KEY QUESTIONS

- How did the actions of individual princes affect the course of the First Crusade?
- Why did the leaders of the Second Crusade fail?
- What effect did the leaders of the Third Crusade have on its outcome?

INTRODUCTION

On 20 August 1191, Richard the Lionheart, the hero of the Third Crusade, was faced with a choice. He had 2,700 Muslim prisoners after his successful capture of Acre. He had kept them as hostages to ensure his enemy, Saladin, stuck to the terms of his surrender. However, when the conditions were broken, the prisoners were a useless bargaining token. He could not release them, because they would join the enemy's forces. He could not keep them indefinitely, as he would have to spend the rest of his life guarding them at Acre. Instead, he did what he had to do. They were murdered, in cold blood, in full view of Saladin's army. The crusaders were free to advance their campaign and Saladin retreated from Ascalon.

Almost 100 years before, Bohemond of Taranto, one of the leaders of the First Crusade, faced defeat on the plains of Antioch. His forces, along with the supporting armies of six other princes, had made little progress in the capture of Antioch. The Turks always seemed to be one step ahead and Bohemond suspected this was due to espionage. In order to stop this, Bohemond ordered the bodies of any Muslim killed to be brought before the city walls. The bodies were cooked and preparations were made to eat them. The crusaders, at this stage, did not resort to cannibalism but the spies had been scared off.

The leaders of the crusades did what they had to do. They would go to extraordinary lengths to achieve their goals and, in a time before the idea of basic human rights, often did so. This chapter will look at the impact the key leaders had on the course of each crusade. It will explore how the eight princes of the First Crusade, each with a different goal in mind, shaped the crusader landscape of Outremer. It will explain why the leaders of the Second Crusade failed so utterly to retake the land lost to Zengi. Finally, it will outline the progress King Richard I made in the Third Crusade, but also examine why he, along with two of the most powerful rulers in Europe, was unable to recapture Jerusalem.

1096 – The armies of the eight princes set off on their journey to the Holy Land

July 1099 – Jerusalem is captured by Godfrey of Bouillon

| 1095 | 1100 | 1105 | 1110 | 1115 | 1120 | 1125 | 1130 | 1135 | 1140 | 1145 |

March 1098 – Baldwin of Boulogne leaves the First Crusade and establishes his own county in Edessa

June 1098 – Bohemond of Taranto defeats the forces of Kerbogha and takes possession of Antioch

May 1147 – The German army, under Conrad III, sets off to Outremer on the Second Crusade; a month later the French follow

HOW DID THE ACTIONS OF INDIVIDUAL PRINCES AFFECT THE COURSE OF THE FIRST CRUSADE?

The eight princes and their changing priorities

Who were the leaders of the First Crusade?

The First Crusade had no single commander-in-chief who could direct the campaign to Jerusalem with a sense of common purpose. Instead, its leaders were a mixed bag of princes from different parts of Europe, with different political backgrounds and different expectations of what they would gain from the crusade. The main **contingents** of crusaders were:

- Germans and Lotharingians, led by Godfrey of Bouillon and his brother, Baldwin of Boulogne

- northern French, led by Hugh of Vermandois, Robert of Normandy, Robert of Flanders and Stephen of Blois

- Italian Normans, led by Bohemond of Taranto and his brother, Tancred of Hauteville, although the latter was not of princely status

- southern French and Provençals: led by Raymond of Toulouse (or Saint-Gilles).

> **KEY TERM**
>
> Contingent
> A group of armies with a shared sense of purpose or identify. For example, the northern French contingent of the First Crusade contained at least four armies.

> **EXTEND YOUR KNOWLEDGE**
>
> The first wave: the People's Crusade
> The first wave of crusaders left much earlier than the **contingents** of the eight princes. This wave contained a 40,000-strong, mainly peasant army from all across Europe. Its two most famous leaders were Peter the Hermit and Walter Sansavoir. Their journeys began in spring 1096 and Peter's forces reached Constantinople on 1 August 1096. There they caused so much trouble that they were shipped across to Asia Minor within a week. The crusaders established a camp at Civetot and began raids on the surrounding countryside. One such raid, at the fort of Xerigodos, ended with the slaughter of the crusaders by Turks. In a revenge attack, Walter Sansavoir and a force of 500 knights set out on 21 October 1096. They were defeated and the Turks proceeded to massacre the crusaders encamped at Civetot. The few that remained escaped to Constantinople. They joined the main army, under the guidance of Peter the Hermit, at Nicomedia in May 1097.

Main priorities: the aims of the princes

It is very difficult to work out the precise aims of each of the princes, as the various chroniclers tended to focus on their own leader's divine motive and shied away from any other. However, the outcome of the First Crusade for each leader can reveal something about their main priorities. The table on the next page, divided by contingent, lists the outcome of the First Crusade for each of the eight leaders. It is important to note that some continued to campaign after the final battle at Ascalon, while others returned in a later crusade. However, this is only referred to in the case of Raymond, as it had an impact on his actions in the First Crusade. These outcomes, their cause and effect, are discussed throughout this chapter.

June 1148 – The Kings of Germany, France and Jerusalem meet at the Council of Acre; they decide to attack Damascus

July 1148 – The siege of Damascus fails; the Second Crusade is over

June 1190 – Frederick Barbarossa dies while swimming in the River Göksu; the German forces are demoralised and only a few continue the journey to Acre

July 1190 – King Philip II of France and Richard I of England meet and set off from Vézelay together on the Third Crusade

1150	1155	1160	1165	1170	1175	1180	1185	1190	1195	1200

May 1189 – The German Emperor, Frederick Barbarossa, sets out on the Third Crusade to help at the Siege of Acre

July 1191 – The Siege of Acre finally comes to an end and the garrison of Acre surrenders

July 1192 – Rather than launch an attack, the crusaders decide to withdraw from Jerusalem; the Third Crusade is over

The aim and achievements of the eight princes

Contingent	Prince	Stated aim of the First Crusaders	Did they contribute to the stated aim of the crusade?
German and Lotharingian	Godfrey of Bouillon	To capture Jerusalem from the Muslims.	Yes – became ruler of Jerusalem.
	Baldwin of Boulogne		Partially – conquered Edessa but priorities changed after this. He established himself in northern Syria as the Count of Edessa.
Northern French	Hugh of Vermandois		Partially – he helped to secure possession of Antioch, but abandoned the crusade after this.
	Robert of Normandy		Yes – he fought to the end at the Battle of Ascalon.
	Robert of Flanders		Yes – he fought to the end at the Battle of Ascalon.
	Stephen of Blois		Partially – he took part in the early stages of the siege of Antioch but deserted when it looked like failure was imminent and he feared for his own safety.
Italian Normans	Bohemond of Taranto		Partially – he helped to capture and secure Antioch. His priorities then changed and he established himself as Prince of Antioch and left the crusade.
Southern French	Raymond of Toulouse		Yes – he fought to the end of the Battle of Ascalon, although his priority, to secure his own territory, slowed the crusade. He achieved this after the First Crusade when he became Count of Tripoli.

Divisions: the political background of the princes

The seeds of conflict between the leaders were sown long before their journey began in 1096. There were three significant issues that would later cause delays, separation of the crusading army and outright violence between the princes.

The first was the attitude towards the pope, with some princes being long-time supporters of the papacy, whilst others had been in direct conflict with it. For example, Raymond of Toulouse led his contingent jointly with the pope's representative, Adhemar of Le Puy. In contrast, Godfrey of Bouillon, a supporter of Henry IV of Germany, had taken part in the siege of Rome in the early 1080s. His attitude to the pope, though no longer overtly hostile, would certainly have influenced his relationship with Raymond.

A more significant issue was the diverse range of relationships with Alexius I, the Byzantine Emperor. Some crusaders, notably Bohemond and the Italian Normans, had led campaigns against Alexius, and in June 1081 to February 1082, Bohemond had laid siege to the Byzantine city of Durazzo. This was to result in both tension and a concerted effort by Alexius to get the leaders to swear an oath of **vassalage** to him. This would have been much easier for Robert of Flanders, whose father, Robert I of Flanders, had sent 500 knights to support Alexius earlier in the 1090s. However, it was a measure, discussed below (see page 39), that would cause delay and later result in disunity amongst the crusaders.

(see page 39)

KEY TERM

Vassalage
This was a formal commitment to acknowledge someone as your overlord in return for land. In the context of the First Crusade, this meant any land the crusaders acquired they held on behalf of Alexius I.

The final issue between the eight princes was their attitude to power. This was to have the biggest impact on their priorities throughout the crusade. Some leaders wanted to establish their own principalities rather than campaign all the way to Jerusalem. The most notable example was Bohemond of Taranto (see Chapter 1), who went to extraordinary lengths to secure the principality of Antioch. Other leaders wanted control and glory, such as Raymond of Toulouse who sought, without success, to become commander-in-chief of all the crusading armies. Finally, there were others, such as Stephen of Blois, who had no desire for more power, which led to a somewhat lukewarm commitment to the campaign.

The first priority: getting to the Byzantine Empire

Naturally, the four contingents chose different routes across Europe to reach their rendezvous point in Constantinople. However, the fact they chose departure times that would not result in a common arrival time illustrates how disconnected they were from the start. Hugh of Vermandois, without his fellow French princes, departed in August 1096 and travelled via the port of Bari, in Italy, but had to be rescued by the Byzantines when he was shipwrecked on the way to Durazzo. He was thus the first to arrive.

The Germans and Lotharingians, with a long distance and troublesome territory to traverse, set off next. Godfrey of Bouillon left in the early autumn of 1096 and, in order to cross Hungary without violence, had to temporarily surrender his brother as a hostage. They were followed by the Italian Normans, who lived close by the borders of the Byzantine Empire and crossed the Adriatic in October 1096. Finally, the southern French and Provençals departed in late November 1096, but chose a long south-eastern route that slowed the pace of their journey.

The short-term impact of their staggered departures was to delay the beginning of the crusade itself, but did have one beneficial side effect. It prevented any single place in Europe having to feed and provision the entire army of the First Crusade at the same time.

Early divisions: the journey through the Byzantine Empire

The princes' armies arrived at Constantinople between late 1096 and early 1097. Alexius, fearful of disorder and distrustful of some of the leaders, decided to force them to take an oath. This was a very serious undertaking for any medieval person, because it was considered an act of extraordinary sin to break an oath. Each prince who encountered Alexius was made to promise the return of any land they captured that had once been part of the Byzantine Empire as part of an oath of vassalage. In return, Alexius guaranteed help and supplies.

The decision to take the oath divided the crusaders. Some, like Godfrey of Bouillon, took it very seriously. He entered into a long negotiation with Alexius and only took the oath after the emperor temporarily cut off his supplies. When he swore it, on 20 April 1097, he understood the seriousness of his commitment. He was followed by the northern French, Hugh of Vermandois, Duke Robert of Normandy, Count Robert of Flanders and Count Stephen of Blois, who all took the oath without objection. This suggests that the priority of these crusaders from the start was not to grab land that formerly belonged to the Byzantine Empire but to stick with the primary aim of the First Crusade: the capture of Jerusalem.

In contrast, the following three princes took a very different attitude to the oath.

- Bohemond of Taranto: he took the oath on 10 April 1097, but had no intention of keeping it. This is illustrated by his actions during the siege of Antioch.

- Raymond of Toulouse: he arrived in Constantinople on 21 April 1097, but refused to take the oath Alexius demanded. Instead, he took an oath to maintain the emperor's life and honour. This suggests he also planned to claim former Byzantine territory, such as Antioch, for himself.

- Baldwin of Boulogne: he, along with Tancred of Hauteville, avoided the oath altogether and bypassed Constantinople. He was the first to abandon the crusaders to establish his own **county** in Edessa.

These decisions set the tone for the rest of the expedition. They highlighted the division between those who were prepared, at least in theory, to go all the way to Jerusalem, and those who had more limited goals in mind.

KEY TERM

County
An area of land ruled by a count. In Outremer a count was a member of the upper nobility and held their land from the king of Jerusalem.

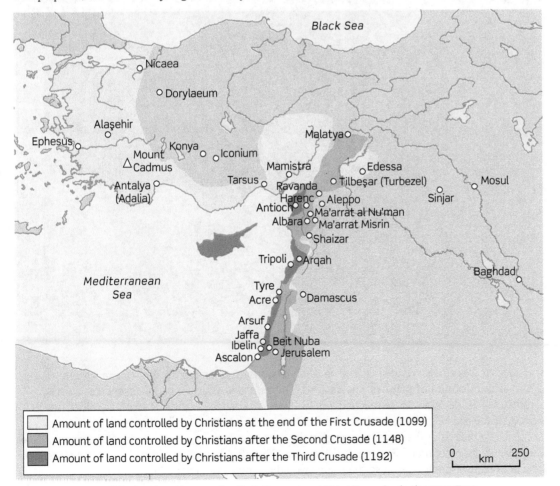

Amount of land controlled by Christians at the end of the First Crusade (1099)
Amount of land controlled by Christians after the Second Crusade (1148)
Amount of land controlled by Christians after the Third Crusade (1192)

0   km   250

Figure 2.1 A map of the key locations on the First, Second and Third Crusades in the Near East.

Turning point: the siege of Nicaea

The siege of Nicaea was the first time the leaders of the crusade realised that they would have to work together. In May 1097, they began to arrive at Nicaea. Godfrey of Bouillon, Robert of Flanders, Hugh of Vermandois and Tancred of Hauteville arrived in early May, followed by Bohemond's forces on 14 May and the rest two weeks later. This meant the assault to take the city did not really begin until all the armies had arrived. However, by 18 June, they had taken the city through a combined strategy. On the one hand, they blockaded the Askanian Lake that surrounded Nicaea, which cut off the city's main supply route, and at the same time they maintained a siege using their land forces.

SOURCE

1 An illustration of the siege of Nicaea from a medieval manuscript. It shows the most common type of warfare that crusaders engaged in, which was to lay siege to a town. It also graphically illustrates the savage tactics crusaders would use to defeat a town's garrison. In this case the heads of slain Muslim soldiers are thrown back into the city using a trebuchet.

KEY TERM

Council of princes
The term for the group that met to make command decisions during the First Crusade. It included the key princes who led the crusade, such as Bohemond of Taranto.

This success was a result of the leaders' decision to work together. During the siege, a system known as the **Council of princes** was devised. This provided a forum, in the absence of a single commander, for decisions to be reached jointly. It was this council that decided on the blockade strategy. They also realised, as a result of the delays at Nicaea, that they needed to plan their journeys together. After the siege they divided the army into two waves, one under Bohemond of Taranto and the other under Raymond of Toulouse. This, they hoped, would make it easier to collect, steal or purchase supplies because the troops would be spread out over a larger area.

The council also decided to maintain frequent and close communication between the two waves. This joint planning helped the crusaders to survive their journey through Asia Minor. For example, at Dorylaeum, Bohemond of Taranto and Robert of Normandy were attacked by the Turks. The two princes took up a defensive position, communicated with the second wave, which then joined them and made the Turks retreat. This illustrates that the leaders' priorities, at least in Asia Minor, had combined. They needed to survive to meet their goals and they were prepared to work together to achieve this.

ACTIVITY
KNOWLEDGE CHECK

The priorities of the eight princes

1 Construct a table with two columns labelled 'The crusade leaders were divided' and 'The crusade leaders were united'.

2 Read back through the material in this chapter so far, and then add evidence to your table to support each view.

3 On the basis of the material in your table alone, do you think the First Crusade was more likely to succeed or fail?

Baldwin's conquest of Edessa, 1097

Why was Baldwin tempted east to Edessa?

On 10 September 1097, Tancred of Hauteville and Baldwin of Boulogne left the main crusading army to journey through Cilicia on their way south to Antioch. They both used this as an opportunity to gain land for themselves, which led to conflict between them. For example, when Tarsus was taken by Tancred his banners were raised, which meant that the town was his to control. However, Baldwin, whose army outnumbered that of Tancred, had the banners pulled down and replaced with his own.

An even more serious conflict occurred in Mamistra, of which Tancred took control and then fought over with Baldwin. This was the first example of fighting between the crusading armies themselves, but did not last long. Once both sides had cooled off, Baldwin took the decision to abandon the competition, allow Tancred's occupation of the Cilician towns and went in search of territory further east in Edessa. This enabled Tancred to garrison his conquests, resume his journey south and rejoin the crusaders.

In the meantime, Baldwin began his journey east with the successful capture of Ravanda and Tilbeşar. By the time he reached the city of Edessa, which was under Armenian rule, his reputation as a powerful military leader had preceded him. On 6 February 1098, he was invited by Toros, the ruler of Edessa, to become his son and heir. However, Toros was deeply unpopular and was murdered on 9 March. This meant that Baldwin was now the ruler of Edessa and he set about the task of taking complete control of his new county.

SOURCE

An account of Baldwin's conquest of Edessa from Fulcher of Chartres. Fulcher was the chronicler of the northern French, but became Baldwin of Boulogne's chaplain during the crusade. He witnessed the events first hand and wrote up his chronicle in 1101, 1106 and 1124–27.

Then, trusting in the Lord and in his [Baldwin's] own strength, he collected a few soldiers, and set out toward the Euphrates River, and there seized many forts both by force and cleverness. Among these, he took the very best one, which was Turbezel [Tilbeşar]. The Armenians who lived there granted it to him peaceably, and many others were subjected to him...

...Baldwin was invited to go there [Edessa], so that they would become mutual friends like father and son as long as both should live. If, by chance, the Edessan duke should die, immediately Baldwin, as if he were his son, would possess the city and his whole land in inheritance forever. For he had neither son nor daughter. And because they were unable to defend themselves from the Turks, that Greek [Toros] wished to have himself and his land defended by Baldwin and his soldiers, who he had heard were very brave warriors.

The effects of the acquisition

The events during the Cilician passage had several important effects for the armies of the First Crusade.

- The loss of Baldwin of Boulogne and his army: he did not complete his vow to travel to Jerusalem until 21 December 1099, which was after its capture.

- Money: Edessa was a prosperous county and Baldwin was able to give his brother, Godfrey of Bouillon, 50,000 gold bezants to fund the campaign south to Jerusalem, via Antioch.

- Distraction: the Muslim army, led by Kerbogha, which was headed to Antioch to stop the siege in May 1098, was distracted for 3 weeks by an unsuccessful attempt to capture Edessa. This gave the main Crusader army more time to break into Antioch.

Baldwin's decision to leave the First Crusade showed that his chief priority was to gain land for himself, which weakened the overall strength of the crusaders. However, his selfish actions did at least contribute to the crusaders' first significant success in the Holy Land: the capture of Antioch.

Bohemond's seizure of Antioch, 1098

Stage 1: the siege of Antioch

The main body of the crusader army reached Antioch in October 1097 and began to lay siege to the city. It had a formidable garrison, led by Yaghi Siyan, which meant that the siege dragged on for 7½ months. This drained the crusaders' strength, but also gave figures like Bohemond and Raymond a chance to hone their military leadership skills and strengthen their position as leaders. Bohemond rose to especial prominence, because he was responsible for the victory of the Lake of Antioch in February 1098 where 1,500 of the 5,000-strong garrison were killed. He also helped the crusaders to gain access to the city in June 1098 through his negotiations with an Armenian, or possibly a garrison captain, who let them sneak in.

The effects of the siege

The lengthy siege of Antioch placed an incredible strain on the crusading armies and their leaders. It resulted in considerable loss of life and damage to morale. During the famine of December 1097, while the other leaders were on **foraging** campaigns, Raymond of Toulouse and the remainder of the crusading army were attacked by Yaghi Siyan. This led to around 35 deaths, but more significant for morale the banner of Adhemar of Le Puy was captured. The loss of this banner, which the garrison delighted in waving around, sapped the morale of the starving crusaders.

SOURCE 3

An account of Bohemond's victory at the Lake of Antioch, also known as the Lake Battle, in the *Gesta Francorum*. This was written by an anonymous southern Italian Norman. The chronicler, although a supporter of Bohemond, reveals the effect a strong leader could have on the battlefield.

Our army joined battle successfully and fought hand-to-hand; the din arose to heaven, for all were fighting at once and the storm of missiles darkened the sky. After this the main army of the Turks, which was in reserve, attacked our men fiercely, so that they began to give back a little…

…So Bohemond, protected on all sides by the sign of the Cross, charged the Turkish forces, like a lion which has been starving for three or four days, which comes roaring out of its cave thirsting for the blood of cattle, and falls upon the flocks careless of its own safety, tearing the sheep as they flee hither and thither. His attack was so fierce that the points of his banner were flying right over the heads of the Turks.

The other troops, seeing Bohemond's banner carried ahead so honourably, stopped their retreat at once, and all our men in a body charged the Turks, who were amazed and took flight. Our men pursued them and massacred them right up to the Orontes Bridge.

THE SIEGE OF ANTIOCH

October 1097
The siege of Antioch begins

29 December 1097
Raymond of Toulouse, left to defend the crusading army, is attacked by the Antioch garrison

February 1098
The victory of the Lake of Antioch; Bohemond plans to divide the army into six squadrons, which helps him to defeat part of the garrison

2 June 1098
An insider lets Bohemond and his forces past the walls of Antioch before Kerbogha reaches them

December 1097
The army suffers from severe famine; Bohemond and Robert of Flanders are sent to attack Ma'arrat Misrin in order to gain supplies

January 1098
The Byzantine general Taticius leaves the crusaders

May 1098
A large Muslim army, under Kerbogha, stops off to besiege Edessa (unsuccessfully) before heading to Antioch

4 June 1098
The siege is complete, but Kerbogha takes up a position outside, in the Tower of the Iron Bridge, which traps the crusaders inside

KEY TERM

Foraging
An attempt to search and steal food supplies. These were a common feature of the crusades, because they could not travel with enough supplies to sustain their army for long periods.

The siege also caused the First Crusade to lose two of its leaders who, out of fear, retreated from Antioch back to Constantinople and did not return. In January 1098, for example, Taticius, a Byzantine general who had provided vital tactical advice during the siege of Nicaea and journey through Asia Minor, headed back to the empire. Even more significant was the desertion of Count Stephen of Blois who, on his journey back to Constantinople, convinced Alexius and his army to turn back from their plan to help the crusaders at Antioch.

EXTEND YOUR KNOWLEDGE

General Taticius

Taticius was a Byzantine general who was known for his distinctive physical appearance, as he wore a replacement metal nose. He made a vital contribution to the First Crusade as both a military advisor and commander. He travelled with the armies of the princes in command of around 2,000 **turcopoles**. He was also an invaluable guide and helped to plan the itinerary of the crusaders to Antioch. This ensured they were well supplied and arrived at an appropriate time of year. However, despite the support he offered during the march, at the siege of Nicaea and at the Battle of Dorylaeum, Taticius left the First Crusaders during the siege of Antioch. There are two versions of why he did this. These said it was either out of fear for his life or to collect supplies. Regardless of which version is closest to the truth, once Taticius had left he did not return.

KEY TERM

Turcopole
The light cavalry troops used by the Byzantine Empire. They were paid mercenaries with mixed Greek and Turkish heritage.

Why did the capture of Antioch succeed?

The city of Antioch was successfully captured by the crusaders in June 1098 in spite of the beseigers' poor supply of food, the loss of two of their leaders and the resolve of Yaghi Siyan's garrison. There were three main reasons for this.

The foraging strategy: the leaders knew that to survive the siege they would need plentiful supplies. This led to a plan in which Raymond of Toulouse would forage in the Ruj Valley and Tancred in the areas surrounding Harim. This helped to ensure supplies in the early stages of the siege.

Financial support: Raymond of Toulouse was exceptionally wealthy. He was able to use this money to help the crusaders. For example, it was used to fund the building of La Mahomerie in May 1098, a fort to block access to Antioch at the Bridge Gate.

Secret negotiations: Bohemond of Taranto entered into secret negotiations with someone inside the city, who one chronicler called Firouz. This allowed the crusaders access to Antioch just before the relief force under Kerbogha arrived.

Stage 2: securing Antioch

By 4 June 1098, the crusaders had not simply secured access to Antioch; they had, in fact, become imprisoned within it. The forces of Kerbogha had abandoned their siege of Edessa and as a result around 35,000 Turks were encamped outside Antioch. This was a major challenge for the leadership of the crusades, because morale was at an all-time low. On 12 June, Bohemond had to order the closure of the city's gates in order to stop crusaders escaping. However, the victory that they were about to achieve showed how strong the princes had become.

EXTEND YOUR KNOWLEDGE

The Holy Lance

One event that helped to improve morale was the discovery of the Holy Lance. On 10 June, a peasant called Peter Bartholomew reported that he had seen a vision of St Andrew and Christ. He said that the two figures had revealed the location of the Holy Lance to him. This was a very high profile relic, because it was believed to be the spear that Longinus, a Roman soldier, had thrust into Christ's side on the cross. On 14 June, when the siege of Kerbogha was at its height, the search for the Holy Lance began. It was found in the Basilica of St Peter, within the church of Antioch. This had an extremely positive effect on morale, because relics were believed to have huge power and significance. It partly helps to explain why the crusaders managed to stave off defeatism during this period.

On 28 June, the battle for Antioch began. The army was now under the control of Bohemond, who had been elected by the Council of princes to replace Raymond, who was ill, as the supreme commander of the First Crusade. He faced a huge challenge, as he only had around 200 horses and the city was surrounded by Kerbogha's troops. Nevertheless, Bohemond was able to win the battle and force Kerbogha to retreat for several reasons.

- He arranged for his troops to leave Antioch via the Bridge Gate. Its position meant that Kerbogha's troops, stationed at the other gates, would not be able to reach him quickly because the river blocked their path.

- He broke his army up into seven divisions, each with a clear leader. This would help to keep the army in formation during Kerbogha's counter-attack.

- He was able to convince Kerbogha, through the relatively small size of each division, that this was not an all-out offensive. Kerbogha did not respond until most of the troops were gathered on the plains outside the city.

- He kept back extra troops in a separate division. They were used as a **rearguard** and countered Kerbogha's first relief force, which never reached the main divisions. In the meantime, the main divisions were able to hold their ground against the troops already stationed around Antioch.

All of these measures meant that when Kerbogha finally realised that Bohemond had arranged for a decisive battle, the crusaders were ready for him. Kerbogha's first relief force was repelled by the extra division. During their retreat, they encountered Kerbogha's main force and threw them into disarray. They joined the retreat and Kerbogha, though not decisively beaten, was forced into a withdrawal by his now uncontrollable troops. The Turks were thus defeated and the reputation of Bohemond secure.

Stage 3: the possession of Antioch

Antioch had been seized thanks to Bohemond, but he was not prepared to give it up to Alexius I under the obligations of his oath. This was a problem because Raymond, who recalled the oath made to Alexius I, wanted to rule it in the name of the Byzantine emperor. He held on to two strategically important locations: the Palace of Yaghi Siyan and the Tower of the Iron Bridge. This led to a six-month long stalemate over what to do with Antioch, which was perpetuated by Raymond's recovery from illness and refusal to accept Bohemond's overall leadership. Instead of progress, Bohemond busied himself consolidating control over Tancred's Cilician towns and Raymond attempted to establish himself in the towns to the south, such as Albara and Ma'arrat al Nu'man.

The First Crusade was not just delayed; this time it faced paralysis and potential collapse. No single leader seemed able to enforce a decision. Instead, an embassy, including Hugh of Vermandois, was sent by Raymond to Alexius to appeal for his help. His reply did not arrive until the following April and thus did nothing to help. In fact, it made the situation worse, because Hugh chose to stay in Constantinople, which deprived the crusade of yet another leader. This delay was compounded by the death of Adhemar of Le Puy in November 1098, whose leadership of the Council of princes had helped to bring an element of cohesion to the crusaders.

By December 1098, the crusade seemed to have ground to a halt. Both Raymond and Bohemond had attacked the town of Ma'arrat al Nu'man, which fell on 12 December, and again both argued over what to do with their new possession. At the end of the year, little had changed since June, as no new leader had established control. However, the patience of the bulk of the crusading armies had begun to run out. The popular backlash that was to follow finally shocked the leaders into action.

In January 1099, while Raymond made a failed attempt to bribe the other leaders to support him, the remainder of his contingent took actions into their own hands. They believed Raymond would try to **fortify** Ma'arrat and continue his conflict with Bohemond. In order to prevent this, a mob pulled down the walls of Ma'arrat and destroyed its fortifications. This forced Raymond's hand and under intense popular pressure he was the first to set off for Jerusalem on 13 January 1099. The crusaders' final journey was now under way, but they had left one more prince, Bohemond, behind them.

SOURCE

4

A description by Raymond of Aguilers of the events that followed the capture of Antioch. He was a chronicler from the southern French and Provençal contingent and acted as Raymond of Toulouse's personal chaplain. The source illustrates the effect the crusaders believed the dispute over the possession of Antioch had on the course of the First Crusade.

Internal strife worried our leaders and further undermined friendly relations, so that only a few avoided disputes with their comrades or servants over theft or violence. In the absence of a judge who could or would discuss lawsuits, each person became a law unto himself. In these conditions the ailing Count [Raymond] and Bishop [Adhemar] offered little protection to their followers. But why trifle with such petty details? Luxuriating in idleness and riches, the crusaders, contrary to God's commands, postponed the journey until the Kalends of November. We believe that, if the Franks had advanced, not one city between Antioch and Jerusalem would have thrown one rock at them so terrified and weakened at this time were the **Saracen** cities following the defeat of Kerbogha.

> **KEY TERM**
>
> **Saracen**
> The name used by Christian crusaders to refer to followers of Islam.

Emergence of Godfrey of Bouillon as leader and the capture of Jerusalem, 1099

The fall of Raymond of Toulouse

Raymond began his march south with the support of Tancred of Hauteville, who was at the rear of his contingent, and was joined two days later by Robert of Normandy. These powerful men were crucial to Raymond's continued dominance over the crusading armies. However, Raymond stretched their support to breaking point when, upon arrival in Arqah, he began to besiege the city on 14 February 1099. His motivation for doing this was not to help capture Jerusalem. Instead it was part of his plan to take control of nearby Tripoli and establish his own county there. He was joined, at the end of March, by Godfrey of Bouillon and Robert of Flanders.

At this point, despite the support of the hardened core of crusaders that had survived the journey, Raymond finally lost control. On 13 May 1099, he heard that the caliph of Baghdad was on his way with a powerful relief force. Raymond's nerve had broken and he gave up on the siege of Arqah. Tancred, who could see that Raymond's commitment to the crusade had faltered, shifted his allegiance to Godfrey of Bouillon. The march to Jerusalem began again on 16 May and, as they approached Jerusalem, Robert of Normandy also transferred his support to Godfrey. Raymond's hopes of leading the crusaders to victory had been shattered by his attempt to take power for himself.

The siege of Jerusalem

The attack on the walls of Jerusalem took five weeks. The crusaders divided their efforts between Godfrey of Bouillon's followers, which included Robert of Flanders, Robert of Normandy and Tancred, in the west and Raymond of Toulouse's contingent in the south. Despite the fact that Godfrey and Raymond were now at odds with one another, the siege was a success. On 15 July 1099, Godfrey's men, who had shifted their focus to the east of Jerusalem, now broke through the walls. The garrison withdrew to the citadel and surrendered after Raymond offered it protection. However, many of the city's remaining Muslim population were indiscriminately massacred. For example, Tancred offered protection to 300 Muslims sheltering in al-Aqsa Mosque, but other crusaders murdered them shortly afterwards. Jews were also targeted and, according to one Muslim chronicler, some were even burnt to death in their synagogue when it was set alight. These were brutal measures, but through them the crusaders' hold on Jerusalem was secured.

The attack, rather than taking the 7½ months the crusaders had endured at Antioch, had been achieved in a short time for the following reasons.

- They used a range of strategies. At first Godfrey focused on the western wall, but when this did not produce results he shifted the attack to the northern wall as well. This did not work either, so he tried the eastern wall, which they managed to cross using a **siege tower**. The crusaders' flexibility helped to speed up the siege.

- Godfrey of Bouillon was prepared to take part in the heart of the attack. This helped to raise the morale of his troops and to maintain their commitment to yet another siege.

- The crusaders were a hardened core. Aside from Raymond of Toulouse, the crusaders who had reached Jerusalem were an experienced force of united and loyal soldiers that had endured long marches, protracted sieges and faltering leadership. They were fully prepared for the task of besieging Jerusalem.

> **KEY TERM**
>
> **Siege tower**
> A large tower made of wood and protected by animal skins to prevent it being set alight. These were used, along with ladders, to break into a fortified town or city.

Securing control: Godfrey of Bouillon

Jerusalem had been captured, but the First Crusade had one last crisis to tackle before their task of securing the Holy City was complete. A Muslim counter-attack was on its way from Egypt and by 4 August the Muslims were encamped outside Ascalon. Godfrey quickly contacted the forces of Robert of Flanders, Robert of Normandy and, in spite of their ongoing conflict, Raymond of Toulouse. They gathered on 12 August 1099 at Ibelin and launched a surprise attack. The result, thanks largely to Raymond's quick thinking, was that the Egyptian camp was captured and the threat extinguished.

In the meantime, the dispute between Godfrey and Raymond rumbled on and their argument reached a crescendo on 22 July 1099 when Godfrey was elected ruler of Jerusalem. Raymond was not happy with this and, with memories of Antioch in mind, held onto the strategically significant Tower of David. This time, however, the conflict did not drag on, as Raymond was betrayed by one of his followers and the Tower was handed over. However, the bitterness between the two men came to the fore once more. After the Battle of Ascalon, the crusaders were divided again and unable to get surrender terms from the town of Ascalon itself. This important city remained in enemy hands, leaving a base for future Muslim counter-attacks to the south of Jerusalem.

The First Crusade had come to an end. Jerusalem was secure, despite the fact that there was a base for future counter-attacks to its south. Robert of Normandy and Robert of Flanders began their journey home and Raymond continued to try to take further towns, but failed. He decided to make his way back to Constantinople and was later to head the Crusade of 1101 with limited success.

ACTIVITY
KNOWLEDGE CHECK

The success of the First Crusade

1 Produce a timeline of five key events in the First Crusade from the victory at Dorylaeum to the Battle of Ascalon.

2 Add to your timeline the leader who had the biggest effect on the outcome of each event.

3 Identify the leader who you feel had the biggest effect on the course of the First Crusade. This could be the one you have labelled most frequently.

4 In no more than 100 words, explain the effect your chosen leader had on the course of the First Crusade.

WHY DID THE LEADERS OF THE SECOND CRUSADE FAIL?

Personal and political rivalries and tensions

Who were the leaders of the Second Crusade?

The Second Crusade was called for in December 1145 after the capture of Edessa by Zengi, and its leaders were very different from those of the First Crusade. They were powerful rulers in their own right. Louis VII was the king of France and now possessed a sizeable kingdom thanks to his marriage to Eleanor of Aquitaine. There are several theories as to why he agreed to lead the French in a crusade, which include that it was an act of penance for burning a church at Vitry, or that he wanted to fulfil his dead brother's vow to go to Jerusalem. Whatever his motivation, Louis was committed to the crusading cause at Vézelay during Bernard of Clairvaux's sermon at Easter 1146 and set his departure date for 15 June 1147.

Louis VII was joined by another powerful ruler, Conrad III, the king of Germany. He had the support of an army of around 30,000 to 35,000 soldiers and used the call to crusade to consolidate his power in the empire. His rivals, such as Duke Welf VI of Bavaria, who had already made their desire to go on crusade public, were forced to support Conrad when he made a formal commitment at Speyer on 18 December 1146. This was again in the presence of his senior nobles and Bernard of Clairvaux. He set his departure date for May 1147, which gave him 6 months to prepare for the journey to Outremer.

The journey to Constantinople

The routes both kings chose to get to Constantinople were affected by their political rivalries, but also showed willingness on their part to try to work together. Conrad's route went through Hungary in order to reach the borders of the Byzantine Empire. He chose this path with caution, as he had recently been defeated in a war with Geisa II, King of Hungary. However, it was his only real option, because his poor relationship with Roger of Sicily meant that he could not travel via the sea route. This was a result of his campaigns against Roger to protect the papacy in Rome.

Louis's choice of route showed considerable sensitivity to Conrad's circumstances, as well as his own personal situation. For example, Louis rejected Roger of Sicily's offer to ship the French to the Byzantine Empire. This decision was made for two reasons. It was partly because he did not want to antagonise his new ally, Conrad III, but it was also because Roger had made it clear he wanted control of Antioch. However, this principality was under the control of Eleanor of Aquitaine's uncle. Louis's wife, who was very powerful in her own right, therefore played an important part in his decision to follow a similar land route to Conrad.

Their journeys therefore began with a spirit of friendly relations between Conrad and Louis, in spite of the tricky issue of Louis's earlier negotiations with Roger over transporting troops. Louis had met with Conrad's ambassadors at Châlons-sur-Marne in the middle of 1147 and had reacted positively to their requests. In return, when Louis arrived in German territory he found preparations had been made for his journey. For instance, when he arrived at Regensburg there were ships ready to take his troops along the River Danube. There were occasional conflicts between French soldiers and Germans along the way, but the Second Crusade had got off to a promising start.

Louis and Conrad's relationship with Manuel I

Why was a good relationship important?

In 1095, Alexius I had invited crusaders into the Byzantine Empire to help him tackle the Muslim threat. However, there was no such invitation in 1147 from the new Byzantine emperor, Manuel I. This was very significant because the key to the success or failure of the crusade depended on the relationship between the leaders and the emperor. This relationship would affect several aspects of the crusade.

- The level of military support: during the First Crusade, Alexius had provided a Byzantine general, Taticius, both to act as a guide and to provide crucial support in battle. The crusaders would not have made it very far into Asia Minor without him.

- The amount of supplies and provisions: it was within Manuel's power to provide markets for the crusaders to buy goods from and ensure reasonable prices. If these were unavailable the crusaders would struggle to provision their troops. The emperor could also make ships available at ports under Byzantine control in Asia Minor.

- The loyalty of the Byzantines: Manuel had a treaty with the Turks, which was signed at Konya. A poor relationship might lead to betrayal of the crusaders' location or plans to their enemy.

- The level of delay: the First Crusaders had been held up at Constantinople in order to get them to swear an oath to Alexius I. The same delays could be imposed on Louis and Conrad if the emperor had reason to distrust them.

Conrad III's relationship with Manuel I was strong, however, and the two had formed an alliance against the southern Italian Normans. This relationship came under strain, though, when Conrad's forces began their march through Hungary and the Byzantine Empire to Constantinople. This was because Manuel had the Byzantine army, commanded by Prosuch, follow the Germans in order to prevent any efforts to capture territory. This led to several violent incidents, which included an attempt to burn down a monastery by Frederick of Swabia after a Greek soldier killed a German. Perhaps as a result of actions such as these, Conrad was made to swear a limited oath not to act against Manuel I's wishes.

The relationship between Manuel I and Louis VII was somewhat more strained because of the latter's close association with Roger of Sicily. This was partly a result of Roger's Norman origins, but mainly because Roger and Louis had originally planned to crusade together. Louis and the pope therefore tried to build bridges with Manuel, in the autumn of 1146, when they sent him a letter to explain their intentions. Manuel's reply, which referred to an oath of **homage**, showed that he was mistrustful of the French.

This mistrust was not helped when, in the autumn of 1147, Roger's admiral, George of Antioch, began to attack parts of the Byzantine Empire. Therefore, when Louis arrived in Constantinople on 4 October 1147, he was, after protracted negotiations, made to swear an oath of homage and to guarantee not to take Byzantine lands. In return he would receive guides and supplies.

The German campaign: September 1147 to June 1148

Conrad's plan was to get to Antioch as quickly as possible so that the operation to recapture Edessa (see page 49) could begin. His idea was to split the army into two parts with the fastest contingent, made up of soldiers, led by Conrad from Nicaea along an inland route via Iconium to pick up supplies. Otto of Freising would lead the rest along the supposedly safer coastal route. They were to depart with 8 days of supplies for a journey that Conrad estimated would take 20 days, because he assumed supplies could be acquired on route to Iconium. This plan was put into action on 25 October 1147.

However, in reality events did not go as planned, largely a result of Conrad's overconfidence. He believed they could acquire supplies as they travelled, but they struggled to do so because Manuel actually had little control of the area they journeyed through. The result was that, as the crusaders neared the site of the battle of Dorylaeum, they were ambushed by the Turks and had to retreat to Nicaea. They suffered a casualty rate of around 17 percent and many Germans gave up and headed back home. The other force, under Otto, also suffered raids, but little is recorded of their journey.

SOURCE

5

A description of the journey of the German contingent from Constantinople into Asia Minor by Odo of Deuil who travelled with the French army. In this source he reveals the attitude of the French to the Germans, as well as their mistrust of Manuel I.

Meanwhile the king of the Franks [Louis], whose wont was always to season majesty with humility, enjoined upon the German emperor with urgent entreaty that he should wait for him on this side of the Arm and those whose common will had undertaken a common task should also use a common plan of action. The German emperor [king], however, was hastening ardently toward the place for which he had set out, and when he had received a guide for the journey (or, rather, for wandering and death) from the Greek emperor, he went across. Although I have written before, and it is true, that an infinite number of his men had already perished, we heard from the Greeks who counted them as they crossed that he went across with 900,566 men [inaccurate]. Accordingly, he came to Nicomedia, where his men divided into groups because of a disagreement. The emperor went to Iconium; his brother, Bishop Otto of Freising, and many nobles took the shore route. We shall refer to their lamentable and swift misfortunes at the proper time and place...

Conrad himself, with the remnants of his army, joined up with the French when they arrived at Nicaea in mid-November 1147. However, Conrad fell ill when they reached Ephesus and left, with his army, for Constantinople to recover. He did not arrive in Acre until April 1148 and travelled there directly by ship. He joined the crusaders at the important Council of Acre on 24 June 1148, which was to decide the future of the Second Crusaders. His relationship with Manuel I had enabled him to make it there safely, but his impatience and overconfidence had lost him a large part of his army.

The French campaign: December 1147 to March 1148

Louis left for Outremer in late 1147 and initially met with more success than Conrad and his army. He chose to march along the Maeander valley towards Antalya where, Manuel assured Louis, ships would be waiting to take him to Antioch. It was during this march that Louis showed himself to be a talented leader. He ensured that his army kept in formation, which limited the opportunities available for the Turks to attack. When they did attack, in December 1147, Louis made effective use of a cavalry charge on steep ground to overcome the raid. However, the same difficulties the Germans faced as a result of their relationship with Manuel were soon to beset the French.

The first major problem was logistics. From around 3 or 4 January the French were extremely short of supplies. They had struggled to get provisions from the locals and when Manuel's guides did make markets available, they also passed on the movements of the French to the local Turks. This was partly a consequence of the treaty Manuel had signed at Konya and made it very easy for the Turks to track the crusaders. Even when they reached the well-established Byzantine town of Antalya, the markets that the guides secured were very expensive. This caused a heavy drain on Louis's limited financial resources.

However, Louis did not just lose money and suffer the consequences of shortages; his army also came under intense pressure. Around mid-January the French began to march across Mount Cadmus. They had planned to complete the journey over 2 days, but the vanguard decided to carry on from the summit, which left the baggage train some distance behind and unguarded. The Turks, who saw this break in formation, attacked. Louis was forced to hand over authority to the Templars, who had travelled at the rear, in order to reform his troops. The main body of the army survived, thanks to the Templars, but Louis's reputation as a military leader was damaged.

By the time the French reached Antalya, on 20 January 1148, their morale had taken a serious hit. They had lost support from the German army, their leader had lost authority and they had either been betrayed or exploited by the Byzantine Greeks. The final challenge they faced on their journey was that the fleet Manuel had promised was too small to carry the whole army. Only Louis and his officers could travel by ship; the other 7,000 had to endure a long march to Tarsus during a harsh winter with many difficult river crossings. When Louis, and what remained of his army, finally made it to Antioch on 19 March 1148, they could breathe a sigh of relief. They had survived the journey but at considerable expense in both money and lives.

The failure to consult the leaders of the crusader states

Neither Conrad nor Louis had consulted with the leaders of Outremer in advance of the Second Crusade, which had several negative effects on the course of their campaign.

The crusaders' stated goal was the recapture of Edessa, but this had been completely destroyed in 1146. However, as late as February 1148, Conrad wrote a letter explaining his intention to take Edessa, showing the leaders still had no knowledge from the leaders in Outremer that their objective was unrealistic. Having eventually found this out, the crusaders then took 4 months, from March to June 1148, to establish a new goal for the campaign, delaying their progress into Outremer. Keeping the crusading army together was an expensive business, and these delays did not help their cause. Finally, the crusaders did not respond to the needs of all of Outremer. Instead, they were presented with a plan in Antioch, which reflected northern interests, and a plan in Jerusalem, which reflected the threat that kingdom faced from the south.

The Antioch plan

Prince Raymond of Antioch made a military proposal to Louis, alongside the nobles of Antioch, in May 1148. His plan was that the crusaders could help to capture Aleppo and Shaizar, which would neutralise the Muslim threat to Antioch in the north. This was important because the threat had begun to increase ever since Nur ad-Din had replaced Zengi as the leader of Aleppo. It was also a fairly realistic aim because Shaizar had nearly been captured in a previous campaign with the Byzantines in 1138. The Antioch plan would have been a sensible move for Louis and his forces.

However, Louis, much to Raymond's chagrin, rejected the plan out of hand. William of Tyre, the medieval chronicler, claims that Louis's only interest was to finish his journey to Jerusalem to fulfil his vow. The result of this decision was that Raymond tried to use Louis's wife, Eleanor, as a pawn to get, or possibly force, Louis's support. Louis remained steadfast in his objection to the Antioch plan and the attempt to use his wife created a permanent rift between the two rulers. When Louis resumed his journey southwards, he left behind any hope of Antiochene military support for the Second Crusade.

EXTEND YOUR KNOWLEDGE

The affair of Prince Raymond of Antioch and Eleanor of Aquitaine
The lack of Antiochene support for the Second Crusade, as well as the unwillingness of Louis VII to pursue a campaign in the north, were both central to its failure. At the heart of the matter was an alleged affair between Eleanor, Louis's wife, and Raymond, her uncle. The allegation is largely based on chronicle material from William of Tyre and John of Salisbury. They claim that Raymond lured Eleanor into an intimate relationship, which she chose to pursue. The story goes that Eleanor sought a divorce, but Louis denied her this. His reputation had already been damaged along the journey to Antioch, and he could ill afford the embarrassment of an unfaithful spouse. Louis therefore forced Eleanor to continue with him on the crusade. This allegation has been used to explain the breakdown in relations between the two rulers that led to the adoption of the Jerusalem plan, but it is important to note that it is not a record of fact.

The Jerusalem plan

SOURCE

6 An illustration from William Tyre's *A History of Deeds Done Beyond the Sea* written in the 12th century. It shows the Council of Acre (top) and the siege of Damascus (bottom). This event marked the turning point of the Second Crusade and this was perhaps why it was chosen for illustration. It shows that the Council of Acre was an important gathering of powerful rulers and that their choice to target Damascus created a formidable challenge for the crusaders.

On 24 June 1148, an array of important nobles gathered at the Council of Acre to debate an objective for the Second Crusade. The most significant representatives were the French barons under Louis VII, the German dukes under Conrad III, and the nobles of Jerusalem chiefly represented by Queen Melisende. They had a choice of three plans, which included a northern campaign to Edessa, a southern campaign to capture Ascalon or an eastern campaign to take Damascus. The representatives chose the Damascus plan. It appeared to be a sensible choice because:

- there was no point in a northern campaign; Edessa had been razed to the ground and Prince Raymond had withdrawn his support

- Ascalon was not an immediate threat and was surrounded by crusader castles

- the truce between Jerusalem and Damascus, which up until this point had limited the threat to Jerusalem, had come to end with the rise of Nur ad-Din in Aleppo.

The choice was made with the interests of Jerusalem at the forefront and preparations began for the attempt to capture Damascus in July 1148.

Failure at Damascus in 1148 and the end of the crusade

The siege of Damascus

The siege of Damascus started out well under the troops of King Baldwin III, who launched an attack on 24 July 1148 through the orchards in the west, which was supported by Louis VII's soldiers. However, Conrad III, who had an army made up of those soldiers who had sailed via Lisbon and a further 2,000 horses that Manuel I had given to him, made the most gains. It was thanks primarily to his efforts that the river was won and the crusaders were able to establish a camp outside the city. They now had a ready water supply from the river and a food source from the orchards. All that remained was to begin the lengthy process of an attack on the city walls and to defeat its garrison.

However, on 27 July 1148, the crusaders changed their plan. They decided to shift their attack to a weak point in the eastern walls of the city. They hoped it would speed up the siege, which was important because Nur ad-Din had begun to mobilise troops from Mosul and Aleppo to stop the attack on Damascus. Unfortunately, the strategy change was a very bad decision. There was no access to water or food on the eastern side of the walls and the crusaders were quickly exhausted. After 3 days they retreated and the siege of Damascus was at an end.

 THINKING HISTORICALLY   Cause and consequence (3c&d)

Causation and intention

1 Work on your own or with a partner to identify as many causes of failure of the Second Crusade as you can. Write each cause on a separate card or piece of paper.

2 Divide your cards into those which represent:

   a) the actions or intentions of people

   b) the beliefs held by people at the time

   c) the contextual factors or events (i.e. political, social or economic events)

   d) states of affairs (long- or short-term situations that have developed in particular ways).

3 Focus on the intentions and actions of the key people in the run-up to the failure of the Second Crusade. For each person draw on your knowledge to fill in the table below, identifying:

   a) their intentions

   b) the actions they took to achieve these

   c) the consequences of their actions (both intended and unintended)

   d) the extent to which their intentions were achieved.

Key figure	Intentions in 1147	Actions taken	Consequences	How far intention achieved
Manuel I	To ensure the Germans did not capture any land in Hungary. To protect Byzantine land from the French. To ensure the Turks did not launch a reprisal attack on the Byzantine Empire.	The Byzantine army followed the Germans through Hungary. Louis was made to swear an oath of homage and provided guides and supplies. A treaty was made with the Turks at Konya.	The German army clashed with the Byzantines in Hungary. The French and Germans were rushed through the Byzantine Empire, which led to supply problems. The Byzantine guides betrayed Louis and his forces suffered heavy losses.	Short term – the Byzantine Empire was safe from attack. Long term – the Second Crusade was weakened and ultimately failed.
Louis VII				
Conrad III				
Raymond of Antioch				

4 Discuss the following questions with a partner:

   a) Did any one party intend for the Second Crusade to fail?

   b) How important are people's intentions in explaining the failure of the Second Crusade?

SOURCE

7 William of Tyre's explanation of why the siege of Damascus failed. He was a contemporary of the Second Crusade and interviewed participants as part of his research, but was not present at the siege itself. He rose to the position of archbishop of Tyre in 1175 and had been the tutor of Baldwin, son of King Amalric I of Jerusalem. His account reveals the attitude of contemporaries to the leaders of the Second Crusade.

At this crisis [the success of the western attack] ... the Damascenes began to work upon the cupidity of some of our people. By offering inducements, they attempted to capture the hearts of those whose bodily strength they could not hope to overcome. Skilful arguments led certain of our nobles to assume the role of the traitor Judas and induced them, on assurance of receiving a great sum of money already collected, to endeavour to raise the siege...

...Their wicked suggestions persuaded the king and the pilgrim princes, who fully relied upon their loyalty and assiduity, to leave the orchards and move the armies to the opposite side of the city. In order to conceal their guilt under some plausible pretext, they said that on the opposite side of the city which faced south and east there were no protecting orchards and neither river nor moat to hinder the approach to the fortifications...

...Their sole purpose in presenting these arguments was to cause the removal of the army from its present position, for here the city was particularly hard pressed and powerless to hold out, while on the other side the siege could not possibly be long maintained. This specious talk was believed by the kings and all the principal leaders of the united host. The position which had been won with great toil and loss of men was abandoned...

There was some discussion, at a new council, that the crusaders should now attack Ascalon, but nothing happened. On 8 September, Conrad realised the Second Crusade was over and began his journey home via the Byzantine Empire. In the meantime, Louis stayed in Jerusalem until April 1149 to fulfil his vow to spend a year there. When he finally returned home, with a fleet sent by Roger of Sicily, he was attacked by Byzantine forces, which soured their relationship still further. Finally, Prince Raymond of Antioch was killed in June 1149 at the Battle of Inab and the northern crusader states began to buckle. By the end of the 1140s, the king of Jerusalem had arranged to sell off the castles in Edessa and the rest of the county was abandoned for good.

ACTIVITY
KNOWLEDGE CHECK

The failure of the Second Crusade

1 Create a spider diagram called 'The failure of the Second Crusade' and add the following branch titles to it.

- The retreat of the Germans at Dorylaeum
- The rejection of Prince Raymond of Antioch's plan
- The unsuccessful siege of Damascus

2 Annotate each branch with an effect the event had on the course of the Second Crusade and a reason why the event occurred.

3 Look at your reasons why each failure occurred. Then, using the information from your diagram, explain which of the following statements is more accurate:

- 'The Second Crusade failed because of poor leadership.'
- 'The Second Crusade failed because of circumstances beyond the control of Louis VII and Conrad III.'

AS Level Exam-Style Question Section B

To what extent was the leadership of the First and Second Crusades responsible for their different outcomes? (20 marks)

Tip

This is asking you to explain two different outcomes. You must refer to the fact that the First Crusade succeeded whereas the Second Crusade did not.

WHAT EFFECT DID THE LEADERS OF THE THIRD CRUSADE HAVE ON ITS OUTCOME?

Background to the Third Crusade

The years that followed the Second Crusade witnessed the gradual erosion of the crusader states of Outremer. After the Battle of Hattin in 1187, Jerusalem was taken by the Muslim forces of Saladin. Christian control of Outremer had been reduced to the county of Tripoli, a pocket of land surrounding Tyre and the principality of Antioch. In 1189, the crusader states were in a fight for their lives. The king of Jerusalem, Guy, had begun to besiege Acre in August 1189, but made little progress in 2 years. It was in this context that the three most powerful rulers of Europe emerged to attempt to retake Jerusalem by force.

SOURCE

8 A scene from the Luttrell Psalter produced in England in the 14th century. It shows King Richard I knocking Saladin off his horse. The fact that this scene was chosen for the Luttrell Psalter, despite the fact the two never met face to face, illustrates the central role that leaders, and their strong personalities, played in medieval warfare.

The Emperor Frederick Barbarossa of Germany, aged 70, was the oldest and most experienced of the leaders of the Third Crusade. He had taken part in the Second Crusade and had an army of around 15,000 soldiers at his disposal. His initial campaign was followed by the forces of King Richard I of England and King Philip II of France. Richard was the wealthier of the two thanks to his father Henry II's successful collection of the Saladin Tithe. This enabled him to outfit his force much more fully for the English journey. Despite his comparative lack of finance, however, Philip had the largest army, with 2,000 mounted men to Richard's 800. These leaders set in motion the last crusade of the 12th century that could claim to have been a success.

EXTEND YOUR KNOWLEDGE

The Saladin Tithe

The Saladin Tithe was an innovation in the organisation of a crusade. The terms of the tax were agreed by King Henry II of England and King Philip II of France on 22 January 1188. It was imposed on those who had not taken a crusade vow and required the taxpayers to part with a tenth on their **movables**. The collection was successful in England, in spite of heavy opposition, because of the innovations Henry II had made to government administration. However, in France, which did not have the same developed institutions as England, only a small part of the tax was collected and Philip promised never to impose it again.

KEY TERM

Movable

An item of property that is not land or buildings. In the medieval period a tax on movables usually involved animals, monetary assets and supplies.

The significance of the death of Frederick Barbarossa

German participation in the Third Crusade had begun and come to an unsuccessful conclusion before Richard I and Philip II had even arrived at Outremer. On 11 May 1189, Frederick's army marched out of Regensburg towards the Byzantine Empire on its way to Asia Minor. It was about to face many challenges, because in the years since the Second Crusade the Byzantine Greeks had grown much closer to the Turks. For example, the emperor, Isaac Angelus, had come to an agreement with Saladin to delay the German journey. However, it was largely thanks to Frederick that Isaac struggled to fulfil that agreement.

Upon entering the Byzantine Empire it became clear that Frederick's army was not welcome. Isaac, contrary to an agreement he made with Frederick back in September 1188, prevented markets from being set up. This cut off supplies to the Germans, so Frederick took radical action. On 26 August 1189, his troops seized control of Plovdiv and began a military campaign. This resulted in a decisive victory against the Byzantines at Dhidimotikon on 22 November, which enabled the German army to use Adrianople as a rest stop for the winter. Isaac realised on 14 February 1190 that his conflict with Frederick was not worth the effort and returned to the September agreement. Frederick's troops were allowed to cross the Dardanelles in March.

However, the problems did not end there. The march across Asia Minor from Alaşehir towards Konya was a serious challenge for the crusaders and they faced the same problems as their First Crusade counterparts. During the journey they quickly ran out of food and many horses and supplies were lost. It was not until they reached Konya, which was captured from the Turks on 18 May 1190, that they had the opportunity to recover. Unfortunately, once they had resumed their journey and reached the River Göksu on 10 June, Frederick either decided to go for a swim or tried to cross the river on horseback and was swept off his horse. The water was extremely cold and the shock killed him.

Frederick's death had a profound effect on the army. Some of them went home, others sailed to Antioch and Tripoli, and the rest marched overland. Many died during the journey, as disease was rife in Antioch in 1190. Those who finally made it to Acre in early October 1190 were few in number and in weakened condition and their help at the ongoing siege of Acre was minimal. They were further demoralised by the death of Duke Frederick of Swabia on 20 January 1191. The German campaign, for the most part, was over. Emperor Frederick's death had fractured his army, preventing it from turning the tide of the siege.

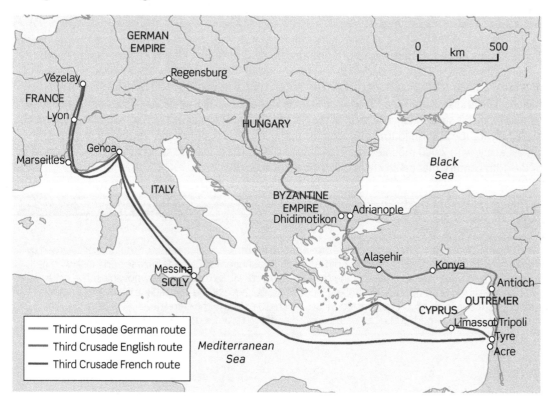

Figure 2.2 A route map of the Third Crusade. It shows the various routes the Third Crusaders took to join the siege of Acre.

SOURCE

9

A description of the effects of the death of Frederick Barbarossa on the soldiers present at the siege of Acre from the *Itinerarium peregrinorum et gesta regis Ricardi*, which was written by Canon Richard de Templo between 1216 and 1222. This excerpt gives a broader view of the effects of Frederick's death.

Climbing up the towers, Turks yelled insults at the besieging Christians outside [Acre]. 'What are you doing, wretches? What more are you hoping for? You were expecting the imminent arrival of your emperor, but he's drowned! Your hope has disappeared and you can do no more to resist, as you see!'

Shouting these insults, they led a dance around the city, blowing trumpets, cawing as is their custom, with drums crashing and declaring the joy of their hearts in as many ways as they could. So they mocked and derided the Christians and aroused confidence and rash joy in their own side.

The Christians were shattered by this news. They were afflicted with incredible grief, almost desperate, mortally wounded by this bitter disaster, because it was true that they had expected to achieve their end with the emperor's help. So they could hardly believe what the Turks had said, but the latter claimed that it was true and that Saladin had told them. For there were not enough Christians to control the entrances to the city or to prevent Turks from going in and out secretly.

The rivalries of Richard I and Philip II

On 30 December 1189, King Richard I of England and King Philip II of France met at Nonancourt. There they both swore an oath to protect the crusaders and that they would work together to achieve this. They met again at Vézelay in July 1190 and agreed to share any spoils of the crusade equally between them. They then set out together on their journey to Outremer. However, beneath the surface of this apparent co-operation was a series of contentious issues that would not only slow the progress of the Third Crusade, but also minimise their chance of recapturing Jerusalem. A timeline of the Third Crusade is provided below, in stages, to illustrate the effects of their rivalry.

Issue 1: the betrothal of Richard and Alice

The first issue that divided the kings of England and France was the tricky matter of Richard's engagement to Philip's sister, Alice. It would be a matter of national embarrassment for Philip if Richard went back on the engagement. However, Richard wanted to marry Berengaria of Navarre in order to form an alliance against his old enemy, Raymond, the Count of Toulouse. He hid this plan from Philip until he knew that he too had taken a crusade vow. This was because he feared it might provoke a war that Richard could not fight if he was in Outremer. When the engagement to Berengaria was made public, Philip eventually released Richard from his commitment for 10,000 marks.

However, the cost to the crusade itself was even more substantial. It had created tension between the leaders, which caused problems during early conflicts. For example, when Richard besieged Messina in order to collect his own sister's **dowry** and fund the crusade, Philip was present but did not help. In fact, the chronicler Ambroise claimed that Philip's men actually defended Messina against Richard's attack. In addition to tension, it also caused delay. Richard was anxious to secure the succession before he went on crusade and therefore had to wait until Philip released him from his engagement to Alice. He then delayed until Berengaria could reach him in Cyprus and they could marry, which they did on 12 May 1191.

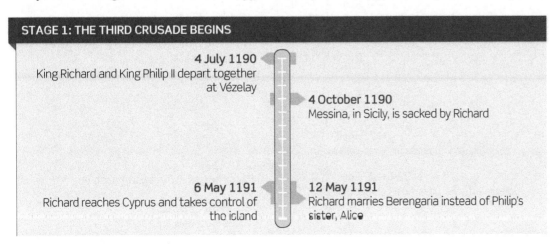

STAGE 1: THE THIRD CRUSADE BEGINS

4 July 1190
King Richard and King Philip II depart together at Vézelay

4 October 1190
Messina, in Sicily, is sacked by Richard

6 May 1191
Richard reaches Cyprus and takes control of the island

12 May 1191
Richard marries Berengaria instead of Philip's sister, Alice

Feudatory
A person that held land from a lord under the feudal system. For example, King Richard also ruled the county of Poitou where Guy's family held its land.

Issue 2: the rival claims to Jerusalem

The relationship between Richard and Philip was further complicated by their connections to the kingdom of Jerusalem. There were two rival claimants to the throne of Jerusalem who were each supported by a different crusade leader:

- Conrad of Montferrat was Philip's cousin and held the garrison at Tyre in Outremer
- Guy of Lusignan was a **feudatory** of Richard in Poitou; Guy led the siege against Acre and held the title of king of Jerusalem in the name of his late wife Sybil, queen of Jerusalem. Sibyl was also Richard's cousin.

The effect of these links to Conrad and Guy were two-fold. First, it increased the strain on the crusaders. For example, when Richard arrived at Tyre on 6 June 1191, Conrad refused to allow him entry. Richard was therefore forced to sail directly to Acre and begin the siege without any respite. Secondly, it caused delay in the attempt to retake Jerusalem, because it took so long to make any decisions. For instance, when Acre surrendered on 12 July 1191, it took until 28 July to decide who the ruler of the kingdom of Jerusalem would be. Guy was chosen, but after his death Conrad was to inherit the title.

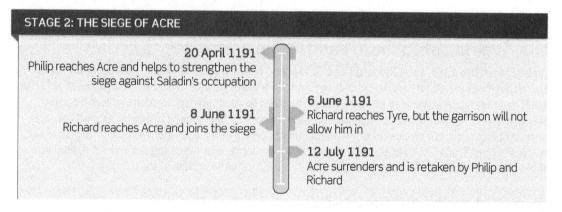

STAGE 2: THE SIEGE OF ACRE

20 April 1191
Philip reaches Acre and helps to strengthen the siege against Saladin's occupation

8 June 1191
Richard reaches Acre and joins the siege

6 June 1191
Richard reaches Tyre, but the garrison will not allow him in

12 July 1191
Acre surrenders and is retaken by Philip and Richard

Issue 3: European politics

Philip returned to France before the Third Crusade was over, which extended the rivalry back into Europe. In April 1192, Richard received news that Philip was threatening the border of his territory in Normandy. He received further news in May 1192 that Philip had been openly conspiring against him with his brother John. This had a profound impact on Richard, who was deeply troubled by a threat to his kingdom that he could do nothing about. It was also one of the reasons why he ultimately chose to withdraw rather than besiege Jerusalem in July 1192.

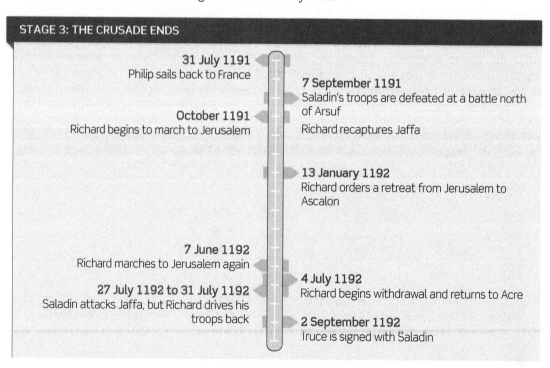

STAGE 3: THE CRUSADE ENDS

31 July 1191
Philip sails back to France

October 1191
Richard begins to march to Jerusalem

7 September 1191
Saladin's troops are defeated at a battle north of Arsuf
Richard recaptures Jaffa

13 January 1192
Richard orders a retreat from Jerusalem to Ascalon

7 June 1192
Richard marches to Jerusalem again

27 July 1192 to 31 July 1192
Saladin attacks Jaffa, but Richard drives his troops back

4 July 1192
Richard begins withdrawal and returns to Acre

2 September 1192
Truce is signed with Saladin

ACTIVITY
KNOWLEDGE CHECK

The troubled leadership

According to the *Itinerarium*, the Turks said: 'Your hope has disappeared and you can do no more to resist.'

1 What effect does this suggest Frederick's death had on the course of the Third Crusade?

2 Do you think his death had a more serious impact than the rivalries of Richard I and Philip II? Explain your answer with reference to the goal of recapturing Jerusalem.

AS Level Exam-Style Question Section B

To what extent did the quality of crusade leadership improve in the years 1147–92? (20 marks)

Tip

This question is asking you to consider both continuity and change. Even though Richard I was a strong leader, some of the weaknesses that troubled the Second Crusade leaders continued.

Richard's decision to attack Sicily and Cyprus

Richard's first stop on the crusade was in the city of Messina in Sicily. He arrived there on 22 September 1190 with the express purpose of collecting his sister's dowry from Count Tancred of Lecce. When Tancred refused to pay, Richard attacked Messina to force his hand. On 4 October, Messina was under Richard's control and Tancred paid up. By the time Richard set sail from Sicily, with an estimated force of 17,000 troops, he had extorted 40,000 gold ounces from Tancred to finance the crusade.

On 10 April 1191, Richard's army left Sicily. Its journey proceeded peacefully until 25 ships went missing. Three of these had run aground on the island of Cyprus and Isaac Comnenus, its independent Greek ruler, had imprisoned their crews. This prompted Richard to invade the island on 6 May. He took the coastal town of Limassol immediately and then began a campaign inland. By 1 June, after the capture of Kyrenia, where Isaac's wife and daughter were hiding, Isaac had surrendered. The island was now at Richard's disposal and he chose to sell it immediately. The Templars bought it for 100,000 bezants.

Richard's leadership at Acre and Philip's return to France

SOURCE 10

A section of a map of Outremer drawn by the medieval chronicler Matthew Paris in the mid 13th century. It is a drawing of Acre's walls (left) and the fortifications at Jerusalem (centre). It shows how important ships were to the survival of this coastal strip of Christian territory and how heavily fortified each city was.

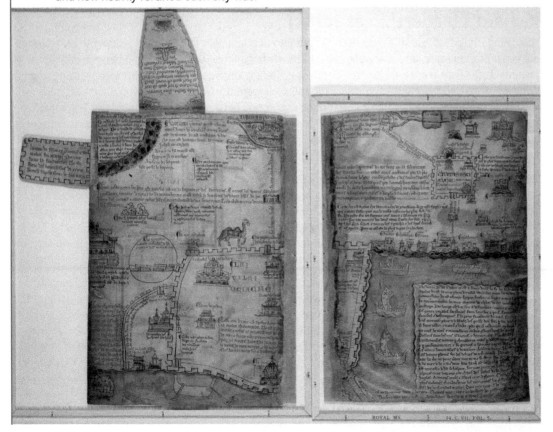

Philip was the first to arrive at Acre on 20 April 1191, while Richard was still busy collecting funds. The arrival of the French king provided vital support for the siege on Acre. It had made very little progress since 1189. However, Philip provided six full supply ships and began to construct siege weapons to attack the walls of the city. He was joined by Richard on 8 June, who travelled with 25 ships from his fleet of 200, and began to construct his own siege weapons. Together their combined forces gradually destroyed the walls of Acre and by 12 July 1191 the Muslim garrison surrendered.

SOURCE

11 A chronicle account of the siege of Acre from the *Itinerarium peregrinorum et gesta regis Ricardi*. The chronicle is full of stories about Richard I and his skilled leadership. This one illustrates the impact of Richard on morale as the siege of Acre entered its third year.

> The king considered the difficulties which they had encountered; how warlike their enemies were, and that courage is needed at critical junctures. He decided that the best way to arouse enthusiasm in the young was to offer a reward rather than force them by commands, because everyone is attracted by the smell of money. So he resolved that a public crier should announce that everyone who took one stone from the wall next to the aforesaid tower would receive two gold coins from the king. Later he promised three gold coins, finally four: so that for each stone that anyone took from the wall they received four gold coins in payment.
>
> You would have seen youths leap forward, and men-at-arms of great valour rush to the wall and eagerly keep on pulling out stones, as greedy for glory as for gain. Even among the darts of their adversaries they boldly pressed on with the destruction of the wall. A great many of them were wounded and had to abandon the work...However, men of valorous spirit overcame the danger and took a great many stones from the body of the wall.

The surrender provided a genuine morale boost for the crusaders. However, it also caused the campaign to falter. Progress was delayed due to a month-long argument over who would be king of Jerusalem. It was eventually decided that Guy Lusignan would be king for life. After that Conrad of Montferrat would inherit the kingdom. Once this was resolved King Philip decided to return to France, because Philip of Flanders had been killed at the Acre campaign, which left his land in the Vermandois vulnerable to French expansion. Philip journeyed home on 31 July to claim his land and left the Duke of Burgundy in charge of the French forces that remained. The crusade had lost another leader, but at least it now had one clear commander: King Richard I of England.

Richard's leadership at Jaffa

After King Philip had left for home, Richard put into action a plan to take back all the territory along the coast of Outremer. On 22 August 1191, his army began the 70-mile march down the coastline towards Jaffa. They were a huge force and were carefully organised. The knights were separated into three divisions and marched in columns. On their left were the infantry, who would fight off raids and surprise attacks from the Turks. On their right, cushioned between the knights and the sea, marched the baggage train. This meant the baggage train was protected and the knights, except those at the back, were not troubled greatly by Turks. The result of this careful and well-ordered journey was that the crusaders arrived safely at Jaffa.

Richard's leadership was the key reason why this journey succeeded. He had planned the march formation and monitored it closely. He also made preparations to ensure it held firm. For example, he allowed the infantry who were exposed to the Turks to alternate with those marching alongside the baggage train. This gave them rest and helped sustain morale. The king also ensured that if the formation was broken, it would quickly be reformed. For instance, on the first day when the rearguard fell behind and was attacked by Turks, Richard rushed to help them and the enemy were repelled.

His other contribution was at the Battle of Arsuf, which occurred on 7 September when Saladin's troops attacked the marchers. Richard showed strong leadership at this battle because he acted quickly to ensure success. At the start the Turks had tried to force the Franks into action by constant attacks on the Hospitallers in the rearguard. Richard had ordered them to wait until the army were ready for a general attack, but they could not and charged too early. Richard reacted immediately and launched a full-scale attack to support them. He was then able to stop the attack when it had made progress and reform the army before a counter-attack was launched. Saladin's troops gave up and Jaffa was theirs for the taking.

Reasons for Richard's decision not to attack Jerusalem

The first march to Jerusalem

SOURCE

12 A letter written by King Richard I at Jaffa on 1 October 1191 to the Abbot of Clairvaux, Garnier of Rochefort. This was written before Richard set off for Jerusalem and reveals the king's state of mind prior to his decision to abandon the march.

Because the inheritance of the Lord is already partly recovered, and because to further its recovery we constantly endure the heat of day and have already exhausted all our money – and not only our money but both our strength and our body also – we have to tell your fraternity that we can in no way remain in Syria beyond next Easter. The duke of Burgundy, with the French under his command, and Count Henry with all his men ... have spent all their wealth in the service of God and will return to their own lands unless by the ingenuity of your preaching thoughtful provision may be made for people to populate and defend the land and for more money to be spent in God's service.

So, throwing ourselves at your holiness's feet with profuse tears, we offer up our affectionate prayers, asking ever more earnestly that you ... will make every effort to induce princes and nobles ... throughout the Christian world to share in the service of the living God. Call upon them that from next Easter they will uphold and defend the Lord's inheritance which we, with God's favour, will by then have fully obtained.

The Third Crusade's goal was to recapture Jerusalem and in late October 1191 Richard's army began a slow advance to the city. It took its time because Richard wanted to secure castles as it went in order to maintain a supply line. The army reached Beit Nuba, 12 miles from Jerusalem, on 3 January 1192 and then stopped. On 13 January, it turned around and headed back to the abandoned city of Ascalon to refortify it. The chief reason for this change of heart was the advice Richard received at an army council on 6 January. The Templars and Hospitallers, who had local knowledge, said that the army could not win. It might take the city, but Saladin's forces would take it back. The crusaders therefore had to deal with Saladin first.

The second march to Jerusalem

There was no further action, other than the refortification of Ascalon, until May 1192. This was because the crusaders were divided over the issue of who would rule the kingdom, which had reappeared in February 1192. After the siege of Acre, Guy had been made king of Jerusalem, but Conrad had the combined support of the French and the local lords (see page 56). His supporters decided to take action and tried to seize control of Acre for Conrad in February. This internal dispute threatened to plunge the kingdom into civil war.

In order to avoid this, the barons of Jerusalem and the French crusaders, in spite of Richard I's wishes, pressured him to revise the agreement of 28 July 1191 and replace Guy with Conrad. Richard accepted this and gave Guy Cyprus to rule instead, but Conrad still refused to help the crusaders. It was not until his assassination on 28 April 1192 and his replacement by Count Henry of Champagne, who both Richard and Philip were related to, that the crusade could continue. The effect of this dispute had been both to cause delay and to weaken Richard's resolve to fight for the kingdom.

The joint English and French forces set out to Darun in May 1192. Their plan was to take the coastal town, which would extend the coastline of Outremer and block Saladin's communication link with Egypt. This was achieved on 22 May. The crusaders then resumed the journey to Jerusalem and reached Beit Nuba on 7 June. Here they began a long wait for Henry of Champagne's forces to arrive and bolster their numbers. It was during this wait that the crusade finally disintegrated.

In mid-June, a committee of 20 gathered to agree the next stage in the crusader's campaign. It recommended, with the full support of Richard, that the combined forces launch an Egyptian campaign and strike at the heart of Saladin's territory. However, despite the merits of this plan, the French refused. They even threatened to begin an attack on Jerusalem without English support. Richard was anxious, especially after he received news about the troublesome situation back in England. He also knew that they could not hold Jerusalem and, in an atmosphere of disunity, recommended withdrawal. This began on 4 July 1192.

THINKING HISTORICALLY Cause and consequence (3a&b)

The might of human agency

1 'Our lack of control'. Work in pairs.

Describe to your partner a situation where things did not work out as you had intended. Then explain how you would have done things differently to make the situation as you would have wanted. Your partner will then tell the group about that situation and whether they think that your alternative actions would have the desired effect.

2 'The Tyranny of failed actions'. Work individually.

Richard I set out on the Third Crusade with the intention to recapture Jerusalem. He failed to achieve this goal.

    a) Write down three ways in which Richard I could have acted differently.

    b) Now imagine that you are Richard I. Write a defence of your actions. Try to think about the things that you would have known about at the time and make sure that you do not use the benefit of hindsight.

3 'Arguments'. Work in groups of between four and six.

In turn, each group member will read out their defence as Richard I. Other group members suggest ways to reassure the reader that they were not a failure and that in some ways what happened was a good outcome.

4 Think about Baldwin of Boulogne and the conquest of Edessa.

Baldwin of Boulogne had abandoned the First Crusade to secure land for himself. He replaced his brother as king of Jerusalem in 1100.

    a) In what ways were the consequences of the conquest of Edessa not anticipated by Baldwin of Boulogne?

    b) In what ways did the conquest of Edessa turn out better for Baldwin of Boulogne than his intended consequences?

5 Think about Conrad III and the plan to travel to Antioch during the Second Crusade.

Conrad III began his journey from the Byzantine Empire to Antioch in order to recapture Edessa in October 1148. He retreated after an ambush near Dorylaeum. Answer the following questions:

    a) In what ways were the consequences of the planned journey not anticipated by Conrad III?

    b) In what ways did the planned journey turn out worse for Conrad III than his intended consequences?

6 To what extent are historical individuals in control of the history they help to create? Explain your answer with reference to specific historical examples from this topic and others you have studied.

The final battle: Jaffa

Before the Third Crusade came to an end, there was one last twist in the story. Once Saladin heard that the crusaders had begun to withdraw from Jerusalem, he decided to attack Jaffa before Richard's forces made it back. Saladin's siege began on 27 July 1192 and Jaffa surrendered on 30 July, although its **citadel** still held out. However, Richard arrived before Saladin could secure control and, according to the chronicler Ambroise, heroically jumped from his ship into the water and launched a counter-attack. Jaffa was retaken and secured by 5 August. Saladin could have cut Outremer's coastal strip in half, but he had been stopped just in time.

By September 1192, Richard was ill and anxious to return to England. He sought a truce with Saladin and the following terms were agreed.

- The Christians would retain control of the territory from Tyre down the coast to Jaffa.

- The Christians would relinquish control of Ascalon to Saladin.

- Saladin would allow Christian pilgrims access to Jerusalem to visit its holy shrines.

With the coast secure and the truce signed, Richard set sail from Acre on 9 October 1192. The Third Crusade had not recaptured Jerusalem, but it had regained Christian control of the coast.

KEY TERM

Citadel
A fortified castle built within medieval cities to protect and control them.

ACTIVITY
KNOWLEDGE CHECK

The Third Crusade in Outremer

Use the information in this chapter to explain whether the Third Crusade was a success or a failure. Try to explain your answer thoroughly by referring to different individuals or groups.

ACTIVITY
SUMMARY

The leadership of the Crusades

1 Choose three ways to assess the significance of a crusade leader on the course of a crusade from the following list:

- How successful were they in battle?
- How committed were they to the stated goal of their crusade?
- How much land did they capture?
- How effectively did they work with other leaders?
- How much support did they have?
- How responsive were they to changing circumstances?
- How far did they speed up or slow down the course of their crusade?
- How well did they prepare for their crusade?

2 Create a table with four columns, one headed 'Leader' and the rest headed by the three criteria you selected in 1. Then list the following leaders down the left-hand side of your table:

- Bohemond of Taranto
- Godfrey of Bouillon
- Conrad III
- Louis IV
- Frederick Barbarossa
- Richard I
- Philip II

3 Use the material in this chapter to assess each of the leaders against your chosen criteria.

4 Explain who you think had the most significant impact on the success of a crusade.

5 Explain who you think had the most significant impact on the failure of a crusade.

WIDER READING

Asbridge, T. *The First Crusade: A New History – The Roots of Conflict Between Christianity and Islam*, Oxford University Press (2004)

Madden, T. *The New Concise History of the Crusades*, Rowman & Littlefield (2005)

Nicolle, D. *The Third Crusade 1191: Richard the Lionheart, Saladin and the struggle for Jerusalem*, Osprey Publishing (2005)

Phillips, J. *The Second Crusade: Extending the Frontiers of Christendom*, Yale University Press (2010)

A Level Exam-Style Question Section B

How far do you agree that the Third Crusade in the years 1189–92 was more effectively organised than the First Crusade in the years 1095–99? (20 marks)

Tip
This question is asking you to reach a judgement on the extent to which each crusade was organised, rather than which was more successful. It is important to move beyond the fact that the First Crusade achieved a lot more than the Third Crusade.

1.3 The crusader states of Outremer, 1100–92

- What effect did the geography and economy of Outremer have on the history of the crusader states?
- How did the defence of Outremer change over time?
- How effective was the government of Outremer?

INTRODUCTION

William of Tyre, a chronicler of events in Outremer, told a story of a young king who was once in his care. This boy had deeply impressed William because of both his intellect and his character. One day William watched him play a game with a group of other boys. The game became violent and the boys pinched and dug their nails into each other's arms. Most of them screamed and cried with pain, but not the young king in William's care. He endured it all without complaint. It was clear to William that he would one day make a great ruler.

Tragically, the opposite was the case. Reports kept arriving of the boy's inability to feel pain and it became apparent that he had no feeling at all in his right arm and hand. The royal physicians took immediate action, rubbed oils and even poisons into the boy's arm, but they had no effect. His father and William now had to face the truth that the boy, soon to be King Baldwin IV, had begun to show signs of leprosy, a then incurable disease that would cause a fracture so deep in the politics of Outremer that the door was open for a Muslim invasion.

This chapter will explore a world in which Frankish settlers lived out their entire lives in a conquered landscape, a world that one day would be shattered by the events that followed Baldwin IV's diagnosis. It will examine the different states the Franks established and how they utilised the landscape and their position in the eastern world to sustain them. It will look at how this group, whose everyday lives were dominated by the need for protection, looked to their rulers, then military orders and even former allies to provide this. Finally, it will chart the course of a government at first led by strong and effective rulers that over time became divided and weak.

WHAT EFFECT DID THE GEOGRAPHY AND ECONOMY OF OUTREMER HAVE ON THE HISTORY OF THE CRUSADER STATES?

Outremer was divided into four separate crusader states: Edessa, Antioch, Tripoli and Jerusalem. The first three were subordinate to a greater or lesser extent to the authority of the kings of the fourth (see Figure 1.2, page 28).

November 1100 – Baldwin, Count of Edessa, is crowned King Baldwin I of Jerusalem

1115 – A castle called Montreal is built to increase control over the kingdom of Jerusalem; it is later able to hold out against attack for a year and a half

April 1131 – Queen Melisende and King Fulk become the rulers of Jerusalem

1095	1100	1105	1110	1115	1120	1125	1130	1135	1140

1101 – The consolidation of Outremer's territories begins with the acquisition of Arsuf and Caesarea

1119 – The Templar movement begins under the leadership of Hugh of Payns

1136 – The Hospitaller movement becomes militarised and is given the Castle of Beitgibelin

A summary of the crusader states

State	Government system	Communities	Chief economic activities
Edessa	County	A small number of Frankish settlers and a large Armenian population.	Agricultural: grain crops around the River Euphrates. Animals reared on the highlands and in the forest.
Antioch	Principality	Diverse ethnic groups: Franks, **eastern Christians** and Muslim Arabs.	Chiefly agricultural but had an important port at St Simeon.
Tripoli	County	Diverse ethnic groups: Franks, eastern Christians and Muslim Arabs.	Agricultural and industrial: sugar cane production and olive cultivation. Large weaving community in Tripoli. Two important ports at Tortosa and Tripoli used by traders from Homs and Damascus.
Jerusalem	Kingdom	Diverse ethnic groups: Franks, eastern Christians, Jews, Samaritans, Druzes, Arab Muslims, Bedouins.	Agricultural: variety of crops including olives, wheat and citrus fruit. Very reliant on trading cities of Acre and Tyre for sugar and spice trades.

KEY TERMS

Principality
An area of land ruled by a prince. Antioch was the only principality in Outremer and its rulers claimed they were independent of Jerusalem, even though in practice they were not.

Eastern Christian
A general term used to describe a member of the Greek Orthodox Church, also known as Melkites, the indigenous Syrian Orthodox Church, also known as Jacobites, and the Armenian Orthodox Church.

Edessa

The state of Edessa, located to the north-east of Antioch, was the first county to become a part of Outremer and the first to be abandoned. Its earliest Frankish ruler was Count Baldwin I, who acquired the county through his capture of prominent fortresses like Turbessel. He so impressed the Edessans, who lived in fear of Muslim conquest, that he was welcomed as their ruler in March 1098. In his new role, he took on a county with a largely Armenian population, most of which either farmed on the fertile areas around the Euphrates River or kept horses, sheep and cattle on Edessa's dry, high plateaux. Armenians also dominated the upper echelons of society and, in the early days, most of the nobility remained the same.

This consistency, which Baldwin was careful to insure, was a result of political necessity. Edessa was a county under threat of invasion from the Turks, a threat which only increased as Zengi began to consolidate Muslim territory from 1127 (see pages 97–98). This shaped its history and it was the reason that, when Baldwin I became king of Jerusalem, his successor, Count Baldwin II, was happy to pay homage to him. Baldwin and his successors needed practical assistance, which is illustrated by three key moments in the county's short history.

- The Battle of Harran in 1104: Baldwin II, then Count of Edessa, was captured and during this time a **regent** was needed. Tancred de Hauteville, regent of Antioch and nephew to Bohemond of Taranto, took on this role, but was not willing to relinquish it. Baldwin I of Jerusalem had to use force to remove him.

- Control of Antioch: the principality of Antioch was Edessa's nearest Frankish neighbour. When Antioch was without a leader, Joscelin I, the Count of Edessa from 1119, joined forces with Baldwin II, who had then become king of Jerusalem. They worked together, as regents, to repel the Turkish threat.

- The increased pressure from Zengi: Joscelin II faced an increased threat from the Turkish ruler Zengi when the Byzantine emperor, who had halted Zengi's attacks, died in 1143. At this moment the county's future hung in the balance and would be decided by the support it received from Jerusalem.

KEY TERM

Regent
A person, usually of noble birth, who rules on behalf of a minor or an absent ruler. In Outremer the regent was selected by either the king of Jerusalem or the absent ruler.

1152 - Baldwin III forces his mother, Melisende, out of power

July 1174 - Baldwin IV, a leper, is crowned king, but Raymond of Tripoli acts as regent on his behalf

1186 - Sibyl is crowned queen and she crowns her husband, Guy, as king; this is at the height of an ongoing dispute over the succession

| 1145 | 1150 | 1155 | 1160 | 1165 | 1170 | 1175 | 1180 | 1185 | 1190 |

1153 - The last important port of Jerusalem, Ascalon, is captured by the Franks with the help of pilgrims from Europe

1180 - A new Byzantine emperor, Andronicus I, is replaced by Manuel Comnenus and turns the empire against the crusader states

May 1187 - Saladin uses his truce with Raymond of Tripoli to begin a campaign to attack Acre; the campaign ends with the Franks' defeat at Hattin in July

Battle of Harran, 1104

The battle that took place at Harran on 7–8 May 1104 played a significant role in halting the crusader advance into northern Syria. It was an early example of a combined Muslim force restricting the expansion of the crusader states. Count Baldwin II of Edessa had been pursuing an aggressive policy to extend the county southwards towards Aleppo. However, the Seljuk rulers of Mosul and Ardin, who had been rivals, joined forces to attack Baldwin after he attempted to take Harran. Baldwin sought help from Joscelin I of Courtenay, as well as from Bohemond and Tancred in Antioch. They came to his aid, but were resoundingly defeated and Baldwin and Joscelin were captured at Harran. Ridwan of Aleppo, another Muslim emir, took advantage of their setback and reacquired Artah from Antioch, as well as other border fortresses in the area. The Byzantine Empire also seized the opportunity to retake some of its former possessions, such as Latakia. Tancred won much of this territory back in the years that followed and managed to diminish the threat from Ridwan. Nevertheless, the Battle of Harran demonstrated that, if necessary, the Turks could contain the crusader states.

Joscelin I of Courtenay (d.1131)

Joscelin is a good example of an ambitious ruler of a crusader state. He was cousin to Count Baldwin II of Edessa who made him Lord of Turbessel. This was a very prosperous and well-defended area. However, he was expelled by Baldwin II who wanted the land back when he fell on hard times. This gave Joscelin's career a boost because the king, Baldwin I, made him Lord of Tiberias. On Baldwin II's accession to the throne of Jerusalem, Joscelin returned to favour and was made Count of Edessa in 1119. In this role he showed himself to be an active ruler. He attacked Aleppo and established extensive, but not complete, control of the area surrounding it. He also helped to defend Antioch when its regent, King Baldwin II, was imprisoned in April 1123. However, once he had tasted power he did not want to give it up. In 1126, when the new Prince of Antioch, Bohemond II, arrived to take control, Joscelin attacked Antioch in order to establish his own control over the principality. The king had to step in and force Joscelin to back down, but once again had to rely on his support in Antioch when Bohemond died in 1130. Joscelin died shortly afterwards when a tower fell on him during a siege in 1131.

Unfortunately the death of King Fulk of Jerusalem in 1143, and the subsequent tensions between Queen Melisende and her son Baldwin III, provided an opportunity for Zengi to attack Edessa while prompt and full military support from Jerusalem for its **vassal state** was unlikely. This led to the capture of the city of Edessa in the same year. By 1150, after the failure of the Second Crusade to reverse the situation, all hope for the county was lost. On the advice of King Baldwin III of Jerusalem, Beatrice, wife of the Count of Edessa, sold the county to the Byzantine Empire.

Vassal state

An area of land, for example a county, that is held from a king in return for military service and allegiance. In the kingdom of Jerusalem, Edessa and Tripoli were vassal states.

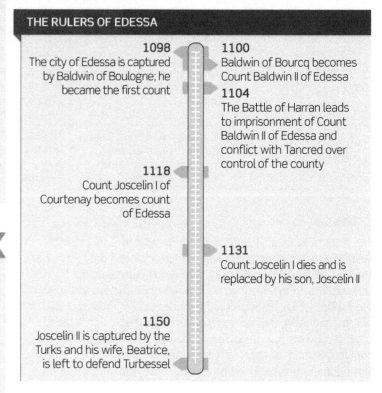

1098
The city of Edessa is captured by Baldwin of Boulogne; he became the first count

1100
Baldwin of Bourcq becomes Count Baldwin II of Edessa

1104
The Battle of Harran leads to imprisonment of Count Baldwin II of Edessa and conflict with Tancred over control of the county

1118
Count Joscelin I of Courtenay becomes count of Edessa

1131
Count Joscelin I dies and is replaced by his son, Joscelin II

1150
Joscelin II is captured by the Turks and his wife, Beatrice, is left to defend Turbessel

Antioch

The principality of Antioch was an important barrier for Outremer against Byzantine influence and invasion. It was acquired by Bohemond of Taranto after a lengthy struggle and he remained there in January 1099 when the other crusaders marched south to Jerusalem. Bohemond was now prince of a large territory wedged between the County of Edessa and the sea (see Figure 1.2, page 28). It was split up into provinces, which were ruled by lords who owed **feudal** allegiance to the prince. In contrast to Edessa, the princes of Antioch did not hold their title from the king of Jerusalem. This gave them a considerable measure of freedom to organise their government and the distribution of land. However, their freedom was limited by the severity of the threats they faced. The first came from the Byzantines in the north, who claimed overlordship of the principality, and the second from the Turks on its south-eastern frontier, who tried to recapture it.

Feudal

A system whereby a vassal owed obligations to his lord in return for land or the right to collect a tax. In Outremer these obligations were usually in the form of military service.

Antioch was therefore under immense pressure and, despite its claims to independence, had to accept the authority of the king of Jerusalem in order to survive. In fact, between 1110 and 1137, the kings of Jerusalem helped out Antioch on at least 15 separate occasions. The first problem was that the principality needed a clear ruler otherwise it would disintegrate in the face of military threats. Two examples of Jerusalem's intervention are related to regency and succession.

- Regency: Prince Bohemond I had been absent from Antioch since 1100 due to his capture, attempt to restart the crusade and subsequent embarrassment at its failure. He died in the West in 1111 and was succeeded by his infant son, Bohemond II. By 1119, both the regents from Antioch's nobility were dead. King Baldwin II of Jerusalem therefore filled the gap until Bohemond II was ready to rule in 1126.

- **Succession**: in February 1130, Bohemond II was killed and his widow, Alice, wanted to rule on her own. However, King Fulk of Jerusalem, fearful that a female ruler would not be able to defend Antioch, intervened. He arranged for Alice's daughter, Constance, to be married to Raymond of Poitiers in 1136, making Raymond prince of Antioch.

KEY TERM

Succession
A system by which a deceased ruler was replaced. In Outremer the next ruler was usually the eldest son or closest male relative.

The second problem, which forced Antioch to submit to the primacy of Jerusalem, was the level of threat it faced. The Byzantine Empire had wanted to reclaim Antioch ever since its loss in 1084, and the earliest years of its Frankish history were therefore marked by conflict over strategically important areas like Tarsus and Latakia. The princes needed help from King Baldwin I to reclaim their frontier towns and protect their border. This was offered on numerous occasions throughout the 1100s. For instance, in the early conflict, troops and supplies were sent to Antioch in 1110, 1111 and 1115. This helped to sustain the Frankish influence in the north.

However, it was not always possible for Jerusalem to send help because of the Turkish threat elsewhere. This meant that the princes of Antioch had to use other means to maintain control. For example, in 1137, 1145 and 1159 they paid homage to the Byzantine emperor in order to gain military support against the Turks. Unfortunately, by the end of the 12th century, this support had also waned (see pages 79–82). As a result, Saladin was able to capture Latakia in 1188, which meant Antioch was now physically separated from its Frankish neighbours. In spite of this, after the Third Crusade, Antioch was included in the truce Richard III negotiated with Saladin. Its dependence and relationship with the kingdom of Jerusalem, unlike Edessa, survived the 12th century.

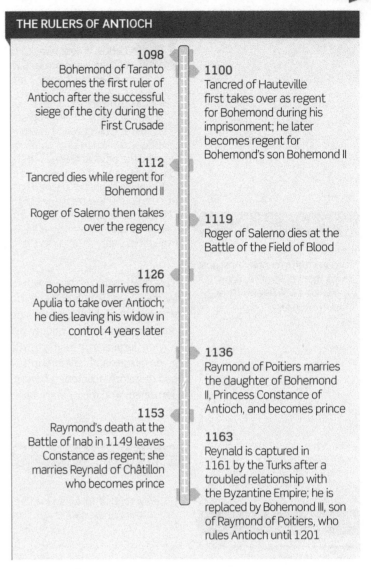

THE RULERS OF ANTIOCH

1098
Bohemond of Taranto becomes the first ruler of Antioch after the successful siege of the city during the First Crusade

1100
Tancred of Hauteville first takes over as regent for Bohemond during his imprisonment; he later becomes regent for Bohemond's son Bohemond II

1112
Tancred dies while regent for Bohemond II

Roger of Salerno then takes over the regency

1119
Roger of Salerno dies at the Battle of the Field of Blood

1126
Bohemond II arrives from Apulia to take over Antioch; he dies leaving his widow in control 4 years later

1136
Raymond of Poitiers marries the daughter of Bohemond II, Princess Constance of Antioch, and becomes prince

1153
Raymond's death at the Battle of Inab in 1149 leaves Constance as regent; she marries Reynald of Châtillon who becomes prince

1163
Reynald is captured in 1161 by the Turks after a troubled relationship with the Byzantine Empire; he is replaced by Bohemond III, son of Raymond of Poitiers, who rules Antioch until 1201

Tripoli

The last state to join Outremer was the County of Tripoli, which was established principally through the efforts of Raymond of Toulouse. After the crusade of 1101, Tortosa was the first area of what would become the County of Tripoli to be captured. Then Raymond's forces captured Gibelet in 1104 and established a siege camp 3 miles north of the city of Tripoli. This city, which formed the centrepiece of the county, was taken in 1109, shortly after Raymond's death, and the county continued to expand until the late 1120s. At its greatest extent, the county that Raymond's successors controlled included not only Provençal and Languedocian settlers and nobles but also communities of Greek Orthodox Christians, other eastern Christians and pockets of Muslim settlement.

In contrast to Antioch and Edessa, the County of Tripoli, despite its position as a vassal state of Jerusalem, tried to maintain a large measure of independence. For example, during the succession crisis of 1109, King Baldwin I negotiated a settlement and divided the county between William Jordan, count of Cerdagne, and Bertrand, son of Raymond of Toulouse. However, upon William's death, Bertrand ignored the terms of the settlement and took control of Tripoli with the support of his son, Pons, who succeeded him in 1112. The county was still a vassal state of Jerusalem, but it was not prepared to bow to Jerusalem's every wish.

SOURCE 1

An account from William of Tyre's *History of Deeds Done Beyond the Sea*, written in the early 1180s. It describes Count Pons of Tripoli's resistance to the authority of King Fulk in 1131. William was born to a French family that had settled in Syria and at the height of his career was archbishop of Tyre.

Mindful of the affront offered him [Fulk] on his journey when Pons refused to allow him to pass through the land of Tripoli, the king agreed to their [people of Antioch's] request. He mustered as large a force as possible and proceeded towards his adversary. The forces met near Rugia. Both sides were drawn up in battle array, and a fierce combat ensued. For a long time the result was doubtful. Finally, however, the king gained the advantage and put the count and his men to flight. Many of the latter's soldiers, exhausted by the fight, were captured and led in chains to Antioch. Eventually, however, through the earnest efforts of loyal advocates of peace, the king and the count were reconciled. The captured knights were restored to the count, and the affairs of the land of Antioch seemed to have been put into better condition. Nevertheless, the wiser men of the province feared that after the king returned to his own land the country might be shaken by internal sedition, which would afford the **infidels** a better chance to attack. They therefore earnestly implored him to remain longer among them. To this the king graciously consented…

KEY TERM

Infidel
A generic term for non-Christians. It was most commonly used by crusaders to refer to their Muslim enemies.

This relationship changed when, as with both Edessa and Antioch, the Turkish threat began to increase and Tripoli became more reliant on Jerusalem. For example, Raymond III, count of Tripoli, was imprisoned in Damascus between 1164 and 1172 by the Turks. In his place, King Amalric became regent of the county until the ransom of 80,000 bezants could be paid. Tripoli also came to rely on Jerusalem's military orders to defend its key possessions. For example, the Hospitallers were given castles and territory in 1144 and 1177, and the Templars in 1167 (see pages 75–77). Tripoli had therefore developed from a large measure of independence into yet another territory the kings of Jerusalem and the military orders within it had to sustain.

KEY TERM

Master
The title for the leader of a military order.

THE RULERS OF TRIPOLI

1102
Raymond of Toulouse establishes the county through his capture of Tortosa in 1101; he becomes its **Master** in 1102

1109
Bertrand, Raymond's eldest son, becomes the ruler of Tripoli despite a dispute with his cousin, William Jordan

1112
Pons, son of Bertrand, becomes count; he gains Tancred's support to unify the county

1137
Pons is killed in Damascus and Raymond II becomes count

1152
Raymond II is murdered and Raymond III takes over; he rules until 1187, but between 1164 and 1172 Amalric is regent due to Raymond's imprisonment

1148
Raymond II uses support from Nur ad-Din to stop a rival claimant, Bertram, the grandson of Raymond of Toulouse, from taking control

The primacy of Jerusalem

Jerusalem, the primary target of the First Crusade, was to become the heart of the Frankish states of Outremer. However, when Godfrey died on 18 July 1100 and Count Baldwin became king on Christmas Day, he inherited a fragmented collection of territories that could hardly be called a kingdom. This included the city of Jerusalem and its surrounding area of southern Judea, a coastal strip around Jaffa and a territory around Galilee. It was also an extremely mixed community, which included separate villages populated by Muslims, eastern Christians and Jews, as well as nomadic Bedouins. The Franks, under Godfrey and then Baldwin, joined this diverse population from 1099 onwards, but only as a ruling minority, supported by urban and rural settlers, not as a replacement.

Over the 12th century, the kings of Jerusalem became the primary power in Outremer. However, this was a power built on dependence. In order to achieve control throughout the kingdom of Jerusalem, it was divided into palatinates. These were areas ruled by lords who, despite being royal vassals, could act without royal assent to defend their territory. For example, Count Garner of Grez, who had appealed for Baldwin to become king, was given control of an area around Nablus in the north of the kingdom. The kingdom of Jerusalem therefore relied on a system of **marcher lords** who, in return for power, protected the border regions and provided military service when called upon by the king.

However, the level of power given to the lords of Jerusalem was also a threat to the king's power. For instance, by 1175, ten families controlled 24 of the most important lordships in Jerusalem. This meant they had enough control to overpower the king. The king tried to limit this by keeping some of the most powerful areas, or **fiefs**, for the **royal demesne**, such as Jerusalem and Acre. He also confiscated fiefs if a vassal rebelled, such as Hugh of Le Puiset in 1132. This skilled application of feudalism, which worked as long as the kingdom remained under stable leadership, helped to maintain control. It was the same principle that led to Jerusalem's primacy amongst the states of Outremer.

Religious reasons for the primacy of Jerusalem

The religious importance of Jerusalem to Christians also helped to ensure that the kingdom of Jerusalem became the most important crusader state. The main reasons for its importance were the following.

- It was home to an array of holy sites and relics, such as the Church of the Nativity at Bethlehem and the relic of the True Cross. This meant it was the main destination for pilgrims.

- Many new religious foundations in the other crusader states were attached to churches in Jerusalem, such as the Church of the Holy Sepulchre.

- It had the most powerful **patriarchate**. There were patriarchs in both Jerusalem and Antioch, but in 1111 substantial parts of Antioch's patriarchate were given to Jerusalem by Pope Paschal II.

ACTIVITY
KNOWLEDGE CHECK

The crusader states

1 Bullet point one unique feature for each crusader state (Edessa, Antioch, Tripoli and Jerusalem).

2 Explain how each unique feature you have identified made the crusader state different from the other crusader states.

3 Why, in view of their differences, do you think Jerusalem's primacy emerged over all of them? Try to give two reasons in your answer.

The absence of natural boundaries to the east

Outremer had some natural boundaries, which included the Taurus mountain range in the north and the Lebanese mountains to the east. It also had rivers like the Jordan, which protected the kingdom of Jerusalem before its expansion. However, these boundaries were inadequate because there were huge gaps with large plains between the mountains and the rivers were easily crossed at shallow fords. The only other possibility for a boundary was desert, which is why the Franks tried to extend control over Aleppo and Damascus. Their lack of success in these cities meant that even the possibility of the desert as a natural boundary to the east was never realised.

This had a profound effect on the geography of the crusader states, because it meant they had no fixed political boundary lines that could be drawn on a map. Instead, it is better to view Outremer as a collection of Frankish centres of power. For example, the population of Edessa was heavily reliant on fortified towns, like Turbessel, to protect it. The closer the inhabitants were to the fortified town, the more secure they were from attack. This explains why, instead of a long border of castles along the eastern edge of Outremer, many are located deep within the states themselves. It was not a modern, clearly defined kingdom; rather it was a fragmented collection of lordships, each centred on some form of fortification.

The geographical situation had a number of effects on the history, organisation and development of the Frankish states, as follows.

- Edessa: the county was vulnerable to attack from Mosul to its east and Aleppo to its south. This is why it was one of the first states to fall to Muslim control.

- Antioch: the principality was incredibly reliant on help from the kingdom of Jerusalem, and later the Byzantine Empire, to fend off attacks from the Turks.

- Tripoli: it was vulnerable to the **Assassins** who populated the Nosairi Mountains and the Muslim inhabitants of Homs to the east. This is why Raymond II granted so much territory to the Hospitallers.

- Jerusalem: its distribution into separate fiefs, each held by a Frankish noble, was carefully organised to ensure the kingdom was well protected.

The importance of the seaports

Economic links

The principal seaports of Outremer were Acre, captured in 1104, and Tyre, which capitulated in 1124. They were a lifeline for the crusader states because they created a relatively secure and speedy route for goods and people to arrive. This was in stark contrast to the long and arduous land journey the First and Second Crusaders embarked upon. The new route made possible a number of opportunities to boost the Levantine economy, which could not have been achieved on foot or horseback.

First, the seaports helped Outremer to become a part of a large, pre-existing trade network, which linked the West, Byzantium and Egypt together. The ports provided an outlet for exports, such as sugar and spices, and a means to import goods, such as cotton, metals and certain foods that were not available in the crusader states.

Secondly, they ensured a connection to the thriving world of Italian commerce, which had already begun to prosper in the lead up to the First Crusade (see page 12). The Italians were in search of new ways to bolster their economic power and therefore established lucrative trading communities in key seaports. For example, Acre had a Genoese quarter that formed an entirely separate community, with different rights, privileges and judicial processes. These communities were usually established as part of a deal, whereby an Italian **Commune** was formed in territory granted to it in return for military support. The siege of Tyre (1124), to take one example, was supported by a Venetian fleet, which received rights to one-third of the city as well as certain privileges in payment for its service.

The benefits of Outremer's seaport links were considerable. They provided revenues for settlers, service industries and local lords. Profits from trading were generated from a number of sources, which included:

- the cost of reaching the east by ship

- the fees payable at the harbour, which included mooring at the outer harbour and access to the inner harbour

- the wage paid to have goods transferred from the ship to the shore

- the tax paid to the port official, set somewhere between 4 and 25 percent, for the import of goods

- the rent paid on the storage of goods

- the tax, which the purchaser paid, to take the goods out of the city.

Another source of income, especially for Acre, was the service industry provided for the influx of pilgrims on their way to Jerusalem. They needed food, rest and guidance before they could continue their journey. The seaports therefore helped Outremer to stand side by side with prosperous ports like Alexandria and begin to share in their wealth.

KEY TERM

Assassins
A tribe of Shi'a Muslims who lived in the Nosairi mountains near Tortosa.

KEY TERM

Commune
A form of government in which a group who shared common aims and activities joined together. These groups selected their own consuls to govern them and protect their interests.

Military links

The seaports not only made living in the East a realistic prospect, providing an income and a connection back to the West, but also helped to make it a safer place for the Franks. This was because after the capture of Ascalon in 1153, there was no longer a safe place for an Egyptian fleet to stop and get fresh water. This limited their ability to harass Franks living along the coast and prevented attacks on European ships as they made their way to Outremer.

In addition to protection, the ports also created a means for outside help to reach the Frankish settlers. For example, in 1104 a Genoese fleet helped to capture Gibelet and attack Acre. This help continued throughout the 12th century and came from other sources too. In 1169 and 1177, the Byzantine Empire provided naval backing for Outremer's military campaigns. This was especially important because Outremer never possessed a sizeable fleet of its own, although it did attempt to build one in the kingdom of Jerusalem in the 1160s. The seaports helped to plug this gap with outside support, which was perhaps best illustrated by the successes of the Third Crusade.

Trade between Muslim and Christian cities

Trade was one of the single most important generators of revenue for the crusader states. It was vital for settlers to have an outlet for their goods in order to make money and sustain their basic needs. It was equally important for Muslim-held cities near Outremer, which included Damascus and Aleppo, to have a means to trade their goods with Byzantium and western Europe. This means was provided by the ports of Acre and Tyre, which were home to communities of both Christians and Muslims. The following are some examples that illustrate this diversity.

- In both Tyre and Acre there were mosques provided for Muslims to worship in. There is even evidence that a converted mosque was shared by both Christians and Muslims at Acre.

- Royal protection was granted by Baldwin III to Abu Ibn Izz ad-Din, a Muslim from Tyre, to trade with Egypt.

- In 1180, Ibn Jubayr said that two Muslim traders who dominated business on the coast of Outremer were from North Africa and lived in Damascus.

These examples of accommodation and tolerance appear to be a little out of place in a community that had forced Muslim rulers out of the region. However, it happened because it created profit for the traders and revenue for the local lords. This is illustrated by the laws of the kingdom of Jerusalem, which outlined the taxes that were imposed on traders:

- sugar, which was highly sought after in the Mediterranean world, had a duty of 5 bezants imposed on it for every 100 bezants traded

- shoes, if bought by a Saracen, had a 10 percent duty added to them

- cardamom, a spice, had a duty of 10 bezants and 5 **karoubles** imposed on it for every 100 bezants traded

- any product that was exported to non-Christians had an additional 1 karouble duty for every 1 bezant traded.

These laws, which are of 11th-century origin, even go as far as to describe the procedure by which a Frank could recover a debt from a Saracen. They indicate, at least on paper, that Outremer was a vibrant trading community that relied upon connections from well beyond its Christian settlements.

> **KEY TERM**
>
> Karouble
> A Greek coin. It was worth around one twenty-fourth of a gold bezant.

SOURCE

2 An extract of the laws of the kingdom of Jerusalem developed in the 12th and 13th centuries, which outlines debt collection procedures. This is a translation of a 13th-century Old French manuscript and provides a valuable insight into the existence and nature of the trade between Muslim and Christian groups.

If a Frank makes a claim in court against a Saracen to have what the latter owes him, and the Saracen denies owing it, and the Frank has no guarantor for it, it is right that the Saracen must swear on the law that he owes the Frank nothing, and thereupon he must be acquitted. Likewise, if a Saracen makes a claim against a Frank in court to have what the Frank owes him, and the Frank does not have it for him, and the Saracen has no guarantor for it, the law decrees that the Frank should not make an oath to the Saracen, if he does not acknowledge the debt at all.

Patterns of settlement and migration from Europe

One of the first problems the leaders of Outremer faced after the First Crusade was that Franks were in the minority. Godfrey, the first ruler of Jerusalem, was only left with around 300 knights after the Battle of Ascalon in 1099. This meant it was very difficult to impose his authority and organise his defences. Fortunately, over time a substantial number of settlers were attracted to the crusader states, which helped to secure a long-term western presence in the Near East.

Reasons for settlement in Outremer

There were a variety of reasons that attracted settlers to Outremer. The very earliest was a consequence of the crusade itself, as some crusaders felt obliged to stay with their lords if they chose to settle. Others decided to stay of their own volition after they had fulfilled their vow to go to Jerusalem. They were joined by fresh migrants who had a desire to live in the Holy Land for spiritual benefit, with some of their number choosing to live as hermits in the caves near Jerusalem and Galilee. This population was bolstered each year by a temporary influx of pilgrims who came to visit the holy sites and would stay for several months.

KEY TERM

Labour service
A feudal term that refers to the unpaid work a peasant was expected to do in return for the land they cultivated.

Another motive for settlement was the economic situation in western Europe. Some areas, especially the Low Countries, suffered from overcrowding and frequent famine. In other areas, the level of taxation or demands of **labour service** made life more difficult. For instance, around the year 1150, one cobbler from Châlons-sur-Marne decided to leave for Outremer to escape a restrictive tax regime. Settlers like him were attracted to the idea of a 600-mile strip of land, which was relatively underpopulated, had fertile plains available to farm on and thriving urban communities from which to profit.

However, it would be a mistake to believe that settlers forced out of Europe by economic hardship travelled to Outremer driven on by only a vague hope for a better life. In fact, they were offered concrete benefits to migrate. One example, from the reign of King Baldwin III, is the benefits offered to settlers at Casal Imbert around 1150. These included:

- long-term leases on housing; this provided the migrants with a sense of security

- certain exemptions, such as on rent for housing or plots of arable land

- free facilities; this included the use of a mill and a communal olive grove

- favourable terms, such as a payment of only one-seventh of all crops to Baldwin.

Although these were particularly attractive terms, they reflect the general situation that farmers in Outremer got a better deal than those back home in Europe. This was especially true of labour services, which at their most extreme only took up a day a week and included undemanding tasks such as transporting goods to the lord or repair work on roads and aqueducts. This helps to explain why some were prepared to abandon everything they knew to become settlers in Outremer.

Migration from Europe: who were the settlers?

There is very little evidence from the 12th century of how many chose to settle in rural Outremer and from where they originated. The records that do survive suggest that there were sizeable populations of European migrants in rural villages scattered across the crusader states. For example, in the village of Magna Mahomeria in the kingdom of Jerusalem, a list of 150 names from the middle of the 12th century has survived. Of these names, 74 have the migrant's place of origin listed and 44 of these are from France and other parts of western Europe. This suggests there existed sizeable communities of westerners in rural villages in Outremer.

More evidence exists for urban settlers, in particular the Italian communities that set themselves up in the crusader states. There are records of Italian quarters with residents from the cities of Genoa, Pisa and Venice in Outremer's major towns and cities. In Antioch, the Genoese had a number of communal buildings, which included a church, as well as 13 houses. The rights to these quarters were given to them at the end of the 11th century. Another example was the port of Tyre, which had granted one-third of the port to a Venetian settlement. These mercantile settlers illustrate that France was not the only country migrants travelled from.

Effects: patterns of settlement in Outremer

A study by an archaeologist called Ronnie Ellenblum has found that there were about 200 colonial settlements in Outremer, which ranged from small farms to fully planned developments. These new villages included buildings such as a tower, a courthouse and a church. A good example is the village of Ramot, near the city of Jerusalem, which had the following features:

- a fortified building for storage and the protection of a lord

- construction around a road to transport produce

- uniform strip fields for farming

- houses with wine-making and olive-pressing facilities.

The absence of forced conversions

Villages like Ramot would normally have a church or, if there was an eastern Christian population already there, they would share a church. This idea of living side by side with indigenous Christians is demonstrated by the pattern of known Frankish settlements. Frankish settlers were common in the western areas of Galilee, where there were indigenous Christians, but they were few in number in eastern Galilee where there were no established Christian communities. The rural picture was therefore one of Frankish farmers living and working alongside, or near to, indigenous Christian groups.

However, the urban picture was quite different and communities from different groups did live and work together, albeit in separate quarters. Some examples of cosmopolitan urban areas, where even Muslim groups were allowed to live without conversion, included the following.

- Acre: this had a pilgrim population from the West and Byzantium, traders from across Frankish Outremer, as well as merchants from Alexandria, Damascus and Aleppo.

- Tyre and Tripoli: both had sizeable Muslim populations within their city walls, who lived alongside the Christian communities that had settled there.

- Antioch: this had a significant Byzantine Greek and Armenian population that lived with the newly arrived Frankish settlers.

The make-up of urban areas is significant to an understanding of Outremer's history, because most of the population lived in these environments. For example, of the 150,000 residents of Palestine, around 120,000 lived in towns. Jerusalem's population itself stood at 20,000 in the early 12th century and grew to 30,000 within a few decades. This helps to explain why towns and cities were usually the primary focus of a crusade, or a planned campaign, because they were the centres of Frankish control and settlement.

SOURCE

3

An account of the relationship between Frankish settlers and indigenous communities from Fulcher of Chartres's *Gesta Francorum Jherusalem peregrinantium*, completed by 1127. Fulcher accompanied Baldwin I when he became King of Jerusalem and charts the affairs of the kingdom up to 1127.

For we who were occidentals [westerners] have now become orientals [easterners]. He who was a Roman or a Frank has in this land been made into a Galilean or a Palestinian. He who was of Rheims or Chartres has now become a citizen of Tyre or Antioch. We have already forgotten the places of our birth; already these are unknown to many of us or not mentioned any more. Some already possess homes or households by inheritance. Some have taken wives not only of their own people but Syrians or Armenians or even Saracens who have obtained the grace of baptism. One has his father-in-law as well as his daughter-in-law living with him, or his own child if not his stepson or stepfather. Out here there are grandchildren and great-grandchildren. Some tend vineyards; others till fields. People use the eloquence and idioms of diverse languages in conversing back and forth. Words of different languages have become common property known to each nationality, and mutual faith unites those who are ignorant of their descent. Indeed it is written, 'The lion and the ox shall eat straw together' [Isaiah 62:25]. He who was born a stranger is now as one born here; he who was born an alien has become as a native.

Geography and economy

1 Explain what effect the following features of Outremer's geography and economy would have on a rural Frankish settler:

- a lack of natural boundaries to the east

- access to a seaport

- a trade relationship with a Muslim city

- attractive conditions of labour from some local lords.

2 Explain which of the features listed above would have the biggest impact on the actions of the king of Jerusalem.

3 Bullet point three potential effects of Outremer's geographic features and economic needs on its historical development.

HOW DID THE DEFENCE OF OUTREMER CHANGE OVER TIME?

Baldwin I's consolidation of territory, 1100–18

In 1100, Baldwin's situation as ruler of the kingdom of Jerusalem was not very promising. He held the cities of Jerusalem and Bethlehem, and controlled one port, Jaffa, which had been captured in 1099. He faced threats on several fronts.

KEY TERM

Fatimids
A group of Shi'ah Muslims that dominated Egypt. In the First Crusade they ignored the siege of Antioch because it was controlled by Sunni Turks of the Abbasid group ruled by the caliph in Baghdad.

- The southern frontier: the **Fatimids** of Egypt were a serious challenge to Baldwin's hold on Jerusalem. Between 1101 and 1118, the Egyptians launched ten separate invasions aimed at Baldwin's territory. An example of how dangerous these attacks could be occurred on 19 May 1102 when the Egyptians defeated Christian forces at Ramla. The army was massacred and very few, aside from Baldwin, escaped with their lives.

- The northern states: Baldwin was not just concerned with his own territory in Jerusalem; he also had to help out his fellow rulers in the north. This occupied much of Baldwin's time between 1109 and 1115 when he had to support the defence of Outremer against threats from Mosul, Damascus and Aleppo.

- The eastern territory of Jerusalem: there was very little Frankish control of the territory on the interior of Outremer. There were Bedouin tribes and Muslim trade routes that ran through the areas to the east of the Sea of Galilee, which could be a staging post for an invasion.

Acquisition of territory

Regardless of the threats from the land borders, Baldwin's first priority was to secure coastal areas. This would generate a route for further western help to arrive and prevent a naval attack on Outremer from Egypt. His acquisition of key coastal towns is outlined in the timeline below, which also illustrates the degree to which Baldwin relied on foreign support.

BALDWIN'S CONSOLIDATION OF TERRITORY

1101
Arsuf and Caesarea are captured with the help of a Genoese fleet

1102
Tortosa and Gibelet are successfully taken, again with support from a Genoese fleet

1104
Haifa and Acre fall under Baldwin's control with help from Venice and Genoa respectively

1110
Beirut and Sidon are captured; this time naval support is provided by a Norwegian fleet led by King Sigurd

1124
Tyre falls after the death of Baldwin I in 1118

The Franks, under Tancred of Hauteville, also made gains on their eastern frontier. The area to the east of the Sea of Galilee was garrisoned up to the Red Sea between 1115 and 1116. In the north, Baldwin II of Edessa and Roger, the regent of Antioch, met with success against threats to their territory. The year 1115 was a particularly good one as a Muslim force was taken by surprise and defeated at Tell Danith. This attack did not help to gain territory, but did in the short term help diminish the threat to the northern states.

Effects of Baldwin's defence strategy

The most successful element of Baldwin's defence strategy was that the Egyptians did not succeed in their almost annual invasion attempts from the south. In the years these were launched, particularly in 1105, 1107 and 1111, they were repulsed. In fact, his policy of consolidation led to a substantial growth of his influence over coastal towns and the areas to the east. However, on his death in 1118, there were still a number of threats that future rulers would have to tackle, including the following.

- The expansion eastwards beyond the Sea of Galilee had created tension with Damascus. This led to a defeat at Al-Sinnabra in 1113 and ongoing conflict after Baldwin's death.

- The roads, used chiefly for trade and pilgrim traffic, were more secure. For instance, in 1108 Baldwin and 60 knights successfully attacked a **caravan** that had not paid the toll, which indicates his control of trade routes. However, pilgrims still faced raids on their journey through Outremer along the roads into Jerusalem.

- Most of the ports were now under Frankish control. However, Tyre did not fall until after Baldwin's death and Ascalon remained in Egyptian hands until 1153. This explains why the Egyptians were able to launch so many attacks into Outremer.

KEY TERM

Caravan
A group of traders who travelled together across the desert. A Muslim caravan was usually permitted to travel through Outremer if it was unarmed and paid appropriate duties.

Adoption of local methods of fortification and the building of castles

The land of Outremer, largely as a consequence of its lack of natural boundaries to the east, was never truly secure against threats from the Byzantine Empire to the north, the Turks to the east and the Egyptians to the south. This meant that Franks relied upon defended settlements for security. There was an array of different types of fortification, many of which the Franks had taken over or rebuilt for their own purposes. The purpose of a castle often reflected its geographic location.

- Edessa: the county was sparsely populated and under constant threat of invasion. The inhabitants relied on fortified towns like Turbessel to retreat into when an enemy attacked.

- Antioch: it was important to safeguard access to its main port, Latakia. The castle at Margat defended coastal access and Saone protected the routes from the interior.

- Tripoli: castles were used for acquisition. A castle was built at Mount Pilgrim, just to the south-east of the city of Tripoli itself. It was used to sustain the siege on Tripoli until 1109.

- Jerusalem: the kingdom was threatened by the Egyptians. Chastel Hernault was built in the 1130s to defend the road into the city of Jerusalem. The Egyptian threat also meant key cities, such as Jaffa, had walls built in case of invasion.

The main types of fortification in Outremer

Fortification type	Description	Example
Fortified towers	A simple tower, constructed of stone and with two floors.	Malregard was built during the siege of Antioch in 1098.
Enclosure castles	A walled enclosure with towers on each corner.	Tamara in eastern Negev (origins in third century).
Enclosure and keep	Similar to an enclosure castle, but with an extended corner tower or a tower built within.	Gibelet built in Tripoli by the Franks.
Concentric castle	A castle within a castle.	Belvoir built along the River Jordan in Jerusalem.
Spur castles	A castle built with three cliffs surrounding it and defences at the front.	Krak des Chevaliers in southern Syria built to defend the Homs valley.
Fortified towns	A town surrounded by city walls with a number of gated entrances.	Turbessel in Edessa, which was captured in the First Crusade.

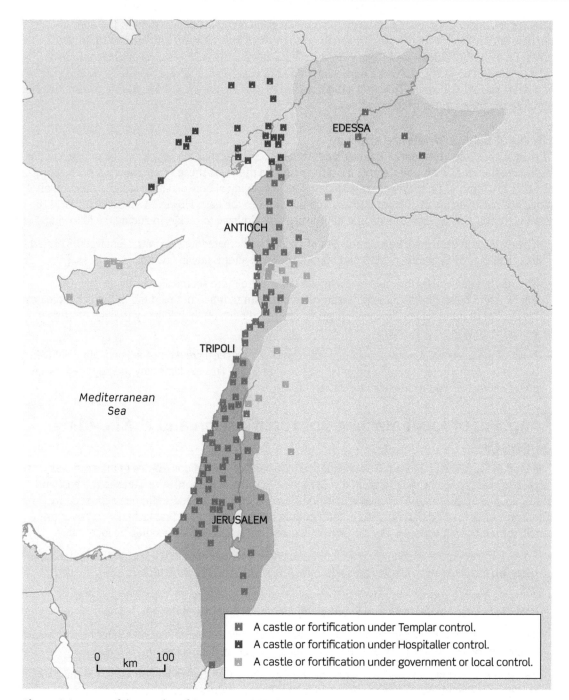

Figure 3.1 A map of the castles of Outremer, 1100–87.

The changing purpose for castles in Outremer corresponded with advances in their design. At first, they were largely fortified towers built quickly in order to establish control. These developed into more sophisticated forms, such as concentric and spur castles, as the 12th century progressed (see the table on main types of fortification in Outremer on page 73).

SOURCE 4

A photograph of Krak des Chevaliers. This was a spur castle and so had three sides that were surrounded by a steep cliff or drop. The photograph shows the commanding view that Krak had over the surrounding Homs Valley.

The changing use of castles

The purpose of castles in Outremer changed over time.

- Consolidation and submission: castles were used to establish control over newly captured territory. They were built, or taken over, for this purpose until around 1115.

- Administration: once Frankish control was more secure, castles were built at the centre of a rural territory as symbols of a local lord's authority. The neighbouring population would be obliged to pay rent or a part of their crops to the garrison in the castle.

- Defence: from the late 1160s, castles were again used primarily for their defensive purpose. This was because the Muslim threat was once again on the increase.

ACTIVITY
KNOWLEDGE CHECK

Establishment of control

- Construct a strengths-and-weaknesses table on the defensive situation in Outremer at the end of Baldwin I's reign.

- Study the map of the distribution of castles in Outremer in Figure 3.1. Select three that you think were built for different reasons and explain what their purposes might have been.

- Would the building of these castles have resolved any of the weaknesses identified in your table? If so, explain how a castle might resolve one of these.

AS Level Exam-Style Question Section A

Were castles and fortified settlements the main reason for the survival of the crusader states in the years 1100–44? Explain your answer. (20 marks)

Tip
This question draws on material from two sections in this chapter. Consider both defensive measure and the influx of settlers.

The protection of the military orders of Templars and Hospitallers

The two main military orders in Outremer were the Templars and the Hospitallers. Their origins have already been explored in Chapter 1.1 (see page 30) and here the discussion will focus on their military function.

Full members of both of the military orders had taken equivalent vows to members of a monastic community. However, their primary function was far more practical than spiritual. The Hospitallers were formed in the late 11th century and were named for the Hospital of St John, which they ran in Jerusalem. They were joined by the Templars, formed around 1120, to defend pilgrims and named after their base at the Temple of Soloman. Throughout their 12th-century history, the Hospitallers had 300–500 members and the Templars about 500. This number was supplemented by crusaders, administrators and paid mercenaries.

Military roles

Neither order started off as a sophisticated fighting force ready to defend the Holy Land. Instead, this was a function that developed from the late 1120s onwards. First, the Hospitallers shifted from their exclusive role as care-givers to a military order at some point between 1130 and 1140. They had acquired their first fortified site in 1128 at Calansue, which was along the coast to the south of Tyre. However, it was not until they were given the Castle of Bethgibelin by King Fulk in 1136 that they began to play an important role in the defence of Outremer. This castle was in the south of the kingdom of Jerusalem and was close to Muslim-held Ascalon, which meant it was at greater risk from a Muslim assault. After this, the Hospitallers' process of militarisation continued and sped up rapidly in the 1160s when they were given around 12 castles and asked to defend the entire city of Sidon.

In contrast to the Hospitallers, the Templar movement was set up with a military role in mind. Initially, it relied on the support of volunteers like Count Fulk of Anjou, who according to Orderic Vitalis became a temporary brother for one year in the East in 1120. However, they soon gathered sufficient funds to maintain knights from their own resources and by 1129 had been given formal approval at the Council of Troyes. This decision meant the Church had accepted that its members were permitted to commit violent acts in God's name. It was perhaps the next logical step in terms of holy violence after the First Crusade, but it was not without its critics. This is why Bernard of Clairvaux was asked to write *Liber ad milites Templi de laude novae militiae* ('Book to the Knights of the Temple: In Praise of the New Knighthood'), which formed a rigorous defence of the lifestyle and actions of the Templars.

EXTEND YOUR KNOWLEDGE

In Praise of the New Knighthood – De laude novae militiae

This treatise was written by Bernard of Clairvaux in the 1130s and can provide an understanding of why westerners were increasingly willing to donate to the orders and how they were able to grow. It demonstrated that the concept of a military order was a completely new one and Bernard gave a justification for their existence. It was written in response to three requests from Hugh of Payns to encourage people to support or at least accept the Templars in the West. Bernard outlined the key features of a member of the Templar movement by comparison with a conventional secular knight. He stressed the good intention of the Templar knights when they went to fight in the name of Christ, which he said was in contrast to secular knights, who were obsessed with their appearance and other frivolities. He repeated the arguments for the use of violence for a holy purpose, but went further than this through his exploration of the nature of the Templar movement itself. He described their order as egalitarian, but with clear obedience to a leader and a disciplined lifestyle. For example, excessive laughing and growing their hair too long were both frowned upon by the Templars. His sermon closed with an enthusiastic description of the Holy Land itself and, by implication, the importance of its proper defence.

KEY TERM

Seneschal
An officer within the Templars who looked after the administration of the order's land and possessions.

Role in military campaigns

Both orders took on an important role in military campaigns designed to crush a potential threat to Outremer. This can be shown by the actions of the Templars after the Second Crusade. In 1149, Antioch was forced to face the threat from Nur ad-Din head on and the Templars lent their support. A letter from the **seneschal** of the Temple suggests the order sent a force of 120 knights and around 1,000 soldiers, which included a significant number of paid mercenaries. Another example of Templar support for a military campaign comes from 1177, when 80 Templars joined other Frankish forces to defeat Saladin at Montgisard.

The Hospitallers also became heavily involved in military campaigns in the late 1100s and were keen to help remove the threat Outremer faced from Egypt. In 1167, the Hospitallers offered to provide 500 knights and 500 turcopoles for the campaign. This level of participation was so extraordinary that it brought the Hospital to the brink of bankruptcy. After the campaign the Hospitallers owed around 100,000 bezants thanks to further promises made by Gilbert of Assailly, the master of the Hospital. However, this did not prevent their continued involvement in battles between 1170 and 1187 to try and halt the Muslim invaders.

Defence of settlements

The military orders did not just provide knights to support planned campaigns. They also took on formal responsibility to defend key urban sites. At different points in the 12th century, they were given the task of manning the ramparts at places like Acre, Tripoli and Tyre. In other Frankish settlements they were even entrusted to govern and defend entire towns or cities. These included Tortosa, which was given to the Templars to govern in 1152, and Sidon, which was granted to the Hospitallers in the 1160s. The picture that emerges is one of Outremer's rulers, with insufficient resources to defend their states, turning to the military orders for support.

The effect of this reliance on the orders meant the burden on their brother knights grew heavier as the Muslim threat increased. By the end of the 12th century, they were expected to be able to leap to the defence of the crusader states. There is evidence in 1164 of 60 Templars killed when Artah was attacked. However, by 1187, the number who lost their lives in battle had grown considerably. At the Battle of Hattin the Templars lost around 230 brothers in an attempt to stop Saladin from reaching Jerusalem. This shows just how much Outremer's defensive strategy was dependent on the military strength of the Templars and Hospitallers.

The control of border castles by Templars and Hospitallers

The Templars and Hospitallers were not only required to bolster troop numbers and provide military advice, but also to run or build a substantial number of Outremer's castles. There were a number of reasons for this.

- They had the resources to garrison them: in 1178, Baldwin IV gave the Templars the castle at Jacob's Ford. In return they were expected to garrison it with 80 knights and have 900 troops ready to call on.

- Rulers felt they could be trusted: when Raymond III of Tripoli became the regent for Baldwin V in 1185 the castles were put under the control of the military orders. This was to minimise the capacity for Raymond to overpower the rulers of Jerusalem permanently.

- The orders had the necessary resources to build fortifications: the Hospitallers were given Platta in the 1140s on the condition that they had to fortify it within a year.

- The government had grown weaker due to the Muslim threat: in 1157, half of the Hospitallers were given Banyas by Baldwin III because he thought it would be captured.

- The states needed more money: Raymond III of Tripoli gave the Hospitallers the fortress of Tuban and other territories in 1180 to pay off his debt to them of 80,000 bezants, which had been accrued to pay for Raymond's release from a Muslim prison.

Key strongholds

By the 1180s, the military orders controlled a considerable number of castles, as a result of the government's increased reliance upon them to provide for Outremer's defence. The Hospitallers had about 25 castles and the Templars around 17. Some of these were exceptionally powerful castles, which had a substantial amount of land under their control. For example, the Hospitallers were given the Castle of Margat by Bernard Le Mazoir in 1186. This gave them the jurisdiction to conduct their own negotiations with Muslim invaders without the need to consult the ruler of Antioch. Their acquisitions confirmed their social status and power was equal to that of a lord.

Their castles were also very important for the control of access to Outremer. It was crucial that key passes through mountainous territory were monitored by a castle. This was because they could provide front-line defence against an invasion force and impose local duties on traders. The Castle of Gaston (Baghras), which was placed under Templar control in the 1130s, was built for this purpose. It controlled the Belen Pass, in the Amanus Mountains, which provided access from the north-east into Antioch. This meant any invaders from Armenian, or later Edessan, territory could be cut off in the mountains.

The Templars were given larger castles for an offensive purpose as well. The gift of Jacob's Ford from Baldwin IV, under the conditions outlined above, carried with it the expectation that the castle would apply pressure on Damascus and help to take the city. On the other end of the scale, they ran smaller outposts at places like Destroit and Yazur, to meet the original aim of their military order, which was to protect the pilgrim roads. Both orders had therefore, by the 1180s, come into possession of an array of different castles, of different sizes and for different purposes (see Figure 3.1, page 74).

However, the events of Saladin's incursions in the 1180s were to transform this situation. By the close of the decade, the military orders had lost control of the majority of their castles. The only significant fortresses left in the hands of the Hospitallers were Krak des Chevaliers and Margat, while the Templars were left with Tortosa and Roche Guillaume, which were all in the northern part of the crusader states. This was a reversal of fortunes that demonstrated how much responsibility the military orders had for defence, because without their castles the situation had become desperate enough finally to convince the rulers of Europe to launch the Third Crusade.

Financial support for the military orders by European nobles

Both military orders had property in western Europe, which they used to fund their activities in Outremer. This property was often gifted to them by a sponsor who asked for spiritual support, such as prayers after their death, in return. This helped the orders to develop large estates that had a commandery building at the centre to run them. These commanderies were expected to pay a tax, called a responsion, of around one-third of their revenue, to their counterparts in Outremer. In order for this responsion to get to the crusader states, the orders developed an international network that could transfer messages, money and materials across wide distances. The orders therefore had a sophisticated infrastructure, which the Templars made one further use of. They began to offer financial services in the west, which helped them to raise even more money. It was thanks to these sources of revenue, coupled with the work of the estate managers, that both the Templars and Hospitallers were able to contribute so much to the defence of the crusader states.

SOURCE

5

A charter from 1168 in which Raoul, lord of Coucy, the son of a crusader, arranged for a donation to the canons of the cathedral of Nazareth. The charter, although not an example of financial support for the military orders, reveals the strong presence of the Templars in the West and their regular contact with Outremer. The signatories also show how highly regarded donations to Outremer were.

I, Raoul, lord of Coucy, caused it to be officially put into writing that from the gift of my father, Enguerran, I gave and granted to the church of Nazareth in which his body rests, for his soul and for mine, and for the souls of my ancestors and successors, ten *libras* [Roman pounds] of Provins from my wionage at Lion [the Coucys taxed merchants who used the road for trade in and near Laon], to be received each year on the feast of the Blessed Rémi by the hands of the brothers of the Temple...

...I have signed it with my seal and the signature of the witnesses. The sign of Louis, king of France. The sign of Henry, archbishop of Reims. The sign of Henry, bishop of Silvanectensis. The sign of Eustace Canis, brother of the Temple... Issued at Noyon, in the years of the Incarnate Word, 1168.

Early support for the military orders

The Templars quickly gained support for their order as a result of the work of their first leader, Hugh of Payns. He held his knighthood from Count Hugh of Champagne who became a Templar in 1125. After Hugh of Champagne's death his family began to make donations of property and money to the order. However, this was just the start for Hugh of Payns, who went to Europe to try and get more financial support in 1127. During this tour he was able to attract further support from nobles like King Henry I of England who made donations of silver and gold. He also raised the profile of the order and helped to encourage future patronage of the Templars. Some examples of this included:

- in 1133, Laureta, from southern France, gave all her inheritance to the Templar agent, Hugh Rigaldi; it was only a small amount of property, but it demonstrated support at a local level for the orders

- in 1139, Eleanor of Aquitaine, wife of Louis VII of France, gave the Templars a house in the port of La Rochelle, which became a very important base for the order

- in 1141, the Duke of Brittany gave the Templars an island and a part of his own income along with a place to live in the city of Nantes.

These one-off noble donations were supplemented by regular donations of smaller amounts from local village landholders. For example, a charter from Toulousain dated from the late 1120s lists 44 individual donations, ranging in size from several properties to small amounts of cash. All of these gifts would have helped to build castles, pay mercenaries and provide garrisons with supplies in Outremer.

The Templars were not the sole recipients of donations from European nobles. The Hospitallers were also able to attract the support of wealthy patrons. Their first European estates actually pre-date those of the Templars, with the first examples found in France in 1100 and England in 1128. They attracted donations from nobles like Atton, the archbishop of Arles, who donated sizeable amounts of property to the Hospitallers in Provence between 1115 and 1126. Their income, like that of the Templars, was also supplemented with smaller donations. In Essex, 135 12th-century grants to the Hospitallers are recorded, of which most are for less than nine acres of land. It was the accumulation of gifts like this that helped the Hospitallers to work alongside the Templars to protect Outremer.

How did these donations develop over time?

The first half of the 12th century was a period of establishment for the military orders in Europe. This paralleled the establishment and consolidation period that Outremer had experienced prior to 1144. Then, in the crusader states, a period of increasing threat began after the Second Crusade. This was paralleled in Europe by a substantial increase in donations to the military orders, which itself was perhaps a result of a distinct lack of willingness to launch another crusade. The increased support for the military orders is illustrated by the fact that:

- in 1172, King Henry II of England promised to pay for 200 knights to spend a year in Jerusalem

- in 1184, both Henry II and King Philip II Augustus of France agreed to levy a tithe to help Outremer; in England £20,000 was sent to the Templars and Hospitallers in 1186

- in Champagne, the Templars had received substantial holdings (see above); by 1191, their power and wealth had grown to such an extent that they were prohibited from the acquisition of more property in the county.

A Level Exam-Style Question Section B

How far do you agree that the defensive situation was transformed between the First and Second Crusade? (20 marks)

Tip

This question is asking you to reach a judgement on the extent of change. Make sure you are clear how the situation had changed before you begin writing.

These donations were supported by the actions of other European nobles and powerful churchmen who helped to generate an environment of patronage for the military orders. Some tried to encourage donations, such as Pope Celestine II. He published a **bull** in 1144, which granted a one-seventh indulgence to anyone who donated to the Templars. Others, like King Stephen of England, granted rights and privileges to help the orders generate an income. He allowed the Templars to hold a market at Witham in Essex. Later, King Henry II gave the order the right to **assart** 2,000 acres of woodland and let them off paying the fine for already assarting 2,164 acres. Thanks to all this support the European estates were able to grow and meet the burdens placed on their brothers in Outremer in the late 12th century.

Lack of support for the states from Byzantium and Europe

Byzantine support, 1099–1144

The crusader states, however, did not receive the same level of support from the Byzantine Empire as they did from western Europe. The relationship between Outremer and the Byzantine Empire was soured by the issue of ownership and control of the principality of Antioch. Both Emperor Alexius Comnenus and his successor, John Comnenus, believed that they were overlords of the prince of Antioch. Alexius had forced Bohemond I of Antioch to acknowledge this in the Treaty of Devol in 1108. However, the Frankish rulers often ignored or paid no attention to their supposed loyalty to the Byzantine emperor. In 1137 an attack was launched by John Comnenus on Antioch because he was angry at his exclusion from discussions about who would wed Princess Constance. This was just one example of the six invasion attempts through Cilicia and then into Antioch between 1099 and 1144.

In spite of this poor relationship, both the Byzantines and the Franks were united in their desire to prevent a Turkish invasion. This resulted in an alliance of convenience between Raymond of Poitiers, Prince of Antioch, and John Comnenus in 1137. This led Raymond, John and Joscelin II, the Count of Edessa, to launch an attack on the Turks in 1138. They reoccupied Cerep and Kafr Tab and almost succeeded in the capture of Shaizar. However, this union came to a sudden end when John died in 1143 and was replaced by Manuel Comnenus, who was angry about the Frankish occupation of fortresses in Cilicia.

Improving relations with Byzantium, 1158–80

After 1158, relations with the Byzantine Empire began to improve once more. This is indicated by the fact that Baldwin III, King of Jerusalem, sold off the remainder of the fortresses in Edessa to them in the late 1150s. The positive feeling between the two was cemented by a series of marriage alliances:

- 1158, King Baldwin III married Theodora, who was Emperor Manuel I's niece

- 1161, Manuel himself married a Frankish bride, Maria of Antioch

- 1167, King Baldwin III's successor, Amalric, also married a member of Manuel's family called Maria Comnena.

In a spirit reminiscent of the First Crusade, the warming up of relations led to practical support and co-operation between the Byzantines and the Franks. Manuel offered his support for at least two Frankish campaigns that would not have a direct impact on Byzantium or significantly further their territorial interests:

- on 25 October 1169 an army of Frankish and Byzantine forces met on a joint Egyptian campaign; they reached Damietta on 27 October and began to lay siege to it but gave up in December 1169

- in 1177 a Byzantine fleet arrived to help in another Egyptian campaign, but due to lack of support from the European contingent for the plan it came to nothing.

Reversal of relations, 1180–92

The good relationship between the Byzantine Empire and the crusader states came to an abrupt end when Manuel died in 1180 and was replaced by Emperor Andronicus I in 1182. Andronicus had no desire to cultivate a relationship with the Franks, as his empire faced serious riots and dissent after a disruptive period of regency. He needed to focus on the consolidation of his own position and therefore entered into an alliance with Saladin at some point in the mid-1180s. This decline in Franco-Byzantine relations meant that no further support was forthcoming from the empire and Saladin could now pursue his campaign against Outremer with renewed vigour.

Change and continuity (5b)

Impetus and disruption

Changes in the years leading up to the complete breakdown of Franco-Byzantine relations in 1185

Bohemond of Taranto refused to hand Antioch over to the Byzantines (1098).	Emperor Alexius I Comnenus forced Bohemond I of Antioch to accept his overlordship (1108).	Emperor John Comnenus temporarily occupied Antioch's Cilician towns (1137–42).
Emperor Manuel signed a Treaty with the Turks during the Second Crusade.	King Baldwin III married a member of the Byzantine imperial family (1158).	Emperor Manuel married Maria of Antioch (1161).
Lord Andronicus betrayed Amalric and ran off with the widow of King Baldwin III, Queen Theodora (1166–67).	King Amalric's and Emperor Manuel's forces joined together on an Egyptian campaign (1169).	Emperor Andronicus made a truce with Saladin in June 1185.

Patterns of development consist of changes which at given times converge and have a bearing on one another, and at other times diverge and have little in common. In the above example, the changes come together to form a pattern of development that tends towards a breakdown of Franco-Byzantine relations by 1185.

Group work

Write each change on a small piece of paper and arrange them on an A3 piece of paper as you think best. Then link them with lines and write along the lines what it is that links those changes. Try to make sure that you think about how those links may have changed over time.

Answer the following questions individually or in pairs:

1 Why is 1108 an important year in changing relationships between the Franks and Byzantines?
2 Which changes were significant in Byzantium's increasingly anti-western attitude in the years leading up to 1185?
3 What changes were important in helping Muslim forces to resist the Christians of Outremer?
4 The foreign policy of which emperor represents a divergence from the general pattern?

European support between the crusades

Europe was the lifeline of the crusader states and without their support Frankish control of Outremer would have been impossible. It was, after all, the Europeans who took part in the First Crusade that established Christian rulers in the region. However, their help for Outremer's defence was very limited between the main crusades of 1096–1102, 1147–49 and 1189–92. The help they did offer is outlined in the table below.

European support between the First, Second and Third Crusades

Date	Campaign details	Outcome
1122–24	Pope Calixtus authorised a crusade. In 1122, a Venetian fleet headed to Outremer, via Corfu, to help Baldwin II's consolidation programme.	Tyre captured on 7 July 1124.
1129	A campaign launched without the pope's authorisation. Count Fulk of Anjou led a force to Outremer.	An unsuccessful siege of Damascus.
1153	The pilgrims that arrived were intercepted by Baldwin III who offered them money to help attack Ascalon.	Ascalon, the last Muslim port on the edge of Outremer, captured in August 1153.
1157–58	Count Thierry of Flanders headed to the Holy Land with a contingent of knights.	Removed the blockade of the castle of Krak des Chevaliers, almost conquered Shaizar, took Harenc in February 1158 and defeated the Damascenes at Butaiha.
1177–78	Count Philip of Flanders, the count of Champagne and Peter of Courtenay.	Participated in campaigns in Homs, Hama and Harenc.
1183	Duke of Brabant and Ralph of Mauleon arrive with a small force from the West.	Occupied and secured Tubania after Saladin had left and tried to retake it in October 1183.

However, there were numerous examples in the 12th century of European deafness to an appeal for help from the crusader states. After the Second Crusade, the principality of Antioch faced the threat of an imminent Muslim invasion. Reynald of Châtillon appealed for help to King Louis VII of France, but this was ignored. The battle that ensued, at Inab, led to the death of the Prince of Antioch, Raymond of Poitiers, and several important strongholds were lost. In the years that followed, many more appeals for help were acted on by the pope, but ignored by European nobles and their knights. Between 1157 and 1184, at least seven crusade letters were authorised, but there was no Third Crusade until 1189.

Even when the rulers of Outremer sent out embassies to appeal personally for help to European rulers, little was done to bolster their defences. In 1169, Archbishop Frederick of Tyre was sent to ask for the help of Louis VII of France and Henry II of England. He was authorised to offer Louis the keys to the kingdom of Jerusalem, but this symbolic gesture achieved little when the murder of Thomas Becket led to political turmoil in England. Three years later, the rebellion of Henry's family in 1173 put an end to any hope that he would become deeply involved in helping the crusader states. Instead, the rulers of Outremer realised they would have to find ways to handle the Muslim threat themselves. For example, in 1171, King Amalric sent an embassy to the West, but this failed and led him to try and establish relations with a local Muslim group called the Assassins. It was clear that only dramatic events, like the capture of Jerusalem, would trigger large-scale help.

The main effect of European support for Outremer was that their borders, in the second half of the 12th century, began to contract. By the 1170s, the Christians had lost control of any land east of the River Orontes as a result of repeated Muslim invasions. Two examples of losses that resulted from an insufficient defence force include the following.

- In Tripoli, in the 1160s, the castles of Moinetre, Akkar (Gibelcar), Chastel Blanc and Aryma were lost to Nur ad-Din, while Count Raymond III was imprisoned in Aleppo.

- In 1174, when the king of Jerusalem was on a campaign in Egypt, Nur ad-Din attacked and captured Banyas.

- In 1179, the Franks were defeated in the forest of Banyas and Marj Ayun. Saladin was able to use this opportunity to destroy the castle at Jacob's Ford.

These examples illustrate that, without substantial support from Europe, the rulers of Outremer simply did not have enough forces to maintain their defences. The feudal lists that survive suggest that in total they could call up around 2,000 knights to defend the whole of Outremer, which pales in comparison with the estimate that 6,000 set off on the First Crusade. These inadequate knightly resources, combined with European unwillingness to help and a frosty relationship with the Byzantines, no doubt helped Saladin to penetrate the defences of Outremer in the 1180s.

HOW EFFECTIVE WAS THE GOVERNMENT OF OUTREMER?

ACTIVITY
KNOWLEDGE CHECK

Developments in the defence of Outremer

The list below is one way that the time period between the major crusades could be divided:

1100-18: A period of consolidation

1118-47: The lead up to the Second Crusade

1153-77: The Egyptian campaigns

1177-87: The lead up to the Third Crusade.

1 At which point did the military orders begin to contribute to the defence of Outremer? List two things they contributed.

2 At which point was the contribution of support from the military orders most important? Explain two reasons why.

3 At which point did both Byzantine and European support contribute to the defence of Outremer? List two things they contributed.

4 In no more than 100 words, sum up the essential changes in the defensive situation after 1177.

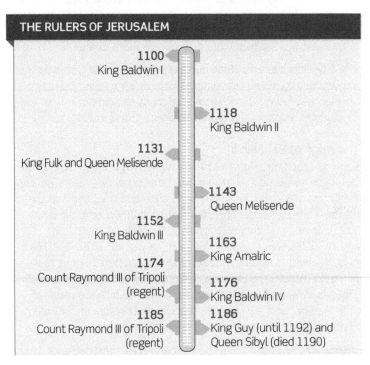

THE RULERS OF JERUSALEM

1100 King Baldwin I

1118 King Baldwin II

1131 King Fulk and Queen Melisende

1143 Queen Melisende

1152 King Baldwin III

1163 King Amalric

1174 Count Raymond III of Tripoli (regent)

1176 King Baldwin IV

1185 Count Raymond III of Tripoli (regent)

1186 King Guy (until 1192) and Queen Sibyl (died 1190)

The rule of Baldwin I and Baldwin II

The reign of Baldwin I

Godfrey of Bouillon was elected the first ruler of Jerusalem on 22 July 1099, but rather than take on the title 'King of Jerusalem' he was known as 'The Advocate of the Holy Sepulchre'. This suggested a measure of humility, which his successor did not share. Godfrey died almost a year later and his replacement, Baldwin I, began to make his journey southwards from Edessa. In contrast to his predecessor, he was to be referred to as a king, rather than an advocate or prince. He was quick to justify this title, as even before his reign had technically begun he took decisive action on his journey to Jerusalem. He installed a new count in Edessa and prevented a Danishmend Turk capture of Antioch. He was crowned king on 11 November 1100.

His reign over Jerusalem was both strong and effective, because he consolidated the territories of Outremer (see pages 72–73) and established a clear system of overlordship over his vassals in the kingdom of Jerusalem. Some examples of his actions to establish his authority include the following.

- Authority over the church: the patriarch of Jerusalem, Daibert of Pisa, had tried to prevent Baldwin from becoming king. He preferred the candidacy of Bohemond I of Antioch. Baldwin managed to get Daibert deposed in 1102 and eventually, in 1112, got his own candidate in place, Arnulf of Chocques.

- Intervention in the affairs of the kingdom: numerous examples of this are evident and even if his actions were unsuccessful, such as his intervention in the succession dispute in Tripoli in 1109, they showed he was an active ruler prepared to tackle issues directly.

- Defence of the kingdom: Baldwin not only consolidated territory, but also actively defended against the Turkish threat. For instance, in 1113, Galilee was invaded by the Turks from the east, but Baldwin managed to force them to retreat.

- Castles: the intensive castle building programme that Outremer was eventually to rely so heavily upon for its defence began in Baldwin's reign. Montreal, built deep into the south-eastern territory of the kingdom, was constructed on Baldwin's orders in 1115.

The reign of Baldwin II

Baldwin I died on 2 April 1118 and named his brother, Eustace of Boulogne, as his heir. At around the same time, Baldwin of Bourcq, the Count of Edessa, arrived in Jerusalem and tried to claim the throne. This triggered a crisis over who would become the next king. The main contender, supported by many of Jerusalem's senior nobles, was Eustace. However, he was still in Europe. His rival, Baldwin of Bourcq, had some key supporters such as the patriarch, Arnulf, and Joscelin of Courtenay, who was the lord of Tiberias as well as Baldwin's cousin. It was mainly as a result of their support, and the fact that Baldwin was present in Jerusalem to press his case, that he was able to secure the kingship.

He quickly proved himself to be an able and effective defender of Outremer. This was evident in his treatment of the situation in Antioch. After the Battle of the Field of Blood, Antioch had been left without a regent for Bohemond II. Baldwin II stepped into the breach and acted in this role until 1126, which involved six trips of 280 miles to Antioch in order to resolve political issues and provide defence.

He also continued Baldwin I's strategy of territorial expansion in order to minimise the Muslim threat to Jerusalem. In fact, during his entire reign, Baldwin II led around 19 military campaigns, including attempts on Damascus and its surrounding territory in 1126 and 1129.

SOURCE

6 A description of Baldwin II's arrival in Antioch after he had dealt with a Turkish invasion force elsewhere, while another force had attacked the city of Antioch itself. It is from Walter the Chancellor's *The Antiochene Wars*, written around 1122. Walter was a member of the government of Antioch and can therefore give us an Antiochene view of Baldwin.

Not long afterwards Baldwin arrived, the renowned king; to all the Christian people he was great in prospect, greater in arrival, greatest in the protection he brought. When he realized how the infidels' tyranny had burned into our men, penetrating beneath their skin and flesh and to the very marrow, and the Turks had not been held back by any knight, but only by the yawning waters at the sea, he was stricken by very great sorrow, and hurried to enter the city, not to rest, but first to seek God's kingdom and, since he was about to fight for his fatherland, to pray devoutly to God, as befits a king, in the church of St Peter in order that … he could confidently take on the infidels…

…He sent out scouts in advance, quickened the pace and drew up the battle-lines, then he hurried on his way in pursuit; but when he fully realized, from the reports of messengers, that the Turks were a long way off and not halting in any place for sure, but riding more rapidly than usual, as if impelled by fear, and he perceived this his own men were tired from the journey … he reconsidered and returned to Antioch.

However, Baldwin's aggressive policies, coupled with the shady circumstances in which he became king of Jerusalem, meant cracks began to show in the government of Jerusalem. The main challenges Baldwin II faced, which he met with mixed success, were as follows.

- Rebellion: in 1123, Baldwin II was captured in a military campaign in the northern states and was imprisoned until 1124. During his imprisonment, some of Jerusalem's nobles tried to get Count Charles of Flanders installed as king. Charles refused their request.

- The church: the patriarch of Jerusalem tried to claim Jaffa and wanted control of the city of Jerusalem, because he said it had been promised by Godfrey of Bouillon. These claims were unsuccessful thanks to Baldwin's refusal to acquiesce to them.

- Succession: Baldwin II only had daughters and was therefore unable to secure a male line for the succession. He married his daughter, Melisende, to Count Fulk of Anjou and they had a baby called Baldwin. Baldwin II resolved the issue of his dynasty being overtaken by Fulk's, as he named Melisende, Fulk and Baldwin III as joint heirs to the kingdom.

The origin of these three challenges to effective government was Baldwin's long period of absence in Antioch. This gave the nobles an opportunity to rebel, but another issue was at the heart of their opposition. It was Baldwin's actions when he took the throne that had led to discontent in the first place. In order to secure his rule he had put his own supporters into key positions. For example, Joscelin of Courtenay was made count of Edessa and another cousin, William Bures-sur-Yvette, was given the lordship of Galilee. It was this favouritism that destabilised, but never overwhelmed, the rule of Baldwin II.

Baldwin III and the conflict with Queen Melisende

Baldwin II died on 21 April 1131 and was succeeded by his daughter, Queen Melisende, her husband, King Fulk, formerly of Anjou, and their son, Baldwin III. Their accession to the throne of Jerusalem provoked a conflict between two factions:

- the Montlhéry family; Baldwin II, Melisende and Count Hugh of Jaffa were all members of this family, who held a powerful influence over the nobility in Outremer

- the Angevins; they were newly represented in the East by Count Fulk of Anjou, who was already a powerful ruler in his own right when he arrived in Outremer.

Conflict arose once Fulk became king, as he chose to put Angevins into key positions within the nobility of Jerusalem. This was crucial to help consolidate his position but angered the established lords. He also tried to sideline Melisende and rule without her input. These two factors combined led to a revolt, almost on the scale of civil war, by Count Hugh of Jaffa in 1134.

Hugh, through his support for Melisende's cause to have more power, had already been accused of treason against Fulk prior to 1134. In fact, he was due to take part in a trial by combat when he chose to retreat to Muslim-held Ascalon. Once in Ascalon he made an agreement with the Muslims against Fulk. The effect of this was to turn some of his supporters against him and he was forced to give up his rebellion. Hugh's punishment was exile, but on his way out of the kingdom he was stabbed and died in Apulia. Fulk was implicated in the murder of Hugh, but the evidence for this is largely speculative.

SOURCE 7

An account of how Queen Melisende reacted to the murder of Count Hugh, which Fulk was implicated in. It is from William of Tyre's *A History of Deeds Done Beyond the Sea*, which was written in the early 1180s. William, as archbishop of Tyre, probably wanted to mask the discord between European settlers and those already in Outremer.

Some said that the king cherished a deep mistrust of the count who was rumoured to be on too familiar terms with the queen, and of this there seemed to be many proofs. Hence, spurred on by a husband's jealousy, the king is said to have conceived an inexorable hatred against the man...

[After a discussion of the events of the rebellion and Count Hugh's murder] From that time, all who had informed the count and thereby incited the king fell under the displeasure of Queen Melisende and were forced to take diligent measures for their own safety... Even the king found that no place was entirely safe among the kindred and partisans of the queen. At length, through the mediation of certain intimate friends, her wrath was appeased, and the king finally, after persistent efforts, succeeded in gaining a pardon for the other objects of her wrath – at least to the extent that they could be introduced into her presence with others. But from that day forward, the king became so uxorious that, whereas he had formerly aroused her wrath, he now calmed it, and not even in unimportant cases did he take any measures without her knowledge and assistance.

SOURCE 8

A report of the effect of Fulk's alterations to the nobility of Jerusalem from Orderic Vitalis's *The Ecclesiastical History*, which was written between 1114 and 1141. It is unlikely Orderic would have been present at these events and his account would have been based on reports from visitors to Outremer.

To begin with he [Fulk] acted without the foresight and shrewdness he should have shown, and changed governors and other dignitaries too quickly and thoughtlessly. As a new ruler he banished from his counsels the leading magnates who from the first had fought resolutely against the Turks and helped Godfrey and the two Baldwins to bring towns and fortresses under their rule, and replaced them with Angevin strangers and other raw newcomers to whom he gave his ear; turning out the veteran defenders, he gave the chief places in the counsels of the realm and the castellanships of castles to new flatterers. Consequently great disaffection spread, and the stubbornness of the magnates was damnably roused against the man who changed officials so gauchely. For a long time, under the influence of the powers of evil, they turned their warlike skills, which they should have united to exercise against the heathen, to rend themselves. They even allied on both sides with the pagans against each other, with the result that they lost many thousands of men and a certain number of fortresses.

THINKING HISTORICALLY   Change and continuity (4a)

Significance
Look at the two accounts of Hugh of Jaffa's rebellion in Sources 7 and 8.

1 In what ways does the archbishop, William of Tyre, think that the rebellion might be significant?

2 How significant does William seem to think the rebellion might be in the long run?

3 Compare this to the account of the English chronicler Orderic Vitalis. What significance does Orderic ascribe to Hugh of Jaffa's rebellion?

4 Why do you think these views might differ so greatly?

The power of Queen Melisende

Melisende was understandably angry that her closest male relative had been murdered when he appeared primarily to be defending her interests. This put Fulk in a tricky position, because he could not afford to generate any more animosity towards his leadership at the same time as attempting to resolve Antioch's problems. He was therefore forced to give Melisende a greater role in the day-to-day government of the kingdom. This was a role that she continued actively to fulfil after Fulk's death in 1143, with the support of her cousin, Manasses of Hierges.

When Baldwin III came of age in 1145, his mother, who ruled as a queen rather than as a regent, was not prepared to give up the kingdom. Baldwin III tried to resolve the issue in 1152 and requested a formal division of the kingdom between him and Melisende. This request was ignored by Melisende and Baldwin III was forced to take action. Manasses was besieged in Mirabel, captured and then sent into exile. At the same time, Melisende was besieged in Jerusalem and forced back to her lands in Nablus. As a result, Baldwin III had finally become the undisputed ruler of Jerusalem.

The rule of Baldwin III

The effect of the infighting between Baldwin III and his mother was that the southern campaign had stagnated and no progress had been made in the south. This quickly changed once Baldwin III's position was secured. He built a castle at Gaza, which cut a vital road link between Ascalon and Egypt. He also succeeded in the acquisition of Ascalon itself in 1153, a key port for control of Outremer's coast. In fact, for the remainder of Baldwin III's reign he demonstrated in the following ways that his government could be effective.

- The crusader states bowed to his primacy: Joscelin II of Edessa had been captured in 1150, Raymond II of Tripoli murdered in 1152 and Princess Constance of Antioch had lost her husband in battle in 1149. All of the crusader states therefore looked to Baldwin III for help to restore stability.

- His lords were forced to submit to him: some of the lords of Jerusalem ruled over vast fiefs and began to ignore the judgements of the king of Jerusalem. For example, Gerard, Lord of Sidon, ignored Baldwin's authority and was forced to return his fief to the king as a result.

- He ensured a stable succession: his brother, Amalric, who was well established in Jaffa and Ascalon, succeeded him without dispute after his death on 10 February 1163.

The rule of the 'leper king' Baldwin IV

When King Amalric I died on 11 July 1174, he left behind a government heavily divided by factionalism. This was a result of the fact that Amalric had married twice. One faction gathered around his first wife, Agnes of Courtenay and her children, the other around his second wife, Maria Comnena and the nobles who were popular with Amalric in his later years.

The factions of Baldwin IV's government: Baldwin's paternal line

Name	Additional information
Count Raymond III of Tripoli	Baldwin's cousin
Prince Bohemond III of Antioch	Baldwin's cousin
Balian of Ibelin	There were other Ibelin family members in this faction
Isabel	Daughter of Amalric's second wife, Maria Comnena
Humphrey of Toron	Married to Isabel and stepson to Reynald of Châtillon's stepson

The factions of Baldwin IV's government: Baldwin's maternal line

Name	Additional information
Agnes of Courtenay	Baldwin's mother
Sibyl	Daughter of Agnes of Courtenay and brother to Baldwin IV
Guy of Lusignan	The second husband of Sibyl
Baldwin V	The son of Sibyl and her first husband, William Longsword
Count Joscelin III of Courtenay	Sibyl's uncle
Patriarch Heraclius	Head of the Catholic Church in Outremer
Gerard of Ridefort	Master of the Temple

Thirteen-year-old Baldwin IV had to face the effects of factionalism as soon as he took the crown on 15 July 1174. He was too young

to rule the kingdom and so one of Amalric's most trusted advisors, Miles of Plancy, was appointed to act as regent. However, Miles of Plancy was murdered towards the end of 1174, which allowed Count Raymond III of Tripoli to take over as regent and begin to establish his power base. This set in motion a series of disputes that at times were to paralyse the government of Baldwin IV.

Baldwin's leprosy

The leprosy that Baldwin IV suffered from was the backdrop to the 12 years of argument that began with the regency of Raymond III. Leprosy is a disease that affects the skin, nervous system, nose, throat and eyes. For Baldwin this meant that his feet and hands were disfigured, he suffered from a loss of sensation and eventually he went blind. Towards the end of his life he was unable to walk or ride and had to be carried around by servants. However, the most important consequence of Baldwin's leprosy was his inability to have children. This had two effects on his reign.

1 Baldwin IV prioritised the issue of his sister's marriage. He needed Sibyl to have a male child to secure his royal line.

2 The king's mother, Agnes of Courtenay, was active in the government in her role as queen mother as Baldwin was unmarried.

SOURCE 9 A French illumination from William of Tyre's *History of Deeds Done Beyond the Sea* written in the early 1180s. It accompanies William's story of the discovery of Baldwin IV's leprosy outlined in the introduction to this chapter.

Factions in action, 1174–85

Before Raymond III's regency came to an end, Sibyl was married to William Longsword of Montferrat in 1176 and they had a child called Baldwin (V). Unfortunately, Baldwin V's father died before he was born. This meant that once Baldwin IV had assumed control of the government in 1176, his first task was to find a new husband for Sibyl. This was important because Baldwin IV knew that his leprosy would kill him in early life and he needed to find a king to rule alongside Sibyl until Baldwin V came of age.

Meanwhile, Raymond III was worried that Sibyl's new husband would diminish his power and influence over the government still further. He decided to intervene before Baldwin IV's chosen candidate, Duke Hugh III of Burgundy, reached Jerusalem. In 1180, Raymond, along with Bohemond III of Antioch, began an invasion of the kingdom. They wanted to marry Sibyl to someone they could exercise influence over and chose Balian of Ibelin as their puppet. In order to prevent this match, Baldwin acted quickly and, on his mother's advice, encouraged Sybil to marry Guy of Lusignan.

EXTEND YOUR KNOWLEDGE

Guy of Lusignan (1129–94)

Guy was the son of Hugh VIII of Lusignan, which made him part of a noble family subject to Richard I. His brothers, Geoffrey and Almaric, called him to Outremer and suggested him as a potential second husband for Sybil. Sybil's mother, Agnes of Courtenay, persuaded her to marry him in 1180. It is evident that Sybil grew to like him, as the couple had four children and she rejected attempts by Baldwin IV, and later the nobles of Jerusalem, to get her to divorce him. Guy went on to play an important role in the succession crisis of 1185 (see below) and the Third Crusade (see 'What effect did the leaders of the Third Crusade have on its outcome?' pages 53–61). After the death of Sybil and the events of the Third Crusade, Guy was removed from his position as king of Jerusalem and made lord of Cyprus. He ruled the island until his death in 1194.

The situation now looked pretty grim for Raymond III, whose aborted attempt to raise the status of his faction had been scuppered by Sybil's marriage. However, the balance of power shifted once again in 1183. In August, Baldwin IV had gathered his troops in Galilee to repel Saladin's invasion force. Unfortunately, before the battle began, Baldwin IV caught a fever and was unable to fight. Guy was appointed as regent to act in his place, but struggled to get the lords under his command to obey his orders. This meant Saladin was free to plunder Galilee because the army took no action, although its presence prevented any territory from falling into Saladin's hands. After this Baldwin lost faith in Guy's abilities and he took back control of his kingdom.

The desire for power expressed principally by Raymond III, which at times brought him into open conflict with the faction headed by Agnes, weakened the government. The timeline below illustrates four moments when Saladin was able to take action due to Baldwin's ineffective government.

REIGN OF BALDWIN IV

1174
Saladin is able to annex Damascus with no opposition from the kingdom of Jerusalem

1175
Raymond III of Tripoli makes peace with Saladin; this allows Saladin to focus on uniting different Muslim groups

1180
Baldwin IV makes a truce with Saladin, which lasts until 1182

1183
Saladin launches an invasion from Damascus into Galilee; the area is plundered but the army refuses to meet him in battle

ACTIVITY
KNOWLEDGE CHECK

Look at the timeline on the reign of Baldwin IV and read back through the material above. Then explain why the government of Jerusalem took no decisive action against Saladin in 1174, 1175, 1180 and 1183.

Growing divisions: the succession crisis of 1185

The animosity between the two factions had intensified by 1183. By then both sides had tasted power and both had had it snatched back from them. In November, Baldwin IV, whose bouts of illness had become more frequent and more crippling, laid the groundwork for a succession crisis. He had his infant heir, Baldwin V, son of Sibyl, crowned king and co-ruler. Baldwin IV now began to plan his final years, which he wanted to spend in Tyre. This proposal, which would have involved an exchange of territories with Guy, had to be abandoned because of the growth of animosity between Baldwin and Guy in 1183.

Guy was furious with Baldwin IV, as a result of the coronation of Baldwin V and his reaction to the events of the 1183 campaign. He was certainly not prepared to help him enjoy a comfortable retirement. Instead, when Baldwin tried to bring about a reconciliation, he was refused access to the port of Ascalon. The breach between them had become impossible to bridge. This was good news for Raymond III because his faction was once again popular with the king. When Baldwin IV began to fade away at the start of 1185, Raymond III was appointed regent once more. He remained in this role after Baldwin IV's death in March as he then became regent for Baldwin V. Unfortunately for Raymond III, Baldwin V's reign was to be a short one. The boy king died in August 1186 and one last round in the succession dispute began.

Raymond's fall from power

After Baldwin V's death, Joscelin III of Courtenay was somehow able to convince Raymond to retreat to his lordship territory of Tiberias. The two sides gathered together, one around Isabel, the other around Sibyl, to consider their position. There were three possible outcomes to the succession crisis in 1185.

1 Henry II of England could have become the regent until the issue of succession was resolved. Baldwin IV had sent an embassy in 1184 to Henry with this idea in mind.

2 Raymond III's faction could have maintained their grip on power through the coronation of Isabel and Humphrey.

3 Sibyl and Guy could have been crowned the rulers of Jerusalem. This would have been a victory for Agnes's faction, although not one Agnes would have witnessed as she died in 1185.

Sibyl's faction was the first to take action. The barons of Jerusalem wanted Sibyl to be queen, but only if she agreed to divorce Guy. Sibyl did as she was asked, was crowned queen and then chose Guy as her king. The nobles had been deceived and were angry, especially Reynald of Châtillon, who had turned his support to Sibyl from his own stepson. Around the same time that Sibyl and Guy were crowned, Raymond III's faction met at Nablus and planned to crown Isabel and Humphrey. It looked like the kingdom would slip into civil war, but this was prevented by the actions of Humphrey. Instead of accepting the crown, Humphrey heard of Guy's coronation and rushed to Jerusalem to pay homage to him.

Effect of the divisions

Raymond III was furious with Humphrey, whose actions had put paid to the idea of Isabel and Humphrey's coronation.

His grip on power had been lost for the second time and another two years of infighting had exposed the following weaknesses in the government of Outremer.

- A divided nobility: at the end of 1186, even though Guy and Sibyl were now king and queen, the two factions still existed. This meant any response to the Muslim threat from Saladin would be difficult to organise.

- An inactive government: the government had been crippled by the dispute between the factions. They had been unable to disrupt Saladin's preparations for war or convince the West to help them.

- A cease in hostilities: Raymond III had made a truce with Saladin in 1185. This was an alliance Saladin would later exploit to help his 1187 invasion to succeed.

The significance of Raymond of Tripoli's truce with Saladin

The first hostilities

Raymond III of Tripoli made a truce with Saladin in 1185 while he was still regent for Baldwin V. This was a logical action because the kingdom was too divided to take any decisive action against Saladin. Unfortunately, it was this very division that caused the truce to break down. Towards the end of 1187, Reynald of Châtillon launched a raid on a Muslim caravan, stole its booty, and imprisoned the traders and escort. King Guy tried to salvage the truce with Saladin and requested that Reynald return what he had taken. Reynald, still bitter about the succession dispute that had disadvantaged his stepson, ignored Guy and gave Saladin the excuse to begin hostilities. In March 1187, Saladin attacked Kerak and Montreal.

This was just the prelude to one of Saladin's most successful years in Outremer. He now decided to exploit another internal division. At some point between 1186 and 1187, Raymond had asked Saladin for help against Guy's forces. Raymond was afraid that Guy would attack because he refused to pay homage to him. In return for Saladin's support, Raymond allowed a force of around 7,000 men to journey through Galilee on their way to besiege Acre in May 1187. This was a move that made Raymond a traitor.

In the same month, another force of around 130 knights with 300 men in support, including the Masters of the Templars and Hospitallers, were on their way to Tiberias. They had been sent to encourage Raymond to restore his relationship with King Guy and Queen Sibyl. However, their priorities changed when they

THINKING HISTORICALLY Cause and consequence (4a&b)

Fragile history

Nothing that happens is inevitable. There are causes of change which did not have to develop as they did. Something could have altered or someone could have chosen differently. What actually occurred in the past did happen but it did not have to be like that.

Work on your own and answer the following questions. When you have answered the questions, discuss the answers in groups.

Perceived reasons for the succession crisis of 1185–86

Development	Event	State of affairs	Event	Trigger event
The deterioration of Baldwin IV's health due to leprosy	Baldwin IV's decision to marry Sibyl to Guy of Lusignan in 1180	Tension within Baldwin IV's court between the paternal and maternal factions	The coronation of Baldwin V as co-ruler	The death of the infant Baldwin V

1 Consider Baldwin IV's decision to marry Sibyl to Guy and the political tensions of the time.

  a) How did Baldwin IV's decision to marry Sibyl to Guy of Lusignan affect the tension between the factions?

  b) Had there been no tension would the marriage still have been important?

  c) What other aspects of the situation existing in 1180 would have been affected had there been no political tension?

2 Consider the deterioration of Baldwin IV's health and the events involving the infant Baldwin V.

  a) How important is the deterioration of Baldwin IV's health as a causal factor of the two events?

  b) What might have happened had Baldwin IV decided not to crown Baldwin V while he was still alive?

3 What other consequences came about as a result of the information in the table? Try to identify at least one consequence for each.

4 Choose one factor. How might the succession crisis of 1185–86 have developed differently if this factor had not been present?

discovered Saladin's advance force was in the area. Raymond strongly advised them to hide out with him until the force had passed through. This was ignored as Raymond was now viewed as a traitor. Instead, they launched an attack on Saladin's force of 7,000 and were defeated.

Saladin was quick to capitalise on this success and gathered a huge invasion force together. On 2 July 1187, Saladin abandoned his agreement with Raymond and laid siege to his town of Tiberias. Raymond could see that the situation was desperate and advised Guy to repeat his actions of 1183 and wait for the Muslim forces to retire. Raymond's earlier treachery by coming to an agreement with Saladin meant that Guy was simply not prepared to listen to his main rival. Guy took his army to face Saladin's forces and suffered a heavy defeat at the Battle of Hattin. Jerusalem fell shortly after and the stage was now set for the Third Crusade to begin.

EXTEND YOUR KNOWLEDGE

Saladin's pretext for an invasion

Saladin had a longstanding hatred for Reynald of Châtillon, who controlled the south and east of the kingdom of Jerusalem. In the early 1180s, Reynald first came to Saladin's attention when he broke a two-year truce and raided Tabaka and Taima, which were on the pilgrim road between Damascus and Mecca. He was also alleged to have attacked a Muslim caravan during this campaign when they had stopped near Montreal. This made Reynald a nuisance to Saladin, but in 1183 he became a potential threat. In this year, Reynald arranged for five galleys to be transported to the Red Sea and used them to attack the Muslim pilgrim ports along the coastline. It was even believed by some Muslim contemporaries that Mecca itself might have been a target. The attack did do some damage, but did not seriously threaten Mecca and was stopped by forces from Egypt. The situation calmed for a time, but when Reynald captured a caravan during a period of truce in late 1186/early 1187 tensions flared up once more. Reynald felt that he had every right to seize the caravan. He had not negotiated, nor supported, Raymond's four-year truce with Saladin. The caravan had been travelling from Cairo to Damascus across his territory and had avoided paying his dues. However, Saladin did not see it this way and used it as an excuse finally to launch a full-scale invasion of the crusader states.

A Level Exam-Style Question Section B

How accurate is it to say that, in the years 1152–87, the crusader states became unstable and ineffectively governed? (20 marks)

Tip

This question covers a time span that does not simply go from strong governance to weak. You will need to consider change over time in your answer.

ACTIVITY
KNOWLEDGE CHECK

The rulers of the kingdom of Jerusalem

1 What three criteria would you use to assess the effectiveness of a ruler of the crusader states?

2 Apply these criteria to each of the rulers of the kingdom of Jerusalem from 1100 to 1187.

3 Use your three criteria to explain who was, in your view, the least effective ruler of the kingdom of Jerusalem.

ACTIVITY
SUMMARY

Developments in *the crusader states*, 1100–87

1 Create a timeline from 1100 to 1187 divided by the major events in the different reigns of the rulers of the kingdom of Jerusalem (see page 81).

2 a) Choose one colour. Annotate the timeline with one action taken to:
   - help Edessa
   - help Tripoli
   - help Antioch
   - assert Jerusalem's primacy.

   b) Choose a different colour. Annotate the timeline with one example of:
   - reliance on a military order to help win a battle
   - reliance on a military order to defend a fortification
   - support from a foreign power to remove a threat to Outremer's defence
   - a defensive measure taken by a ruler of Jerusalem.

   c) If appropriate, add a label underneath each ruler in brackets:
   - Strong and effective government
   - Weak and ineffective government.

3 List any connections between a strong and effective ruler of Jerusalem and intervention in the other states.

4 List any connections between a strong and effective ruler of Jerusalem and the security of Outremer.

5 Refer to your timeline and the material in the rest of this chapter. Explain the consequences of weak and ineffective government.

WIDER READING

Barber, M. *The Crusader States*, Yale University Press (2012)

Ellenblum, R. *Crusader Castles and Modern Histories*, Cambridge University Press (2009) particularly chapters 10 and 11

Morton, N. *The Medieval Military Orders 1120–1314*, Routledge (2012)

Phillips, J. *The Crusades: 1097–1197*, Routledge (2014)

Riley-Smith, J. *The Oxford Illustrated History of the Crusades*, Oxford Paperbacks (2001)

1.4

The changing Muslim response to the crusades, 1095–1192

KEY QUESTIONS

- Why did the Muslim opposition to the First Crusade fail?
- To what extent did Muslim power increase between 1144 and 1169?
- What impact did Saladin have on the Muslim response to the crusaders?

INTRODUCTION

On 3 July 1192, tears rolled down the face of the Muslim ruler Saladin as he performed his Friday prayer in the Aqsa mosque in Jerusalem. The army of Richard I was camped a short distance from the city and Saladin knew that, despite his lifelong fight to capture Jerusalem, within a day it could easily be snatched from his hands. His tears fell upon a city that had experienced a turbulent history. Over a century before, it had been captured by one Muslim group, the Seljuks, from another, the Fatimids. Then, with the First Crusade well underway, the Fatimids had recaptured it, only to lose it months later to the crusaders.

Saladin may have taken this moment to reflect upon his own life. It was a life that he had dedicated to uniting all the Muslims in Syria, Egypt and northern Iraq under his rule. He perhaps thought back to 1169 when he had claimed the title of the Egyptian vizier and it first became possible for him to lead the Islamic world in the Near East. He might even have allowed himself to recall with a little pride how, in 1187, with the divisions of the Seljuk and Fatimid world gone, Jerusalem was recaptured from almost a century of Frankish rule. He had completed the journey begun by Zengi, who launched the Muslim counter-crusade, and Nur ad-Din, who brought together much of Muslim Syria under one ruler.

This chapter will examine how the deep divisions between different Muslim groups not only allowed the First Crusade to capture much of the Holy Land, but even helped some of the crusader efforts along. It will explore how the Muslim world first began to unite under Zengi, and then Nur ad-Din, in order to challenge the Frankish presence in Outremer. Finally, it will analyse the manner in which Saladin strengthened this unity in order to conquer a large part of the crusader states.

However, this chapter will also discuss the limits to the growth of Muslim power under Zengi, Nur ad-Din and Saladin. They may have used diplomacy and coercion to force their authority upon the Near East, and then reversed many of the successes of the First Crusade, but their power was never absolute. After all, Saladin, fearful for his own life, left Jerusalem after his tearful Friday prayer session. He knew the Muslims under his control or in alliance with him were not quite strong enough or united enough to capture and hold all of the crusader states. On 4 July, he must have felt an overwhelming sense of relief when he heard the news that Richard I, a man consumed by his own doubts and worries, had abandoned his plans for a siege.

969 – The Fatimid Dynasty takes control of Egypt and parts of Syria and Palestine

| 965 | 970 | 975 | 980 | 985 | 990 | 995 | 1000 | 1005 | 1010 | 1015 | 1020 | 1025 | 1030 | 1035 | 1040 | 1045 | // | 1090 |

1037 – The Seljuk tribe emerges and takes control of Khorasan; it begins to take territory from the Fatimids

WHY DID THE MUSLIM OPPOSITION TO THE FIRST CRUSADE FAIL?

The split between Sunni Seljuk Turks and the Shi'ah Fatimids of Egypt

In the 11th century, Islam was split into two different traditions: Sunni and Shi'ah. This division had led to the rise of rival dynasties, with different claims to power and a strong desire to rule over the entire Islamic world. It meant that when the first crusaders arrived at the doorstep of Asia Minor in 1097, they entered into a world that had been divided by centuries of conflict. It was this disunity that prevented an effective Muslim counter-attack and allowed the crusaders to march hundreds of miles south, through enemy territory, to take Jerusalem in 1099. There were two principal groups, whose enmity caused this to happen, the Shi'ah Fatimids and the Sunni Seljuk Turks.

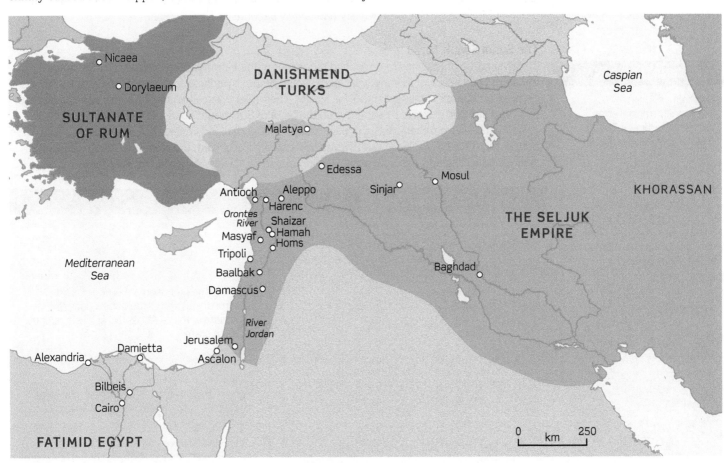

Figure 4.1 Map of the Muslim territories on the eve of the First Crusade.

1099 – Jerusalem is seized from Fatimid control by the leaders of the First Crusade

1144 – Zengi captures Edessa from the Franks; this triggers the Second Crusade

1154 – Nur ad-Din takes control of Damascus by force

1174 – Nur ad-Din dies and Saladin begins to take control of his former territories

1187 – The Battle of Hattin and the capture of Jerusalem by Saladin

| 1095 | 1100 | 1105 | 1110 | 1115 | 1120 | 1125 | 1130 | 1135 | 1140 | 1145 | 1150 | 1155 | 1160 | 1165 | 1170 | 1175 | 1180 | 1185 | 1190 |

1097 – The Siege of Nicaea and the Battle of Dorylaeum mark the first major defeat of Islamic forces in the First Crusade

1127 – Zengi becomes the governor of Mosul; he begins to take control of important Muslim cities

1146 – Nur ad-Din comes to power as ruler of Aleppo after the murder of Zengi

1169 – Saladin becomes the vizier of Egypt after power is usurped from the Fatimid vizier, Shawar, by Saladin's predecessor

1183 – Saladin takes control of Aleppo from Zengi II

The Shi'ah Fatimids

Shi'ah Muslims believe that authority to be a political and religious leader comes directly from the Prophet Muhammad. His descendants, through his wife Fatimah and son-in-law 'Ali, are known as imams. Different Shi'ah groups believe that the line of descent from the prophet followed different paths and ended at different stages. However, the Fatimid dynasty did not believe the line had disappeared at all. They claimed that they were direct descendents of 'Ali and that a Fatimid caliph could therefore rule with his authority. The position of caliph was primarily a symbolic one and much of the day-to-day running of government was in the hands of a vizier.

By 969, the Fatimids had control of Egypt and had established an empire that until the 1060s also covered much of Syria and Palestine. Over a century later, they had held onto possession of Egypt but had lost control of most of their territory further north. In fact, by 1095, they could only claim authority over Tyre, Sidon and Acre. This was thanks to the work of the Egyptian vizier Badr al-Jamali. He fought to maintain a Fatimid presence outside Egypt, but due to the threat from a rival group of Muslims, the Fatimid dynasty had largely become an Egyptian one.

The Sunni Seljuk Turks

The rival group of Muslims that reduced the power of the Fatimids were followers of the Sunni tradition. They believed that a government should be run by adhering to **Sunna**, the customs of the prophet, and **Shari'a**, the legal basis for a state. Their ruler was called a caliph, with **sultans** beneath him, who had power to enforce the law on the basis of Sunna and Shari'a. The most powerful Sunni caliph had been from the Abbasid dynasty based in Baghdad. However, after 1059, the Abbasids were puppet rulers for the Seljuk Turks. They were nomadic Turks from the steppe of the Aral Sea that established a sultanate covering parts of Iran, Iraq, Syria, Cilicia, Anatolia and Palestine.

THE RISE OF THE SELJUK TURKS

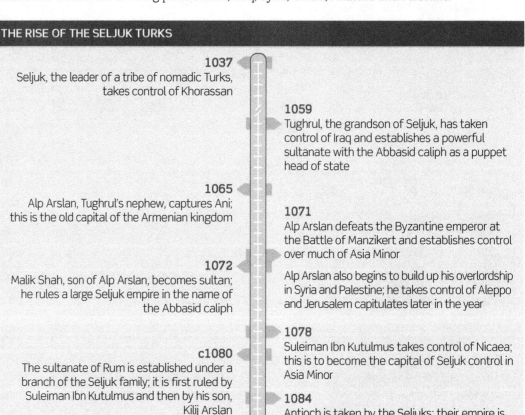

1037
Seljuk, the leader of a tribe of nomadic Turks, takes control of Khorassan

1059
Tughrul, the grandson of Seljuk, has taken control of Iraq and establishes a powerful sultanate with the Abbasid caliph as a puppet head of state

1065
Alp Arslan, Tughrul's nephew, captures Ani; this is the old capital of the Armenian kingdom

1071
Alp Arslan defeats the Byzantine emperor at the Battle of Manzikert and establishes control over much of Asia Minor

Alp Arslan also begins to build up his overlordship in Syria and Palestine; he takes control of Aleppo and Jerusalem capitulates later in the year

1072
Malik Shah, son of Alp Arslan, becomes sultan; he rules a large Seljuk empire in the name of the Abbasid caliph

1078
Suleiman Ibn Kutulmus takes control of Nicaea; this is to become the capital of Seljuk control in Asia Minor

c1080
The sultanate of Rum is established under a branch of the Seljuk family; it is first ruled by Suleiman Ibn Kutulmus and then by his son, Kilij Arslan

1084
Antioch is taken by the Seljuks; their empire is now at the height of its power

SOURCE

1 An image of the Seljuk sultan Malik Shah from a 14th-century manuscript. The image depicts Muslims from different areas under his control, shown by the different styles of headwear. It suggests that he was a powerful ruler. However, his death marked a turning point in the power of the Seljuk Turks.

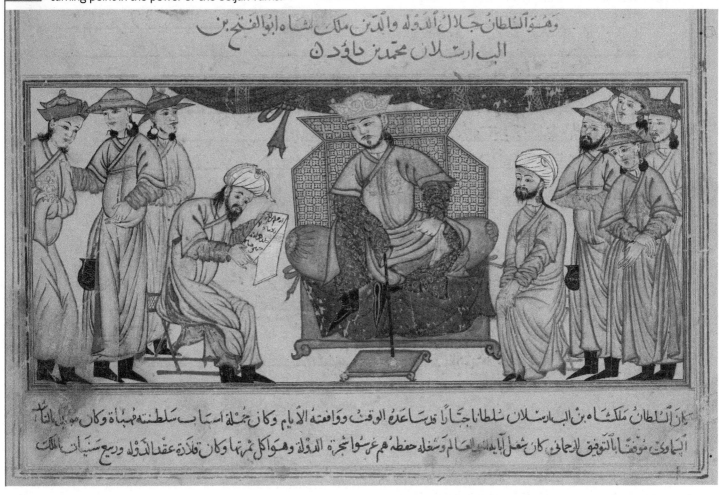

Weaknesses in 1095

The Seljuk Turks might have been strong enough to face the crusading armies in 1095 if the powerful rule of Malik Shah had continued and the Fatimid dynasty had either provided support or stayed out of the way. Unfortunately, several prominent figures died in the 1090s and transformed the political landscape of the Muslim empires.

- In 1092, Malik Shah's vizier, Nizam al-Mulk, was murdered. Malik Shah himself died a month later. This set the stage for a succession crisis that crippled the Seljuk Empire.

- In 1094, the Egyptian vizier, Badr al-Jamali, died. The Fatimid caliph al-Mustansir died shortly afterwards. This triggered a succession crisis among the Fatimids as well.

The Fatimids had lost a powerful vizier in Badr al-Jamali, as he had been responsible for the resurgence of their power in the 1080s. His death temporarily halted their incursions into Palestine, but a few years later the political situation in Egypt stabilised. They resumed their attacks against the Turks and retook Jerusalem in 1098. This action made it clear they were not going to support the Seljuks or co-operate with them. Instead, they were going to exploit the crusader attacks for their own political gain.

In contrast to the temporary effect of al-Mustansir's death on the Fatimid government, the death of Malik Shah had a profound effect on the Seljuk Turks. They had lost an exceptionally strong ruler whose empire began to collapse into rival territories ruled by different **atabegs**. Their political situation was not only threatened from the outside by the Fatimids and the crusaders, but also from the inside by their own rulers. The following issues divided the Seljuks.

KEY TERM

Atabeg
A military ruler similar to the position of a general in the West. An atabeg could both lead an army and rule a city or territory.

- Malik Shah had left Aleppo to his nephew, Ridwan. He was very unpopular with the Aleppans.

- The Atabeg of Mosul threatened Ridwan's hold on Aleppo as he wanted to extend his power over northern Syria.

- Ridwan's brother, Duqaq, had been left Damascus. He opposed Ridwan and tried to stop him from increasing his possessions in Syria.

- The **emir** of Antioch joined Duqaq of Damascus in an alliance against Ridwan of Aleppo.

- Malik Shah's brother, who ruled Syria, was killed by his nephew in the fighting that followed.

> ### KEY TERM
>
> **Emir**
> The Islamic equivalent of a lord. Emirs had some degree of independence, but held their power from a sultan or caliph. They tended to rule over cities, like Homs or Shaizar, and usually commanded an army.

> ### EXTEND YOUR KNOWLEDGE
>
> **Malik Shah (1035-92)**
> The Seljuk sultan Malik Shah was the son of Alp Arslan. He was a powerful ruler who extended his empire in the east against rival Muslim groups and in the west against the Byzantines and Fatimids. It was under his guardianship that rule over Anatolia extended to such an extent that the sultanate of Rum was established with his cousin, Suleiman Ibn Kutulmus, and his son, Kilij Arslan, as its rulers. He was a ruthless leader who tackled threats to his authority swiftly. For example, he put down rebellions from his brother, Tekish, in 1081 and 1084. However, it was this strength that created a power vacuum, which the First Crusade took advantage of. He died in somewhat mysterious circumstances shortly after the murder of his vizier. The result was a period of Seljuk civil war for his sultanate between three rivals, which included his sons, Mahmud and Barkyaruq, and his brother, Tutush.

The effect of all of this infighting was the disintegration of the Seljuk Empire. It had gone from having a strong sultan with loyal atabegs beneath him, to a group of rival atabegs, loosely related to each other, who desperately began to try and establish their own sultanates. For example, Homs was under the control of a Turk called Janah al-Dawla, Tripoli was governed by a group called the Qadis and Jerusalem was ruled by the **Artuqids**. This disintegration meant it was no surprise that the Fatimids were able to take Jerusalem in 1098, or that the counter-attack against the crusaders took a long time to organise and ultimately proved ineffective. The Muslim rulers were simply too divided to stop them.

> ### KEY TERM
>
> **Artuqid**
> A member of a tribe of Turks from eastern Anatolia and Iraq founded by Artuq. They were supposed to be under the control of the Seljuk sultan, but they came into conflict with one another. They later supported Nur ad-Dın and Saladın.

SOURCE 2

A treatise on holy war written by al-Sulami. In it he argues that disunity weakened Muslim Syria and led to great losses during the First Crusade. It was written around 1105 and formed an attempt, which was unsuccessful, to call for a jihad against the Franks.

When the reports confirmed for them that Syria suffered from the disagreements of its masters and its rulers' being unaware of its deficiencies and needs, they confirmed their resolution to set out for it, and Jerusalem was their dearest wish... They looked out over Syria, on separated kingdoms, disunited hearts and differing views linked with hidden resentment, and with that their desires became stronger and extended to everything they saw. They did not stop, tireless in fighting the jihad against the Muslims. The Muslims were sluggish, and were reluctant to engage in combat until the enemy conquered more than their greatest hopes had conceived of the country, and destroyed and humiliated many times the number of people they had wished. Still now they are spreading further in their efforts, assiduous in seeking an increase in their profits. Their desires are multiplying all the time because of what appears to be the Muslims' abstinence from opposing them, and their hopes are invigorated by virtue of what they see of their enemies' contentedness with being unharmed by them, until they have become convinced that the whole country will become theirs and all its people will be prisoners in their hands. May God in his generosity humble their ideas by bringing together everyone and arranging the unity of the people...

The significance of Kilij Arslan's defeat at Nicaea, 1097

Background to the siege of Nicaea

Kilij Arsan was the Seljuk sultan of Rum, ruler of a large territory in western Anatolia carved out by his father, Suleiman Ibn Kutulmus. His sultanate was surrounded by enemies: the Byzantines to the west, the Danishmend Turks to the north and the Greater Seljuks of Iraq and Iran to the south. The city of Nicaea itself, on the north-western edge of his sultanate, was the first target of the crusaders in 1097. It was also Kilij Arslan's capital and was well guarded and well defended. For the crusaders, securing Nicaea would mean access to an old military road eastwards into Asia Minor. For Kilij Arslan, preventing a successful siege could end the crusade before it had even reached the Holy Land.

May 1097 was the month Kilij Arslan could have repeated his success against the People's Crusade (see page 37) and destroyed the princes' armies. He had the opportunity to strike at the individual contingents rather than the whole force of the crusader army, as the contingents arrived by separate routes at separate times. Godfrey of Bouillon's forces arrived on 6 May 1097. They waited until 14 May for Bohemond's contingent before they launched an attack. They then had to wait until 3 June for the northern French to arrive. Kilij could have attacked the crusaders before they had begun their siege on Nicaea and may have forced them to retreat. The effect would have been to slow or perhaps even stop the crusade.

The siege of Nicaea

In reality this opportunity for a show of Muslim strength was missed as Kilij was occupied elsewhere (see page 93). By 14 May, around 7,500 knights and 5,000 infantry began to besiege Nicaea. The crusaders adopted a dual strategy with a land-based blockade of the city's gates and the use of siege weapons against its towers and walls. Kilij arrived on 16 May, while the siege was in full force. He tried to break through the army surrounding his capital city, but was hugely outnumbered. On 21 May, he gave up and fled south. The city's garrison was to hold out another month, as it continued to receive supplies through its western entrance, which was on a lake.

The crusaders finally managed to force Nicaea to surrender on 18 June 1097, as a result of an ingenious strategy to block the western entrance to the city and reinvigorate the siege on the walls at the same time. A request was sent to Emperor Alexius Comnenus for ships to be carried overland to Lake Ascanius. These would be used to blockade the water side of Nicaea. The fleet arrived on 17 June and was deployed on 18 June outside the city. The garrison, which had long since been abandoned by Kilij Arslan and was surrounded by the full might of the First Crusade, gave up. This was a huge success for the crusaders, but the first of several missed opportunities for the Turks.

Why did Kilij Arslan fail?

Kilij had arrived at the siege after it had already begun. He had been busy in a conflict with the Danishmend Turks over Malatya. This delayed his arrival until 16 May 1097, which gave the bulk of the crusader army time to arrive, discuss strategy, secure supplies and launch its offensive. When Kilij reached the city, he found it surrounded by the crusaders. This left him in a difficult position. He would have to break through first and then defend the city from the rest of the army. His forces, weakened by the campaign they had just left, were insufficient and could not break through. When Kilij gave up on 21 May, he left behind his capital, his family and the bulk of his money. The loss of Nicaea was a costly first mistake.

The significance of Kilij Arslan's defeat at Dorylaeum, 1097

After the siege of Nicaea, the crusader numbers had dropped. There were now around 50,000 in the army with about 7,000 knights. Kilij Arslan decided to make one more attack on the crusaders and he hoped that even with a small force of 6,000 Muslim troops he might be able to halt or slow their progress. He tried to increase his chances of success with a diplomatic effort to unite with fellow Muslims and made an alliance with his former enemy, the Danishmend emir. His plan was to pick a moment when the full force of the crusading army was divided into smaller contingents and then launch a surprise attack with his mounted archers on one of these. He could then withdraw and attack the next time the crusaders split up.

Kilij's first opportunity arose on 1 July 1097, when Bohemond's contingent marched on ahead of the main army en route to its rendezvous point at Dorylaeum. Before they reached their destination, the combined troops of the Seljuk Turks of Rum and Danishmend Turks surrounded the crusaders and attacked. The crusaders held their ground and waited for the other contingents to arrive. In the meantime, thousands of Christians faced wave after wave of arrow attack, but managed to stay in formation.

The risk was that if they began to charge or try to escape, the Turks would have been able to break into the heart of the contingent and massacre the Christians.

Fortunately, before this happened, at around midday and after five hours under attack, Godfrey's contingent arrived. Kilij was now outnumbered and stood very little chance of victory. He knew his only chance of success was to attack small parts of the crusader army, rather than the whole. Kilij's army took the only option left open to it and chose to flee. It had inflicted heavy losses, as around 4,000 Christians were killed, but the crusader army was undefeated. It continued on its journey through Anatolia and towards the Holy Land.

ACTIVITY
KNOWLEDGE CHECK

The divisions in the Muslim world of the Near East

1 Look at Source 2 by al-Sulami. Identify two claims he makes to explain why the Muslims were defeated in the First Crusade.

2 Re-read the material above. What evidence can you find to back up the claims made by al-Sulami?

Why was the Battle of Dorylaeum significant?

The principal outcome of the Battle of Dorylaeum was that Kilij Arslan's reputation as a powerful Sultan was shattered. The crusader army faced very little opposition from the other towns and cities of western Anatolia and most surrendered without a fight. By the time the crusaders reached their next stopping point at Konya, they found the town had been abandoned ahead of their arrival. The locals, many of whom were eastern Christians, realised that Kilij did not have the strength to defend his territory and the initial resistance to the West had failed. The main consequences of Kilij's defeat were as follows.

- Byzantine reoccupation: the Byzantine Empire had, until recently, ruled over much of Anatolia. With Kilij's forces weakened, the Byzantine army took the opportunity to reoccupy Nicaea and its surrounding towns. The Muslim threat from western Asia Minor had been removed.

- Turkish forces temporarily wiped out: around 3,000 Muslims were killed during the counter-attack at Dorylaeum. This was fortunate for the crusaders because as a result of the summer heat, lack of supplies and intense tiredness, they were only able to march around five to ten miles a day. The army was in no fit state to defeat a large Turkish force.

- Education: the crusaders had witnessed the tactics the Turks were to deploy in later battles. They had seen how powerful the mounted archers were and learnt how the Turks would pretend to retreat in order to get the army to break formation.

At the end of 1097, the initial attempt to prevent the First Crusade had failed. The Muslims had not presented a united front against the Christians, nor had they acted with sufficient speed to stop them. By the time they did begin to work together it was too late; Nicaea had surrendered, the authority of the Turkish rulers was weakened and the Byzantine Empire had re-established its grip on the region.

The defeat of Kerbogha's force at Antioch, 1098

Early attempts

The Franks began to lay siege to Antioch in October 1097 but it took until December for the Turks to organise a relief force to help the city's garrison. This force was led by Duqaq, king of Damascus, and was supported by his atabeg, Tughtegin, and his ally, Janah-ad-Daulah, the emir of Homs. They surprised the crusaders, who were on a foraging expedition, on 31 December, but were unable to achieve a decisive victory against them.

Many knights survived because Bohemond of Taranto managed to hold his cavalry in formation in order to escape, although he suffered heavy losses in his infantry. The next day Robert of Flanders led an attack against the Turks to try and take back their supplies. The Turks forced Robert to retreat, but then chose to take no further action. Their inaction, which is unexplained by contemporary sources, meant the crusaders survived to continue the siege.

A new force of around 12,000 men, under Ridwan of Aleppo, set out for Antioch in February 1098. They had every chance of success because the crusaders only had around 700 mounted knights available to intercept the Turks. This would leave the siege camp with only infantry for protection. Nevertheless, in spite of their numerical superiority, the Turks were once again defeated. This time it was through Bohemond's skilled leadership that the Franks were able to use surprise and a cavalry charge to force Ridwan's troops to retreat. In the end they fled all the way back to Harim after a prolonged chase by the crusaders. They had once again been defeated by the crusaders and the siege of Antioch continued.

Kerbogha's final attempt

By May 1098, the crusaders had been able to attack Antioch, without effective opposition, for over seven months. Kerbogha, the governor of Mosul, knew that the garrison could not hold out indefinitely against the crusaders and would soon run out of supplies. His fear of a crusader victory led him to gather around 35,000 Turks to try and bring an end to the siege. He drew on allies from across the Turkish world, which included powerful rulers like Tughtegin of Damascus and Sulayman of Mardin. When this huge force arrived at Antioch on 5 June and began its assault on the crusaders on 9 June, it had sufficient manpower to bring an end to the First Crusade once and for all.

Unfortunately for the Turks, troop numbers were not enough to defeat the crusaders. Bohemond's sophisticated strategy (see pages 43–44) led to a crusader victory on 28 June 1098. This was not only a result of crusader skill but also of weakness in the Muslim forces. The Turks contributed to their own downfall in a number of ways.

- **Time wasting:** Kerbogha's forces spent three weeks in Edessa as part of an attempt to take control of the city from Baldwin of Boulogne. This was unsuccessful and meant that by the time the Turks arrived at Antioch, the crusaders had already broken into the city.

Kerbogha (d.1102)

Kerbogha was a powerful ruler of northern Iraq whose leadership was partly responsible for the disunity of the Seljuk Empire. He first came to prominence in the Seljuk civil wars as a supporter of Barkyaruq and acted as a commander on his behalf. He was captured in May 1094 and only obtained his freedom when Barkyaruq met with some success against his enemies. After his release, Kerbogha embarked upon a campaign to increase his own power and influence. He besieged Mosul and captured the city in 1095. He then looked westwards to extend his empire. It is in this context that his actions during the First Crusade should be viewed. His attempts on Edessa and on Antioch were opportunistic and part of his empire-building plans. They were borne out of the potential the Seljuk civil war had created for a new, powerful Muslim ruler to emerge. His failure at capturing both cities led him to leave campaigning in Syria for elsewhere. He died in 1102 with little by way of achievement other than the capture of Mosul.

- **Division among allies:** Kerbogha gathered troops from across the territories of the Seljuk Turks, but he did not have complete authority over them. As the governor of Mosul, he was powerful, but he did not command their absolute loyalty. He was also unable to get Ridwan of Aleppo to join him.

- **Poor generalship:** Kerbogha made bad decisions on the battlefield that led to his defeat. For example, he chose to spread his troops around the whole city rather than concentrate his attack forces. He also lacked the power to rally his troops. This meant that when the crusaders defeated the first wave of Turks and they began to flee, Kerbogha was unable to prevent the rest of his army from joining them.

- **The Seljuk Fatimid divide:** in February 1098, the Fatimids had approached the crusaders with a proposal for peace. The result was that the Fatimids did not send an army to support Kerbogha. It also encouraged the crusaders to focus on the capture of territory in the north rather than the towns and cities near to Egypt in the south.

SOURCE 3

Ibn al-Athir's description of the Muslim attack on the Franks at Antioch and its results. It is recorded in his *Universal History*, which was written in the early 13th century. Al-Athir was noted for the breadth of his source material.

On the fifth day they went out of the gate in scattered groups of five or six or so. The Muslims said to Karbughā, 'You ought to stand at the gate and kill all that come out, because now, when they are scattered, it is easy to deal with them.' He replied, 'No, do not do that. Leave them alone until they have all come out and then we can kill them.' He did not allow his men to engage them. However, one group of Muslims did kill several that had come out but he came in person and ordered them to desist.

When the Franks had all come out and not one of them remained within, they drew up a great battle line. At that, the Muslims turned their backs in flight, firstly because of the contempt and the scorn with which Karbughā had treated them and secondly because he had prevented them from killing the Franks. Their flight was complete. Not one of them struck a blow with a sword, thrust with a spear or shot with an arrow. The last to flee were Suqmān ibn Artuq and Janāh al-Dawla because they were stationed in ambush. Karbughā fled with them.

SOURCE

4 An account of Bohemond's victory against Kerbogha from the *Gesta Francorum*. This was written by an anonymous southern Italian Norman knight or cleric, c1101.

After Curbara saw the lines of the Franks, so beautifully formed, coming out one after the other, he said: 'Let them come out, that we may the better have them in our power!' But after they were outside the city and Curbara saw the huge host of the Franks, he was greatly frightened …

…Curbara began immediately to retreat little by little toward the mountain, and our men followed them little by little. At length the Turks divided; one party went toward the sea and the rest halted there, expecting to enclose our men between them. As our men saw this, they did likewise. There a seventh line was formed from the lines of Duke Godfrey and the Count of Normandy, and its head was Reinald. They sent this (line) to meet the Turks, who were coming from the sea. The Turks, however, engaged them in battle and by shooting killed many of our men. Other squadrons, moreover, were drawn out from the river to the mountain, which was about two miles distant. The squadrons began to go forth from both sides and to surround our men on all sides, hurling, shooting, and wounding them. There came out from the mountains, also, countless armies with white horses, whose standards were all white. And so, when our leaders saw this army … they recognized the aid of Christ, whose leaders were St. George, Mercurius, and Demetrius. This is to be believed, for many of our men saw it. However, when the Turks who were stationed on the side toward the sea saw that that they could hold out no longer, they set fire to the grass, so that, upon seeing it, those who were in the tents might flee. The latter, recognizing that signal, seized all the precious spoils and fled.

THINKING HISTORICALLY Evidence (3a)

The value of evidence

Read the evidence from Ibn al-Athir (Source 3) and the Norman knight/cleric (Source 4) about the battle for Antioch on 28 June 1098, then work through the tasks that follow.

1 Write down at least three ways in which Ibn al-Athir's *Universal History* is useful for establishing the sequence of events during the battle for Antioch, and three ways in which the *Gesta Francorum* is useful.

2 Compare your answers with a partner, then try to identify at least two limitations of each source for establishing the sequence of events in the battle.

3 Discuss with a partner whether you think Ibn al-Athir or the anonymous crusader's account is more useful for establishing the sequence of events on 28 June 1098.

4 Suppose the sources were used to answer the question 'What was the role of Kerbogha in the battle for Antioch?' Complete the diagrams below to show the usefulness and limitations of the two sources for answering this question and two questions of your own.

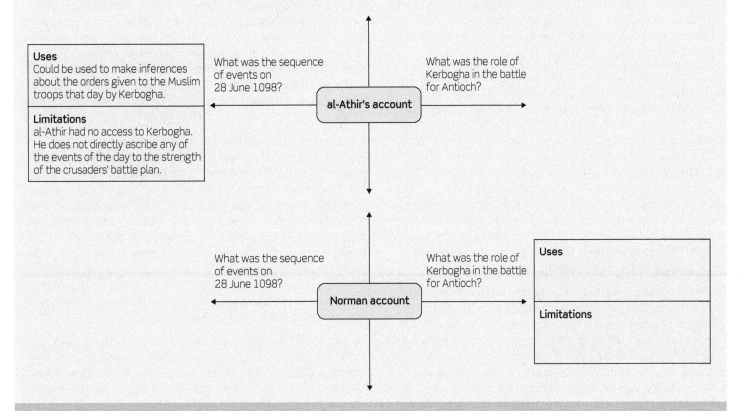

The fall of Jerusalem, 1099

A view of Jerusalem with the Dome of the Rock in the foreground. This was the most well-known Muslim mosque in Jerusalem and symbolised the importance of the city to Muslims. The loss of the city was of huge religious significance to Muslims.

The march south

The fundamental reason for the crusader victory over the Muslim forces at Jerusalem was that they were able to reach the Holy City with very little opposition along the way. The Arabs, Turks and Egyptians could have attacked, ambushed or obstructed the march south. This would have reduced the numbers in the crusader army, placed greater strain on its supplies and sapped the morale of the troops. It would also have given the Egyptians more time to prepare a rigorous defence of Jerusalem. The failure to provide opposition proved to be yet another missed opportunity for the Muslim forces.

At the heart of this failure were the divisions that had allowed the crusaders to march through Asia Minor and successfully take Edessa and capture Antioch. First, the rivalry between the rulers of Aleppo and Damascus had grown in intensity. The two rulers were more interested in fighting each other than facing the crusader threat. Secondly, this Seljuk division was exacerbated by the fact that it did not control all of Syria and Palestine. There were Arab emirs who ruled over Shaizar, Homs and Hamah that had little interest in helping either the Seljuks or the Fatimids. Finally, there was a tension between the rulers and the ruled. Most of the native Syrians were Shi'ah Muslims, but were ruled by Sunni Seljuks. This made it unlikely the local population would unite under a Seljuk banner to oppose the crusaders.

The impact of these divisions was that the Muslim towns and cities the crusaders travelled past preferred to negotiate rather than fight. For instance, the emir of Homs gave the crusaders money in return for the city's safety. He was joined by several other leaders, such as the ruler of Caesarea, who ransomed their towns to avoid conflict. Some even went as far as to help the crusaders along their journey. In order to encourage the crusaders to bypass their towns, emirs such as the emir of Shaizar offered guides to help their enemy navigate through Muslim territory. The result was a peaceful, well-supplied and relatively easy journey southwards.

However, it was the biggest division among the Islamic rulers that helped the crusaders the most. The Egyptian Fatimids, now in control of Jerusalem, had been in negotiation with the crusaders for around two years. Talks were only abandoned when the Egyptian vizier al-Afdal presented his final offer in June 1099. By this time, the crusaders were already at Bethlehem and no Fatimid army had marched north to defend Jerusalem or intercept them. In fact, the only significant delay the crusaders encountered was of their own making, when Raymond of Toulouse had embarked upon the siege of Arqah. The crusaders therefore reached Jerusalem with their army intact and their forces ready to attack.

The failure to defend Jerusalem

When the crusaders arrived outside Jerusalem in June 1099, they had reached a city that had only just been captured by another group: the Egyptian Fatimids. They had taken advantage of the Seljuk preoccupation with the First Crusade and recaptured the city from their Muslim rivals. This helped the crusaders in two ways.

1 The Fatimids had little time to refortify Jerusalem and prepare it for a lengthy siege.

2 The siege machines they had just used to take the city had been disassembled and the wood hidden. The crusaders found it in a nearby cave and used it to make their own siege tower.

The crusaders' position was further strengthened by the reliance of the Fatimids on their peace negotiations. In June 1099, the Egyptian embassy had presented a final offer. The proposal was that the Fatimids would be allowed to keep Jerusalem, but they would permit 200 unarmed Christians to enter the city as pilgrims. Unfortunately, al-Afdal had not realised how central the Jerusalem objective was to the crusaders and his offer was refused. The talks collapsed and the crusaders felt justified to begin their siege. In the meantime, the Fatimid commander of Jerusalem, Iftikhar ad-Daulah, faced a daunting task with no immediate support from Egypt.

The siege of Jerusalem was a success for the crusaders (see page 45) and one of the reasons it fell was that Iftikhar faced too great a challenge. The crusaders attacked the city on two fronts, but the garrison commander did not really have enough troops to defend them both. This strain clearly affected him because he allowed himself to be duped by the crusaders. They constructed their siege tower outside the Quadrangular Tower in order to lure Iftikhar's troops into the defence of that point. When the crusaders moved their siege tower during the night of 13–14 July to St Stephen's Gate, the garrison was in the wrong place. This helped the crusaders to make rapid progress in their attack on the city and secure control of it by 15 July.

By the time the Fatimid vizier, al-Afdal, had reached Jerusalem it was already too late. He arrived in early August with a force of around 20,000, which outnumbered the crusaders. However, he had been slow to act and this gave the crusaders the upper hand. They were able to catch the Egyptians by surprise while they were still in their camp around Ascalon, and they forced them to disperse with a powerful cavalry charge. The Fatimids, delayed by overconfidence and rivalry with their Muslim counterparts in Syria and Palestine, had failed to prevent the crusaders from the achievement of their final goal. Jerusalem was to remain out of their hands for almost a century, until another Egyptian ruler, Saladin, eventually took it back.

ACTIVITY
KNOWLEDGE CHECK

The fall of Antioch and Jerusalem

Use the information above on the failures at Dorylaeum, Antioch and Jerusalem to answer the following questions:

1 What was the most significant effect of the loss at the Battle of Dorylaeum? Why?

2 To what extent did Antioch and Jerusalem fall from Muslim control for the same reasons?

TO WHAT EXTENT DID MUSLIM POWER INCREASE BETWEEN 1144 AND 1169?

Zengi and the seizure of Edessa, 1144

The rise of Zengi

Zengi, the Sunni governor of Mosul, was the first Muslim ruler effectively to present himself as the leader of a jihad. Sunni Muslims in the 12th century believed this meant that he was striving to spread Islam until the whole world was under its influence. In their tradition the authority to lead a jihad came from the caliph, who was based in Baghdad. However, Zengi appropriated this idea for his own use. He claimed that the Islamic world needed to be brought under the control of one ruler first so that it could then launch an attack on the Franks. The caliph would be the symbolic head of this offensive, but Zengi was to exercise practical power. His governorship thus marked the first attempt to consolidate the power of the rival Turkish warlords.

EXTEND YOUR KNOWLEDGE

Jihad

The literal translation of jihad is a 'struggle'. Within medieval Islamic doctrine there were two types of jihad. One was an internal jihad, which meant to improve oneself and become more pious. The other was an external jihad, fought against the Franks and other non-Muslim groups and as such was the Muslim answer to a crusade. This was the justification that Sunni rulers used to motivate supporters to join their attacks on the crusader states. It rose to prominence in anti-crusader rhetoric during the reign of Zengi after his attack on Edessa in 1144. Another feature of the jihad was that it should be fought by a pious leader. This is why figures like Zengi and Saladin were keen to show themselves as generous and deeply religious. Zengi, for example, founded *madrasa*, which were theological colleges, and *khanqas*, which provided homes for Sufi preachers.

It was an attempt that met with considerable success, as Zengi managed to use force and diplomacy to carve out a large principality in Syria and northern Iraq between 1127 and 1146. The timeline below illustrates how Zengi was able to spread his power from the city of Mosul to neighbouring Aleppo and then begin to challenge the authority of Damascus. It also shows his successful reduction of the threat from the Franks through the capture of castles and territory near Tripoli. Before the seizure of Edessa, Muslim power had already begun to gather into the hands of one man and the stage was set for Zengi's jihad against the Franks.

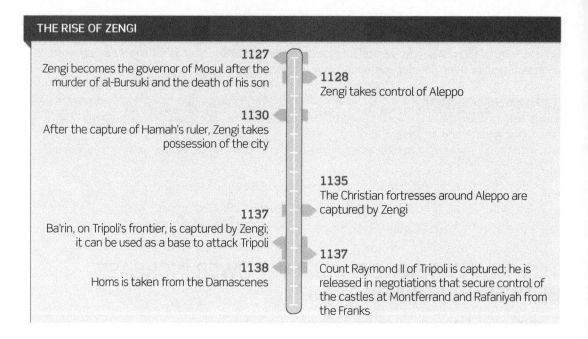

THE RISE OF ZENGI

1127
Zengi becomes the governor of Mosul after the murder of al-Bursuki and the death of his son

1128
Zengi takes control of Aleppo

1130
After the capture of Hamah's ruler, Zengi takes possession of the city

1135
The Christian fortresses around Aleppo are captured by Zengi

1137
Ba'rin, on Tripoli's frontier, is captured by Zengi; it can be used as a base to attack Tripoli

1137
Count Raymond II of Tripoli is captured; he is released in negotiations that secure control of the castles at Montferrand and Rafaniyah from the Franks

1138
Homs is taken from the Damascenes

Limits to Zengi's power

Zengi was a powerful ruler, who was later able to use his power to begin a counter-crusade against the Franks. However, his authority had limits and he faced a number of rivals who restricted his influence. These included the following.

- The Damascene Turks: Damascus was under the control of a powerful atabeg called Muin al-Din Unur. In 1140, Unur's power was strengthened through an alliance with the Franks against Zengi.

- The Artuqid Turks of Diyr Bakr: they limited Zengi's control of the territory surrounding his principal cities of Aleppo and Mosul. He attempted to defeat them in 1134 when he launched an attack on the ruler of Hisn Kayfa, but failed to secure the region.

- The Seljuk Turks of Anatolia: they were a block to the spread of his influence to the north-west of his territories.

- The Franks: Zengi was threatened by the Christians, usually from Tripoli, on a number of occasions. For example, Count Bertrand of Tripoli launched an unsuccessful attack in the mid-1130s.

- The Byzantines: in April 1138, the Byzantine emperor, John Comnenus, attacked Shaizar and almost succeeded in its capture.

The seizure of Edessa

The attack on the city of Edessa by Zengi was a reaction to the political situation in both the Islamic and Christian territories. It had been triggered by an alliance between Count Joscelin II of Edessa and the Artuqids of Diyr Bakr. This alliance threatened Zengi but at the same time gave him an opportunity. In late 1144, Joscelin II had responded to a request for help from the Artuqid Qara Aslan, which meant that Edessa was vulnerable to attack.

This was a chance for Zengi to weaken the Artuqids through the removal of an ally and also to restore his reputation as the leader of a jihad. This reputation had come under question because of Zengi's primary focus on war against fellow Muslims, rather than incursions against the Christians. For example, in 1139, Zengi had seized control of Ba'albek from a fellow Muslim ruler and taken many prisoners. He promised to free the prisoners, but ultimately decided it was better to have them executed.

His actions at Ba'albek had damaged Zengi's popularity and threatened to undermine his authority as the leader of a jihad. Any attempt to take power from the Franks could only work to his benefit. This was especially true because Zengi's territory was vulnerable to the Franks. When he first came to power in the 1120s, cities like Aleppo and Shaizar had only recently stopped the payment of tribute to the Franks. This showed how susceptible these cities were if the Franks were allowed to retain or increase their strength. An attack on Edessa would be Zengi's chance to restore his reputation, reduce a rival Turk's power and limit Frankish influence in the region.

In late November 1144, Zengi began to lay siege to Edessa. He had tunnels dug under the northern walls of the city and built siege towers to attack the walls at their weakest points. The attack reached its climax on 23 December when Zengi ordered the wooden props of the tunnels to be set on fire. This caused the tunnels and the walls above to collapse. The city was entered on 24 December and the citadel captured by 26 December. The city had been taken by force and around 15,000 Edessans had been killed in the process. It was a huge victory for Zengi and a startling defeat for the Franks.

SOURCE

6

An account of the seizure of Edessa in *The Damascus Chronicle* written around 1160 by Ibn al-Qalanisi, a Syrian chronicler. It provides an Islamic perspective on Zengi and how the idea of the holy war was used by him to gather supporters. His success, described in the source, helps to explain how he emerged in the Islamic world as the leader of the first significant jihad against the Franks.

He [Zengi] wrote to the tribes of **Turkmens**, calling upon them to give support and assistance against it and to carry out the obligation of the Holy War, and a great host and vast multitude of them joined him, so that they surrounded the city on all sides and intervened between it and those who sought to bring supplies and foodstuffs to it. Even the birds could scarce approach it, in fear of their lives from the unerring shafts and watchfulness of the besiegers. He set up **mangonels** against its walls, and while these unceasingly bombarded the city, he engaged in constant and persistent fighting with its people. The men of Khurāsān and of Aleppo ... set to work and made saps [tunnels] at a number of places...They then shored these up with stout timbers and special appliances ... When fire was applied to the shoring it caught the timbers and destroyed them, and immediately the walls fell down. The Muslims forced their way into the city, after a great number on both sides had been killed over the ruins; so many of the Franks and Armenians were killed and wounded that they were compelled to abandon the town and the Muslims took possession of it by the sword...

KEY TERMS

Turkmen (a.k.a. Turcoman)
A group of nomads who converted to Islam in the 10th century.

Mangonel
A siege weapon that was used to hurl rocks at a castle or fortified town.

SOURCE

7

An account of the seizure of Edessa in William of Tyre's *A History of Deeds Done Beyond the Sea*, which was written in the early 1180s.

Zengi found the town bereft of defenders and was much encouraged. He encircled the town with his forces, assigned the officers of his legions to appropriate stations, and dug in. The catapults and siege engines weakened the fortifications; the continual shooting of arrows tormented the citizens incessantly; and the besieged were given no respite...

... He ran the gamut of attacks and left nothing untried which could harass the citizens and aid him in gaining control of the city. He sent sappers through trenches and underground tunnels to undermine the walls. As they dug passages beneath the walls, they buttressed these with posts, which were afterward set on fire. A great part of the wall was thus broken down ... Their forces rushed together into the city. They slew with their swords the citizens whom they encountered, sparing neither age, condition, nor sex. of them it might be said: 'They murder the widow and the stranger, they slay the orphan, the youth, and the virgin, together with the old man.' The city, therefore, was captured and delivered to the swords of the enemy.

Consistency in claims

Sources 6 and 7 could be used by a historian to build up a picture of Zengi and the conquest of Edessa in 1144.

Answer the following questions:

1 Explain why Sources 6 and 7 offer two views of Zengi's conquest of Edessa. How might this affect their value as pieces of evidence in appraising the situation? Explain your answer.

Discuss the following questions in groups:

2 Suppose the historian had ten independent accounts that agreed broadly with Source 6 and only four that agreed with Source 7. What would that tell them about the event?

3 How far should the balance of the evidence play a role in constructing written history? What else must a historian consider about the evidence being used before drawing conclusions?

AS Level Exam-Style Question Section B

To what extent did the Muslim response to the crusades change in the years 1095 to 1149? (20 marks)

Tip

This question is asking you to make a judgement on the extent of change between the First and Second Crusades. Remember that Muslim unification was still far from complete by 1149.

The effects of the seizure

The capture of Edessa restored Zengi's status as the leader of a jihad against the Franks. He immediately tried to consolidate this victory and captured Sürüc in January 1145. He also began to attack Birecik in March 1145, but had to abandon the siege in May due to the murder of his deputy in Mosul. Regardless of this setback, Zengi had set the stage for a Muslim counter-attack and power began to slip from Frankish hands. Unfortunately, Zengi was unable to see the fruits of his victory because he was killed by one of his Frankish slaves in 1146. This meant he did not witness the events of the Second Crusade and the failure of the Christians to extend or even to re-establish their control in the Near East.

Nur ad-Din's consolidation of power, 1146–54

Nur ad-Din's goals

On 14 September 1146, Zengi was stabbed to death and his sons, Sayf al-Din Ghazi and Nur ad-Din, inherited his territories. Sayf inherited the lands to the east which were centred on Mosul and Nur inherited Aleppo to the west close to the Frankish border. This division meant that Nur ad-Din's priorities were focused on Syria, rather than spread across both Syria and northern Iraq. His two initial goals were a result of this:

1 to unite Syria under one Muslim ruler

2 to reduce the threat from the Franks on his western border.

These goals were more limited than his father's and, as such, had a much greater chance of success. In order to unite Syria, he would need control of the principal cities of Damascus, Homs and Ba'albek. However, these would only be secure if the Frankish influence in Edessa was removed and the immediate threat from Antioch, his closest Frankish neighbour, was minimised.

Tackling the Frankish threat: Antioch

After the fall of Edessa in 1144, Antioch was now the biggest threat to Aleppo and Nur ad-Din's power in the surrounding region. In 1146, Nur ad-Din decided to form an alliance with the Seljuk sultan of Rum who, as their northern neighbour, also stood to benefit from the weakening of Antioch. The pair made a tentative move almost immediately and captured Hab and Kefer Lata, which would secure access to Aleppo. They followed this up in June 1149, with additional support from a Damascene force, with a direct assault on Antioch's key strongholds. This led to the Battle of Inab on 29 June 1149, at which the Antiochenes were defeated and Raymond of Poitiers, the prince of Antioch, was beheaded.

The Battle of Inab was a hugely significant victory for Nur ad-Din. He took advantage of his success through a continued campaign in Antioch before he negotiated a treaty with the Franks. His follow-up actions allowed him to take Apamea, Harenc, Albara and Artesia from the Antiochenes. He also captured the castle at Tortosa in Tripoli, which he destroyed and then abandoned. This meant that, by the summer of 1150, in which he took control of the region around Bira, Nur ad-Din had successfully extended his border westwards to the line of the Orontes River valley.

Tackling the Frankish threat: Edessa

Alongside his campaigns against Antioch, Nur ad-Din also had to quell the unrest in Edessa that followed Zengi's death. In November 1146, the people of Edessa tried to take back control of their city from Islamic rule. However, on 9 November, Nur ad-Din arrived with his Aleppan troops and forced the Edessans to surrender or flee their city. In total, around 30,000 were killed in the massacre that followed. This was to ensure that there were no further uprisings against Nur ad-Din's authority in the city.

He then, after providing support for Damascus in the siege that formed the centrepiece of the Second Crusade, rekindled his alliance with the sultan of Rum. Together they subdued the rest of Edessa's fortress towns after they had been sold to the Byzantines. The last major stronghold, the fortified town of Turbessel, was captured on 12 July 1151 by Nur ad-Din. The threat of an invasion by the Franks, or the Byzantines, via Edessa had now been removed and he could focus on the unification of Muslim Syria.

The unification of Syria under one Muslim ruler

In 1149, Nur ad-Din's brother, Sayf al-Din Ghazi, died. This was an opportunity for Nur ad-Din to try to capture Mosul and expand his empire eastwards. Unfortunately, this came at the same time as the death of the ruler of Damascus, the campaign in Antioch and the capture of an important Edessan noble. Nur ad-Din did make a half-hearted claim on Mosul, but it was given to another brother to control and Nur ad-Din settled for Homs as compensation. Instead of the extension of his land eastwards, he had begun to lay claim to land in the south and had set in motion his consolidation programme in Syria.

The next step was to acquire the powerful city of Damascus. The ruler, Mu'in al-Din, died in August 1149 and Nur ad-Din tried to convince the inhabitants of Damascus to accept him as their ruler. However, control was in the hands of the Burid dynasty and passed instead to Abaq. He formed an alliance with the Franks to help prevent Nur ad-Din's forces from taking the city. Nur ad-Din tried to capture Damascus again in June 1151, but the Damascenes turned to the Franks once more and they forced him to retreat in July. It was not until Abaq was deposed in April 1154, and Nur ad-Din began an attack and intensified the blockade of the city, that it was finally taken.

SOURCE

8

An explanation of why Damascus was captured by Nur ad-Din in *The Damascus Chronicle* written around 1160 by Ibn al-Qalanisi, a Syrian chronicler. It provides an insight into why the ruler of Damascus was deposed as a result of Nur ad-Din's actions.

> In Dhu'l-Qa 'da [Islamic month – beginning 18 January 1154] prices rose in Damascus owing to the absence of the usual grain convoys from the north, Nur al-Din, lord of Aleppo, having issued orders preventing and prohibiting traffic. This measure caused great distress among persons of humble condition and the poor and weak. The price of a sack of wheat reached twenty-five dinars and even more. A large number of persons withdrew from the town, and they suffered such hardship, distress and weakness that a great many died on the roadsides, and the supply of provisions was cut off on all sides. It was said that Nur al-Din was determined to proceed to the siege of Damascus and hoped to capture it by this means, since it was difficult for him to break down its resistance owing to the strength of its sultan and the number of its troops and auxiliaries – we pray God for speedy release from distress and to look upon His creatures with compassion and mercy, as He hath ever shown goodness and bounty to them in the past.

The last step in the unification of Muslim Syria was to take the only remaining stronghold of the Burid dynasty. This was achieved in June 1155 when Nur ad-Din captured Ba'albek. This meant that, for the most part, Muslim Syria was now in the hands of one Muslim ruler. Nur ad-Din was now free to focus his efforts on the reduction of the crusader states, the conquest of Egypt and, eventually, the acquisition of Mosul.

Nur ad-Din's growing rift with Saladin

The growth of Nur ad-Din's power, 1154–69

The successful unification of Muslim Syria, and the campaigns against the Franks in both Edessa and Antioch, had helped to cement Nur ad-Din's image as the leader of a jihad. By 1154, he had earned his place as Zengi's successor, but it was a position he was now forced to defend as the power of the

Franks grew under King Baldwin III and King Amalric. He rose to the challenge and was able to contain the threat to Syria on a number of occasions.

- In 1156, he began to resolve the ongoing issue of Harenc. It had been disputed by the Franks and Turks ever since the Battle of Inab. Nur ad-Din negotiated a treaty that shared the revenues of Harenc between both sides.

- In 1157, he successfully repelled an attack on Shaizar by the Franks.

- In August 1164, he defeated the Christian forces at Artah. He was supported by the Artuqid Turks and at the Battle of Harim captured several Frankish nobles, including Bohemond III of Antioch and Raymond III of Tripoli. He also established complete Muslim control of Harenc.

These examples illustrate that Nur ad-Din continued to act in role as the leader of a jihad. However, his power was not without limits and he was prepared to turn on his Muslim allies if necessary. For example, in 1159, the Byzantine emperor, Manuel Comnenus, threatened Aleppo with an invasion. Nur ad-Din chose to join Manuel in a truce against Kilij Arslan, the sultan of Rum, rather than fight with the odds stacked against him. Nur ad-Din's image as a shield against the Franks was also questionable, because he did not win every battle. For instance, the Franks defeated him during an attack at al-Buqay'a in 1163. This suggests that whilst Nur ad-Din's power had increased, it was far from ready to launch an all-out assault on the Franks.

The issue of Egypt

One of the main reasons Nur ad-Din was unable to pursue an all-out jihad against the crusader states was that Muslim Syria simply did not have enough resources to defeat them. However, Egypt could provide the answer to this problem. It was immensely wealthy and had a world-renowned port at Alexandria. It was also a powerful country that could provide Nur ad-Din with enough troops to launch an attack on the crusader states from both the south and the east. The only problem was that Egypt was still under Fatimid control and did not fall within the influence of Nur ad-Din's Abbasid caliph.

The temptation to launch an invasion of Egypt was strengthened by the threat it faced from the Christians. It would be a catastrophe for Nur ad-Din if Egypt fell to Baldwin III or Amalric, because they would then be able to use its wealth to turn on him. This was a very real threat because the Franks launched five attempts on Egypt in the 1160s, which included attacks on Bilbeis, Alexandria, Cairo and Damietta. Nur ad-Din's situation was endangered still further by an alliance against him between the Egyptian vizier, Shawar, and the Franks. In 1167, Shawar offered the Franks 400,000 dinars if they would stay in Egypt until Nur ad-Din's forces had been defeated. It was clear immediate action had to be taken to avoid Egypt's fall into Frankish hands.

The Egyptian campaign: the rise of Saladin

Saladin began his rise to prominence in Nur ad-Din's Egyptian campaign. The commander of Nur ad-Din's invasion force was Shirkuh and his nephew, Saladin, acted as his second in command. The first recorded action in Saladin's military career

SOURCE 9

A photograph of the minbar (a platform from which a sermon is delivered by an imam or religious leader) of Nur ad-Din, which he commissioned in 1168–69. It was his intention to place this in the Aqsa Mosque once he had conquered Jerusalem. This task was completed by Saladin once Jerusalem was captured. The minbar is a powerful symbol of Nur ad-Din's emphasis on his role as the leader of a jihad against the Franks.

occurred in 1167. In this year, Shirkuh's forces attacked and captured Alexandria, after which Shirkuh split his troops. He took part of his army out of the city to avoid all his forces being trapped in a lengthy siege. Saladin remained behind and took charge of defence. The campaign then descended into a stalemate situation and was resolved by peaceful means. Shirkuh and Amalric agreed that they would both leave Alexandria, which they did in August 1167.

However, the withdrawal was only a short pause in the Egyptian campaign. In November 1168, the Franks seized the initiative, attacked Bilbeis and massacred its inhabitants. Their former ally, Shawar, turned to Nur ad-Din for help. Shirkuh, along with Saladin, marched in response to Cairo, where his army made camp in order to defend the capital from the Franks. Amalric, rather than entering into another siege, decided to count his losses and withdrew on 2 January 1169. Unfortunately, from Shawar's point of view at least, Shirkuh and Saladin remained encamped outside Cairo.

By 8 January 1169, Shirkuh had entered Cairo. He then began to position himself as Shawar's replacement as vizier. This was an important position, because the caliph was the symbolic leader of the country, but his vizier acted on his behalf as the actual ruler. On 18 January, Shawar was murdered, probably by a supporter of Shirkuh or perhaps even at his request. Regardless of guilt, Shirkuh was installed as the new vizier by the caliph, although his rule was to be a brief one. On 13 March 1169, Shirkuh himself died and, even though there were rumours of the use of poison, it is most likely that it was the result of a poor diet and illness associated with this. His replacement, invested on 26 March, was none other than Saladin.

The rift between Nur ad-Din and Saladin

At first sight the investment of Saladin with the title of Egyptian vizier appeared to be a tremendous victory for Nur ad-Din. His power was now spread across Abbasid Syria and Fatimid Egypt. He should have been in a position finally to launch a definitive assault on the Franks. However, Saladin's actions made it clear that, rather than bolster the position of Nur ad-Din, he planned instead to build his own power base. Saladin would not exactly challenge Nur ad-Din's power, but nor would he act as a mindless puppet to exploit Egypt for Nur ad-Din's ends.

In order to consolidate Saladin's position, he first placed his family in key positions within the Egyptian government. His brother, Turan-Shah, joined him almost immediately on 7 July 1169; his father, Ayyub, arrived soon after and was appointed Egypt's treasurer. The rest of his brothers and his nephews quickly followed. With his family around him, he could feel more secure against rival claims to his leadership and minimise the risk of a rebellion within his government. He strengthened his position still further through the creation of a military corp, the Salhiyya, which was directly responsible to him. By the time a force of Franks and Byzantines renewed their offensive in Egypt in October 1169, Saladin was ready to defeat them.

Despite Saladin's theoretical challenge to Nur ad-Din's power, it was not until the 1170s that this had any practical effect on Nur ad-Din. There were at least three instances before Nur ad-Din's death in May 1174 when Saladin failed to act in accordance with his wishes.

- In September 1171, Saladin and Nur ad-Din planned a joint offensive against the Franks. The plan was for Saladin to attack Shaubak and Nur ad-Din to attack Kerak. Then the pair would meet up in the middle. Saladin took Shaubak but then retreated before Nur ad-Din reached him. He may have feared the very real potential for Nur ad-Din to order him back to Syria.

- In 1173, Saladin began an attack on the castles at Montreal and Kerak. Nur ad-Din planned to join him, but once again Saladin decided to leave before his arrival. Saladin chose instead to consolidate the territories around Egypt. Nur ad-Din was thus denied another opportunity to confront his supposed servant in Egypt.

- Nur ad-Din wanted to use Egypt as a financial resource to fund his campaigns further north. However, Saladin knew that if Egyptian resources were extracted from the country's population, his own strength and perhaps even his position would be threatened. When Nur ad-Din ordered a financial audit of Egypt in 1173, Saladin replied with extravagant gifts rather than the promise of an annual tribute.

Ibn al-Athir's description of the deep difference between Nur ad-Din and Saladin. It is from his *Universal History*, which was written in the early 13th century. It shows that, at this point in history, the belief was that Saladin would have to submit to Nur ad-Din if the pair met face to face.

When Nur al-Din heard what Saladin had done [attacked Shaubak], he left Damascus, also making for Frankish territory to enter it from another direction. Saladin was told: 'If Nur al-Din enters the lands of the Franks while they are in this situation, you on one side and Nur al-Din on another, he will conquer them and when the Franks are cleared from his route and their king taken, with Nur al-Din there will be no place left in Egypt. If Nur al-Din comes to you here, you will have to meet him and then he will exercise his authority over you as he wishes. If he wishes, he will leave you alone and if he wishes, he will dismiss you and you will be unable to resist. Your politic course is to return to Egypt.'

Saladin then withdrew from Shawbak to return to Egypt, without taking it from the Franks... He made his excuses at length but Nur al-Din did not accept them. His attitude towards him changed and he resolved to enter Egypt and expel him.

ACTIVITY
KNOWLEDGE CHECK

The power of Zengi and Nur ad-Din

1 Look back at the goals of Nur ad-Din between 1146 and 1154 on page 100. Try to think of a third goal for the period from 1154 to 1169.

2 Create two spider diagrams entitled 'Zengi's power' and 'Nur ad-Din's power'. Add the three goals to each diagram, then find evidence for them. Try to include both achievements and limitations.

3 After reviewing your spider diagrams, do you think Nur ad-Din could have launched a full-scale attack aimed at Jerusalem in 1169?

THE POWER OF SALADIN, 1169–92

Consolidation of Saladin's power in Egypt and Syria, 1169–84

Control of Egypt

The previous section detailed how Saladin strengthened his hold on power in Egypt between his appointment as vizier in 1169 and the death of Nur ad-Din in 1174. His actions are summarised below.

- He placed his family into key positions within Egypt's government.
- He created a military unit directly responsible to him.
- He prioritised Egypt's needs over those of Nur ad-Din.

During this period, Saladin also needed to strengthen his position over the Egyptians themselves. He could not simply use force and coercion; he also had to be accepted in order to avoid rebellion. The first step in this process was to legitimise his authority as the vizier of Egypt. The problem was that Saladin's authority came from the Abbasid caliph al-Mustadi, based in Baghdad, not the Fatimid caliph in Cairo, al Adil. Saladin resolved this when al Adil became ill in August 1171 and it became apparent he would soon die.

He decided to have the Sunni Abbasid caliph proclaimed as the caliph of Egypt at Friday prayers on 10 September 1171. This marked the end of the Fatimid dynasty and a challenge to Saladin's power was neutralised.

The death of al-Adil a few days later on 13 September 1171 was a turning point in Saladin's control of Egypt. Nevertheless, he still needed to improve his popularity amongst the Egyptians. He was, after all, a conqueror who had usurped power from the longstanding Fatimid dynasty. In order to tackle this, Saladin decided to cancel an unpopular trading tax called the mukus in Fustat and Cairo. This measure came into force on Friday 6 October 1174. It showed that Saladin was not, at this stage, going to act as a foreign ruler who had come to steal from Egypt. Instead, he worked hard to construct his image as a leader who would look after the Egyptians, rather than simply use the country for his own ends.

The death of Nur ad-Din

On 15 May 1174, a new chapter in Saladin's career began that broadened his horizons beyond Egypt's borders. Nur ad-Din had died and his empire, which now covered Egypt, Syria and the Jazira region in northern Iraq, was up for grabs. However, this would not be a quick and easy task because Nur ad-Din's death split up his possessions. The table below provides a summary of Nur ad-Din's empire in 1174.

The situation in Nur ad-Din's empire after his death

Country/ region	Key stronghold(s)	Date acquired by Nur ad-Din	Situation after his death
Egypt	Cairo	1169	Saladin was still in control as the Egyptian vizier.
Syria	Aleppo and Damascus	1146 and 1154	Aleppo was inherited by Nur ad-Din's son, al-Salih. The Damascenes tried to remain independent and formed an alliance with the Franks.
Jazira	Mosul	1170	Nur ad-Din's nephew, Said ad-Din, inherited Mosul.

> **A Level Exam-Style Question Section B**
>
> To what extent was Nur ad-Din personally responsible for the growth of Muslim power? (20 marks)
>
> **Tip**
> *Other explanations should take account of the role and importance of Saladin, but it should be remembered that his influence on Muslim power was not wholly positive.*

Saladin aimed to be the most powerful leader in the Islamic Near East and model himself as the next leader of the jihad against the Franks. This was a task that took him over 10 years and would involve:

- the reconstruction of Nur ad-Din's territories under one leader through the use of force and diplomacy

- the legitimisation of Saladin's authority outside of Egypt through negotiation with the Abbasid caliph

- the maintenance of loyalty to his predecessor's claims through a slow acquisition of power, rather than a full-blown offensive campaign into the territories of Damascus, Aleppo and Mosul.

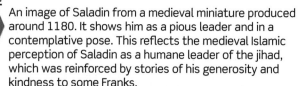

SOURCE 11

An image of Saladin from a medieval miniature produced around 1180. It shows him as a pious leader and in a contemplative pose. This reflects the medieval Islamic perception of Saladin as a humane leader of the jihad, which was reinforced by stories of his generosity and kindness to some Franks.

Stage one: Damascus

Damascus was Saladin's easiest conquest. On 28 October 1174, with al-Salih occupied in Aleppo and Said ad-Din busy with Mosul, Saladin marched peacefully into Damascus. The Franks did not come to the Damascenes' aid and Saladin proclaimed himself ruler of the city. He strengthened his claim through his marriage to Nur ad-Din's widow in late 1176 in Damascus. By this time, the city had submitted itself to him and had already provided troops for his campaign against Aleppo. Saladin now had control of Egypt and southern Syria. The next step was to conquer the north.

SOURCE

12 Baha ad-Din Ibn Shaddad's account of the sultan's march to Syria and his taking of Damascus. Baha ad-Din Ibn Shaddad entered the service of Saladin in 1188 and wrote his *Life of Saladin* in praise of his master before his death in 1234.

When the sultan [Saladin] received confirmation of Nur al-Din's death, aware that his son was a child unable to shoulder the burdens of kingship and incapable of taking on the defence of the lands against God's enemies, he made his preparations to march to Syria, since it is the cornerstone of Muslim territory. He set out with a large force of troops, leaving in Egypt some to assume its protection and defence...

...The followers of al-Salih were not united and their policies were in disarray. They were fearful of one another and several of them had been arrested... The sultan arrived in Syria demanding that he himself should take on al-Salih's guardianship, direct his affairs and set straight what had gone awry. The sultan reached Damascus, without having renounced allegiance, and entered the city after a peaceful hand-over ... and he took over the citadel.

He went straight to his father's house and people flocked to him rejoicing at his coming. That same day he distributed huge sums of money to the people and showed himself pleased and delighted with the Damascenes, as they did with him.

Stage two: Aleppo

The acquisition of Aleppo proved a far more difficult task. Instead of a simple, peaceful march into a leaderless city, Saladin had to take it by force from a legitimate heir. The timeline below outlines the key stages in the Aleppo campaign. It shows how long it took for Saladin to take the city, because he faced a strong leader, an alliance between Aleppo and Mosul against him and struggled to get the Abbasid caliph of Baghdad to support him. The eventual submission of the city on 11 June 1183 was a hard-fought victory for Saladin.

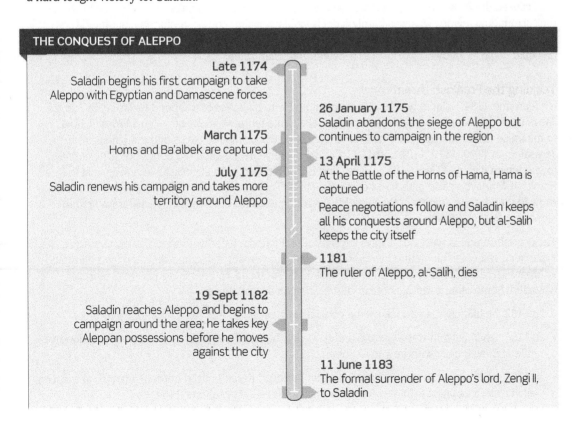

THE CONQUEST OF ALEPPO

Late 1174
Saladin begins his first campaign to take Aleppo with Egyptian and Damascene forces

26 January 1175
Saladin abandons the siege of Aleppo but continues to campaign in the region

March 1175
Homs and Ba'albek are captured

13 April 1175
At the Battle of the Horns of Hama, Hama is captured

July 1175
Saladin renews his campaign and takes more territory around Aleppo

Peace negotiations follow and Saladin keeps all his conquests around Aleppo, but al-Salih keeps the city itself

1181
The ruler of Aleppo, al-Salih, dies

19 Sept 1182
Saladin reaches Aleppo and begins to campaign around the area; he takes key Aleppan possessions before he moves against the city

11 June 1183
The formal surrender of Aleppo's lord, Zengi II, to Saladin

Stage three: Mosul

The final stage in Saladin's attempt to recreate Nur ad-Din's empire was to capture Mosul. This would give him control of the Jazira region of northern Iraq. He began his campaign against the city in 1185 and adopted the same approach he had taken to Aleppo. He first tried to take over the territory around the city before he began to besiege it. He took control of the area to the south around the rivers of the Great and Little Zab. He also conquered Mayyafariqin to the north in August 1185. Mosul was effectively surrounded.

However, its new king, Izz al-Din, refused to be drawn into a battle and Saladin became seriously ill. This led to the decision to make a permanent peace with Mosul. In February 1186, Izz al-Din accepted the overlordship of Saladin and agreed a peace treaty in March. This new alliance meant that Mosul would now provide Saladin with troops to fight the Franks. He may not have taken direct control of the Jazira, but he had now reached the peak of his power as a Muslim ruler.

Securing his position

Saladin had already used one method to secure control of his newly acquired territories through his marriage to Nur ad-Din's widow in 1176. Another method to legitimise his authority was to encourage the Abbasid caliph of Baghdad, al-Mustadi, formally to invest him as the city's ruler. In 1175, al-Mustadi invested Saladin with Egypt, Yemen and most of Syria. Unfortunately, the new caliph in 1180, al-Nasir, was not so keen to help Saladin and refused to invest him with Mosul. This was one of the reasons why Saladin ultimately accepted overlordship of Mosul instead of direct rule. Nevertheless, Saladin's emirs could now be safe in the knowledge that their power flowed from a legitimate ruler.

An equally important step in Saladin's journey to power was to quell any personal threats to his life. He was a prominent political figure and as such could be a target for an assassination. For example, in 1174, al-Salih's supporters sponsored 13 Assassins to murder Saladin. They approached his tent during a mealtime and one attacked Saladin, but before the Assassin had time to launch a deadly blow a loyal emir beheaded him with a well-timed swing of the sword. Several of Saladin's men were killed, including an important lord called Khumartekin, but Saladin himself survived.

Saladin chose to take revenge in August 1176, after he faced another attempt on his life by the Assassins. He took his army to the Assassins' castle at Masyaf and pretended to besiege the castle. This caused the Assassins to gather around the castle, which allowed Saladin's men time to plunder the surrounding region. This was hardly a decisive blow against the Assassin tribe, but it did show them that Saladin was not to be trifled with. After this, there were no serious attempts on his life and he could begin to enjoy his position as a powerful Muslim ruler.

Tackling the Frankish threat

Until around 1184, Saladin was largely preoccupied with his attempt to bring Muslim Syria and the Jazira under his control. Nevertheless, he did take some tentative steps between 1170 and 1184 to minimise the threat from the Franks. He launched successful offensives into the kingdom of Jerusalem in 1170, 1179, 1182 and 1183. During these years, he acquired control of some small towns, which included Gaza, Aila (Aqaba) and Buria. He also led a successful attack against the Franks at Marjayoun and plundered parts of Galilee. These successes, while hardly ground-breaking, showed that despite an overall focus on Muslim conquests, his consolidation programme required him to confront the Franks.

These confrontations were not always successful and Saladin faced setbacks. The most notable of these occurred when he planned a raid on Ascalon, but was surprised and defeated by the Franks at Mont Gisard on 25 November 1177. He lost 1,000 men and 750 of his troops were seriously wounded. Some other examples of his failures include the following.

- In 1182, he launched an attack on the coastal town of Beirut, but failed to capture it.

- In 1183, while Saladin was able to plunder Galilee, he failed to bring the Franks out to a decisive battle and eventually withdrew in October.

- In 1183, and then again the next year, Saladin besieged Kerak but did not managed to take it. This was in spite of support from the Artuqids. He withdrew in September 1184.

Saladin's campaigns against the Franks therefore provided a backdrop to his period of consolidation, but were more of a distraction than a primary goal. This explains why he was willing to negotiate a truce with the Franks in 1180 and then again in 1185. The 1180 truce, for example, gave him time to intervene in an argument between the Seljuks and the Artuqids. The 1185 truce gave him the breathing space he needed to attack Mosul and force Izz al-Din to support him. His last truce of the period, which was made with the Byzantine emperor, was negotiated with border security in mind. Saladin knew he needed to tackle one threat at a time and, with his consolidation programme complete, he was now ready to take on the Franks.

Muslim challenges to Saladin

It is popular to view Saladin as a powerful figure who united the Muslim world in the Near East. This was an image that Saladin himself was careful to construct with the help of historians like Baha ad-Din Ibn Shaddad. However, he was not universally popular in the Islamic world and this was one of the reasons he struggled to capture Outremer in its entirety. His biggest rival was the caliph of Baghdad, al-Nasir, who did not trust Saladin. This fear was shared by the Seljuks of Iran and Anatolia, as well as Muslim groups elsewhere, such as the Almohads in North Africa. It developed because Saladin spent a much greater proportion of his life in the fight against fellow Muslims, rather than the Franks. In fact, he only really spent the final years of his life, 1187–93, focused exclusively on the holy war. The result was a lack of Muslim support from outside his territories and a struggle to gain naval supremacy, which in turn explains why Tyre remained in the hands of the Franks after the Third Crusade.

ACTIVITY
KNOWLEDGE CHECK

Saladin's consolidation programme

1 In what ways did the death of Nur ad-Din signal a new beginning for the growth of Muslim power?

2 Write three sentences giving one example in each of the methods used by Saladin to break down the barriers to his rule by (i) Muslims in Egypt, (ii) Muslims in Syria, (iii) the Franks.

The attack on Tiberias

In 1187, Saladin finally took up the role established by Zengi and then Nur ad-Din as the leader of a jihad. Up until then, he had come under fierce criticism for his focus on conflicts against fellow Muslims, rather than Christians. This policy, while unpopular with the current Abbasid caliph, was a sound one. It had given Saladin time to build up the resources required to defeat the crusader states. By this year, he had the combined forces of three countries to call upon, while the crusaders struggled to get any support from the West at all.

The invasion of the kingdom of Jerusalem began with a small Muslim force numbering around 7,000 led by Saladin's son, al-Afdal. He entered Galilee under the treaty negotiated with Raymond III of Tripoli (see page 86) and planned to attack the coast

A small Christian force of around 130 knights decided they would try and stop al-Afdal. However, in what would prove to be the first example of the Franks' numerical inferiority, they were defeated and killed at Cresson. Numbers were to play a central role in the successes Saladin was about to enjoy. The estimated sizes of the two forces were as follows.

- In May 1187, Saladin gathered around 30,000 men together, which included around 12,000 cavalry.

- In June 1187, King Guy of Jerusalem assembled around 20,000 men, which included around 1,200 mounted knights.

SOURCE 13 Ibn al-Athir's description of Saladin's call to jihad in 1187. It is from his *Universal History*, which was written in the early 13th century. It reveals the broad range of troops Saladin could now draw on to give him numerical superiority in the conflict with the Franks.

In 583/1187 Saladin wrote to all the provinces to call them to arms in the Holy War. He wrote to Mosul in the Jazira, to Arbela and other eastern states, to Egypt and to the Syrian domains, calling them to arms and exhorting them to fight in the Holy War, and commending as many as possible to arm themselves for battle. At the end of muharram/April 1187 he and his army and the Damascene guard left Damascus and marched to Ras al-Ma', where the Syrian contingents joined them. He gave his son al-Malik al-Afdal 'Ali command of them and marched with a contingent of his own troops to Busra. This was because he had heard that Arnat of al-Karak was going to attack the pilgrims [a group of Saladin's relations on a pilgrimage] and cut off their advance, making it clear that once he had dealt with them he would return to bar the way to the Egyptian army and prevent its joining up with the Syrians. Saladin therefore marched on Busra to prevent Arnat's attack on the pilgrims and to make him stay quietly at home for fear of the Sultan.

In July 1187, the invasion began in earnest. Saladin's plan was to try and draw the Franks into battle. His experience in 1183 had taught him that if he allowed them to stay in a defensive position, it would lead to a lengthy, costly and morale-sapping campaign. The Franks would simply move from one castle or fortified city to another and would never join Saladin in a large-scale battle. He wanted a big confrontation because only then would his superior numbers give him the advantage he needed to achieve a decisive victory.

On 2 July, a small contingent from Saladin's forces attacked and captured the town of Tiberias, but its citadel held out. The trap had now been laid and Saladin hoped that King Guy of Jerusalem would choose, somewhat unwisely, to take his entire army down the treacherous steep path that descended into Tiberias to confront him. Fortunately for the Muslim forces, this is exactly what Guy decided to do. On the night of 2–3 July, Guy began the march to Tiberias. This was a huge mistake and the scene was now set for the battle Saladin had hoped for.

The Battle of Hattin

Guy's poor decision, perhaps a result of his belief that Saladin had a relatively small force, became apparent on his journey down to Tiberias

On 3 July, Guy's forces descended 1,500 feet towards the town. During this descent, Muslim forces launched countless small attacks on the Frankish army. This sapped the strength of the Christians, but was less significant than their passage through the village of Turan. This was the last point at which they would have access to a water supply. Nevertheless, Guy's army marched on.

When night began to fall, the Frankish army, slowed by the Muslim attacks, had not reached its destination. Instead, Guy ordered it to stop at Meskenah and camp there for the night. Saladin, who had arranged for water to be brought to his troops via a camel transport from Lake Tiberias, prepared for the final battle. His troops raided Guy's camp on and off throughout the night. Meanwhile, the Franks were left without water and were denied sleep. The next day would be a very tough one for them.

On 4 July, Guy decided to change his strategy because his troops were now desperate for water. They began to head to the springs at Hattin, but Saladin's army stood in their way. The only practical choice left was for the Franks to make a stand from the best position they could reach. Guy therefore gathered his troops on the hills at the Horns of Hattin among the remains of an ancient fortification. It was here that the Franks made their last attempt to defeat Saladin.

After a lengthy fight, which lasted well into the day and saw a small force under Raymond III of Tripoli escape, Guy made his final move. He launched two cavalry charges against Saladin, but these had little effect. Guy and many other important nobles including Reynald of Châtillon were taken prisoner. The True Cross, captured in the First Crusade, was also taken from them. The battle was over and the Franks, exhausted and desperate for water, had been defeated in the decisive victory Saladin had hoped for.

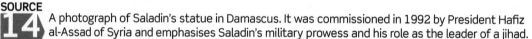

SOURCE

14 A photograph of Saladin's statue in Damascus. It was commissioned in 1992 by President Hafiz al-Assad of Syria and emphasises Saladin's military prowess and his role as the leader of a jihad.

The effects of the Battle of Hattin

Victory in battle had opened the way for Saladin to take control of the kingdom of Jerusalem, but first he settled an old score. Reynald of Châtillon and King Guy were brought before him and Guy was offered water. This was an old ritual and suggested that Guy would be allowed to live. When he tried to pass the water to Reynald he was reprimanded. The pair were sent away and only Reynald was asked to return. Saladin, who was angry about Reynald's earlier attack on a Muslim caravan, took his revenge. Reynald was offered conversion, which he rejected, and Saladin beheaded him. The message was clear: Saladin would show little mercy to those who crossed him.

Fear of Saladin, coupled with the more important fact that most city garrisons in the kingdom had sent their men to help Guy, meant most cities quickly capitulated due to a lack of forces. The timeline below, which lists when key Frankish strongholds fell to Saladin, is evidence of his lightening strike approach. If any city offered significant resistance and threatened to bog him down in a siege, such as Tyre, he passed it by. The result of this strategy was that, at the end of 1187, a few cities, such as Tortosa and Antioch, and a handful of castles, such as Krak des Chevaliers and Beaufort, remained under Frankish control.

SALADIN'S CONQUEST OF OUTREMER

4 July — Saladin defeats King Guy at the Battle of Hattin

5 July — Tiberias is the first to capitulate. The citadel, under the control of Raymond III of Tripoli's wife, Eschiva, surrenders

9 July — The important coastal town of Acre capitulates

19 July — Another coastal town, Sidon, is taken by Saladin

6 August — Further north, Beirut surrenders to Saladin

5 September — In order to complete the coastal conquests, Ascalon is taken; only Tyre survives Saladin's coastal invasion force

The fall of Jerusalem to Saladin, 1187

Jerusalem itself was defended by Balian of Nablus, but the city's defence was desperately undermanned. In an attempt to provide an effective force against Saladin, Balian knighted any nobleman over the age of 16. However, without an army in the field or a fully manned garrison, Balian stood little chance of success. The city fell after a short siege on 2 October 1187. In a show of mercy, which improved Saladin's reputation considerably, he allowed the citizens of Jerusalem to ransom themselves. For example, 7,000 of the poor were granted their freedom for 30,000 bezants. Few were allowed to remain behind as free men and the Franks left the city they had held for almost a century.

AS Level Exam-Style Question Section A

Was the strength of Muslim leadership the main reason for crusader losses between the fall of Edessa (1144) and the capture of Jerusalem by Saladin (1187)? (20 marks)

Tip
Balance your answer against reasons from other chapters, such as the weaknesses in the government of Outremer.

Consolidation

After the fall of Jerusalem, Saladin had captured most of the coast and a significant inland city. However, the landscape of Outremer still contained a number of castles in Frankish hands and cities that remained under their control. Muslim forces now had to slow down and commit themselves to a range of sieges in order to consolidate their position. Saladin occupied himself with the following movements for the next 3 years.

- The southern approach to Antioch: Saladin took Jabala and Latakia in July 1188.
- Defences further north: Saladin took the fortress at Baghras and Darbsak in September 1188. These were to the north of Antioch.
- Long sieges of isolated castles: Saladin targeted a number of castles between 1188 and 1190. For example, Kerak fell in November 1188, but it took until April 1190 for Beaufort to surrender.

Saladin, in a repetition of his policies in Egypt, Syria and the Jazira, dedicated his time to a consolidation programme. This helped to ensure that Jerusalem would remain in Muslim hands, rather than fall to the participants of the Third Crusade.

EXTEND YOUR KNOWLEDGE

Saladin's humanity
There are countless stories of Saladin's generosity towards his enemies, which all helped to establish his status as a pious leader of the jihad. For example, one story tells how, after the capture of Jerusalem, a group of female Franks approached Saladin. They wanted his help to find their husbands and fathers. He agreed and began an investigation. Their male relatives, who had been captured in the Battle of Hattin, were released back to them. If they were found to have been killed in the battle, Saladin gave the women presents instead. Another story tells of an old pilgrim who was captured when Saladin took Acre. He had come to Outremer on a pilgrimage to Jerusalem. After an appeal to Saladin, the old man was allowed to go free and travel on to fulfil his vow. However, Saladin's generosity sometimes worked against him. For instance, after the Battle of Hattin, he eventually released King Guy of Jerusalem on a promise never to fight against Saladin's interests again. However, Guy, who had made the promise under duress, was released from it and led the vigorous assault that resulted in the Franks retaking Acre. Saladin's kindness may have bolstered his status in the eyes of some of his fellow Muslims and made the truce that ended the Third Crusade more palatable to the Franks, but it did not always help his cause.

The strands of complex change

Changes leading up to the fall of Jerusalem to Saladin in 1187

Strands	Explanation of how the strand links to the fall of Jerusalem
Divisions in the government of Outremer	Stable succession from Baldwin III to Amalric (1163). Baldwin IV took the crown (1174). Raymond III and Bohemond III invaded the kingdom of Jerusalem (1180). Raymond III's truce with Saladin (1185). Succession crisis (1185–86).
Decline in support from the Byzantine Empire	The Frankish and Byzantine forces joined together in an Egyptian campaign (1169). Emperor Manuel I died (1180). Emperor Andronicus made an alliance with Saladin (1185).
Decline in support from Europe	European pilgrims helped to capture Ascalon (1153). Frederick of Tyre was refused help by Louis VII and Henry II (1169). King Amalric turned to the Assassins for help after European embassy failed (1171).
Growth of Saladin's power	Saladin became vizier of Egypt (1169). Nur ad-Din died (1174). Aleppo submitted to Saladin (1183). Mosul accepted Saladin's overlordship (1186).

Make two copies of the graph below. On the first copy, plot the individual strands on the y-axis. Use a different colour for each. You don't need to label the events. On the second copy, plot a single line which is a combination of all four strands. For example, at a given point two of the four strands are plotted high up on the y-axis while two are plotted lower. The combined strand would have to be plotted somewhere in the middle to represent a summary of those four individual strands.

Loss of Jerusalem likely

Loss of Jerusalem unlikely

1150 1155 1160 1165 1170 1175 1180 1185 1190

Answer the following questions:

1 How have the strands combined to make change less or more likely?

2 Why did Jerusalem fall in 1187, but not before?

The siege of Acre and the Battle of Arsuf, 1189–91

Saladin's position after 1187

The year 1187 had been one of extraordinary accomplishment for Saladin. The consolidation programme that followed also met with some success. However, after the fall of Jerusalem, Saladin began to face a number of problems that would ultimately help the Third Crusade to victory at Acre.

- Loss of troops: after the lightening pace of the 1187 campaigns, things began to slow in 1188. Many of Saladin's allies wanted to go home. For example, Taqi al-Din went back to Mosul with troops from the surrounding region, al-Adil returned to Egypt and al-Zahir to Aleppo.

- Funding: it cost Saladin's emirs a lot of money to stay out in the field. Imad al-Din complained in early 1189 that he faced serious financial difficulties.

- Frankish resistance: Jerusalem may have quickly capitulated, but other Christian possessions continued to fight and forced Saladin to abandon certain areas. For example, in 1188, a Sicilian fleet arrived and prevented Saladin from the capture of Tripoli.

1189: the beginning of the siege of Acre

Acre was an important port that Saladin had captured in 1187. It was important because it could provide a naval base for the Franks to supply a campaign to regain the kingdom of Jerusalem. In August 1189, King Guy began the siege of Acre with the troops that had survived or avoided the Battle of Hattin. They camped outside the city walls and began to besiege it.

Saladin prevaricated, worried that the siege was a deliberate trick or diversion, but came to Acre's rescue in September. On 15 September 1189, the Muslim forces launched an attack on Guy's camp, but failed to destroy it. The crusaders responded in kind and attacked Saladin on 4 October, but they too made no progress. By 23 October, with both sides entrenched in their positions, Saladin requested help from his allies in northern Syria and Iraq. They did not arrive until early summer 1190 and Saladin delayed further action.

Why did the 1190 campaign to relieve Acre fail?

In November 1190, after another year of campaigning, Saladin was in the same situation as in October 1189. Both sides were trapped in a stalemate. The main reason for this lack of progress was the failure to co-ordinate the Muslim allied forces. Zangi of Sinjar arrived too early in 1190 for Saladin to make use of his troops so they were sent back. Kilij Arslan, who had been forced to redirect his troops northwards due to the threat from Frederick Barbarossa's German crusaders, did not arrive until October 1190. Even Saladin slowed down progress through his focus on the conquest of Beaufort Castle first, which kept him out of the Acre campaign until the castle was captured on 2 April 1190.

The effect of the delays was two-fold. First, it cost Saladin a lot of money to keep his troops in the field. He reckoned, in a letter to an ally, that his expenditure was around 20,000 dinars a day.

Secondly, no major action began until July 1190. In May, a somewhat irritated Zangi rejoined Saladin, but troop numbers were still small. It was not until 25 July that action restarted due to the aggression of the Franks. They launched an attack on the Muslim camp, but were repelled. In the battle that followed, one Muslim reported that around 12,000 Franks were killed. However, Saladin failed to take advantage of this victory and the camp around Acre was given the time it needed to recover.

By the close of the campaigning season, it was clear that Guy's siege would continue. Saladin began to withdraw on 20 October 1190 to a more secure position. However, the Franks made one last attempt to make progress before the season closed. On 13 November, they began a march to take Haifa, but this was intercepted by Saladin's forces. Most of the Franks managed to escape, but Haifa was safe. By 14 November, it was clear that nothing more could be achieved by either side. Saladin had given the Third Crusade another year to arrive.

The fall of Acre

In late May 1191, Saladin received news that the siege at Acre had intensified. He took immediate action and, although he was some distance from Acre, he made the journey there within a week. This would be his third year encamped around the city, but it would also be his last one at the siege. By 12 July 1191, the Muslim garrison had surrendered. The main causes of Saladin's failure to stop the Franks are given below.

- The 2-year breathing space had allowed Guy to strengthen his troops after the disasters of 1187.

- Guy now had support from King Philip II of France and King Richard I of England, which gave him the strength to capture Acre.

- In contrast, Saladin had fewer troops. In 1191, not all rejoined Saladin. For example, the army from Diyr Bakr was occupied elsewhere and could not come back.

- The Christian blockade of the city, chiefly by land and partly by sea, prevented supplies from entering Acre. The Muslim garrison began to starve, whereas the Franks had fresh troops and a regular supply line.

Saladin's fortunes had changed and he was forced to seek terms from the Franks. He had to pay 200,000 dinars, return the relic of the True Cross and free his prisoners. For their part, the Christians promised to release their Muslim prisoners. This was the truce that led to Richard I's infamous massacre of 2,700 prisoners, but it was also the start of a new chapter for the Franks in Outremer.

The Battle of Arsuf

King Richard I's crusaders, supported by King Guy and his other Frankish allies, began their march to retake Jaffa in late August 1191. They were intercepted by Saladin near Arsuf and were forced into a battle, after which Saladin's army retreated. The Frankish victory that followed (see page 58) was largely a result of Richard I's leadership during the battle itself. The effects, for Saladin, were profound. Richard I's army was undefeated, despite Saladin's use of his entire force of around 30,000 men. In consequence, Saladin was unable to stop Richard from the recapture of Jaffa and the Christian hold on the coast was secured.

Saladin's success in keeping Muslim control of Jerusalem in 1192

Saladin had suffered in 1191 because he had divided his efforts across the remnants of Outremer and this had given the Franks the time they needed to capture Acre and Jaffa. In order to prevent the same outcome in Jerusalem, Saladin focused his efforts solely on the defence of the city. It was a result of this almost exclusive emphasis on Jerusalem's protection that it remained in Muslim hands.

Preparation for Richard I's first attempt on Jerusalem

Saladin's first move was to prevent the Franks from the acquisition of any more Muslim strongholds. This led him to destroy the fortifications at Ascalon and the castle at Ramla. He then began to build up Jerusalem's defences. Izz al-Din sent Saladin 50 masons to help build a defence to the north of the city. They were supported by 2,000 prisoners who provided the main labour force. At the same time, Saladin began to request troops to assist in their defence. The first arrived from Egypt on 22 December 1191 and helped to improve the morale of Saladin's army, which had been drained by nearly six years of campaigning.

These preparations, in part, explain why Richard I withdrew from his first march to Jerusalem on 3 January. Richard had other concerns as well (see page 59), but he realised that Saladin's rigorous defensive measures would make the city difficult to take. He also knew that if he took the city it would be very difficult to hold on to it. Saladin's focus on one objective had paid off. He now had to wait it out until Richard I returned to England.

Richard I's second attempt

Not content simply to wait for Richard to begin a second march to Jerusalem, Saladin took further action to strengthen the Muslim hold on the city.

- He allowed his troops to return home in early 1192, which would give them time to rest. They were ordered to return in May.

- He deployed his field army sensibly. They were spread out along the line of the Jordan Valley to the north and south of Jerusalem. This meant there was no single point for Richard to target, but the army could also regroup quickly if the city required help.

- He developed his intelligence network. It was thanks to his spies that he knew what the Franks were planning. This enabled him to poison the water supplies outside of Jerusalem when he heard a second march had begun.

In spite of all these plans, when the second march approached Jerusalem, Saladin was profoundly worried. He called his senior emirs to a meeting on 2 July 1192 and decided that the threat to Jerusalem was now too great for him to remain. On 3 July, Saladin left the city, but he departed safe in the knowledge that if Richard did capture Jerusalem, he would not hold it for long. There were reinforcements on their way from al-Adil and al-Afdal, which calmed Saladin's nerves. In the event, he need not have worried. Richard approached the city, but then departed on 4 July (see page 59). Jerusalem was safe.

EXTRACT

 A description of the climax of the Third Crusade when Richard approached Jerusalem for the second time. It is from a biography of Saladin called *Saladin: The Politics of the Holy War*, written in 1982 by M.C. Lyons and D.E.P. Jackson, and is based on contemporary correspondence and chronicle accounts translated from Arabic. This excerpt shows the level of anxiety Saladin suffered in early July 1192.

Saladin had particular reason to be anxious about Egypt. At the start of the Crusade he had been warned that the Frankish effort would be divided between Syria and Egypt and Richard had several times been heard threatening to march south ... 'Uthman, who had been left in charge, had never had to face a serious emergency and if Richard moved Saladin would almost certainly have to leave Jerusalem and follow him. In that case ... the Franks could double back ... [and] he could find the Hattin position reversed and his own army cut off without supplies.

Jerusalem, however, was still too strong a magnet for the Franks ... On 2 July al-Afdal arrived with al-Zahir ... and in the evening Saladin held a council ... Ibn Shaddad was asked to address them and he suggested that they should meet by the Rock and bind themselves to fight to the death. Saladin remained silent for a long time and the emirs stayed motionless, 'as though birds were perched on their heads.' He then told them that all the Muslims were depending on them...

On 3 July Saladin performed the Friday prayer ... and Ibn Shaddad wrote: 'I saw him prostrating himself and repeating words with the tears pouring down on to his prayer mat.'

ACTIVITY
KNOWLEDGE CHECK

The campaigns of Saladin in Outremer 1187–92

1 Summarise the main stages of Saladin's campaign between 1187 and 1192.

2 Identify the period when Saladin was most successful and the period when he was least successful.

3 To what extent was Saladin's campaign in Outremer a success? Use three criteria to explain your answer.

The truce

The city of Jerusalem was no longer a target for the Third Crusade. After a short-lived attempt on 27 July 1192 by Saladin to capture Jaffa, a truce was negotiated with the Franks (see page 60). It was signed on 2 September 1192 and secured a long-term Frankish presence on the coast. It also confirmed that Jerusalem was now under Muslim control. The truce lasted for over 3 years, but Jerusalem itself remained under Muslim rule until 1229. When Saladin died on 4 March 1193, he had both become a powerful Muslim ruler and launched a jihad that destroyed much of the legacy of the First Crusade.

ACTIVITY
SUMMARY

The changing Muslim response to the crusades

1 Create a living graph with two axes. Label the x-axis with dates from 1095 to 1192 and the y-axis with a scale of 1 to 10 ranging from 'Muslim failure' to 'Muslim success' in response to the crusades.

2 Plot the following events onto your living graph:

- 1097 the Battle of Dorylaeum
- 1099 the fall of Jerusalem
- 1144 the seizure of Edessa
- 1153 the capture of Ascalon
- 1169 the protection of Cairo from Amalric
- 1177 the defeat at Mont Gisard
- 1187 the capture of Jerusalem
- 1192 the siege of Acre.

3 Explain the reasons behind the following decisions you made in the construction of your graph:

- the placement of events from the First Crusade
- the extent of success you awarded the seizure of Edessa
- the pattern of rankings between 1144 and 1169
- the level of similarity between your ranking for the siege of Acre in 1192 and the fall of Jerusalem in 1099.

4 Describe the general pattern of the Muslim response to the crusades.

5 Look back through the chapter and add eight more events to your living graph. Explain whether this would cause you to qualify your judgements in response to (4) or not.

A Level Exam-Style Question Section B

How far do you agree that the Muslim defence in the years 1189–92 was more effectively organised than their efforts in the years 1096–99? (20 marks)

Tip
Before you reach a judgement, consider the parallels between the delayed response from the Turks to the First Crusade and Saladin's response to the siege of Acre.

WIDER READING

Cobb, P. *The Race for Paradise: An Islamic History of the Crusades*, Oxford University Press (2014)

Hillenbrand, C. *The Crusades: Islamic Perspectives*, Edinburgh University Press (1999)

Hindley, *G. Saladin: Hero of Islam*, Pen & Sword Military (2010)

Irwin, R. 'Islam and the crusades, 1096–1699', in Riley-Smith, J. *The Oxford Illustrated History of the Crusades*, Oxford University Press (2001)

Lyons, M. and Jackson, D.E.P. *Saladin: The Politics of the Holy War*, Cambridge University Press (1984)

Maalouf, A. *The Crusades Through Arab Eyes*, Saqi Books (1984)

Tyerman, C. *God's War: A New History of the Crusades*, Penguin (2007)

1.5 What explains the failure of the Fourth Crusade?

KEY QUESTIONS

- How significant was Innocent III's role in the failure of the Fourth Crusade?
- How did the size and leadership of the crusading forces contribute to the failure of the Fourth Crusade?
- What impact did Doge Enrico Dandolo have on the course of the Fourth Crusade?
- How did Prince Alexius's failure to keep his promises cause the Fourth Crusade to collapse?

INTRODUCTION

On 12 April 1204, in the midst of an intense siege, a churchman called Aleaumes began to crawl through a small gap in the walls of Constantinople. His brother, Robert of Clari, tried desperately to pull him back, but Aleaumes kicked him away. He was the only one brave enough to squeeze through the hole that would allow the crusaders access to the city. Once through he ran at the stunned defenders, who must have been surprised by a single armed churchman, and they began to back away. In the meantime, 70 crusaders under the leadership of Peter, lord of Amiens, followed Aleaumes through the gap. This was a big enough force to begin to attack the people of Constantinople and release one of the city gates.

With the gate opened, a surge of crusaders entered the city. They were not there to seek advice, rest or provisions, as crusaders had in previous campaigns, but to take the city of Constantinople by force. A few hours later they had succeeded thanks to the bravery of a single cleric. He cared little for the rules against churchmen bearing arms and, like the rest of the crusaders present, did not seem to mind that he was attacking fellow Christians. As a result, the Fourth Crusade was the first to end, not on the shores of Outremer, or at the gates of Jerusalem, but in the capital of a defeated Christian empire.

The course of the Fourth Crusade

The capture and subsequent sack of Constantinople, which involved the sacred theft of much of the city's treasured relics, was not what Pope Innocent III had in mind when he first called for a crusade in August 1198. He had hoped for a force of kings, or leading nobles, who would travel to Outremer, pick up where the Third Crusade had left off and recapture Jerusalem.

In November 1199, this outcome appeared possible, as the nobility of France and Flanders, which included influential figures like Thibault III of Champagne, signed up to the Fourth Crusade at a tournament in Écry. These men began to plan the crusade and sent representatives to Venice to begin to work out the detail of their journey in March 1201.

August 1198 – Pope Innocent III issues the call for the Fourth Crusade

March 1201 – The plans for the transportation and destination of the crusade are negotiated with the doge of Venice, Enrico Dandolo

1198	1199	1200	1201

November 1199 – A tournament is held at Écry at which many crusaders are recruited

May 1201 – Count Thibald III of Champagne, an important French leader, dies and the Fourth Crusade loses a considerable amount of support from France

At this stage, however, things started to go wrong for the crusaders. First, Thibault III died in May 1201, and secondly, many other crusaders began to make their own plans to travel to Outremer. This meant that only a small force of crusaders gathered in Venice in June 1202 to begin the campaign. Their number was too few to pay the fee that had been promised to the Venetians and the situation looked bleak. The leader of Venice, **Doge** Enrico Dandolo, offered a solution. He asked the crusaders to delay their campaign and help him recapture the Adriatic port city of Zara (modern day Zadar, Croatia) for the Venetians.

In November 1202, the Fourth Crusaders thus began their first diversion and captured Zara, but they still lacked the funds to pay the Venetian fee. Dandolo's proposal had only allowed for the postponement of the debt, not its cancellation. Under these circumstances, they accepted an offer to help an ousted prince, Alexius, claim the throne of the Byzantine Empire. This would provide them with the money, funds and troops they needed to carry on.

On 17 July 1203, the crusaders, now on their second diversion, forced the emperor to flee Constantinople. Then they helped Prince Alexius claim the throne, but it soon turned out he had promised more than he could deliver. The Fourth Crusaders became desperate and by April 1204 took decisive action. They attacked the city of Constantinople and took by force what Prince Alexius had failed to deliver.

EXTEND YOUR KNOWLEDGE

Constantinople

The city of Constantinople was the capital of the Byzantine Empire, which spanned a huge territory from Greece to Asia Minor. It was founded in the 4th century by the Roman emperor, Constantine, and it became the centre of the eastern half of the Roman Empire. By the 13th century, it was the largest city in Christendom and was home to a population of around 500,000 people within the walls of the city itself. It was renowned for its lavish buildings, such as the Hippodrome, the Great Palace and the church of Hagia Sophia. Its location, at the point where the West met Asia, was also exceptionally well defended. It had the Sea of Marmara and the Golden Horn to protect its southern and northern boundaries. The rest of the exposed boundary was protected by a huge, thick, high wall. It would therefore be a difficult city to capture, but a powerful, strategic and immensely wealthy one to control.

By 16 May 1204, the crusaders were in possession of the capital of **Byzantium**. They appointed Baldwin of Flanders to be the ruler of their empire, which they renamed Romania, but they now had a huge task on their hands. They had an empire to secure and in April 1205, while many rank and file crusaders returned home, the rest began to set themselves up as the rulers of Romania.

The Fourth Crusade's objective to recapture Jerusalem, as set out by Innocent III, was never met. Diverted twice and then preoccupied with events in the former Byzantine Empire, the crusade had failed in the eyes of its architect.

June 1202 – The crusaders begin to gather in Venice; it quickly becomes apparent that their numbers are inadequate to pay for the treaty negotiated with Dandolo

September 1202 – Dandolo agrees to postpone payment of the treaty if the crusaders agreed to help him attack Zara; they accept his terms

January 1204 – Murtzuphlus is imprisoned by the Byzantine emperors Alexius IV and Isaac II; he has himself crowned Alexius V

1205 – Peter of Capuano absolves the crusaders from their vow to travel to Jerusalem; the pope is furious, but the Fourth Crusade is over

1202	1203	1204	1205

December 1202 – Prince Alexius proposes an alternative destination for the Fourth Crusade; he offers incredible incentives in return for help to restore his father to the throne of Constantinople

July 1203 – The crusaders attack Constantinople and force its emperor, Alexius III, to flee

April 1204 – The crusaders, in response to the overthrow of Alexius IV, attack and ransack the city of Constantinople

May 1204 – Baldwin of Flanders is crowned emperor of Romania, the former Byzantine Empire

EVALUATING INTERPRETATIONS OF HISTORY

This chapter explores a variety of different interpretations to explain why the Fourth Crusade failed to reach Outremer. These have been presented by different historians from the 19th century onwards and include discussion of a number of aspects.

- The influence of Innocent III: some blame Innocent III due to his ill-thought-out plan, while others focus on the part his lack of influence played in the failure to stop the crusade diversion.

- The leadership: perhaps, it has been suggested, the leadership lacked the necessary clout to achieve the goals they set themselves. The detail of the plan, which they devised, was beyond them.

- The Venetians: others suggest it was not the whole crusade leadership that was to blame, but rather that it was one leader, Doge Enrico Dandolo, who shaped the crusade according to his own priorities.

- Prince Alexius: finally, there is a case to be made that the crusade would have succeeded if Prince Alexius had never made his outlandish and, as it turned out, unrealistic promises to the crusaders.

All of the arguments above share one key feature: they are opinions, rather than simple dates or descriptions of an event. They are examples of the mainstay of the work of historians, who for the most part do not simply narrate stories but also present arguments. These arguments, which may identify and explain important causes, assess the impact of changes in the past or explore the significance of an individual, are interpretations. They are important because they help people to understand the past beyond simplistic knowledge of what happened and when.

Historians construct these interpretations from different perspectives and apply different methodologies to the evidence they use. However, as long as their methodology is logical, their investigation thorough and their evidence marshalled carefully, completely different interpretations can be equally valid. This chapter will help you to consider the evidence that has been used to construct particular interpretations. It will also encourage you to see how and why historians have attributed more weight to certain pieces of evidence and sources of information than others. Finally, it will give you the opportunity to analyse the quality of the reasoning that has been used to create an interpretation.

Reading the extracts

Before you approach some of the extracts in this chapter, it is important to appreciate that they are interpretations based largely on the evidence of medieval chroniclers. As such, you should try to have the following questions in mind when you read them.

- Consider the evidence they choose and why: whose accounts have they utilised to construct this narrative or explanation? Has their perspective, such as their nationality, influenced this choice? (Look at Extract 5 on page 131 for a French historian's attempt to blame the Venetians.)

- Consider the weight they apply to certain sources of information: have they privileged a chronicler who was a member of the leadership over one who gives the view of the rank and file? (Consider how Extract 8 uses the *Life of Innocent III* chronicle for the basis of its claims.)

- Consider their methodology: how, if at all, have they attempted to deal with discrepancies between the accounts of the different chroniclers? Is there a sense of evidence being marshalled in their arguments? (Look at how the historian in Extract 3 makes effective use of one chronicler's account of events.)

- Consider the quality of their reasoning: have they made the origin of their evidence clear? Are the claims they have made on the basis of this logical? (Explore the careful way in which letter evidence is used to reach valid conclusions in Extract 2.)

It may help to read some of the original chroniclers' accounts of the Fourth Crusade in order to understand how these interpretations have been constructed. References to these can be found at the end of this chapter.

EXTEND YOUR KNOWLEDGE

The chroniclers of the Fourth Crusade

The most well-known chronicler of the Fourth Crusade is Geoffrey of Villehardouin. He was the **marshal** of Champagne and as such was a major player in the Fourth Crusade. For example, he helped to devise the original plan in Venice. His chronicle, *La Conquête de Constantinople* (*The Conquest of Constantinople*), provides the view of a leader. In contrast, Robert of Clari, whose chronicle has the same name as Villehardouin's, was a knight from the Picard region. His work gives the perspective of a rank-and-file crusader, which helps historians to understand the motivations of the ordinary crusaders and their awareness of events and decisions that shaped the crusade. Other notable sources of information, which have been used to construct the extracts in this chapter, are:

- *Devastatio Constantinopolitana*: this provides the view of a German crusader from the Rhineland

- *Gesta Innocentii III*: this is the official papal view of the crusade; it contains a collection of papal correspondence as well

- Nicetas Choniates's *History*: this is the view of a Byzantine historian who had an important job in the imperial government; it gives an eastern perspective on the siege and sack of Constantinople.

KEY TERM

Marshal

A military office that, in the context of Champagne, made its holder the most important adviser on matters of war. Geoffrey of Villehardouin, the famous chronicler, held this position from 1185.

HOW SIGNIFICANT WAS INNOCENT III'S ROLE IN THE FAILURE OF THE FOURTH CRUSADE?

The call for a crusade, 1198

Little had changed in the geography of Frankish Outremer since the disastrous loss of Jerusalem to Saladin and the few gains that the Third Crusade made on the coast. Perhaps the most significant development was Saladin's death in 1193 and the division of the Muslim Empire. Nevertheless peace remained, as the two sides maintained Richard I's truce, which the Muslim rulers used to dispute the issue of Saladin's legacy. Meanwhile, the Franks took the opportunity to resume a 'business as usual' approach to life in Outremer. Even when the truce expired, there was only a small, aborted attempt at a crusade in 1197, which captured a few coastal towns. It appeared that the zeal to regain Jerusalem had finally faded away.

Pope Innocent III

SOURCE

1

A 13th-century Italian fresco portrait of Pope Innocent III. It demonstrates how young Innocent III was when he became pope and therefore his potential to take an active role in crusade management.

This atmosphere of apathy was transformed on 8 January 1198 when Lothar of Segni was elected pope. At the relatively young age of around 37, Lothar, who took the name Pope Innocent III, approached his new role with great personal vigour. This was demonstrated by his early attempts to interfere in the appointment of a new Holy Roman Emperor after the death of Henry VI in 1197. He hoped that through his actions he could secure the territory of the papacy from the political threats it had faced throughout the last two centuries. This was a task he spent much time on, but it was not his sole aim.

His other great concern was, like so many of his predecessors, the fate of Outremer and the Holy City of Jerusalem. Neither faced any immediate threat, as the coast was secure and Jerusalem, though not in Frankish hands, had been open to Christian pilgrims under the terms of Richard I's truce. However, as far as Innocent III was concerned, no new threat was necessary. He wanted to be the pope who recaptured Jerusalem, and even expressed a desire personally to lead a crusade. This desire to lead, though somewhat unrealistic, had its foundation in the instability of crusades led by secular leaders.

A year before Innocent III's election, in 1197, a crusade had set out from the German Empire led by Henry VI, but had crumbled after his death in Messina and the succession crisis it caused. It was in this context that the new pope had made the decision to take as big a role as possible in the next crusade. This is why in August 1198 he issued a lengthy crusading bull called *Post miserabile*, which set out in detail the organisation of the Fourth Crusade. This crusade was going to be different because it would not be the campaign of a great European king or emperor. Instead it would be Innocent III's, shaped by his aims, his plans and his legates.

THINKING HISTORICALLY Interpretations (5a)

What I believe is how I see

In this chapter, you will explore a variety of interpretations of the reasons for the failure of the Fourth Crusade. These interpretations are often shaped by the background of the historian who wrote them. Below are three descriptions of the perspectives of very famous historians. They have been written for the purposes of this exercise.

Herodotus

- His research consisted of conversations

- He identified that accounts had to be judged on their merits

- Some believe that certain passages in his writing are inventions to complete the narrative

Leopold von Ranke

- He believed in an evidence-based approach and relied heavily on primary sources

- He desired to find out the 'facts' and discover the connections between them

- He stressed the role of the individual in shaping history

Karl Marx

- He believed that history would go through stages leading to a state where everybody was equal

- He believed that historical changes were ultimately determined by changes to the economy

- He was often driven by political considerations and looked for evidence to support his point of view

Work in groups of between three and six. Each member or pair will take the perspective of one of the above historians and argue from that perspective. Work through the questions as a group and answer the last one individually.

1 Herodotus did not use written evidence to construct his history. Does this mean that his history is less useful than that of the others?

2 Von Ranke based his writing almost exclusively on primary sources from the time he was investigating, rather than secondary sources. How might this affect his ability to see larger patterns in history as opposed to the others?

3 Marx put his philosophy of history, and perhaps politics, first and research second. Would this make his history weaker than that of the others?

4 'Colourful' individuals populate the writing of Herodotus and von Ranke, while Marx concentrates on the difference between classes. Write three historical questions that each historian might ask.

5 The three historians mentioned above all had different methods and motivations and yet their writing has been valued ever since it was created. Explain how the prior knowledge that we bring to the history that we write does not invalidate it.

Innocent's crusade reforms

Attracting crusaders

Several reforms were introduced by Pope Innocent III to maximise the number of participants who would sign up to the Fourth Crusade. His first task was to improve the incentive on offer. In the past, crusaders could expect a *remissio peccatorum* (the terms of which are explained in Chapter 1, see page 14), but Innocent III was prepared to go further. He offered crusaders a plenary indulgence, which was designed to be a guarantee that all sins would be forgiven, regardless of whether the individual concerned had done enough in the eyes of God to deserve this.

The incentive was improved still further as the pope decided to make it available to a wider range of people. *Post miserabile* explicitly stated that an indulgence, of varying degrees, was now on offer to the following groups of people:

- a self-funding crusader; this was the traditional type of participant who had always received an indulgence

- a crusader whose journey was being funded by someone else; again this type of crusader would have received a *remissio peccatorum* in the past

- a non-crusader who paid for another to go on crusade or paid what they could; this was a new group to receive an indulgence.

The new indulgence, it was hoped, would have two benefits. First, it would help bolster the funding for the crusade, and secondly, it would discourage non-combatants from taking part. These groups, such as the old or infirm, could now provide funds for spiritual benefit instead.

The last measure Innocent III put in place was designed to remove an obstacle to potential crusaders. In September 1201, two years after the original call for a crusade, the pope decided to abandon a long-standing doctrinal position about the powers of a wife. In the past, a crusader had to seek the permission of his wife before he could accept the crusade vow. However, Innocent III decided to abandon this stricture in the hope that it would provide a boost to crusade recruitment. This may seem like a relatively minor measure, but it was seen as a dramatic change in doctrine and revealed that the pope would bend Church law to improve the Fourth Crusade's chance of success.

Maximising recruitment

In the 12th century, many more crusades were called for by the papacy than actually came to fruition in a fully manned campaign to Outremer. Pope Innocent III was not prepared simply to issue a crusading bull and then see what effect it had. Instead, he formalised the recruitment measures of the most successful popes of the 12th century. His first action, in 1198, was to set up a general executive office for 'the business of the cross'. This office would ensure that a named individual was responsible for the different areas under the control of Rome. Those appointed would help organise crusade recruitment and spread papal influence throughout western Christendom.

The second measure followed the example of Pope Eugenius III, who had attempted to control who preached the crusade through official appointment. Those appointed, like Bernard of Clairvaux, would spread an approved message and, it was hoped, would attract the right sort of participant to the crusade. The most notable preachers appointed under the authority of Innocent III's new office for the business of the cross were Fulk of Neuilly and Abbot Martin of Pairis. These were influential men, who could be trusted to present *Post miserabile* with the emotional flair needed to excite commitment. Abbot Martin, for example, achieved considerable success after his heartfelt sermon at Basel Cathedral in May 1200.

Pope Innocent III also borrowed from the most successful feature of Pope Gregory VIII's Third Crusade, which was the strength of its leadership. He appointed legates to prepare the ground for the Fourth Crusade. The first, Peter of Capuano, was sent to England and France to establish a truce between King Richard I and King Philip II. This would then allow two of the most important kings in the West to lead the crusade out in the field, but under the watchful eye of the papal legate. The second appointee, Soffredo, was sent to Venice to begin to make practical arrangements for the journey to Outremer. In this way, through his legates, Innocent III could control the crusade from his relatively secure base in Rome.

Ensuring success

The benefit of the recorded history of the 11th- and 12th-century crusades allowed Innocent III to take steps to ensure the mistakes of the past were not repeated. The main problems had been the following.

- The poorly defined nature of what counted as a commitment to the crusade meant that several leading nobles and their followers abandoned the First Crusade before it even reached Jerusalem.

- The lack of communication with the leaders of Outremer prior to the Second Crusade led to inaction and disputes about the most logical goal when the crusaders finally arrived.

- The cost of participation in the Third Crusade had been prohibitive to some potential crusaders. This was because expensive sea travel was commonly seen as the only realistic transportation method.

In order to overcome the first problem, *Post miserabile* stated that a crusader had to commit themselves to two years of service to fulfil their vow. The second problem was tackled through the use of papal legates, who were dispatched to Outremer in advance of the Fourth Crusade. Finally, the solution to the third problem built upon the principle of the Saladin Tithe. Innocent III tried to raise funds in the following ways.

- He initially encouraged bishops, at a council in Dijon in 1198, to commit one-thirtieth of their incomes to the crusade.

- He then, on 31 December 1199, issued *Graves orientalis terrae*, which was a general tax of one-fortieth on the Church.

- Finally, in a move designed to encourage lay donation, the pope ordered chests to be placed in churches. Donors would receive indulgences in return for their support.

The problems with Innocent III's plans

Leadership

It could be argued that the Fourth Crusade had failed before it even started, because Innocent III did not succeed in his plan to secure powerful secular leadership. Richard I of England was the first king to be approached by the papal legate, Peter of Capuano. His recruitment would have brought both funding and the full might of the English nobility. Unfortunately, Peter of Capuano's approach to negotiation failed to impress Richard. The legate asked for a five-year truce between Richard I and Philip II of France, which Richard indicated he might support, but Peter of Capuano also asked for the release of Bishop Philip of Beauvais from imprisonment.

The second demand made upon Richard I was too much for him. He hated Bishop Philip of Beauvais with a passion and was not prepared to release him. Peter of Capuano was reprimanded by Richard I for his unrealistic request and the chances of securing Richard's support were weakened. By April 1199, any hope of Richard leading the Fourth Crusade was gone, after the king died from a crossbow wound at the siege of the castle of Châlus-Chabrol. The succession crisis that followed his death ensured that the English would be too busy to repeat the commitment they had shown to the Third Crusade.

Nevertheless, there were still other kings to whom Innocent III could appeal. Philip II of France would be a powerful leader if his support was secured. However, politics stood in the way of his appointment to the leadership of the Fourth Crusade. The first stumbling block was the papal legate's poor diplomacy, as Peter of Capuano once again alienated a prospective crusader. He insisted that Philip II should restore his lawful wife, Ingeborg of Denmark, to his court and send away his new wife, Agnes of Meran. When Philip II refused, Peter of Capuano placed the country under **interdict** and the negotiations collapsed.

> **KEY TERM**
>
> **Interdict**
> A ban on a person or a place to claim ecclesiastical privileges and perform church functions, such as public prayer and baptism. It was often used against monarchs to force them to follow the pope's commands.

The second issue was that Philip II was really too busy to find the opportunity of crusade leadership an attractive prospect. The death of Richard I had sparked a succession crisis in England, which gave Philip II the opportunity to enlarge his own kingdom at the expense of English possessions in France. This campaign continued until May 1200 when a treaty was signed with King John, but by this time it was too late and the crusade plans were already under way. The only other possible candidate of similar status, the German Holy Roman Emperor-Elect, Philip of Swabia, was not even approached because Innocent III disputed his claim to the imperial title. This left the Fourth Crusade without a king or emperor at its head.

Early recruitment problems

One of the biggest problems the Fourth Crusade faced when it assembled in Venice in June 1202 was the small number of crusaders who turned up. This, in part, can be blamed on Innocent III because the preachers he appointed failed to stir up sufficient recruits. Some were mired in controversy, like Fulk of Neuilly whose reputation was tarnished by rumours of embezzlement of funds. Others, like Eustace, abbot of St Gerner de Flay, focused their sermons on the idea of **vita apostolica** and moral reform, which masked the crusade message they were supposed to spread. Eustace, for example, talked more about breaches of the Sabbath than the crusade.

> **KEY TERM**
>
> *Vita apostolica* (apostolic life)
> This was the idea of returning the Church to a purer form and following examples of conduct from its earlier days. It was an element of the Gregorian Reform Movement (see page 15).

The inadequate efforts of the pope's preachers were compounded by Innocent III's failure to appreciate the fact that conceptions of chivalry had shifted in the 12th century (see page 31). The Third Crusade had done much to associate crusading with chivalry, because Richard I and his followers were idolised by the knightly classes. At first sight this would suggest that it should have been easier to recruit crusader knights. However, the new chivalric values placed prominence upon following overlords like Richard I rather than the old physical ideals of brute strength and warlike deeds. Knights would not simply support Innocent III as a chance to show off, as some did for Urban II; instead they would have to follow their leader.

Innocent III's failure to recruit the top strata of secular society was therefore fundamental to the problems that followed. Indeed, his actions even exacerbated the recruitment problem. For example, in 1198, Innocent III was deeply involved in the succession crisis that followed Henry VI's death. He was regent for Henry VI's son, Frederick, but Philip of Swabia had taken the imperial throne. While Innocent III entered into talks with Philip of Swabia, another noble, Markward of Anweiler, began to take land in southern Italy and Sicily. By November 1199, Innocent III was so afraid that Markward might threaten the papal state that he offered a plenary indulgence to soldiers who fought him. He thus diverted recruits away from the Fourth Crusade.

Logistics

The final charge that can be laid against Innocent III was that he changed the features of a crusade too much too quickly. For example, his attempt at a Church-wide crusade tax in 1199 was largely unsuccessful and had to be reformulated for Innocent III's later crusade in the bulls *Quia maior* and *Ad liberandum*. In his demand for one-fortieth of Church income he had to fight the conservative tide of Church thinking. Most still held firm to the idea that payment to go on a crusade should be made by the individual, rather than the Church. One papal bull was not going to radically transform their beliefs.

Equally problematic was Innocent III's deadline. He gave the crusaders until March 1199 to depart on the Fourth Crusade, which was only six months after he had first published *Post miserabile*. This was hardly enough time for recruitment of crusaders, leadership decision making and the arrangement of transportation to Outremer. Jerusalem, to take one example, was captured in October 1187 and *Audita tremendi* was issued within the month, but Richard I and Philip II did not depart until 4 July 1190. Innocent III's expectations exceeded what was realistic and his plans for the Fourth Crusade, flawed as they were, were in part responsible for the crusaders' failure ever to reach Outremer.

ACTIVITY
KNOWLEDGE CHECK

The plans for the Fourth Crusade

1 Create a strengths-and-weaknesses table with the title: 'Pope Innocent III's plans for the Fourth Crusade'.

2 Based on the contents of your table, how far do you agree with the view that it was probable the Fourth Crusade would fail?

Innocent's determination to lead the crusade: attempts and failures

On the one hand, Innocent III could be blamed for the failure of the Fourth Crusade because he was responsible for the initial plans and went ahead with them without support from kings or emperors. On the other hand, it could be argued that Innocent III's impact on the course of the Fourth Crusade once it had begun was minimal. If this was the case, he could hardly be completely culpable for its failure to reach Outremer. There were three key turning points in the crusade that led to its eventual collapse. These will be explored in greater detail later, but in summary they were:

- November 1202: the crusaders attacked the Christian city of Zara, on behalf of the Venetians, rather than travel to Outremer

- Summer 1203: the crusaders were diverted to Constantinople to reclaim the city for the ousted Prince Alexius rather than journey on to Outremer

- April–May 1204: the crusaders attacked Constantinople, took the city and established a new empire called Romania; Peter of Capuano officially absolved the crusaders from their vow in mid-1205.

Failure to influence the Zara campaign

The first test of Innocent III's ability to influence the events of the Fourth Crusade occurred when the crusaders decided to attack Zara, a Christian city under the authority of the king of Hungary. Innocent had two methods at his disposal to try and prevent the attack. The first was his papal legate, Peter of Capuano, who had the authority to make decisions on behalf of the pope out in the field. The second was through the communication of his views to the crusade leadership. Innocent III heavily disapproved of the attack on Zara and so sent a letter that forbade it and threatened excommunication to any Christian who took part.

Unfortunately, for Pope Innocent III at least, the attack did take place and this demonstrated how impotent the pope was in controlling the actions of the crusaders. His papal legate, rather than condemn the attack, chose to endorse it out of fear that the forces of the crusade might disintegrate. In effect, Peter of Capuano had given the crusaders approval for the attack and then travelled to Rome before the siege began. He had gone out of the desire to seek papal approval, but this meant that the primary figure of papal authority was not even on the crusade. The pope had, in the short term, lost any hope of directing the course of the campaign.

The papal letter did not fare much better. It arrived at Zara in November 1202 via Abbot Peter of Lucedio and was read to the crusade leaders. After consideration of the pope's opinion and the effect it might have on the rank and file, the leadership chose to suppress it rather than release it into general circulation. This sent a clear message to Innocent III. He may have been the instigator of the Fourth Crusade but he was not its commander-in-chief.

Failure to prevent the diversion to Constantinople

After the capture of Zara, Pope Innocent III was keen for the crusade to continue on to Outremer. He certainly did not want the crusaders to attack any more Christian cities, especially Constantinople, the home of the patriarch of the Greek Orthodox Church. Innocent III's opinion is clear from his actions up until 1202.

- From the beginning of his papacy until 1202, Innocent III was in ongoing diplomatic talks with the Byzantine emperor Alexius III over the reunification of the eastern and western churches.

- Innocent III used diplomatic means to encourage Emperor Alexius III to leave the Fourth Crusade alone and allow it to proceed to Outremer without any Byzantine opposition.

- In February 1202, when Prince Alexius presented Innocent III with a plan to overthrow Emperor Alexius III, the pope opposed it. He was unlikely to support the cause of an ally of his imperial rival, Philip of Swabia.

Despite the pope's opposition to the diversion of the Fourth Crusade to Constantinople, all his attempts to stop it failed. First, in early 1203, he sent a letter that banned any attack on Christian lands without just cause. Another letter clarified the position about who was excommunicated and who would be absolved. Alongside this, he sent a message with an envoy of bishops that any attack on Constantinople was prohibited. All of these messages were suppressed. Even the ultimate weapon in the pope's arsenal, excommunication, was of little use if very few crusaders actually knew they were excommunicants.

Innocent III's inability to shape the course of the crusade was further limited by his decision in April 1203 to order Peter of Capuano to head straight to Acre. Before he went, Peter sent a bull of excommunication for all Venetians to Boniface of Montferrat, one of the crusade leaders, and then set off to Outremer. The bull, somewhat unsurprisingly, was suppressed. The pope, who had now removed even the symbol of papal authority from the crusade, was powerless. He sent yet another letter around May or June of 1203, which repeated the prohibition on the trip to Constantinople. However, by this time it was too late; the crusaders were en route to Constantinople. The pope could not stop them.

The neglect of the Holy Land

In May 1204, Constantinople had been captured and a new western emperor, Baldwin of Flanders, had been elected. The crusaders, rather than use their newfound position to finally launch their attack on the borders of Outremer, stayed in Romania. The pope may have wanted them to continue on the Fourth Crusade, but any influence he might have had was gone. In mid-1205, the papal legate, Peter of Capuano, returned to the Fourth Crusaders in Constantinople. There he granted them **absolution** from their crusade vow without the consent of the pope. Innocent III had not even been given the opportunity to abandon his own crusade. His crusade was over, but when it ended it was hardly his crusade at all.

KEY TERM

Absolution
A sacrament of the Catholic Church. It means that a sin has been forgiven. However, it can also mean a formal release from a vow or commitment, as simply to break a vow would be considered sinful.

An interpretation: the role of Innocent III

Extract 1 is a recent historical interpretation of Innocent III's role in the Fourth Crusade. It suggests that the pope bears a considerable degree of responsibility for the course of the crusade because he planned it. However, this argument is tempered by the idea that he was disobeyed by the crusade leadership.

EXTRACT

1   From Jonathan Riley-Smith, *The Crusades: A History*, published in 2014.

...The inclusion of Innocent's name among those responsible for the diversion is particularly unkind, but there is a kind of justice in it. It is likely that the strategy which went awry was his own. He certainly knew and approved of the plan to attack Alexandria and he came to an agreement with the Byzantines over provisions for the fleet on the way.

If he was responsible for the idea, it must rank as another of his wildly over-ambitious ones. From the start the crusade proceeded in a way that was galling for him. One act of disobedience led to another. Most of the crusaders, however divided and personally distressed, ignored his advice and prohibitions.

EXTRACT

2   Marco Meschini's explanation of the role of Innocent III in 'The Four Crusades of 1204', from *The Fourth Crusade*, published in 2008.

In a word, by building himself up as the theoretical craftsman of the crusade, Innocent necessarily subordinated himself to the will of others. The same may be said regarding his subsequent attempts to take the political wheel of the expedition by means of his envoys, whose influence on the events of the crusade was very limited.... Innocent [also] had a static conception of the aims of the crusade, offset by a certain elasticity as to the means to achieve them. Among those means may be counted three important milestones. The first stands in the redefining of the time period of the vow in the Holy Land necessary to attain the indulgence of the crusade, a period which, in the letter of 1199, changed from two years to one. This was a clear concession to prospective participants determined by the scarcity of recruits up to that point. The second indication is found in the famous *consilium sine bulla* sent by the pope to the armada around the middle of 1203, containing a dispensation of sorts allowing the crusaders to remain with the Venetians despite their excommunication. In the very same letter, one can also find the third indicator of that behaviour, when the pope permitted the crusaders to outfit themselves at the expense of the Greeks, using force if necessary. In all three cases, Innocent lowered his own standards in an attempt to control the conditions unfolding on the ground and direct the will of the principal crusaders. Such political choices, generated precisely by the aforementioned elasticity, were perceived nevertheless by the commanders of the crusade and by Venetian commanders as signs of weakness, with the consequence that the crusade became ever less 'Innocent's' and thereby remarkably less 'innocent'.

THINKING HISTORICALLY Interpretations (3a)

Differing accounts

Carefully read the two historical interpretations of the role of Innocent III in the Fourth Crusade (Extracts 1 and 2) before completing the activities that follow.

1 For each of the historians, create a summary table of their views, as below:

   a) Make a note of how they address the key issues.

   b) Make a note of the evidence they give in support of this claim.

   c) Use your notes and knowledge to give evidence that supports or challenges their interpretation.

HISTORIAN:_____	Interpretation of the issue	Evidence given	Evidence which supports or challenges this view
How influential was Pope Innocent III in the course of the Fourth Crusade?			
How active was Innocent's participation in the crusade?			
To what extent was the outcome of the Fourth Crusade the fault of its leaders rather than the pope?			

2 In pairs discuss which historian's interpretation of Pope Innocent III's role in the Fourth Crusade seems to best fit with the available evidence. Which seems the most convincing?

3 Make a note of any issues which made it difficult to compare the two interpretations directly.

4 Challenge: seek out another historical interpretation of the role of Pope Innocent III in the Fourth Crusade and compare this with the views you have explored already.

HOW DID THE SIZE AND LEADERSHIP OF THE CRUSADING FORCES CONTRIBUTE TO THE FAILURE OF THE FOURTH CRUSADE?

Recruitment

Who was recruited to lead the Fourth Crusade?

The earliest leaders of the Fourth Crusade were not kings but a collection of barons from northern France and the region of Flanders. The most influential of this group, recruited by the pope's official preachers, were:

- Thibault III of Champagne
- Louis of Blois
- Simon of Montfort
- Reynald of Montmirail
- Baldwin of Flanders
- Hugh of Saint Pol.

These leaders were a tightly knit group. The first four were all recruited together at a tournament at Écry on 28 November 1199. Baldwin of Flanders, who took the vow shortly after them, was Thibault's brother-in-law and close family ties appeared to dispose them towards crusading. Thibault's grandparents were the Second Crusaders, King Louis VII and Eleanor of Aquitaine. Four of them also shared a connection to the Third Crusader, King Richard I, who was the uncle of Louis of Blois and Thibault, as well as an ally of Hugh of Saint Pol and Baldwin.

The link to Richard I perhaps encouraged them to follow in his crusading footsteps. However, of even greater importance was the fact that the Fourth Crusade also gave them the chance to escape the threat to their lands from King Philip II. This threat, although nothing new, was intensified by the death of Richard I, because he had acted as their protector. The leaders were therefore connected by geography, family and a shared political situation. They may not have been kings, but they were a powerful group who brought both their wealth and their loyal vassals to the crusading cause.

EXTEND YOUR KNOWLEDGE

Baldwin of Flanders (1171–1206)

Baldwin, one of the crusaders to see the campaign through from start to finish, provides an excellent case study of a typical leader of the Fourth Crusade. He had been an ally of Richard I against Philip II and had regained much of the county of Flanders from Philip's hands in battle. After he had committed himself to the crusade, he had sent a representative to Venice and therefore played a key role in the planning process. He was an enthusiastic crusader and his forces were among the earliest to reach Venice in July 1201.

He also supported many of the decisions that led to the crusade's failure to reach Outremer. For instance, he backed the proposals of Prince Alexius to travel to Constantinople. Baldwin ended his career as a leader with his remarkable election to the imperial throne in Constantinople. Unfortunately, in this role he faced many challenges. For example, in March 1205, there was a rebellion in Thrace supported by the ruler of Bulgaria. Baldwin was captured in April at Adrianople, while attempting to tackle the rebellion. By 1206, he was assumed dead and replaced by Henry of Flanders as emperor.

Early warning signs: recruitment problems

Even at this early stage, as the Fourth Crusaders took their vows in late 1199, there were signs of the problems that would eventually divert the crusade away from Outremer. These included the following.

- The inability to recruit kings: the death of Richard I in April 1199 and the controversy that surrounded Philip II's marriage ensured the crusade would not be led by a monarch.

- The need for baronial support: recruitment was dependent on the personal decision of leading nobles. If a baron decided not to take the vow, it was unlikely his lords would join up.

- The need for mercenaries: in the 12th century it became increasingly common for mercenaries to be hired to supplement a crusading force. Without a king in charge, hired troops would be essential to bulk up the numbers.

On their own these issues were not enough to prevent the crusade, but they did have an impact. The lack of royal leadership meant there were no royal coffers, countrywide taxes or naval fleets to utilise. It also meant some leading barons, such as Duke Eudes III of Burgundy, felt able to ignore the call to the crusade. This restricted the number of lords who chose to join up from the area. The final effect was a financial one, as the actions of the leaders would need to reflect their financial position. Thibault III of Champagne believed it would cost him 25,000 livres to fund his own troops, but he also knew he would have to pay roughly the same again for mercenaries. Without cash to pay them, the crusading forces would quickly crumble.

Leadership decisions: the plan for the Fourth Crusade

Whose plan was it?

The Fourth Crusade was essentially based around a plan devised by three counts from northern Europe. Thibault III of Champagne, Louis of Blois and Baldwin of Flanders met in the summer of 1200 to discuss their shared priorities. Once decided, they planned to send six representatives, who would include Geoffrey of Villehardouin, John of Fraise and Conon of Béthune, to make arrangements based on their decisions. This envoy would have the power to negotiate a legally binding agreement on behalf of its overlords.

The key features of the plan

In their second meeting of the summer at Compiègne, the leaders agreed that sea travel would be an essential feature of the crusade. It was quick, it would avoid the Byzantines and it would ensure that only crusaders with sufficient means, or in the pay of nobles, took part.

However, it also meant that without a national fleet to call upon, they would need to pay for a fleet from the Venetians. With this plan in mind, the envoy was sent to Venice in early 1201.

The envoy was also informed of the target for the campaign, although it was under orders only to reveal this detail on a 'need to know' basis. The fleet was not to head straight to Outremer to support Jerusalem or Antioch, but instead to sail to the port of Alexandria in Egypt. From there it would capture the rest of Egypt from the Muslims. The chosen destination was kept secret because the leaders felt it might discourage recruitment.

However, it was a sound choice and was made on the basis that Egypt had been considered as a target before. Richard I had wanted to divert the Third Crusade there, attempts had been made by Amalric, the king of Jerusalem, to take it in the late 12th century and a Sicilian attack in 1174 had met with some success. It was also more logical to take Egypt first and then use this as a base to attack Muslim Syria, especially as the Christians of Outremer had negotiated a five-year truce with the Muslims in 1198. The Franks of Outremer would not want to risk a breach of the truce unless they felt confident of success.

The flaws in the plan

Problem 1: the price of reliance on the Venetians

EXTEND YOUR KNOWLEDGE

Doge Enrico Dandolo (1107–1205)
Enrico Dandolo was elected doge of the city state of Venice in 1192. In this capacity he ruled over a city that controlled its own affairs and was in competition with other Italian city states such as Pisa and Genoa. His earlier career prepared him well for government service. For example, he had served as both a judge and then an ambassador for Venice to Byzantium. Some claim that it was during his time at Constantinople as ambassador, in the anti-western riots of 1171, that he was blinded by the Byzantines. These rumours are unfounded and it is now thought that he developed cortical blindness, caused by a problem in the brain, in the late 1170s. In fact, Dandolo was on favourable terms with the Byzantines prior to the Fourth Crusade and had negotiated a treaty that secured a privileged trading position for Venice in 1198. His subsequent role in the attack on Constantinople, and the foundation of Romania, were unlikely to have been part of a personal vendetta, but due to the opportunities the city offered to the crusaders. He died in Constantinople, shortly after leading a rescue force against the Bulgarians, aged around 98.

The negotiations that led to the Treaty of Venice in April 1201 began when the envoy reached the city of Venice and met the doge, Enrico Dandolo. The terms it devised were both grand in scale and in cost. In total, it was assumed that the Venetians would provide transport for 33,500 men, which included:

- 4,500 knights
- 9,000 squires (two per knight)
- 20,000 additional troops on foot.

In addition, arrangements were made for:

- the transportation of 4,500 horses (one per knight)
- 9 months' food supply for all of the troops
- a Venetian escort made up of 50 galleys and a crew of around 30,000 Venetians.

These preparations would be ready by 29 June 1202, when the crusaders were expected to arrive, and in return they would meet the following terms of payment:

- 85,000 marks (around £60,000 currently) to be paid in instalments
- an initial deposit of 5,000 marks
- half of the booty and land acquired by the crusade to be given to the Venetians.

These terms meant that this was one of the most ambitious transportation treaties of the medieval period. It would take the efforts of an entire city over a year to prepare, and would involve a tremendous amount of labour to adapt and build ships to house knights, horses and supplies. The fact that the envoy had secured Venetian support was in part a success, but it came at a tremendous price. This could be considered reasonable if broken down into individual costs, but it still involved payment of an amount that was double the annual income of King John of England.

However, of greater significance for the outcome of the crusade was the fact that the treaty was based on some very optimistic guesswork on the part of the envoy. It had been forced to estimate the size of the army that would require transportation and its arrival at the figure of 33,500 was more in line with the ambition of its leaders than the reality of crusading. In the Third Crusade, for example, Frederick Barbarossa had only travelled with around 15,000 troops and his contingent had been considered one of the largest in crusading history. The envoy had therefore taken a huge gamble, as the Venetians were guaranteed 85,000 marks but they were not guaranteed 33,500 troops.

Problem 2: the size of the forces

Unfortunately for the leaders of the Fourth Crusade, their gamble failed to pay off. In fact, out of the 33,500 troops they had committed themselves to pay for, only around 12,000 had arrived by August 1202. Of these, up to 1,800 were knights and the rest were support troops or squires. This disappointment was compounded by the tardiness of the prospective crusaders. They were supposed to be ready to leave Venice by 29 June 1202, but many important figures arrived late. Even the papal legate, Peter of Capuano, did not arrive until 22 July, and it took until August for the Germans to arrive under the leadership of Abbot Martin of Pairis. The most punctual troops were therefore forced to wait at Lido, a small island near Venice.

The effect of the death of Thibault III of Champagne

The relatively small force that gathered on the island was a result, in part, of circumstances beyond the control of the leadership team. A year before, on 24 May 1201, Thibault III of Champagne had died and passed on the responsibility to fulfil his crusade vow to Reynald of Dampierre. His death had a profound effect because it left the Fourth Crusade without its principal leader.

Steps were taken to try to rectify this and the position was first offered to Duke Eudes of Burgundy, but he refused. The leaders finally settled on the selection of Boniface of Montferrat after some persuasion from the chronicler Geoffrey of Villehardouin.

In many ways Boniface was the ideal candidate for the job, as he came from a family with strong crusading traditions. His brother, William Longsword, had fathered King Baldwin V, while another brother, Conrad of Montferrat, had held the garrison at Tyre during the Third Crusade. Boniface accepted the position at a meeting at Soissons in June 1201 and the other leaders swore an oath to acknowledge him as the head of the crusade forces. From there he travelled to Hagenau and spent the Christmas period with Philip of Swabia and his guest, Prince Alexius Angelus. Eventually he arrived in Venice on 15 August 1202, as one of the last leaders to join the forces gathered at Lido.

Boniface's poor punctuality was, however, only one of a number of problems that arose after Thibault III's death and the change of leadership, and included the following.

- The loss of support from some knights in the Champagne region. For example, Reynald of Dampierre wanted to fulfil his promise to Thibault as quickly as possible. He chose to sail directly to Outremer rather than wait for the Venetian gathering.

- The nationality of Boniface created friction between the crusade leadership. He was Italian, whereas the rest of the leaders were from France, or were connected to it through ties of overlordship with the French king. As an outsider, it would take time for the others to trust and respect him.

- The connections of Boniface were somewhat controversial. He was friends with Philip of Swabia, an enemy of the pope in the imperial succession crisis. He also had a close relationship with the Byzantine Empire, as his wife, Irene Angelus, was the daughter of the deposed emperor, Isaac Angelus.

The effect of the decision to avoid Venice

Another reason for the small size of the forces that gathered at Lido was that some contingents simply avoided Venice altogether. This was not because they objected to Boniface's leadership, but rather that only the knights of Champagne, Flanders, Blois, Saint-Pol and, after his acceptance of the Treaty of Venice, Montferrat had formally agreed to meet in Venice. The other crusaders were free to travel by whatever method and route they preferred. Indeed, if they had the means and it was easier to sail from closer ports, such as Marseilles, it made perfect sense for the crusaders to make their own way to Outremer. Historical precedence was on their side, because this is precisely what had happened during the Third Crusade.

The choice of some to avoid Venice was also a result of the leadership's secret decision to attack Egypt first. The consequence of a hidden objective was that the other contingents had little appreciation of why it was important to meet in Venice, a natural port to choose for an attack on Alexandria. In fact, even some of those who were aware of this secret, such as Louis of Blois, tried to back out of the Treaty of Venice. He had to be convinced by a personal visit from Villehardouin and Saint-Pol to bring his forces to the city. This suggests that even those who signed up to the original plan had limited faith in it and helps to explain why other groups bypassed Venice and the commitment that came with it.

The effect of the flaws in the Treaty of Venice on the size of the forces that gathered is hard to gauge, but in total it is thought around 300 knights arrived in Outremer rather than travelling with the Fourth Crusaders. This figure also includes those who left the Fourth Crusade at a later stage, such as at the siege of Zara. The following were some notable absentees from the Venetian gathering.

- Reynald of Dampierre: he felt obliged to fulfil the request from Thibault III of Champagne to complete his crusade vow. He travelled directly to Outremer and provided help to Prince Bohemond IV of Antioch in his fight against the threats to the principality.

- John of Nesle: he was supposed to join Baldwin of Flanders. He sailed from Flanders, but was delayed and ended up sheltering at Marseilles for the winter. He then chose to sail directly to Outremer from the French port, which deprived Baldwin of up to half of his potential forces.

- Walter of Brienne: he helped Pope Innocent III deal with a threat in southern Italy. After this was resolved, he sailed straight on to Acre. This was another example of papal involvement that hindered the Fourth Crusade.

The effect of finance on the size of the forces

The final factor that limited the size of the gathering was the financial capacity of the crusade leaders who had sworn their loyalty to Boniface of Montferrat. In their commitment to the Treaty of Venice, they had clearly overreached themselves. They simply could not afford to pay for up to 20,000 soldiers to join the Fourth Crusade and were overly optimistic to assume noble support from across Europe would cover the funding gap. Their resources and limited power meant the lofty goal they had set for the size of the crusade was beyond their means.

The problem of inadequate financial resources was worsened by the actions of the papal legate, Peter of Capuano. On 22 July 1202, with the desire to improve the efficiency of the crusading army, he decided to absolve all the non-combatants from their crusade vow. This would certainly help the chances of the army to win battles free of the burden of the old or infirm. However, it also deprived the crusade of fee-paying personnel, which meant there was less money for the provision of hired troops as it was instead required to pay the Venetian fee of 85,000 marks.

Consequences: in debt to the Venetians

The Venetians, the chronicler Robert of Clari recorded, had stopped all commercial activities for 18 months in order to prepare for the Fourth Crusade. By the June 1202 deadline, they had 500 ships ready to leave port. However, as a result of the size of the crusading force that had gathered in Venice, the leading nobles were unable to pay the entire fee (see above). The signatories of the Treaty of Venice had relied on the fact that other nobles, who brought their vassals with them, would cover the cost for their own troops. Without the additional fee-paying nobility, the average fee per crusader was simply unaffordable.

In this context, with just over one-third of the anticipated forces at Lido, it was remarkable that the leaders were able to raise 51,000 marks to pay off part of the treaty. This money, for the most part, had to come from their own pockets, because the other main source, Innocent III's tax of one-fortieth, had gathered little in the way of funds. In England, for example, it was not even collected until 1217. The crusaders were thus left penniless encamped upon the island of Lido, completely dependent upon the generosity of the Venetians to continue to supply them. They then had little choice but to rely on the governors of Venice to find a solution that would allow them to pay off their 34,000 mark debt and resume the Fourth Crusade.

An interpretation: weakness of the leadership

Extract 3 is an interpretation of the role the leaders played in the failure of the Fourth Crusade. It argues that the leaders were too weak to force troops to assemble in Venice and the plan was an unrealistic one. The account of Geoffrey of Villehardouin is also quoted below (see Source 2) and helps show how Phillips's interpretation has been constructed on the basis of a sophisticated reading of contemporary chronicle evidence.

EXTRACT 3 From Jonathan Phillips, *The Fourth Crusade and the Sack of Constantinople*, published in 2004.

Crusaders ... who did take part were under no compulsion to sail from Venice. Blinded, perhaps, by the prospect of the wonderful Venetian navy, and believing ... that in pure military terms this was the best way for the crusaders to reach Egypt, [the leaders] had assumed that all the holy warriors would wish to join the same fleet. Crucially, the only signatories to the treaty with Venice were the representatives of Champagne, Flanders, Blois and Saint-Pol. Beyond these contingents there was no obligation for any of the crusaders to travel with the Venetians. Likewise, there was no papal directive ordering such a course of action and none of the expedition's nobles had sufficient authority to compel everyone to gather at the head of the Adriatic...

Most previous crusading expeditions had travelled in a fragmented and ad hoc manner... Sometimes these groups gathered together for convenience or, once in Asia Minor, joined together for safety, but to ask such a polyglot force as the Fourth Crusade to meet in Europe was unprecedented.

ACTIVITY
WRITING

The language of historians

Re-read Extract 3 and then answer the questions below:

1 Identify words and phrases used to express degrees of doubt and certainty. Write them out in order of most to least certain.

2 Identify words that are used to introduce new evidence to develop and strengthen the historian's argument.

3 Extract 3 goes on to conclude: 'As the summer of 1202 wore on, the plan for the expedition to travel in one enormous fleet looked increasingly implausible'. Find two points the author has made earlier in the extract to reach this conclusion.

SOURCE 2 Geoffrey of Villehardouin, marshal of Champagne, was an important participant in the Fourth Crusade. He was part of the envoy that was sent on behalf of Thibault of Champagne to Venice and helped to negotiate the Treaty of Venice. His chronicle blames low numbers on the actions of the leaders who chose to avoid Venice.

About the same time a fleet of ships, which carried a very large contingent of men-at-arms, had set sail from Flanders to travel round by the coast. The men in charge of this fleet were Jean de Nesles, Governor of Bruges, the Comte [count] Philippe de Flandre's [Flander's] son Thierry, and Nicolas de Mailly... This fleet was very fine and well equipped; the Comte de Flandre and his fellow Crusaders had relied greatly on it, because it carried most of their best sergeants. But the men in charge, and all the people with them, broke the promise they had made to their lord, because, like so many others of their sort, they were afraid to face the great perils of the enterprise that the army in Venice had undertaken.

In much the same way the Bishop of Autun also failed to keep faith with us, as did the Comte Guignes de Forez ... all of whom avoided coming to Venice because of the great risk involved, and sailed instead from the port of Marseilles.

AS Level Exam-Style Question Section C

Study Extracts 1 and 3 on pages 122 and 127 before you answer this question.

Historians have different views about the reasons for the failure of the Fourth Crusade. Analyse and evaluate the extracts and use your own knowledge of the issues to explain your answer to the following question.

How far do you agree with the view that the Fourth Crusade failed because of weaknesses in the crusade leadership? (20 marks)

Tip
Extract 3 focuses on the inability of the leaders to gather a large force together. You should try to use your knowledge of their other weaknesses, and the implications of these, in assessing the view.

The weakness of the leadership

Interpretations of the past, such as Phillips's explanation in Extract 3 of why the requirements of the Treaty of Venice were not met in the summer of 1202, are based on a broad range of contemporary evidence. This activity will help you to understand the basis for the claims made in Extract 3.

1 Find evidence from this chapter to support the following arguments in Extract 3:

- the total number of crusaders was overestimated

- 'none of the expedition's nobles had sufficient authority to compel everyone to gather at the head of the Adriatic'

- it was unlikely that the entire 'polyglot force' would meet in Venice.

2 Some information that Phillips used to construct his interpretation has been omitted from Extract 3. Find two pieces of evidence from Source 2 that Phillips might have used to support his interpretation.

3 Explain why Phillips does not agree with Villehardouin's argument in its entirety.

WHAT IMPACT DID DOGE ENRICO DANDOLO HAVE ON THE COURSE OF THE FOURTH CRUSADE?

The doge's plan

SOURCE

3

A 13th-century image of Venetian ship builders from a medieval Venetian manuscript. This was the type of work that Venice was famed for and was one of the main reasons why the crusaders chose to negotiate a transportation treaty with the city in the first place.

In some ways it could be argued that the doge of Venice, Enrico Dandolo, actually rescued the Fourth Crusade rather than contributed to its failure. In September 1202, it was clear that the crusade leadership was not going to be able to pay off the debt to the Venetians. This left it in a state of limbo, unable to continue the crusade and not willing to disband it after the payment of 51,000 marks to the Venetians. Under these circumstances, Dandolo suggested a solution.

The doge proposed to offer a moratorium on the remaining debt of 34,000 marks, but in return he asked for the army's help to achieve one of Venice's military objectives. His plan was that the crusaders would set off to the port of Zara, which was under Hungarian control, and help re-establish Venetian authority over it. The army could then spend the winter in Zara, supplied by the prosperous port, and sail on to Egypt early in 1203.

Why did Dandolo propose an attack on Zara?
The proposal to attack Zara gave the Fourth Crusade a way to continue. Nevertheless, it also served the best interests of Dandolo and the Venetians. Dandolo's priorities were influenced by the following factors.

- The value of Zara: the Venetians had lost control of the port in 1186. It was a valuable possession because it was a key stop-off point on the journey to Outremer. It also supplied Dalmatian oak that was used to construct Venetian ships.

- Personal investment: Dandolo had been the primary supporter of the Treaty of Venice. He had convinced the governing bodies of Venice to accept it and was therefore responsible for the huge commitment the city had made to the enterprise. The Zara plan provided a means to begin to recover the debt that was palatable to the city's government.

- The risk of violence: a force of around 12,000 crusaders was on Venice's doorstep and they had just paid 51,000 marks to the city. There was a serious risk, if the crusade was halted, that the crusaders might, at best, request their money back or, at worst, attack the city itself.

- The desire for salvation: Dandolo was an old man. He took the crusade vow himself before the fleet set off in October 1202. This meant he was able to take advantage of the plenary indulgence that Pope Innocent III offered to fully fledged members of the Fourth Crusade.

Dandolo's proposal therefore reflected his own priorities and the needs of his city. It was a way to meet a religious goal, through the plenary indulgence for his sins, as well as a political and economic one, through an attack on a rebellious Zara and then the capture of the lucrative port of Alexandria.

How did Dandolo's proposals weaken the crusade?
Some leading figures of the Fourth Crusade opposed the plan to attack the port of Zara because it was a Christian city. It was also under the control of a Christian king, Emeric of Hungary, who had himself taken the crusade oath. It did not appear to be an oath he took very seriously, as he repeatedly tried to excuse himself from action in the crusade. Nevertheless, the vow meant, in theory at least, that all of his lands were under the legal protection of the pope. The Fourth Crusaders had therefore accepted a controversial proposal to attack fellow Christians who were themselves under papal protection.

Divisions in the crusading force
The decision to travel to Zara did not critically wound the Fourth Crusade, but it did begin the process of division that was to sap troops from its ranks. Prior to the departure from Venice to Zara, both Boniface of Montferrat and Peter of Capuano travelled to Rome to convey news of the crusade to the pope. Boniface did not return until Zara had fallen and Peter was absent until the capture of Constantinople. The forces that were about to attack Zara had therefore lost their commander-in-chief and papal authority for their actions. In fact, upon hearing the news of the attack, Innocent III dispatched a letter to the crusaders which made it clear that he would not sanction the use of force at Zara (see 'Failure to influence the Zara campaign', page 121).

The papal letter itself was never publicly shared with the whole crusading host, but it did cause further disruption in the ranks of the leadership. Two key leaders, Abbot Guy of Vaux-de-Cernay supported by Simon of Montfort, used the letter to quell enthusiasm for the siege (see the timeline on page 130). When they failed to halt the attack on the port, they chose to abandon the crusade as well.

Their actions had highlighted the early tension between those who wanted the crusade to proceed at any cost and those who were wary of ignoring the pope's advice. However, the majority of the barons and the Venetian force still supported the attack and the crusade continued.

The crusaders at Zara

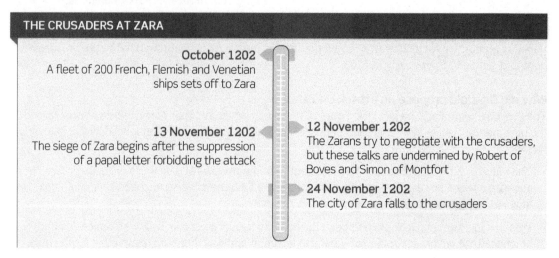

THE CRUSADERS AT ZARA

October 1202
A fleet of 200 French, Flemish and Venetian ships sets off to Zara

13 November 1202
The siege of Zara begins after the suppression of a papal letter forbidding the attack

12 November 1202
The Zarans try to negotiate with the crusaders, but these talks are undermined by Robert of Boves and Simon of Montfort

24 November 1202
The city of Zara falls to the crusaders

How did the siege of Zara weaken the crusade?
The Fourth Crusade had found a way to continue and, in a sense, had been saved by Dandolo. Nonetheless, the siege also contributed towards the crusade's eventual failure. First, it delayed the journey to Alexandria, because it was now too late in the year to embark on a long voyage. The crusaders would have to spend winter encamped outside Zara. Secondly, it led several leading nobles to abandon the cause. Simon of Montfort and others associated with him distanced themselves from the crusade. In the meantime, leaders from other contingents began to question their actions taken against papal command. For example, Abbot Martin of Pairis asked the pope if he could be freed from his vow, but this request was denied.

There were now unwilling participants on the Fourth Crusade and morale began to worsen. This was not helped by the actions of Innocent III who had decided to excommunicate all the crusaders at Zara. In order to appeal the sentence, an embassy was sent to Rome with prominent leaders from the French contingent. Innocent III's response came in February 1203. He asked for the crusaders to take an oath to avoid any further attacks on Christians without just cause, which the French and their allies took willingly, but the Venetians did not. The French were thus released from their punishment but the Venetians remained excommunicants.

The Venetian decision to ignore the papal request for an oath was just one manifestation of the gap that had begun to grow between the original crusading force and their Venetian allies. On 27 November 1202, just before the dispatch of the embassy to Rome, there had been violent riots between the French and the Venetians that led to around 100 deaths. The reaction to the oath, and the rioting that had preceded it, were two clear signs that the objectives of one large and essential part of the army differed considerably from the original crusaders. The latter wanted to reach Alexandria and ultimately recapture Jerusalem in order to fulfil their vow, whereas the former wanted to secure the interests of their city and its commercial power.

ACTIVITY
KNOWLEDGE CHECK
The doge's plan and the capture of Zara
1 Identify three problems the crusaders faced between September 1202 and December 1202.
2 For each problem, explain how it could be linked to Dandolo.
3 Then try to find a limitation for your argument. Consider his positive effects on the crusade, or the indirect nature of his responsibility for the problem.
4 In light of your answers to 2 and 3, do you think it would be fair to blame one man for the failure of the Fourth Crusade? Explain your answer.

An interpretation: the key role of Venice and Dandolo

Extract 4 is an assessment of the part the Venetians, under the leadership of Dandolo, played in the direction of the Fourth Crusade. John Fine's interpretation rests on the principle that the priority of Venice was material gain. It was in its economic interests to take Zara, and then Constantinople, which meant the Venetians were happy to divert the crusade along those lines. They also had the power to do so because they controlled the crusaders' primary method of transportation. Fine thus privileges the role of Dandolo as the 'prime mover' of the Fourth Crusade, which can be justified by the pivotal role he played in the events that followed his involvement.

However, there is a controversy over the precise motivation of this 'prime mover' and hence his impact on the Fourth Crusade. In Extract 5, Louis de Mas Latrie argues that there was a secret treaty between Dandolo and Sultan Malik al-Adil to sabotage the Fourth Crusade. In contrast, in Extract 6, Christopher Tyerman makes the case that Dandolo genuinely supported the goals of the original plan because they would satisfy the material interests of Venice. Extract 5 would therefore suggest Dandolo caused the Fourth Crusade to fail, whereas Extract 6 challenges this allegation but maintains the important role money played in Dandolo's actions.

EXTRACT 4

From John Fine, *The Late Medieval Balkans: A Critical Survey from the Late Twelfth Century to the Ottoman Conquest*, published in 1987.

The Venetian doge Dandolo, over eighty and blind, became one of the prime movers for the crusade, but one who never lost sight of Venice's material interests. He hated the Byzantines and felt that Venetian trade was in danger as long as the empire survived. He feared that at any time some emperor might repeat the 1171 arrests and property seizures. Furthermore, in an attempt to escape from Venice's stranglehold on its economy, trade, and naval defense, the empire had been granting privileges to other Italian cities – Genoa and Pisa, Venice's rivals. A conquest of Constantinople by a Venetian-led crusade could give Venice a monopoly over Eastern trade. Thus the Germans, Normans, and Venetians, the manpower being mobilized for the new crusade, were all hostile to Byzantium.

Venice rapidly acquired a leading role in the crusade through its role in transport. After the failures of recent crusades that had taken the overland route across Anatolia, a territory divided between the empire and various Muslim states, it made sense to travel to the Holy Land by sea. Venice, however, expected the other crusaders to pay their passage. Not surprisingly, the crusaders did not have the cash to pay Venice's high prices; so, unknown to the pope, Venice sought services in lieu of debt.

KEY TERM

Lateran Council
A council of Church officials held by the pope in the Lateran Palace. It dealt with matters of Church law and contemporary political issues.

EXTRACT 5

Louis de Mas Latrie's analysis of the reason why the Venetians were keen to divert the Fourth Crusade away from the goal of Alexandria. It was written between 1852 and 1861.

The redactors of the compilations annexed to the French text of the *Chronicle* of William of Tyre all recall that Malik al-Adil [Sultan of Egypt], learning of the armaments prepared by the Christians in the wake of the failure of the crusade of Emperor Henry VI, sent an embassy to Venice in the hope of warding off the new danger which threatened Egypt. The details of the negotiation are missing. The objective and the price of the service requested, however, are clearly indicated. 'The sultan chose envoys and servants,' says one chronicle. 'He gave them fine presents and sent them to Venice. He charged them to say to the doge and the Venetians that, if they could bring it about that the Christians would not go into the land of Egypt, he would give them rich goods and great franchises in the port of Alexandria.'

The archives of Venice contain indirect confirmation of this audacious bargain, which foreign chroniclers have ignored, and which a contemporary Venetian writer, having access to the sources, has implicitly recognized, but without sufficient emphasis. There exists in the official collection of the Pacts of the Republic a series of privileges of Sultan Malik al-Adil from the year 1205 to the year 1217, granting to the Venetians the favor of conducting commerce in his states in security, of enjoying exceptionally advantageous tariffs freely ruled by them at Alexandria.

EXTRACT 6

Christopher Tyerman's exploration of the attitude of Venetians towards the goal of capturing Alexandria, from *God's War: A New History of the Crusades*, published in 2006.

Egypt and the great entrepôt of Alexandria presented a very different option, a greater risk for a much greater potential profit. The centre of the hugely lucrative spice trade, handling the spices that had been shipped from south east Asia to the Red Sea ports and thence to the Nile before forward transit to Europe, as well as a source of wheat, sugar and alum (used in dyeing and leather making) and a market for timber and metals, Alexandria had accommodated western traders since the eleventh century. However, compared with Genoa and Pisa, Venice maintained only a modest presence there, trade with Egypt constituting perhaps 10 per cent of the city's eastern business. Dandolo had seen the opportunities at first hand during a visit to Egypt in 1174. In 1198, perhaps in response to Cardinal Soffredo's mission, the pope granted a license to Venice to continue trading with Egypt in non-military materials (i.e. non metal and timber) despite the general, and largely ignored, ban decreed by the Third **Lateran Council**. A successful crusade presented Venice with the chance to expand its share of the richest market in the Levant. The stipulation in the 1201 treaty for equal shares in any conquests recognized Venice's enormous risk as well as its huge material and human contribution, with the war galleys and numbers of crew amounting to only little less than the estimated crusader army. It also echoed the so-called *Pactum Warmundi* of 1124, under which the Venetians had agreed to assist the Franks under Patriarch Gormund of Jerusalem capture Tyre in return for a third of the city. In a new Frankish Alexandria, Venice would control most of the trade. Thus the crusade presented Venice with a unique commercial opportunity, a chance to assert civic patriotism and the undying glory of winning back Jerusalem, which the city's Genoese and Pisan rivals had failed to achieve ten years before.

THINKING HISTORICALLY | Interpretations (4a)

The weight of evidence

Work in pairs. Read Extracts 5 and 6, do the activity and answer the questions below.

1 Use highlighter pens to colour code the extracts. Use one colour for 'evidence', another colour for 'conclusions' and a third colour for 'language that shows the historian is reasoning' (e.g. 'therefore', 'so' or the gaps where these words are implicit).

2 How do the extracts differ in terms of the way that the evidence is used?

3 Which of these extracts do you find more convincing? Which has the best-supported arguments?

4 What other information might you want in order to make a judgement about the strength of these claims?

5 Write a paragraph of 200 words explaining the importance of using evidence to support historical claims.

HOW DID PRINCE ALEXIUS'S FAILURE TO KEEP HIS PROMISES CAUSE THE FOURTH CRUSADE TO COLLAPSE?

Prince Alexius's plan for the crusade

In late 1202, the Fourth Crusade had once again stalled, as the armies waited outside Zara for winter to pass. Around this time, a new figure with a new problem and some extraordinary promises made an offer to the crusaders. He was Prince Alexius Angelus, the son of the former Byzantine emperor, Isaac II. In 1195, Isaac II had been deposed and then blinded by his own brother, who became known as Alexius III. The new emperor-elect then placed Isaac II and his son under house arrest, perhaps under the impression that his position was secure because blindness barred an emperor from ruling Byzantium.

EXTEND YOUR KNOWLEDGE

Isaac II Angelus (c1135–1204)

Isaac II succeeded the Byzantine emperor, Andronicus I, who was murdered after his anti-western policy had placed the city of Constantinople in grave danger in September 1185. Isaac II was a relatively weak ruler, in comparison with his predecessors, and struggled to enforce his authority in the empire. For example, he failed to control Isaac Comnenus, the ruler of Cyprus, before it was taken by Richard I. He was also an unlikely ally of the Fourth Crusaders, because his policies were decidedly anti-western. He had been at war with the Normans as a result of their invasion of Thessalonica. He had also tried to form an alliance with Saladin to protect himself from the Third Crusade forces of Frederick Barbarossa. Towards the end of his life, Isaac II was deposed from his role as emperor twice, by Alexius III and then Murtzuphlus. He died in a prison cell shortly after his son's death in February 1204.

However, Alexius III had not counted on young Prince Alexius's ingenuity. By 1201, the prince had escaped his prison with the help of some Pisan allies. He headed west and began to drum up support in the courts of western Europe for his father's restoration to the imperial throne. His proposal stood at least some chance of success, because the walls of Constantinople were weak and the naval fleet numbered only 20 old ships. In fact, the only major stumbling block was its army, which stood at an impressive 30,000 troops. It also had a contingent of Varangian guards, who had a distinguished reputation as skilled warriors. The prince was going to need an army of his own to reverse the events of 1195.

The intervention of Prince Alexius: his proposal

Prince Alexius made an appeal to the crusaders via Philip of Swabia, the German king and the emperor of the western Empire, in December 1202. The prince had a close connection with the emperor, as Philip was married to the prince's sister, Irene Angelus. The envoy Philip sent to Zara, on behalf of his brother-in-law, offered a means to strengthen the Fourth Crusade. It asked for the crusaders' help to restore the prince's father to the Byzantine throne and crown the prince as co-emperor. In return for their help to either intimidate Alexius III into submission or use force to re-take Constantinople, the prince offered:

- 200,000 marks
- 10,000 troops to join the Fourth Crusade
- to pay for 500 knights who would defend Outremer for the lifespan of Prince Alexius
- to bring the eastern Christian Church of Byzantium back under the control of Rome.

The supporters

The promises Prince Alexius offered were truly incredible and were generally greeted with enthusiasm by the crusade leadership. This included groupings from across the different nationalities of the Fourth Crusade:

- the Venetians under the leadership of Dandolo
- the French with support from the counts of Blois and Saint Pol
- the supporters of Philip of Swabia, which included Boniface of Montferrat and the Bishop of Halberstadt.

Their support for the scheme was understandable, because it gave the crusade a fighting chance of success. First, they were much more likely to recapture Jerusalem with an extra 10,000 troops. Secondly, the plan appealed to historical precedence. Crusaders had used Constantinople as their base for an attack on Syria and Palestine ever since the First Crusade. Thirdly, it would alleviate the problem of the Venetian contract, which had only six months left on it. Once those six months were up, the crusade would lose a fleet and most of its supplies. The prince's proposal meant the crusade could pay off the contract and be assured of supplies once its task in Constantinople was complete. It could then continue on to Outremer.

However, there are some 19th-century historians who see in the crusade leadership's enthusiasm a more sinister motive. They believed that the Fourth Crusade was an elaborate conspiracy, which had been used from the very beginning by Philip of Swabia to help the young prince.

EXTRACT

Donald Queller and Thomas Madden analyse the idea of a plot laid by Philip of Swabia to divert the Fourth Crusade to Constantinople all along. It is from *The Fourth Crusade: The Conquest of Constantinople* (second edition), published in 1997.

Historians who attribute the Latin conquest of Constantinople to a plot laid primarily by Philip of Swabia see in the election of Boniface of Montferrat to head the crusade precisely the instrument required by the Hohenstaufen to achieve his ends. The author of the Gesta Innocentii, desiring not only to clear his hero of any responsibility for the sack of Constantinople, but also to cast blame upon the hated house of **Hohenstaufen**, states that Boniface 'was said' to have treated with Philip concerning the installation of Alexius in Constantinople by means of the crusading army. Such a discussion surely took place. Historians, however, sometimes leap too readily from discussion to deeds, from idle talk to careful plans, to successful execution... Philip, it is agreed, was powerless; so, these historians contend, he worked his way by wile through Boniface. But neither Philip nor Boniface had any way of foreseeing the fortuitous concatenation of circumstances that ultimately led the crusade to Constantinople. Boniface did not have a crusading army at his disposal just because he had been elected commander. A crusading army was not like a modern army, disciplined, and ruled by a fixed and well-organized chain of command... Boniface would have been not only arrogant, but foolish, if he believed at Christmas of 1201 that he had power to manage the crusade according to his will.

EXTRACT

From Eduard Winkelmann, *Philip von Schwaben und Otto IV von Braunschweig*, published in 1873–78. Winkelmann proposes the theory that the outcome of the Fourth Crusade was a conspiracy plotted by Philip of Swabia.

At the court of Philip of Swabia now [July 1201] emerged for the first time the idea of making use of the imminent crusade in the interest of the dynasty of the Angeli, and soon an appropriate intermediary was found. It was the marquis Boniface of Montferrat, a man who, along with Philip, had sought to promote this affair as early as 1200. He was related to the king of France and also to the Angeli, since his brother, Conrad of Tyre, had taken as a wife a daughter of Isaac. But the marquis was particularly suitable since the French crusaders with the consent of their king elected him their leader in September 1201. On 14 September he was still at Citeaux [motherhouse of the Cistercian Order]. From there he went to Germany to Philip, through whom he was won for the cause of the Byzantine pretender. Gesta Innocentii [Life of Innocent III], c. 83: 'He travelled from France to Germany; there he was said to have agreed with Philip that he would bring about the return to Constantinople by means of the Christian army of Alexius, Philip's brother-in-law, who had fled from captivity, for the purpose of gaining the Roman Empire.'

KEY TERM

Hohenstaufen
A dynasty of German rulers of the Holy Roman Empire. They ruled it from 1138 to 1208 and from 1212 to 1254 and included Philip of Swabia.

Interpretations (4b)

Method is everything
A spectrum of historical methodology

Bad history	Good history
• Based on gut feeling • Argument does not progress logically • No supporting evidence	• Based on an interpretation of evidence • Argument does progress logically • Evidence deployed to support argument

Work in pairs.

Historical writing can reveal much about the methods by which it was constructed. Read Extracts 7 and 8 and answer the following questions.

1 Look carefully at the spectrum of methodology above.

   a) Where would you place each source on the spectrum of historical practice?

   b) What evidence would you use to support your choice?

2 Look at Extract 8. How would you change it to make it the same quality of historical writing as Extract 7?

3 Use a dictionary. Explain the following words in their relation to historical writing: substantiation, deduction, inference, cross-reference.

4 How important is it that historians understand and evaluate the methods used by other historians?

How did the proposal weaken the Fourth Crusade?

Despite the strong case to accept Prince Alexius's proposal to help his father reclaim the imperial throne, the view of the leaders was not shared by the entire crusading host. Many of the crusaders were not prepared to endure any further delays on their journey to Outremer. As a result, around 1,000 were allowed by the leadership to leave and another 1,000 left without permission. This meant that, after the losses at Zara, and the decision to travel to Constantinople the crusading contingent itself had been reduced to around 3,000 troops by August 1203.

The main host may have haemorrhaged troops, but for the most part, the crusade leadership remained intact. The only departure of note was Renauld of Montmirail, who took several important French knights with him to travel directly to Outremer. Other leaders, such as Simon of Montfort and Guy of Vaux-de-Cernay, who had already distanced themselves from the action at Zara, now made the decision to abandon the Fourth Crusade for good. They began to make preparations to travel from the port of Apulia to Outremer. The crusade had therefore lost a few important figures, but if Prince Alexius was able to fulfil his promises this was a small price to pay.

Nevertheless, it was not a price that the pope was prepared to accept. His influence on the course of the Fourth Crusade had already begun to erode after the diversion to Zara. By the summer of 1203, Innocent III had decided he would oppose Prince Alexius's

proposal. He may have been tempted by the offer of Byzantine submission to the control of Rome, but his opposition to any plan associated with Philip of Swabia held firm (see 'Failure to prevent the diversion to Constantinople', page 121). Ultimately, he had decided to resist a plan that appealed to the leadership and this meant he was permanently sidelined. The pope now stood little chance of success in forcing the crusaders to continue onto Outremer.

The crusaders at Constantinople

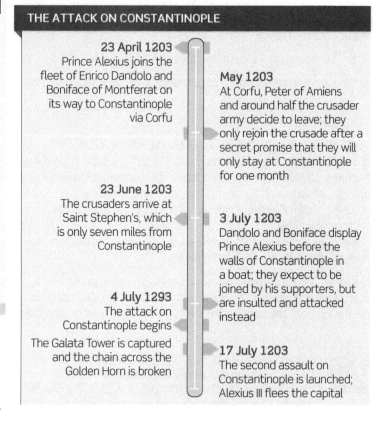

THE ATTACK ON CONSTANTINOPLE

23 April 1203 Prince Alexius joins the fleet of Enrico Dandolo and Boniface of Montferrat on its way to Constantinople via Corfu

May 1203 At Corfu, Peter of Amiens and around half the crusader army decide to leave; they only rejoin the crusade after a secret promise that they will only stay at Constantinople for one month

23 June 1203 The crusaders arrive at Saint Stephen's, which is only seven miles from Constantinople

3 July 1203 Dandolo and Boniface display Prince Alexius before the walls of Constantinople in a boat; they expect to be joined by his supporters, but are insulted and attacked instead

4 July 1293 The attack on Constantinople begins The Galata Tower is captured and the chain across the Golden Horn is broken

17 July 1203 The second assault on Constantinople is launched; Alexius III flees the capital

Short-term achievements of the attack

In the short term this plan for their onward journey looked like it might actually happen. On 18 July 1203, Isaac II was restored to the imperial throne by the Greek nobility. The crusade leaders were invited into the city, along with Prince Alexius, and entered into a discussion with Isaac II. He agreed, despite considerable reservations and with the knowledge that the promises could not be fulfilled, to the commitments Prince Alexius had made. The crusaders, no doubt wary their new ally would turn on them, forced him to accept the coronation of Prince Alexius as well. As a result, on 1 August 1203, Prince Alexius became Alexius IV.

The westerners' closest Byzantine ally was now in a position to carry out his side of the bargain. He gave the crusaders 100,000 marks, 50,000 of which were given straight to the Venetians. The other half was given to the rest of the forces who had signed up to the Treaty of Venice. However, they had to pay 36,000 marks to the Venetians in order to settle the terms of this treaty once and for all. They were left with the rest to provision and maintain their forces, which were encamped in Galata. Here they waited, with a combined force of around 3,000 troops, for their leaders to arrange the next stage in the journey.

The failure of Prince Alexius and its significance

Unfulfilled promises

The crusaders' optimism that they would join the autumn shipping passage to Outremer did not last long. It quickly became apparent that Alexius IV had promised far more than he could actually deliver. For example, he had managed to pay 100,000 marks out of the treasury of Constantinople to the crusaders, but this fell far short of his promise to give 200,000 marks to them. In fact, Alexius IV would struggle to raise any more money, because the rulers of the rest of his empire had not submitted to his authority and therefore could not be taxed. He was an emperor but he did not yet have full control of an empire.

Instead of taxation, Alexius IV had to try and raise money within the city itself in order to provision the crusaders at Galata. The only way to do this quickly was to take extreme measures. He ordered the world-renowned relics of Constantinople to be melted down for money. However, even this measure was not enough and in November 1203 he was left with little practical choice but to stop the payments to the crusaders. In one fell stroke he had alienated both his allies, through his decision to withhold further funding, and his own people, as a result of his order to melt down their precious holy relics.

However, it was not just a lack of capital that frustrated the crusaders. There was also the matter of the religious justification for their diversion to consider. Alexius IV had promised that the eastern Church would submit to the pope's authority and end the schism that had begun in 1054. This promise was acted upon, as Alexius IV managed to persuade Patriarch John X Camaterus to submit to the pope's authority, but it was hardly fulfilled. The patriarch did not try and change the doctrine of the Church to match the West, nor would he travel to Rome to take part in a ceremony in which he would be granted the **pallium**. It was evident to the crusaders that Camaterus's promise was mere lip service, rather than a genuine submission.

KEY TERM

Pallium
A woollen band worn about the neck. It is a badge of office as well as a symbol of recognition of papal authority.

At the heart of both of these problems was a weak and inexperienced emperor. He could not fulfil his promises because he did not have the power to do so. The Byzantine Empire was unstable and Alexius IV's position insecure. He faced a serious threat from the nobles that ruled the rest of his imperial territories and it was with the risk of rebellion in mind that Alexius IV reached out to the crusaders. On 29 September 1203, he made a request that was to have a profound effect on the future of the Fourth Crusade. He asked the principal leaders, along with their armies, to remain at Constantinople until March 1204.

The crusade leaders had little choice but to agree. They wanted to carry on to Outremer, but it was impractical to do so without more money, the provisions Alexius IV had promised and the additional troops he would provide. They were caught in a trap, because their initial commitment to Alexius IV had made them completely reliant on his promises. In order for him to deliver on them, they would have to strengthen his position as emperor. The crusaders therefore joined Alexius IV on a tour of the Byzantine Empire and once again the crusade was delayed. Those who had been assured of a one-month limit on their stay in Constantinople were furious as the ships of the autumn passage came and went without them on board.

The fall of Alexius IV

On the night of 27 January 1204, both Isaac II and Alexius IV were imprisoned by a senior nobleman, Alexius Dukas, who was known as Murtzuphlus by his contemporaries. Alexius IV was therefore no longer in a position to fulfil his promises to the crusaders. His fall from power occurred for several reasons.

- Alexius IV was too closely associated with the crusaders. He had relied on their help to regain power and during his tour of the Byzantine Empire.

- The hostility between the crusaders and the citizens of Constantinople had grown. For example, on 19 August 1203, a fire was started by the crusaders that destroyed 440 acres of the city; 15,000 westerners who lived in the city decided to flee to the crusader camp at Galata.

- Diplomatic relations between the crusaders and the Byzantine government had broken down. In December 1203, a French and Venetian embassy was thrown out after it tried to demand that the emperor should stick to his earlier promises.

- The rise of Murtzuphlus, who was promoted to **chamberlain** by Alexius IV. His popularity grew after he launched a brave, but unsuccessful, land assault against the crusaders on 7 January 1204. This helped him become an anti-western figurehead with the populace of Constantinople. With their support, he was able to overthrow Isaac and Alexius IV and have himself crowned Emperor Alexius V.

KEY TERM

Chamberlain
An important official in the administration of the Byzantine Empire, who was also referred to as the *protovestiarius*.

The effects of the fall of Alexius IV

On 8 February, Alexius IV was murdered and then, on 28 February, Isaac II died. The fall of Alexius IV was of profound significance. The Fourth Crusade had reached an impasse for several reasons, which included the following.

- The crusaders were about to break another deadline: after Alexius IV's request for ongoing crusader support, the main body of the crusaders had agreed to stay until March 1204. This deadline was only one month away and, if allowed to pass by without action, would cause anger among an increasingly impatient force.

- Lack of provisions: until Alexius IV had begun to take formal military action he had continued to provision the crusaders.

Alexius V, however, made it clear he would not carry on this support. The crusaders would have to risk raids in hostile territory, such as the king of Bulgaria's lands, to sustain their soldiers.

- The aggression of Alexius V: one of his earliest actions as emperor was to ambush Henry of Flanders's troops outside Constantinople. It was clear he wanted the crusaders gone and would use force to try and remove them from Galata.

- The failure of negotiations: on 7 February 1204, Alexius V and Dandolo met to try to reach a negotiated solution to their mutual problem. Alexius V wanted the crusaders to leave and Dandolo wanted money and provisions. These negotiations achieved nothing except increased tension.

By March 1204, almost all their options had been exhausted. The main body of the crusading forces wanted to join the spring passage to Outremer, but the leaders lacked the capital and provisions required to do this. Faced with an impatient army and a hostile emperor, the leaders felt there was only one way to get the provisions and other resources necessary to continue. They decided to attack and capture the city of Constantinople, take by force what they could not get through diplomacy and finally begin their journey to Outremer.

The sack of Constantinople and its significance

Preparations for the attack

Before the invasion of Constantinople, the crusade leadership met to prepare a pre-attack agreement. It was designed to ensure that once Constantinople was captured the western forces did not turn on one another. The following were the principal terms of the March Pact of 1204, as decided by Dandolo, Boniface, Baldwin and the French leaders.

- Money: the Venetians were to take most of the booty until their debt of 200,000 marks, accrued over the year since the Treaty of Venice expired, was settled. The rest would be split half and half between the Venetians on the one hand and the crusaders on the other.

- Leadership: a new emperor to replace Alexius V would be chosen by 12 electors. The emperor would have limited power, because he would rule over one-quarter of the former Byzantine Empire.

- The former Byzantine Empire: the remaining three-quarters of the empire would be divided into various titles and fiefdoms. These would be handed out to the Venetians and the crusaders by a commission.

In many ways, the March Pact of 1204 was a sensible move by those who wanted the Fourth Crusade to continue. It would ensure the crusaders and Venetians remained united, help them to replenish their funds in a fair way and give the crusaders access to the horses and other resources needed to carry on. Its terms helped to galvanise a force that now numbered around 20,000, which included the 3,000 original crusaders alongside the Venetian troops and some of the western evacuees of Constantinople. However, it also contained one crusade-crippling feature.

It was agreed that all the signatories of the March Pact would stay in Constantinople for one more year to secure the empire. The crusade would be delayed once again.

The capture and sack of Constantinople

The attack began on 9 April 1204 and, by the night of 12 April, a terrified Alexius V took flight under cover of darkness. His escape marked the start of a three-day raid of the city by the invaders, referred to as 'the sack of Constantinople' due to its infamy in the history of the crusades. In addition to looting money and precious metals, they also took part in a city-wide **_furtum sacrum_**. Many of Constantinople's relics and treasures were stolen and some of the most famous of these, such as the statues of four horses, still reside in St Marks in Venice today.

> **KEY TERM**
>
> _Furtum sacrum_
> A sacred theft of relics from one place to take them to another. It was justified by the idea that the saints they were attached to wanted their relics to be moved.

SOURCE

The four horses on display above St Mark's Cathedral in Venice. This was just one example of the treasures stolen from Constantinople and transported abroad during the sack of the city.

The effects of the sack of Constantinople

This act of city-wide burglary had a substantial impact on the future of the Fourth Crusade, because it provided a means for it to carry on. For example, the invaders gathered:

- 300,000 marks from the treasury that was split between the Venetians and the crusaders; the Venetians got the lion's share of this in settlement of their debt, but there was still plenty to replenish the coffers of the crusading contingents

- 10,000 horses that would help the crusaders who, after years of waiting, foraging and occasional sieges, had few horses left at their command.

Despite the level to which the Fourth Crusaders were replenished, the theft of Constantinople's relics also had a negative consequence on the crusade's prospects. It poisoned the relationship between the native inhabitants of the Byzantine Empire and the westerners. This meant that if the crusaders and the Venetians wanted to keep control of Constantinople, they would have a lot of work to do in order to win the citizenry over. It would also make one of their goals set in 1203, the reunification of the churches of the East and West, much more difficult because of the scale of the *furtum sacrum*. A new patriarch of Constantinople, no matter how strong willed, would struggle to get his clergy to submit in both heart and mind to the pope in Rome.

The establishment of Romania

The sack of Constantinople was soon followed by the foundation of a new crusader state that would replace Byzantium. It was called Romania and May 1204 marked the start of a process that would keep the crusaders very busy indeed. They had to:

- elect an emperor; Baldwin of Flanders and Boniface of Montferrat were the chief contenders for this position, but Baldwin won and was elected emperor on 16 May 1204

- divide up Byzantine land; this led to military conflict between Baldwin and Boniface

- tackle external threats from former rulers like Alexius III and Alexius V.

The establishment of Romania became an all-consuming task for the crusaders. By mid-1205, the majority of them had abandoned any plans to travel on to Outremer. Some were disheartened, such as the 7,000 westerners who, according to Villehardouin, went back to Europe in April 1205. The rest were simply too busy and were fortunate that, in the summer of 1205, Peter of Capuano travelled to Constantinople. There, without permission from the pope, he declared the crusade over and absolved the crusaders of their vow.

Peter of Capuano's action was a practical move, as he could not have realistically restarted the Fourth Crusade, despite the pope's wishes. Innocent III simply had to reconcile himself with the truth. The crusade he had started six years previously was not going recapture Jerusalem. It had, in fact, failed.

Prince Alexius and the fall of Constantinople

The Fourth Crusade's primary objective was to reach Outremer and then attempt to recapture Jerusalem. Any diversion away from this goal helped to contribute to its failure.

1 Create a table with three columns headed 'Event', 'Leader's justification', 'Effect on Fourth Crusade'. Down the left-hand side of the table list the following events:

December 1202: Prince Alexius's proposals are discussed and accepted

July 1203: First attack on Constantinople

September 1203: The crusaders accept Alexius IV's request to stay in Constantinople until March 1204

April 1204: Second attack and sack of Constantinople

May 1204: The establishment of Romania.

2 For each event explain:
   a) how the leader justified the event
   b) whether it would strength or weaken the Fourth Crusade.

3 Which event do you think had the biggest impact on the failure of the Fourth Crusade to achieve its objective? Explain your answer.

An interpretation: Prince Alexius to blame

Extract 9 outlines the important part Prince Alexius played in the redirection of the Fourth Crusade from Outremer to Constantinople. Thomas Asbridge argues that the diversion to Constantinople changed the priorities of the crusade for good and that, once there, the events that unfolded kept the crusaders there. His interpretation makes the point that Prince Alexius's promises were simply too lavish. They had the dual qualities of being attractive but also extraordinarily difficult to fulfil. The interpretation suggests that, as a result, Prince Alexius was to blame, because his own failed proposal led to the sack of Constantinople and the end of the Fourth Crusade.

EXTRACT
9 From Thomas Asbridge, *The Crusades: The War for the Holy Land*, published in 2010.

Once there [Constantinople], the expedition rapidly lost sight of its 'sacred' goal to recapture Jerusalem. After a short-lived military offensive, the existing imperial regime was toppled in July 1203 – at only limited cost in Greek blood – and Alexius was proclaimed emperor. But when he proved unable to redeem his lavish promises of financial reward to the Latins, relations soured. In January 1204 Alexius' grip on power faltered and he was overthrown (and then strangled) by a member of the rival Doukas family, nicknamed Murtzurphlus (or 'heavy-brow', on account of his prominent eyebrows). In spite of their own recent estrangement from the late emperor, the crusaders interpreted his deposition as a coup and characterised Murtzurphlus as a tyrannical usurper who must himself be removed from office. Girded by this cause for war, the Latins prepared for a full-scale assault on the great capital of Byzantium.

On 12 April 1204, thousands of western knights broke into the city and, in spite of their crusading vows, subjected its Christian population to a horrific three-day riot of violence, rape and plunder. In the course of this gruesome sack the glory of Constantinople was smashed, the city stripped of its greatest treasures – among them holy relics such as the Crown of Thorns and the head of John the Baptist.

AS Level Exam-Style Question Section C

Study Extracts 4 and 9 on pages 131 and 137 before you answer this question.

In the light of differing interpretations, how convincing do you find the view that the Fourth Crusade failed because Dandolo 'never lost sight of Venice's material interest' (Extract 4, lines 2–3)? (20 marks)

To explain your answer, analyse and evaluate the material in both extracts, using your own knowledge of the issues.

Tip

You will need to find evidence to support the view that Dandolo was one of the 'prime movers' of the Fourth Crusade, but do not get tricked into following the 19th-century theory that he planned to divert it from the start. This is not what the author of Extract 4 is suggesting.

EXTRACT 10

From Edwin Pears, *The Fall of Constantinople: Being the Story of the Fourth Crusade*, published in 1885. This was the first work of history on the Fourth Crusade written in English and accepted the inaccurate view that the Venetians had always planned to redirect the crusade to Constantinople. Each of the following questions has been and is still the subject of controversy:

1) The conduct of Venice; as to which the questions to be settled are:

   a. Was there a treaty with Malek Adel like that described by Charles Hopf, by which, in return for benefits conferred on the republic, Venice undertook not to convey the crusaders to Egypt?

   b. Did Dandolo intentionally make difficulties while the Crusaders were on the Island of Lido, in order to carry out his part in such a treaty?

   c. Was the expedition to Zara part of Dandolo's design for a diversion of the crusade, or was it due to accidental circumstances, without premeditation on the part either of Dandolo or Boniface?...

2) ...The design and conduct of the Crusaders:

   a. What was the destination desired by the crusaders, and were they agreed that this should be Egypt?

   b. Were the Crusaders duped into violating their vows by acquiescing in the diversion upon Zara, or did they willingly accept the proposal as the best under the circumstances?

   c. Was Villehardouin cognizant of the treachery of Venice, if there were treachery, and does he conceal facts which were within his knowledge?...

3) ...The conduct of Boniface.

4) The conduct of Philip of Swabia.

5) The conduct of Innocent the Third.

In reference to these latter subjects the principal questions under discussion are:

   a. Was there an undertaking or an understanding between Philip, Boniface, and Dandolo, previous to the departure of the expedition from Venice, that it should be diverted from its purpose as a crusade into an expedition directed against Constantinople?

   b. How far was Innocent cognizant of the designs of Philip and the leaders?...

   c. ...When did Philip first entertain the idea of an attack upon Constantinople for the benefit of young Alexis?

ACTIVITY
SUMMARY

Interpretations: what explains the failure of the Fourth Crusade?

Read Extract 10 from Edwin Pears, *The Fall of Constantinople*. It lists the questions he felt needed answering before a decision can be made about why the Fourth Crusade failed.

1 What are the flaws in his questions (e.g. what do they presuppose)?

2 Choose one question he poses that you think is valid. Explain why you think it might be a good starting point for constructing an interpretation.

3 Try to construct your own interpretation, in no more than 400 words, in answer to your chosen question.

4 Reflect: what are the strengths of the interpretation you have constructed? How could you improve it?

WIDER READING

Angold, M. *The Fourth Crusade Event and Context – The Medieval World*, Routledge (2003)

Phillips, J. *The Fourth Crusade: And the Sack of Constantinople*, Pimlico (2005)

Queller, D. and Madden, T. *Fourth Crusade: The Conquest of Constantinople*, University of Pennsylvania Press (1999)

Some primary sources can also be found in translation on the World Wide Web:

The Sack of Constantinople (1204), Nicholas Choniates

The Chronicle of the Fourth Crusade and the Conquest of Constantinople (c1207), Geoffrey Villehardouin

The Conquest of Constantinople, Robert of Clari

Preparing for your AS Level Paper 1 exam

Advance planning

1. Draw up a timetable for your revision and try to keep to it. Spread your timetable over a number of weeks, and aim to cover four or five topics each week.
2. Spend longer on topics that you have found difficult, and revise them several times.
3. Above all, do not try to limit your revision by attempting to 'question spot'. Try to be confident about all aspects of your Paper 1 work, because this will ensure that you have a choice of questions in Sections A and B.

Paper 1 overview:

AS Paper 1	Time: 2 hours 15 minutes	
Section A	Answer 1 question from a choice of 2	20 marks
Section B	Answer 1 question from a choice of 2	20 marks
Section C	Answer 1 compulsory interpretations question	20 marks
	Total marks =	60 marks

You should familiarise yourself with the layout of the paper by looking at the examples published by Edexcel. The questions for each section are followed by eight pages of lined paper where you should write your answer.

Section A questions

Section A questions ask you to analyse and evaluate either cause or consequence. You should consider either the reasons for, or the results of, an event or development. You will be asked for coverage of a period of around ten years, possibly a little longer. For example, a question for Option 1F might be 'Was the involvement of President Truman the main reason for the changing status of black Americans in the years 1945–55?' Your answer should consider the reason(s) given in the question, then look at other relevant points and reach a conclusion.

Section B questions

Section B questions cover a longer timespan than in Section A, at least one-third of the period you have studied. The questions take the form of 'How far...', 'How significant...', 'To what extent...' or 'How accurate is it to say...'. The questions can deal with historical concepts such as cause, consequence, change, continuity, similarity, difference and significance. Again, you should consider the issue raised in the question, consider other relevant issues, and then conclude with an overall judgement.

Section C questions

There is no choice in Section C, which is concerned with the historical interpretations you have studied linked to the question 'What explains the failure of the Fourth Crusade?' You will be given two extracts totalling around 300 words (printed separately) and the question will take the form 'How far do you agree with the view that...?' There is no need to use source analysis skills such as making inferences or considering provenance for Section C answers. You will need to use the extracts and your own knowledge to consider the view given in the question.

Use of time

This is an issue that you should discuss with your teachers and fellow students, but here are some suggestions for you.

1. Do not write solidly for 45 minutes on each question. For Section A and B answers you should spend a few minutes working out what the question is asking you to do, and drawing up a plan of your answer. This is especially important for Section B answers, which cover an extended period of time.
2. For Section C it is essential that you have a clear understanding of the content of each extract and the points that each extract is making. Read each extract carefully and underline important points. You could approach your answer by analysing the first extract, then the second, and then using your own knowledge before reaching an overall judgement. You might decide to spend up to ten minutes reading the extracts and drawing up your plan, and 35 minutes writing your answer.

Preparing for your AS Level exams

Paper 1: AS Level sample answer with comments

Section A

These questions assess your understanding of the period in breadth. They will ask you about the content you learned about in the four key themes, and may ask about more than one theme. For these questions remember to:

- give an analytical, not a descriptive, response
- support your points with evidence
- cover the whole time period specified in the question
- come to a substantiated judgement.

Was the succession crisis of 1185–86 the main consequence of Baldwin IV's leprosy in the years 1174–86?
Explain your answer. (20 marks)

Average student answer

Baldwin IV was crowned king in 1174, but he had leprosy. There were many effects of Baldwin IV's leprosy because it meant he would die young. It also meant that he could not have children. This had lots of other effects on his reign.

In 1185–86 there was a succession crisis. The new king was called Baldwin V and was too young to rule Jerusalem so Raymond III of Tripoli was his regent. This meant that Raymond III was in control of the kingdom. However, in 1186 a succession crisis began. Baldwin V died in August and another couple managed to take over. They were Guy and Sibylla and they distracted Raymond III in late 1186. When he was distracted they had themselves crowned as rulers. This was a big consequence of Baldwin IV's leprosy because he died young.

Another main consequence was that Baldwin IV's leprosy meant that he could not have children and was often too ill to rule. This meant that there were lots of arguments over who was in charge of the kingdom. Early on in his reign, Baldwin's first regent was killed. There were also two groups who tried to control him. One was made up of people on his mother's side and the other was made up of people on his father's side. These two groups argued a lot. In 1180, his father's side even tried to invade the kingdom to make sure they were in control. They were stopped by the other group who managed to stay in control by quickly arranging a marriage. This was a major consequence of Baldwin IV's leprosy because it was these two sides that argued in the succession crisis of 1185–86.

This is a weak opening paragraph because it only provides a little bit of relevant context. It could be improved by a suggestion of what the other effects were. This would provide a focus for the answer.

The paragraph contains accurate material, but there is limited development of the points made. There is a brief link to Baldwin's leprosy, but it is weakly developed. The answer would be greatly improved by a clearly established connection to Baldwin IV's leprosy from the start of the paragraph.

There is a stronger link to the question in this paragraph and an attempt to link the consequence to the previous one. However, the material included in the paragraph is very general. It needs specific examples to develop some of the points made.

It also contains two distinct points: the government split up into two sides at the start of his reign and the two groups had a major dispute around 1180. The answer could be improved by exploring these in two separate paragraphs.

Another consequence was that Saladin took a lot of land and was able to build up his Muslim empire. Saladin took over Damascus and made it a part of his empire in 1174. This made him a more powerful ruler. In 1175 Raymond III decided to make a truce with Saladin. He had more time to take control of more Muslim cities during this time. By 1183 Saladin was much more powerful. He began to invade the Kingdom of Jerusalem and raided the area of Galilee in 1183.

The last big consequence of Baldwin IV's leprosy was that Raymond of Tripoli decided to make a truce with Saladin in 1185. He was able to do this because he was regent for Baldwin V at the time. This gave Saladin the opportunity he needed to finally deal with the threat from the Christians. In May 1187 he used the truce to his advantage. He forced Raymond to allow him to send 7,000 troops through Raymond's lands on their way to the port of Acre. This was the first serious threat the kingdom had faced in many years. The Templars and Hospitallers felt that Saladin had to be stopped. They tried to attack Saladin's troops, but they were defeated. Saladin was very pleased with this success. He decided it was now time to launch a full scale invasion of Outremer. He started this in July 1187 and the first stage of his invasion ended with the capture of Jerusalem in October. This was a huge consequence of Baldwin's leprosy, because it gave Saladin the opportunity to attack.

In conclusion, one of the main consequences of Baldwin IV's leprosy was a succession crisis at the end of his reign. However, there were other main consequences as well. There were lots of arguments during his reign about who was in charge. At the same time, Saladin built up his empire and began to invade Baldwin's kingdom. This led to another consequence, that from 1185 onwards Saladin was able to invade the kingdom.

This is a very descriptive paragraph, but does contain relevant and specific examples of Saladin's empire building. It could be developed through a link to previous paragraphs as well as how it relates to Baldwin IV's leprosy.

This paragraph contains the beginnings of a good explanation of the seriousness of the consequence under discussion. However, it relies mainly on material outside the timescale in the question. It could be improved through a greater focus on the truce and its potential consequences, as these fit within the timescale.

The concluding paragraph lacks focus. It is important to avoid simply restating everything you have said in the rest of the answer. Pick out the key arguments and then come to a reasoned judgement on what you believe the main consequence was.

Verdict

This is an average answer because:

- it does not always establish any link between the issue (Baldwin IV's leprosy) and the consequences
- the consequences are not all backed up with specific examples
- it relies on material from outside the timescale in the question
- the conclusion restates the points, but does not give a judgement on what the main consequence was and why.

Use the feedback on this answer to rewrite it, making as many improvements as you can.

Paper 1: AS Level sample answer with comments

Section A

These questions assess your understanding of the period in breadth. They will ask you about the content you learned about in the four key themes, and may ask about more than one theme. For these questions remember to:

- give an analytical, not a descriptive, response
- support your points with evidence
- cover the whole time period specified in the question
- come to a substantiated judgement.

Was the succession crisis of 1185–86 the main consequence of Baldwin IV's leprosy in the years 1174–86?
Explain your answer. (20 marks)

Strong student answer

In 1174 Baldwin IV was crowned king of Jerusalem. His reign was marked by problems caused by his leprosy and ended with a truce agreement with Saladin and a prolonged succession crisis after his death in March 1185. The reason his medical condition could have serious consequences was that Baldwin IV could not father children and those around him knew he would lead a short life. As a result his government split into factions that argued over who would rule. The main consequences of his leprosy were the emergence of these factions at the start of his reign, the influence that the maternal faction had over events in the late 1170s and a period of inactivity in Baldwin's government in the 1180s that Saladin could take advantage of. The main consequence, out of all of these, was the one that had the most influence on the effectiveness of Outremer's government.

Baldwin IV suffered from leprosy and this meant he was extremely weak towards the end of his life. By early 1185 he was unable to rule and asked Raymond III of Tripoli to become his regent. This weakness forced him to take drastic action and have his infant heir, Baldwin V, son of his sister, crowned king and co-ruler of his kingdom. When Baldwin IV died, in March 1185, Raymond III remained as regent, but now ruled on behalf of the young Baldwin V. This meant the kingdom had two weak rulers between 1185 and 1186 that required someone else to rule on their behalf. In fact, Baldwin died too soon to properly secure the succession as he did not live long enough for Baldwin V to reach maturity. If he had, he could have influenced the events of August 1186. In this month Baldwin V died and a full blown succession crisis began. Raymond III of Tripoli wanted one set of rulers in charge, Isabella and Humphrey of Toron, but there were rival claimants to the throne, Sibylla and Guy of Lusignan. This meant there was a serious risk that the country could end up in a civil war. This was only prevented by a mixture of luck and speedy action on behalf of Sibylla and Guy. Their chief representative, Joscelin III of Courtenay, managed to convince Raymond III to retreat to Tiberias for his own protection. This gave Sibylla and Guy a chance to be crowned in Jerusalem before Raymond III could have his own candidates crowned. However, Raymond was not put off by events and tried to hold a coronation where he was. This failed because Humphrey, when he heard the news of Sibylla and Guy's marriage and coronation, refused to support Raymond's plan and paid homage to Guy instead. The succession crisis was therefore a major consequence of Baldwin's leprosy, because the government of Outremer was nearly split in half, but it was perhaps not the main consequence because this was avoided.

> This is a strong introduction because it provides context for the timescale in the question and the potential consequences Baldwin IV's leprosy could generate. It also provides focus because it lists a series of consequences and suggests a criterion for assessing which the main one was. This could be improved through an indication of what the main consequence was.

> The paragraph is a detailed discussion of the main consequence in the question. It clearly establishes the link between Baldwin IV's leprosy and how the succession crisis resulted from that. It also evaluates whether this was the main consequence or not. However, there is a lot of material on the succession crisis here and this could be shortened in order to provide time for better coverage of the other consequences.

Another consequence of Baldwin IV's leprosy, as well as his youth, was that he struggled to rule Outremer on his own. This created a power vacuum at the very start of his reign and the government divided into two factions. The first was connected to his paternal line and was led by his cousin, Raymond III of Tripoli. The other was linked to his maternal line and was led by his mother, Agnes of Courtenay. His government was less effective as a result because each faction wanted power, which they thought they could get by securing their own candidate for the succession. They could then exercise influence over their candidate who would provide them with land and wealth, or perhaps a part in important decisions. This was a more significant consequence than the later succession crisis because it occupied much of Baldwin's time and distracted him from the government of Outremer.

However, factionalism also allowed Baldwin IV to show strength and so had positive consequences. Baldwin IV favoured his mother's faction and wanted his royal line to continue through his sister, Sibylla. He showed strength in 1180 when Raymond III wanted to marry Sibylla to his preferred candidate, Balian of Ibelin, instead of Baldwin's. Raymond III started an invasion of the kingdom to try to get his own way, but Baldwin quickly arranged for Sibylla to marry one of his supporters, Guy of Lusignan. His leprosy had the consequence of making Baldwin IV fight for and achieve his goal.

The final consequence was that Saladin was able to take action when Baldwin's government was inactive. For example, in 1183, Saladin raided the area of Galilee but little action was taken against the threat. The regent, Guy of Lusignan, seemed unable to get the lords to obey his commands and fight. In the end there was little choice but to make peace with Saladin. This is why, in 1185, Raymond III signed a truce with Saladin. This was a significant consequence, because it gave Saladin time to prepare his troops for a large invasion and made the government appear weak.

In conclusion, the succession crisis of 1185–86 was a major consequence of Baldwin's leprosy because it rendered the government ineffective, whilst the succession was secured. However, the crisis itself was not the main consequence because it came at the end of a series of arguments over the succession that had all been serious. In reality the most serious consequence was the emergence of factionalism at the start of his reign. This had the biggest influence on effective government because it created the environment for a succession crisis in 1185, forced Baldwin to make a show of strength in 1180 and prevented his government from tackling the Muslim threat.

> This is a shorter paragraph than the first, but demonstrates evidence of expert thinking. It makes connections between the concept of factionalism, power and the important part succession played in this. It would benefit from more specific examples to develop the problems factionalism created to help substantiate the final claim.

> This paragraph links well to the previous one and evaluates the overall argument that all the consequences of his leprosy were negative and caused ineffective government. This paragraph would benefit from greater explanation of the evidence used.

> The paragraph has several specific examples of the gains Saladin made as a result of Baldwin's illness. However, it requires a clearer connection to be made with Baldwin's leprosy and a greater range of evidence. It could be improved with references to Saladin's achievements in the early 1170s as well.

> This is a strong conclusion because it evaluates the consequence proposed in the question, but suggests that another consequence was the main one. It also refers back to the introduction in order to give the argument coherence.

Verdict

This is a strong answer because:

- the introduction provides the backbone for the answer with both context and focus
- a range of consequences is covered; each is supported by accurate specific examples
- the argument is developed throughout, although the first issue has been explored in much greater depth than the rest; this has left less time to explore other consequences and so these are less well supported
- there is evidence of good conceptual understanding of concepts related to power and government
- the conclusion reaches a clear judgement on the main consequence and substantiates it.

Paper 1: AS Level sample answer with comments

Section B

These questions assess your understanding of the course in breadth and will cover a period of 30 years or more. They will ask you about the content you learned about in the four key themes, and may ask about more than one theme. The questions will also require you to explore a range of concepts, such as change over time, similarity and difference, as well as significance. For these questions remember to:

- identify the focus of the question
- consider the concepts you will need to explore
- support your points with evidence from across the time period specified in the question
- develop the evidence you deploy to build up your overall judgement
- come to a substantiated judgement that directly addresses the question set.

How significant were political motives in the decision to call for the First and Second Crusades? (20 marks)

Average student answer

The First Crusade was proclaimed at the council of Clermont in 1095 by Pope Urban II and the Second Crusade was started by Pope Eugenius III in 1145. They both had a motive. There were some political motives, but there were lots of other reasons to start a crusade as well.

> This is a weak introduction because it only provides a small amount of information about the topic in the question. It could be improved by identifying other factors to assess the significance of political motives against. This would help to sharpen the focus of the answer.

The main political motive for the First Crusade was that the Byzantine Empire was under threat from the neighbouring Muslim Turks. In 1095 one tribe called the Cumans attacked Adrianople. This was part of the empire. In 1095 the Byzantine Emperor Alexius I asked for help from the pope. Alexius I wanted to take back the city of Nicaea from the Turks. He asked for help to do this because he wanted to create a buffer zone between his empire and the Turks. Another political threat came later because Outremer needed to be protected from the Turks. In 1144 Edessa was taken by Zengi. This led to the call for the Second Crusade.

> There are several points in this paragraph, which are each supported with a small amount of evidence. The second point, Alexius's request for help, is the only one that shows a weak attempt at development. This paragraph could be improved by explaining in greater detail how each piece of evidence led to the call for a crusade.

There were also religious motives for both crusades. Jerusalem was a very special place to Christians. It was the home of holy sites like Calvary and the Holy Sepulchre. Many people went on pilgrimage to Jerusalem. In the 1060s, 7,000 German pilgrims went there. Empress Helena also went there in the 4th century. She was the mother of Emperor Constantine. The other religious motive was the indulgence. This was an offer of a remission of sins. It meant that anyone who went on a crusade would be forgiven for all their sins and could go straight to heaven. This was a new idea by Pope Urban II. This led to the call for a crusade because the pope wanted to help people get to heaven and a crusade would give them a chance to do this.

> This is a very descriptive paragraph, which contains some material from outside the timeframe. There is limited development of the idea of an indulgence but the explanation does not make much sense. It could be improved by a stronger focus on, and explanation of, the connection to Jerusalem in the First and Second Crusade.

The political motive of the threats to the Byzantine Empire and Outremer were linked to the political motives of the pope. Pope Urban II had a lot of his own political problems. He was in a fight with the Emperor of the German Empire who wanted to get rid of Urban II and replace him. In 1095 Urban II managed to show the emperor, who was called Henry IV, that he was strong. He allowed Henry's wife, Praxedis, to separate from him at her request. This meant the pope had successfully embarrassed Henry IV. He needed to find another way to show he was stronger than Henry IV. The First Crusade was a good way. Urban II would be in charge of it and it would show how much power and support he had. This is why he asked for a crusade.

> The factor in this paragraph is linked to a previous one and it contains one piece of specific evidence that is developed and linked back to the question. It could be improved with more specific pieces of evidence, which show an awareness of change over time.

The last reason for a crusade was that knights wanted to fight. In the First Crusade, 10 percent of the crusaders were knights. These were men who fought on horseback and were well-known for their use of a heavy lance in a cavalry charge. They wanted a chance to fight. There were other reasons for knights as well. In 1120 Hugh of Payns started the Templars. He did this to protect pilgrims from Muslim raids. In 1120 there was a Muslim raid from Tyre and Ascalon, which killed 300 pilgrims. This meant that knights wanted to go and protect people. At its height, about 500 knights were in the Templars.

> There is a partial attempt in this paragraph to develop the point that knights wanted to fight, but no clear connection is made to the crusades. The other point does not relate at all to the First or Second Crusade. An alternative choice of factor would help to focus this paragraph on the question.

The main cause for the First Crusade was political because Alexius wanted help and then Edessa wanted help. However, there were lots of other main causes as well. Both crusades were called because Jerusalem was a special place and the pope wanted to give out indulgences to people. He also wanted more power for himself and to give the knights something to do. Ultimately the two popes called for crusades because they met all of their different needs.

> This is a poor attempt at a conclusion. It restates the points from the answer and hints at material that has not been discussed in the main body of the argument. It would benefit from a clear judgement on how significant political motives were in comparison to the other factors that have been discussed.

Verdict

This is an average answer because:

- it does not consistently explain how the evidence under discussion led to the call for a crusade
- some paragraphs rely heavily on one specific example or on very general/irrelevant material
- parts of the argument reach illogical conclusions
- there is little reference made to the similarities and differences between the two crusades
- the conclusion restates the points and the judgement reached is vague and poorly substantiated.

Use the feedback on this answer to rewrite it, making as many improvements as you can.

Paper 1: AS Level sample answer with comments

Section B

These questions assess your understanding of the course in breadth and will cover a period of 30 years or more. They will ask you about the content you learned about in the four key themes, and may ask about more than one theme. The questions will also require you to explore a range of concepts, such as change over time, similarity and difference, as well as significance. For these questions remember to:

- identify the focus of the question
- consider the concepts you will need to explore
- support your points with evidence from across the time period specified in the question
- develop the evidence you deploy to build up your overall judgement
- come to a substantiated judgement that directly addresses the question set.

How significant were political motives in the decision to call for the First and Second Crusades? (20 marks)

Strong student answer

In 1095 the First Crusade was called in response to a plea from the Byzantine Emperor, Alexius I. Almost 50 years later the Second Crusade was proclaimed after an envoy was sent to seek help following the fall of Edessa in 1144. The two men who made this call were Pope Urban II and Pope Eugenius III and it is their motivations that need to be explored. These motives include political ones, such as the threat to their allies and the chance to increase their power, but also religious motives and the need to respond to the demands of the knightly classes. Ultimately, the most significant group of motives will be the ones that most strongly influenced the decision of the two popes to call for a crusade, rather than those which motivated others to join the crusades.

Both the First and Second Crusade were politically motivated because they were called in response to a real political threat. In the 11th century, the Byzantine Empire faced threats from the Muslim Turks in Asia Minor. In the long term Byzantine land had been captured from them. In 1078 the Seljuks had taken Nicaea, which was only 100 km away from Constantinople. This threat had increased by 1095 when other Muslim tribes, such as the Cumans, attacked Adrianople. This led the Byzantine Emperor to appeal for the pope's help at a church council in Piacenza in early 1095. The fact that Urban II agreed to support Alexius I suggests that the call for the First Crusade later that year was an attempt to put his promise into action. A similar political threat existed in 1145 when Eugenius III called for the Second Crusade. This time Outremer itself was under threat. The Muslim ruler, Zengi, had captured Christian fortresses, such as Rafaniyah in 1137, and had taken an entire Christian city called Edessa in December 1144. An envoy was sent to the pope, which reached him in November 1145, and asked for his help. The pope called for the Second Crusade in his *Quantum praedecessores* in response to this. This meant that political motives were significant because both popes made the decision to call for a crusade as a direct response to a threat and an appeal for their help.

Another political motive was the pope's desire for power. Urban II launched the First Crusade because he thought it would increase his political power. He was in an argument with the German Empire over investiture and the German emperor had even set up an antipope. If Urban II was able to get European nobles to support him in a crusade, it would show the German emperor how powerful he was. Urban II's power was also limited because he did not control the Eastern Christian Church in the Byzantine Empire. A successful crusade might also improve relations with the Byzantines and therefore help to bring their patriarch back under his control. However, this motive for a crusade was less apparent by the Second Crusade. Pope Eugenius III

This is a strong introduction because it shows that the question has been closely read. It provides context for the timescale of the answer, but also background to the outcome under examination. It is focused, because it lists alternative factors and proposes a criterion to assess their significance. It could be improved through a suggestion of whether or not political motives were the most significant factor.

This is a good paragraph because it directly addresses the factor given in the question. It has two developed points and uses examples from across the timescale of the question to support them. It begins to draw out the similarities between the political motives for both crusades, but this could be explored further if some excess detail, which is not crucial to the points being made, was left out.

did not try and assert his control over kings and emperors, but instead let the German and French kings lead the crusade. He had also abandoned any references to reuniting the Eastern and Western churches in his sermons and letters, because relations with the Byzantines had been so badly damaged during the First Crusade. This all suggests that the desire for power, in order to establish a papal monarchy, may have strongly influenced Urban II, but not Eugenius III because he knew a crusade was unlikely to improve his position.

However, there were also religious motives for both crusades. Jerusalem was of immense religious significance and thus an important goal. It was home to holy sites, such as Calvary and the Holy Sepulchre, which meant it was attractive to pilgrims. For example, in the 1060s, 7,000 German pilgrims went there. The pope may have wanted to help pilgrims to continue to travel there and so called for the First Crusade. His call was certainly influenced by the idea that Jerusalem was under some sort of religious threat. This is shown in two of the surviving accounts of Urban II's sermon at Clermont, which claim that he said Muslims were polluting Jerusalem. This theme is referred to again in the Second Crusade when Bernard of Clairvaux, who had a big influence on Eugenius III, pointed out the potential threat to Jerusalem in his recruitment letters. The importance of Jerusalem must have been significant for both crusade popes, but it provided an aim rather than directly cause them to call for a crusade.

Finally, the demands of knights might have influenced the pope. Some knights wanted an opportunity for power and wealth. A good example is Bohemond of Taranto, because he evidently wanted to be a prince. He refused to hand over Antioch to the Byzantines in 1098 and even led an unsuccessful attempt to attack Alexius I and protect his new principality in 1107. It is possible that Urban II was aware that some knights wanted more land, which is why he referred to the scarcity of wealth and land in Europe in his Clermont sermon. However, it is unlikely he called the crusade to help knights, but instead used it as a recruitment device to attract men like Bohemond.

In conclusion, political motives, in the form of a response to threats, were the most significant cause of the call for both crusades. In the First Crusade, the threat was to the pope's ally, in the Second Crusade it was to the pope's crusader kingdom itself. However, religious motives provide an essential backdrop for the decision of both popes. They did not provide the trigger, but they did give an aim for both crusades without which the call would have been meaningless and have lacked appeal. This appeal was improved by other motives, such as opportunities of land and wealth, but they did not actually influence either pope's decision. Both popes lived in a political world, alongside kings and emperors, and it was this world that had the greatest influence on their decision.

This paragraph's main strength is the level of expert thinking it displays. There are references to various concepts related to power and control, as well as a clear explanation of change over time. The evidence used is a little general and could be developed through greater use of specific examples to support the argument.

Another factor is explored in this paragraph, which helps to provide the argument with balance. There is also some exploration of continuity over time. The development of the argument at the end of the paragraph could be improved through greater explanation and an explicit link back to political motives.

This is a short, but promising paragraph. It explores a further factor and judges its possible impact on Urban II. It could be improved with greater coverage of the timescale.

The conclusion directly addresses the question and reaches a substantiated judgement. It assesses one factor against the others with reference to the criterion in the introduction. It could be improved through discussion of change over time, as it only explores the continuities.

Verdict

This is a strong answer because:

- the introduction provides relevant context and establishes the focus for the argument succinctly
- a range of factors is covered; each is supported by accurate specific examples
- each point is developed, but earlier factors are developed to a greater extent; this has meant alternative factors are explored in less detail
- there is evidence of good conceptual understanding of concepts related to power and the relationship of the pope to secular rulers
- the conclusion reaches a clear judgement on the most significant motive, balances this against the other motives and demonstrates good conceptual understanding.

Paper 1: AS Level sample answer with comments

Section C

These questions require you to read and analyse two extracts carefully in order to develop a response which examines and makes an informed judgement about different interpretations. The best answers:

- need to show an understanding of the extracts and identify the key points of interpretation
- deploy own knowledge to develop points emerging from extracts and provide necessary context
- develop a judgement after developing and weighing up different interpretations.

Study Extracts 1 and 3 on pages 122 and 127 before you answer this question.

Historians have different views about the reasons for the failure of the Fourth Crusade. Analyse and evaluate the extracts and use your own knowledge of the issues to explain your answer to the following question.

How far do you agree with the view that the Fourth Crusade failed because of weaknesses in the crusade leadership? (20 marks)

Average student answer

The first extract from Jonathan Phillips talks about the failures of the crusade leadership. There were lots of problems with the leadership. This was partly because they were nobles rather than kings. It was also because the plan that they helped to create was very poor. In order for it to work, they would have to gather a lot of crusaders together. If they could not do this, the Fourth Crusade would struggle.

> This is not really an introduction. It is a brief reference to the overall topic of the first extract and a list of problems with the leadership. It would benefit from outlining the argument of both extracts.

One of the main reasons the Fourth Crusade failed was the size of the forces that gathered in Venice. The original plan was that 33,500 crusaders were supposed to meet in Venice. This was a difficult number to reach because the leaders had a lot of problems. For example, Thibault III of Champagne died. In the end, only around 12,000 crusaders had turned up in Venice by 1202.

> This provides some relevant contextual knowledge, but there is no attempt to link this with Extract 1. This could be improved with a direct reference to an issue raised in Extract 1.

The crusade leadership also came up with a poor plan. It was expensive because they would have to pay the Venetians 85,000 marks. In return they would get transportation, 9 months' worth of supplies and an escort of Venetian soldiers. The main part of the plan, which was to travel to Alexandria first, was kept secret. These arrangements would all be ready by June 1202 and the crusaders were supposed to gather then.

> This is a largely descriptive paragraph with no developed points. This detail could be used to develop the issue about the leaders' assumptions in Extract 1.

The fundamental reason for placing blame on the leadership was that 'crusaders ... who did take part were under no compulsion to sail from Venice'. This meant that it was unlikely that all the crusaders would go to Venice to join the Fourth Crusade. They were more likely to follow the easiest route to reach Outremer. This would mean less people were in Venice.

> The paragraph contains the first direct quotation from an extract, which it begins to explain. It could be developed further through links to earlier material in the answer, such as the requirement for high numbers in Venice.

The second extract covers the role of Innocent III in the failure of the Fourth Crusade. Innocent became pope in 1198. He was only 37 years old, which is very young for a pope. He wanted to make his mark and so he launched a crusade as soon as possible. In August 1198 he announced the Fourth Crusade in *Post miserabile*.

> This is another descriptive paragraph, which provides little information about the interpretation in Extract 2. It could be improved through development of the different emphasis of this extract in comparison to the first.

Pope Innocent III played a key role in the failure of the Fourth Crusade. He initiated it and he came up with the initial plans. His first failure was an inability to recruit powerful leaders, because his legate seemed to upset them. He arranged for both King Richard I and King Philip II to be approached. However, neither would join the Fourth Crusade. This meant it lacked strong leaders, with the resources of entire kingdoms, to boost the size of the forces. The pope also chose some inappropriate preachers to go and recruit knights to the cause. They were inappropriate because they tended to give sermons on moral reform, as well as the crusade message. This had the effect of hiding the crusading message and damaging recruitment. Finally, his logistics were poor. His initial plan only allowed the crusaders 6 months to get ready.

> This paragraph is the first substantial attempt to provide context in order to build up the case that Pope Innocent III was to blame for the failure, not the leaders. It could be improved by a reference to the element of Extract 2 under development.

Finally, Extract 2 is different to Extract 1 because it says the Fourth Crusade failed because the crusaders 'ignored his advice and prohibitions'. This means that the crusade did not fail because of the main crusade leaders, but because the pope could not really control them. If he could not control them, he was partly to blame for his lack of power. However, it was also the crusaders' fault for ignoring him.

> There is limited development of one quote from Extract 2 and this is used to highlight a difference between the extracts. It would benefit from less paraphrasing of the quote, which could be replaced with direct comparison to the argument in Extract 1.

In conclusion, it is clear that the Fourth Crusade failed because 'none of the expedition's nobles had sufficient authority'. This meant that they would find it difficult to lead and then control the crusade. In fact, it meant that they could not even get enough people to join the crusade, which led to all sorts of problems. They are certainly more to blame than Pope Innocent III. They were the ones who came up with the details of the plan, which was what caused the crusade to fail in the end. However, the blame cannot entirely be laid at the door of the crusade leadership, because the pope did start it and took the first steps in the planning process. He is partly responsible for the failure as well.

> The conclusion is basic, but does at least make a reference to an extract and reach a judgement. The judgement is poorly explained and could be improved by reference to specific context from the main argument or the extracts.

Verdict

This is an average answer because:

- it makes very few direct references to the extracts
- the contextual information is mainly used to describe rather than develop the debate related to the diversion of the Fourth Crusade
- the construction of the argument is poor; it lacks an introduction that outlines that establishes the focus of the debate and the context that surrounds it
- the conclusion reaches a judgement, but it is poorly substantiated.

Use the feedback on this answer to rewrite it, making as many improvements as you can.

Paper 1: AS Level sample answer with comments

Section C

These questions require you to read and analyse two extracts carefully in order to develop a response which examines and makes an informed judgement about different interpretations. The best answers:

- need to show an understanding of the extracts and identify the key points of interpretation
- deploy own knowledge to develop points emerging from extracts and provide necessary context
- develop a judgement after developing and weighing up different interpretations.

Study Extracts 1 and 3 on pages 122 and 127 before you answer this question.

Historians have different views about the reasons for the failure of the Fourth Crusade. Analyse and evaluate the extracts and use your own knowledge of the issues to explain your answer to the following question.

How far do you agree with the view that the Fourth Crusade failed because of weaknesses in the crusade leadership? (20 marks)

Strong student answer

The extracts emphasise the role of the crusade leadership and Pope Innocent III in the failure of the Fourth Crusade. The first suggests that the assumptions of the crusade leadership, the poorly thought out plan that resulted from these and their relative lack of authority led to the failure of the crusade. In contrast, Extract 2 highlights the role of Innocent III as the individual who had the greatest responsibility for the failure of the crusade. It suggests that he came up with the overall plan, but lacked the authority to see it through. These are two alternative interpretations, but both are trying to explain the same result, which was that the Fourth Crusade lacked numbers and so were forced to rely on the Venetians, follow their plan and be diverted away from Outremer. It is this outcome that the two interpretations can be judged against.

Extract 1 from Phillips argues that the leaders were to blame, because they 'had assumed that all the holy warriors would wish to join the same fleet'. It was this assumption that created the fundamental flaw in the plan for the Fourth Crusade because it led the leadership to make arrangements for a huge fleet of crusaders. In order for their plan to work the crusaders would all have to share this 'wish'. The number that was agreed in the Treaty of Venice in April 1201 was 33,500 men with 4,500 horses, who would be supplied for 9 months by the Venetians at a cost of 85,000 marks. The leaders had therefore negotiated an expensive treaty that relied on the assumption a huge number would turn up. If they did not then the leadership would have to find another way to pay.

Another key issue that Phillips's interpretation emphasises is authority. He argues that 'none of the expedition's nobles had sufficient authority to compel everyone'. This suggests that the crusade failed because the leadership could not get enough crusaders to gather in Venice because they were not kings or emperors. They certainly did struggle with numbers, as only 12,000 turned up, and the leaders did lack authority. There were no kings, as Richard I was put off by the pope's demand for the release of Bishop Philip of Beauvais and, more importantly, was killed in April 1199. In addition, their own leadership team faced difficulties, such as the death of Thibault of Champagne in May 1201, which meant there were fewer crusaders from the large Champagne region. The death of influential potential leaders meant that the leadership lacked the 'authority' it needed to gather sufficient forces for the crusade.

This is a strong introduction because it identifies the issues in both extracts and provides relevant context to help reach a conclusion at the end. It could be strengthened through a suggestion of the answer's overall argument.

This paragraph focuses on one quote from Extract 1 and develops the point that the historian has made. It also support this issue with details from own knowledge. It could be improved with more development of the broader debate on how this would lead to failure.

This paragraph focuses on one quote from Extract 1 and develops the point that the historian has made. It also support this issue with details from own knowledge. It could be improved with more development of the broader debate on how this would lead to failure.

Extract 2 builds up the case that rather than weak leadership of the crusade itself, it was the pope who was to blame for the failure of the Fourth Crusade. Riley-Smith points out that 'the strategy which went awry was his own', which suggests that the pope was responsible for the overall direction of the crusade. Any flaws that developed in the plan the leadership created resulted from his initiative, rather than their own weaknesses. This is supported by the fact that the pope set up the crusade in August 1198 and his strategy guided them. It was his legate who failed to get support from kings like Philip II of France. It was also his strategy that was 'over-ambitious'. He tried to change too much too quickly, such as the financing and indulgences, and he made unrealistic requests, such as a 6 month deadline. This suggests that the crusade was poorly planned and implemented from the start and would struggle as a result.

> The argument outlined in Extract 2 is developed here with a focus on one key issue within it. It stresses the differences in the interpretation confidently, but would benefit from indicating the links/similarities between them as well.

Another key difference in this interpretation is that Innocent III was responsible for the failure because he lacked control of the crusade. Riley-Smith states that 'one act of disobedience led to another', which suggests that, like the leaders inability 'to compel everyone to gather' in Extract 1, the pope lacked the ability to get them to follow his plan for the crusade to reach Outremer. His views were certainly ignored in the decision to attack Zara and then discounted in the plan to attack Constantinople. The meant the crusade never reached Outremer because he lacked the authority to control the leadership. They followed a path that allowed them to pay the Venetians, rather than to help Jerusalem.

> This is a slightly briefer paragraph, but it explores a difference confidently and, to a weaker extent, a similarity between the extracts. It would benefit from development of the similar theme of authority in both extracts.

In conclusion, the Fourth Crusade failed because it was forced to follow a series of diversions. Extract 1 privileges the role of the leadership in constructing an unrealistic plan, whilst Extract 2 stresses the role of the pope in creating the climate for this plan. However, it was the specifics of the plan that the crusade leadership created that led to failure, because they were too weak to see it through. The pope could be responsible for the initiative and his overambition may have fuelled their plan, but the treaty was ultimately a leadership decision, not the pope's.

> The conclusion is short, but gives a clear judgement, which builds on the overall argument of the answer. It considers the argument in Extract 1 relative to the argument of Extract 2 in order to reach a conclusion. It would benefit from further substantiation for the conclusion's final point.

Verdict

This is a strong answer because:

- it makes direct references to the extracts and explores a couple of key issues raised in both
- the contextual information is used to develop the issue that the historian has raised, although the material deployed varies in level of depth
- it has a clear introduction that establishes the boundaries of the debate, which are then developed in the main body of the argument
- the conclusion reaches a supported judgement.

Preparing for your A Level Paper 1 exam

Advance planning

1. Draw up a timetable for your revision and try to keep to it. Spread your timetable over a number of weeks, and aim to cover four or five topics each week.
2. Spend longer on topics that you have found difficult, and revise them several times.
3. Above all, do not try to limit your revision by attempting to 'question spot'. Try to be confident about all aspects of your Paper 1 work, because this will ensure that you have a choice of questions in Sections A and B.

Paper 1 overview:

AL Paper 1	Time: 2 hours 15 minutes	
Section A	Answer 1 question from a choice of 2	20 marks
Section B	Answer 1 question from a choice of 2	20 marks
Section C	Answer 1 compulsory interpretations question	20 marks
	Total marks =	60 marks

You should familiarise yourself with the layout of the paper by looking at the examples published by Edexcel. The questions for each section are followed by eight pages of lined paper where you should write your answer.

Section A and Section B questions

The essay questions in Sections A and B are similar in form. They ask you to reach a judgement on an aspect of the course you have studied, and will deal with one or more historical concepts of change, continuity, similarity, difference, cause, consequence and significance. The question stems which will be used will include 'To what extent…', 'How far…', 'How significant was…' and so on. You should consider the issue raised by the question, develop your answer by looking at other relevant points, and reach a judgement in your conclusion.

The main difference between Section A and Section B questions will be the timespan of the questions. Section A questions will cover a period of ten years or more, while Section B questions will be concerned with at least one-third of the period you have studied.

A Section A question for Option 1E might read 'How far was high expenditure on the armed forces responsible for economic decline in the USSR in the years 1964–82?' Your answer should consider the issue of expenditure on the armed forces, look at other issues such as agricultural decline, falling productivity in industry, and Brezhnev's reluctance to undertake economic reforms, before reaching an overall judgement on the question.

A Section B question on the same paper will cover a longer period of time, but have a similar shape. For example, 'How successful were the government's social policies in improving the lives of the Soviet people in the years 1917–64?' Here you should consider various successes, such as full employment, education and healthcare, but also point out policies which were less successful, such as housing and different policies towards women over time. You should conclude by reaching a judgement on the question.

Section C questions

There is no choice in Section C, which is concerned with the historical interpretations you have studied linked to the question 'What explains the failure of the Fourth Crusade?' You will be given two extracts totalling around 400 words (printed separately) and the question will take the form 'How convincing do you find the view that…?' There is no need to use source analysis skills such as making inferences or considering provenance for Section C answers. You should approach your answer by analysing both extracts separately, and then use your own knowledge to support, and to counter, the view given in the question, before reaching an overall judgement.

Use of time

This is an issue that you should discuss with your teachers and fellow students, but here are some suggestions for you.

1. Do not write solidly for 45 minutes on each question. For Section A and B answers you should spend a few minutes working out what the question is asking you to do, and drawing up a plan of your answer. This is especially important for Section B answers, which cover an extended period of time.
2. For Section C it is essential that you have a clear understanding of the content of each extract and the points that each extract is making. Read each extract carefully and underline important points. You might decide to spend up to ten minutes reading the extracts and drawing up your plan, and 35 minutes writing your answer.

Preparing for your A Level exams

Paper 1: A Level sample answer with comments

Section A

These questions assess your understanding of the period in breadth. They will ask you about the content you learned about in the four key themes, and may ask about more than one theme. For these questions remember to:

- give an analytical, not a descriptive, response
- support your points with evidence
- cover the whole time period specified in the question
- come to a substantiated judgement.

To what extent was Nur ad-Din personally responsible for the growth of Muslim power between 1146 and 1174? (20 marks)

Average student answer

Muslim power began to grow after Zengi came to power in 1127 as the ruler of Mosul. He quickly took control of much of Muslim Syria, as well as parts of northern Iraq. His power grew so strong that by 1144 he was able to capture Edessa from the Franks. Muslim power grew from these foundations thanks to the efforts of Nur ad-Din, who followed Zengi, and his Muslim supporters.

> This is a weak introduction because it only provides context from before the timescale in the question and it barely hints at other factors for growth. It could be improved with context exploring the outcome in the question.

Nur ad-Din started to gain power in 1146 when he inherited Aleppo from Zengi. This was the first step in his journey to power. It increased when he took control of Damascus in 1154 from a rival Muslim ruler. It was so strong by 1156 that he was able to defeat the Franks in that year, as well as in 1157 and 1164. However, it reached its height in 1169 after his forces took control of Egypt. Under Nur ad-Din Muslim power had therefore grown a lot between the start of his rule and 1169.

> The material in this paragraph is largely descriptive. There is a weak attempt to link the material to the question in the concluding statement. A key area of improvement would be to link the example of Nur ad-Din's action to how it increased Muslim power.

Nur ad-Din's power would never have grown so dramatically if he had not received help from other people. He formed alliances with fellow Muslim rulers to attack the Franks in Antioch and Edessa. He needed the extra support because he did not rule all of the Muslim territories in and around Syria, which meant he did not have enough forces to seriously threaten the Franks. However, with supporters he could both attack and defend against them. Nur ad-Din also used alliances to stop his power from being reduced. He formed an alliance with the Byzantine Empire against a rival Muslim ruler. This meant his power remained strong, thanks to the protection and support of his neighbours, and could continue to grow in the way described earlier.

> The paragraph explores an alternative factor to the one in the question and develops a couple of points in relation to the question. However, it would benefit from specific examples to substantiate the points under exploration.

Another important reason why Muslim power grew was that Nur ad-Din's rivals were too weak and he could take advantage of their weakness. For example, his brother, Sayf ad-Din Ghazi, was the ruler of Mosul and died in 1149. He could have taken his territory and this would have enabled him to strengthen his hold on the Muslim world. However, he did not do this because he was too busy dealing with Damascus and Antioch at the time. If he had not been so busy, more Muslim power would have been in one person's hands.

> The factor chosen for this paragraph is a relevant one, but the evidence chosen does not develop or even effectively illustrate the point being made. It could be improved with a relevant specific example to develop it.

Saladin was also responsible for the growth of Muslim power. He took on a crucial military role in the capture of Cairo during the Egyptian campaign in 1169. He was the nephew of Shirkuh, who led the campaign, and helped Shirkuh to become Egyptian Vizier. When his uncle died, Saladin replaced him as Vizier but was still under the authority of Nur ad-Din. This meant Muslim power had grown dramatically because Egypt and Syria were now under the authority of Nur ad-Din and it was thanks to Saladin that this happened. He also helped to secure this power when Nur ad-Din died in 1174. Saladin immediately took control of Damascus and in 1183 he conquered Aleppo. In effect, both Nur ad-Din's former lands, and the lands Saladin had taken control of, were now under one Muslim ruler and so Muslim power was greatly strengthened through this unity.

> Another key factor in the growth of Muslim power is explored here, but substantial parts of the supporting evidence are outside the timescale in the question. The paragraph needs to be refocused on the events before 1174.

In conclusion, Muslim power had grown a lot between 1146 and 1174. This was mainly a result of the actions of Nur ad-Din. He was able to build on the successes of Zengi and extend his control over much of Muslim Syria and Egypt. He did this through the formation of alliances, taking advantage of the weakness of other rulers and with the help of men like Saladin. When he died in 1174, Muslim power was more unified than it had ever been which meant it was ready to take on the Franks.

> This gives the impression of a satisfactory conclusion, but it is let down by an attempt to force the other factors to support the main one, which is in contrast to the argument in the rest of the answer. It would benefit from a clear judgement on the relative significance of the factors, which would match the approach taken to the question throughout.

Verdict

This is an average answer because:

- it does not clearly explain the link between the evidence and the outcome in the question (a growth in Muslim power)
- some points are not substantiated with specific examples
- parts of the argument are developed with evidence from outside of the timescale

- the conclusion reaches a judgement, but it does not clearly relate to the argument developed in the answer.

Use the feedback on this answer to rewrite it, making as many improvements as you can.

Paper 1: A Level sample answer with comments

Section A

These questions assess your understanding of the period in breadth. They will ask you about the content you learned about in the four key themes, and may ask about more than one theme. For these questions remember to:

- give an analytical, not a descriptive, response
- support your points with evidence
- cover the whole time period specified in the question
- come to a substantiated judgement.

To what extent was Nur ad-Din personally responsible for the growth of Muslim power between 1146 and 1174? (20 marks)

Strong student answer

Muslim power grew considerably under the rule of Nur ad-Din. In 1146, Nur only inherited Aleppo from Zengi, which had an unstable border with the Franks of Antioch and Edessa. In contrast to this weak position, when Nur died in 1174 he could rightly claim to be the leader of an Islamic empire. His control was now partly extended into the Frankish territories of Antioch and Edessa, fully established over Muslim Syria, parts of northern Iraq, and much of Egypt. This was a result of his personal efforts, but was not done alone. He also relied on allied support, the weakness of his Muslim rivals to power and the help of Saladin. Nur's personal responsibility can therefore be measured in terms of how pivotal a role he played in the growth of Abbasid Muslim control, which this essay will demonstrate was more significant in the consolidation of power, rather than its growth.

Nur ad-Din played a central role in securing Muslim power from the Frankish threat. Firstly, he ensured that control of the city of Edessa remained in Muslim hands. He used Aleppan troops to subdue an uprising against Muslim control after Zengi's death. Around 30,000 of the city's inhabitants were killed. This was a drastic measure, but it ensured that Nur's authority over conquered territory was assured through fear of a similar reprisal. Nur also made sure that Antioch did not threaten Aleppo's borders. After the Battle of Inab in 1149, his troops took territory from the Antiochenes, such as Apamea and Artesia. This helped to create a buffer between the Franks and Nur's Aleppan territory. However, it was not Nur's only goal. He was also responsible for a general strategy to bring Abbasid Syria under one ruler's control. In this goal he was successful, as he captured Damascus in August 1154, after aborted attempts in 1149 and 1151, and he conquered Ba'albek in June 1155. The effect of his military strategy was that a major Muslim rival, the Burid dynasty, was gone and Abbasid Syria was under Nur's control and influence. Nur was thus personally responsible for securing his own power as well as consolidating Muslim power in Syria under one ruler.

By 1155 Nur ad-Din had been responsible for the consolidation of power in Syria, but how personal this responsibility was can be challenged by the fact that he had to rely on allies to achieve it. For example, the Battle of Inab in 1149 was crucial to the destruction of resistance from Antioch. In this battle Nur relied upon an alliance with the Sultan of Rum, as well as a Damascene force, in order to defeat the Antiochenes. Without their help, he would not have been able to use his Aleppan troops to take further territory from the Antiochenes. Nur also had to use alliances to prevent the growth of his power from being restricted or even reduced. In 1159 he formed an alliance with Manuel Comnenus against the Sultan of Rum. This helped to prevent a Byzantine invasion, but it also showed that the power Nur had tried to gather still relied upon the agreement and support of others, rather than his own ability to make and enforce his own decisions.

This is a strong introduction because it provides relevant context for the outcome in the question. The focus for the answer is also established and covers the key factors to be explored, the criteria for analysis and a hint at the overall argument. It could be improved with further exploration of what 'Abbasid' control means, which would show stronger conceptual understanding.

This paragraph has a strong focus on the key factor proposed in the question. It explores a number of points, supported with specific examples. The breadth of the evidence is almost ten years, but the quality of the argument could be strengthened if evidence from throughout the timescale was used.

There is a careful consideration of extent in this paragraph, which helps to limit the argument presented in the previous paragraph. It could be improved with further links developed between the two paragraphs for the later period of his rule.

Another reason Nur ad-Din was able to consolidate Muslim power was that he faced some weak Muslim rivals. In Damascus, which was a key city to control in order to unite Abbasid Syria, there was a weak ruler called Abaq. He had inherited the city in August 1149, but relied on alliances with the Franks for protection against Nur. His repeated calls for help from the Franks made him very unpopular with his own people and he was deposed. This meant that Nur ad-Din could take control with little opposition, which clearly limits his personal responsibility for the success. However, in other circumstances when his rivals were weakened, Nur did not take action if he thought it would damage his position. For example, when his brother died in 1149, he could have marched into Mosul, but he sensibly chose not to do so. This action would have overstretched him at a time when he was preoccupied with Antioch and Damascus, which shows he made sensible, responsible decisions in the consolidation of his power.

> The argument presented in this paragraph is a balanced one, as it presents both a limitation to Nur ad-Din's personal responsibility and evidence to support it. It could be improved with a clearer development of the overall argument at the end of the paragraph.

Finally, whilst Nur was responsible for the actions of his military officers, he did not personally take part in all the campaigns to extend Muslim power. He relied on men like Saladin, who helped to capture Egypt in 1169 and had himself installed as the vizier on 26 March. It was in this position that Saladin secured Abbasid control over Egypt in 1171 when he ensured that the Fatimid caliph, al-Adil, was succeeded by the Abbasid caliph, al-Mustadi. Nur's personal responsibility for Saladin's actions is further limited by the fact that Saladin felt able to act on his own initiative, even against Nur's will, to increase Abbasid power over Egypt. For example, Nur wanted Saladin to send him regular payments from Egypt to fund campaigns elsewhere, but Saladin refused in order to gain the support of Egyptians for Abbasid rule. Clearly, there was not a straightforward power relationship between the ruler and the ruled because Saladin could not be ordered around. Abbasid power had grown massively from 1169 onwards, but Nur's role was more of a figurehead as Saladin's overlord, than a powerful dictator with Saladin at his side.

> There is strong conceptual understanding in this paragraph, because it carefully considers elements of the relationship between the ruler and the ruled in the Muslim empires. There is also a sense of change over time, as it covers the later period in the timescale. It could be improved through greater evaluation of Saladin's role in the growth of Muslim power, which could also be limited.

In conclusion, Nur ad-Din was personally responsible for the consolidation of Muslim power because it was his decisions that made it happen. By the mid-1150s, Nur's consolidation of Abbasid Syria had created a springboard from which others, like Saladin, could extend Muslim power in the 1160s into Egypt. However, despite Nur's pivotal role as a decision maker, he relied upon alliances and opportunities to achieve his goals. Without alliances to support his offensives and the weaknesses of his rivals to exploit, it is unlikely Muslim power would have grown as it did.

> This is a short conclusion, but presents a clear and substantiated judgement. It considers change over time and the relationship between the different factors. It could be developed with further exploration of the limitations to Nur ad-Din's 'personal' responsibility for later growth, which was suggested in the introduction.

Verdict

This is a strong answer because:

- it explores a range of key factors, which both support and challenge the factor in the question
- each point is supported by specific examples that are developed
- the entire timescale is explored, but this is an area of the answer that could be improved
- the conceptual focus of the question is fully explored, as the idea of 'personal responsibility' is developed throughout
- a strong and substantiated overall judgement is reached, but extent in the conclusion could be explored a little further.

Paper 1: A Level sample answer with comments

Section B

These questions assess your understanding of the course in breadth and will cover a period of 30 years or more. They will ask you about the content you learned about in the four key themes, and may ask about more than one theme. The questions will also require you to explore a range of concepts, such as change over time, similarity and difference, as well as significance. For these questions remember to:

- identify the focus of the question
- consider the concepts you will need to explore
- support your points with evidence from across the time period specified in the question
- develop the evidence you deploy to build up your overall judgement
- come to a substantiated judgement that directly addresses the question set.

How far did the fundamental problems faced by the leadership of the Second Crusade remain in place during the Third Crusade? (20 marks)

Average student answer

The First Crusade was divided because there were eight different princes, who each had different priorities and goals for their campaign. This is why it took such a long time for them to capture Jerusalem. The Second Crusade also had a divided leadership because the French and the Germans struggled to work together effectively. Ultimately the Second Crusade failed at the siege of Damascus. Finally, the Third Crusade was divided as both Philip II and Richard I could not get on with each other. In the end Jerusalem was abandoned to Saladin because of the leadership.

The biggest problem faced by the leadership of both crusades was the personal rivalry between the main leaders. In the Second Crusade, the French and German leaders did not work together effectively. This problem remained in place during the Third Crusade, as Richard I and Philip II were political rivals. For example, there were serious problems created by Richard's betrothal to Philip's sister, Alice. It became clear during the early planning of the crusade that Richard intended to go back on this betrothal, which would embarrass Philip. This was partly why Philip II decided that after Acre had been captured in July 1191, he would not join Richard I on the march to Jerusalem. As a result, Richard I lacked the forces to capture Jerusalem and had to abandon the crusade. The rivalries between leaders in all the crusades remained as strong as ever in the Third Crusade.

Another huge problem for both crusades was their poor relationship with the Byzantine Emperor. The First Crusade had benefited from the fact that Alexius I had requested their help and so he was prepared to provide troops and supplies. However, neither the Second nor Third Crusade was requested by the Byzantines. In the Second Crusade, the Byzantine army clashed with Conrad III, as they were under orders to watch him closely on his journey through Hungary. There was also tension between the French and the Byzantines, because Louis VII was an ally of Roger of Sicily who began to attack parts of the Byzantine Empire in 1147. On the crusade itself, Manuel I's guides would not make markets available to the Second Crusaders, nor did he provide the fleet for an entire army that he had promised. In the Third Crusade, there were still problems. For example, the new emperor, Isaac II, had an agreement with Saladin to delay the Germans. This did not go down well with the Germans. The German emperor, Frederick Barbarossa, seized Plovdiv in August 1189 and began to attack the Byzantine Empire. It was clear that this problem remained fundamental in both crusades.

This is a weak introduction because it provides context, parts of which are relevant to the question, but the focus is only hinted at. It could be improved with a clear explanation of what the fundamental problems were, as well as any changes over the time period.

There is some appreciation of similarity across the period in this paragraph, but the material is unbalanced and heavily focused on the Third Crusade. It would benefit from the use of specific examples from the Second Crusade to explore the similarities further.

This is a largely descriptive paragraph, which draws on specific examples from both crusades, but does not develop them and instead wastes time exploring the First Crusade. There is an attempt to link the material to the question in the concluding statement, but this would require some clear, developed explanation to be effective.

The final problem that both crusades faced was the strength of their Muslim opponents. In the Second Crusade they faced Nur ad-Din, who controlled a small territory but was able to call on allies to help at Damascus. This meant that the crusaders struggled to attack Damascus because of the amount of support that Nur had. This fundamental problem continued in the Third Crusade. By the time of Saladin, the Muslims controlled a huge territory and so Saladin had large resources to call upon. This made Saladin a very difficult enemy to defeat. This was a fundamental problem for both crusades and actually got worse between the Second and Third Crusades because of the increasing power of Saladin.

> This paragraph develops a couple of points and begins to consider difference, but relies upon very general material. It needs specific examples to substantiate the points raised.

Some of the problems did not remain in place. One change was problems with strategy. In the Second Crusade there was no clear strategy. They did not make up their mind as to what to do on the crusade until they reached Acre in 1148. Then at the siege of Damascus in 1148 they changed strategy halfway through the attack. Conrad III had made gains to the west of Damascus, but they decided to shift their strategy to a weak point in the eastern walls which lacked a water and food source. This all changed in the Third Crusade, as they had a clear strategy from the beginning to recapture Acre. This meant that the Third Crusade actually achieved something and one crusade succeeded in a goal because a fundamental problem was fixed.

> This is the only example of an attempt to explore the other side of the argument, which will help to reach a judgement. One point is developed in this paragraph. The answer would benefit from the discussion of more elements of difference in order to make a judgement on extent.

In conclusion, both crusades failed because the fundamental problems remained in place. The rivalries between the main leaders meant that they did not work together, both crusades lacked support from the Byzantine Empire and both faced strong Muslim resistance. This is why they made little or no progress.

> There is an attempt to substantiate a judgement, but it only restates similarities and links with little sense of difference between the two crusades. It would benefit from a greater exploration of difference.

Verdict

This is an average answer because:

- the introduction only provides some relevant context for the question
- there are descriptive passages where the material is not developed
- some points lack specific examples and rely on very general evidence, or material from outside of the period in question, to support them
- there is a sense of similarity over time, but the differences are weakly explored and so the judgement is weak as a result.

Use the feedback on this answer to rewrite it, making as many improvements as you can.

Paper 1: A Level sample answer with comments

Section B

These questions assess your understanding of the course in breadth and will cover a period of 30 years or more. They will ask you about the content you learned about in the four key themes, and may ask about more than one theme. The questions will also require you to explore a range of concepts, such as change over time, similarity and difference, as well as significance. For these questions remember to:

- identify the focus of the question
- consider the concepts you will need to explore
- support your points with evidence from across the time period specified in the question
- develop the evidence you deploy to build up your overall judgement
- come to a substantiated judgement that directly addresses the question set.

How far did the fundamental problems faced by the leadership of the Second Crusade remain in place during the Third Crusade?
(20 marks)

Strong student answer

The Second Crusade involved a difficult, dangerous journey through Asia Minor for both of its leaders. They survived this, but the crusade still ultimately failed in its attempt to take Damascus in July 1148. The Third Crusade was different as it did succeed in the capture of Acre and Jaffa, but it ultimately failed to capture Jerusalem. In many ways they both faced the same fundamental problems, which included personal rivalries, a poor relationship with the Byzantine Empire and a strong Muslim opposition. In others, such as planning and preparation, problems were largely resolved. However, this essay will argue that despite these changes, the fundamental problems of the Second Crusade not only remained in place, but had intensified by the time of the Third Crusade.

The personal rivalry between the leaders of the Second Crusade meant that they failed to work together effectively. Louis VII and Conrad III were not enemies, but they were kings and each believed they were powerful enough to act alone. This sense of pride meant that they failed to work together. For example, Conrad did not wait for the French to arrive in the Byzantine Empire, but instead set off through Asia Minor on his own. The effect of this was that, with fewer troops, he was victim to an ambush near Dorylaeum and had to retreat back to Nicaea to wait for the French. This was a fundamental problem because the Second Crusade lost troops as a result. It remained a problem for the Third Crusade because there was intense rivalry between Richard I and Philip II. This meant Philip II felt no need to support Richard I when it did not suit him to do so. On 31 July 1191, after the capture of Acre but before any attempt on Jaffa or Jerusalem, Philip left because he thought he stood a chance of taking land in Europe after the death of Philip of Flanders. This left Richard with a smaller army and contributed towards his decision to abandon the march on Jerusalem. In both crusades, a lack of unity reduced the size of the fighting force and therefore weakened their chance of success.

Another fundamental problem for the Second Crusade was the relationship between the crusade leaders and the Byzantine Empire. This was poor because Manuel I failed to support the Second Crusaders and had even made a treaty with the Turks at Konya. This meant that the Byzantine guides betrayed the French, allowing the Turks to track them, and attack whenever they appeared weak, such as the crossing of Mount Cadmus. This relationship seriously hampered the speed and progress of the Second Crusade. However, it was not as fundamental to the Third Crusade.

This is a strong introduction because it provides a small amount of context to illustrate that both crusades faced problems. It also clearly presents the focus of the argument, suggesting criteria through a summary of the fundamental problems of the Second Crusade, and a sense of the overall argument. It might benefit from a fuller discussion of what would make a problem 'fundamental'.

A strong paragraph, because it draws out the similarities between the two crusades. It could be improved with a sharper sense of difference. The Second Crusade's leaders were arguably not as clearly divided as they were in the Third Crusade.

It remained in place because Frederick of Barbarossa had to fight the Byzantines at Dhidimotikon on 22 November 1189 in order to gain passage through the empire. However, it was no longer fundamental, because the German army was affected far more by the unrelated death of Frederick Barbarossa than they were by the delay caused by Byzantine opposition. A problem fundamental to the Second Crusade remained, but it was not fundamental to the Third Crusade.

> This paragraph considers the extent of similarity carefully as it provides balance to the argument that fundamental problems remained in place. It also considers the nature of what a 'fundamental' problem was. It would benefit from more material on why the problem was not fundamental to the Third Crusade of Philip II and Richard I.

The Second Crusade also faced a new problem, which was the strength of Muslim opposition. When the Second Crusaders attacked Damascus, Nur ad-Din was able to help protect it with his Aleppan troops and his brother's support from Mosul. It was the threat of these reinforcements that led the crusaders to abandon the siege. By the time of the Third Crusade this problem had grown much stronger. Saladin had united Muslim Syria and Egypt, which meant he was more able to resist the Third Crusade. For example, he could quickly call on troops from Egypt to help protect Jerusalem, which he did on 22 December 1191. This meant Richard I, with no additional troops nearby to call upon, had little choice but to abandon his first march on Jerusalem. A problem fundamental to the events that ended the Second Crusade had intensified over the 40 years leading up to the Third Crusade.

> This is a shorter paragraph, but it considers the changing nature of the problem faced by both crusades. It would benefit from more specific examples of why the problem was 'fundamental' to the Third Crusade to strengthen the argument.

Finally, one of the most fundamental problems of the Second Crusade was largely resolved by the Third. The First Crusade was poorly planned as the leaders left at different times, many died on the long land journey which itself was delayed by diversions and disputes over territory. There were marginal improvements by the Second Crusade, such as the fact that Louis VII's ambassadors met Conrad III's beforehand to plan the crusade. However, it was still poorly planned because Outremer's leaders played no role in the planning. This is why it took from March to June 1148, after the crusaders had arrived in Outremer, to decide upon a goal for the Second Crusade. This gave the Muslim counter-attack plenty of time to prepare. Fortunately, the trend towards improved planning continued and the Third Crusade no longer faced this problem. Richard I and Philip II met twice, in 1189 and 1190, to plan the crusade and journey. This is why they arrived within 2 months of one another and joined together at Acre, which was recaptured through a joint attack by July 1191. At least one fundamental problem, that had threatened the First Crusade with collapse and had barely been resolved by the Second Crusade, had been tackled by the Third Crusade.

> There is a good example of expert thinking in this paragraph, as there is a discussion of patterns and trends over the whole period. However, the material on the First Crusade should be replaced with material about improved planning of the smaller scale crusades or campaigns between 1148 and 1189.

In conclusion, the fundamental problems that beset the Second Crusade, especially rivalry and poor relationships, troubled the Third Crusade as well. However, their impact was felt less in the Third Crusade because of the intensification of a problem that had first appeared during the Second Crusade. This was the strength of Muslim opposition which, even after the fundamental problem of poor planning was resolved, could not be overcome. The Third Crusade therefore faced a narrower range of fundamental problems, but their effect was just as severe.

> This is a short conclusion, but it clearly considers the extent of similarity as well as the changing nature of the fundamental problems of the two crusades. It could be improved with further explanation of the relative significance of the similarities compared with the differences.

Verdict

This is a strong answer because:

- it explores a range of similarities and differences in order to reach a balanced judgement
- each point is supported by specific examples that are developed, but the range of these could be improved
- the entire timescale is explored throughout the answer
- the conceptual focus of the question is fully explored and there is evidence of expert thinking
- a clear and substantiated overall judgement is reached, but the conclusion could be explained in greater depth.

Paper 1: A Level sample answer with comments

Section C

These questions require you to read two extracts carefully to identify the key points raised and establish the argument being put forward. For these questions remember to:

- read and analyse the extracts thoroughly remembering that you need to use them in tandem
- take careful note of the information provided about the extracts
- deploy own knowledge to develop the points and arguments that emerge from the extracts and to provide appropriate context
- develop an argument rooted in the points raised in the extracts and come to a substantiated conclusion.

In the light of differing interpretations, how convincing do you find the view that the Fourth Crusade failed because Dandolo 'never lost sight of Venice's material interest' (Extract 4, lines 2–3)? To explain your answer, analyse and evaluate the material in the extract, using your own knowledge of the issues. (20 marks)

Average student answer

Venice had a long history of involvement in the crusades. Venetians had not been on the First Crusade, but they began to take an active role in Outremer soon afterwards. In 1104 they sent a fleet to help capture Haifa and they took a very active role in the siege of Tyre in 1124. In return for this, they received a third of the city and set up a Venetian outpost there. Venice had also been involved in the Byzantine Empire. In 1198, Dandolo had arranged for Venice to have a privileged trading position in Constantinople. It was therefore no surprise when Venice agreed to the Treaty of Venice in April 1201 to transport the Fourth Crusaders to Alexandria.

> This is a weak introduction because it provides context for Venetian involvement in crusading, but this does not help to establish why the Fourth Crusade failed and its link to 'material interest' is implicit. It also makes no reference to the extracts. An improved version of this context would refer explicitly to the failure of the crusade.

The Venetians played a substantial role in the failure of the Fourth Crusade. This was because they demanded a high fee for their services and insisted that it had to be paid in full. When it became clear that not enough crusaders had arrived in Venice to pay the fee, the Venetians would not back down. The effect of this was that the crusaders were made to attack Zara instead of head straight to their destination. This meant many crusaders left. After this, Dandolo encouraged the crusaders to support the claims of Prince Alexius. The result of this was that they ended up at Constantinople rather than their destination. On two occasions Venice had caused the Fourth Crusade to head off course.

> This paragraph has still not referred directly to the extracts and provides some general points about the problems that the Venetians created. This needs to be linked to material in Extract 1.

Extract 2 differs from Extract 1 because it blames a different person for the failure of the Fourth Crusade. It suggests that it failed because the crusaders were distracted by Constantinople and so they stayed there instead. In fact, it goes further and suggests that they had been tricked into going there and were let down when they finally arrived. This is why, instead of heading on to their destination, they ended up attacking the city of Constantinople instead. In the end this attack was brutal, but they picked up a lot of relics and prizes.

> The reference to Extract 2 strengthens the answer, because it is now more rooted in the extracts. However, it contains very general material that does not develop the opening point. It would benefit from the use of relevant specific examples from the extract.

A key reason why the Fourth Crusade failed was that Prince Alexius was 'unable to redeem his lavish promises', which the crusaders had relied upon. They had been promised that he would help the crusade continue, pay off any remaining debts and would provide extra food and soldiers. This would be necessary because the crusade had taken longer than expected and had already lost time and men elsewhere. However, he was unable to do this because he was too weak. This meant that the help that the crusade was counting on did not appear and so led to its failure to continue.

Another cause of the failure of the crusade was the small size of the forces available. In August 1202, only 12,000 crusaders turned up in Venice. Out of these 12,000, only around 1,800 were knights. Lots of crusaders were also late, such as the Germans who arrived 2 months after the deadline. In the meantime, the rest of the forces had to wait. The reason the numbers were so small was that some, like Reynald of Dampierre, chose to avoid Venice altogether. This situation was made worse by the fact that an important leader, called Thibault III of Champagne, had died in 1201. This led to a small number of crusaders meeting up in June to August 1202.

Overall the evidence suggests that the Fourth Crusade failed for many reasons. It is true that Dandolo did make a lot of important decisions, which were based on Venice's interests, and this was why the crusade did not follow its original plan. However, there were lots of other reasons that were not down to Dandolo and Venice. The fact that only a small number of soldiers turned in Venice, the crusaders decided to attack Constantinople, as well as the lack of support from Prince Alexius that followed, all help to explain why the Fourth Crusade failed. It was not just because of Dandolo, but he did not really help either.

This is a promising paragraph because it refers directly to a quote from the extract and begins to develop the issue with some general material, although the quote has been taken a little out of context. It could be improved with a closer reading of the quote in order to make more accurate use of it.

This is a very descriptive paragraph, which suggests another factor, but does not attempt to link it to the extracts or explain how the material answers the question. It would benefit from an explanation of how it links to the issue of 'material interest' or how it challenges its significance.

There is some attempt to outline the relative significance of the factor proposed in Extract 1, but there is no attempt to directly compare or measure this. It could be strengthened by adding support to the closing statement.

Verdict

This is an average answer because:

- it only refers to the extracts directly on one occasion; other links are implicit
- the explanation relies on vague contextual material to explore Extract 1 and generalised references to information in Extract 2 to explore difference
- there are descriptive passages that are not linked directly to the debate
- the argument is poorly organised; the introduction provides contextual material that leads up to the issues in the Fourth Crusade, but does not explore them
- the conclusion reaches a judgement, but it is contains a limited amount of substantiation.

Use the feedback on this answer to rewrite it, making as many improvements as you can.

Paper 1: A Level sample answer with comments

Section C

These questions require you to read two extracts carefully to identify the key points raised and establish the argument being put forward. For these questions remember to:

- read and analyse the extracts thoroughly remembering that you need to use them in tandem
- take careful note of the information provided about the extracts
- deploy own knowledge to develop the points and arguments that emerge from the extracts and to provide appropriate context
- develop an argument rooted in the points raised in the extracts and come to a substantiated conclusion.

In the light of differing interpretations, how convincing do you find the view that the Fourth Crusade failed because Dandolo 'never lost sight of Venice's material interest' (Extract 4, lines 2–3)? To explain your answer, analyse and evaluate the material in the extract, using your own knowledge of the issues. (20 marks)

Strong student answer

Both extracts focus on the importance of individual leaders in shaping the course of the Fourth Crusade and its eventual failure. The first argues that Dandolo had the strongest influence on the crusade and that, as a Venetian, he prioritised their financial needs from the start. John Fine emphasises the idea that these needs could be served by Byzantine conquest, which is why the Fourth Crusade ended up at Constantinople rather than Outremer. In contrast, Extract 2 privileges the role of Prince Alexius and suggests that it was not until the crusaders actually reached Constantinople that the diversion away from Jerusalem seemed certain. It was only at this stage, rather than from the start, that the crusaders became embroiled in Byzantine politics. Asbridge also broadens the scope of 'material interest' beyond the Venetians and suggests that all the crusaders' needs were served by an attack on the city. These alternative interpretations are both exploring the same outcome, which was that the Fourth Crusade became trapped in the Byzantine Empire. It is their importance in causing this outcome that the two arguments should be evaluated against.

> This is a strong introduction because it identifies the issues in both extracts and provides relevant context to help reach a conclusion at the end. It could be improved with a little more clarification of the 'material interest' point that has been briefly applied to Extract 2.

Fine presents the case that Dandolo 'never lost sight of Venice's material interests' on the basis that their trade in the east was under threat by the situation in the Byzantine Empire. It is certainly true that Dandolo's action were consistent with the desire to protect Venice's financial position. For example, the Treaty of Venice promised the Venetians 85,000 marks to transport the Fourth Crusaders, but they could only pay 51,000 marks. In order to protect their interests, Dandolo proposed that the crusaders divert to Zara, which was an important port on the route to Outremer that Venice had lost control of in 1180. This suggests that 'material interests' and the receipt of something instead of immediate payment were of paramount importance to Dandolo. This view is also supported by the fact that Dandolo was keen to accept Prince Alexius's request for help, because the Fourth Crusaders would receive 200,000 marks in return, which they could pay off their Venetian debt with. Both examples show that money was crucial to the decisions Dandolo encouraged the crusaders to make. The result of this was that after the second agreement to divert the crusade their numbers had dropped from 12,000 troops to around 3,000. The Fourth Crusade had therefore been weakened by financially motivated choices.

> This paragraph explores the key interpretation in the question and uses contextual detail to add weight to the claim. It would benefit from greater focus on the exploration of the long-term material interests Venice had in Byzantine trade, because this is the focus of the extract.

However, this argument relies upon the assumption that Dandolo was 'one of the prime movers for the crusade', which suggests that the Venetians were in control of the course of the Fourth Crusade. This is supported by the fact that the Venetians did control the transport, because under the Treaty of Venice they provided 500 ships for the crusaders and an escort of 30,000 Venetians. This meant the crusaders had to rely upon them, especially when they could not pay their 34,000 mark debt for the transport. The result of this reliance was that the leadership of the Fourth Crusade were effectively forced to accept Dandolo's proposal to attack Zara in return for a moratorium on their debt and then later add to his support for Prince Alexius's proposal. This supports Fine's view that Dandolo was a 'prime mover', as doge of Venice, and could force his will upon the crusaders. Nevertheless, this view privileges the agency of one individual when there were other powerful decision makers too, such as Boniface of Montferrat, the papal legate and the northern French counts. This interpretation therefore rests on their relative insignificance.

> This is a strong paragraph because it uses specific contextual material to support the key assumption in Fine's interpretation. It also begins to evaluate this assumption, but this evaluation would benefit from further explanation.

In contrast to the view that Venetian interests shaped the Fourth Crusade on its path to failure from the start, Asbridge argues that it was only when the crusaders reached Constantinople that 'the expedition rapidly lost sight of its "sacred" goal to recapture Jerusalem'. The central feature to his argument is that the situation the crusaders encountered in Constantinople prevented them from making any further progress. For example, after the crusaders had fought to put Prince Alexius on the imperial throne, they were given great rewards, which included 100,000 marks, and were allowed to see the wealth and prosperity of Constantinople first hand. This increased the desire of all the crusaders, not just the Venetians, to stay near a source of such potential wealth. However, a more significant pull towards Constantinople was that the new Alexius IV still needed their help. In September 1203 he asked them to stay until March 1204 and join him on a tour of the empire. This not only delayed the crusade, but increased its obligations to the Byzantine Empire instead of Jerusalem and the crusade.

> This paragraph explores the differences in the argument between Extract 1 and Extract 2. It uses a range of contextual details to explore the key point in Extract 2. It could be improved through an exploration of some of the similarities in this interpretation to the first, such as the continued Venetian material interest in this situation.

Asbridge's argument therefore presents Prince Alexius as the prime mover for the crusade, instead of Dandolo. It was Alexius, after all, who brought the Fourth Crusaders to Constantinople. He was also primarily responsible for the fact that the crusade was forced to stay there because 'when he proved unable to redeem his lavish promises of financial reward to the Latins, relations soured'. These poor relations contributed to the coup that forced him from power and, in turn, forced the crusaders to take control of the city. Once they had done this, in April 1204, they had to remain in their new kingdom of Romania to secure it. The crusade was therefore stuck in the Byzantine Empire in order to sort out a problem that Prince Alexius had created.

> There is a strong sense of evaluation in this paragraph, because it uses Extract 2 to challenge the assumption at the heart of Extract 1. It would benefit from more specific contextual details to support this alternative argument.

In conclusion, both of these arguments are largely based on the evidence of medieval chroniclers, who present differing explanations for the events of the Fourth Crusade, and can therefore support different interpretations. Whilst Extract 1 suggests Dandolo was the 'prime mover' and so pushed Venice's needs from the start, Extract 2 suggests the expedition was not on course to fail until it ended up at Constantinople. There is something to be said for both of these views. Venice's interests did play a prominent role in both of the diversions and so their 'material interests' were always a part of the picture. However, the idea that this alone caused the crusade to fail places too much responsibility on Dandolo and excludes the interests of others leaders and the attraction of Constantinople to all. Dandolo certainly pushed it in the direction of failure, but Venetian interests alone did not trap the Fourth Crusade in the former Byzantine Empire.

> The answer reaches a strong conclusion. It could be improved through further analysis of the first point related to the nature of the historical debate on this topic.

Verdict

This is a strong answer because:

- it makes direct references to the extracts and compares the key arguments presented in both
- the basis for the issues raised in each extract is established through the use of detail from the extract and contextual detail
- the introduction is focused on the key issues in each extract, which helps to provide a clear boundary for the answer to explore
- the conclusion reaches a supported judgement based on an evaluation of the views in both extracts and a consideration of the nature of historical debate.

Anglo-Saxon England and the Anglo-Norman kingdom, c1053–1106

As Edward the Confessor lay dying at the start of 1066, Anglo-Saxon rule had just ten months of existence left. Instead of the brutal Dark Age kingdom of popular imagination, late Anglo-Saxon England was a vibrant and prosperous land. It possessed a sophisticated government, the envy of its European rivals and created largely out of the terrifying struggle against the Vikings. For the everyday people there was also a growing reliance on the law in order to settle disputes. It was a time of magnetic personalities in an age when individuals could shape history. Centre stage was the warrior–statesman Harold Godwinson, his reputation built on charm, inherited wealth and, above all, military success in Wales. Behind him stood the shadowy and troubled figure of Edward the Confessor. With no children to follow on after his death, and having been far too generous in promising the throne to others, Edward's deathbed anointment of Earl Harold meant only one thing for Anglo-Saxon England. War was on its way.

Duke William of Normandy was another giant of the age. The night he was conceived, his mother, Herleva, is said to have dreamt of an oak tree erupting from her. Growing quickly, it soon overshadowed Normandy, before throwing its branches across the water to England. In truth, the future king of England was lucky to survive his youth in the rebellious and violent duchy. By 1066, however, he was a warrior in his prime, determined to press a doubtful claim to the English throne. Having prepared a vast army and gained widespread European support, William put to sea in September and embarked on what must have been the greatest adventure of his life. The Norman invasion had begun and with it a clash between the old Anglo-Saxon world and the brutal efficiency of the Normans. At the bloody climax on Saturday 14 October 1066, the cream of Anglo-Saxon nobility lay either slaughtered on the slopes of Senlac Hill near Hastings or dying in the thick forest beyond.

Norman victory that day had been a close-run thing and rested on the command decisions made by Harold and William. Different choices might well have resulted in very different outcomes. In the aftermath of battle, men and women across England had to decide whether to accept or fight the new regime. There was never a unanimous answer and this provided William with the advantage he needed to defeat a series of rebellions, which saw him campaigning the length and breadth of England for five years. By the time the last substantial revolt had been crushed in the East Anglian fens, the occupation was already beginning to change England. It had become a nation locked down by castles, a new elite and knights.

1042–66 – Edward the Confessor king of England	1042–66
January 1066 – King Edward dies and Earl Harold becomes king of England 14 October 1066 – Duke William of Normandy defeats King Harold at Hastings	1066
1067–71 – A series of nationwide uprisings against Norman occupation	1067–71
1071 – The last English rebels at Ely surrender	1071
1075 – Three disgruntled earls attempt to seize England from William I	1075
1079 – William I is defeated at Gerberoy by his son, Robert Curthose	1079
1082 – William I arrests his half-brother, Bishop Odo of Bayeux	1082
9 September 1087 – William I dies shortly after fighting in the Vexin region of France and power passes to his sons 1087–1100 – William II king of England 1087–1106 – Robert Curthose becomes duke of Normandy	1087–1106
1093–1109 – William II appoints Anselm as archbishop of Canterbury	1093–1109
1096 – Robert Curthose pawns Normandy to William II to fight in the crusades	1096
28 September 1106 – Robert Curthose is imprisoned by his brother, King Henry I, after losing the Battle of Tinchebrai 1106–35 – Henry I becomes duke of Normandy, re-uniting the Anglo-Norman realm	1106–35

Central government was expanding, private land ownership was at an end, while towns were becoming more cosmopolitan. England was also being transformed by a new religious idealism championed by Rome and expressed most visibly in the construction of dominating cathedrals. Some vestiges of the Anglo-Saxon system would survive, however, and still manage to shape our world today.

By the time William died in 1087, his rule had also been felt in Scotland, Wales, Maine, Brittany and the Vexin. His end, though, was pitiful. Fearing instability, the assembled magnates immediately departed William's deathbed to safeguard their estates, leaving the servants to strip the Conqueror's body of everything valuable in a frenzy of looting. William's political legacy was a deathbed division of Normandy from England, while his personal one was three sons, all intent on out-achieving him and each other. His favoured middle child, William Rufus, would die first. Bequeathed England, he would prove his skills as a warrior but incur the lasting wrath of the Church by driving the archbishop of Canterbury into exile. William's eldest and most disloyal son, Robert, while becoming a hero of the Crusades, would preside over serious misrule in Normandy and spend the last 28 years of his life a prisoner. It would be Henry, the youngest and most overlooked, who would emerge as the true heir of the Conqueror, with his own climactic battle at Tinchebrai taking place exactly 50 years after the Battle of Hastings.

1063

1063 – A united Wales collapses after its king, Gruffydd, is defeated by Harold, earl of Wessex

1066–78

1066–78 – William I king of England

1070–89

1070–89 – The reformer Lanfranc is appointed archbishop of Canterbury

1072

1072 – William I invades Scotland, receiving the submission of King Malcolm III

1076

November 1076 – Shock defeat of William I at Dol, Brittany, by King Philip I of France

1081

1081 – William I leads his army to the most westerly point of Wales

1086

1086 – The Domesday survey records England's land holding and economic assets

1088

1088 – William II defeats a plot to install his brother, Robert, on the throne

1094

1094 – English power collapses in Wales

1100

2 August 1100 – William II is killed in the New Forest

Henry, William I's youngest son, seizes the English throne and becomes king of England

2a.1 Late Anglo-Saxon England, c1053–66

KEY QUESTIONS

- How was Anglo-Saxon England governed?
- How advanced was the Anglo-Saxon economy?
- Why was the Godwin family so powerful?
- What were the early threats to Harold's throne?

INTRODUCTION

Anglo-Saxon England had emerged from the chaos of successive Viking invasions to become a prosperous and well-governed land under Edward the Confessor. While pious and respected, he was also responsible for plunging England into a succession crisis by failing adequately to appoint an heir. Three great warriors saw this as their moment to seize the English throne, but with fatal results for a society already 500 years old.

Who were the Anglo-Saxons?

The story of the Anglo-Saxons begins with the collapse of the Roman Empire in the fifth century. In AD 410, the last Roman legions were withdrawn from Britain to help defend the imperial city of Rome from invading barbarians. After 350 years of colonial rule, they left behind a sophisticated Romano-British culture, but also a largely defenceless island. There followed a century and a half of immigration by Angles, Saxons and Jutes from northern Germany and southern Denmark and four great independent Anglo-Saxon kingdoms emerged as East Anglia, Mercia, Northumbria and Wessex. The native Britons were either pushed out to the fringes of Cornwall and Wales or assimilated with the incomers. From this fusion the tentative beginnings of a new English identity began to form, reinforced by the gradual spread of Christianity following St Augustine's missionary work in 597. By the ninth century, the Anglo-Saxons themselves had begun to use the word 'Angli' or 'English' to refer to themselves.

1042 – Edward succeeds to the throne, restoring the Royal House of Wessex after 30 years of Danish rule

1051 – Godwin, earl of Wessex and his sons rebel against Edward and are exiled

1051–52 – Edward possibly promises the throne to William of Normandy

1052 – Godwin returns and forces Edward to restore his earldom

1053 – Godwin dies and his son Harold becomes earl of Wessex

1040	1045	1050	1055

1055 – Harold's brother Tostig becomes earl of Northumbria after the death of Earl Siward

Gruffydd of Wales sacks Hereford

1055–57 – Harold's brothers Gyrth and Leofwine become earls of East Anglia and Kent

1057 – Edward the Exile returns from Hungary but dies, leaving the infant Edgar as his heir

Death of Earl Leofric of Mercia; the earldom is

Anglo-Saxon dominance received its greatest challenge from the Vikings. At first, in the 790s, they only came for plunder, but by the 860s they came to stay. At its lowest point in 878, Anglo-Saxon control was reduced to only a few square miles of Somerset and Alfred, king of Wessex, was forced to hide out in the marshes. From this point, however, Alfred was able to reorganise his forces and he set about constructing a series of fortified towns across Wessex called *burhs*. This allowed him to defeat a renewed Viking onslaught in 892 and then the gradual rollback of Viking control could begin. Alfred's son, Edward the Elder, reconquered Danish Mercia and East Anglia as far as the River Humber, while his great grandson, Athelstan, completed the advance by taking Northumbria and securing the submission of Scotland and Wales. In the process of defeating the Vikings, Alfred and his successors had created the idea of England as a distinct political entity with defined borders, a central government, laws, taxation and local administration. The West Saxon kings had now become the kings of England and overlords of Britain. Their dominance was not to last. In 1013, King Sweyn of Denmark invaded the North of England, defeating King Aethelred II and his son Canute, then completed the conquest over the whole of England. The survivors of the royal house of Wessex fled abroad, including Aethelred's young son and heir, Edward.

For the next 20 years, Edward grew up as an embittered exile in Normandy and the English Crown must have seemed a distant prospect. When King Canute died in 1035, he left behind two sons, Harold and Harthacanute, to continue the Danish line. An attempted invasion by Edward and his younger brother, Alfred, only ended in tragedy when Alfred was captured and executed. However, when Harold and Harthacanute died in quick succession, Edward found himself able peacefully to take the English throne in 1042 and restore Alfred's royal line.

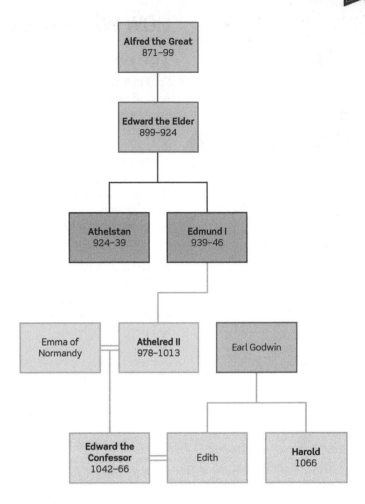

Figure 1.1 The line of the royal house of Wessex, dates show years of rule.

1062 – Edwin, son of Earl Aelfgar, becomes earl of Mercia on his father's death

1064 – Harold visits Normandy and possibly swears an oath to William

1065 – Northumbrians revolt against Earl Tostig

1060

1065

1070

1063 – Harold and Tostig lead forces by land and sea to defeat Gruffydd of Wales

1066 – King Edward dies and Harold becomes King

Battles of Gate Fulford, Stamford Bridge and Hastings

HOW WAS ANGLO-SAXON ENGLAND GOVERNED?

The power of the king

For Edward the journey to be king had been a difficult one but the prize was worth waiting for. Late Anglo-Saxon England possessed a well-ordered and sophisticated system of government and at its heart lay a monarchy vested with huge powers and responsibilities. As the commander of the nation's army and the only one with the right to raise an army, the king's most important duty was protecting the country from all external and internal threats. In addition, the king, divinely appointed, had a key religious function, as he controlled the running of the Church and appointed its leaders. As England's chief arbiter of justice, he had to settle disputes between his leading subjects and increasingly keep his people safe from criminal acts. The king was also England's supreme decision-maker, with the sole right to make laws and decide on foreign and domestic policy. In return he was expected to govern in the best interest of his people. Finally, the king alone possessed the right to mint coins and his main economic function was to ensure that the integrity of the currency was maintained.

Anglo-Saxon kings exercised their power through the institution of the royal household. This was constantly on the move as the king sought to project his power across the kingdom and visit his scattered estates. The closest thing England had to a capital was Winchester, where the royal treasure was held. The household itself was made up of the king's immediate family and the domestic servants and priests who looked after them. There was a basic bureaucracy known as the **chancery**. Staffed by royal clerks who could read and write, it issued the royal **writs**, which were one of the principal instruments used to control the provinces. Source 1 contains one of the few surviving examples of a writ from Edward the Confessor's time. It denotes the existence of an administrative machine which could produce and distribute orders and also an underlying expectation that these would be obeyed. Also in the household were a group of elite soldiers called **housecarls**, who formed the king's bodyguard and the core of the royal army in times of war. Forming part of the wider royal court and helping advise the king were the great men of the nation: earls, **thegns**, archbishops, bishops and abbots. Government in late Anglo-Saxon England was a personal business. As a result, the king rarely found himself alone and was central to all the decisions being taken.

KEY TERMS

Chancery
A writing office where royal writs were produced.

Writ
A short, sealed document with a standard greeting. It crisply communicated the king's orders to his provinces.

Housecarl
A member of the household troop or an Anglo-Saxon king or noble.

Thegn
A member of the Anglo-Saxon nobility.

Itinerant
Anglo-Saxon kings were constantly on the move. The itinerary of the king listed the places he visited.

SOURCE 1

A sealed writ of Edward the Confessor, announcing that he has granted the land of Perton in Staffordshire to Westminster Abbey, probably from December 1065, for the dedication of the Abbey.

King Edward sends friendly greetings to Bishop Leofwine and Earl Edwin and all my thegns in Staffordshire. And I inform you that I have given to Westminster, to Christ and to St Peter, the land at Perton and everything belonging thereto, in woodland and in open country, with sake and with soke, as fully and as completely as I myself possessed it in all things, for the sustenance of the abbot and the brethren who dwell in the monastery. And I will not permit anyone to alienate there any of the things that belong to that foundation.

This centralisation of power in the hands of the king set England apart from its neighbours. France, for example, was under the control of the Capetian royal line but their authority was weak and confined to a small area around Paris. The rest of the kingdom was firmly in the control of powerful lords such as Duke William of Normandy. The distinctiveness of the English model lies in its origins. As the West Saxon kings defeated the Vikings and advanced beyond Wessex in the tenth century, so too did the idea that the whole of England should be governed as a single entity rather than being divided into separate kingdoms. This evolution can be traced through the titles the kings used on charters and coins. Whereas Alfred was styled *rex Saxonum* or king of the Saxons, a 931 charter from his grandson, Athelstan, called him *rex Anglorum*, king of the English.

The power of late Anglo-Saxon kings like Edward the Confessor should not be exaggerated, however. By modern standards his government was basic. There is no evidence of separate government departments and the fact his household was **itinerant** limited its capacity. There were also various checks on the king's power, which made him far from an autocrat. Edward had little authority in the fiercely independent North and never visited this region. Above all, Edward had to work in co-operation with his leading subjects if he wanted the country to be well governed and the army to fight for him willingly. The collective power and influence of the Anglo-Saxon nobility far outstripped his own. As well as being present in the royal court, they exerted influence through the **witan,** which discussed and sanctioned laws, approved key appointments and helped settle disputes. To keep his nobles onside, the king could deploy various strategies, including dominating them by force of personality as partly suggested in Source 2. He could also win their support through the power of patronage by granting land, titles and offices. In this Edward was helped by being the largest single landowner and richest individual in England. He could also flatter by bringing his nobles into the decision-making process. As will be seen, Edward was not particularly successful at asserting himself over his leading men and ended up being dominated by one noble family in particular, the Godwins.

SOURCE 2

From *Vita Edwardi Regis* ('The Life of King Edward'), an anonymous work written c1065–67 and dedicated to Queen Edith, daughter of Earl Godwin and wife of Edward the Confessor. It gives a **hagiographical** account of Edward's saintly qualities as well as focusing positively on the Godwin family.

King Edward was a very proper figure of a man – of outstanding height, and distinguished by his milky white hair and beard, full face and rosy cheeks, thin white hands, and long translucent fingers; in all the rest of his body he was an unblemished royal person. Pleasant, but always dignified, he walked with eyes down-cast, most graciously affable to one and all. If some cause aroused his temper, he seemed as terrible as a lion, but he never revealed his anger by railing. To all petitioners he would either grant graciously or graciously deny, so that his gracious denial seemed the highest generosity. In public he carried himself as a true king and lord; in private with his courtiers as one of them, but with royal dignity unimpaired.

Earldoms, shires and local government

From the centre, the king's authority could be transmitted downwards through a hierarchical system of regional and local government. Directly below the king were the earls, who governed vast areas of England. The four principal earldoms were Wessex, Mercia, Northumbria and East Anglia. Acting in the king's name, the earls were responsible for keeping the peace in their territories, exercising justice and raising armies. While they exercised a good deal of autonomy, they were not independent rulers. They could not mint their own coins or hold their own courts and ultimately they owed their position to the king.

The principal administrative units of the late Anglo-Saxon state were the almost 40 counties or shires. These mattered because this was where day-to-day government took place. The royal official responsible for implementing the king's will in the shire was the sheriff. He supervised the collection of taxes, dispensed justice and settled disputes in shire courts. In times of national emergency, he also organised and led military forces. The sheriff would have been drawn from the thegnly class. Consisting of around 5,000 landed gentry, thegns formed the solid backbone of England. To deal with local matters, shires were then subdivided into units of a dozen or so villages known as hundreds. These were administered by reeves, another type of royal official. Below this was another smaller subdivision, the vill, overseen by its own reeve as well. Although vills and hundreds would not be so enduring, the system of shires laid out by the late Anglo-Saxon kings would remain largely unchanged until local government reorganisation in the 1970s and they are of course still recognisable today.

The legal system

Late Anglo-Saxon England also saw the beginnings of a hierarchical nation wide legal system. At the top, the king presided over disputes between his earls or thegns as well as some of the most serious criminal cases, such as murder, treason, arson and rape. Under the concept of the King's Peace, it was regarded as the monarch's duty to keep his people safe from these types of offences. The next level were the shire courts. They met about twice a year, normally at Easter and Michaelmas (October) and were presided over by the earl or sheriff. Significant legal cases from across the shire would be heard, such as theft, violence, and land and family disputes. In addition, royal writs and charters would be read and discussed. As a result, these courts were an important public event and were attended by the all the notable families of the shire. Most of the routine legal cases were heard in the hundred courts. As the lowest public court in the land, they dealt with local land disputes and issues of law and order. They were important because for most people this was their main experience of royal government.

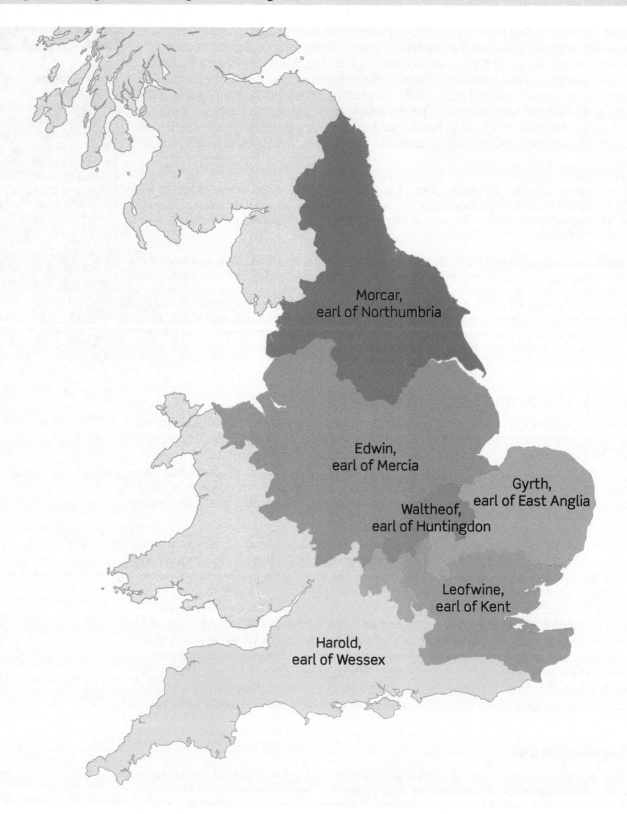

Figure 1.2 The Anglo-Saxon earldoms at the start of 1066.

When a case was put to trial, common methods of deciding guilt or innocence were used across the country. People of good character could swear on oath that they were telling the truth or else bring in oath helpers to back them up. In criminal cases the judgement of God was called upon through ordeals. In trial by cold water, a person was shown to be guilty if they floated in water blessed by a priest. This was on the basis that holy water would not receive a sinner. In trial by hot iron, the accused had to carry a piece of red hot iron for three paces. The hand was then bound and inspected three days later. The presence of infection would lead to a guilty verdict.

To help maintain law and order, late Anglo-Saxon kings also became enthusiastic legislators and their legal codes give a vivid insight into contemporary concerns, assumptions and organisation. Edward the Confessor seems to have been the exception by not passing any new codes of his own, instead relying on the rich body of laws inherited from his predecessors, including Athelstan who passed ten codes. One of these stated that all buying and selling had to be carried out in a trading centre and witnessed by a reeve. This was to try and clamp down on the sale of stolen property, most notably cattle. To provide some kind of basic policing structure, another of Athelstan's codes set out that all freemen over the age of 12 had to belong to a tithing. It was the duty of each member of a tithing, made up of ten people, to police the behaviour of its other members and ensure they did not commit crimes. They also had to be prepared to form a posse to ride after cattle rustlers. Twice a year the sheriff had to tour his shire to ensure that each tithing was functioning correctly. Over the course of his reign, Edward developed a reputation as a great giver of justice and, as can be seen in Source 3, a document purportedly detailing the laws current in his kingdom became extremely influential among a later generation of scholars. Although its precise origins are dubious, it does help shed some light on early medieval attitudes to law and order.

SOURCE 3

From *Leges Edwardi Confessoris* ('The Laws of Edward the Confessor'). Written c1140 by an anonymous writer, this claims to be based on a 1070 source recording Edward's laws and customs for the benefit of William I. However, the existence of this document seems highly doubtful.

When anyone anywhere was found murdered, the slayer of this person was sought in the vill where the body was found; and if he could be found, he was handed over to the king's justice within eight days of the dying. If, however, he could not be found, they had a month and a day as respite to locate him. If he was not found, 46 marks were collected from the vill. And if the vill did not suffice for the payment of so much money, what could not be collected in the vill was collected throughout the hundred.

However, it would be wrong to say that a uniform, coherent system of justice existed across the country. Each region had its own legal customs and traditions. Canute's law code accepted that different laws existed in Wessex, Mercia and the old **Danelaw,** and a code produced by Henry I as late as 1115 made the same admission. It was also a time when many people saw the settling of justice as a private affair and preferred to take matters into their own hands. This was especially the case in remote regions like Northumbria where the lack of central authority meant **blood feuds** were a key part of life.

EXTEND YOUR KNOWLEDGE

Working with the evidence

Reconstructing the Anglo-Saxon world is a difficult task for the historian. Very little evidence has survived the passage of nearly 1,000 years, while the principal accounts that remain tend to be Norman. The works of William of Poitiers and William of Jumieges as well as the stunning **Bayeux Tapestry** stand out, but they represent a victor's version of events, produced after the conquest to justify the invasion. To provide an alternative viewpoint, there are not many sources to turn to. The principal English view is provided by the *Anglo-Saxon Chronicle*, while *The Life of King Edward*, produced for the Confessor's widow, provides further detail. In addition, the later generation of Anglo-Norman historians, such as William of Malmesbury and Orderic Vitalis, were able to look back on the past with less partisan eyes and so they in turn provide us with fresh perspectives.

The task of discovering the economic, social and legal world of Anglo-Saxon England hinges on a few key documents. Chief among them is the Domesday survey, while a small number of writs, charters and wills are also available for study. They are very scarce, though, with less than 100 charters and writs from the Confessor's time and only one from Harold's. This in turn raises its own questions. For example, does this low number mean the state was not very active or merely reflect the fact that so few have survived?

Archaeology can also play a role through the excavation of Anglo-Saxon settlements, burial sites and the chance discovery of hoards. The scarcity of evidence, as will be seen, means this period of history is rich in debate and speculation with historians having to hedge their conclusions with terms like 'possible' and 'probable'.

KEY TERMS

Danelaw
An area of northern and eastern England that had been under Viking control from the ninth century. It had different laws from the rest of England, which reflected the difference in the ruling classes in the two territories.

Blood feud
A method of settling disputes whereby relatives and friends avenged those who were murdered or injured.

Bayeux Tapestry
A visual account of the final months of Edward's reign, Duke William's preparations for invasion and the Battle of Hastings. It is generally thought that the tapestry was designed and made in Kent in about 1070–80 on the orders of Bishop Odo of Bayeux, Duke William's half-brother. Harold Godwinson is not sympathetically portrayed.

ACTIVITY
KNOWLEDGE CHECK

1 What were the main duties of an Anglo-Saxon king?

2 What qualities does Source 2 identity in Edward the Confessor? What important attributes for a king are not mentioned?

3 Write down five ways in which the Anglo-Saxon system of government could be described as efficient and well run.

4 How useful is Source 3 for finding out about the Anglo-Saxon legal system?

HOW ADVANCED WAS THE ANGLO-SAXON ECONOMY?

Edward the Confessor's England was a rich and prosperous land. Following its conquest in 1066, the scale of its wealth become the envy of Europe. This was helped in part by William's spectacular return to Normandy in March 1067 laden with Anglo-Saxon treasure. Although William's rule would ruthlessly exploit England for its wealth, he also created the means for later historians to analyse it. In 1086, William ordered the making of the Domesday Book. This detailed record describes the state of the country before and after the conquest and at the time of the survey. Although not perfect, as London and Winchester were left out, it does allow the Anglo-Saxon economy to be reconstructed, as seen in Sources 4 and 5. While the backbone of the economy was farming, it also reveals a flourishing non-agricultural sector. There were 112 towns, 6,000 watermills and thriving industries. These ranged from lead mining in Derbyshire, tin mining in Cornwall, the Worcestershire salt industry centred on Droitwich, and pottery-making in Norwich and Stamford.

KEY TERMS

The Domesday survey is full of technical terms, some of them no longer in use today.

Carucate/hide
The standard unit of assessment used for tax purposes. It was meant to represent the amount of land that could support a household, roughly 120 acres. In the old Danish areas of England, the hide was known as the carucate.

TRE
An abbreviation for *tempore regis Edwardi*, 'at the time of King Edward', meaning from before the Norman Conquest.

Villan
The most numerous class of unfree peasants. A villan owed his lord labour services, normally of two to three days a week, but also farmed land for himself. While the Domesday Book refers to this group as villans, they were also known as villains or villeins.

Bordar
A class of unfree peasants below **villans** but above slaves.

Demesne
Land held directly by the lord.

Berewick
An outlying holding of a manor.

Messuage
The unit of land tenure within a borough, typically comprising a house and property.

£/s/d
Pounds, shillings and pence.

Burgess
Townspeople.

Moneyer
A person licensed to strike coins.

Geld
A national land tax, assessed on the number of hides a person owned.

SOURCE 4

Part of the Domesday entry for Grimshoe Hundred, Norfolk, c1087.

Methwold was held by (Archbishop) Stigand as 20 **carucates** of land **TRE**. Then there were 28 **villans**, afterwards 24, now 18. Then there were 4 **bordars**, afterwards 8, now 13; there have always been 24 slaves and 30 acres of meadow; then there were 6 ploughs in **demesne**, afterwards and now 5. Then there were 23 ploughs belonging to the men, afterwards 13, now 7; there have always been 2½ mills, 7 fisheries in demesne, 4 horses, 12 head of cattle, 84 pigs, 800 sheep and 27 beehives. To this a **berewick**, Weeting, has always belonged; there have always been 3 villans and 1 bordar and 3 slaves and 1 acre of meadow. Then there were 2 ploughs in demesne, afterwards and now 1; then there was 1 plough belonging to the men; then as now there were 2 horses. In Feltwell there are 60 acres of land. And in Thetford there was half a carucate of land, and 5 bordars TRE, now there are 3, and 2 **messuages** are vacant and there is 1 church; and 1 church of St Helen with 1 carucate and 1 villan, and there could be 1 plough.

SOURCE 5
Part of the Domesday entry for the city of Shrewsbury, Shropshire, c1087.

IN THE CITY OF SHREWBURY IN THE TIME OF KING EDWARD there were 252 houses, and as many burgesses in these houses, rendering **£7.16s 8d** of rent a year. There King Edward had these undermentioned customs.

If any person wittingly broke the king's peace imposed by the king's own hand he was made an outlaw; he who broke the king's peace imposed by the sheriff paid a fine of 100s; and he who committed highway robbery or housebreaking gave as much... When the king stayed in the city, 12 of the better citizens mounted watch for his protection, and likewise when he went hunting there the better among the burgesses possessing horses guarded him with arms. For heading off game the sheriff sent 36 men on foot as long as the king was there. When the sheriff wishes to march into Wales, anyone who after being summoned by him did not go gave a fine of 40s. A woman taking a husband in any way, gave to the king 20s if she was a widow, 10s if an unmarried woman, in whatever way she took the man. Should the house of any **burgess** be burnt by misfortune or accident or by negligence he gave 40s to the king by way of fine and 2s to each of his 2 nearest neighbours. When a burgess who was in the king's demesne died, the king had 10s by way of relief... When the king was leaving the city the sheriff sent 24 horses for him from Leintwardine and the king took these with him as far as the first house in Staffordshire.

The king had there 3 **moneyers** of the kingdom, who, after they purchased the money-dies, like other moneyers of the kingdom, on the fifteenth day gave to the king 20s each, and this was done when the coinage was changed.

All together this city rendered £30 a year. The king had 2 parts, and the sheriff the third. In the year before this survey it rendered £40 to Earl Roger. TRE this city paid **geld** for 100 hides.

A Level Exam-Style Question Section A

How far could the historian make use of Sources 3 and 5 together to investigate the Anglo-Saxon legal system?

Explain your answer, using both sources, the information given about them and your own knowledge of the historical context. (20 marks)

Tip

Remember to discuss both sources equally and together as a package.

Royal mints and the silver penny

Underpinning the strength of the Anglo-Saxon economy was a stable national currency based on silver pounds, shillings and pence. The pennies, bearing the king's head and so also acting as a powerful symbol of royal authority, were of relatively high value. One silver penny would be equivalent to a day's labour, a sheep could cost five silver pennies, an ox 30. Although it would be wrong to assume England had a fully monetised economy as barter was still the mainstay for many local transactions, this system of currency was widely used and trusted and as a result it made extensive trade possible. Around nine million pennies were in circulation by 1066. Of the stray coin losses found by archaeologists today, as many as two-thirds were not produced by the local mint, showing that once in circulation they passed from hand to hand rapidly and spread across the country through trade.

To maintain the integrity of the currency, royal control was absolute. Dies were produced in London and silver pennies of standard design were then cast by royally licensed moneyers in 60 mints spread across the country. Foreign coins were forbidden and had to be handed in to the mints, where they were melted down and recoined. Every five years all coins in circulation ceased to be legal tender by royal decree and had to be exchanged for the new design. For this privilege, people had to pay 15 percent of the value of their old coins. This helped maintain the integrity of the currency and made a profit for the king. The coinage system is regarded as one of the greatest achievements of the Anglo-Saxon state and was far superior to anything else seen in north-west Europe at the time. It is also comforting to know that the Anglo-Saxon system of pounds, shilling and pence proved so strong it lasted until 1971 and the advent of decimalisation. The pound in your pocket today is one of the last echoes of that distant world.

Figure 1.3 The main towns and ports of late Anglo-Saxon England.

Urbanisation and the growth of trading centres

As well as a stable currency, other factors are regarded as important for the development of towns. These include a relatively stable political environment, a settled population, a well-farmed hinterland to ensure regular supplies of food and raw materials, and a network of trading contacts, all of which were to be found in Anglo-Saxon England. Their presence helps explain the high degree of urbanisation seen by 1066. Ten percent of the population lived in towns, with London's population reaching around 10,000 and Norwich, Winchester and York 5,000–10,000. Although this may not sound high, no English city, with the exception of London, exceeded 14,000 until the 16th century.

Most of the major towns in England developed from the fortified *burhs* built by King Alfred and his successors to fight the Vikings. In Wessex, nowhere was more than about 30 kilometres or a day's march away from the safety of one. With many laid out according to a common town plan, the *burhs* were also planned from the outset to be places of permanent habitation, trade and manufacture, as well as the administrative centres of the shires. By the late Anglo-Saxon period, they were fulfilling this function, helped by law codes that stated that all trade had to take place in urban markets. These provided everyday items which could not be bought or made in villages, including wool clothing, leather footwear, clay pottery, metal pots, tools, salt and candles. Streets in Winchester in this period included those named for butchers, goldsmiths, shoemakers, shieldmakers and tanners. Archaeologists digging in the Coppergate area of late Anglo-Saxon York have found evidence of bone and antler work, jewellers producing amber and jet rings, beads and pendants. Some towns developed specialisms. Norwich bought herrings from Yarmouth, smoked them and sold them on. Town markets and fairs were also the place to acquire luxury goods from abroad.

Coastal towns and overseas trade

Edward the Confessor's England was tied into a complex European trading system. Merchants from Scandinavia, Flanders, Rhineland, Normandy, France and Spain have all been mentioned in Anglo-Saxon records. They brought with them, among other things, cloth, pottery, gloves, wine, amber and millstones. Particularly prized were swords of tempered steel from Spain and coats of mail from Germany. More exotic spices and gems reached England from the trade routes opened by the Vikings. These ran the length of the Baltic and then down the waterways of Russia to the Black Sea and Constantinople. England exported far more than it imported, including cheese, ham, salt, meat, smoked herrings, wool and leather. Indeed, as money flowed in from the continent to purchase these goods, late Anglo-Saxon England became a net importer of silver due to a favourable balance of trade, giving the thegnly class a steady supply of ready money.

The main Anglo-Saxon ports were Southampton, London, Lincoln, Cambridge, Norwich and York, all ideally placed for continental trade. These had developed from the main trading ports of the eighth and ninth centuries known as the Emporia and shared the common characteristic of being located slightly inland on river estuaries, which offered shelter, a sloping beach on which boats could be hauled and good communications inland. Archaeologists in the 1980s found evidence of a late Anglo-Saxon wharf complex at Billingsgate, London. In the West, Bristol developed possibly to take advantage of trade with southern Ireland, then a Norse outpost. Ports actually on the coast, such as Orwell, Dunwich and Boston, began their development at the time of the conquest or later.

The system of taxation

Thanks to the sophisticated system of local government, the king was able to tap into England's wealth to raise very large sums of money. This was achieved through a geld administered by the shires and hundreds. It was typically collected annually and amounted to two shillings per hide, enough to raise around £6,000. In times of emergency it could also raise much more. According to the **Anglo-Saxon Chronicle**, between 991 and 1012 £137,000 was paid to buy off Danish invaders. The ability to raise such large sums at short notice underlines the wealth of the kingdom and strength of the state.

KEY TERM

Anglo-Saxon Chronicle
A year-by-year account of English history, in English, from Julius Caesar up to the mid 12th century. It was probably started in Wessex at the end of the ninth century and then continued in a number of monasteries. The most important surviving manuscripts are those written at Abingdon (text C) Worcester (D) and Canterbury (E). Although all probably based on a common source, they contain differences of fact and interpretation, reflecting local sympathies. The 'C' version is royalist in tone and hostile to the house of Godwin, whereas the 'E' version is Godwinist. Version 'D' from further north is largely neutral. Collectively they provide a unique English account of events before 1066. After William's conquest, the *Chronicle* was continued at Peterborough only.

With the decline of the Viking threat during Edward the Confessor's rule, money no longer had to flow outwards to Scandinavia in the form of protection payments to avoid attack. It instead stayed in the hands of the nobility and went to support their increasingly luxurious lifestyles. Many were building lavish compounds with large wooden halls, private chambers and stone churches. Harking back to the splendour of imperial Rome, purple cloth was also a favoured item. As shown in Source 6, the opulent gifts made in wills during this period provide an insight into the scale of personal wealth some of England's several thousand thegns enjoyed.

SOURCE

6 The will of Wulfsige from c1043.

Here in this document it is made known to whom Wulfsige grants his possessions. First, for his soul, two-thirds of the estate at Wick to Bury St Edmunds and the third part to Bishop Elfric, except one yardland and mast for twelve swine which Wulfwyn shall have for her life, and after her death it shall go to Bury St Edmunds; and all the men are to be free for the sake of the souls of us both.

And I grant to my royal lord two horses and a helmet and a coat of mail, and a sword and a spear inlaid with gold. And I grant to my lady half a mark of gold, and to my niece an ore's weight of gold. And Stanhand is to have everything which I have bequeathed to him, and my brother's children their own land, and two horses with harness, and one coat of mail and one cloak.

And he who alters my will, may Almighty God turn away his face from him on the Day of Judgement unless in this life he will quickly make amends for it.

ACTIVITY
KNOWLEDGE CHECK

1 Find five pieces of evidence that support the view that Anglo-Saxon England had an advanced economy.

2 How useful is Source 4 for investigating the late Anglo-Saxon economy?

3 What factors encouraged the growth of towns in Anglo-Saxon England?

4 What can you learn from Source 5 about how the Crown sought to control towns?

5 Assess the significance of Source 6 in exploring the level of personal wealth in the late Anglo-Saxon period.

WHY WAS THE GODWIN FAMILY SO POWERFUL?

Earl Godwin

The story of the Godwin family is one of power and ambition. Starting out as the son of an obscure Sussex thegn, Godwin's political skill turned him into one of King Canute's chief advisors, also earning him the ancient earldom of Wessex. This would form the basis for his and his family's subsequent dominance over Anglo-Saxon England. Godwin needed to call on all his ability when Danish control ended with the return of Edward. Implicated in the brutal murder of Edward's brother Alfred, Godwin was able to avert disaster by becoming king-maker. He secured Edward the support of the wider English nobility, allowing a smooth transfer of power. Godwin was rewarded in 1043 when his eldest son, Swegn, and second son, Harold, were granted earldoms in Hereford and East Anglia. In 1045, Godwin arranged for Edward to marry his daughter Edith, cementing his dominance over the new king who was still finding his way in a country largely unknown to him.

Edward, though, must have found this reliance on his brother's murderer galling. To reduce Godwin's power, Edward began bringing in allies from his time in exile in Normandy, after developing a Norman faction in court. In 1051, he acted. Backed by Siward, earl of Northumbria, and Leofric, earl of Mercia, Edward exiled the Godwin clan and sent Queen Edith to a nunnery. Edward's bitterness was clear when he stated that Godwin would only be forgiven when Edward's brother, Alfred, was restored to him alive. The next year, however, the Godwin family returned in force, pillaging the South West and landing an army in London. With his own army reluctant to fight, Edward was forced to capitulate, banish most of his Norman advisors, who were publicly blamed for the trouble, and restore the Godwin family to power. Edward's humiliation must have been total.

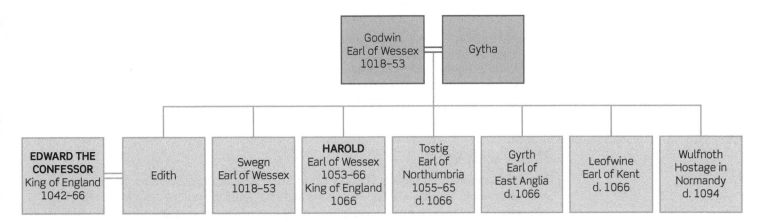

Figure 1.4 The Godwin family tree.

The rise of Harold

Godwin, the great political survivor, died in 1053 and his son, Harold, became earl of Wessex. Harold's brother, Tostig, was handed the great province of Northumbria in 1055 and his other brothers, Gyrth and Leofwine, subsequently became earls of East Anglia and Kent. At its height in the 1060s, only Mercia was not under the control of the Godwin family. Enormous political power was therefore concentrated in its hands. Adding to this was its sheer wealth. Domesday shows that the family estates amounted to around £7,000 in 1066, with Harold's share at £5,000. No-one else could come close, including the king, whose estates stood at £5,000, while Leofric's family was worth £2,400 and Siward's £350. The Godwins were able to use their huge resources to fund large bodies of housecarls and also to build up a network of supporters across the country by granting land. It is not hard to see why Harold, foremost of the Godwins, was being described as *subregulus* or deputy king.

SOURCE

From *Vita Edwardi Regis*, an anonymous work written c1065–67 and dedicated to Queen Edith, daughter of Earl Godwin and wife of Edward the Confessor.

The King appreciated (Harold and Tostig) and with them thus stationed in his kingdom, he lived all his life free from care on either flank, for one drove back the foe from the south and the other scared them off from the north. Also the king did not suffer their younger brother, Gyrth, to be left out of the honours, but gave him a shire at the extremity of East Anglia, and promised to increase this when he was older and had thrown off his boyhood years… And so, with the kingdom made safe on all sides by these princes, the most kindly king Edward passed his life in security and peace, and spent much of his time in the glades and woods in the pleasures of hunting … In these activities he sometimes spent the day, and it was in these alone that he seemed naturally inclined to snatch some wordly pleasure. Otherwise this man, of his free will devoted to God, lived in the squalor of the world like an angel.

This does raise the question of why Edward allowed the aggrandisement of the Godwin family. In truth, Edward had little choice in the 1040s. After having spent a long exile in Normandy, he knew very little of the English political system. He had no entrenched supporters in court and, as his lands were scattered throughout the kingdom, no real power base. As a result, he had to rely on Earl Godwin as the most powerful man in England in his early days, only to attempt to remove the family in 1051 once he was more established on the throne. After Godwin's death, Edward seems to have established a more positive working relationship with Harold and he developed a strong attachment to Tostig, perhaps encouraged by Queen Edith who favoured this brother. This no doubt helped Edward come to terms with his domination and he must have realised that Godwin strength also ensured peace and stability in his kingdom, as seen in Source 7.

EXTEND YOUR KNOWLEDGE

PASE Domesday is a powerful database created by the Department of History and the Centre for Computing in the Humanities at King's College, London and in the Department of Anglo-Saxon, Norse, and Celtic at the University of Cambridge. It allows users to interrogate the data contained in the Domesday survey and display it in a variety of forms. It is particularly useful for finding out who held land in a particular region or the extent of their lands nationwide.

Search for PASE Domesday and then select 'Domesday' from the menu at the top of the page. Follow the instructions in the Step-by-step guide (PDF format) to learn how to use the database and then carry out searches for Earl Harold Godwin and King Edward. Use the map display tab to see how their landholdings compare in size and geographical spread. You could repeat this for the rest of the Godwin family and the other earls of late Anglo-Saxon England.

The Welsh wars

Harold Godwinson had presence. The *Vita Edwardi* describes him as tall, handsome, graceful and remarkably strong. The Bayeux Tapestry shows him singlehandedly pulling a Norman knight from quicksand during the 1064 Brittany campaign, while a second saved man is carried over his shoulder. The *Vita Edwardi* continues that he had an easy-going confidence and positive temperament, although it frowns on his promiscuity. However, it also states that Harold won the respect of those around him by being prepared to discuss his policies and battle plans and listen to criticism. Above all, it portrays him as a formidable warrior, able to endure hardship, lead men and kill. This reputation was earned in the bitter Welsh wars, although Harold had a steep learning curve.

KEY TERM

Welsh Marches
The disputed borderlands between England and Wales.

Wales became a major threat to English security with the rise of Gruffydd ap Llewelyn, who declared himself the first king of Wales in 1055. This ended the destructive pattern of bloody feuds between the different principalities and instead focused Welsh energies outwards to the disputed **Welsh Marches**. By this stage, Gruffydd had already gained the upper hand, defeating English forces in 1039, 1049 and 1052. The most serious attack came in 1055 when he formed an alliance with the disgraced earl of East Anglia, Aelfgar, banished from the English court for treason. Their forces invaded Herefordshire, ransacking Hereford itself. King Edward raised an army and sent Harold to deal with the problem. He refortified Hereford and then reached a peace deal, whereby Aelfgar was restored to his earldom and Gruffydd was conceded territory on the border in return for accepting Edward's overlordship. This cautious approach was sensible. It was Harold's first major campaign and so he was still learning to command. Winter was drawing near and so the fighting season was over. Harold had also ended the dangerous alliance between Gruffydd and Aelfgar.

This proved, however, a temporary peace. June 1056 saw Gruffydd defeat the warrior monk Leofgar, bishop of Hereford, who had made an ill-judged raid into Wales. Harold led an army to punish Gruffydd but it failed and only resulted in Harold being forced to concede more terms and recognise Gruffydd as king of all Wales. The English forces proved similarly impotent in 1058 when Gruffydd launched further attacks. He was allied once again with Aelfgar following yet another expulsion of Aelfgar from his earldom, but this time he was also joined by Magnus, the son of the king of Norway. Harold secured peace by restoring Aelfgar to his earldom, while Gruffydd was granted more land and Magnus was bought off. This once again showed Harold's preference for compromise and diplomacy.

Harold would finally prove his martial abilities following further raids by Gruffydd in 1062. Aiming for the element of surprise, Harold led a small cavalry force through harsh winter conditions to try and capture the Welsh king at his palace at Rhuddlan on the River Clwyd in North Wales. Tipped off, Gruffydd escaped just in time and Harold vented his rage by burning the palace. After careful preparation, in May 1063 Harold launched a full-scale campaign. While the English fleet blockaded and ravaged the Welsh coastline, Harold took an army into South Wales and Tostig invaded North Wales. The two brothers met in mid Wales and began devastating the land. For the next three months, the fighting was savage, as the brothers relentlessly hunted Gruffydd and gradually wore the Welsh fighters down through countless skirmishes. Harold also turned his forces into the equivalent of medieval commandoes. With no real supply lines, they lived off the land. To aid mobility in difficult terrain, Harold's men replaced their heavy mail with leather jerkins and they also started fighting with javelins like their Welsh counterparts. Welsh morale finally broke and, in August, Gruffydd's men turned on him, delivering his head to Harold.

This victory mattered because following Gruffydd's death Wales once again degenerated into warring principalities and so ceased seriously to threaten England. It also showed that the Anglo-Saxon military machine was extremely effective and led by a man of considerable ability. Harold had planned and implemented a complex land and sea operation and proven willing to adapt new tactics in the field. For Harold the conquest of Wales was his finest hour. He personally delivered Gruffydd's head to the king and his reputation stood at its peak.

EXTEND YOUR KNOWLEDGE

Military earls

Primarily concerned with religious devotion and administering justice, as well as lacking the hard skills needed to command troops in the field, Edward never led his army into battle. As well as Harold, another earl who won martial glory by acting on the king's behalf was Siward of Northumbria. He helped Malcolm of Scotland defeat Macbeth in 1054, a story later retold by Shakespeare.

Earl Harold's oath to Duke William

Some time in the spring of 1064, Harold made a trip to France and this event highlights the difficulty of establishing truth in history. As seen in Source 8, William of Poitiers provides a detailed Norman view of the visit. According to this version, Harold was travelling on Edward's behalf to confirm the offer of the English throne to Duke William, which had originally been made at some point in 1051 or 1052. En route he was shipwrecked and held captive by the count of Ponthieu for ransom, before being rescued by William and taken to his court. While there, Harold took an oath of loyalty to William. Of his own free will, William of Poitiers continues in his account, he also promised to help Duke William secure the English throne on Edward's death. Before Harold returned to England, William and Harold campaigned in Brittany as brothers in arms. The Bayeux Tapestry provides a visual account of this story including the crucial oath-taking scene, as seen in Source 9.

SOURCE

 8

From *Gesta Guillelmi ducis Normannorum et regis Anglorum* ('The Deeds of William Duke of Normandy and King of England') by William of Poitiers, c1070s. This is a well-informed insider's account of the Norman Conquest. Its main purpose was to celebrate William the Conqueror and provide justification for the invasion. In his youth, William of Poitiers had served as a knight for Duke William before turning to God and becoming his chaplain.

About the same time (1064), Edward King of the English, who had already established William as his heir and whom he loved as a brother or a son, gave a guarantee more important than anything hitherto. He resolved to forestall the inevitability of death, for whose approaching hour this holy man, seeking heaven, made ready. To confirm his former promise by a further oath he sent to him Harold, of all his subjects the greatest in riches, honour and power...

At a council convened at Bonneville Harold publicly swore fealty to him by the sacred rite of Christians. And according to the entirely truthful relation of certain most notable men of utter integrity who were present at the time, at the end of the oath he freely added the following clauses; that he would be the agent of Duke William at the court of his lord King Edward as long as the latter lived; that he would strive with all his influence and power to bring about the succession of the English kingdom to William after Edward's death; that he would meanwhile hand over to the custody of William's knights Dover castle, fortified by him at his own expense...

Therefore we address these few words to you, Harold. How, after these things, do you dare rob William of his inheritance and wage war upon him whom by sacred oath you have recognised as of your race, and to whom you have committed yourself by hand and mouth? You should have suppressed the opposition which you perniciously incited. Accursed were the favourable winds which filled your ill-omened sails on your return! Wicked was the unruffled sea which could endure to bear you, basest of men, to the shore! Doomed was the peaceful port which received you who were bringing so great a calamity to your country!

AS Level Exam-Style Question Section A

How much weight do you give to the evidence of Source 8 for an enquiry into the strength of William's claim to the throne?

Explain your answer using the source, the information given about it and your own knowledge of the historical context. (12 marks)

Tip

When weighing up a source, remember to look at both sides of the debate and consider its reliability as a source of evidence.

SOURCE 9 A scene from the Bayeux Tapestry, probably produced in Kent around 1070 on the orders of Bishop Odo of Bayeux. The text states 'Where Harold made an oath to Duke William'.

However, it is hard to accept fully version of event of William of Poitiers. If Edward did want Duke William as his successor, it raises the question of why he did not follow up Harold's trip by announcing it formally, summoning William to his court, granting him land or hostages or even crowning William in his own lifetime. It also seems highly unlikely that Harold would have been prepared to make such a trip and offer. As the most powerful man in a country that lacked a direct heir and as a king in all but name, it seems natural to assume that Harold would be casting his own eyes over the throne by this stage. There is also no corroboration of William of Poitiers's version of the story in the two main English sources, the *Anglo-Saxon Chronicle* and *Vita Edwardi*. Finally, the oath-taking scene in the Bayeux Tapestry does not provide complete confirmation of William of Poitiers's account. The commentary in the border states 'Where Harold made an oath to Duke William' but is silent as to what the oath was about, even though there is room for an explanatory phrase. This omission must be seen as deliberate and perhaps reflects doubts on this key part of William of Poitiers's story. The tapestry also places the oath-taking at Bayeux whereas William of Poitiers puts it as Bonneville. Such inconsistencies undermine overall credibility.

Instead, rather than an accurate retelling of history, this Norman version of events may have been produced in order to justify the Norman invasion. In it Harold conveniently becomes a perjurer and usurper by accepting the crown in 1066. These were serious charges and Duke William could have used them to win papal support for the invasion. It would, however, be unrealistic to think this was all a complete fabrication by the Norman court and no visit or oath took place. It is possible to imagine other reasons for Harold's visit to Normandy, such as ascertaining if William would support his own bid for the throne or trying to secure the release of two of his nephews and his brother. They had been held hostage in Normandy following the short-lived exile of the Godwin family in 1051. While in William's court, it is possible that an oath could have been extorted from Harold. After all, he was in a weak position. He had been freed from imprisonment by William who also held members of his family hostage and he might only have been able to escape from Normandy by agreeing to William's demands. If this was the case, according to the standards of the day, the oath would not have been binding.

Alternatively, Harold may have made some other kind of promise to William, such as an oath of friendship between England and Normandy. Significantly, the *Vita Edwardi* does state that Harold was too free with oaths. As we will never know for certain what happened, it is instead better to think in terms of possibilities and probabilities.

The Northumbrian uprising

In a fascinating section, the *Vita Edwardi* compares Harold and Tostig. Both brothers were strong, brave and handsome. It praises Tostig for his loyalty to his wife but offers no comment on Harold, a silent admonishment of his womanising. Where Harold was open, Tostig was secretive. Harold aimed at happiness and acted in a prudent way politically, whereas Tostig aimed for success and acted vigorously. In a telling phrase, it also states that Tostig was sometimes overzealous in attacking evil and this is what proved his undoing in Northumbria. A wild and lawless kingdom, strangers had to travel in groups of 30 or more to avoid being attacked. Blood feuds were endemic and local nobles acted as crime lords. After being appointed earl of Northumbria in 1055, Tostig attempted to bring this region under control, but in so doing he acquired a reputation as a tyrant. He employed brutal tactics and funded his efforts by raising taxes. The fact that he was a southerner ruling over the fiercely independent North only added to his unpopularity. It proved too much when Tostig arranged the murder of three local magnates and, in 1065, the Northumbrians rose up. Tostig's housecarls were slaughtered, his treasure plundered and Morcar, son of Earl Aelfgar of Mercia, was installed as the new earl. The rebels then began to march south, sacking Lincoln, Nottingham, Derby and Northampton and threatening the stability of England. The king placed Harold in charge of finding a solution but also made it clear at a royal council in Britford near Salisbury that he wanted the rebels defeated and his favourite, Tostig, restored. Harold argued that this would result in civil war and foreign enemies would take advantage. The king was overruled and no army was raised. At a full assembly at Oxford in October, Morcar was elected as earl and Harold sent his brother into exile. Tostig fled to Flanders, vowing revenge.

EXTEND YOUR KNOWLEDGE

Morcar

Morcar was grandson of Earl Leofric of Northumbria and son of Aelfgar, the rebellious earl of Mercia who joined forces with Gruffydd ap Llewelyn. Morcar's elder brother, Edwin, became earl of Mercia on their father's death in 1062, while Morcar became earl of Northumbria in 1065. As will be seen, both brothers would be brought to ruin by the Norman Conquest.

Harold could be viewed as acting for the good of the nation by putting his country before his brother. Alternatively, by not fighting too hard for Tostig he may have been removing a rival for the throne. At the most extreme, Tostig charged Harold with fermenting the rebellion himself, something which Harold strongly denied. The uprising mattered because Harold now had a dangerous enemy and the unity of the Godwin family had been shattered. This unity had been the key to its success and its loss would play a large part in Harold's downfall in 1066.

ACTIVITY
KNOWLEDGE CHECK

1 Write down five reasons to explain why the Godwin family was so powerful.

2 To what extent can Edward the Confessor be criticised for not limiting the power of the Godwin family?

3 How useful is Source 7 for explaining the dominant position of Harold Godwinson?

4 Why did it take Harold so long to defeat Gruffydd ap Llewelyn?

5 Do you agree with Source 8 that Harold took an oath of loyalty to William?

6 Do you think Harold made the correct choice in expelling his brother Tostig from his earldom?

WHAT WERE THE EARLY THREATS TO HAROLD'S THRONE?

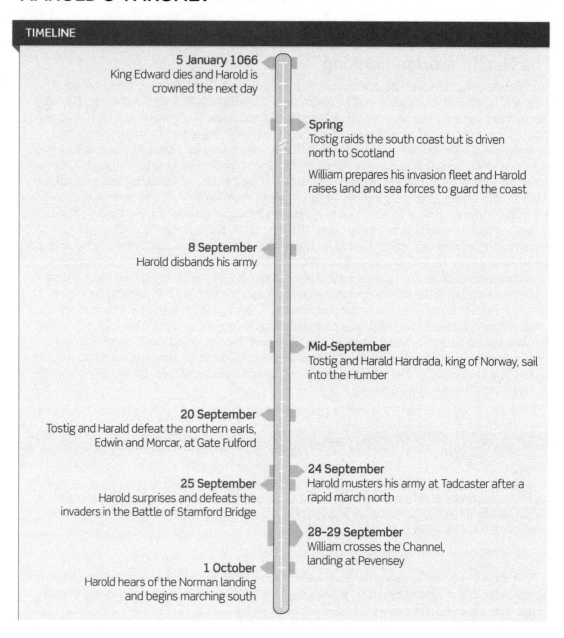

TIMELINE

5 January 1066
King Edward dies and Harold is crowned the next day

Spring
Tostig raids the south coast but is driven north to Scotland

William prepares his invasion fleet and Harold raises land and sea forces to guard the coast

8 September
Harold disbands his army

Mid-September
Tostig and Harald Hardrada, king of Norway, sail into the Humber

20 September
Tostig and Harald defeat the northern earls, Edwin and Morcar, at Gate Fulford

24 September
Harold musters his army at Tadcaster after a rapid march north

25 September
Harold surprises and defeats the invaders in the Battle of Stamford Bridge

28–29 September
William crosses the Channel, landing at Pevensey

1 October
Harold hears of the Norman landing and begins marching south

Edward's death

While exiled in Normandy from around 1016, Edward made a promise to complete a pilgrimage to Rome if he ever returned to England. When he did return, Edward soon found that the pressures of ruling gave him no time to keep his promise and so he sought atonement by building Westminster Abbey. It was consecrated on 28 December 1065. By this stage, Edward was dying and the leading figures of Anglo-Saxon England gathered. A vigil was kept by his favourites including Queen Edith, Archbishop Stigand and Harold. Perhaps due to a vow of celibacy or an inability of Queen Edith to conceive, there was no son in attendance. Slipping in and out of consciousness, Edward spoke of terrible prophecies in which England was consumed by fire and abandoned to the devil. What happened next is crucial. Did Edward offer the throne to Harold? As Sources 10–17 show, both Norman and Saxon accounts, in varying degrees of firmness, seem to suggest that Edward's last act was to appoint Harold as successor. This mattered, because according to the standards of the time a dying man's last words were the most solemn that could be spoken. On 5 January 1066, Edward died. Edward was buried in Westminster the next day. His shrine can still be visited today, although in a much adorned state following the rebuilding of the abbey under Henry III.

A scene from the Bayeux Tapestry, probably produced in Kent around 1070 on the orders of Bishop Odo of Bayeux. The text reads 'Here King Edward in bed addresses his faithful friends; and here he is dead'.

From *Vita Edwardi Regis*, an anonymous work written c1065–67 and dedicated to Queen Edith, daughter of Earl Godwin and wife of Edward the Confessor.

Let us describe how this gem of God stripped off the corruption of his earthly body and obtained a place of eternal splendour in the diadem of the heavenly king. When he was sick unto death and his men stood and wept bitterly, he said 'Do not weep, but intercede with God for my soul, and give me leave to go to Him.' ... Then he addressed his last words to the queen who was sitting at his feet, in this wise, 'May God be gracious to this my wife for the zealous solicitude of her service. For she has served me devotedly, and has always stood close by my side like a beloved daughter. And so from the forgiving God may she obtain the reward of eternal happiness.' And stretching forth his hand to his governor, her brother, Harold, he said, 'I commend this woman and all the kingdom to your protection. Serve and honour her with faithful obedience as your lady and sister, which she is, and do not despoil her, as long as she lives, of any due honour got for me. Likewise I also commend those men who have left their native land for love of me, and have up till now served me faithfully.

The claimants

The vacillating Edward must accept a measure of responsibility for the succession crisis that followed his death. There were, by this stage, numerous contenders to the throne. Aside from the deathbed offer to Harold, Edward had possibly pledged the crown to William in 1051, reconfirming the offer in 1054, although the unreliability of the Norman accounts makes the truth of this hard to establish. For a time he also seems to have pinned hopes for an heir on surviving members of the royal house of Wessex. While Edward's half-brother, Edmund Ironside, had been killed by Canute

An entry for 1065 from the *Anglo-Saxon Chronicle*, Abingdon Manuscript C. The same verse also appears in the Worcester Manuscript D.

The blameless king was ever blithe of mood,

Though long before, bereft of land,

He lived in paths of exile widely through the world,

After Cnut had overcome the race of Aethelred

And Danes ruled the dear Kingdom

Of England for 28 years

In number, dispensed riches.

Afterwards came forth, noble in array,

A king good in virtues, pure and mild;

The princely Edward defended homeland,

Country and nation, until the very bitter death

Suddenly came and seized so dear

A prince from the earth. Angels conveyed the

Righteous soul into heaven's light.

However, the wise man committed the kingdom

To a distinguished man, Harold himself,

A princely earl, who at all times

Loyally obeyed his superior

In words and deed, neglecting nothing

Of which the nation's king was in need.

in 1016, Edmund Ironside's child Edmund the Atheling, meaning 'the man of royal descent', had survived, growing up in the court of the king of Hungary. In 1054, Edward charged Ealdred, bishop of Worcester, with the task of bringing Edmund out of exile. Although initial attempts at persuasion failed, the prince finally returned in 1057, only to die soon afterwards in mysterious circumstances. The king took Edmund's young son, Edgar, into his care and, by 1066, aged 15, he had the strongest bloodline claim to the throne. While the hereditary principle carried great weight in Anglo-Saxon England, the lack of any fixed laws governing the process of succession meant that it was not absolute. Adding to the complexity was a slender claim from King Harald III Sigurdsson of Norway, otherwise known as 'Hardrada' or 'Hard ruler'. Hardrada was an opportunist for sure, but he was also a legend in his own lifetime. Reputedly just over two metres tall and built like a bear, he had honed his marshal skills fighting for the Byzantine imperial guard in Constantinople.

The Coronation

The task of sorting out this dangerous tangle fell to the nation's leaders in the witan. It was this body that had endorsed Edward's own ascent to kingship in 1042 and it met on the same day as the funeral to decide his successor. This meeting is therefore a crucial event in the story of 1066, although there are no detailed accounts of who attended or what was discussed. It seems likely, though, that all the leading magnates and clergy were present. They had already assembled in Westminster for the abbey's consecration as well as the traditional Christmas witan and would no doubt have stayed on when it became clear that Edward was dying. This is also backed up by the names on the witness lists of charters issued around this time. At the meeting it is probable that Edward's dying words would have been given prominence. They would also have discussed the strengths of Harold, the youth of Edgar the Atheling and the dangers posed by outsiders. The outcome is, of course, known and Harold was crowned later the same day.

Historians are still undecided about how to view the witan's decision and the rapid coronation. It could be seen as a ***coup d'état*** by Harold but once again it is a matter of possibilities and probabilities. A convincing case can be made that the witan positively approved Harold becoming king rather than just acquiescing to it. Representing the combined weight of the English political nation, it was not a group to be easily overawed. It had seen Harold's track record in government as sub-king and it also knew that, unlike Edgar the Atheling, Harold was a warrior in his prime capable of protecting England. By now the threat of invasion from the rival claimants in Normandy and Scandinavia was a dawning possibility. Capping it all, Harold had the blessing of the outgoing king.

The principal Norman and English sources are equally divided over the events of 6 January. Sources 13 and 14 show that, for the Normans, Harold's coronation had no legitimacy. It represented first and foremost a betrayal of his sacred oath to William. In Norman eyes, this should have led Harold to reject all offers of the crown. They also portrayed it as a *coup d'état*, further undermined by associating his crowning with the controversial Stigand, who was both archbishop of Canterbury and bishop of Winchester, and thus condemned by the pope for holding two offices. In stark contrast, the English monk John of Worcester raised the possibility (Source 15) that Harold was crowned by Archbishop Ealdred of York, who, unlike Stigand, was in possession of a valid **pallium** from the pope. As Sources 16 and 17 show, there are also subtle differences in the different versions of the *Anglo-Saxon Chronicle*, with version E giving Harold the backing of the political nation, unlike versions C and D.

SOURCE

13 From *Gesta Guillelmi ducis Normannorum et regis Anglorum* by William of Poitiers, c1070s. William of Poitiers was chaplain to William the Conqueror at the time of the Norman invasion.

And now unexpectedly there came a true report, the land of England was bereft of her king Edward, and his crown was worn by Harold. Not for this insane Englishmen the decision of a public choice, but, on that sorrowful day when the best of kings was buried and the whole nation mourned his passing, he seized the royal throne with the plaudits of certain iniquitous supporters and thereby perjured himself. He was made king by the unholy consecration of Stigand, who had been deprived of his ministry by the justified fervour of papal anathema. Duke William took counsel with his vassals and determined to avenge the wrong by arms and in arms to claim his inheritance, although many magnates argued persuasively against the enterprise as too hazardous and far beyond the resources of Normandy.

SOURCE 14
A scene from the Bayeux Tapestry showing the coronation of Harold by Archbishop Stigand. The tapestry was probably produced in Kent around 1070 on the orders of Bishop Odo of Bayeux.

SOURCE 15
From *The Chronicles* by John of Worcester, c1140. He was a monk from Worcester who based his work on a now lost version of the *Anglo-Saxon Chronicle*.

[Edward] met his death at London, and was royally buried the next day, most bitterly lamented, not without tears by all who were present. When he was entombed, the underking Harold, son of Earl Godwin, whom the king had chosen before his demise as successor to the kingdom, was elected by the primates of all England to the dignity of kingship, and was consecrated king with due ceremony by Ealdred, archbishop of York, on the same day.

SOURCE 16
An entry for 1065 from the *Anglo-Saxon Chronicle*, Worcester Manuscript D. The Abingdon C version is broadly similar.

And King Edward came to Westminster towards midwinter, and had consecrated there that minster which he himself built to the glory of God and St Peter and all God's saints; and the church consecration was on Holy Innocents' Day; and he passed away on the eve of Twelfth Night, and he was buried on Twelfth Night in the same minster. And here also Harold became consecrated as king, and he experienced little quietness in it while he ruled his kingdom.

SOURCE 17
An entry for 1065 from the *Anglo-Saxon Chronicle*, Peterborough Manuscript E.

In this year [1065] the minister at Westminster was consecrated on Holy Innocents' Day, and the king Edward passed away on the eve of the Twelfth Night and was buried on Twelfth Night inside the newly consecrated church in Westminster. And Earl Harold succeeded to the kingdom of England just as the king granted it him – and also men chose him for it – and was blessed as king on Twelfth Night.

EXTRACT 1

From *In Search of the Dark Ages* by Michael Wood, published in 2005.

Earl Harold seized the throne and was crowned in the abbey. It was alleged by some that on his deathbed Edward had put his kingdom in Harold's protection, and the Bayeux Tapestry portrays such a scene. But the unseemly haste of the earl's consecration indicates the true nature of the changeover: an all powerful dynasty, not of royal blood, had effectively usurped the throne... It was a coup d'etat carried off with great speed and purpose.

EXTRACT 2

From *1066: A New History of the Norman Conquest* by Peter Rex, published in 2011.

It was not a matter of undue haste and there was nothing improper about it. It was a matter of simple convenience and a response to the need for a King to be chosen as soon as possible... Everyone of importance was present. It was not a Witan liable to be overawed by the prestige of Earl Harold. Given the constant threat presented by the Scandinavian kings, aware that the exiled Earl Tostig could well attempt a come back, and possibly aware also ... of the ambitions of William the Bastard, it was essential that a King be chosen.

With powerful forces circling, England's new king issued coins with the inscription '*PAX*' ('Peace') and an image of himself wearing the crown and clutching his rod of justice. Harold, though, could not relax. Aside from the threat from Hardrada and William, his vengeful brother, Tostig, was sheltering in the court of Flanders. On England's northern border was the opportunist Malcolm, king of Scotland. Although Edwin and Morcar had given him their support in the witan, he also knew there was still a danger of internal division. This is why Harold travelled north at Easter to warn of the dangers of a house divided. Around this time Harold also made another political move by marrying Eadgyth, the sister of the two northern earls.

> **AS Level Exam-Style Question Section A**
>
> How accurate is it to say that Harold Godwinson was able to dominate Edward the Confessor because of his military reputation? (20 marks)
>
> **Tip**
> *Beside the outcomes of the Welsh wars, consider why else Harold was in a strong position.*

The Battle of Gate Fulford

The Bayeux Tapestry shows King Harold sitting uneasily on his throne. Above him blazes Halley's Comet, below are the ghostly portents of invading ships. Harold suspected that he would have to fight and kill in 1066 but he did not expect the first blow to be from his brother. Emboldened by a joint invasion pact with Hardrada for later in the summer, Tostig appeared off the Isle of Wight in May. With a fleet of 60 vessels, he pillaged the south and east coasts, before sailing into the protection of Scottish waters.

It had not been a successful foray, as losses and desertions left Tostig with only 12 ships. Crucially though, as seen in Source 18, Harold interpreted the raid as a precursor to a full-scale Norman invasion. This corresponded with intelligence he had received of a developing Norman fleet and as a result he mobilised the **fyrd** and summoned his elite housecarls.

> **KEY TERM**
>
> Fyrd
> Freemen who were called up to serve in the army for a set period of time when the king needed them. The Anglo-Saxon army consisted of lightly armed peasants led by thegns who were well armed with helmets, chain mail coats, swords or battleaxes. While the thegns also had horses, these were used for riding to the battlefield, where they would then dismount. Both groups normally fought on foot.

The normal period of fyrd service was two months. Now, with an army of perhaps 10,000 and a fleet of 700 ships to support, the logistical clock began to tick. Calculating that Normandy rather than Norway was the real danger and believing the defence of the North could be left to Edwin and Morcar, Harold chose to base his forces on the south coast. Throughout the summer, the navy made regular patrols, hoping to intercept and potentially destroy the Norman fleet. It did not appear. Unfavourable northerly winds kept William at bay and on 8 September, with supplies running low and having kept his forces in the field for an unprecedented four months, Harold was forced to demobilise.

SOURCE 18

An entry for 1066 from the *Anglo-Saxon Chronicle*, Abingdon Manuscript C.

Earl Tostig came from overseas into the Isle of Wight with as large a fleet as he could muster and both money and provisions were given him. And then he went away from there and did damage everywhere along the sea-coast wherever he could reach, until he came to Sandwich. When King Harold, who was in London, was informed that Tostig his brother was come to Sandwich, he assembled a naval force and a land force larger than any king had assembled before in this country, because he had been told as a fact that Count William from Normandy, King Edward's kinsman, meant to come here and subdue this country... Then King Harold came to Sandwich and waited for his fleet there, because it was long before it could be assembled; and when his fleet was assembled, he went into the Isle of Wight, and lay there all that summer and autumn; and a land force was kept everywhere along by the sea, though in the end it was no use. When it was the Feast of the Nativity of St Mary [8 September], the provisions of the people were gone and nobody could keep them there any longer. Then the men were allowed to go home, and the king rode inland, and the ships were brought up to London.

A week later and powered by the same wind that had curtailed William, Hardrada arrived off the coast of north-west England. His 300 longships full of warriors joined Tostig's much smaller fleet in rowing up the River Ouse before disembarking at Riccall. Their destination was the old Viking stronghold of York, about 16 kilometres away.

Tostig had promised Hardrada that the North would rally to their banner but at Gate Fulford, about three kilometres short of their target, Edwin's and Morcar's men formed up and blocked the road. It was 20 September and the first of the year's three great battles was about to begin.

To the right flank of the English army lay the river, with marsh to the left. Numbers stood at around 6,000 men apiece, all on foot. The battle commenced with a Saxon charge into the Viking right under the command of Tostig, successfully pressing it back. Experience now told and Hardrada sensed an opportunity. He wheeled his left forces round and smashed into the side of the advancing English. After a short but intensive fight, the Saxons broke and in trying to escape the pincer movement many lost their lives in the marsh. In truth the outcome was not surprising. Edwin, the eldest at around 18, and Morcar were both inexperienced. Many of their fyrdmen who made up the bulk of their army were just as green. They faced hardened warriors well used to fighting together and a leader of exceptional quality. Finally, as seen in Source 19, the confined geography of the battlefield meant that any Viking surge would have fatal results. The battle cost the English around 1,000 lives, including many of the experienced housecarls. Although both northern earls lived to fight another day, they now had no immediate capacity to supply Harold with fresh troops.

SOURCE

19

From *The Saga of Harald Sigurtharson* by Snorri Sturluson, c1230. Sturluson was an Icelandic historian, poet and politician. Although historians cast doubt on the validity of much of his writing as it mixes fact with mythology, it is still considered a useful source for highlighting otherwise little-known aspects of history.

King Harald lay in the Ouse when the army of the earls (Edwin and Morcar) came down from the land to oppose him. Then the king went on land and began to array his army for battle. One wing stood on the bank of the river, the other was arrayed further up on land, and extended to a ditch. There was a swamp, deep and broad and full of water. The earls deployed their army down along the river with the whole body of their men. The royal banner was close by the river. There the king's men stood thickest, and the lines were thinnest by the ditch, with the troops he could least rely on. Then the earls proceeded down along the ditch. There the wing of the Norwegian army extending to the ditch gave way, and the English followed them up, thinking that the Norwegians were about to flee. That part of the English army was led by Morcar.

But when King Harald saw that the battle array of the English had come down along the ditch right opposite them, he had the trumpets blown and sharply urged on his men to the attack, raising his banner called Landwaster. And there so strong an attack was made by him that nothing held against it. Then there was a great slaughter among the earl's men. Soon their army took to flight. Some fled up or down along the river, but most leapt into the ditch. There the bodies of the fallen lay so thick that the Norwegians could walk dry-shod over the swamp.

EXTEND YOUR KNOWLEDGE

Sources of narrative

Source 19 helps demonstrate how historians work. As the only detailed account of the Battle of Gate Fulford, it forms the basis for almost all later writing on this subject. In several different history books that feature the Battle of Gate Fulford, it is possible to recognise parts of this source being reused with perhaps additional layers of analysis being added.

AS Level Exam-Style Question Section A

Why is Source 19 valuable to the historian for an enquiry into the outcome of the Battle of Gate Fulford?

Explain your answer using the source, the information given about it and your own knowledge of the historical context. (8 marks)

Tip

What useful information does the source provide and what is significant about its provenance?

The Battle of Stamford Bridge

Beacon fires would first have brought the news of the Viking invasion to Harold. Still with a credible Norman threat, Harold also knew the Vikings had to be stopped and he at once began raising a new army. Assembling his housecarls in London, he commenced a forced march along the old Roman road of Ermine Street and covered a spectacular 300 kilometres in five days. Along the way his numbers were swelled by local recruits. It was a bold strategy as it risked tiring his men, but Harold wanted to prevent Hardrada from having the chance to consolidate his hold. He was also planning on taking the Vikings by surprise. Reaching Tadcaster, about 24 kilometres from York, late on 24 September, Harold heard the enemy was camped at Stamford Bridge and decided to attack the next day.

The first the Vikings knew of the Anglo-Saxon's presence was an approaching cloud of dust. By then, the Anglo-Saxons were around one and a half kilometres away. Surprise was total. Many Vikings did not even have their protective mail coats on. The fighting that followed was ferocious and had three phases.

The first was an initial delaying action by a small group of Vikings on the west bank of the River Derwent, the task eventually falling to a lone Viking on the bridge itself. He cut down perhaps 40 Anglo-Saxons singlehandedly. Once the Anglo-Saxons were through onto the east bank, the main phase took place on ground now called Battle Flats. The Norsemen formed a traditional shield wall and a battle of attrition ensued as the Anglo-Saxon housecarls launched sustained attacks. It was during this stage that Hardrada was cut down by an arrow to the throat. The final phase was entered when Viking reinforcements arrived from Riccall where they had been protecting the fleet. This brought an initial boost but by dusk the Viking shield wall had disintegrated and they were being ruthlessly hunted down.

SOURCE 20

The Battle of Stamford Bridge (1870) by Peter Nicolai Arbo, a Norwegian historical painter who specialised in scenes from Norwegian history and Norse mythology. This painting captures the final moments of Hardrada and shows the Anglo-Saxons fighting on horseback, something that is widely accepted as not happening.

Why an experienced Viking force was overcome is a key question. Harold's tactic of surprise worked. It is doubtful that Hardrada had time to form his army up properly. His troops were also vulnerable in close combat as many had left their mail coats at Riccall with the fleet, due to the warm weather and a complacent belief that there was no immediate threat. Although exact numbers are not known, Harold certainly had the advantage. This was possibly in the order of two to one as Hardrada made the fatal mistake of dividing his forces by leaving a significant part to protect his fleet. When these reinforcements did arrive, they were exhausted after a march in full kit. In terms of equipment and tactics, though, both sides were very similar, fighting on foot in a shield wall with the battleaxe as the weapon of choice. The loss of Hardrada so early on in the fight was a severe blow and Tostig was killed soon after. Finally, the underlying Anglo-Saxon military system must also be given credit as it allowed Harold to mobilise and deploy a force at very short notice.

The Battle of Stamford Bridge deserves to be better known. The forced march and surprise attack represented outstanding military skill. It was one of the heaviest defeats suffered by the Vikings at the hands of the English and it put an end to any further Norse invasions. It is said that even a century later unburied Viking bones still littered the battle site. Most importantly, one day after the battle the wind shifted and the Norman fleet could depart. Landing 400 kilometres to the south at Pevensey, Harold now had to face his most deadly opponent with an exhausted and depleted army.

ACTIVITY
KNOWLEDGE CHECK

1 To what extent could it be said that Edward the Confessor had no clear policy for his succession?

2 To what extent do you agree with the historian Michael Wood's view in Extract 1 that Harold seized power in a *coup d'état*?

3 What does Source 18 reveal about the problems King Harold faced in the summer of 1066?

4 Use Source 19 to create a sketch map of the Battle of Gate Fulford, showing the position of the armies, geographical features and key lines of movement.

5 How useful is Source 20 as a depiction of the Battle of Stamford Bridge?

6 In what ways was Stamford Bridge a significant battle?

ACTIVITY
SUMMARY

1 Create a diagram showing the structure of Anglo-Saxon government from the king down to the vill. Make sure you include the role and powers of each level. Then add in any limitations on the king's power.

2 Create a second diagram showing the structure of the legal system. Add separate annotations showing ways in which the legal system was still basic.

3 For each of the following headings, record two pieces of evidence to demonstrate the complexity of the Anglo-Saxon economy: Agriculture, Industry, Towns, Trade, Currency, Tax.

4 Create a spider diagram showing all the reasons why Harold was in a strong position on taking the throne in January 1066. Then add to it all the threats he faced. Where does the balance lie?

5 Provide a summary of the military engagements in this period by completing the table below.

Engagement	Main commanders	Who won	Key reasons for the outcome
Wales			
Gate Fulford			
Stamford Bridge			

WIDER READING

Barlow, F. *Edward the Confessor*, Yale University Press (1997)

Bartlett, R. *England under the Norman and Angevin Kings: 1075–1225*, Oxford University Press (2002)

Rex, P. *1066: A New History of the Norman Conquest*, Amberley Publishing (2011)

Williams, A. *The English and the Norman Conquest*, Boydell Press (1995)

Wood, M. *In Search of the Dark Ages*, BBC Books (2005)

A Level Exam-Style Question Section B

'The Anglo-Saxon kingdom was both strong and successful in the years 1053–66.' How far do you agree with this statement? (20 marks)

Tip
Remember to define the two key terms.

2a.2 The Norman Conquest of England and extension of control in Wales and Scotland, 1066–93

KEY QUESTIONS

- Why was William able to win the Battle of Hastings?
- How did William deal with opposition to his rule?
- How effectively did the Normans deal with the threat posed by Wales and Scotland?
- How did the Normans militarise English society?

INTRODUCTION

William, duke of Normandy, was lucky to survive his youth. He was the product of a tryst between Robert, duke of Normandy and Herleve, the daughter of a Rouen merchant. In 1035, when William was aged around seven, his father embarked on a pilgrimage to the Holy Land. Before leaving and in the absence of a legitimate son, Robert made his leading men swear an oath of loyalty to William. He also took the precaution of appointing guardians to watch over him, including Robert, archbishop of Rouen, Alan, count of Brittany, and Gilbert, count of Brionne. When Duke Robert died on the journey home, it was these men who handed the duchy to William. For the young boy, however, it was far from a blessed inheritance. Normandy descended into violence as leading families sought to capitalise on the lack of central authority to expand their own power. They also struggled to gain control over William and in the process three of his guardians were murdered. On one occasion an assassin stole into William's bedchamber and slit the throat of his steward, Osbern. 'Many times', William is reported to have said by the chronicler Orderic Vitalis, 'I was smuggled secretly out of the castle at night by my Uncle Walter and taken to the cottages and hiding places of the poor, to save me from discovery by traitors who sought my death.' This chapter will examine how the young duke developed into one of the most formidable and ruthless warriors of the age. When he died in 1087, his second son, William Rufus, succeeded to the English throne, while his eldest son, Robert Curthose, became duke of Normandy. William Rufus in particular would attempt to build on William the Conqueror's legacy and this chapter will look at his exploits in Scotland and Wales.

28 September 1066 – William's fleet sails into Pevensey Bay

14 October 1066 – Battle of Hastings
Death of Harold II

1068 – Siege of Exeter
First revolt in the North
Harold's sons raid South West England

1071 – Harrying of the North
King Malcolm III of Scotland raids Northumbria
Hereward the Wake leads rebellion in East Anglia
East Anglian rebels surrender at Ely

1065 — 1070 — 1075

October–December 1066 – William's march to London

25 December 1066 – William I crowned at Westminster Abbey

1067 – Uprising in Kent
Eadric the Wild attacks Hereford

1069 – Two significant uprisings in the North
Further rebellions in the South West and Welsh borders
Danish invasion fleet arrives

1075 – Revolt of three earls against William I

1072 – Peace of Abernethy between William I and King Malcolm

WHY WAS WILLIAM ABLE TO WIN THE BATTLE OF HASTINGS?

William's military experience

William saw his first battle at Val-es-Dunes in 1047, aged 18. By then he was an impressive man, above average in height at 1.75 metres, strongly built and with a harsh, guttural voice. Fighting alongside the French king, Henry I, against rebels in western Normandy, William won praise for his valour. Almost two decades of combat followed as William brought the unruly duchy under his control and dealt with repeated invasions. In the process he was prepared to play the long game. When the rebel leader from Val-es-Dunes, Guy of Burgundy, fled to his near impenetrable castle at Brionne, William besieged it for three years. At other times he realised the effectiveness of sudden violence, as seen in Source 1. When the town of Alençon rebelled against him in 1051 and the castle defenders hung out hides 'for the tanner's son' in reference to his illegitimacy, he captured the fortress, took 32 men captive and cut off their hands and feet. Alençon promptly surrendered and in fear the neighbouring fortress of Domfront, also under siege, gave up as well.

SOURCE

1 From *Gesta Normannorum ducum*. Written c1070 by William of Jumieges and dedicated to William the Conqueror, whose achievements it celebrates.

On the pretext of various disputes, he (Count Geoffrey) began to attack the duke, destroying Normandy by violent pillage and gaining control of the castle of Domfront. The duke came up, ready for war, to reconnoitre Domfront and saw it encircled with steep and lofty crags and inaccessible to assault. Without delay he summoned his Norman forces and constructed strong siege-castles about it to block all access and egress. While he was for some time delayed in these preparations, lo! Scouts arrive and report that the castle of Alençon can be taken without loss. At once the duke set off, leaving a force to man the siege-castles and rode through the night with his army to reach Alençon at dawn. There he found, in a certain castle on the other side of the river, those who mocked him with insults. Whereupon, having roused the ardour of his troops, he took the castle, put it to the flames and burnt it. At his command the mockers had their hands and feet cut off under the eyes of the populace of Alençon. They, dismayed at such severity, fearful lest similar penalties should be inflicted upon them, threw open the gates and surrendered the town.

EXTEND YOUR KNOWLEDGE

Gesta Normannorum ducum ('The Deeds of the Dukes of the Normans') by William of Jumieges, c1070.

A Norman monk and chronicler, William of Jumieges was from the influential and well-connected monastery of Jumieges in Normandy. He wrote the first part of his history about the earlier Norman dukes c1060, updating it with a triumphal account of the Norman Conquest by 1070-71. This makes it the earliest Norman literary source on the events of 1066. The work is dedicated to William the Conqueror and should be viewed as a piece of Norman propaganda. Its main purpose was to legitimise Duke William's succession to the English throne and celebrate his achievements. Mixed in with the obvious bias, however, are many useful observations about events in England and Normandy on either side of 1066. Occasionally, William of Jumieges does make factual errors, saying for example that Harold fell at the beginning rather than the end of the battle, and he seldom gives dates in his writing. Together with William of Poitiers, although not as detailed in his writing, William of Jumieges is the principal Norman source on the Norman Conquest.

William's two greatest enemies during this period were the count of Anjou, Geoffrey Martel, and Henry I of France, who had soon become aware of the threat the duke of Normandy posed. In 1054, they invaded the duchy in a two-pronged assault. In dealing with this, William, in common with most military leaders at the time, displayed a reluctance to fight directly, knowing the grave risks involved. Instead, he divided his forces in two, shadowed the enemy as they advanced and waited for a moment to strike. When Geoffrey's forces were widely scattered while pillaging in the town of Mortemer, William's knights launched a surprise attack. This ambush was so devastating it proved enough to end the invasion. Geoffrey was forced to withdraw, as did Henry when he heard the news that his ally had retreated. A second two-pronged assault came in 1057 and once again William allowed it to penetrate unopposed before picking his moment to respond. This came when Henry was crossing a ford on the Dives River near Varaville and the incoming tide left his army split in two. In a classic ambush William descended on the rearguard and massacred it. This was the last time a French king invaded Normandy in William's lifetime.

1080 – Robert, son of William I, campaigns in Scotland against King Malcolm

9 September 1087 – Death of William I; he is succeeded by his son William Rufus

1092 – William II campaigns in Cumbria

| 1080 | 1085 | 1090 | 1095 |

1081 – William leads military expedition into Wales

1093 – Norman control in Wales is at its height

November 1093 – King Malcolm of Scotland is ambushed and killed

In 1060, both Henry I and Geoffrey Martel died. The new French king, Philip I, was a minor and the county of Anjou lapsed into civil war. William could now take the initiative. In 1063, he took the province of Maine after carrying out a policy of deliberate destruction to spread terror. In 1064, Brittany was subdued. These victories meant that William had fully secured the borders of Normandy, which would be of crucial advantage to him in 1066. By now he was also a formidable warrior, who knew how to co-ordinate complex campaigns, build, take and defend castles, lead lightening raids and ambushes, and waste land. Around him he had assembled a loyal and dependable body of men. His closest friends were William fitzOsbern, the son of William's murdered steward, Osbern, and Roger of Montgomery, the son of the man who had arranged that murder. Although an unlikely pairing, like William they were young, ambitious and warlike. Put simply, William and his followers were good at fighting because they liked it. The one weakness was that, apart from the battle at Val-es-Dunes, William had little experience of set-piece battles.

Invasion preparations

On hearing the news of Harold's coronation, William began preparing for war. His first step was to secure the backing of his nobility. Many needed persuading, believing that it was too hazardous and beyond the resources of Normandy. Through force of personality and promise of great rewards, he won them over in a series of assemblies. Meanwhile, as part of a diplomatic assault, a formal protest was sent to Harold, while the Norman case was set out before Pope Alexander by Lanfranc, abbot of St Stephen in Caen. Although the exact details are not known, it is probable that he stressed Harold's perjury as well as the moral corruption of the English Church, as exemplified by the pluralism of Archbishop Stigand (see page 186). The pope was convinced and sent William his papal banner as blessing. This mattered because the venture now had the blessing and support of the head of the Church. Soldiers from outside Normandy and especially from Brittany, Ponthieu and Flanders flocked to join his banner, also lured by the promise of riches and William's outstanding military reputation.

William then began the immense logistical task of mustering his invasion force. The Ship Lists shown in Source 2 give an idea of the sheer size of the invasion fleet, as well as its significant leaders. By August it was ready, lying off Dives-sur-Mer, while an army of perhaps 10,000 men lay in camp. It has been calculated that to maintain this force for one month would have required 9,000 cartloads of food and fuel and 5,000 cartloads of waste going the opposite way. The 2,000 war horses alone would have needed 13 tonnes of both grain and hay a day. It is therefore a significant achievement that William kept his army provisioned from around August to October without the need to pillage the surrounding countryside. William also seems to have avoided the other curses of large military encampments: ill-discipline and disease. In September, he moved his fleet to the mouth of the River Somme, to exploit the shorter crossing, and then waited for a favourable wind.

SOURCE 2

The Ship Lists of William the Conqueror detailing the contributions of ships and soldiers made by his magnates in 1066. It dates from c1067 to 1072 and was probably drawn up in the abbey of Fecamp. As a coastal monastery, Fecamp must have had a particular interest in the maritime crossing, while monks also acted as the chief archivists of the age, helping preserve what was deemed significant information.

When William, duke of the Normans, came to England to acquire the throne, which by right was owed to him, he received from William fitzOsbern the steward sixty ships; from Hugh, who later became earl of Chester, the same; from Hugh of Montfort fifty ships and sixty soldiers; from Remigius, almoner of Fecamp who later became bishop of Lincoln, one ship and twenty soldiers; from Nicholas, abbot of Saint-Ouen fifteen ships and one hundred soldiers; from Robert, count of Eu, sixty ships; from Fulk of Anjou forty ships; from Gerald the steward the same number; from William, count of Evreux eighty ships; from Roger of Montgomery sixty ships; from Roger of Beaumont sixty ships; from Odo, bishop of Bayeux, one hundred ships; from Robert of Mortain one hundred and twenty ships; from Walter Giffard thirty ships and one hundred solders. Apart from these ships which all together totalled one thousand the duke had many other ships from his other men according to their means. The duke's wife Matilda, who later became queen, in honour of her husband had a ship prepared called 'Mora' in which the duke went across. On its prow Matilda had fitted a statue of a child who with his right hand pointed to England and with his left hand held an ivory horn against his mouth.

EXTEND YOUR KNOWLEDGE

Why did William wait to invade?
The huge logistical challenge of maintaining an army in the field does raise the question of why William waited so long before putting to sea. The traditional explanation put forward by Norman chroniclers is that the wind was in the wrong direction. This is plausible given the basic state of sailing vessels at the time, while for the Normans it also has the advantage of placing the ultimate responsibility in God's hands. Alternatively, it may be that William, aware of how risky a landing would be, deliberately delayed so that the English fyrd guarding the coast would run out of provisions.

The fleet of ships arrived off the shingle beach at Pevensey on the morning of 28 September. Landing on hostile terrain, the success of the whole enterprise now depended on William's military leadership and judgement. His first steps onto English soil could not have been more inauspicious. Stumbling, William loudly proclaimed to his aghast soldiers that he was seizing England with both hands, as related by William of Poitiers. In truth William could not have been more lucky. Had he landed in summer he would have been met with immediate resistance. From Pevensey William quickly moved to Hastings, which had the benefit of a large harbour as well as a defensible location in the event of a retreat. Strategically astute, William knew that it was in his interest to fight a tired Harold quickly and in a place of his choosing. A long delay would open up problems of provisioning and maintaining morale. At its worst, William could find himself facing winter blockaded in the Hastings peninsula by the Saxon fleet on one side and a reformed Saxon army on the other. William's plan was simple, to tempt Harold into early battle. William therefore sent his armies to ravage the surrounding lands, which formed part of Harold's Wessex earldom. The Bayeux Tapestry shows houses and huts being burnt to the ground while terrified occupants cower outside.

The choices Harold now made in response to William's provocation would provide the context in which the Battle of Hastings was fought. The new king did not hesitate. From York, he raced his army down the old Roman road of Ermine Street, stopping on the way at his foundation of Waltham Abbey to pray for victory. He covered the 305 kilometres in eight days. Five days were spent in London gathering what forces he could before a further 149 kilometres forced march south took him to the enemy. Harold's decision to force an early confrontation can be seen as reckless in the extreme and the result of his personal desire to avenge the damage done to his Wessex lands. While Harold can be seen as falling into William's trap, there is some rationale to his decision. He did not know whether William was receiving reinforcements from the continent and so growing stronger by the day. As lord and king he felt morally bound to help his subjects. It also presented Harold with attractive military options. He may have been thinking of launching a Stamford Bridge style surprise attack or else bottling William up in the Hastings peninsula, where he would soon run out of supplies. Both scenarios required him to move fast. Ultimately, though, it was a poor choice. It meant that Harold arrived for battle with exhausted troops and, crucially, reinforcements still on their way. A few more days would have resulted in a much more formidable army, including the archers he was forced to leave behind at Stamford Bridge as well as housecarls from Edwin and Morcar. In addition, he could have brought his fleet to bear by cutting off William's supply lines. William's plan had, however, worked and these options were closed down.

Late on Friday 13 October, the Saxon arrival in the Hastings peninsula was spotted by Norman scouts, removing Harold's option of a Stamford Bridge style surprise attack. Both sides knew the morning would bring battle. Norman sources claim the Saxons spent that night drinking and feasting and the Normans in silent prayer. There is little truth in this. Instead, like all soldiers preparing for battle, it would have been a tense and nervous time. At first light, initial manoeuvring saw Harold occupy the high ground on Senlac Hill. For William the challenge was clear. For him to march on London and secure the crown, Harold had to be removed from the hill and defeated that day. For Harold a simple draw would suffice.

The armies of Harold and William

Harold formed his army up along the crest of the ridge occupying a front just under one kilometre in length. At the crown lay his own position and the two standards, the Dragon of Wessex and the Fighting Man. Although estimates vary, his army probably stood at between 7,000 and 8,000 men. His infantry was organised in ten ranks, all on foot, with the well-armed and equipped housecarls and thegns at the front, forming a protective shield wall and assuming the place of greatest danger. Behind them were the fyrdmen, lightly armed with spear or battleaxe and shield.

Harold's plan seems to have been to hold this strong position where the Norman cavalry would be least effective and take any opportunities that were offered. He spoke to his men, stressing their invincibility if they stood firm. Shouting the English war cry of 'Ut, ut' ('Out, out') and beating their shields, these troops now fired for battle were able to look down the slope towards the assembling Normans. The Norman army was similar in size but contained a higher proportion of professional fighting men. It also had a very different composition. William placed his archers and crossbowmen in the front line, then the heavy infantry in hauberks (chain mail tunics) carrying spears and at the rear the elite **knights** on war horses. This reflected the sequence of planned attack. William also divided the army into three divisions. On the left were the Bretons, in the centre the Normans, on the right the French. Finally, William placed himself at the centre, armed with a mace and riding his Spanish warhorse 'so that he could direct operations on all sides with hand and voice', as William of Poitiers writes. William warned his men that retreat was impossible and defeat would mean death. He spoke of Harold's broken oath and reminded them that God was on their side and the pope had blessed their crusade. Alongside him flew the papal banner.

KEY TERM

Knight
A mounted soldier with arms and armour. In battle knights were organised into conroi or squadrons, each having its own distinctive pennant or banner known as a gonfanon.

Senlac Hill would therefore see a clash between two distinct armies. The Anglo-Saxons represented the old guard, fighting on foot in the style of the Vikings. This had disadvantages. In particular, it was hard for a leader on foot truly to command his army once battle had commenced, although his presence in the battle line must have boosted the morale and fighting spirit of his men. The Norman use of mounted knights and archers represented the future of medieval warfare and these assets would prove crucial in William's ultimate victory. However, it is wrong to assume that the outcome was inevitable. Both armies were capable of carrying the day. Although Harold was weakened by the loss of so many trained fighters at Stamford Bridge and limited in his ability to command, he had the advantage of holding the high ground, the shield wall was extremely powerful in defence and he did not need to deliver a knockout blow. In order to determine the outcome at Hastings, it is necessary to look at the course of the battle and in particular the decisions made by the two commanders.

The course of the battle

The battle began at nine o'clock with an aggressive plan of attack from William. While his strategy of ceaselessly taking the fight to Harold would ultimately win the day, it took time to bring results. Archers fired into the shield wall but the line held firm. William then sent the infantry up the slope. Brutal hand-to-hand fighting ensued but still the English line refused to break. It also held out against the first assault by cavalry. William of Poitiers stated that the English 'were so tightly packed together that there was hardly any room for the slain to fall'. This pattern of attack continued for several hours before reaching a crisis point at around noon. The Bretons broke, fleeing back down the slope in the face of mounting losses. Sensing victory, the English fyrdmen poured after them. To avoid becoming isolated and also in response to the spreading panic, the centre and right of William's line also began to pull back. Rumour then spread that William himself had been killed. The Norman army was on the cusp of collapse. It was at this point that leadership on both sides played a critical role. Harold failed to capitalise on the ensuing Norman chaos by ordering a general charge. The potential to sweep the Normans from the hill was lost. On the other side, William, pushing back his helmet, rode across his troops showing them that he was alive. The Norman line began to solidify and then turned on the now isolated English peasants. Here the difference in the troops in the two armies became evident, as outside the protection of the shield wall the more poorly armed and armoured fyrdmen were no match for the Norman knights, who cut them down with relative ease.

SOURCE 3

A scene from the Bayeux Tapestry showing the fleeing Breton cavalry floundering in the marshy ground. Then the pursuing Englishmen are themselves cut down by reinvigorated Norman units. Dating from c1070, the Tapestry was most probably created in Kent on the orders of Bishop Odo of Bayeux, Duke William's half-brother.

By now it was around two o'clock. Both sides paused to reform and then William once more sent his infantry and cavalry up the slope and fighting resumed. Due to the steep sides, flanking or going around the enemy was not an option and direct assaults on the shield wall continued. As described by William of Poitiers in Source 4, the Normans began using the tactic of feigned retreats to weaken the shield wall. This claim has generated intense controversy among historians. The debate is continued in Extracts 1 and 2, but the idea of deliberate retreats seems plausible given the highly trained nature of William's knights and the wider examples of this tactic's use. As a result, the actions of William's cavalry were responsible for significantly degrading Harold's forces. They would also help deliver the final blow.

SOURCE

From *Gesta Guillelmi ducis Normannorum et regis Anglorum* ('The Deeds of William, Duke of Normandy and King of England') written by William of Poitiers, c1070s. He was not present during the battle but his history is based on the eyewitness accounts of others.

The Normans and their allied forces, realizing that they could not overcome an enemy so numerous and standing so firm without great loss to themselves, retreated, deliberately feigning flight. They remembered how, a little while before, flight had been the occasion of success. The barbarians exulted with the hope of victory. Exhorting each other with triumphant shouts, they poured scorn upon our men and boasted that they would all be destroyed then and there. As before, some thousands of them were bold enough to launch themselves as if on wings after those they thought to be fleeing. The Normans, suddenly wheeling their horses about, cut them off, surrounded them, and slew them on all sides, leaving not one alive.

Twice they used the same stratagem to the same effect, and then attacked more furiously than ever the remaining enemy, still a formidable force and extremely difficult to surround. It was now a strange kind of battle, one side attacking with all mobility, the other enduring, as though rooted to the soil. The English began to weaken, and as if confessing their guilt by their submission, suffered the punishment. The Normans shot, smote and pierced: it seemed as if more movement was caused by the falling dead than by the living. Those who were only wounded could not withdraw, but died in the press of their companions. Thus fortune sped to accomplish William's triumph.

EXTRACT

From *The Field of Hastings* by Lt Col Charles Lemmon, published in 1956.

According to the Norman chroniclers, the retreat of the Norman cavalry was a feint designed to draw the Saxons out, after which they wheeled about and destroyed their pursuers. Apart from the fact that no allegation of a retreat 'according to plan' carries conviction, there is the serious military objection that such a manoeuvre is contrary to the principle that troops once committed to the attack cannot be made to change their direction. The impossibility of passing orders to hundreds if not thousands of individuals, all engaged in separate hand-to-hand combats; and of the simultaneous timing of such an operation should also be sufficiently apparent: yet the incident of the 'Feigned Retreat' has been almost universally accepted, given great prominence in all narratives as the cunning ruse whereby William won the battle, and will die hard. The reason why the chroniclers made up this story is fairly obvious: they dared not record that the Norman cavalry ran away.

EXTRACT

From *Hastings 1066* by Christopher Gravett, published in 2000.

There would have been many occasions when squadrons were grouping on the valley floor to recover breath while comrades fought on the hilltop, presenting opportunities for the strategy to be agreed. The fact that a number of knights fought in a conroi made up of men trained together in arms over the years meant that they were supremely capable of enacting a concerted manoeuvre when necessary. They only needed to wheel and follow the gonfanon of their lord as he led them in the pre-arranged feigned flight. Thus there would be no need to involve large numbers in the exercise, though this may have been done simply by instructing several conrois to act in unison. Such flights are well testified in warfare; Normans used them near Arques in 1052-3 ... as well as at Messina in Sicily in 1060.

At about 4pm with light fading and the shield wall severally weakened, William's leadership skills came to the fore. He had the determination to rally his troops and order one last assault to break the enemy line. He co-ordinated this last attack so that his archers fired high this time in order to ensure the arrows would land on top of the Anglo-Saxons. His cavalry, followed by infantry, then smashed through the shield wall. William was in the thick of the fighting and narrowly escaped death, losing his third horse that day. The Bayeux Tapestry shows that King Harold was not so lucky. When he was initially struck by an arrow, a four-man 'hit squad' took advantage of the general battle confusion to reach him. The first knight ran Harold through the chest with a lance, the others decapitating and disembowelling the king before hacking off his leg. Harold's death saw English resistance crumble. Loyalty meant the housecarls gathered around their dead king and went down fighting. Elite losses that day included Harold's two brothers, Gyrth and Leofwine. The once-mighty Godwin family had collapsed completely. As seen in Source 5, for the Normans this was a just outcome.

EXTEND YOUR KNOWLEDGE

Gesta regum Anglorum ('The Deeds of the Kings of the English') by William of Malmesbury, c1125, revised c1140.

William of Malmesbury was a monk at Malmesbury Abbey in Wiltshire and is considered, along with Orderic Vitalis, one of the foremost scholars of his age. William was a prolific historian, also producing *Gesta pontificum Anglorum* ('The Deeds of the Bishops of England') and many other works. His father was a Norman and his mother English and this mixed upbringing must have helped give him a less partisan view of events than the Norman chroniclers such as William of Poitiers. William recognised this in the prologue to the *Gesta regum Anglorum*, stating 'Many both Norman and English have written about King William for different reasons: the former have praised him to excess … the latter, out of national hatred, have heaped upon their ruler undeserved reproach. I for my part, as the blood of either people flows in my veins, shall steer a middle course.' However, although William of Malmesbury belonged to an English monastery, he could not escape the Norman world view as his first abbot was a monk from Jumieges, Normandy.

William of Malmesbury's usefulness is increased by the fact that in compiling the *Gesta regum Anglorum* he visited many English religious centres in search of sources, including the significant archival collections held at Worcester and Glastonbury. William started writing the *Gesta* at the request of Queen Matilda II, wife of Henry I and herself of mixed Anglo-Scottish parentage. He completed it in c1125 and later revised the text several times. William of Malmesbury's writing contains a strong moral message. He believed Anglo-Saxon England fell because of its own decadence. While he believed the Normans were fulfilling God's duty, he was also prepared to condemn them when they allowed avarice and power to get in the way of this.

SOURCE

From *Gesta regum Anglorum* by William of Malmesbury, c1125. This extract describes Anglo-Saxon society before the Norman Conquest and how its flaws helped lead to defeat at Hastings.

The desire after literature and religion had decayed for several years before the arrival of the Normans. The clergy, contented with a very slight degree of learning could scarcely stammer out the words of the sacraments and a person who understood grammar was an object of wonder and astonishment. The monks mocked the rule of their order by fine vestments and the use of every kind of food. Their nobility, given up to luxury and wantonness, went not to the church in the morning after the manner of Christians, but merely in a careless manner heard matins and masses from a hurrying priest in their chambers amid the blandishments of their wives. The common people left unprotected became a prey to the most powerful who amassed their fortunes by either seizing on their property or by selling their persons into foreign countries... Drinking in parties was a universal practice in which occupation they passed entire nights as well as days. They consumed their whole substance in mean and despicable houses unlike the Normans and the French who in noble and splendid mansions live with frugality. The vices attendant on drunkenness which enervate the human mind followed. Hence it arose that when they engaged William, more with rashness and precipitate fury than military skill, they doomed themselves and their country to slavery by a single and that an easy victory.

EXTEND YOUR KNOWLEDGE

Counter-factual history

The Battle of Hastings is full of 'what ifs'. Had William been unable to rally his troops following the Breton collapse or had he been killed in one of his numerous close shaves, would the outcome have been very different? What would have happened if Harold had not been cut down and had instead lasted the remaining hour before darkness closed that day's fighting? Exploring alternative possibilities is known as counter-factual history and it can be a useful way of assessing the relative importance of factors. It can also be applied to any of the events contained in this book. What if the weather had been cold on the morning of the Battle of Stamford Bridge, for example? What other counter-factual questions can you think of?

Assessment of the Battle of Hastings

William's victory at Hastings is due to a combination of factors. The challenge is to decide where the balance lies. Was the battle won by the Normans or lost by the Saxons?

William's leadership

William's victory stemmed from his careful preparation. While in Normandy he built up a broad coalition of support, ranging from Norman magnates to the pope. His logistical organisation was meticulous, allowing an army to be maintained in the field throughout the summer and then successfully transported across the Channel. Once in England, William chose to stay in a defensive pocket and ravaged land to provoke Harold into battle. The strategy paid off. It was William rather than Harold who picked the time and place of battle, helping neutralise Harold's natural advantage of fighting on home soil. This superior generalship, honed by a youth campaigning in France, came to the fore during the battle. William took the fight to Harold and throughout the day relentlessly attacked. He saw the potential for victory in the chaos of the Breton retreat and proved his skill by rallying wavering troops.

Harold's mistakes

Harold's rush to engage William meant that he threw away all the advantages that stemmed from his position as the sitting king and leader of the Godwin family. Waiting would have allowed Harold to assemble an overwhelming army but by not taking the long view Harold faced William with an under-strength force lacking the experienced housecarls. The folly of this became apparent when the untrained peasants repeatedly broke the shield wall during the feigned retreats. During the battle, Harold lacked inspiration. He did not order a general charge but nor was he able to keep his army on the hill in their defensive position, which would have allowed him to see the day out.

Unequal armies

William gained a decisive edge in the battle from his heavy cavalry and archers. Furthermore, Harold was severely limited in his ability to command his troops by fighting on foot in the Viking style. Compare this with William's horse-borne prominence, which allowed him to rally his troops following the Breton collapse. However, the outcome of the battle should not be viewed as inevitable. Despite the undoubted advantage William's highly trained and mobile force gave him, the battle was a close-run thing until the key moment of Harold's death.

> **AS Level Exam-Style Question Section B**
>
> How accurate is it to say that Duke William of Normandy won the Battle of Hastings because of the mistakes of King Harold? (20 marks)
>
> **Tip**
> *Remember to explore the other side of the question and all the examples of excellent leadership by Harold too.*

> **ACTIVITY**
> **KNOWLEDGE CHECK**
>
> 1 What military attributes does William display in Source 1?
>
> 2 Do you think Harold made the right choice in deciding to confront William quickly?
>
> 3 What were the main differences between the Saxon and Norman armies at Hastings?
>
> 4 Do you think the feigned flights described in Source 4 could have taken place?
>
> 5 Write down five reasons to explain William's victory at Hastings.
>
> 6 How useful is Source 5 for explaining the Norman victory at Hastings?

HOW DID WILLIAM DEAL WITH OPPOSITION TO HIS RULE?

The submission of the earls

The following morning, camped among the debris of war, William must have reflected on his position. He now found himself with a battle-damaged army in a hostile land of two-and-a-half million Anglo-Saxons. The great city of London blocked his advance, while the North was largely unknown to him. Beyond England's frontiers lay the Welsh princes and the Scottish king, all of whom had the capacity to generate trouble. Despite the defeat of Hardrada, there also remained a potent threat from Scandinavia, whose leaders had long-standing claims on the country.

Furthermore, the English who had not fought at Hastings showed no signs of submitting. Instead, Edwin and Morcar had reached London with their forces, while Archbishop Stigand put Edgar the Atheling, Edward the Confessor's great-nephew, forward as the new king, although the northern earls refused to agree to this. Until all these dangers had been addressed, William's victory was far from complete.

William now had to take the offensive and his immediate priority was to gain control of the South East. Employing terror tactics, he staged a savage attack on the town of Romney before marching on the key port of Dover and the religious centre of Canterbury. Both surrendered without resistance. London, England's most populated city and the nodal point for roads to the rest of the country, was the most important prize. Aware from scouting parties that it contained soldiers ready to fight, and not wanting to risk a direct assault, William instead set out to isolate and intimidate the city by a brutal circular march through the surrounding shires. As he knew from his experience on the continent, this could be carried out at minimal risk to his own forces. Moving westwards he **wasted** parts of Surrey and Hampshire before receiving the submission of Winchester, the ancient capital of Wessex. Pushing northwards, William crossed the River Thames at Wallingford and established a castle to prevent relief reaching London from the West. As a sign that his strategy was working, Stigand left London to offer his surrender. William then finished the encirclement by blocking the two great roads of Ermine Street and Watling Street and in so doing cut London off from the North. He then established a castle at Berkhamsted and waited. Panic hit London and the remaining English leaders surrendered, including Edgar Atheling and the two northern earls.

On Christmas Day, William was crowned king of England in a ceremony deep in symbolism. Taking place at Westminster Abbey and following an order of service that dated back to the coronation of King Edgar in 973, William wanted to reinforce the point that he was the true heir and successor of King Edward. When he was anointed by Archbishop Ealdred of York, he also gained the aura of being blessed by God, while he could now tap into the Anglo-Saxon's inherent loyalty to the Crown, no matter its wearer. The coronation also showed just how insecure the Normans felt. Mistaking English shouts of acclamation for William as signs of revolt, the guards panicked and set fire to nearby houses and fighting broke out outside the Abbey itself.

Rebellion in the South 1067–69

New Year 1067 saw no signs of English resistance and in spring William felt confident enough to return to Normandy. His ship left from Pevensey and in a classical reference bore the white sails of victory. William then staged a triumphal tour around Normandy, showing off the English prisoners, including Edgar the Atheling, Edwin, Morcar and the infamous Stigand. Running England in his absence were William fitzOsbern and Odo, bishop of Bayeux, although the harshness of their rule encouraged the first stirrings of revolt. In the summer, a small rebellion broke out in Kent. It was made slightly more threatening when Eustace of Boulogne, William's standard bearer at Hastings, crossed the Channel from France to become its leader. While the Kentishmen no doubt wanted an end to Norman rule, Eustace himself appears to have been motivated by a personal desire for more power and reward following his service in 1066. The rebels were easily cut to pieces by the Dover Castle garrison. Eustace fled back across the Channel, later reconciling himself with William. The initial lack of English resistance can be put down to the shock of defeat and the heavy losses suffered by the warrior class in the battles of 1066. Above all, though, there was an absence of leadership. Edgar Atheling, the northern Earls and Harold's children were all too young and inexperienced to unify the nation in revolt. Many of the thegns were prepared to accept the new regime in the hope of preserving their estates. This was encouraged by William's initial policy of conciliation, where he promised to rule in accordance with the laws of Edward the Confessor and in conjunction with the traditional elites.

The Normans were becoming aware that the comparative calm would not last. Intelligence was reaching them that English exiles were seeking help from overseas and were especially active in the court of King Sweyn of Denmark. Then, at the end of the year, the first true rebellion began in Exeter. This was partly in response to increased taxation to fund the Norman occupation but it was also possibly inspired by the presence of Harold's mother, Gytha, in the city. William must have considered it a serious threat as he made a dangerous sea crossing from Normandy back to England in December 1067. He was also aware that the South West in general had been a Godwinson stronghold and had made no official submission to him. In January 1068, despite the harsh winter conditions, he marched his forces into Devon. Significantly, these included English troops that had been raised under the Anglo-Saxon levy system without any apparent difficulties. This shows that even at this early stage many English men and women were adjusting to the new reality and seeking to make the best of it. As described in Source 6, William's Norman troops laid siege to the English rebels in Exeter, suffering heavy losses in assaulting the city walls. The men of Exeter attempted to rally support from across the region but when they found none forthcoming they submitted to William and ended the 18-day siege.

EXTEND YOUR KNOWLEDGE

Historia ecclesiastica ('The Ecclesiastical History') by Orderic Vitalis, c1114–41

Orderic Vitalis was a monk, English by birth but writing in Normandy at the well-connected and influential monastery of St Evroul. His 13-volume Church history was written over a 30-year period and includes a description of the events of 1066, largely based on the works of William of Poitiers and William of Jumieges. Writing 50 years after the event, Orderic Vitalis himself was not in a position to gather eyewitness accounts. However, he is far less partisan than the early Norman sources and includes some additional material from charters and monastery archives. While never questioning the legitimacy of the Norman Conquest, he did seek to redress the clearest examples of anti-English sentiment put forward by the Norman chroniclers. Whereas William of Poitiers described Harold as 'a man soiled with lasciviousness, a cruel murderer', for example, in Orderic Vitalis's work he became a 'brave and valiant man, strong and handsome'. Like William of Malmesbury, Orderic Vitalis also saw the conquest as a moral story, illustrating the dangers inherent in not pursuing a godly life.

SOURCE

 6 Orderic Vitalis describes the Norman attempts to take the city of Exeter in his *Historia ecclesiastica* ('The Ecclesiastical History'), written c1114–41.

First of all he [King William] rode nearer with 500 knights to reconnoitre the ground, examine the fortifications, and learn what measures the enemy were taking. The gates were closed, and a great force manned the ramparts and the whole circuit of the walls. So by the king's command the whole army closed in on the city, and one of the hostages was blinded within sight of the gates. But neither fear nor pity for the remaining hostages could shake the resolution of the angry citizens; instead their obstinate determination to defend themselves and their homes grew all the stronger. The king, however, closely besieged the city, attempting to storm it, and for many days he fought relentlessly to drive the citizens from the ramparts and undermine the walls. Finally the citizens were compelled by the unremitting attacks of the enemy to take wiser counsel and humbly plead for pardon.

William gave them lenient terms but established a castle to ensure his future control over the city. He also staged a march through the rest of Devon and Cornwall to underline his strength, as well as receiving the submission of Bristol and Gloucester. Gytha, meanwhile, fled to the island of Flat Holme in the Severn Estuary, where the wives of many noblemen were hiding out, and then on to Flanders. The South West was still not completely secure, however. In the summer of 1068, three of Harold's sons crossed over from Ireland to raid. They attempted to storm Bristol but were beaten off by local English forces and were then routed by English thegns in north Somerset. Trouble returned in the summer of 1069, which, as will be seen, was a critical time for William. Men from Somerset and Devon lay siege to a new castle at Montacute, while Harold's sons launched a second raid from Ireland, this time with a superior force of 60 ships. William, hard pressed in the north, relied on Count Brian of Brittany and Bishop Geoffrey of Coutances to restore order. They did not disappoint him and this was history's last sight of Harold's sons.

EXTEND YOUR KNOWLEDGE

This textbook has organised the rebellions by geographical location. Can you think of a different way of categorising them?

The harrying of the North, 1068–70

TIMELINE

Summer 1068
First rebellion in York

William conducts his first northern campaign

Castles are built in Warwick, Nottingham and York

January 1069
Earl of Northumbria and his men are massacred at Durham

Edgar the Atheling besieges York

February–March 1069
William defeats rebels and builds a second castle in York

Summer 1069
New risings in Devon, Cornwall, Shropshire, Staffordshire and Cheshire

August 1069
Danish fleet first appears off the east coast and starts heading north

September 1069
Danes and rebels led by Edgar the Atheling storm York and a new uprising begins

Autumn 1069
William marches north, seizes York and defeats rebels

Danes avoid battle

December 1069
William holds Christmas in York

January–February 1070
Harrying of the North

February 1070
William advances across the Pennines in midwinter

February–March 1070
William surprises rebels in Chester

Shrewsbury and Stafford are relieved by royal forces

March 1070
Royal army is dismissed at Salisbury

The greatest threat to William's rule came from the North and he would be forced to take to the field three times in extended campaigns between 1068 and 1070. The first sign of impending trouble was Edgar's defection from William's court to Scotland, followed by Edwin and Morcar, who fled back to their earldoms. Having been restored to some of their lands following their enforced trip to Normandy in 1067, these nobles had realised that, despite William's initial promises to rule in conjunction with the Anglo-Saxon elite, in reality they wielded little power and influence. Edwin also felt personally embittered that William had broken a promise to marry one of his daughters to him. William, aware that resistance was beginning to build in the North, centred on York, acted to head off trouble. He staged a series of lightning raids into Warwickshire, Nottinghamshire and Yorkshire, blazing a trail of destruction. As the *Anglo-Saxon Chronicle* says, 'he allowed his men to harry wherever they came'. The policy worked. He received the surrender of Edwin and Morcar and established a castle in York before returning southwards.

If 1068 had been tough for William, 1069 was critical. In January, rebels attacked Durham, killing the Norman earl Robert of Commines and his knights. The news quickly spread to York, where local insurgents lay siege to the castle. Edgar the Atheling then moved into the region from Scotland to assume leadership of the rebellion. In a lightning march comparable to Harold's advance on Stamford Bridge, William was able to relieve the garrison at York, although Edgar escaped back to Scotland. After establishing a second castle in a clearly troublesome city, William returned south to celebrate Easter at Winchester.

Events once again spiralled out of control in the summer, when a Danish fleet of 240 ships containing an army of trained warriors appeared off Kent. It was led by King Sweyn's sons, Harold and Canute. The appeals by the English exiles had finally borne fruit. The fleet raided its way up the east coast of England before anchoring off the River Humber. Yorkshire now descended into rebellion and Edgar the Atheling arrived with a force to join the Danes in support of the rebellion. They jointly seized York in September. This was the most dangerous point for William. He was now facing a rebellion in a fiercely independent region which resented rule from the South, as the rebellion against Tostig in 1065 demonstrated. The rebels had a figurehead in the form of Edgar Atheling, who had a powerful claim to the English throne. Above all, they were backed by a Danish army. Hanging over William was also the threat of a Scottish invasion, as Malcolm III had strong links with Edgar the Atheling and a desire to control Northumbria. Finally, William's forces were now being stretched, as events in the North encouraged a fresh round of uprisings in the South West and along the Welsh border. William reacted with speed and brutality and headed north. He staged a march from Nottingham to York, devastating the land as he went before reoccupying the city for a third time. He also went in search of the Danish army but they refused to give battle. William celebrated Christmas amid the empty, burnt-out ruins of York. To show his authority, he wore the crown, which had been specially brought up from Winchester. William then undertook one of the most brutal acts of his reign. He split his troops up into smaller war bands and they set about the systematic destruction or harrying of Yorkshire and the surrounding areas.

According to the usually restrained *Anglo-Saxon Chronicle* the king went 'with all his army that he could collect, and utterly ravaged and laid waste to that shire'. Orderic Vitalis's account in Source 7, written when it was safer to voice criticism, gives a more vivid insight into the scale of violence. The region did not recover for generations. In 1086, the Domesday Book designated one-third of Yorkshire as 'waste'.

SOURCE

 7

Orderic Vitalis describes the harrying of the North in his *Historia ecclesiastica*, written c1114–41. Believing that it was morally wrong to target those who bore no responsibility for the rebellions, his condemnation of William was unusually strong.

He [King William] himself continued to comb forests and remote mountain places, stopping at nothing to hunt out the enemy hidden there. His camps were spread over an area of 100 miles. He cut down many in his vengeance; destroyed the lairs of others; harried the land and burned homes to ashes. Nowhere else had William shown such cruelty. Shamefully he succumbed to this vice, for he made no effort to restrain his fury and punished the innocent with the guilty. In his anger he commanded that all crops and herds, chattels and food of every kind should be brought together and burned to ashes with consuming fire, so that the whole region north of Humber might be stripped of all means of sustenance. In consequence so serious a scarcity was felt in England, and so terrible a famine fell upon the humble and defenceless populace, that more than 100,000 Christian folk of both sexes, young and old alike, perished of hunger.

My narrative has frequently had occasion to praise William, but for this act which condemned the innocent and guilty alike to die by slow starvation I cannot commend him. For when I think of helpless children, young men in the prime of life, and hoary greybeards perishing alike of hunger, I am so moved to pity that I would rather lament the grief and sufferings of the wretched people than make a vain attempt to flatter the perpetrator of such infamy.

To deal with the rebellions in the North West, William crossed the rugged Pennines in the teeth of winter. As Source 8 shows, it pushed some of his troops to the point of mutiny but William drove them on through force of personality. The march achieved its objective. The rebels were completely unprepared for a winter assault and William was able to take Chester and Stafford without difficulty. After establishing castles, William unleashed his army to ravage the wider region. William still had to deal with the danger posed by the Danish fleet, which had wintered in the River Humber. When they saw that their English allies had been routed, however, William was able to disperse them with a bribe. The king returned south and celebrated Easter in lavish style, knowing that the rebellious spirit of the North had been crushed.

SOURCE

8

From *Historia ecclesiastica* by Orderic Vitalis, written c1114–41.

They urged in defence of their conduct that they could not obey a lord who went from one hazard to another and commanded them to do the impossible – The king continued on his way, leaving behind those who would not follow – along a road no horseman had attempted before, over steep mountains and precipitous valleys, through rivers and rushing streams and deep abysses. As they stumbled along the path they were lashed with rain and hail. Sometimes all were obliged to feed on horses which had perished in the bogs. The king himself, remarkably sure-footed, led the foot-soldiers, readily helping them with his own hands when they were in difficulties. So at last he brought his army safely to Chester and suppressed all risings throughout Mercia with royal power.

EXTEND YOUR KNOWLEDGE

For a greater insight into how the first three generations of chroniclers attempted to come to terms with the ferocity of the Norman takeover, from an initial stunned silence to a gradual, restrained criticism, read Elizabeth van Hout's article 'The trauma of 1066', in *History Today*, volume 46, issue 10 (1996).

AS Level Exam-Style Question Section A

How much weight do you give to the evidence of Source 7 for an enquiry into the methods used by the Normans to defeat the rebels?

Explain your answer using the source, the information given about it and your own knowledge of the historical context. (12 marks)

Tip

Remind yourself why Orderic Vitalis is considered a pre-eminent historian.

Foreign intervention and the East Anglian rebellion 1070–71

With the North subdued, East Anglia became the last bastion of resistance to the Normans, centred on the Isle of Ely. English rebels began collecting there from spring 1070, when it was occupied by a section of the Danish fleet, clearly showing that Viking promises counted for little. It is during this period that Hereward the Wake emerged as the chief rebel leader. While his life has become clouded in legend, it seems likely that he was a local thegn whose lands had been confiscated by the Normans, leaving him with few other choices besides taking up arms. This composite force had a number of advantages. As a main operating base, Ely was an ideal location. Surrounded by vast marshland, it was easily defensible, while the stone walls of the abbey provided a stronghold. In addition, it was strategically located to allow the mobile Danish fleet to strike northwards to Lincolnshire and Yorkshire, east into the Midlands and south to London. Furthermore, the sea access also meant Ely could potentially receive reinforcements from the thousands of English exiles on the continent. The danger the rebels posed to Norman control was shown when Hereward, backed by the Danes, launched a devastating raid on Peterborough in early June.

SOURCE

9 From *Gesta Herewardi* ('The Deeds of Hereward') by an unknown author, c1109–31. It claims to be a translation of an earlier and now lost work.

> William moved his whole army to Aldreth where the surrounding water and swamp were narrower, the breadth there extending to four furlongs [800m]. Having brought there tools and fitments of timber and stone, and heaps of all kinds they built a causeway through the swamp, although it was narrow and quite useless to them. Moreover, close to the wide river near this place, that is to say Aldreth, they assembled in the water large tree-trunks joined together with beams, and underneath tied whole sheep-skins, flayed and reversed and fully inflated so that the weight of those going over might be better borne. When this was finished such a multitude rushed on to it all at once, greedy for the gold and silver and other things, not a little of which was thought to be hidden in the Isle, that those hurrying in front were drowned together with the road itself they had made. Those who were in the middle of the company were swallowed up in the watery and deep swamp as well. A few of those who were following at the rear got away with difficulty, flinging down their weapons, wallowing in the water and making their way through the mud. Thus in this way, with hardly anybody pursuing them, great numbers perished in the swamp and waters, And to this day many of them are dragged out of the depths of those waters in rotting armour. I have sometimes seen this myself.

William successfully dealt with this threat through diplomacy and force. Realising the Danes were the most important factor, he bought them off again and they sailed home in midsummer 1070. He then initially entrusted the capture of the rebel base to his deputies, but Hereward was able to use the challenging geography and his superior military skill to ambush and hold off the Norman attackers. The longer the rebels held out, the more Ely became a beacon of resistance. In 1071, Earl Morcar was one of the many warriors who arrived to make a stand. His brother, Edwin, was probably killed somewhere in the North around this time while trying to flee to Scotland. In the summer of 1071, William took command of the operation. He sent a fleet to blockade the island on which Ely stood and then constructed a causeway through the marsh. This allowed his army to advance and launch a successful assault although, as Source 9 reveals, it was not without its own difficulties. Hereward disappeared into legend while Morcar was imprisoned for the rest of his life.

EXTEND YOUR KNOWLEDGE

Hereward the Wake

Hereward the Wake was rescued from obscurity in Victorian times when romantic tales of heroic Anglo-Saxons fighting the tyranny of the Normans became popular. This was a theme first developed by Walter Scott's *Ivanhoe* and continued in Charles Kingsley's 1865 novel *Hereward the Wake: The Last of the English*. Today he is once again reaching a wider audience through novels such as the *Hereward* series by James Wilde and Laurence Brown's *Cold Heart, Cruel Hand*. Read one of the fictional depictions of Hereward and produce a book review. Does the novel offer a convincing account of Hereward's life and how accurately does it portray the wider historical setting? What does it suggest about Hereward's reasons for rebelling, why he was able to fend off the Normans for so long and ultimately what happened to him?

THINKING HISTORICALLY   Cause and consequence (5b)

Causation relativity

Historical events usually have many causes. Some are crucial, while some are less important. For some historical questions, it is important to understand exactly what role certain factors played in causing historical change.

Significant factors in the timing and nature of the East Anglian rebellion, 1070–71

In 1070, Hereward, a Saxon thegn, entered into armed rebellion following the seizure of his lands by the Normans.	The conquest of England by King Alfred and his heirs in the tenth century had helped develop an English national identity.
The period 1067–70 saw a series of unco-ordinated rebellions across England. The northern uprising was savagely put down by William during the winter of 1069–70.	After the Battle of Hastings, England's natural leaders proved unequal to the task of leading a co-ordinated uprising. Many skilled warriors went into exile.
The East Anglian Fens gave the rebels defensive advantages, while Ely acted as a fortified base. Initial Norman attempts to storm Ely failed.	A section of the Danish fleet arrived at Ely in the spring of 1070, although it was soon bought off by William and took no part in the action beyond sacking Peterborough.

Answer the following questions:

The timing of the East Anglian rebellion

1 How important were Hereward's personal circumstances in explaining the timing of the uprising in East Anglia?

2 In what ways did the arrival of the Danish fleet transform the situation in the North of England? How far did this precipitate the East Anglian rebellion?

3 How could William have reduced or prevented the level of resistance seen at Ely?

The nature of the East Anglian rebellion

4 How far do you think attitudes of patriotism motivated the warriors who were involved in the stand at Ely?

5 What role did the above factors play in determining the way that William responded to the uprising at Ely?

6 Would the nature of the Ely uprising have been the same if the Anglo-Saxon elite had provided a greater level of leadership to the rebellions?

7 What roles did each of the causal factors above play in determining the nature and timing of Hereward the Wake's uprising at Ely?

The revolt of the earls, 1075

The last echo of Anglo-Saxon resistance took place in 1075 while William was in Normandy. Although not an uprising of the people, its power lay in the identities of its three conspirators: Ralph de Gael, earl of Norfolk; Roger de Breteuil, earl of Hereford; and Waltheof, earl of Northumbria. These were significant members of the ruling class. Ralph was the son of a Breton who had served William loyally as earl of East Anglia. Roger was the son of William's lifelong friend and ally, William fitzOsbern. Waltheof, son of the great Earl Siward, was one of the most powerful Anglo-Saxons still surviving. With Breton, Norman and English backgrounds respectively, they also had the potential to cause trouble for William, both in England and on his borders in Normandy. The trio had everything to lose by taking on someone as ruthless as William. Clearly, though, they thought victory was a real prospect. Hatching their plan at a wedding feast, they aimed to divide the kingdom into three, with one of them becoming king. The trump card was securing the support of the Danes.

Waltheof, earl of Northumbria, 1050–76

Despite his tender age of just 15, in 1065 Waltheof became earl of Northamptonshire and Huntingdonshire. Following the Battle of Hastings, he submitted to William and was allowed to keep his pre-Conquest title and possessions. In 1069, Waltheof joined forces with Edgar the Atheling in the northern rebellion but after its failure made fresh submission to William. He was restored to his earldom and went on to marry William's niece, Judith of Lens. In 1072, he was appointed earl of Northumbria, a title previously held by his father, Siward. In 1075, he became involved in the revolt of the earls against William and was executed the following year.

However, despite its potential, in the end the rebellion failed to pose a significant risk to the king. William remained in Normandy and relied on his regent, Lanfranc, who was now archbishop of Canterbury, to organise its destruction. Lanfranc was helped in this by gaining advanced warning of the plot when Waltheof had cold feet, which led him to confess all. Despite being compromised, the two remaining earls pressed ahead with their plan. Ralph de Gael took to the field and advanced west from Norwich, while Roger de Breteuil advanced east from Hereford, the aim being to join forces and isolate the North of England. However, they failed to gain much local support and crucially the Danish army never materialised.

SOURCE

Archbishop Lanfranc's first letter to Roger, earl of Hereford, in 1075. In writing this letter, the archbishop was acting in his capacity as the king's regent while William was away in Normandy.

Lanfranc, by the grace of God archbishop, greets his dearest son and friend earl Roger and sends him his blessing.

Our lord the king of the English greets you and all of us as his faithful subjects in whom he places great trust, commanding us to do all in our powers to prevent his castles from being handed over to his enemies: may God avert such a disaster. I urge you then, as I must urge the dearest of my sons – whom God knows I love wholeheartedly and long to serve, whose father too I loved like my own soul – to be so scrupulous in this matter and in all your duty as a vassal of our lord the king that you may have praise of God and the king and all good men. Never forget your father's distinguished career: the faithful service he gave his lord, his zeal in winning great possessions and how honourably he held what he had won.

On another point, the king has ordered his sheriffs not to hold any courts within your lands until he himself returns to England and can hear personally the matters in dispute between you and those sheriffs.

I wish that I could speak to you in person. If that is your desire too, let me know where we can meet and discuss both your affairs and the interests of the king. For my part I am ready to meet you at whatever place you may name.

You are asked to see that Beringer, who brings you this letter, has a just settlement with those men whom he accuses of having stolen his horse.

The Lord almighty bless you and direct your whole life in righteousness.

The earls were therefore in no position to take on the two powerful Norman armies raised against them and led by men of the highest calibre, including Odo, bishop of Bayeux. As a result, the rebellion quickly unravelled. Ralph de Gael was forced back to his castle and, when this came under siege, he left the defence of it to his redoubtable wife and fled to Brittany to continue the fight. Unable to exact revenge on Ralph de Gael, William ensured that his followers were captured and mutilated. Roger de Breteuil, meanwhile, was captured and spent the rest of his life in prison. Obstinate and proud, perhaps there he had time to reflect on Lanfranc's initial effort to neutralise the rebellion through diplomacy, as seen in Source 10, as well as the stark warning contained in Source 11. Waltheof, last of the Anglo-Saxon earls, despite confessing all, was executed the following year. When the Danes finally arrived with 200 ships, the revolt was effectively over. They sacked York Minister in the traditional fashion before departing.

SOURCE

11

Archbishop Lanfranc's third letter to Roger, earl of Hereford, in 1075. No replies, if any were made, have been preserved. While in his second letter Archbishop Lanfranc continued to implore Earl Roger to end his rebellion, in this third letter the tone has markedly hardened.

Lanfranc, by the grace of God archbishop, to his one-time dearest son and friend earl Roger: may he have sound judgement and some concern for his soul's welfare.

I grieve for you inexpressibly, for God knows I loved you and desired with all my heart to love and serve you. But because the Devil's prompting and the advice of evil men have led you into an enterprise which under no circumstances should you have attempted, necessity has forced me to change my attitude and turn my affection not so much into hate as bitterness and the severity of justice. I have sent messengers, I have sent letters not once but a second time inviting you to come to me: to receive my counsel for your soul from me your father in God and true friend, and on better advice to abandon the foolish undertaking which you had planned. You would not do so. Therefore I have cursed and excommunicated you and all your adherents by my authority as archbishop; I have cut you off from the holy precincts of the Church and the assembly of the faithful, and by my pastoral authority I have commanded this to take effect throughout the whole land of England. I can free you from this bond of anathema only if you seek my lord the king's mercy and if you render satisfaction to him and the other men whose property you have unjustly seized.

ACTIVITY
WRITING

Analyse Source 11 in which the archbishop of Canterbury attacks Earl Roger for his disloyalty.

1. Identify any words or phrases you do not understand and research their meanings.

2. Identify words and phrases that show Lanfranc's feelings towards Earl Roger. Write a short paragraph explaining his views, using quotes from the extract to back up your points.

This was the last revolt William would face with an English element. Determined resistance to Norman rule had now come to an end. William's ability to defeat a succession of rebellions stems partly from their lack of co-ordination. At no point did William have to face a general revolt across the whole country. Furthermore, he had able and loyal supporters scattered throughout the country, entrenched in powerful castles. As has been seen, they won important battles for him. William, though, led from the front when the threat was at its greatest and he would rapidly and decisively move into the danger zone. He also benefited from the ineffectiveness of the Danes and Scots in helping the rebels. Above all, he was prepared to be completely ruthless and the widespread tactic of wasting proved extremely effective at deterring further uprisings.

ACTIVITY
KNOWLEDGE CHECK

1 Why do you think William initially faced so little opposition from the English?

2 What does Source 6 reveal about William as a military leader?

3 How useful is Source 7 for explaining the failure of the rebels to remove William from power?

4 What are the three main reasons to explain the failure of Hereward the Wake's uprising?

5 How does Archbishop Lanfranc in Source 11 attempt to dissuade Earl Roger from rebelling? Why do you think Earl Roger would not be persuaded?

6 In the period 1067-75, which was the most dangerous point for William's control over England?

HOW EFFECTIVELY DID THE NORMANS DEAL WITH THE THREAT POSED BY WALES AND SCOTLAND?

Imposing Norman control in Wales

Offa's Dyke is a 193-kilometre earthwork running from Liverpool Bay in the north to the Severn Estuary in the south. Constructed by the eighth-century king of Mercia, it officially demarked the border between England and the Celtic tribes of Wales. As seen in the last chapter, in reality this border was fluid, as both sides were always seeking to expand their territory and influence. As a result of Harold's defeat of Gruffudd ap Llywelyn in 1063, the English gained the upper hand and the briefly united Wales once again split into the warring kingdoms seen in Figure 2.1. The most important of these were Gwynedd in the north, Powys in the centre and Deheubarth in the south. In this divided state, Wales did not pose a significant long-term threat to William.

In the short term, however, it soon became apparent that some of the Welsh princes were intent on taking advantage of England's post-conquest chaos. In August 1067, Bleddyn ap Cynfyn, prince of Gwynedd and Powys, and his brother Rhiwallon allied with the English thegn, Eadric the Wild. Having been dispossessed of his Shropshire estates by the Normans, Eadric had been fighting

a low-level war against the Normans with some success. With Welsh help, Eadric could now expand his ambitions and they jointly invaded Herefordshire, ravaging the land and laying siege to Hereford Castle. Unable to take it, they withdrew back to Wales with their booty. In 1069, revolt flared again. Prince Bleddyn and Eadric the Wild led their men in ravaging Shropshire, Cheshire, Staffordshire and burning Shrewsbury town after failing to take the castle. Eventually, this threat receded when Eadric the Wild made his peace with William in 1070, no doubt realising the futility of continued resistance.

To ensure stability on the border, William created three new earldoms, centred on Chester in the north under Hugh d'Avranches, Shrewsbury in the centre under Roger of Montgomery, and Hereford in the south under William fitzOsbern. This in effect created a buffer zone between England and Wales. All men of aggression, the earls were soon expanding their power westwards. Earl Hugh extended his boundaries into the kingdom of Gwynedd as far as the River Conwy, and by the end of William's reign was raiding as far west as Snowdonia.

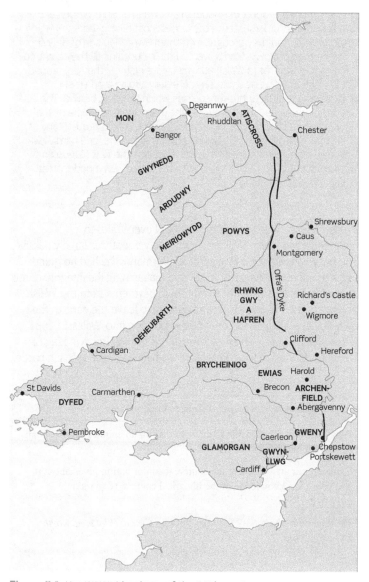

Figure 2.1 The Welsh kingdoms of the 11th century.

Orderic Vitalis says that 'He went about surrounded by an army instead of a household.' What this meant for the Welsh people is captured in Source 12, as well as how the Normans used the rivalries of the Welsh kingdoms to their advantage. Roger of Montgomery pushed across Offa's Dyke and founded a castle and town named Montgomery after his home in Normandy, while his men advanced along the Severn Valley, setting up castles of their own. William fitzOsbern started extending Norman control into the kingdom of Gwent. He most notably established towns and castles at Chepstow and Monmouth. This process was continued by his son but the advance westwards was temporarily halted by the 1075 revolt of the earls.

SOURCE

12 From *The Life of Gruffydd ap Cynan* by an unknown author, c1160. Gruffydd ap Cynan was prince of Gwynedd from 1081 to 1137. Most of his career was spent in warfare against Welsh rivals and the Normans. He was imprisoned by the Normans at Chester from 1081 to 1093.

Then there grew much evil and grief in Gwynedd. And during that time, after a little while, Hugh earl of Chester and many other leaders, namely Robert of Rhuddlan and Warin of Shrewsbury, and Walter of Hereford, mustered the largest host ever of horsemen and footsoldiers. And they brought with them Gwrgenau son of Seisyll and the men of Powys and traversed the mountains till they came to Llyn. In that cantref [a Welsh administrative district] they encamped for a week, causing destruction there daily and ravaging it and inflicting a great slaughter of corpses which they left behind. The land then remained desolate for eight years and the people of that land were scattered over the world despised and destitute. Many of them went into exile to other lands over many years, and hardly did any of them return to their land. And that was the first plague and fierce advent of the Normans first to the land of Gwynnedd, after their advent to England.

While the earls extended English control over Wales to unprecedented levels, William's own involvement was largely passive. Too busy with affairs in England and Normandy, he had no grand plans of conquest. As a result, beyond maintaining the integrity of the border and ensuring he received tribute payments from the Welsh princes as their overlord, he was content to leave the earls to their own devices. William led only one expedition into Wales, in 1081. It was designed as a show of force after Rhys ap Tewdwr, king of Deheubarth, had defeated his Norman-backed Welsh rivals in battle.

AS Level Exam-Style Question Section A

Why is Source 12 valuable to the historian for an enquiry into Norman expansion into Wales?

Explain your answer using the source, the information given about it and your own knowledge of the historical context. (8 marks)

Tip
The source is about the life of Gruffydd ap Cynan. Why is he worth knowing about?

Advancing the length of Wales, William brought his army to a halt at St Davids, its most westerly point. Once there and with his point made, William recognised Rhys ap Tewdwr as ruler of Deheubarth in return for an oath of loyalty and an annual tribute of £30.

Under William II, this policy of steady expansion driven largely by the earls continued until Norman control reached a high point in 1093. As a result of having built castles in Bangor, Caernarfon and Anglesey, Norman control extended over the north coast, while in the south the kingdoms of Brycheiniog, Morgannwg and Dyfed had been taken, with a castle being established as far west as Pembroke. Soon after, however, the harshness of Norman rule brought about a fight back from the Welsh, led by the princes of Powys and Gwynedd. By 1100, the Normans in the north had been driven back to Conwy, while much of Powys in the centre and Dyfed in the south had been lost. William II was forced to invade twice – in 1095 and 1097 – but with little impact.

William the Conqueror and Scotland

Malcolm III of Scotland and the northern rebellion

Rival claims of lordship over the North meant Scotland posed a far greater threat to England's stability than Wales. Tensions between England and Scotland were long standing, with the flash points being the disputed border territories of Lothian, Northumbria and Cumbria. In 973, King Edgar of England and King Kenneth of Scotland had reached an agreement whereby Lothian was ceded to the Scots while the English took Northumbria. Since 1018, the Scots had also held Cumbria. When William assumed the crown in 1066, he faced a Scottish king, Malcolm III Canmore, with growing southerly ambitions. Despite coming to power in 1058 with English help, King Malcolm had launched a raid on Northumbria in 1058, a further attack in 1061 to recover southern Cumbria and then in 1066 he had provided support to the exiled Tostig. In the chaos after the Battle of Hastings, Malcolm saw the opportunity to weaken England's hold over Northumbria. The northern rebellion of 1068 provided the first chance, although its swift collapse discouraged Malcolm from sending aid. Recognising the danger from Scotland, William, working through emissaries, secured an oath of loyalty from Malcolm and a promise not to assist the rebels. Much to Norman anger, however, this did not stop the Scottish king from providing a safe haven for the likes of Edgar the Atheling. The following year, the North was engulfed by a far more deadly Danish-backed uprising. Although Malcolm chose not to intervene with an army of his own, presumably preferring to see how events would develop, the threat of a Scottish invasion hung over William and helps explain his urgency in crushing the revolt. That Malcom was firmly on the rebel's side was made clear by his marriage to Edgar the Atheling's sister, Margaret, in late 1069. With the fall of Northumbria to William's forces in early 1069, rebels once again sought sanctuary in Scotland. Malcolm now also faced the prospect of a hostile English neighbour uncomfortably close to Cumbria and Lothian. As a show of force and in order to destabilise the region, he launched a devastating raid into Northumbria that summer, sacking Durham and Cleveland. A glimpse of how the Normans viewed his actions is provided in Source 13.

SOURCE
13

From *Gesta regum Anglorum* ('The Deeds of the Kings of the English') by William of Malmesbury, c1125. An Anglo-Norman monk, William of Malmesbury believed the Anglo-Saxons lost at Hastings because of their moral corruption.

Perhaps I should not be out of order were I severally to commemorate their deaths [Malcolm III, Edgar, Morcar and Waltheof] though I might risk the peril of creating disgust, while I should not be easily pardoned as an historian if I were led astray by the falsities of my authorities. Malcolm willingly received all the English fugitives affording to each every protection in his power but more especially to Edgar whose sister he had married out of regard to her noble descent. On his behalf he infested the adjacent provinces of England with plunder and fire. Not that he supposed by so doing he could merely annoy William who was incensed that his territories were subject to Scottish invasions.

By summer 1072, William was ready to deal with the Scottish threat. While his fleet blockaded the coast, he personally led his army, chiefly made up of horsemen, across the River Forth, ravaging as he went. This must count as one of William's great military expeditions but very little is known about it. One of the few references is contained in the *Anglo-Saxon Chronicle*, shown in Source 14, but this is typically sparse in detail. Certainly the invasion was full of risk. It was late in the campaigning season. William was 400 kilometres from his nearest base at York, in unknown terrain. He was also only the second English king to invade Scotland, the first being Athelstan in 934. However, Malcolm, fully aware of Harold Godwinson's fate, refused to give battle, the two kings instead concluding a treaty at Abernethy. For William it was a success. The Scottish king made homage to him and so officially recognised the new regime in England. This, though, was more likely a personal pledge of allegiance rather than an acceptance of William's overlordship over Scotland. William had also neutralised a rebel safe haven by securing the expulsion of Edgar the Atheling and the other exiles.

SOURCE
14

From the *Anglo-Saxon Chronicle*, Worcester Manuscript D, for the year 1072. The monks compiling it were most interested in events in northern England and Scotland.

Here King William led a ship-army and land-army to Scotland, and beset that land to seaward with ships, and himself travelled in with his land-army over the Forth, and there he found nothing he was the better for. And King Malcolm came and made peace with King William, and was his man, and gave him hostages, and afterwards he turned home with all his army.

For Malcolm, it was also far from negative. He had survived an invasion with his kingdom intact and, in 1079, clearly unbowed, he launched another raid into Northumbria. This led to a further English invasion the following year, led this time by William's son, Robert Curthose. As in 1072, Malcolm avoided battle and escaped lightly by offering his submission. On his return to England, Robert Curthose established a castle called Newcastle, strategically sited high on the northern border to allow future incursions into Scotland. Meanwhile, Northumbria remained uncontrollable and lawless and so fulfilled Malcolm's policy of maintaining a buffer between him and England.

William II and Scotland 1091–93

William II was the fourth English king Malcolm had dealt with, but this brought him little benefit. He raided into Northumbria in 1090, bringing a reprisal march from William Rufus the following year. Once again, Malcolm refused to give battle and submitted. However, in 1092, William Rufus went on the offensive and marched into Cumbria, seizing Carlisle and fortifying it. Signalling his intention that Cumbria was going to be fully incorporated into England, peasant settlers were brought from the South and it was placed under Durham's ecclesiastical jurisdiction. The loss of Cumbria was a huge setback for Malcolm. Further humiliation followed in 1093 when he travelled south to Gloucester to discuss Cumbria but William Rufus refused to meet him. In anger, Malcolm staged a raid into Northumbria and was ambushed and killed.

It can therefore be seen that, between 1066 and 1093, the Normans treated Wales and Scotland very differently. While the private actions of Norman lords saw significant sections of Wales steadily brought under English rule, William I and II and their lords never aimed at a similar takeover of Scotland. This is partly because its remoteness from the centre of power in the South of England made a conquest a near impossible proposition. As Scotland was a long-established kingdom ruled over by a king, unlike Wales which was divided into warring factions, it also encouraged the use of the more routine tools of statecraft, including diplomacy and military incursions to punish rather than conquer.

SOURCE
15

From the *Anglo-Saxon Chronicle*, Peterborough Manuscript E, for the year 1093. By this point, Peterborough was the last monastery maintaining a chronicle. It was also still being written in the English language.

He [Malcolm] gathered his army, and travelled into England, raiding with greater folly than behoved him, and then Robert, the earl of the Northumbrians with his men, by surprise trapped and killed him. Morel of Bamburgh, who was the earl's steward and King Malcolm's godfather, killed him. With him was also killed his son Edward, who would have been king after him if he had lived. Then when the good queen Margaret heard this – her dearest lord and son thus betrayed – she became anguished in mind to the point of death and went to church with her priests, and received her rites and prayed to God that she might give up her spirit.

ACTIVITY
KNOWLEDGE CHECK

1 When and where did Eadric the Wild cause trouble for the Normans and what made him stop?

2 To what extent did Wales pose a threat to Norman control of England?

3 How does Source 12 help explain the steady conquest of Wales by the Normans?

4 How useful is Source 13 for understanding why there was continual tension between England and Scotland between 1067 and 1093?

5 How useful is Source 14 for learning about William's invasion of Scotland in 1072?

6 Was Scotland a serious threat to England during the reigns of William I and II?

HOW DID THE NORMANS MILITARISE ENGLISH SOCIETY?

The feudal system

Late Anglo-Saxon England had been largely peaceful. When Edward the Confessor expelled Godwin in 1051, for example, no side went to war and, in 1065, Harold preferred to exile his brother, Tostig, rather than fight the Northumbrians. This lay in stark contrast to Normandy, where William spent two decades engaged in armed struggle. To ensure full control over England after 1066, William imported the aggressive Norman model and created a society geared towards war. As part of this, he introduced a new social and legal system among the upper classes known as 'feudalism'. This saw William grant land to a small elite known as the tenants-in-chief in exchange for military service from knights. As a result of **subinfeudation** a similar relationship could exist between a tenant-in-chief and tenant. Oaths made the arrangement binding and formal. Underpinning this was the principle, established by William as conqueror, that all the land belonged to him. As a result, the idea of **freeholding** disappeared, with land being held from others and not owned.

The tenants-in-chief

The tenants-in-chief were the powerful Anglo-Norman elite made up of earls, archbishops, bishops, abbots and **barons**. Together they were granted almost three-quarters of England by William. Within this elite was an inner circle numbering only 11 and they held one-quarter of all land. This close-knit group, many of them recognisable from the Ship Lists in Source 2, were the Norman magnates who had played such a pivotal role in the invasion. Land was their reward. These included William's boyhood allies, William fitzOsbern and Roger of Montgomery, as well as his two half-brothers, Odo of Bayeux and Robert of Mortain. In exchange for land, each tenant-in-chief had to provide a certain number of knights to carry out the pressing military tasks of occupation, such as garrison duty in the royal castles, fighting rebels or campaigning in Scotland and Wales. This was a quota known as the *servitium debitum* or 'service owed' and could in theory produce an army 4,000–5,000 strong. Unfortunately, there are not many sources relating to this due to the passage of time and the fact that a lot of contracts were agreed orally. The few in existence tend to be from ecclesiastical archives and demonstrate that the Church, which was handed control of one-quarter of England, was not exempt from military obligation. Source 16 is regarded as one of the clearest examples of the feudal process in action. In this the abbot of Evesham is instructed to supervise the feudal levy as well as fulfilling his own obligations.

SOURCE 16 A writ issued by William I c1072, summoning knights from the abbot of Evesham, presumably to take part in the Scottish campaign. It shows that under the feudal system religious institutions had clear military obligations.

> William, king of the English, to Ethelwig, abbot of Evesham, greeting.
>
> I order you to summon all those who are subject to your administration and jurisdiction that they bring before me at Clarendon on the Octave of Pentecost all the knights they owe me duly equipped. You, also on that day, shall come to me, and bring with you fully equipped those 5 knights which you owe me in respect of your abbacy.
>
> Witness Eudo the steward. At Winchester.

The knights

Once quotas had been established, a tenant-in-chief could maintain his knights either by granting them land in exchange for service or by keeping them in his household and providing food, lodging and pay. Landholding knights were **enfeoffed** with their **fief** and, while this allowed them to live off the rents from their land, it was not the road to riches. Their status was only somewhat above that of a well-off peasant. In contrast, household knights were the elite. These were well-trained, professional soldiers, normally young, single and of noble birth. The best migrated to the royal household and formed the nucleus of the Anglo-Norman army, but there were also many openings in the baronial households. William fitzOsbern, for example, kept a household so large that it annoyed the king.

The development of what were in effect private armies throughout the great houses of England was a novel feature of Anglo-Norman society and stemmed from the insecurity the Norman occupiers felt on their estates. Another distinct feature was the close bonds of loyalty between lord and knight. This relationship was reinforced by symbolic acts, such as oath-taking, the granting of arms and armour, and dubbing a man, or delivering a short blow to the back of the neck, to make him a knight. After this the knight became his lord's **vassal**.

KEY TERMS

Vassal
A man who owed allegiance to his lord.

The nature of land tenure

The feudal system is an area of history rich in academic debate. One key question concerns how and when William first introduced the quota system for knights. The traditional view sees it as being imposed uniformly across England in a fairly rapid process during the initial years of the conquest. The 1072 Evesham Summons is one of the main pieces of evidence taken to support this view. However, recent scholarship, based on a study of a wider range of sources, has suggested a more nuanced conclusion. It sees the feudal system as developing slowly in England over many decades. This reflects the fact that, apart from the sudden windfall of the vast Godwin estates, the acquisition of land by William and then its subsequent redistribution was itself piecemeal. It occurred as and when land came to him through death and confiscation. Furthermore, instead of one uniform system, the terms for granting land seem to have depended on local circumstances and past tradition.

In Source 17, the knight William Baynard is taking over land from a Saxon thegn, which indicates that some quotas were perhaps based on pre-conquest obligations of service rather than on a radically new model. This would seem natural, as Anglo-Saxon England did have its own levy system based on the hidage assessment of each estate. This generally saw one soldier serving for every five hides. Source 18 shows that Roger Lacy, son of Walter Lacy, offered to pay for his land, indicating that other arrangements besides knight duty existed. Indeed, after the first generation of the conquest, feudal service was often commuted to payments called scutage. Both William I and William II found this more useful, as in practice they tended to use mercenaries rather than the feudal host in order to save time and ensure they had competent men. Source 19 gives an insight into the traditional view of feudal service and sees Peter, King William's knight, becoming the vassal of the abbey of Bury St Edmunds.

SOURCE 17

An early enfeoffment of a knight by Gilbert, abbot of Westminster c1083.

In the year of the incarnation of our Lord, one thousand and eighty-three. We Gilbert, the abbot, and the convent of Westminster have given to William Baynard a certain farm in the township of Westminster, by name 'Totenhala' to house him, and to be held for him for the whole of his life by the service of 1 knight. This is to be held by him with all the things that pertain to it, as well and freely as ever Wulfric the thegn surnamed 'Bordewayte' held it from the church.

SOURCE 18

A grant of land to be held by military service by Robert Losinga, bishop of Hereford from 1085.

This privilege Robert, bishop of the church of Hereford, ordered to be recorded as agreed between him and Roger Lacy, son of Walter, concerning certain land which is called 'Hamme', and these things which pertain to it. This land belongs to the church of Holy Mary, the Mother of God, and St Ethelbert the martyr; and previously the said bishop held this land as his own demesne and for the sustenance of the church. This land the aforesaid knight, to wit, Roger, asked from the bishop through his friends, and he offered money in respect of it. But the bishop, by the counsel of his vassals, gave him the same land in return for a promise that he would serve the bishop with 2 knights as his father did whenever the need arose. This also was part of the contract: that the men of the bishop belonging to King's Hampton and Hereford, and to the estates pertaining thereto, should be at liberty to take timber from the wood and for the use of the bishop as often as it should be needed for fuel or for repairing houses; and the pigs of these manors should feed in the same wood. This refers to the men belonging to the bishop. And this contract enjoins that if Roger becomes a monk, or dies, neither his mother nor his wife nor his sons nor his brothers nor any of his kinsfolk shall have rights in the aforesaid land, but let the bishop receive whatever in the estates may be to the profit of the holy Church, and his men shall receive the same without any contradiction whatsoever. This instrument was executed in the year of the Incarnation of our Lord 1085.

SOURCE 19

An early enfeoffment on the land of the abbey of Bury St Edmunds from the reign of William I.

Be it known to all of you that Peter, a knight of King William, will become the feudal man of St Edmund and of Baldwin the abbot, by performing the ceremony of **homage**. He will do this by permission of the king and with the consent of the monks, and in return for the service which will here be stated, saving always the **fealty** which he owes to the king, the fief having been freely received except for the six royal forfeitures. Peter promises that he will serve on behalf of the abbot within the kingdom with 3 or 4 knights at their own expense if he has been previously summoned by the king and the abbot to take part in the earlier or later levies of the king's host. If he is bidden to plead on the abbot's behalf at any place within the kingdom, they shall likewise bear their own expense. But if the abbot shall take him anywhere else, then the expense of his service shall be borne by the abbot. Besides this, he shall equip a knight for service without or within the kingdom where and when the abbot shall require to have this knight as his own retainer.

ACTIVITY
WRITING

Use the words in the box to complete the following sentences so that they best describe the nature of the feudal system.

fealty   freehold   homage   knights   landownership   *servitium debitum*   subinfeudation tenants-in-chief   tenants   vassal

The feudal system describes the system of _____ which developed in England during the Norman conquest. As spoils of war, William claimed ownership of the whole of England after the Battle of Hastings. Anglo-Saxons who owned land privately as a _____ therefore lost out. William granted two-thirds of England to his most loyal supporters as a reward for their service. These were his _____. In return they had to supply him with _____. The exact number of knights owed was known as the _____. The _____ were William's vassals and owed _____ to him, which meant loyalty. The bond between the king and his vassal was reinforced by oath-taking and a ceremony in which _____ was made. In a process known as _____, the tenants-in-chief could in turn grant land to _____. The feudal system was not as clear cut as is commonly assumed. It took time to spread over the whole country and land could also be granted in many different ways.

A Level Exam-Style Question Section A

How far could the historian make use of Sources 16 and 18 together to investigate how William raised troops for his army?

Explain your answer, using both sources, the information given about them and your own knowledge of the historical context. (20 marks)

Tip

The feudal system is an area of historical debate. Source 16 fits the traditional view of feudalism.

The power of the castle

As well as creating a new landholding structure geared to war, William militarised the landscape of England with castles. Indeed, one of his first acts on landing was to set up a prefabricated castle at Hastings, as seen in Source 20, and this set the tone for his rule. The motte and bailey castle, having long proved its worth on the continent, became William's key instrument of war in England. Quick to build, it consisted of an earth mound crowned with a wooden tower and surrounded by a ditch and wooden palisades. As has been seen, this was constructed wherever trouble flared. The surrender of Exeter was marked with the establishment of a castle and as the North was quelled further examples were built in Warwick, Nottingham, York, Lincoln, Huntingdon and Cambridge. On the Welsh border, a chain of castles was built to watch over the mountain passes and these became the basis for the Norman penetration of that country. To guard England's northern frontier and provide staging posts for expeditions over the border into Scotland, castles were built at Newcastle and Carlisle.

SOURCE
20
A section of the Bayeux Tapestry showing Norman troops constructing a motte and bailey castle at Hastings. The Bayeux Tapestry was made in Kent in c1080 on the orders of Bishop Odo of Bayeux.

EXTEND YOUR KNOWLEDGE

To view the Bayeux Tapestry in full you can go to Reading Museum's website.

Select five scenes from the Bayeux Tapestry which you think are particularly useful in understanding the background to the Norman invasion and the battle of Hastings.

For the outnumbered and overstretched Normans, castles were vital. They provided points where troops could be concentrated and patrols sent out to dominate the surrounding landscape. Above all they changed the nature of warfare from open battle to sieges. To win, the rebels now had successfully to storm these forts, which, as Eadric the Wild, the northern rebels and the men of the South West found to their cost, was very costly to do. Orderic Vitalis stated that 'the fortifications that the Normans called castles were scarcely known in the English provinces, and so the English – in spite of their courage and love of fighting – could put up only a weak resistance to their enemies'. He regarded the rebels' lack of castles as a key reason for their failure. The importance the Normans attached to the castle can be seen from the high calibre of men installed as castellans or castle leaders. All were significant Norman magnates. In York, that most rebellious of cities, the first castle was entrusted to William Malet of Graville-Sainte-Honorine and the second to William fitzOsbern.

The Norman programme of castle building changed the English landscape and was deeply resented by its people. As Orderic Vitalis lamented, 'they built castles far and wide throughout the land, oppressing the unhappy people, and things went ever from bad to worse. When God wills may the end be good.' It is estimated that over 80 castles had been constructed by 1100. Two-thirds were built in towns, necessitating the demolition of hundreds of homes. Apart from a few examples in Herefordshire to guard against the Welsh, castles had largely been unknown in pre-conquest England.

As such they were also a psychological symbol of conquest and stressed to the English people the permanence of the Norman presence. No better example of building to intimidate exists than the huge White Tower in London, started in the 1070s by William and constructed using stone imported from Caen. It was finished around 1100. In addition, he built a further two stone towers or keeps at Chepstow and Colchester. From the late 11th century onwards, many Norman magnates followed this example, redeveloping motte and bailey fortifications, always meant to be temporary, into solid stone-built structures, As the threat of rebellion died down, the castles became seats of local government and so an inescapable feature of everyday life.

Figure 2.2 The castles of William I and William II.

A Level Exam-Style Question Section B

'William the Conqueror gained full control of England by 1075 mainly through the use of castles.'

How far do you agree with this opinion? Explain your answer. (20 marks)

Tip

While castles were crucial, other factors such as William's leadership, the role of his deputies and the weakness of the rebels and outside forces played a role.

ACTIVITY
KNOWLEDGE CHECK

1 What was the basis of the relationship between a tenant-in-chief and his vassal?

2 How useful is Source 16 for understanding the imposition of the *servitium debitum*?

3 Study Figure 2.2. What explains the positioning of the castles across England and Wales?

4 Bullet point four ways in which castles helped the Normans keep control of England.

ACTIVITY
SUMMARY

1 To understand the outcome of the Battle of Hastings complete the table below.

Key area	Notes
Actions and events that weakened Harold in the period leading up to the Battle of Hastings	
Actions and events that strengthened William before Hastings	
Strengths and weaknesses of Harold's army at the start of the battle, including its composition and position on the battlefield	
Strengths and weaknesses of William's army at the start of the battle	
Mistakes made by Harold and his army during the battle	
Significant actions by William and his army during the battle	

2 Sketch a map of England and add annotations showing the location, date and outcome of the different rebellions between 1067 and 1075. Highlight those that were particularly threatening to Norman control of England.

3 To explore the question of why the rebellions failed to remove the Normans, create two columns. In the first column, list all the actions taken by William that helped to defeat the rebellions. In the second column, list the weaknesses of the rebel groups themselves.

4 Why do you think the Normans expanded into Wales but not Scotland?

5 In a couple of sentences provide a definition of feudalism and then complete the table below.

Source	How does it support or challenge the traditional view of knight quotas in England?
16	
17	
18	
19	

WIDER READING

Douglas, D. *William the Conqueror*, University of California Press (1964)

Gravett, C. *Hastings 1066: The Fall of Saxon England*, Osprey Publishing (2000)

Marren, P. *1066: The Battles of York, Stamford Bridge and Hastings*, Pen and Sword (2004)

Morris, M. *The Norman Conquest*, Hutchinson (2012)

Thomas, H. *The Norman Conquest*, Rowman (2008)

Rex, P. *1066: A New History of the Norman Conquest*, Amberley (2011)

2a.3

State, Church and society, 1066–1106

KEY QUESTIONS

- How innovative was Anglo-Norman government?
- Who were England's new elite after 1066?
- To what extent did town and village life change after the Norman Conquest?
- In what ways did William and his sons reform the English Church?

INTRODUCTION

For English chroniclers, the Norman occupation changed everything. It was a disaster and William of Malmesbury could only reflect on the 'melancholy havoc for our dear country'. In stark contrast, the Conqueror and his followers stressed continuity with the Anglo-Saxon past. Seeing himself as the true heir of Edward the Confessor, William, the *Anglo-Saxon Chronicle* recalled, pledged at his coronation to rule England 'according to the best practice of his predecessors'. In symbolic reflection of this, he employed an order of service that dated back to King Edgar's coronation in 973. The extent to which England changed after 1066 will now be examined and it will be shown that bringing about fundamental change to government, the Church and everyday life involved far more than merely the replacement of one elite by another.

HOW INNOVATIVE WAS ANGLO-NORMAN GOVERNMENT?

The king's household and the chancery

The power of the monarchy

William I gained control of a throne rich in power. Edward the Confessor had been England's supreme decision-maker, head of the Church and chief arbiter of justice. Only he had been able to pass laws, raise an army and mint coins and William saw no need to change this system. He was also aware, from the Confessor's domination by the Godwin family, that these powers were largely illusory unless the great men of the nation could be controlled and brought on side. During the period 1066–1106, William and his heirs successfully achieved this, meaning royal authority in both theory and practice was largely unrestricted. There would be just three baronial revolts, in 1075, 1088 and 1095, all of which were relatively easily put down. Gaining the support of the political nation was achieved, not through drastic innovation, but by applying long-held techniques of kingship.

25 December 1066 – William is crowned at Westminster Abbey

1070 – Stigand and other leading English bishops are deposed

1070-89 – Lanfranc archbishop of Canterbury

1082 – Bishop Odo of Bayeux is arrested

1086 – Information is gathered for Domesday Book

1 August 1086 – Oath of loyalty to William sworn at Salisbury

1065	1070	1075	1080	1085

May 1068 – William's wife, Matilda, is crowned queen

1075 – Unsuccessful revolt of the three earls

1085-86 – Invasion threat from King Canute VI of Denmark

Christmas 1085 – William orders Domesday survey

9 September 1087 – Death of William I

1087-1100 – William II king of England

1087-88 – Domesday Book completed

Force of personality was crucial. As the *Anglo-Saxon Chronicle* said of William, he was 'kind to those good men who loved God, and stern beyond all measure to those men who opposed it'. William II was 'very strong and violent to his country and his men and with all his neighbours, and very terrible' according to the *Chronicle*, while Henry I 'was a good man and people were in great awe of him'. Patronage was a vital lever and, following the spoils of victory; the Anglo-Norman kings had unprecedented amounts of land for distribution. Another important tactic involved bringing the great men into the decision-making process. Domesday, for example, was commissioned by William I only after he had 'deep speech' with his advisers, made up of archbishops and bishops, abbots, earls and barons.

SOURCE

Entry from the *Anglo-Saxon Chronicle*, Peterborough Manuscript E, for the year 1086, in the form of an obituary to William following his death. After 1079, Peterborough was the only monastery maintaining this annual history of England. It was still being written in the English language and as such is one of the few contemporary documents in which the views of the English are represented.

He was also a very stern man, and violent, so that no one dared do anything against his will. He had earls in his bonds who went against his will; bishops he put out of their bishoprics and abbots out of their abbacies and thegns into prison; and finally he did not spare his own brother, called Odo. He was a powerful bishop in Normandy his bishop's seat was in Bayeux and he was the foremost man next to the king. And he had an earldom in England, and when the king was in Normandy he was master in this land. And him he put in prison. Among other things, the good order he made in this land is not to be forgotten, so that a man who was of any account could travel over his kingdom with his bosom full of gold, unmolested; and no man dare kill another man, however great a wrong he might have done the other. And if any common man had sex with a woman against her will, he immediately lost the limbs with which he played.

He ruled over England, and by his astuteness it was so surveyed that there was not one hide of land in England that he did not know who had it or what it was worth, and afterwards set down in his record.

The royal household

While the power of the monarchy reached new heights under the Norman kings, the nerve centre of government located in the royal household remained largely unchanged. As before, the royal household was made up of the domestic household, the *domus*, which looked after the material needs of the king and his family. The *familia* consisted of household knights, acting as the king's bodyguard and the core of the army. Royal administration, including the preparing and issuing of charters and writs, was carried out in the chancery by royal priests. In its most formal and public role, the household also acted as the king's court or *Curia Regis*. This was where the king listened to advisors, received important visitors, made announcements and dispensed justice. It was also an important opportunity to awe subjects through visual displays of majesty. William I started a tradition of formally wearing his crown in court three times a year. At Easter this was in Winchester, at Pentecost (normally in May) in Westminster and at Christmas in Gloucester. All his magnates would be assembled to witness the spectacle and the ceremony would be followed by lavish feasting.

> **AS Level Exam-Style Question Section A**
>
> Why is Source 1 valuable to the historian investigating the power of the monarchy under William I?
>
> Explain your answer, using both sources, the information given about them and your own knowledge of the historical context. (8 marks)
>
> **Tip**
> *This source mentions the arrest of William's half-brother, Bishop Odo of Bayeux. Remind yourself about the changes William made to the structure of earldoms to ensure his leading men did not become overpowerful.*

1088 – Unsuccessful rebellion led by Odo of Bayeux against William II

1095 – Unsuccessful revolt of Earl Robert de Mowbray against William II

2 August 1100 – Death of William II

1100–35 – Henry I king of England

September 1100 – Anselm returns to England

| 1090 | 1095 | 1100 | 1105 | 1110 |

1093–1109 – Anselm archbishop of Canterbury

November 1097 – Anselm leaves England

1107 – Investiture dispute settled in England

As in Anglo-Saxon times, the royal household was mobile, designed to support itinerant kingship (see page 170). After 1066, the government of England also had to adapt to William's frequent absences. He remained duke of Normandy and, after 1072, spent three-quarters of his time outside England. As a result, ways had to be found to ensure the smooth running and stability of the kingdom. William's solution was to employ trusted magnates as regents, including his half-brother, Bishop Odo of Bayeux, his great friend, William fitzOsbern, and later in the reign, Archbishop Lanfranc. During the reign of William II, the royal official, Ranulf Flambard, was similarly entrusted with control of day-to-day government.

Chancery

While the royal household was broadly similar to its counterpart in Normandy, the chancery, which acted as the chief writing office for the king, was a novel institution for William the Conqueror. Recognising its usefulness, William tried to ensure administrative continuity by retaining its head, Regenbald, who had served as **chancellor** under Edward the Confessor and Harold. He was replaced by a Norman official, Herfast, in 1069 and this reflected a wider process underway in the royal household of removing Englishmen from the key posts. This did not damage the chancery's capacity and it proved able to meet the growing demands placed on it by the powerful and energetic Anglo-Norman kings. As an indication of this, although perhaps also indicating poor survival of the earlier records, fewer than 2,000 writs and charters survive from the entire Anglo-Saxon period but from the reign of William II there are on average 15 surviving writs per year and 41 per year for Henry's reign. As well as being issued more frequently, the writs themselves were adapted. Prior to the Norman Conquest, they were only in English, but for a short time afterwards they became bilingual, also being issued in Latin, the administrative language of Europe. From the early 1070s, however, Latin became the standard and reflected the complete take-over of government at all levels by the Normans. The use of writs was also extended. Before 1066, they had largely been a means of announcing grants of land. William and his sons saw their potential and began using them for more general orders and instructions. Source 16 in Chapter 2 (page 210) showed William employing a writ to summon his Evesham knights, for example, while Source 4 (page 220) shows the writ's use in conveying judicial decisions.

KEY TERM

Chancellor
A royal clerk who oversaw the chancery and took responsibility for the royal seal, which was appended to all official documents. The actual term 'chancellor' only seems to have come into common usage in Anglo-Norman times.

EXTEND YOUR KNOWLEDGE

Iconography
Iconography is the use of visual symbols to convey an idea or message. In this period monarchs used royal seals to display a sense of their power. Before the Norman Conquest, both sides of Edward's royal seal depicted him regally enthroned. On one side he held the orb and sceptre and on the other the sword of justice. After the Norman Conquest, William I maintained this tradition by featuring himself enthroned on one side. The reverse, however, displayed him as an armed and mounted knight, firmly underlying the military power behind his rule.

SOURCE 2 The Great Seal of Edward the Confessor.

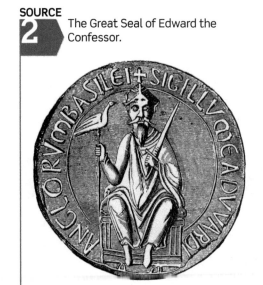

SOURCE 3 The Great Seal of William the Conqueror.

The geld and the silver penny

Kingship was an expensive business. Maintaining the royal household as well as the elite lifestyle meant the treasury at Winchester had regular calls made on it. William I was therefore fortunate in having taken control of a monarchy with established sources of revenue, which included the substantial profits drawn from royal lands. Justice proved lucrative through a share of the fines, while towns generated income for the Crown by taxes on trade, market tolls and other payments stemming from local custom. William also made use of the existing geld system. This was a national tax based on landholding, generally levied at the rate of two shillings per hide of land. William continued the Anglo-Saxon precedent of calling upon this tax in times of crisis. In 1084, for example, when William needed to finance his ongoing war in Maine, he imposed a national levy of six shillings on the hide. Although this was a punitive amount, the geld system was not as lucrative as it once had been. Over the course of his reign, William exempted many individuals and religious institutions from payment, as well as land held in demesne by his tenants-in-chief.

In their financial management of England, William and his sons were keen to maintain continuity in the money supply. The silver penny had been the cornerstone of England's financial success under the Anglo-Saxons, as well as being extremely lucrative for the monarchs themselves (see page 175). While Normandy had its own coinage, it was not up to the same standard, with newly minted coins still bearing the name of the long dead Duke Richard. As a result, few modifications were made after the Norman Conquest. William retained most of the English moneyers, who operated from the same 60 mints as before. As royal authority extended into more remote regions, new mints were opened in Durham and at Cardiff, Rhuddlan and St Davids in Wales. Royal control over the currency, as before, was absolute. No foreign coins were allowed to circulate, while every three years new silver pennies of standard weight and design were issued, with the king taking the profits. The Normans were prepared to be harsh to maintain the system. In 1100, Henry I announced, for example, that anyone found in possession of a fake coin should lose a hand and be castrated. As a result, the coinage system did not break down following the Norman Conquest, with an estimated nine million silver pennies in circulation in 1086, worth £37,500, largely similar to pre-conquest levels.

The office of sheriff

Monarchs, in their administration of both pre- and post-conquest England, faced two important challenges. The first was how to ensure all parts of the kingdom were governed effectively and the second concerned how to communicate orders and directives from the centre to the provinces. The Anglo-Saxons developed an efficient solution by sub-dividing the country into a hierarchy of earldoms, shires and hundreds. The sheriffs were the principal representatives of the king in the localities, while the use of writs was one of the main methods of transmitting instructions. Out of expediency this system was largely maintained by the Anglo-Normans. The royal will continued to be conveyed through writs, put into effect by sheriffs, who operated within the same system of shires and hundreds. Sheriffs also continued with their traditional duties of supervising the collection of taxes and fines, overseeing royal justice in the courts and, in times of war, raising and leading royal armies.

Despite overall continuity, there were a number of important modifications. Initially William tried to work with existing English sheriffs, such as Tofi of Somerset and Edmund of Hertfordshire. After the 1070s, there was a consistent policy of replacing these native incumbents with Norman supporters, in order to emphasise Norman authority. The biggest change, however, stemmed from the dismantling of the great earldoms, which is fully discussed later. Sheriffs had previously been subordinate figures to the earl but when this key check was removed, they saw their own authority increase to fill the power vacuum. This was also encouraged by the high calibre of men appointed. Many were Norman aristocrats and brought this prestige to their posts. Robert Malet, sheriff of Suffolk, possessed a sizeable lordship in Normandy, for example, while Baldwin of Meules, sheriff of Devon, was the son of Count Gilbert of Brionne. These were far from the typical sheriffs of Anglo-Saxon times, who tended to be second-rate landholders, with their status largely derived from their title as a royal official. Even where earls remained, sheriffs still saw an increase in their own authority as a result of royal government dealing with them more routinely. Roger of Hereford's rebellion in 1075 was partly inspired by anger at the growing power of the sheriff in his earldom. For the defeated English, however, the way the Normans reinvigorated the ancient office of sheriff was an unwelcome development. They were at the sharp end of the sheriff's power, which in many cases was used for unscrupulous land grabs.

Codes of law and the local courts

The Anglo-Norman legal system

Within the legal structure there was a good deal of continuity, reflecting both the Norman belief that they were the natural heirs of Edward the Confessor and a healthy dose of pragmatism. The Anglo-Saxon system worked well. As a result, shire and hundred courts were preserved, while the king remained the font of all justice. As before, he or his deputies dealt with the most serious of cases in the king's court. However, there was also some innovation in structure. As a result of the developing feudal system, manorial courts were established, allowing the lord of the manor to maintain order on his estates and settle disputes between his men. The implementation of **Forest Law** demanded its own courts. William signalled the biggest change in a writ issued in the early 1070s, shown in Source 4. In this he bowed to pressure from an increasingly assertive papacy and stated that ecclesiastical cases should not be heard in lay courts or by lay judges but only in Church courts before ecclesiastical judges. He had thus set in motion a train of events, which would end in the fatal disagreement between Henry II and Thomas Becket.

SOURCE

Writ of William the Conqueror concerning spiritual pleas c1072. It was issued in both Latin and English.

> William by the grace of God king of the English to Ralph Bainard and Geoffrey de Mandeville and Peter de Valognes and my other faithful men of Essex and Hertfordshire and of Middlesex, greeting. Be it known to you all and my other faithful men in England that I have determined, with the common counsel and advice of the archbishops, bishops, abbots and all the magnates of my kingdom, to emend the episcopal laws, which were neither satisfactory nor in accordance with holy canon law until my time. Wherefore I command and enjoin by my royal authority that no bishop or archdeacon shall henceforth hold a plea of the episcopal laws in the hundred court, nor bring a case touching the rule of souls before the judgement of laymen, but whoever is summoned according to the episcopal laws concerning whatever cause or offence shall come to that place which has been chosen and named by the bishop for that purpose and there answer concerning his cause or offence and do right to God and his bishop not according to the law of the hundred but according to canon and episcopal law. If, however, anyone, puffed up with pride, shall disdain or refuse to come before the bishop's justice, let him be summoned once, twice, thrice. But if then he will not come to make amends, he shall be excommunicated; and if it is necessary to enforce this, the power and jurisdiction of the king or sheriff shall be brought to bear.

The Normans did not issue any new law codes of their own, although some changes become apparent on reading *The Ten Articles of William I*, a selection of which are included in Source 5. This text was compiled in the early 12th century and historians generally agree that it contains enactments from the king. Article 3 outlines an early version of the *murdrum* fine, which was the main innovation in criminal law. It stated that in the event of a Norman being murdered, a heavy financial penalty would be imposed on a local community if they failed to produce the killer. This law stemmed from the low-level guerrilla warfare being waged against the occupiers in the early stages of the Norman Conquest. It also built on the established principle of communal responsibility for the wrongdoing of individuals. This was familiar to Anglo-Saxons as a result of the tithing system (see page 173). Article 6 concerns methods of proof. Oaths and ordeal by fire and water were Anglo-Saxon practices that continued to be used after 1066 but ordeal by battle was new to England, although common throughout western Europe. It involved fighting with sharpened hammers or staffs and, like all ordeals, was premised on the belief that God would intervene on the right side. Once guilt had been established, the Anglo-Saxon system of compensatory justice began to fall out of favour for the more serious offences and was replaced with death by hanging or physical mutilation, typically the loss of a limb, blinding or castration. This amply reflected the more brutal Anglo-Norman age.

SOURCE 5

From *The Ten Articles of William I*. This was an unofficial compilation of laws attributed to the Conqueror. Written in Latin and compiled in the early 12th century, copies were held by religious institutions such as the priory of Rochester. It is generally agreed by historians that it contains some genuine enactments of the king. As the *murdrum* fine outlined in Article 3 developed, it began to be levied on the community at the outset, rather than on the lord of the manor.

Article 1. In the first place he desires above all that one God should be honoured throughout the whole of his kingdom, and that one Christian faith should be kept inviolate, and that peace and security should be maintained among the English and Normans.

Article 3. I desire likewise that all the men whom I brought with me or who have come after me shall enjoy the benefit of my protection.

i) And if any one of them is slain, his lord shall arrest the slayer within five days if he can. If not, however, he shall begin to pay me 46 marks of silver from the property of that lord as long as it lasts out.

ii) When, however, the property of the lord fails, the whole hundred in which the murder is committed shall pay in common what remains.

Article 6. It has likewise been decreed that, if a Frenchman summon an Englishman for perjury or murder, theft, homicide or ran, by which the English mean open robbery which cannot be denied, the Englishmen shall defend himself by whichever method he prefers, either the ordeal of iron or trial by combat...

ACTIVITY
KNOWLEDGE CHECK

1 List the four main ways in which central government changed after the Norman Conquest of England.

2 What aspects of central government did the Normans maintain and why?

3 Why, and in what ways, did the office of sheriff undergo change in the period 1066–1106?

4 To what extent does Source 5 highlight the main changes to the legal system under the Normans?

WHO WERE ENGLAND'S NEW ELITE AFTER 1066?

The end of the English aristocracy

The conquest of England did not unfold as William hoped. Initially he envisaged ruling with the Anglo-Saxon aristocracy. He allowed Edwin and Morcar to keep their earldoms, and even promised Edwin the hand of his daughter. As a conciliatory gesture to the North following the brutal murder of Earl Robert de Commines in 1069, he handed over this turbulent region to Gospatric and then Waltheof, both sons of great Anglo-Saxon earls. At a lower level, thegns were allowed to retain their lands, as long as they had not fought at the Battle of Hastings, although they did have to buy them back at a price. The high point of co-operation was seen in spring 1068, when William's wife, Matilda, was crowned queen at Westminster Abbey. A witness list attached to a royal charter drawn up on the day shows the mixed nature of William's court. Archbishops Ealdred and Stigand, still holding the great Church offices of York and Canterbury, were signatories, while the other bishops listed were a mixture of Norman and English names. Among the secular magnates, Edwin and Morcar appeared alongside William fitzOsbern and Roger of Montgomery. The charter itself was drawn up in English and Latin.

Shortly after this document was signed, Edwin and Morcar fled north. At heart the English refused to accept their defeat and the resultant rebellions (see pages 200–207) led to a dramatic shift in William's treatment of the native aristocracy. He set out to disinherit and destroy them. Their near total eclipse has been confirmed by more recent computer-aided analysis of the Domesday survey, which has allowed historians to make best use of this often impenetrable document. Of the 1,000 tenants-in-chief it lists, only 13 were English. Furthermore, of the 8,000 subtenants recorded in the survey, only around 10 percent were English. The thegnly class, who once numbered 4,000–5,000, had largely vanished, and the Normans were in charge from the smallest village up to the greatest lordship.

Domesday

The Domesday survey was a kingdom-wide investigation into England's economic assets and land ownership. In around two million words it detailed over 13,000 towns, villages and hamlets, as well as 30,000 manors. It could not have been completed without the Anglo-Saxon system of local government. Commissioners were sent into every county with a detailed list of questions. They needed to find out who owned the land in Edward the Confessor's time, who held it now, how many people lived there, how much livestock, how much money the land generated, what was its tax rating and so on. The landholders had a few weeks to supply the answers, which were then scrutinised in the shire courts by panels of local jurors, itself an Anglo-Saxon innovation dating back to the tenth century. The survey was started soon after Christmas 1085 and completed by August 1086. This speed demonstrated what could be achieved when Anglo-Saxon administration combined with the control and energy of the Normans.

The purpose of Domesday is a matter of debate, as no contemporaries explained why it was undertaken. With so much emphasis on landownership, it has been suggested that William wanted to use the information to reform the geld system. However, no reassessment ever took place and the way the book is constructed makes it unsuitable for individual geld assessment. Instead, it was most probably designed to provide William and his officials with up-to-date information about who owned what land. As will be discussed below, this was needed in order to end the chaos of post-conquest land redistribution. This knowledge would also aid royal administration, which needed to take possession of tenants' land in the event of death or confiscation. The context is also important. The survey was conducted just after a time of acute national crisis, when a Scandinavian invasion seemed imminent. William was forced to raise a massive mercenary army and billet it throughout England. In organising the defence of England, the king must have wanted to know what its resources were and who held them. Domesday supplied him with this information. As will be shown below, it also re-confirmed his landowners' bonds of loyalty to him.

Changes in land tenure

Orderic Vitalis told the story of the Norman knight Gilbert d'Auffay, who fought loyally at the Battle of Hastings and in the subsequent rebellions. William offered him great estates in England as reward but Gilbert returned to Normandy, having 'declined to have any part in plunder. Content with his own, he rejected other men's goods.' This knight was the exception. Land meant wealth and power and for many this was their chief reason in joining William's invasion. The conquest certainly provided the spoils of war, but the way the new Norman elite held their land marked a significant break with the past. Whereas Edward the Confessor had been only one of many landholders, albeit dominant, after Hastings William claimed ownership over the entirety of England. He then granted lands to loyal supporters who, in turn, handed them to their followers, in a process historians call subinfeudation (page 210). The clearest expression of this is the Domesday Book itself. Every county has its own chapter and every chapter begins by listing the king's own lands in the shire. It then details the estates of the bishops, earls, barons and abbots, all of whom are described as holding their land from the king.

The last chapter showed that the terms on which William granted out land varied widely, leading historians to cast doubt on the idea of a single, uniform feudal system across England. As well as tenurial variation, there were also important differences in the way the land was territorially carved up. In the immediate aftermath of the conquest, William granted huge consolidated blocks to his closest supporters, paying no regard to previous patterns of ownership. Odo, bishop of Bayeux, received Kent, William fitzOsbern the Isle of Wight, Roger of Montgomery the country of Shropshire. William's chief concern here was security. This was also seen in the creation of the **rapes**. As new lordships were created in the North of England in the second decade of occupation, consolidated blocks were the preferred method. In total, one-third of England was granted out in this way. Many individual Normans, however, were rewarded for their role in the fighting by a direct transfer of an Anglo-Saxon estate. Domesday shows that the Norman Geoffrey de Mandeville had neatly stepped into the shoes of Ansgar the Staller, for example, who was one of the richest men in pre-conquest England below the rank of earl. Ansgar had fought and been wounded at Hastings, dying soon after. Around 10 percent of properties were allocated in this way.

Rapes

After 1066, Sussex was a strategic gateway between England and France. To ensure its protection, William divided this shire into five separate strips, known as rapes, each under the control of a leading magnate. Hastings was granted to Robert of Eu, for example, while Roger of Montgomery controlled Arundel.

A significant portion of land was also taken illegally through force and intimidation. The Domesday survey is full of tales of disputed land ownership. Richard fitzGilbert, for instance, one of William's great magnates, was accused of seizing three manors in Surrey. Church property was also seen as fair game and the monastery at Ely, as a result of its role in the rebellion, suffered particularly badly. Orderic Vitalis, however, saved his venom for Odo, bishop of Bayeux, comparing him to a 'ravening wolf' for the way he preyed on the estates of Evesham Abbey. So great was the problem that, in 1077, William was forced to write to his leading magnates requiring them and their sheriffs to return any Church property illegally seized. For most English landholders, the only option open to them in the event of illegal seizure was to try and negotiate to have some of it back, most probably on unfavourable terms of service.

It was partly the chaos of ownership that led William to commission the Domesday survey. Many Norman lords had no formal titles to their estates, while the actions of Richard fitzGilbert and countless others meant there were many long-running and bitter legal disputes. The Domesday survey attempted to address this problem by acting as a judicial inquiry. During its process of investigation, as seen in Source 6, special sessions of the shire courts were held in every county and juries were assembled from the local hundreds. As well as being asked to verify the various details collected by the commissioners, they were also asked to state who owned the land. Disputes were common at this stage but the verdicts recorded by Domesday became definitive. As such this document acted as a charter of confirmation, giving the great landowners legal security over their estates. William symbolically marked its completion at an extraordinary ceremony within the confines of an old iron-age fort at Salisbury. The great landholders paid homage to him and swore oaths of loyalty. In so doing, they confirmed the principle that William was the ultimate source of all tenure in England.

SOURCE

6

From the *Anglo-Saxon Chronicle*, Peterborough Manuscript E, for the year 1085. It was compiled by English monks and, although normally cautious in tone, in this example the author's views about Domesday are made evident.

The king had great thought and very deep conversation with his council about this land, how it was occupied, or with which men. Then he sent his men all over England into every shire and had them ascertain how many hundreds of hides there were in the shire, or what land and livestock the king himself had in the land, or what dues he ought to have in 12 months from the shire. Also he had it recorded how much land his archbishops had, and his diocesan bishops, and his abbots and earls, and – though I tell it at too great length – what or how much each man had who was occupying land here in England, in land or in livestock, and how much money it was worth. He had it investigated so very narrowly that there was not one single hide, not one yard of land, not even (it is shameful to tell – but it seemed no shame to him to do it) one ox, not one cow, not one pig was left out, that was not set down in his record. And all the records were brought to him afterwards.

THINKING HISTORICALLY   Evidence (5b)

The importance of context

Documents (texts) are like small pieces torn from a larger tapestry (context). Historians have to reconstruct the larger pattern into which documents might fit in order to use them to construct accounts of the past. The problem is that texts can have multiple contexts. Historians often debate how best to contextualise the documents that they interpret.

Source 6 describes the process of the Domesday investigation.

1 Summarise some key points from the extract above.

   a) Does the document indicate that William was interested in increasing his tax base?

   b) What economic assets were examined by Domesday?

   c) How thorough was the investigation?

The timeline below provides a possible context for the document in the wider story of William's feudal system.

SEQUENCE OF EVENTS 1

1066
Upon conquest, William takes ownership of all land in England.

1066 until his death
William is engaged in a constant process of land redistribution. Its main phase directly after the conquest involves taking estates from rebellious Anglo-Saxons and granting it to key supporters.

During the process of occupation, many Normans seize land illegally. Without proof of ownership, they lack security of tenure and legal challenges are brought against some Norman lords in the hundred and shire courts.

1077
William orders his leading magnates to return land illegally seized from the Church.

Christmas 1085
William, after consultation with his leading magnates, orders the Domesday survey.

1086
Royal Commissioners record who held land in 1066 and who holds it now.

1 August 1086
At a ceremony in Salisbury, the records of Domesday are presented to the king. His leading landholders swear oaths of allegiance to him, confirming their status as his vassals.

2 How does the Domesday survey fit into the pattern of events?

3 How might the Domesday survey have helped William establish order out of the chaos of the post-conquest land grab and reinforce his control over his leading men?

The document might seem to have one kind of meaning when interpreted in the context of land policy. A contrasting interpretation appears if we locate it in another context.

The Domesday survey happened at a time of acute crisis for William. In 1085, England was threatened with Danish invasion.

Consider the second timeline and answer the questions that follow.

SEQUENCE OF EVENTS 2

1084
William's son, Robert, goes into his second exile and attempts to find supporters to further his claim to Normandy.

Autumn 1085
William hurriedly returns from Normandy to England, accompanied by a huge army of mercenary knights and infantry raised from across France.

Upon returning to England, William summons his magnates to debate how to deal with the crisis.

Autumn 1085
News reaches William that King Cnut of Denmark is preparing for an invasion of England.

Autumn/winter 1085
Troops are billeted throughout English castles and towns. Town walls are repaired. The east coastline is closely guarded and is laid to waste to prevent the Danes being able to gain a foothold.

Christmas 1085
Domesday is commissioned.

10 July 1086
King Cnut dies and the threat of Danish invasion recedes.

4 Why might a threat of foreign invasion have acted as a motive for a nationwide survey of England's economic assets and land ownership?

5 Viewed in this context, how can the oath of loyalty made at Salisbury in August 1086 be interpreted?

Consider both timelines together and answer the following questions:

6 Use information from both timelines to construct a possible context for why William ordered the Domesday survey.

7 Why is it important for historians to spend time thinking about possible contexts for a document before they start to use it to draw conclusions about the past?

New earldoms and the growth of Norman influence

William was a good friend. His most loyal supporters became England's new super-rich. Domesday shows that by 1086 half the land in England was held by just 200 Normans and half of that was in the hands of only 10 magnates. Earl Hugh of Chester, for example, owned 300 manors giving an income of £800 a year. William, however, had also learned from the way Edward the Confessor had been dominated by his earls. Wessex was divided up soon after the conquest. Following Edwin's defection and then murder in 1071, the earldom of Mercia was allowed to lapse, as was that of Northumbria after the disloyalty of first Gospatric and then Waltheof. When Ralph de Gael took part in the revolt of the earls in 1075, the same fate befell the earldom of East Anglia. The new earldoms of Kent, Herefordshire, Shropshire and Cheshire were far smaller than their Anglo-Saxon predecessors and were primarily focused on defending vulnerable parts of the kingdom.

This careful management worked and as a result William's magnates enjoyed far less wealth and power than the preceding English earls. At the start of Edward's reign, the collective value of the lands held by Godwine of Wessex, Leofric of Mercia and Siward of Northumbria equalled those of the king. Edward's subsequent lack of power was shown by his inability to remove the Godwin family in 1051, while Aefgar, son of Leofric and one of the poorer earls, had enough resources to rebel against the king on two occasions and fight his way back from exile to reclaim his earldom. Odo, bishop of Bayeux, topped the post-conquest rich list but his wealth was not as great as Aefgar's. Even a coalition of the top ten magnates could not match the resources of William. He had twice as much land as all of them put together and a phenomenal income of £12,600. Roger of Hereford and Ralph of East Anglia found out the implications of this to their cost when they rebelled in 1075. William showed he could deal with even the mightiest of his subjects. In 1082, William ordered the arrest of Bishop Odo. He had finally grown tired of his half-brother's limitless ambition, including designs on the papacy. For Bishop Odo there was no dramatic fight back. He was instead placed on trial and then imprisoned in Rouen.

EXTEND YOUR KNOWLEDGE

Bishop Odo of Bayeux

William gained control of Normandy and then England with the help of a close-knit group of Norman lords, many of them related. Bishop Odo was one of these key men. Born around 1036, he was the son of Herleva, who also bore Duke William, and Herluin of Conteville. Count Robert of Mortain, another leading light, was his younger brother. In a political move and reflecting William's desire to keep important positions within the family, Odo was appointed Bishop of Bayeux in 1049. Bishop Odo, however, was always more interested in military adventure than the Church. In 1066, he contributed 100 ships to the invasion fleet, while the Bayeux Tapestry, which he later commissioned, shows him giving advice to William before the battle. In reflection of Odo's clerical rank, the Tapestry was careful to depict him as providing support from the rear at the Battle of Hastings, rather than directly fighting, with an inscription stating 'Here Odo the Bishop holding a club strengthens the boys.'

Like the other leading nobles involved in the conquest, Bishop Odo found his position transformed by the spoils of war. He became one of the king's elite tenants-in-chief through his appointment as earl of Kent in 1067, with responsibility for protecting this strategic gateway into England. He also acquired numerous estates across the country, giving him an annual income of £3,000 a year, a vast sum second only to the king. Among the English people, however, Bishop Odo became a hated figure. His ruthlessness helped provoke an uprising in Kent in 1067, while Orderic Vitalis likened him to a 'ravening wolf' for illegally seizing lands. For William this did not matter. Odo had played an invaluable part in invading and then securing his new kingdom. As one of William's most trusted deputies, Odo also acted on several occasions as William's regent when he was away in Normandy. In 1075, Bishop Odo led an army to confront Ralph de Gael, earl of Norfolk, during the revolt of the earls.

Motivated by power above all else, in 1082 Bishop Odo incurred his half-brother's wrath by planning an unauthorised military expedition to Italy, possibly in pursuit of the papacy. This was a step too far, leading to his arrest and imprisonment. Bishop Odo was only released following William's death. By this stage, William's eldest son, Robert, was duke of Normandy; his second son, William Rufus, was king of England; while his third son, Henry, was in receipt of £5,000 but no land. Seeking new advantage, in 1088 Bishop Odo joined a coalition of leading magnates determined to install Robert as king of England. William Rufus efficiently defeated the rebels and Bishop Odo was banished from England and disinherited. Perhaps in an attempt to make atonement or in the pursuit of further adventure, he joined Duke Robert on the First Crusade but died on the journey out to the Holy Land in 1097.

The Norman aristocracy

The knights of Anglo-Norman England

While the Norman earls were very different from their Saxon counterparts, a key debate has raged among historians concerning the degree of continuity among the middle-ranking nobility. How different were the countless Ethelberts and Edrics who made up the thegnly class from the Roberts and Ralphs who formed the knightly class? There were important similarities. Both were the principal warriors of the age and would have gone to war equipped with a saddled horse, armour, sword, spear and shield. Both groups also had strong bonds of loyalty to their lord. The epic Anglo-Saxon poem 'The Battle of Maldon', which reflected on their defeat at the hands of the Vikings in 991, made it clear that this included fighting to the death. Cementing these ties with symbolic acts such as the giving of arms and armour was also a consistent feature both before and after the conquest.

In many ways, though, knights were a new social group with a distinct identity and outlook. For the enfeoffed knight (see page 210), land formed the basis of both his military service and loyalty to his lord. It is also probable that among the first generation of conquerors, the bond between lord and knight was far stronger than anything seen previously, as a result of their shared experiences of war and danger. In contrast, a thegn's military service stemmed from his rank rather than the terms of his land tenure. However, the granting of land was only one way of securing loyalty. For example, a thegn might follow a lord as a result of personal commendation. While a thegn had to possess five hides or more, a knight's estate varied in size. There was also a class of landless knights in Norman England who filled the great baronial households. These were more akin to the housecarls of Anglo-Saxon times. Knights, landed or household, typically fought on horseback and their service was more militarily orientated than thegns, involving periods of garrison duty or active service in the royal army. Owing to the relatively peaceful nature of Edward the Confessor's England, thegns were also country gentlemen and military service could form just one part of their wider duties to their locality. When they did fight, it was on foot. Finally, thegns held land for their lifetime, or for three lifetimes if it was granted to them by a charter and so known as 'book land'. In contrast, the estates of the knights became hereditary towards the end of William the Conqueror's reign.

EXTEND YOUR KNOWLEDGE

Primogeniture
During William the Conqueror's reign, the principle of primogeniture become established, whereby the firstborn son inherited the family estate. This had the advantage of ensuring power bases remained intact. In Anglo-Saxon times, lands were often divided widely, the deceased's wishes being set out in a detailed will.

ACTIVITY
KNOWLEDGE CHECK

1 Find four pieces of evidence to show the replacement of the English aristocracy with a new Norman elite after 1066.

2 How does Source 6 help us to understand the system of land tenure in Anglo-Norman England?

3 In what ways did William reduce the power of the Anglo-Saxon earldoms after the conquest?

4 Write down three differences and three similarities between Anglo-Saxon thegns and Anglo-Norman knights.

TO WHAT EXTENT DID TOWN AND VILLAGE LIFE CHANGE AFTER THE NORMAN CONQUEST?

Towns and trading patterns

The flourishing urban communities of Anglo-Saxon England suffered in the immediate aftermath of the conquest. The population of York, fought over and burnt out, was reduced by around half, while countless other towns from Exeter to Durham bore the physical scars of fighting. Some towns were also partly destroyed to make way for new castles. Lincoln saw 166 houses demolished, for example. In addition to this, as Source 7 shows, town dwellers were exposed to the full avarice of the Normans and faced heavy taxation. Despite all of this, Domesday shows that just 20 years after the conquest urban society was once again thriving. This was encouraged by the Normans, who realised that towns were a valuable source of wealth. Indeed, one of the earliest documents issued by William guaranteed Londoners their traditional rights. He was keen to prevent any disruption to commerce. This was repeated for many other towns and the Domesday survey carefully recorded these pre-conquest rights and privileges. Despite the destruction caused by their building, castles also promoted urban growth. They provided a secure environment for trade, while their garrisons required goods and services from the local community. This close relationship helps to explain the development of a town around the fort of Newcastle soon after its establishment in 1080. In fact, most of the 21 new towns founded by the Normans between 1066 and 1100 were next to castles. Similarly, the vast ecclesiastical building programme, which is fully discussed later, brought significant investment to urban centres.

SOURCE
7 Part of the Domesday entry for Shrewsbury, Shropshire, c1087.

> The English burgesses of Shrewsbury say that it is very hard on them that they themselves render as much geld as they rendered TRE, although the earl's castle has occupied the site of 51 messuages and another 50 messuages are waste, and 43 French burgesses hold messuages paying geld TRE, and the earl himself has granted to the abbey which he is building there 39 burgesses formerly paying geld in the same way as the others. All together there are 200 messuages, less 7, which do not pay geld.

The Normans also provided the correct conditions for trade and business to occur. Although there were occasional baronial revolts, England was relatively peaceful after 1071 and this allowed the economy to recover and then flourish. The ports on the south coast, such as Southampton, Pevensey, Sandwich and Chichester, benefited from a strengthening of cross-Channel trade, which was the natural result of England coming into the Norman orbit. As in Anglo-Saxon times, the main exports included tin, surplus grain, hides and herrings. However, English wool was the most important export and this found a ready market in the Flemish textile industry. The conquering Normans also shared the same expensive tastes as the Anglo-Saxon nobility and imports were mainly luxury goods such as silks, spices, furs, wine and finished cloth. As a consequence of this, England's once close trading ties with Scandinavia became less important. This partly explains why York, the one-time Viking capital of England, never fully regained its prominence.

Reflecting this reorientation of trade, urban life soon developed a new continental flavour. Domesday records the presence of French communities in a number of English towns, including 96 Frenchmen in Southampton, settled in an area still known as French Street to this day. They were attracted by new commercial opportunities and favourable trading privileges. Source 8 shows that in Hereford, for example, the French burgesses, unlike their English counterparts, were granted exemption from an extensive list of customs. Although relations between incomer and native must initially have been strained, there are signs of an improvement over time. Source 9 could be questioned as being too optimistic and based on anecdotal evidence only, but its author, Orderic Vitalis, born in 1075, was the product of an Anglo-Norman union. Domesday tells of a Breton settler in Pickenham, Norfolk 'who loved a certain woman on that land and he took her in marriage', although the romance of this story is diminished by the fact that 'afterwards he held that land'. Adding to the cosmopolitan mix, the Normans also introduced a Jewish community into England for the first time. Probably coming from the established community in Rouen, they settled in London, initially dealing in silver and exchanging foreign coins for English ones. Over the next 200 years, their presence across England expanded until their expulsion by Edward I in 1290.

SOURCE 8 Part of the Domesday entry for Hereford, Herefordshire, c1087.

IN THE CITY OF HEREFORD IN THE TIME OF KING EDWARD there were 103 men dwelling within and without the wall, and they had the following customs.

If any of them wished to withdraw from the city he could with the consent of the reeve sell his house to another man who was willing to do the service due from it, and the reeve had the third penny of this sale. But if anyone through his poverty could not perform his service, he surrendered his house, without payment, to the reeve, who saw that the house did not remain empty and the king did not lack his service.

Within the walls of the city each whole messuage rendered 7d, and 4d for the hire of horses, and 3 days reaping in August at Marden, and 1 day gathering the hay where the sheriff pleased. He who had a horse went 3 times a year with the sheriff to the pleas and to the hundred courts at Wormelow. When the king was engaged in the hunt, 1 man from each house by custom went to head off game in the wood.

Other men not having whole messuages provided guards for the hall when the king was in the city.

When a burgess serving with a horse died, the king had his horse and weapons. From him who had no horse, if he died, the king had either 10s or his land with the houses on it. If anyone, overtaken by death, had not bequeathed his possessions the king had all his goods...

From this city the reeve paid £12 to King Edward and £6 to Earl Harold, and he had in his farm all the aforesaid customs.

The king, however, had in his demesne the 3 forfeiture, namely breaking his peace, housebreaking, and highway robbery. Whosoever committed one of these, paid 100s fine to the king, no matter whose man he was.

Now the king has the city of Hereford in demesne, and the English burgesses dwelling there have their former customs; but the French burgesses are quit for 12d from all their forfeitures, except the 3 aforesaid.

SOURCE 9 From *Historia ecclesiastica* ('The Ecclesiastical History') by Orderic Vitalis, c1114–41, in which he describes English towns just a few years after the conquest. Orderic Vitalis was an Anglo-Norman monk, writing in the monastery of St Evroul, Normandy.

English and Normans were living peacefully together in boroughs, towns and cities and were intermarrying with each other. You could see many villages or town markets filled with displays of French wares and merchandise and observe the English, who had previously seemed contemptible to the French in their native dress, completely transformed by foreign fashions.

Village life

For those peasants caught up in the path of the Norman armies, the impact was terrible. They experienced plunder, brutality and murder. Refugees streamed out of combat areas and whole communities were permanently displaced. The Domesday survey has allowed this suffering to be quantified. It recorded the value of manors based on rent returns in 1066, shortly after the conquest, and in 1086. In Yorkshire, where William carried out systematic wasting, the value dropped by 60 percent between 1066 and 1086, suggesting a significant long-term impact. This was by no means unique. In Sussex, the value of manors fell by 40 percent in the time after the conquest, as a result of William's brutal efforts to draw Harold into battle, and had only partially recovered by 1086.

Even in areas less seriously affected by the fighting, life became more difficult. The Normans demanded higher rents and increased obligations, forcing the peasants to work harder. The crushing burden many found themselves under was a frequent lament in the *Anglo-Saxon Chronicle*, as seen in Source 10. Tales of oppressive rents also feature routinely in Domesday. The entry for Marsh Gibbon in Buckinghamshire, for example, states how its English farmer, Aethelric, 'held it in TRE, but he now holds it at **farm** of William [fitzAnsculf] in heaviness and misery'. This also shows a downward move from landowner to tenant. In this respect, Aethelric was somewhat lucky because many freemen saw their lands absorbed into the lord's demesne. This led to a marked decline in the number of high-status peasants and a subsequent rise in landless labourers. The Domesday Book frequently says 'he is now a villain'. This descent into the villan class with its loss of income and status must have been personally tragic. Society's general contempt for this group can be seen from today's modern usage of this word.

KEY TERM

Farm
Land leased at a specific rate. In return, the tenant, known as the 'farmer', received the profits from the estate.

SOURCE 10

From the *Anglo-Saxon Chronicle* for the year 1086. It was produced in Peterborough Monastery by English monks, writing in English, and their sympathy for the ordinary people is evident.

In the twenty first year that William ruled and governed England, as God granted him, occurred a very heavy and pestiferous year in this land. Such a disease came on men that very nearly every other man had the worst illness. Afterwards, through the great bad weather which came as we already told, there came a very great famine all over England, so that many hundreds of men died wretched deaths through the famine. Alas! How wretched and how pitiful a time it was then! Then the miserable men lay well-nigh driven to death, and afterwards came the sharp famine and did for them completely.

Who cannot pity such a time? Or who is so hard-hearted that he cannot weep for such misfortune? But such things happen because of the people's sins, in that they will not love God and righteousness. Just so it was then in those days, that little righteousness was in this land with any man, except with monks alone – there where they behaved well. The king and the principal men greatly loved, and over-greatly, greedy in gold and in silver, and did not care how sinfully it was got as long as it came to them. The king granted his land on such hard terms, the hardest he could. Then a second came and offered more than the other earlier gave, and the king let it go to the man who offered him more. Then a third came and offered yet more, and the king let it go into the hands of the man who offered him most of all, and did not care how very sinfully the reeves got it from wretched men, nor how many unlawful things they did; but the greater the talk about just law, the more unlawful things were done. They levied unjust tolls and they did many other unjust things which are difficult to relate.

While life in the countryside undoubtedly became harder under Norman rule, there was some continuity with Anglo-Saxon England. The Normans did not fundamentally change the basic structure of agriculture or introduce any new innovations. In the South and Midlands, the manorial system predominated, with a **nucleated village**, a manor house for the lord or sheriff, a church and three large common fields. In the North and East, isolated, dispersed settlements were more common, meaning a manor would cover a much larger area. However, here and there were signs of change. In Yorkshire and Durham, many of the peasants displaced by the fighting were resettled in planned, nucleated villages. For their lords, this had the advantage of allowing greater control over the workforce. Unfortunately for the peasants, perhaps the greatest constant was the sheer precariousness of life. The *Anglo-Saxon Chronicle* comments on bad harvests, famines, diseases, storms and fires in 11 of the 34 years between 1066 and 1100. The Anglo-Saxon poem seen in Source 11 would have resonated just as much with the Anglo-Norman peasantry.

KEY TERM

Nucleated village
A settlement pattern in which dwellings were clustered together around a focal point, such as the lord's manor house.

SOURCE 11

From the Anglo-Saxon poem, *The Fortunes of Men*. This poem would have been recited aloud and passed down through oral tradition. Although the precise origins of the poem are unknown, it was recorded in the Exeter Book, a tenth-century anthology of Anglo-Saxon poetry compiled by Benedictine monks.

Often and again, through God's grace,
man and woman usher a child
into the world and cloth him in gay colours;
they cherish him, teach him as the seasons turn
until his young bones strengthen,
his limbs lengthen, So his father and mother
first carry him, then walk with him,
and lavish gifts and garments on him. Only God
knows how years will use the growing child.

One will die young, bringing grief to
his family. The wolf, the grey heath-stalker,
will gorge on him; then his mother will mourn.
Man cannot control his fortune.

Hunger will devour one, storm dismast another,
one will be spear-slain, one hacked down in battle.
One will enjoy life without seeing light,
he will grope about: one with feeble sinews,
a crippled foot, will curse at the pain,
rankled and resentful he will fret at fate.

One will drop, wingless, from the high tree
in the wood; look how he flies still,
dives through the air, until the tree's arms
no longer surround him. Then sadly he slumps
by the trunk, robbed of life; he falls
to earth and his soul flies from him…

One, by God's grace, will overcome
all the hardships that bedevilled his youth
and achieve happiness in old age;
he will welcome the rising sun, and receive
riches, treasures and the mead-cup from his people
as much as anyone can own in the life.

Royal forests and the forest law

The royal forests became one of the most hated symbols of Norman oppression. For Anglo-Saxon kings, hunting had long been a source of pleasure, as well as an essential way to train for war. Edward the Confessor was a keen huntsman, as was Harold Godwinson, frequently depicted in the Bayeux Tapestry with a hawk. However, this pursuit assumed a new importance under William and his sons, who, as rulers in a conquered land, were able fully to indulge their passions. They designated large tracts of Wiltshire, Dorset, Somerset and Essex as royal forest, meaning this land's primary purpose became hunting rather than agriculture. They also, unwittingly, created a lasting legacy through the creation of Sherwood Forest in Nottinghamshire and the New Forest in Hampshire. One chronicler, John of Worcester, claimed that before the latter's creation, it was 'fruitfully planted with churches and people' but on William's command 'men were expelled, homes were cast down, and the land was made habitable only for wild beasts'. There is some exaggeration here, as the New Forest's sandy soil was incapable of supporting any great population density, while Domesday showed that the majority of the area was uncultivated before 1066. However, 20 villages and a dozen hamlets, containing around 2,000 people, were destroyed in its making. Many people continued to live within the boundaries of the various royal forests and bitterly resented coming under their separate legal system, as seen in Source 12. In order to keep the environment suitable for the beasts of the chase, restrictions were placed on farming, grazing cattle and gathering wood. For all except royalty, hunting was prohibited, even on a landholder's own property, and punishments were severe. The death of two of William's sons in hunting accidents was seen by contemporaries as divine retribution.

SOURCE 12

From the *Anglo-Saxon Chronicle*, Peterborough Manuscript E, for the year 1087. An unusually frank assessment of William I by the monks of Peterborough, forming part of the overall obituary to the late king.

He had castles built and wretched men oppressed. The King was so very stark and seized from his subject men many a mark of gold, and more hundreds of pounds of silver that he took by weight, and with great injustice from his land's nation with little need. He was fallen into avarice, and he loved greediness above all. He set up great game-preserves, and he laid down laws from them, that whosoever killed hart or hind he was to be blinded. He forbade hunting the harts, so also the boars; he loved the stags so very much, as if he were their father; also he decreed for the hares that they might go free. His powerful men lamented it, and the wretched men complained of it but he was so severe that he did not care about the enmity of all of them; but they must wholly follow the king's will if they wanted to live or have land – land or property or his good favour.

Alas, woe, that any man should be so proud, raise up and reckon himself over all men. May the Almighty God show mercy to his soul and grant forgiveness of his sins.

A Level Exam-Style Question Section A

How far could the historian make use of Sources 8 and 12 to investigate the extent to which the lives of the English people were transformed by the Norman Conquest?

Explain your answer, using both sources, the information given about them and your own knowledge of the historical context. (20 marks)

Tip
These sources both focus on important aspects of town and village life.

EXTEND YOUR KNOWLEDGE

Forest
Today the term 'forest' is used to describe heavily wooded areas but in Norman times it could be applied to any type of land set aside for royal hunting. It was governed by its own set of laws. The term derives from the Latin word *foris* meaning 'outside', in this case, outside the normal legal system.

The disappearance of slavery

Orderic Vitalis described how the Normans 'arrogantly abused their authority and mercilessly slaughtered the native people' but their role in changing the position of England's most abject group is less widely acknowledged. The evidence richly testifies to the presence of slavery and slave trading in Anglo-Saxon England.

Source 13 from the tenth century is unique in imagining life from a slave's perspective, but this awareness did not translate into efforts to eradicate the practise. It is estimated that around 10 percent of the population were slaves in Edward the Confessor's time, either born into bondage or captured in war or raiding. The *Anglo-Saxon Chronicle* is matter of fact in recounting how the future King Harold raided Porlock, Somerset in 1052 and 'seized for himself whatever came his way in cattle, and in men, and in property'. When the Northumbrians rose in revolt against Tostig in 1065, they marched south seizing 'many hundreds of men, and led them off north with them, so that the shire and other shires which were near there were for many years the worse'. Once sold in England's slave markets, or carried further afield to Ireland and Scandinavia, a slave might fill any number of functions, from heavy agricultural work to domestic service, or even, as William of Malmesbury suggests in Source 14, acting as a concubine.

SOURCE 13

Written by Aelfric, abbot of Eynsham, late tenth century. Aelfric was a highly respected scholar and a prolific writer in the Anglo-Saxon language, the main theme of his work being God's mercy. This extract comes from a grammarian to help young monks learn Latin.

I go out at daybreak, goading the oxen to the field, and I join them to the plough; there is not a winter so harsh that I dare not lurk at home for fear of my master. Throughout the whole day I must plough a full acre or more ... I must fill the stall of the oxen with hay and supply them with water and carry their dung outside. Oh, oh, the work is hard. Yes the work is hard, because I am not free.

SOURCE 14

From *Gesta regum Anglorum*, c1125, by William of Malmesbury, in which he condemns slavery in Anglo-Saxon England by focusing on the sexual licence it gave to the Bristol slave merchants. William of Malmesbury expressed the view that the Norman occupation was a divine punishment of the Anglo-Saxons' corrupt and immoral lifestyle.

They would purchase people from all over England and sell them off to Ireland in the hope of profit; and put up for sale maidservants after toying with them in bed and making them pregnant. You would have groaned to see the files of the wretches of people roped together, young people of both sexes, whose youth and beauty would have aroused the pity of barbarians, being put up for sale every day.

William of Malmesbury, writing in the 1120s, could afford to look back with utmost indignation because by this point slave trading was a thing of the past in England and slavery itself was also largely gone. This was due to the actions of the Normans, who had turned their backs on this institution at around the turn of the 11th century. Part of the reason for this was economic, as many lords found it more profitable to exploit their estates by means of rent-paying tenants rather than slaves who were costly to maintain. However, there was also a moral argument championed by an increasingly assertive Church. Religious leaders were particularly unhappy with how slavery encouraged the keeping of concubines among slave owners, resulting in illegitimate offspring. Although the Normans did not introduce any great emancipation edict, their own set of values was steadily imposed on England. Quantifiable evidence is scarce, but Domesday shows that the number of slaves in Essex, for example, fell by 25 percent between 1066 and 1086. It continued to fall thereafter.

Action against the slave trade came from the highest levels. When Lanfranc became archbishop of Canterbury in 1070, he urged the king to take a stand on the export of slaves from ports like Bristol and Lewes. William was initially reluctant because he gained a share of the profits, however the ninth law from the *Laws of William the Conqueror* stated 'I prohibit the sale of any man by another outside the country on pain of a fine to be paid in full to me.' William had found a way to crack down on slavery while at the same time safeguarding at least some of his income. He showed his opposition to slavery again in 1081 when, as the *Anglo-Saxon Chronicle* says, 'In this year the King led an army into Wales, and there freed many hundreds of men.' While there is an argument that the slave trade was slowly declining in Anglo-Saxon England, the arrival of the Normans dramatically hastened its departure. One English monk, Lawrence of Durham, was able to write 'in this respect they [the English] found that foreigners treated them better than they had treated themselves'.

 THINKING HISTORICALLY Interpretations (5c)

Good questions/bad questions

Below are approaches attributed to three famous historians. They are generalisations for the purpose of this exercise.

Herodotus	Leopold von Ranke	Karl Marx
He looks for the interesting story, the drama and the colourful characters	He is interested in how great men use their influence to bring about change	He is looking underneath the events to see what patterns there are over long periods of time and how ordinary people fit in

Work in groups.

1 Devise three criteria for what makes a good historical question.

2 Consider what you know about the impact of the Norman Conquest on England.

3 Each write a historical question based on that subject matter.

Put the questions you have written into rank order, with the best question first, based on your criteria. Using a piece of A3 paper, write the names of the three historians so they form a large triangle.

Write your questions on the piece of paper so that their positions reflect how likely the historians would have been to be interested by that question. For example, a question about William's domineering style of kingship would interest Herodotus and Ranke but not Marx and so would be somewhere between Ranke and Herodotus but nowhere near Marx.

Add some further questions. Try to think of questions that only one of the three historians would be interested in, for example:

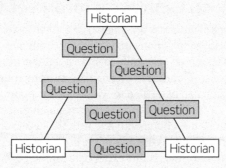

Take it in turns to try to answer the questions you have created in the style of one of the historians. See if the other members of the group can guess which historian it was.

Answer the following questions individually, using the examples created by the above activity:

4 Does one method of constructing history lead to better reasoning than the others? Explain your answer.

5 Explain why all historians who deploy rigorous methodology are, to an extent, useful sources for the study of the past.

IN WHAT WAYS DID WILLIAM AND HIS SONS REFORM THE ENGLISH CHURCH?

Controlling the Church and the deposition of Archbishop Stigand

William was a man of faith and knew that his life as a warrior-statesman frequently risked his soul. Hoping for salvation, he founded the Abbey of St Stephen at Caen in 1063 to act as a powerhouse of prayer. In the 1070s, the abbey of St Martin at Battle near Hastings was similarly created, for 'paying back for the blood shed there by an unending chain of good works' as the *Battle Chronicle* said. Generally, though, he saw no contradiction in blending piety with ruthlessness. At a ceremony marking a grant of land to a Norman monastery, he pretended to plunge a knife into the abbot's hand, saying 'Thus should land be given.' There was little the abbot could say or do in response. William tightly controlled the Norman Church and he wanted to extend this same level of domination to England's ecclesiastical affairs.

William rightly saw the Anglo-Saxon Church as a major source of power and influence. It held over one-quarter of landed wealth, while archbishops, bishops and abbots were important political figures, with long-established roles in advising the monarchy. Although William wanted his men controlling the Church, he at first moved cautiously. This was partly because the backing of the existing establishment was needed to confirm his legitimacy as Edward's rightful successor. Ealdred, archbishop of York, duly complied by presiding over the coronation. William was then diverted by the series of uprisings against his rule. By 1070, these had been largely crushed and the opening of the York **archbishopric** following Ealdred's death in September 1069 pushed the issue of Church leadership into the spotlight.

At a Church council held at Winchester at Easter 1070, the papal **legate**, Ermenfrid, bishop of Sion, had Archbishop Stigand deposed and he was then imprisoned at Winchester. Papal blessing was needed both for the appointment and the removal of bishops, but such an act could not have happened without William's full approval. Successive popes had condemned Stigand for holding two bishoprics and supporting the **antipope**, Benedict X. They had their man at last. Stigand's removal was followed shortly afterwards by the removal of the bishops of Selsey, Lichfield, Durham and Elmham. In their place, William installed loyal supporters from the great churches of Normandy and France. Thomas of Bayeux, one-time chaplain to Bishop Odo of Bayeux and William himself, became archbishop of York while Lanfranc was selected as archbishop of Canterbury. After this purge, only three English-born bishops remained – Leofric of Devon and Cornwall, Siward of Rochester and Wulfstan of Worcester. By William the Conquerer's death, Wulfstan was the last native bishop. It was a similar picture with the great abbeys of England. By 1086, only three Anglo-Saxon abbots remained. The Norman purge did not extend to the lower levels of the Church. English priests, monks and nuns were not figures of importance or capable of posing a military danger and so were largely left alone.

Archbishop Lanfranc's reform of the Church

Lanfranc's appointment as archbishop of Canterbury showed that William's takeover of the English Church was not simply motivated by power. Both men were firm supporters of the papal reform movement that aimed spiritually to strengthen the western Church and, in particular, to remove common abuses of **canon law,** including **simony**, **nepotism**, **pluralism** and **clerical marriages**. Indeed, William had been able to win Rome's support for his invasion by presenting it as an opportunity to take control of, and reform, an outdated English Church, riddled with corruption. In order to bring the Church into line with the latest ways of thinking, Lanfranc convened ten great Church councils during William's reign, itself a new departure, as few had taken place in the Anglo-Saxon period. A formal record exists only for the 1075 Council of London, shown in Source 15. In this Lanfranc is identified as the 'primate of the whole of Britain'. This represented a significant shift in power. While the claim to lead the Church in Scotland and Wales was largely honorific, Lanfranc had, with William's backing in 1070, formally established the primacy of Canterbury over York. Previously these two sees had been considered equal, although in practice the former's wealth and prestige meant this was far from so.

KEY TERMS

Archbishopric
An archbishop's area of authority, with the cathedral church acting as its centre. It could also be referred to as a see or diocese. The chief archbishoprics were Canterbury and York.

Legate
A member of the clergy representing the pope.

Antipope
A rival claimant to the papacy.

KEY TERMS

Canon law
The universal law of the Church.

Simony
The selling of Church posts.

Nepotism
Appointing friends and family to posts.

Pluralism
Holding more than one Church office at once.

Clerical marriage
Priests were meant to be unmarried and celibate, but this was widely flouted.

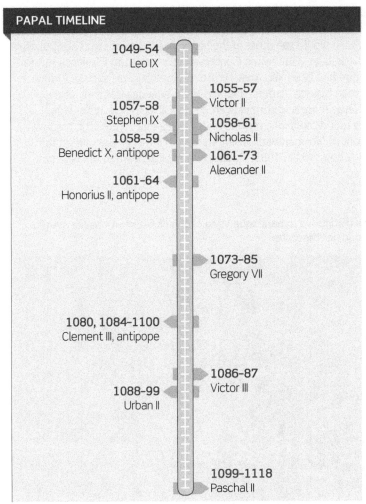

PAPAL TIMELINE

1049-54
Leo IX

1057-58
Stephen IX

1058-59
Benedict X, antipope

1061-64
Honorius II, antipope

1055-57
Victor II

1058-61
Nicholas II

1061-73
Alexander II

1073-85
Gregory VII

1080, 1084-1100
Clement III, antipope

1086-87
Victor III

1088-99
Urban II

1099-1118
Paschal II

SOURCE 15

A formal record of the ecclesiastical synod at London, 1075, from Archbishop Lanfranc's collected letters. It should be viewed as the official minutes of the council, also recording attendance. It was signed by all those present, included two archbishops, 12 bishops and 21 abbots.

In the year of Our Lord 1075, in the ninth year of the reign of William, glorious king of the English, a council of the whole land of England was assembled in the church of St Paul the Apostle in London, namely of bishops, abbots and many ecclesiastics. The council was summoned and presided over by Lanfranc, archbishop of the holy church of Canterbury and primate of the whole island of Britain...

Because the custom of holding councils had been in abeyance in the realm of England for many years, some legislation which is already defined in ancient law was renewed...

iii) Following the decrees of Popes Damasus and Leo and also the councils of Sardis and Laodicaea, which prohibit the existence of episcopal sees in small townships, by the generosity of the king and the authority of the synod, permission was granted to three of the bishops mentioned above to move from townships to cities: Hermann from Sherborne to Salisbury, Stigand from Selsey to Chichester, and Peter from Lichfield to Chester. The case of certain others who remained in townships or villages was deferred until the king, who was at that time fighting overseas, could hear it in person...

(vii) No one shall buy or sell holy orders nor any position in the Church which carries pastoral responsibility. This crime was originally condemned in Simon Magnus by the Apostle Peter; later on it was forbidden and outlawed by the holy Fathers...

(ix) Following the council of Elvira and the eleventh council of Toledo, no bishop or abbot nor any of the clergy shall sentence a man to be killed or mutilated; nor shall he lend the support of his authority to those who are passing sentence.

The London council approved the transfer of three bishop-seats from rural to urban locations, with more to be considered. This brought England into line with the continental view that bishops should be based in large towns close to their flocks. This was also part of a wider reorganisation aimed at creating a uniform, hierarchical Church. The bishoprics themselves were subdivided into smaller territorial units called archdeaconries, each one being headed by an archdeacon. Although this post had existed prior to 1066, few had been appointed and they did not have territorial jurisdiction. By the end of William the Conqueror's reign, almost every bishop had a deputy, policing the localities and ensuring common standards were being maintained. Archdeaconries were themselves divided into rural deaneries, headed by deans, giving yet another layer of control. At the lowest level, the parish was formally recognised, served by a single church and priest.

Many of the reforms introduced by Archbishop Lanfranc were administrative, seeing Church reorganisation as the first step towards the enforcement of higher moral standards. In order to spread the ideas of the reform movement, he demanded bishops hold regular councils of their own, known as synods. Separate Church courts were also introduced, as seen in Source 4 (see page 220).

This was not a complete transformation of pre-conquest patterns, as the writ only applied to hundred courts. Clerical matters could still be heard in shire courts, presided over by bishops. When William tried Bishop Odo in 1083 as a tenant-in-chief rather than a member of his clergy, it demonstrated that the king remained in overall control.

Lanfranc used the synods to speak out on corruption, for example attacking simony at the 1075 Council of London. A year later, at the council of Winchester, he demanded celibacy from the clergy and decreed that in future no-one could be ordained if they were married. Parish priests already married were allowed to remain so, but higher standards were expected of cathedral clergy. They were presented with a choice of either giving up their role or their wives. The English Church was probably no more corrupt than its European neighbours and it had also not been completely isolated from the reforming ideology of the continent. Anglo-Saxon bishops were present at some of the great continental councils, while Earl Harold and his brother, Tostig, went on pilgrimage to Rome in 1061. Although it is impossible to say what direction Church policy would have taken if Harold had stayed king, it is probable that papal reforms would have taken hold. The Normans, motivated by religious idealism, simply speeded up the process.

KEY TERM

Romanesque
The ecclesiastical architectural style that dominated western Europe in the 11th and 12th centuries. Inspired by the Byzantine Empire, it was characterised by thick walls, vaulted ceilings, rounded arches and large towers.

For the ordinary people, the impact of Lanfranc was tangible. Soon after taking office, he ordered the redevelopment of Canterbury Cathedral in the distinctive **romanesque** style. This was the start of an architectural transformation which would see most of the larger Anglo-Saxon churches pulled down and rebuilt, including the cathedrals of Winchester, Canterbury, Durham and Gloucester. Prior to 1066, the only comparable structure had been Westminster Abbey. Nothing was sacred. Lanfranc, together with many of the new Norman Church leaders, doubted the credentials of many of the English saints, such as St Dunstan. Their relics and shrines were removed as the churches were redeveloped. Parts of the liturgy, the round of chants, prayers and masses that formed the mainstay of services, were also altered in favour of Norman versions. For some this was an assault too far, including the monks at Glastonbury who rioted in 1083, leading to a massacre when the Norman abbot sent in knights to restore order.

SOURCE

16 Durham Cathedral, constructed between 1093 and 1133 in the distinctive romanesque style of the Normans. It has survived to this day largely unchanged and as a result is now a UNESCO world heritage site.

William II and Archbishop Anselm

Archbishop Lanfranc died in 1089 and William II showed no interest in appointing a successor, preferring to take the profits of the bishopric instead. Severe illness in 1093 focused his mind, however, and, convinced that he was going to die, William sought to appoint Anselm, the abbot of the great Norman monastery at Bec, to fill the vacancy. At first Anselm rejected the offer, before succumbing to pressure from the king and his assembled magnates. William, however, did not die and soon came to regret his moment of weakness. Intelligent, cruel and cynical, he was unconcerned about piety and saw the Church as an institution to be controlled and exploited. In contrast, Anselm was deeply enthused with the reform movement. There was to be no repeat of the close co-operation that had characterised William's father's relationship with his archbishop.

The most serious clash arose over which of the two rival popes to recognise, Urban II or Clement III. William shared his father's belief that it was the king's right to decide. Unfortunately, while abbot of Bec, Anselm had already recognised Urban II, and out of loyalty refused the king's demand to retract this. Aggravating the situation further was Anselm's insistence that he needed to travel to Rome to collect his pallium from Urban II himself. Over four days in February 1095, the magnates of England held a council at Rockingham to discuss the issue. The bishops were royal appointees rather than theologians and, as a result, were fiercely loyal to the king. They encouraged Anselm to fall in with William's wishes. William de St-Calais, the bishop of Durham, even advised William II to depose Anselm, partly encouraged by his own desire for the office. During the debate, however, the lay nobles swung behind the archbishop, won over by his dignified demeanour in the face of fierce pressure. They also realised that the charges of disloyalty being directed against him were unfair, as Anselm had made clear his recognition of the pope and need to go to Rome from the outset of his appointment. As a result, the conference ended in deadlock. In an attempt to find a solution, William opened secret negotiations with Pope Urban II through his legate, Walter of Albano. In return for recognising the pope, William secured the concession that no legates or papal letters would be sent to England without the king's consent. This was a significant success as it placed the king in firm control of the information flow between the English Church and its centre. Anselm was not informed of these discussions, mainly because William II also attempted to link the recognition of Urban II to the removal of Anselm, although this was rejected by the legate. Anselm received his pallium in May 1095 but he was now fully aware of the king's dislike of him.

Over the next two years, the relationship became strained as William repeatedly refused Anselm permission to organise a reforming council. This mattered to Anselm because he saw it as his godly duty to tackle the corruption evident in the English Church, including William's own practice of selling Church offices and leaving others empty to take the revenues, as highlighted in Source 17. In 1097, both men allowed matters to come to a head. Knowing that it would be a provocation, Anselm asked permission to go to Rome to discuss the matter of Church reform. He was old, in poor health and viewed his office as a burden. William was now in a far stronger position, as a result of the temporary acquisition of Normandy from his brother (see Chapter 4) and the defeat of a rebellion by Robert de Mowbray. Receiving the full backing of the clergy and barons, who were by now tired of what they saw as Anselm's intransigence, William issued an ultimatum. If Anselm left for Rome, William would confiscate his lands and never again receive him as archbishop. Staying would involve Anselm paying a fine and promising not to appeal to Rome again. Faced with a stark choice between exile and submission, Anselm chose the former.

The disagreement between William and Anselm was at a level that had few wider ramifications for the people of England. High politics continued with Anselm's arrival in Rome in April 1098, where he was greeted with honours. There was an exchange of letters between pope and king as each set out their case, although these have not survived. At the Papal Council of Bari in October, William's behaviour was discussed and the prospect of excommunication was raised but not acted on. At Christmas, William's clerk, William Warelwast, arrived in Rome to put the king's case. In truth, Urban II was not prepared to take decisive action in support of Anselm. Urban II's continuing struggle against Clement III meant that he needed England's financial support through the payment of the Peter's Pence tax (a voluntary contribution to the Church). Fate now took over and, before a solution could be found, Urban II died in July 1099 and William in August 1100.

SOURCE

17 From the *Anglo-Saxon Chronicle*, Peterborough Manuscript E, for the year 1100, which reflects on the reign of William II. The monastery's concern for the wider state of the Church is evident.

And through the advice of evil men, who were always agreeable to him, and through his own avarice, he was always harassing this nation with raiding and with excessive taxes, because in his days every justice fell and there rose up every injustice before God and before the world. He humiliated God's church; and in his days, when the elders fell in bishoprics and abbacies he either granted them all in return for money, or held in his own hand and put out at rent, because he wanted to be the heir of every man, ordained and lay. And thus on the day that he fell, he had in his own hand the archbishoprics in Canterbury and the bishopric in Winchester and that in Salisbury and eleven abbacies, all put out at rent. And although I prolong it further, all that was customary in this land in his time – all that was hateful to God and to just men. And therefore he was hated by well-nigh all his nation, and abhorrent to God, just as his end showed, because he departed in the midst of his injustice without repentance and any reparation.

AS Level Exam-Style Question Section A

How much weight do you give the evidence of Source 17 for an enquiry into Church–state relations under William II?

Explain your answer using the source, the information given about it and your own knowledge of the historical context. (12 marks)

Tip

Remind yourself who compiled the Anglo-Saxon Chronicle.

 THINKING HISTORICALLY   Cause and consequence (6b)

Attitudes and actions

Individuals can only make choices based on their context. Prevalent attitudes combine with individual experience and natural temperament to frame the individual's perception of what is going on around them. Nobody can know the future or see into the minds of others.

Context	Action
• Before being appointed archbishop, Anselm had developed a formidable reputation as the abbot of Bec in Normandy. He had known and been respected by William I. • Anselm was an ardent supporter of the papal reform movement. William II repeatedly refused Anselm's requests to organise reform councils or travel to Rome. • Anselm disapproved of the abuses in the English Church and feared that if he did not attempt to tackle them, God would hold him personally responsible. • Both king and archbishop were plain speaking. Anselm was aware of William II's dislike for him but had repeatedly shown his determination to stand up for his beliefs, which saw God put before the king. • Anselm had only accepted the position of archbishop of Canterbury with extreme reluctance and increasingly regarded it as an intolerable burden.	• In November 1097, Anselm went into exile. His aim was to travel to Rome in order to highlight to Pope Urban II the extent of corruption in the English Church and seek counsel. He also wanted to tender his own resignation after four years of what he regarded as fruitless effort. He must have realised, though, that this was unlikely to be accepted, as it would set a dangerous precedent for how monarchs could remove their troublesome bishops.

Answer the following questions individually and discuss your answers in a group:

1 What do you think stopped Archbishop Anselm from choosing exile sooner?

2 Why do you think Anselm finally took the dramatic step of going into exile?

3 What do you think Anselm hoped to achieve by leaving England for Rome?

4 How reasonable was Anselm's course of action given what he understood about the situation at the time?

5 What other information would have been useful to him to help him decide on his course of action?

6 If William II had lived, do you think he would have been prepared to enter into negotiations to secure the return of Anselm?

7 How far should the historian try to understand the context of the beliefs and values of people in the past when explaining why individuals make choices in history?

Henry I, Anselm and the investiture controversy

The issue of England's exiled archbishop now became the problem of Henry I. Possessing none of his brother's disdain for the church, he invited Anselm to return to England in 1100. Although agreeing, the archbishop brought with him the latest ideas from Rome, focused on freeing the Church from secular control. At the papal councils of Clermont and Bari in 1098 and Rome in 1099, **lay investiture** had been specifically condemned because it implied a bishop was dependant for his power on his lay lord, rather than power stemming from the Church. The performance of homage by churchmen to a layman was similarly unacceptable. Anselm dutifully enforced the pope's reforming decrees and, after being greeted by Henry in September 1100, announced that he was unable to perform submission. Furthermore, Anselm warned Henry that if he attempted to invest new bishops himself, they would not be recognised.

This was a direct attack on the monarchy's traditional rights over the Church. William I had maintained the powers of investiture and homage. It was also a strategic problem, because bishops were tenants-in-chief and owing knight-service and homage was a symbolic way of confirming this feudal relationship. Both men, however, did not want the dispute to end bitterly. Henry, still establishing himself on the throne, needed a united Church behind him, as well as the reputation as a god-fearing leader. He was also aware that an exiled archbishop could be exploited by Duke Robert of Normandy, whose own intentions were not yet clear. On Anselm's side was a sense of duty to the English people as their moral guardian, while, as his return to England shows, he also believed that Henry was a monarch with whom he could do business. As a result, the matter of investiture and homage was temporarily put to one side by referring it to Rome, in the hope that Pope Paschal II would soften his stance. In the meantime, Anselm provided good service to his new king by presiding over his marriage to Matilda, also crowning her queen. When Duke Robert landed in England at the head of an army in summer 1101, Anselm played a leading role in persuading many wavering magnates to remain loyal.

In September 1101, the pope's response was received, urging the king to give up the practice of lay investiture but no specific reference was made to homage. While this would form the basis of the eventual settlement between king and archbishop, it would take a further five years to be realised. In Easter 1102, a further mission was sent to Rome, bringing no new solution. Meanwhile, in autumn 1102, Anselm was permitted to hold a reforming council, in which he condemned clerical marriage and simony, among other abuses. Just like William I, Henry had shown that he was in favour of Church reform as long as it did not impinge on his own powers. However, the underlying issues could only be ignored for so long. As Henry's power in England grew, he felt able to exert increasing pressure on Anselm, backed up by his nobles and bishops, to pay him homage and accept lay investiture. In Easter 1103, Anselm again went into self-imposed exile.

Anselm's departure increased the magnitude of the dispute as it brought greater intervention from the pope. In December 1104, Pope Paschal sent Henry a letter, wishing him health, honour and victory but also warning him that those who do not hold the grace of Christ may feel Christ's sword instead. The following March, this was made real when the king's chief advisor, Robert of Meulan, was excommunicated for his role in urging Henry to continue lay investiture. It was obvious that the king would be next and, in order to save his soul, careful negotiations were undertaken. This saw a personal reconciliation between Henry and Anselm in August 1106 in the Norman monastery of Bec, as well as a settlement which was approved of by the pope. The king agreed to give up his right of investiture but he retained the right to receive homage. Anselm returned to England and the compromise was officially sanctioned at a Church council in London in August 1107. While this could be seen as a surrender on Henry's part, his leading churchmen still had to profess obedience and perform their feudal obligations. His influence over appointments was also undiminished, leaving him able to nominate trusted servants such as William Warelwast as bishop of Exeter and his nephew, Henry of Blois, as bishop of Winchester.

The Norman kings and the papacy

For monarchs and princes across Europe, the papal reform movement was a clear challenge. It meant they were not the sole power in their kingdoms or the only focus of loyalty. The results could be destructive. The German emperor, Henry IV, and Pope Gregory VII became locked in a bitter dispute over who had the right to choose and invest bishops. Both sides refused to give way and it ultimately led to open warfare, with Henry IV capturing Rome and deposing Gregory VII in favour of Clement III.

In England, relations never became this strained under William or his sons. It was, however, Edward the Confessor who experienced the first hint of the reforming hand of the papacy. Pope Nicholas II signalled his desire to clamp down on abuses when, in 1061, he granted the pallium to Ealdred, archbishop of York, only on condition that he gave up his Worcester bishopric. Overall, Edward maintained firm control over the English Church and cordial but distant relations with Rome.

William I, too, expected to rule his Church absolutely, although he also managed to enjoy surprisingly positive dealings with the papacy who valued his support for moral reform. As a result, Alexander II provided the papal banner for William at Hastings, while in 1070 he sent legates to re-crown the king and depose English bishops. Early letters between Alexander II's successor, Gregory VII, and William also illustrate warmth. However, this became harder to maintain in the face of Gregory VII's determination to expand papal authority. In particular, he wanted to enforce the regular attendance of English bishops at Rome. In 1080, the pope also called in the favour of his support for the invasion and demanded William pay homage to him for his kingdom. Although William I and Lanfranc were conscientious reformers, they had no desire to diminish their control over the Church. Lanfranc avoided attending papal synods, while William politely rejected any act of fealty, shown in Source 18. William did agree, though, to the payment of Peter's Pence, the ancient tax given to Rome, but made it clear that this did not imply submission. These divisions did not escalate, partly because Gregory VII became too embroiled in the conflict with Henry IV.

SOURCE

18 Letter from William the Conqueror to Pope Gregory VII, summer 1080. This is the king's reply to a letter received from the pope. In this, Gregory VII reminded William of the support provided by the papacy for the invasion of England in 1066. This letter sets out William's official policy towards Rome.

To Gregory, most exalted pastor of Holy Church, William, by the grace of God king of the English and duke of the Normans, sends greetings and the assurance of friendship.

Your legate Hubert, who came to me, holy father, has on your behalf directed me to do fealty to you and your successors and to reconsider the money payment which my predecessors used to send to the Roman Church. The one proposition I have accepted; the other I have not. I have never desired to do fealty, nor do I desire it now; for I neither promised on my own behalf not can I discover that my predecessors ever performed it to yours. As to the money, for almost three years it has been collected without due care, while I was engaged in France. But now that by God's mercy I have returned to my kingdom, the sum, already collected is being sent to you by the above-named legate and the balance will be conveyed, when the opportunity arises, by the legates of our faithful servant archbishop Lanfranc.

Pray for us and for the welfare of our kingdom, for we held your predecessors in great regard, and it is our desire to show to you above all men unfeigned respect and obedient attention.

William II successfully continued his father's policy of resisting papal encroachment. After Gregory VII's death in 1085, the new pope, Victor III, ruled for one year and had no contact with England. His successor, Urban II, was only recognised by William in 1095 on the condition that papal legates sought royal consent before entering England. When Anselm went into exile in 1097, relations deteriorated, although Urban II's own political weakness in Rome prevented him from excommunicating William. Henry I, as has been seen, used tact and diplomacy in his dealings with the papacy and managed to ensure its control over the English Church was not extended during his reign.

A Level Exam-Style Question Section B

How far was the English Church reformed in the years 1066–1106? (20 marks)

Tip

A large focus will be on Lanfranc's efforts, but also consider how all the Anglo-Norman kings resisted the expanding papacy and consider too the breakdown in Church–state relations under William II.

ACTIVITY
KNOWLEDGE CHECK

1 Why did William I want to reform the English Church?

2 How useful is Source 15 to historians seeking to understand Lanfranc's reforms?

3 To what extent does Source 17 explain the Church's hostility to William II?

4 What was the cause of the investiture controversy in England?

5 How did Henry I end this investiture controversy?

ACTIVITY
SUMMARY

1 To gain an overview of the main developments in this chapter, complete the table below. Aim to include at least four pieces of evidence per category.

Category	Evidence of continuity with Anglo-Saxon England	Evidence of a break with Anglo-Saxon England
Anglo-Norman government		
Anglo-Norman elite		
Anglo-Norman towns and village		
Anglo-Norman Church and papal relations		

2 Reviewing the table, where does the balance lie? Which categories changed the most and least? Write a conclusion to the question 'To what extent did the Normans transform Anglo-Saxon England?'

3 To summarise Anglo-Norman papal relations, complete the following table.

King	Reign dates	Popes	Areas of agreement	Areas of dispute
William I				
William II				
Henry I				

AS Level Exam-Style Question Section B

How far were the lives of the English people transformed by the Norman Conquest?
(20 marks)

Tip

This is a broad question and will require information from all four sections in this chapter. In order to gauge the extent of change, remember to include information about Anglo-Saxon England.

WIDER READING

Crouch, D. 'God and the Normans', in *History Today* (October 2002)

Douglas, D. *William the Conqueror*, University of California Press (1964)

Golding, B. *Conquest and Colonisation*, Palgrave (1994)

Golding, B. 'Britain AD 1100', in *History Today* (April 2000)

Gransden, A. '1066 and all that revisited', in *History Today* (September 1988)

Huscroft, H. *Ruling England 1042–1217*, Pearson (2005)

Morris, M. *The Norman Conquest*, Hutchinson (2012)

Thomas, H. *The Norman Conquest*, Rowman (2008)

2a.4

Normandy, 1066–1106

KEY QUESTIONS

- Why did William decide to invade England in 1066?
- How effectively did William deal with the threats to Normandy, 1066–87?
- Why did William Rufus and Robert Curthose fail to restore the Anglo-Norman kingdom, 1087–1100?
- How did Henry I reunite England and Normandy?

INTRODUCTION

The Normans were not quite French. They were instead the descendants of Viking raiders, first attracted to northern France in the ninth century by hopes of slaves, gold and trouble. The Latin for 'Norman' is *normannus*, meaning 'northmen'. A key turning point came in 911 when the powerful Viking leader Rollo signed a treaty with Charles the Simple, king of France, for a grant of land around Rouen. The unruly Norsemen now began channelling their energies into state building, realising a more bountiful source of wealth lay in settled agriculture rather than loot. Rollo and his successors steadily extended their enclave and in the process adopted the language, culture and institutions of their French neighbours, while still retaining their own distinct identity. Normandy's status as a permanent feature of the French political landscape was made clear in 987 when the house of Capet replaced the Carolingians as the ruling royal family. Richard the Fearless formally acknowledged Hugh Capet as his overlord in return for the title of count of Normandy. Almost a century later, William I had achieved unimagined success by raising himself to kingly status with the conquest of England. This chapter will begin by examining the strong military and diplomatic position of Normandy on the eve of 1066 that helped form William's decision to invade England. The subsequent victory at Hastings, however, created its own problems, as enemies and impatient sons alike began casting their jealous eyes over the duchy. The troubled fate of the duchy of Normandy post-1066 will also be detailed.

Why did William decide to invade England in 1066? William's claim to the English throne

William regarded himself as the rightful heir to Edward the Confessor. According to Norman writers such as William of Poitiers, William had first been promised the English throne by King Edward in around 1051. Unfortunately, no English sources mention this pledge, despite its obvious significance. While it could therefore be dismissed as Norman propaganda, Edward did have strong links to the duchy of Normandy from his time in exile (see page 169). It also fits into a period when Edward was

---

1069 – Revolt in Maine against Norman rule

November 1076 – William I is defeated at Dol, Brittany

1078–80 – Revolt against William I by Robert Curthose

1080 – Robert Curthose campaigns in Scotland against King Malcolm

1084–87 – Second exile of Robert Curthose

August 1087 – William I campaigns in the Vexin

| 1065 | 1070 | 1075 | 1080 | 1085 |

1073 – Reconquest of Maine by William I

1077 – King Philip of France regains control of the Vexin

1079 – William is defeated at Gerberoy

9 September 1087 – Death of William I and division of the Anglo-Norman realm

1087–1100 – William II king of England

1087–1106 – Robert Curthose duke of Normandy

attempting to counter the power of Earl Godwin by building up a Norman faction in his court. While an offer by the childless king in 1051 is therefore conceivable, it seems unlikely that Edward held it valid in later years, given his efforts to bring over the remnants of the Wessex royal line from Hungary and his deathbed appointment of Harold (see page 185).

William's claim also rested on Harold's alleged visit to Normandy in around 1064. According to the Normans, this was carried out on Edward's behalf in order to reaffirm his earlier promise of the throne. While in William's court, Harold took a fateful oath to support Duke William in becoming king. Establishing the truth of this story is once again problematic. No contemporary English sources mention the visit, while later English writers, such as William of Malmesbury, give very different versions, arguing, for example, that Harold travelled to Normandy in order to secure the release of family members. These later accounts claim that, once in William's court, Harold was coerced into swearing an oath, although coercion would have rendered it invalid. While the truth will never be known, William's claim to the throne does appear tenuous and certainly far less credible than Harold's, who had the assent of the dying king. However, this did not matter.

England in the mid 11th century was certainly a wealthy prize to be gained and the prospect of elevating his status from duke to that of a king might well have added to the allure for William. In any case, at the outset of 1066, William clearly believed that he had the right to the throne as well as the military might to secure it.

The military position of Normandy

In 1066, Normandy was ready for war. William was a warrior in his prime, with almost two decades of experience of leading men into battle. He had also surrounded himself with an aggressive and tightly knit group of powerful nobles. The inner circle consisted of his two half-brothers, Robert of Mortain and Bishop Odo of Bayeux, as well as his childhood friends, Roger of Montgomery and William fitzOsbern. The wider Norman elite, including Robert, count of Eu, Roger of Beaumont and William de Warenne, were no less tied to him through family or friendship, grants of land and above all a shared desire for wealth and power.

These men were at the top of an aggressive, war-orientated society, keenly aware through oral tradition of their Viking heritage. The Normans were also some of the finest cavalrymen in Europe, with each lord maintaining highly skilled knights. William was able to call upon these in 1066, thereby raising the question of whether his duchy could be described as truly feudal (see page 210). This seems doubtful. Although William was pre-eminent, with his magnates largely accepting the principle that they owned their land and future prospects to him, there does not seem to have been a system of fixed knight quotas. Instead, William used his fearsome personality to draw military service from his vassals. He also made full use of the ties of kinship that directly, or indirectly through marriage, connected him to most of the noble families, as well as the quality of the personal relationships he had built up with them. William's ability to wage war was further strengthened by the fact that Normandy, compared to the standards of the time, was a prosperous and well-administered dukedom, with taxation being collected efficiently by the *vicomtes*, the Norman equivalent to sheriffs. This gave him the financial resources to fund a large mercenary contingent to add to his army.

1091 - William II and Duke Robert reach agreement in the Treaty of Rouen

1096 - Robert Curthose pawns Normandy to William II to fund his crusade

15 July 1099 - Jerusalem is captured by the crusaders

1101 - Robert Curthose invades England

1102 - Robert of Belleme is forced out of England by Henry I

| 1090 | 1095 | 1100 | 1105 | 1110 |

1088 - Unsuccessful rebellion against William II on behalf of Robert Curthose

1094 - William II attempts to conquer Normandy

1097-99 - William II regains Norman influence in Maine and the Vexin

2 August 1100 - Death of William II

1100-35 - Henry I king of England

28 September 1106 - Henry I defeats Robert Curthose at the Battle of Tinchebrai

1106-35 - Henry I duke of Normandy

By 1066, the strategic vulnerability of Normandy, stemming from its lack of natural frontiers, had also been addressed. While protected by the English Channel, on the landward side its forests and rolling countryside merged seamlessly with its neighbours. Although the eastern boundary was marked by the Bresle and Epte rivers, with the Selune and Couesnon rivers performing the same function in the west, in reality these were small, fordable streams. Similarly, the River Avre, a tributary of the River Eure, failed to act as a significant barrier in the south. The one great waterway, the Seine, sliced through the duchy itself, creating a split between upper and lower Normandy. Flowing through both Paris, seat of the Capetian kings of France, and Rouen, William's capital, it also firmly connected Normandy to the heart of France. As a result of its ill-defined geography, the duchy was uncomfortably exposed to surrounding rivals, all with the capacity to make trouble.

As highlighted in Figure 4.1, Flanders and Ponthieu lay to the west and Brittany to the east. The Vexin acted as a buffer to the area held by the French king, while Maine assumed strategic importance by separating Normandy from the great regional power of Anjou. Chapter 2 demonstrates how William overcame this weakness in the lead up to the invasion of England through martial ability, luck and diplomacy. In 1054 and then again in 1057, he defeated a two-pronged invasion by the count of Anjou, Geoffrey Martel and King Henry I of France, while their respective deaths in 1060 brought him room for manoeuvre. The new French king was an infant and Anjou descended into civil war. In 1063, William took Maine and, in 1064, Brittany was subdued.

Flanders at least could be considered a willing ally as a result of William's marriage to Matilda, daughter of its ruler, Count Baldwin. All these events coalesced to give William a vital window of opportunity in 1066, allowing him to leave his duchy and wage a war of conquest across the Channel.

Papal support for William's claim

William was keen to present his invasion as a crusade against a corrupt Anglo-Saxon society. William certainly was a pious man and, under his rule, the Norman Church had flourished, with his own foundation at Caen becoming a centre of monastic learning under its abbot, Lanfranc. Furthermore, William allowed the Norman Church to hold reforming councils to discuss and implement the latest ideas from Rome. It is therefore not surprising that, in preparing for his invasion of England, William appealed to Pope Alexander II for diplomatic support. In early 1066, a mission was sent under the leadership of Gilbert, archdeacon of Lisieux, to explain the Norman case. Although no written records have survived, it is probable that Gilbert focused on Harold's broken oath and the poor state of the English Church under Stigand, archbishop of Canterbury, a man long held in contempt by Rome. This is where Norman and papal interests must have converged, with Alexander II seeing in William a useful tool for bringing religious reform to the English Church and with it greater central control. As a result, Alexander II publicly proclaimed his support for the invasion and in so doing gave William's cause stronger legitimacy. It does not appear that Harold Godwinson was summoned to offer his own defence by the papacy.

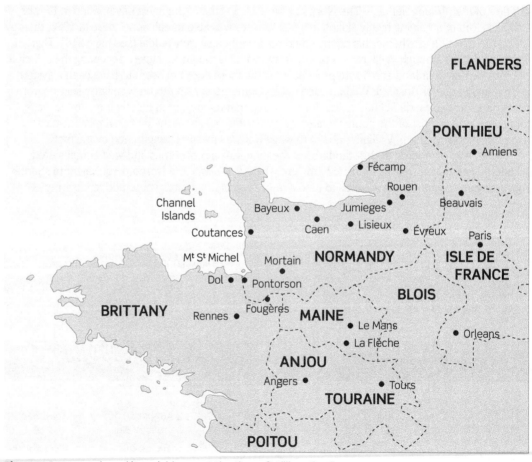

Figure 4.1 Normandy and its neighbours at the time of William the Conqueror.

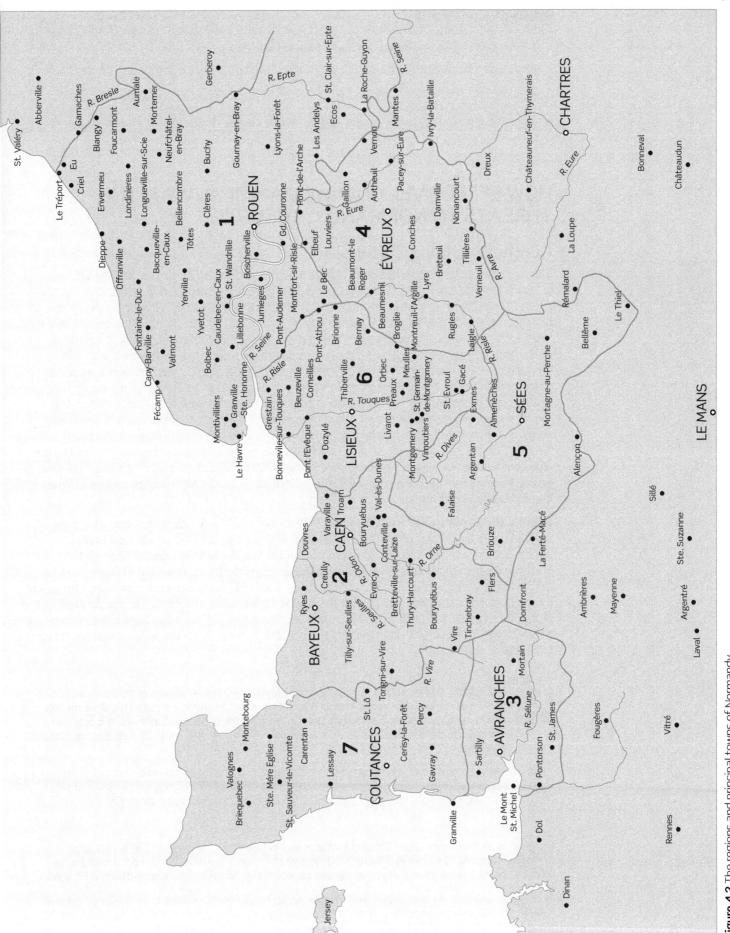

Figure 4.2 The regions and principal towns of Normandy.

HOW EFFECTIVELY DID WILLIAM DEAL WITH THE THREATS TO NORMANDY, 1066–87?

Conflict in Maine, 1068–73

The carefully constructed protection of Normandy from invasion, while vital in allowing William to launch his 1066 expedition to England, proved short-lived. Norman rule over the independently minded Maine had always been precarious. In 1069, the county revolted, falling under the control of one of its own lords, Geoffrey of Mayenne, whose power base lay in the north of the county. William received the news while campaigning in England and was unable to respond. His wife, in charge of Normandy in his absence, lacked the forces or command ability to deal with the crisis herself. Over the next few years, Geoffrey of Mayenne managed to maintain his position over a rebellious population only with difficulty, for example losing control of the city of Le Mans for most of 1070. In 1072, events became more worrying when Maine was seized by Fulk le Rechin, count of Anjou. This also signalled that the bitter succession dispute, which had sapped the strength of Anjou and seen Count Fulk pitted against his brother, was now over. Although not the power it had been under Geoffrey Martel, the reappearance of this traditional enemy on Normandy's border was unwelcome. However, this was just one of several threats facing William and choices had to be made. The need to secure the frontier at the other end of the Anglo-Norman empire proved more pressing and William invaded Scotland that summer.

By 1073, confident that England was secure, William was ready to act. Sources 1 and 2 highlight how this was a near replay of his 1063 conquest of Maine, although William was now Europe's most feared warrior with access to the resources of England, including its troops. Entering the county at the start of the campaigning season, he employed surprise, speed and violence. In quick succession William successfully attacked the strongholds of Fresnay, Beaumont and Sille. Moving on to devastate the countryside surrounding the capital, Le Mans, it surrendered without the need for a protracted siege. By 30 March, just a few weeks after setting out, William was back in Normandy. The ease with which he completed the reoccupation of Maine shows that it was a distraction for William rather than a major crisis.

SOURCE

From *Gesta Guillelmi ducis Normannorum et regis Anglorum* by William of Poitiers, c1070s. William of Poitiers was a royal chaplain to William the Conqueror. He based his *Gesta* mainly on the testimony of those who had been involved in the events and as a result it provides a valuable insider's view of the Normans. In this extract Duke William's 1063 invasion of Maine is outlined.

This then was his chosen method of conquest. He sowed terror in the land by his frequent and lengthy invasions; he devastated vineyards, fields and estates; he seized neighbouring strongpoints and where advisable put garrisons in them; in short he inflicted innumerable calamities upon the land.

SOURCE

From the *Anglo-Saxon Chronicle*, Worcester Manuscript D, for the year 1073. This was produced by monks in the English language at a time when most official documents were being written in Latin. Its purpose was to record significant events which affected England.

In this year King William led an English and French raiding army across the sea and won the land of Maine, and the English greatly despoiled it; they did for vineyards, burned down towns, and greatly despoiled that land, and bent all that land into William's hands, and afterwards they turned home.

EXTEND YOUR KNOWLEDGE

Normandy and Flanders

William's marriage to Matilda was based on love and fidelity. As the daughter of the count of Flanders, Baldwin V, it also brought him strategic advantage. Following Baldwin V's death in 1067, positive relations continued under his son and heir, Baldwin VI. However, on 16 July 1070, Baldwin VI died unexpectedly. In the ensuing succession dispute, the late count's son, Arnulf, and brother, Robert, both vied for power. William backed the principle of primogeniture and to reinforce Arnulf he dispatched William fitzOsbern who, according to Orderic Vitalis, set out for Flanders 'as if to a game'. The reality was far more deadly. At the Battle of Cassel on 22 February 1071, Robert triumphed by killing his nephew. William fitzOsbern also fell. For William, the loss of his childhood friend and closest advisor must have been difficult. He now also had to contend with a hostile power on his eastern flank. The implications of this became apparent when Robert warmly welcomed Edgar the Atheling into his court, following his expulsion from Scotland after William's 1072 invasion.

William's defeat at Dol

The rise of King Philip I of France

Not all dangers could be so easily dealt with. King Philip I of France emerged from his minority determined to oppose Norman dominance. Seeking allies, in 1072 he married Robert of Flanders's half-sister, Bertha of Hainault. Then, as highlighted in Source 3, he offered Edgar the Atheling the Castle of Montreuil-sur-Mer as a base for harassing Normandy. So seriously did William take this threat that he speedily readmitted Edgar the Atheling to his court. It was, however, the fall-out from the 1075 revolt of three earls that gave Philip the opportunity to engage William directly. Earl Ralph de Gael of Norfolk fled back to his native Brittany, establishing himself in the Castle of Dol on Normandy's western frontier. In a provocative move, he was reinforced by troops from Anjou, indicating the speed at which an anti-Norman coalition was forming. William had to act. Advancing into Brittany in September 1076, he harried the land and lay siege to Dol. The castle held out and in November Philip arrived at the head of army, surprising William into retreat.

SOURCE 3

From the *Anglo-Saxon Chronicle*, Worcester Manuscript D, for the year 1074. As a result of their location, the Worcester monks who compiled the chronicle were extremely well informed about the North of England and Scotland.

In this year King William went across the sea to Normandy, and on the Feast of St Grimbald Prince Edgar came from the land of the Flemings into Scotland, and the king Malcolm and his sister Margaret received him with great honour. At the same time Philip, the king of France, sent a letter to him and ordered him to come to him, and he would give him the castle at Montreuil so that afterwards he could daily do ill-turns to those not his friends. Well, then the king Malcolm and his sister Margaret gave him and all his men great gifts and many treasures in furs covered with purple cloth, and in pelisses of marten-fur, and miniver-fur and ermine-fur and in purple cloth, and in golden and in silver vessels, and led him and all his sailors out of his domain with great honour. But on the journey it turned out badly for them when they were out at sea, because very rough weather came on them, and the raging sea and the strong wind cast them on that land so that all their ships broke up, and they themselves came to land with difficulty, and well-nigh all their treasure was lost. And also some of his men were captured by the French men, but he himself and those of his fittest men travelled back again to Scotland, some pitiably walking on foot, and some wretchedly riding. Then the king Malcolm advised him that he send to King William across the sea, and ask for his protection, and so also he did, and the king granted him that and sent for him.

While William had not ceded territory, the defeat at Dol was significant. According to the *Anglo-Saxon Chronicle*, he lost 'both men and horses, and many of his treasures'. Furthermore, he had failed to remove Ralph de Gael. As this was his first military setback, William's reputation for invincibility was tarnished. Most importantly, William's opponents were emboldened. In very late 1076 or early 1077, Fulk Le Rechin attacked John of La Fleche, one of William's strongest supporters in Maine, in order to undermine Norman control. On this occasion, William broke the siege. In 1077, Simon of Crepi, ruler of the Vexin, retired to a monastery and Philip immediately occupied this crucial buffer without serious opposition from William, who was still reeling from his defeat at Dol. This meant that the kings of England and France were now close and hostile neighbours on the River Epte and this was to have fatal results.

The demands of Robert Curthose, 1078–83

It is also possible that William's eldest son regarded these setbacks as a sign of his father's declining power. Up to this point, Robert Curthose had been a loyal son, in return being made count of Maine and recognised as the heir to Normandy prior to his father's departure to England in 1066. When William returned to England in December 1067, Robert assisted his mother, Matilda, in governing the duchy of Normandy and assumed greater responsibility after her departure for her crowning in England in 1068. All, however, was not well in the relationship. William regarded his eldest son as spoilt and irresponsible, often subjecting him to taunts and humiliations in court. In 1077, it seems the 25-year-old Robert, in common with heirs apparent across the ages, began demanding more power. As Source 4 shows, his demands became increasingly angry. His father, in common with rulers across the ages, refused, 'driving the young man away with jeers in that terrific voice', according to William of Malmesbury. Compounding Robert's sense of frustration was the fact that his wish for more power coincided with his father's increased presence in Normandy, directing its defence. This ended what little autonomy Robert had enjoyed. Tensions came to a head late in 1077 or early 1078, when a brawl broke out between Robert and his younger brothers. The next day Robert and his followers signalled open revolt by making a foolhardy attempt to seize Rouen Castle before fleeing into exile.

SOURCE 4

From *Historia ecclesiastica* by Orderic Vitalis, c1114–41. An Anglo-Norman monk from the monastery of St Evroul, Normandy, Orderic Vitalis wrote his Church history over a 30-year period from 1114 onwards. Orderic Vitalis gathered details about the arguments between William I and Robert Curthose from a fellow monk at St Evroul, who had previously been a messenger to Queen Matilda.

I am not prepared to be your hireling forever. I want at last to have property of my own, so that I can give proper wages to my dependants. I ask you therefore to grant me legal control of the duchy, so that, just as you rule over the kingdom of England, I, under you, may rule over the duchy of Normandy.

This was a crisis not only for William but also for the wider Norman elite. Robert Curthose's rebellious entourage embraced the sons of many of the great families, including Robert of Belleme, son of Roger of Montgomery, and William of Breteuil, eldest son of William fitzOsbern and brother of the recently imprisoned Roger de Breteuil, earl of Hereford. As such it revealed a generational divide between the close-knit warriors who had faced danger together and conquered England and their children, who felt shut out from power and had few exploits to their names. It also testified to the magnetism of Robert Curthose's personality, described by Orderic Vitalis in Source 5. He had built up a large and powerful entourage of knights, renowned for their arrogance, sense of entitlement and extravagant lifestyle. The rebellion became significantly more menacing when Robert toured the courts of Flanders and France. Philip I eagerly took the opportunity and supplied Robert with knights, as well as a castle at Gerberoy, near Beauvais. This allowed Robert to begin raiding into the east of Normandy. Testifying to its seriousness, William laid siege in the depths of winter, shortly after Christmas 1078. After three weeks, the rebels sallied out to battle and unexpectedly won. William, before being put to flight, was unhorsed by his son and wounded in the arm. William Rufus, fighting for his father, was also injured, while many others were killed or taken prisoner.

SOURCE 5

From *Historia ecclesiastica* by Orderic Vitalis, c1114–41. Orderic Vitalis is regarded by modern historians as a careful scholar, who based his *Historia* on archival work and, where possible, eyewitness testimony. He could not completely remove personal bias from his writing, which reveals his support for Henry I and dislike of Duke Robert.

He [Robert Curthose] was talkative and extravagant, reckless, very courageous in battle, a powerful and sure archer with a clear and cheerful voice and a fluent tongue. Round faced, short and stout, he was commonly nicknamed 'fat legs' and 'curt hose'.

SOURCE

From the *Anglo-Saxon Chronicle*, Worcester Manuscript D, for the year 1079. Normally cautious in tone, this entry is unusually fulsome in detailing William's defeat at Gerberoy.

Here Robert, the son of King William, ran from his father to his uncle Robert in Flanders, because his father would not let him govern his earldom in Normandy which he himself and also the king Philip with his consent had given him; and the best who were in the land had sworn him oaths and taken him as lord. Here Robert fought with his father, and wounded him in the hand; and his horse was shot under him; and he who brought up another for him was straightaway shot with a cross-bow – that was Toki, son of Wigod; and many were killed there, and also captured; and Robert turned back to the land of the Flemings. We do not want, though, to write more here of the harm which he did his father... [Here a leaf of the manuscript has been cut away.]

Gerberoy was a significant defeat. William of Malmesbury described it as William the Conqueror's greatest humiliation, while the *Anglo-Saxon Chronicle*, as seen in Source 6, refused to dwell on its implications, or if it did the section was destroyed. The sense of betrayal felt by the king must only have increased when he found out about his wife's involvement in supplying Robert with funds, her loving defence eloquently stated in Source 7. Inevitably, the reverse of Gerberoy was followed by an attack from elsewhere. King Malcolm, after hearing the news, took the opportunity to ravage over the border from the River Tweed to the River Tees from August to September 1079. Meanwhile, William's leading magnates, including Roger of Montgomery and Roger of Beaumont, mediated between father and son. Employing, as Orderic Vitalis said, 'fair speech and pleading to soften his harshness', they also knew their own children's futures depended upon a successful outcome. The king shot back 'Which of my ancestors from the time of Rollo ever had to endure such hostility from any child as I do?' Pressure mounted on William, with even the pope urging reconciliation. Finally, he relented and at Easter 1080 welcomed Robert back to Normandy and reconfirmed his inheritance. In autumn, Robert acted as the dutiful son by setting out on his father's behalf to punish Scotland, in the process leaving his own stamp on history by founding Newcastle.

SOURCE

From *Historia ecclesiastica* by Orderic Vitalis, c1114–41. In this extract Matilda explains to William why she helped their rebellious son. While Orderic Vitalis was never an eyewitness to these events, he used his creativity and wider historical knowledge to bring probable conversations to life.

O my lord, do not wonder that I love my first-born child with tender affection. By the power of the most high, if my son Robert were dead and buried seven feet deep in the earth hid from the eyes of the living, and I could bring him back to life with my own blood, I would shed my blood for him and suffer more anguish for his sake than, weak woman that I am, I dare to promise. How do you imagine that I can find any joy in possessing great wealth if I allow my son to be burdened by dire poverty? May I never be guilty of such hardness of heart; all your power gives you no right to demand this of me.

The division of Anglo-Norman territories

The death of King William I

William celebrated Christmas 1085 in Gloucester but it must have been a tense and lonely time. He was in his late fifties, extremely fat and had recently lost his adored wife. His Anglo-Norman empire was surrounded by enemies. King Cnut IV of Denmark, son of Sweyn Estrithson, was threatening invasion of England, while Malcolm stood hostile on the Scottish border, ready to take advantage. On the continent, Philip I, Fulk Le Rechin and Robert of Flanders, buoyed by memories of Dol and Gerberoy, were all looking for opportunities to bring about William's downfall. His half-brother, Bishop Odo, was trying to ferment rebellion from prison, while Robert Curthose was once again in exile, having fled William's court in 1084 following further arguments with his father. Although embittering William the Conqueror, his son's actions were not as threatening as before. Robert Curthose travelled widely rather than attempting a new campaign to gain control of the duchy of Normandy, spending time in Italy and Germany, as well as a stint on the **tournament** circuit in France. Nevertheless, William would spend the last 24 months of his life on the defence.

> **KEY TERM**
>
> Tournament
> The tournaments of this period were fought between rival groups of knights over an area of several square miles. Events could last several days and provided an ideal military training ground, as well as a way to earn prize money through the capture and ransoming of opponents.

While the threat to England from Denmark had diminished by 1086, the other problems remained and, a decade after being taken under French control, the loss of the Vexin began to bite. In summer 1087, the French king's garrison at Mantes began raiding into Normandy. Still a fighter, William assembled his army and went on the offensive. He devastated the Vexin and, as highlighted in Source 8, put Mantes to the torch. This was his last military act. As he rode through the burning streets of the town, his horse took fright, flinging him against the pommel of his saddle. In agony, William retreated to Rouen and then to the priory of Saint Gervase, away from the noise and heat of the city. It was clear that he was dying. William Rufus and Henry gathered by his bedside but Robert stayed away, preferring the court of the French king and achieving one last slight against his father.

SOURCE 8

From the *Anglo-Saxon Chronicle* for the year 1087, Manuscript E. By this date, only the monks at Peterborough were maintaining this record of English history.

King William went from Normandy into France with an army, and raided against his own lord, Philip the king, and killed a great part of his men, and burned down the town of Mantes and all the holy minsters which were inside the town. And two holy men who served God living in an anchorite's cell were burned to death there. This thus done, the king William turned back to Normandy. He did a pitiful thing, and more pitiful happened to him. How more pitiful? He became ill and that afflicted him severely.

What can I say? The sharp death which spares neither powerful men nor lowly – it seized him. He died in Normandy on the day immediately after the Nativity of St Mary, and was buried in Caen at St Stephen's minster; he had built it earlier and afterwards endowed it in many various ways.

Alas! How false and unstable is the prosperity of this world. He who was earlier a powerful king, and lord of many a land, he had nothing of any land but a seven-foot measure; and he who was at times clothed with gold and with jewels, he lay the covered over with earth.

Only two accounts of the last days of William the Conqueror's life have survived. *De obitu Willelmi* ('On the Death of King William') was written by an anonymous monk of St Stephen's in Caen, William's own foundation, shortly after the event. The other account, by Orderic Vitalis, was produced some 50 years later but reflected his careful historical research. His full description includes a long, clearly imagined speech in which William the Conqueror reviews his life. The sorrow for the bloodshed must have been genuine, however. William was pious and after confessing his sins made lavish bequests to the Church. To please God, he also ordered the release of all his prisoners, including Earl Morcar, Earl Roger and even King Harold's brother, Wulfnoth, held hostage since 1051. The one exception was Bishop Odo of Bayeux, but William relented after pleading by his magnates. William then, as shown in Source 9, formally committed the duchy of Normandy to Robert, his firstborn son. As England had been won in conquest and at huge cost, William felt able to bequeath England only to God but hoped that God would grant it to William Rufus. Finally, William gave Henry £5,000, perhaps worth 70–80 times that amount today.

SOURCE 9

From *Historia ecclesiastica* by Orderic Vitalis. Writing between 1114 and 1141, Orderic Vitalis used his obvious literary skill to depict a likely version of William's death, based on the accounts of others. Orderic Vitalis also had the benefit of hindsight in his writing, knowing that Robert Curthose's dukedom would descend into disorder.

I invested my son Robert with the duchy of Normandy before I fought against Harold on the heath of Senlac; because he is my first-born son and has received the homage of almost all the barons of the country the honour then granted cannot be taken from him. Yet I know for certain that any province subjected to his rule will be most wretched. He is a proud and foolish fellow, doomed to suffer prolonged and grim misfortune. I name no man as my heir to the kingdom of England; instead I entrust it to the eternal Creator to whom I belong and in whose hands are all things.

How should this division of William's lands be viewed? Although there were no set laws of inheritance, it could be seen as conforming to the established customs of the Norman aristocracy, whereby the family lands in Normandy passed to the eldest son and the English lands of conquest went to the second son. However, the separation of Normandy from England undid William's finest achievement and divisions like this were not the usual practice for west European kings. A different conclusion is also suggested by the fact that the accounts of the king's final days stress his continuing anger towards Robert Curthose. It is possible that William's intention was not to divide his lands but to disinherit Robert and give everything to his second son. It was only pressure from his magnates, recognised in Source 10, as well as an acknowledgement of the binding nature of previous promises, that forced him to relent and propose a compromise. Viewed in this way, perhaps William's final words to Henry, as reported by Orderic Vitalis, were a way of consoling himself as much as his younger son. 'Be satisfied, my son... Patiently allow your elder brothers to take precedence over you. Robert will have Normandy and William England. But you in your own time will have all the dominions that I have acquired.'

SOURCE 10

From the short text *De obitu Willelmi* c1087. It is thought to have been written soon after the king's death by an anonymous monk from William's foundation of St Stephen's in Caen. Later analysis has shown that the text is heavily based around a pre-existing description of the death of King Charlemagne, although altered enough to fit the events of 1087. Despite this, it still has considerable value as a contemporary record.

And as he thought fit, he decreed what was to be given to churches, to the poor, and, lastly, to his sons. And he allowed William his son to have the crown, sword and sceptre encircled with gold and jewels. Whereupon the venerable archbishop William and the others who were present were afraid lest he should remain implacable towards his eldest son Robert, for they knew that a wound frequently opened or cauterized causes sharper pain to the wounded. Trusting therefore in the indomitable forbearance which he invariably showed, they sought gently to sway his mind through archbishop William whose advice he valued. At first the king showed the bitterness of his feelings. Pondering a little while, and collecting his waning strength, he seemed to be counting the number and degree of the injuries he had received from him. Then he spoke: 'Because', he said, 'he had no wish to come and scorns to come, I must now do my part: as you and God are my witnesses, I forgive him all the injuries he has done me, and I give him all the duchy of Normandy.'

AS Level Exam-Style Question Section B

How effectively did William I deal with the challenges to the position of Normandy after 1066? (20 marks)

Tip
In writing your answer, consider which of William's enemies posed the greatest threat.

ACTIVITY
KNOWLEDGE CHECK

1 Who were King William I's main continental enemies after 1066?

2 List the setbacks William suffered in France between 1066 and 1087.

3 How useful is Source 4 for understanding why Robert Curthose rebelled against his father in 1077?

4 Which do you think was the worst defeat for William, Dol or Gerberoy? Explain your answer.

5 How useful is Source 10 for understanding William's deathbed decision to separate England and Normandy?

WHY COULDN'T WILLIAM RUFUS OR ROBERT CURTHOSE RESTORE THE ANGLO-NORMAN KINGDOM, 1087–1100?

The position of Anglo-Norman nobles

Robert Curthose had something to celebrate. After years of frustrated ambition, his father's death meant that he was at last the undisputed ruler of Normandy. He now set about rebuilding his influence in the duchy after his long period of exile by spending money. Past followers had to be rewarded and new ones bought. This was costly and unsustainable and, soon after Robert took power, the Norman treasury, according to Orderic Vitalis, began to run low. A few months later, his situation was eased with £3,000 from his brother Henry in return for a grant of rights over the Coutances and the Avranchin regions in the west of Normandy. Meanwhile, in England, William Rufus was installing himself as king. Aged 27, he was crowned at Westminster on 26 September 1087. One of his first acts was to take full control of the royal treasury at Winchester, finding it overflowing with gold, silver, jewels, robes and precious objects. Following his father's wishes, he distributed generously to the Church, giving away as much as £8,600. However, at heart suspicious, he refused to release the earls Morcar and Wulfnoth, although the latter, after 36 years in captivity, was a harmless old man incapable of maintaining himself in the outside world.

For the Anglo-Norman magnates, William the Conqueror's deathbed division of his realm was far from welcome. It created a conflict of loyalty, which is neatly summarised in Source 11. With lands on both sides of the Channel, these magnates now faced the impossible task of serving two lords. Wrong decisions on their part would be measured in lost estates. This concern gave way to conspiracy when leading nobles headed by Bishop Odo met to discuss the situation shortly after William the Conqueror's death. They agreed that the only solution was to depose William Rufus and reunite England and Normandy under Robert Curthose. William Rufus's harsh character, which they feared would eventually be turned against them and their estates, counted against him, as well as the fact that few of the magnates were bound to him with oaths of loyalty. After Christmas 1087, Duke Robert was informed of the plot and pledged his full support.

SOURCE

11

From *Historia ecclesiastica* by Orderic Vitalis, c1114–41. In this extract the Anglo-Norman monk gives voice to Bishop Odo of Bayeux, one of the chief plotters against William I. While the exact words may have been imagined, Orderic Vitalis gives an insight to the sentiment.

How can we provide adequate service to two lords who are so different and who live so far apart? If we serve Robert duke of Normandy, as we ought, we will offend his brother William, who will then strip us of great revenues and mighty honours in England. Again, if we obey King William dutifully, Duke Robert will confiscate our inherited estates in Normandy...

Let us form an inviolable league; since King William is the younger of the two and very obstinate and we are under no obligation to him he must be deposed or slain. Then let us make Duke Robert ruler over England and Normandy to preserve the union of the two realms, for he is older by birth and of a more tractable character, and we have already sworn fealty to him during the lifetime of the father of both men.

EXTEND YOUR KNOWLEDGE

Did Duke Robert want to invade England in 1088?
It seems doubtful that, without the intervention of the magnates, Duke Robert would have had the ambition to invade England so early on in his ducal rule. Having only visited the country a few times, he had no deep attachment to it. All his previous struggles with his father, which had been pursued with vigour and single-mindedness, were focused on Normandy and Maine.

THINKING HISTORICALLY   Cause and consequence (6a)

Seeing things differently
Different times and different places have different sets of ideas. Beliefs about how the world works, how human societies should be governed or the best way to achieve economic prosperity can all be radically different from our own. It is important for the historian to take into account these different attitudes and be aware of the dangers of judging them against modern ideas.

Oath-taking
Under William I's feudal system, vassal and lord became bound together through the granting of land, mainly in return for military service. This relationship was reinforced by symbolic acts such as the giving of arms and armour and in particular oath-taking. For Normans, an oath was a sacred bond, which should never be broken. This explains why Harold was condemned as a perjurer and usurper for taking the throne in England, after allegedly making an oath to William over holy relics. Similarly, in August 1086, following the Domesday survey, William was able significantly to strengthen his position by receiving oaths of loyalty from his leading magnates at a ceremony in Salisbury. Following William's death and the division of the Anglo-Norman realm between Robert Curthose and William Rufus, these ties of loyalty placed unique strain on the Anglo-Norman magnates as they faced the difficult task of trying to serve two masters.

Answer the following questions:

1 What attitudes do you think had given rise to the idea that an oath, once given, was a sacred bond?

2 If the Anglo-Norman magnates had known how events would progress, for example that Robert Curthose would be deposed by his younger brother, do you think those that were bound by ties of allegiance to Robert would have changed their attitude?

3 Norman attitudes to oaths are different from current attitudes in England.

  a) Are there any other ways in which Norman attitudes differed dramatically from those that are current in England now?

  b) If so, why do you think that they are different?

4 How important is it for historians to deal with events in the context of the beliefs and values of people in the past as well as seeing them as part of a greater pattern?

The rebellion of 1088

The first sign of trouble was the absence of many leading men from William Rufus's 1088 Easter court. When the revolt came, it struck hardest in Kent. Bishop Odo established himself in Rochester Castle, recognising that its strategic position allowed Canterbury and London to be threatened while it could also receive reinforcements from the continent along the Thames and Medway rivers. By summer, its garrison stood at 500 knights. Further south, Gilbert fitzRichard's castle at Tonbridge and Robert of Mortain's castle at Pevensey ensured the rebels had a secure corridor to Normandy. The other main area of rebellion was in the West where Bishop Geoffrey of Coutances and Robert of Mowbray burnt Bath and Berkeley and raided into Wiltshire, while William of Eu rode north into Gloucestershire. Three Herefordshire barons took Hereford and burnt Gloucester with Norman, English and Welsh troops. Subsidiary revolts took place in Leicestershire, Northampton and Durham. The *Anglo-Saxon Chronicle* provides the most detailed narrative of these events.

SOURCE

12 Entry from the *Anglo-Saxon Chronicle*, Peterborough Manuscript E, for the year 1088. After 1079, Peterborough was the only monastery maintaining this annual history of England. It was still being written in the English language and as such is one of the few contemporary documents putting forward the concerns of the English.

This foolish plan was planned in the spring. Then as soon as it came to the Easter, they travelled and raided and burned and laid waste the king's home-farms, and they did for the lands of all those men who were in the king's service. And each of them travelled to his castle and manned and provisioned it as best they could. Bishop Geoffrey and Robert of Mowbray travelled to Bristol, and raided, and brought the plunder to the castle; and afterwards they went out from the castle and raided Bath and all the land thereabout, and they laid waste all Berkeley. And those men who were the chief in Hereford, and all the shire forth with them, and the men of Shropshire with a great people from Wales came and raided and burned in Worcestershire, on until they came to the market-town itself, and wanted to burn the market-town, and rob the minster, and get their hands on the king's castle. Seeing these things, the revered bishop Wulfstan became very troubled in his mind, because the castle was entrusted to him to hold; however, the men of his court went out with a few men from the castle, and through God's mercy and through the bishop's merits, killed and captured five hundred men, and put all the others to flight. The bishop of Durham did what harm he could everywhere in the north. One of them was called Roger, who ran away into the castle at Norwich, and still did worst of all over all the land. Hugh also was one who did not improve anything, neither in Leicestershire nor in Northampton. The bishop Odo, with whom the business originated, travelled into Kent to his earldom and greatly did for it, and wholly laid waste the king's land and the archbishop's, and brought all the goods into his castle in Rochester.

SOURCE 13 The keep at Rochester Castle in Kent, built after the 1088 revolt to replace the original wooden earthwork castle used by Bishop Odo as his power base.

William II was under threat. Of the ten greatest baronial landholders in the Domesday Book, six were on the rebels' side. The king correctly recognised Bishop Odo as his main opponent. Leaving the smaller problems to local commanders, he marched into Kent in April with the simple plan to seek out and destroy his main enemy. By June, Tonbridge and Pevensey castles had fallen, while out at sea a relief force sent by Robert Curthose was intercepted and destroyed. The royal army then turned on Rochester. Two siege engines were set up and conditions in the castle deteriorated quickly. The rebels sought an honourable way out and in the ensuing negotiations it was the king's magnates rather than the king himself who took the lead. Against his desire for punishment, they sought mercy, pointing out, according to Orderic Vitalis, that he had now shown to all how the 'young William is no less powerful than old William'. This was a clear example of the Norman aristocracy drawing together to protect its own members from the wrath of the king. The king acquiesced, realising he needed their support as much as they needed his.

In early July, Bishop Odo and his allies were allowed to leave, bearing arms and riding their horses, but they were jeered by the English troops who demanded the traitors be hanged. With the collapse of the main rebellion in the East, the other insurrections faded away. In the final balance sheet, the rebels had underestimated the king's strength and overestimated their ability to withstand sieges. Robert Curthose's failure to cross the Channel in support was also a factor. He was an accomplished fighter and his presence would have boosted morale.

William II in Normandy, 1091

William II was not a man to forgive. Once control over England was consolidated, his sights were set on revenge and conquering Normandy. From 1090, William began using the superior resources of the English treasury to win over the nobles of Upper Normandy and, in February 1091, he arrived in the duchy to see what further gains could be made. No fighting is recorded and the brothers soon made peace at Rouen, the terms of the pact outlined in Source 14. The pledge of help against his enemies in Maine was the most valuable clause for Robert Curthose; while ever needful of money, he also benefited from the valuable gifts William brought him as a sweetener. William strengthened his position in Normandy by gaining control of significant territories, including the entry port of Cherbourg in the west and the county of Eu in the north. The real loser was Henry, who at that time was in possession of Cherbourg, while he also faced being shut out of the family inheritance by Robert's and William's decisions to become each other's heir.

SOURCE

 14 From the *Anglo-Saxon Chronicle*, Peterborough Manuscript E, for the year 1091. Compiled by monks, it provides a contemporary insight into events.

At Candlemas [2 February] he [King Henry] travelled, to his brother's discomfiture, out of England into Normandy. While he was there, their reconciliation came about on the condition that the earl handed over to him Fecamp and the earldom of Eu and Cherbourg. And in addition to that the king's men were to be unmolested in the castles which they had earlier got from the earl against his will. And in return the king promised him to make Maine obedient, which their father won earlier, and which had then turned against the earl; and promised him all that his father had over there, except what he had granted to the king, and that all those who in England earlier lost their land in the earl's cause should have it again by this pact – and the earl just as much in England as was laid down in their covenants. And, if the earl pass away without son by lawful wedlock, the king was to be the heir of all Normandy; by this same covenant if the king die, the earl was to be heir of all England. This covenant was sworn by 12 of the best of the king's side, and 12 of the earl's – though it did not last for long.

Once the covenant was concluded, the two brothers then turned on Henry, who had fortified his castles in Coutances and Avranches in protest, before retreating to the island monastery of Mont-Saint-Michel. Surrounded by treacherous sands and tidal waters, a direct assault was impossible. Instead, the elder brothers mounted a siege, lasting from February to April. Skirmishes were frequent and, on one occasion, William was unhorsed by a knight of Henry's, only avoiding a more deadly follow-up blow by roaring that he was the king. Clearly confident in his immunity in battle, he was also single-minded in pursuit of victory. William of Malmesbury records how, in a telling moment, William wanted to reject Henry's request to collect water, arguing that it would only prolong the siege, whereas Robert displayed his commitment to family and chivalric values by stating 'Good heavens should I leave our brother to die of thirst? And where shall we look for another if we lose this one.' In April, Henry negotiated an honourable surrender, eventually finding refuge in Domfront Castle on Normandy's southern frontier. Meanwhile, Robert and William returned to England in August to deal yet again with King Malcolm, who had invaded Northumbria in May.

The peace made between Robert and William at Rouen in 1091 ensured stability in Normandy for the next two years but, by the end of 1093, the brothers' relationship was faltering as William showed no intention of aiding Robert in Maine. Following a meeting in Normandy in March 1094 to settle this issue, William once again went on the offensive, his army's advance only being halted by the timely intervention of King Philip of France on Robert's behalf. The French king knew that a destabilised Normandy posed little threat to his own kingdom and it was in his interest that neither brother should emerge victorious. He later allowed himself to be bought off by William and withdrew his forces. The campaign dragged on inconclusively until William returned to England in December. Unable to return to Normandy the following year as a result of a rebellion by the earl of Northumbria and William of Eu, he arranged for Henry to be supplied with arms and funds to continue the war from his base at Domfront. Before this new front could have any impact, however, the fortunes of Normandy were dramatically changed by Pope Urban II's electrifying call to crusade.

The significance of Robert's decision to go on crusade

At Clermont in November 1095, the pope delivered a sermon calling upon all Christians to retake the holy city of Jerusalem. Duke Robert's motives in taking the cross are complex. Orderic Vitalis, consistently critical of Robert, suggested that it was to escape problems at home. Personal piety, the spirit of adventure and the wish to fight in a cause that surpassed even his father's conquest of England must also have played their part. What is certain is the impact of his decision on Normandy. Robert needed both to raise funds to finance the expedition and to ensure that Normandy was safeguarded in his absence. With the help of a papal legate, a deal was struck during the summer of 1096. William agreed to lend Robert £6,666, taking in return Normandy as a pledge for repayment. In September 1096, William crossed to Normandy with the funds, raised through harsh taxation in England, and Robert departed for the East.

William's activity over the next few years deserves credit. As well as suppressing a Welsh revolt in 1097 and sending an army to Scotland, he took his custodianship over Normandy seriously. By 1099, two campaigns in Maine had restored Norman domination to this county, while he also successfully pushed the power of the French king back in the Vexin. Following his father's death here, this was unfinished business for the loyal son. On the crusades, Robert too had success. Jerusalem was captured on 15 July 1099 and by the autumn Robert was on his way back, covered in glory. The next decisive event to impact on Normandy was not his return, however, but the misfired arrow from Walter Tirel's bow that killed William outright on 2 August 1100.

ACTIVITY
KNOWLEDGE CHECK

1 How does Source 11 help us to understand why many nobles wanted an Anglo-Norman union?

2 How useful is Source 12 for understanding the scale of the 1088 rebellion against William II?

3 Who gained the most from the 1091 treaty at Rouen: Robert, William or Henry?

4 Outline two ways in which Robert's decision to go on crusade impacted Normandy.

The Rufus Stone Memorial in the New Forest, marking the spot where William II died.

HERE STOOD
THE OAK TREE,
ON WHICH AN ARROW
SHOT BY
SIR WALTER TYRRELL
AT A STAG,
GLANCED AND STRUCK
KING WILLIAM
THE SECOND,
SURNAMED RUFUS,
ON THE BREAST,
OF WHICH HE
INSTANTLY DIED,
ON THE SECOND
DAY OF AUGUST,
ANNO 1100.

HOW DID HENRY REUNITE ENGLAND AND NORMANDY?

The defeat of Robert of Belleme

Securing control of England

Henry had intelligence, charm and more than a streak of ruthlessness, while to his advantage he lacked William's temper or Robert's short-sightedness. He had, though, grown up in their shadow. Following William's death and with Robert still away on crusade, Henry decided that it was his turn to shine and he set out to seize the English throne. Speed was of the essence. Many Anglo-Norman magnates felt that England and Normandy should be united under one ruler and the natural figure for this was the elder brother, Robert. Leaving William's corpse in the New Forest, Henry rushed to Winchester to secure the royal treasure. In the absence of Anselm, archbishop of Canterbury, Henry persuaded the bishop of London to crown him king on 5 August. To build support among the magnates, Henry used the coronation to issue a 'charter of liberties', promising to abandon the unjust practices experienced during William's reign. Henry further distanced himself from his unpopular brother by imprisoning the unpopular royal clerk, Ranulf Flambard, in the Tower of London and seeking the return of Anselm. In November, in a move to appease his English subjects, he married Edith, daughter of King Malcolm of Scotland and Queen Margaret, and niece of Edgar the Atheling.

EXTEND YOUR KNOWLEDGE

Ranulf Flambard

Ranulf Flambard was a royal clerk who rose to prominence under William I during his work on the Domesday survey and then as keeper of the king's Great Seal. Under William II he took a lead role in managing the financial affairs of the kingdom and in particular helping increase royal revenues by improving the efficiency of tax collection and raising taxes. He actively pressed lawsuits in the pursuit of unpaid taxes, including bringing a case against the bishopric of Canterbury on the day of Archbishop Anselm's consecration.

Unsurprisingly, Ranulf Flambard was a controversial figure. To his opponents he was cruel, immoral and greedy, using his governmental position to further his own wealth at the expense of others. While he could be ruthless to his opponents, his supporters praised him for his loyalty, generosity and talents as an administrator. His nickname, 'Flambard', meaning 'fiery', probably refers to his sharp wit and forceful personality. In 1099, Ranulf Flambard was rewarded by William II with the bishopric of Durham.

Following the death of William II, Ranulf Flambard became a convenient scapegoat for the perceived corruption of the time and the new king, Henry I, imprisoned him in the Tower of London for embezzlement. As a testament to his dynamism, Ranulf Flambard soon escaped, making his way to Normandy. Within six months of his arrival, he had persuaded Duke Robert to invade England. Ever adaptable, Ranulf Flambard later reconciled himself with King Henry, who realised that Ranulf Flambard's talents could be utilised. He was reinstated as Bishop of Durham, eventually dying in 1128. His legacy is still evident in the building projects he oversaw, including Durham Cathedral and Westminster Hall.

The greatest challenge to Henry's fledgling rule came in summer of 1101. Robert Curthose, recently returned from the crusades and feted as a hero, decided to make a bid for the English throne. As preparations were made, some of England's most powerful magnates signalled their support for him, including Count William of Mortain, nephew of William the Conqueror; William de Warenne, earl of Surrey; Ivo of Grandmesnil, lord of Leicester and the three Montgomery brothers: Robert of Belleme, earl of Shrewsbury and the single most powerful Norman after the royal family; Arnulf of Montgomery and Roger the Poitevin. Outwitting Henry's naval patrols and successfully landing an army at Portsmouth, Robert and Henry confronted each other at Alton near Winchester. Henry was in the weaker position but both sides proved unwilling to fight. As Orderic Vitalis said, 'feelings of brotherly love' overtook them and in the subsequent Treaty of Alton Robert renounced his claim to the English throne while Henry surrendered his claims to Normandy and agreed to pay his brother £2,000 a year. They also agreed not to punish each other's supporters.

TIMELINE OF A TROUBLEMAKER: ROBERT OF BELLEME, THIRD EARL OF SHREWBURY C1056–1130

1056
Born the eldest son of Roger of Montgomery, first earl of Shrewsbury

1073
Knighted by William the Conqueror during his siege of Fresnai Castle, Maine

1077
Joins Robert Curthose's revolt against his father

1088
Takes part in the rebellion to install Robert Curthose on the throne of England

Helps defend Rochester Castle, before being allowed safe passage back to Normandy

Imprisoned on his arrival for allegedly plotting against Robert Curthose, precipitating a short family-wide rebellion against the duke

1090
Restored to favour, he supports Robert Curthose in putting down a revolt by the citizens of Rouen in 1090

1094
On his father's death, Robert de Belleme inherits the Norman properties, while his younger brother, Hugh, becomes the second earl of Shrewsbury

1096
Duke Robert departs for crusade and Robert de Belleme builds favour with William II

1098
On the death of his younger brother, Hugh, Robert of Belleme inherits, on payment of £3,000 in relief, his English titles including the rape of Arundel and the earldom of Shrewsbury; this makes him the wealthiest magnate in both England and Normandy

1098
Campaigns in Maine and the Vexin with William II

1101
Along with his two brothers, Roger and Arnulf, Robert of Belleme supports Robert Curthose's invasion of England

1102
Banished from England by Henry I, Robert of Belleme brings disorder to Normandy

1105
Attempt to make peace with Henry I is rebuffed

1106
Sides with Robert Curthose in the Battle of Tinchebrai

Submitting to Henry shortly afterwards, is allowed to retain his Norman lands

1112
Rebels against Henry and is arrested, spending the rest of his life in prison

Henry had no intention of abiding by the treaty and soon made it clear that the disloyalty of 1101 would indeed be punished. In 1102, he moved against Robert of Belleme. Having had him watched for a year, the earl was summoned to answer 45 charges, including the unauthorised fortification of castles. Robert of Belleme replied by raising revolt. Henry lay siege to Arundel in Sussex, Tickhill in Yorkshire and Bridgnorth in Shropshire, taking each in turn. The latter was secured by offering the garrison an enviable choice between death on capture or lands worth £100 on surrender. By the time Henry advanced on Shrewsbury in the autumn, Robert of Belleme realised the game was up. His lands were confiscated and exile to Normandy followed. He was joined by his brothers after they were offered the choice of becoming Henry's men or leaving. The Montgomerys now became Robert Curthose's problem.

SOURCE

16 Entry from the *Anglo-Saxon Chronicle*, Manuscript E, for the year 1102. This was produced by monks at Peterborough to provide a record of significant events that affected England.

Discord arose between the king and the earl Robert of Belleme, who had the earldom in Shrewsbury here in the land which his father Earl Roger possessed earlier, and great authority besides, both on this side of the sea and beyond. And the king travelled and besieged the castle at Arundel, but when he could not win it so quickly he had castles made in front of it and there set them with his men; and afterwards travelled with all his army to Bridgnorth, and stayed there until he had the castle, and deprived the earl Robert of land, and seized all that he had in England; and so the earl departed across the sea, and the army afterwards turned home.

Misrule in Normandy 1100–06

According to Orderic Vitalis, when Robert Curthose first went into exile in 1077 his mother consulted a hermit living in Germany. He predicted that while Robert would succeed his father to Normandy, his reign would be calamitous. The duchy would be stripped of its beauty and riches, while Robert would give himself up to lust and indolence. This may well be apocryphal. While Orderic Vitalis is the main source on Robert, especially in the period after 1100, his comments, dating from 1127 to 1130, are infused with hindsight. He is also far from impartial. A supporter of Henry, Orderic Vitalis's writing on this period can be seen as carefully building a case for Henry's subsequent invasion of Normandy. In this he had to overcome the fact that the dukedom was held legitimately by a hero of the crusades. Orderic Vitalis also had a personal motive for disliking Robert. Much of the unrest which afflicted Normandy occurred within the vicinity of the monastery he would later join.

Following his return from the crusades in the summer of 1100, it is certainly true that Robert presided over serious misrule. One of the first decisions Robert had to take was whether or not to lead an army to assist the Norman garrison at Le Mans, under siege from the counts of Maine and Anjou. According to Orderic Vitalis, he was 'exhausted by the fatigues of his long pilgrimage and more anxious to enjoy the peace of his couch than the toils of war'. More probably, he was preparing for the invasion of England and refused to help. This led the garrison to surrender and Normandy to lose its hold on this strategic territory. As has been seen, Robert then lacked the ruthlessness to capitalise on his successful landing in England to take the English throne. Further embarrassment followed when Ranulf Flambard secured the appointment of his son, aged 12, to the position of bishop of Lisieux. In response, Pope Paschal II wrote to Robert complaining of his treatment of the Norman Church.

More problematic, Robert Curthose proved unable to prevent his duchy slipping into disorder following the arrival of Robert of Belleme. Henry's labelling of Robert of Belleme as a traitor meant that Duke Robert was forced to move against him under the terms of the Treaty of Alton. Having lost his English lands, however, Robert of Belleme was prepared to fight bitterly to regain his Norman lordships in the diocese of Sees. The region descended into violence and Duke Robert proved wanting. In 1102, he besieged Robert of Belleme's supporters in the castle at Vignats but was unable to keep his own forces united due to latent support for Robert of Belleme. One party led by Robert de Montfort, who opposed the campaign, fired their tents. In the ensuing confusion many of the besiegers fled, forcing the duke to retreat. In June 1103, Duke Robert's allies gathered in the nunnery of Almeneches, stabling their horses in consecrated buildings, itself an insensitive act. Robert of Belleme then burnt the nunnery to the ground, killing or mutilating many of the captured soldiers. Duke Robert was spurred into action but his attempt to deal with the rogue noble, holed up in Exmes

Castle, resulted in defeat when Robert of Belleme launched a surprise attack. After this, further castles fell into rebel hands and the duke was forced to make peace in 1104 by confirming Robert of Belleme's Norman inheritance.

The actions of Robert of Belleme were uniformly negative for Duke Robert. A whole region of Normandy had been destabilised, while, by making peace with his brother's enemy, Duke Robert had broken the terms of the Treaty of Alton. In response, Henry sent his men into Normandy, who set about raiding and burning. Furthermore, while focused on dealing with the threat from Robert of Belleme, Duke Robert had been unable to prevent a baronial war developing in the Evreux (see Figure 4.2 on page 243) over the inheritance of William of Breteuil, son of William fitzOsbern, who died on 12 January 1103. With no legitimate heirs, a violent struggle coalesced around William of Breteuil's illegitimate son, Eustace, and an outsider from Burgundy, Reginald of Grancey. Fully aware that he was the prime beneficiary of Normandy's disorder, Henry fanned the flames by supporting Eustace.

Henry's campaign in Normandy

By 1104, Henry's intention to take over Normandy was fully apparent. Secure in his control of England, he travelled to Normandy in August, berating his brother for poor leadership. Henry was laying out the justification for a future invasion based on Duke Robert's incompetence as ruler. As Source 17 highlights, the violent excesses of Robert of Belleme also provided a way of undermining the duke's reputation, hard-earned on the crusades, as a defender of the Church.

SOURCE

17 From *Historia ecclesiastica* by Orderic Vitalis, c1114–41. Orderic Vitalis was particularly critical of Duke Robert's rule in Normandy because his own monastery of St Evroul suffered from the disorder. Writing during Henry I's rule, he supported and justified Henry's invasion of Normandy.

[Robert was] sunk in lethargy and had abandoned all Normandy to thieves and robbers and other evil doers, and had fecklessly left it to the mercy of the shameless scoundrels by whom he was dominated; that he was a mere figurehead in the seat of prince and pastor, for he did not use the office of government to provide for the Church of God and the helpless people, but abandoned them to the unprincipled persecutors like sheep left behind to be devoured by wolves... All Christians should mourn in their hearts to see the Church trodden underfoot and the wretched people destroyed. It is all too obvious in this church that the population of the Cotentin has been miserably uprooted; indeed that all Normandy, dominated by godless bandits, is without a true ruler. The church of God was once called a house of prayer; now you may see it shamefully crammed with worldly goods and the building which should be devoted exclusively to the Hold Sacraments has been turned into a communal storehouse for lack of a just protector.

With the case for invasion made, Henry's first determined move came early in 1105 when he crossed the Channel with troops and money. He bought the support of many castellans (castle governors), which consolidated his control over the west of Normandy and attracted mercenaries to his side. Before his return to England in August, Henry had also secured a bridgehead into central Normandy by taking the towns of Bayeux and Caen, the latter being burned. Duke Robert was left in a critical situation. He was facing a determined opponent with superior military and financial resources. His own support was dwindling, little money was left and he was increasingly powerless to maintain order. Realising the danger, the duke attempted to negotiate, meeting the king in Northampton in early 1106, but to no avail. In June, Henry invaded for the second time. Although he had the upper hand, Henry must have been aware that Robert was still a formidable opponent. He controlled the important towns of Rouen and Falaise, while his principal supporters, William of Mortain and Robert of Belleme, were holding firm. In September, after a period of inconclusive raiding, Henry took the fight to William of Mortain and placed his castle at Tinchebrai under siege. Robert, camped at Falaise, advanced to offer his ally assistance. As Orderic Vitalis wrote, 'That autumn was a stormy one in Normandy, with thunder and torrents of rains and wars.'

Source 18 below provides a clear description of the resultant Battle of Tinchebrai. Henry formed his army up outside the castle and, contrary to contemporary trends, ordered his knights to fight on foot. This was possibly because the undulating terrain was unsuitable for prolonged cavalry manoeuvres but it was also a statement of intent. Knights on foot were less likely to flee. This battle would be fought to the end. One contemporary put Henry's force at 40,000. While this must be an exaggeration, Robert was certainly outnumbered. The majority of his knights were also dismounted. The front line was commanded by the count of Mortain, with Robert of Belleme in charge of the rear.

> **AS Level Exam-Style Question Section A**
>
> How much weight do you give to the evidence of Source 17 for an enquiry into disorder in Normandy under Robert Curthose?
>
> Explain your answer using the source, the information given about it and your own knowledge of the historical context. (12 marks)
>
> **Tip**
> *Although he was overall an excellent historian, remind yourself why Orderic Vitalis was not a completely impartial witness for Duke Robert.*

THINKING HISTORICALLY   Evidence (5a)

Context is everything

In order to increase the usefulness of Orderic Vitalis's account of Duke Robert's rule in Normandy in Source 17, it is important to know the context in which he was writing. The following exercise will help you with this.

Work in groups and read through Source 17.

Take an A3 piece of paper. In the middle of it draw a circle about 18 cm in diameter. Within the circle is the evidence itself, outside the circle is the context.

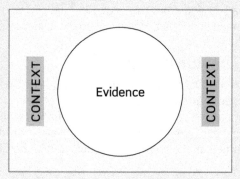

1 Think of a question that the source could be helpful in answering.

2 Inside the circle, write a set of statements giving information that can be gleaned only from the source itself without any contextual knowledge.

3 Outside the circle, write down statements of contextual knowledge that relate to the source.

4 Draw annotated lines to show links between the contextual statements and the information from the source. Does context change the nature or meaning of the information?

Now answer the following question:

5 Explain why knowledge of context is important when gathering and using historical evidence. Give specific examples to illustrate your point.

Beside Duke Robert was his old friend, Edgar the Atheling. During the forming-up stage, Henry sent an emissary with an offer of a compromise. If the duke would hand over all of Normandy's castles, its judicial and administrative business and half of the duchy, he would be provided with a comfortable retirement. 'You can then enjoy feasts and games and all kinds of amusements' as Orderic Vitalis later recorded. It was rejected with scorn. The duke had no wish to be reduced to a dependant. He must also have felt confident enough of victory over a younger brother who lacked his own military experience, otherwise he need not have engaged.

AS Level Exam-Style Question Section A

Why is Source 18 valuable to the historian investigating the Battle of Tinchebrai?

Explain your answer, using the source, the information given about it and your own knowledge of the historical context. (8 marks).

Tip

Remember to look carefully at who wrote this source, as well as the information it contains about the battle.

SOURCE 18

From *Historia Anglorum* ('The History of the English People') by Henry of Huntingdon, c1130. Henry of Huntingdon was the son of an English mother and a Norman father. He became archdeacon of Huntingdon in 1110 and began writing this work around 1123–30, completing it in 1154. He is regarded as a well-informed historian, who used existing sources, as well as adding in his own details.

Upon the king laying siege to the castle of Tinchebrai, the duke of Normandy, with Robert of Belleme and the count of Mortain and all their retinue, advanced against him. The king on his side had with him almost all the chief men of Normandy and the best soldiers of England, Anjou and Brittany. He was therefore not unprepared. After sounding shrill trumpets, the duke with his small force boldly charged the king's more numerous army and since the duke and his troops had been well trained in the wars of Jerusalem, their onslaught upset the royal array. William, count of Mortain, moreover, harassed it at several points and threw it into confusion. The king and the duke, with great part of their troops, fought on foot that they might make a more sustained attack; but the Breton knights bore down upon the flank of the duke's force which, unable to resist the charge, was presently routed.

The battle began at nine in the morning with Duke Robert's smaller army attacking first and pushing back Henry's line, helped no doubt by their crusading experience. Count Helias of Maine, Henry's ally, in combination with the Breton cavalry, then launched an attack on the duke's infantry from the flanks, inflicting heavy losses in the first onslaught. This was enough for Robert of Belleme and his decision to flee effectively brought the battle to an end. It had lasted just over an hour. Casualties were relatively light. One contemporary claimed that Henry had lost only two men dead and one wounded, although this must have been referring to knights only, rather than the rank and file. The duke suffered the indignity of being taken prisoner not by a knight but by Waldric, the king's chancellor. Henry's first experience of pitched battle had therefore been a good one, with a number of factors swinging it in his favour. His superior numbers helped, while a well-timed cavalry charge proved decisive. The duke was let down by Robert of Belleme's retreat, while he also received no external aid. Unlike in 1094, the king of France, old and inactive, was not prepared to intervene.

The significance of Henry's victory at Tinchebrai

The king's victory at Tinchebrai was decisive. Robert was captured and would spend the rest of his life in honourable captivity. Accepting the defeat as total, he released his men from their fealty, which allowed them to surrender honourably rather than continue the fight. With hostilities formally at an end, Henry was now the sole master of two realms. As predicted by his father, he had succeeded in restoring the Anglo-Norman union. This did mean, though, that Henry now faced the same challenges that had repeatedly tested William the Conqueror. In total, he would have to fight three major wars in defence of Normandy between 1106 and 1135. These were against increasingly powerful and aggressive opponents. King Philip of France died in 1108 and was succeeded by his son, Louis VI. In 1109, Count Fulk IV of Anjou died and was succeed by his son, Fulk V, and in 1111 Count Robert of Flanders died and was succeeded by his son, Baldwin VII. The most prominent opponent was William Clito, son of Robert, the now imprisoned duke of Normandy. Born in 1102, William Clito pursued his claims to England and the duchy with vigour and determination.

For the Anglo-Norman nobility, endemic warfare was business as usual. The union of the two realms was more significant because it ended the anguish that went with trying to serve two lords, as well as the resultant insecurity of tenure. Both became pressing issues during the struggle between Robert Curthose and William II. As seen in Source 20 on page 263, William, count of Evreux, eloquently summed up the first dilemma when, in 1104, Duke Robert's lordship over him was transferred to King Henry. The second issue became all too real when, around this time, Duke Robert issued an edict forbidding any man who held land from him crossing to England or serving the English king. Under these circumstances, the maintenance of estates across the Channel became impossible. While Henry's victory at Tinchebrai removed this problem, it was not completely positive. Having two masters had given many a degree of latitude in pursuing their own interests and expressing grievances. If they angered one of the royal brothers, they were always able to travel to the other, who might reward them. After Tinchebrai, this safety valve was removed. Expressing dissent became much more dangerous and, as a result, Henry's power over his nobility increased. This allowed him to extract a greater degree of wealth from his nobility than previous monarchs. It is not surprising to find that in his sole remaining **pipe roll** dating to 1130, a level of royal revenue is recorded that outstripped his father's and would not be exceeded until 1177.

KEY TERM

Pipe roll
An annual record of royal accounts, recording both money paid out and received by the crown.

SOURCE 19 The tomb of Robert, duke of Normandy, in Gloucester Cathedral. He died in 1134 in his early eighties, after nearly 30 years' imprisonment.

SOURCE 20 From *Historia ecclesiastica* by Orderic Vitalis c1114–41, recounting a speech made by William, count of Evreux, when his fealty was transferred from Duke Robert to King Henry. Orderic Vitalis, compiling his history over a 30-year period, used his writing to help justify Henry's invasion of Normandy.

I served your father faithfully all my life, never once compromising my oath to him in any way; likewise I have kept faith with his heir up to now and am resolved to do so always with all the power I have. But since, as God himself says in the Gospel and I have often heard from men of learning, it is impossible to serve in tranquillity two masters who disagree with each other, I elect to place myself under the rule of one, for fear of being unable to satisfy either if I am involved in double loyalty. I love the king and the duke; but I shall do homage to one of them and him I will serve as my lawful lord.

For England, the implications of the union with the duchy were clear. As in the time of William I, its resources and troops were ruthlessly exploited to help protect Normandy. England also experienced long periods of absent kingship. In total 60 percent of Henry's time was spent in Normandy, with the *Anglo-Saxon Chronicle* recording that in 1112, 1117–19, 1124 and 1128 he remained the whole year in the duchy. Source 21 contains a characteristically melancholic entry for these periods. Such was the fate for a country that exactly half a century before Tinchebrai had lost its own king, nobility and independence.

SOURCE

Entry from the *Anglo-Saxon Chronicle*, Manuscript E, for the year 1118. This was produced by monks at Peterborough in the English language to provide a contemporary record of significant events that impacted England.

Here the king Henry stayed all this year in Normandy because of the war with the king of France and the earl of Anjou and the earl of Flanders. And the earl of Flanders was wounded in Normandy and, wounded thus, went into Flanders. Through the hostility of these the king became very troubled and lost much both in money and also in land; and his own men troubled him most, who frequently deserted and betrayed him and turned over to his enemies, and gave up their castles to them to the king's harm and betrayal. England paid dear for all this through manifold taxes which did not leave off all this year.

ACTIVITY
KNOWLEDGE CHECK

1 Why did Henry I expel Robert of Belleme in 1102?

2 Why must some caution be used regarding Orderic Vitalis's comments on Duke Robert?

3 Outline three reasons why Duke Robert lost control of Normandy.

4 How useful is Source 17 for understanding Henry's motivation in invading Normandy?

5 List four ways in which Henry's victory at Tinchebrai was significant.

A Level Exam-Style Question Section B

How far was Henry, in contrast to his brothers, able to reunite the Anglo-Norman realm? (20 marks)

Tip

As well as focusing on Henry's victory in the Battle of Tinchebrai, remember to look at the inconclusive conflicts between William II and Robert Curthose.

ACTIVITY
SUMMARY

1 To gain an overview of the main problems faced by William II in Normandy after 1066, complete the following table.

Problem area	Nature of the problem	Main events	Outcome
Maine			
Vexin			
Robert Curthose			

2 What did William bequeath each of his sons on his deathbed and why did this cause problems?

3 Create a timeline for 1087–1100, summarising the main dealings between Robert, William and Henry.

4 Select eight key events that paved the way for the decisive battle between Henry and Robert at Tinchebrai.

WIDER READING

Barlow, F. *William Rufus*, Yale University Press (1990)

Bartlett, R. *England under the Norman and Angevin Kings*, Clarendon Press (2000)

Douglas, D. *William the Conqueror*, University of California Press (1964)

Green, J. *Henry I*, Cambridge University Press (2009)

Morris, M. *The Norman Conquest*, Hutchinson (2012)

Saul, N. *The Oxford Illustrated History of Medieval England*, Oxford University Press (1997)

Preparing for your AS Level Paper 2 exam

Advance planning

1. Draw up a timetable for your revision and try to keep to it. Spread your timetable over a number of weeks, and aim to cover four or five topics each week.
2. Spend longer on topics that you have found difficult, and revise them several times.
3. Above all, do not try to limit your revision by attempting to 'question spot'. Try to be confident about all aspects of your Paper 2 work, because this will ensure that you have a choice of questions in Section B.

Paper 2 overview:

AS Paper 2	Time: 1 hour 30 minutes	
Section A	Answer 1 compulsory two-part sources question	8+12 marks = 20 marks
Section B	Answer 1 question from a choice of 3	20 marks
	Total marks =	40 marks

You should familiarise yourself with the layout of the paper by looking at the examples published by Edexcel. The questions for each section are followed by eight pages of lined paper where you should write your answer.

Section A questions

Each of the two parts of the question will focus on one of the two contemporary sources provided. The sources together will total around 300 words. The (a) question, worth 8 marks, will be in the form of 'Why is Source 1 useful for an enquiry into…?' The (b) question, worth 12 marks, will be in the form of 'How much weight do you give the evidence of Source 2 for an enquiry into…?' In both your answers you should address the value of the content of the source, and then its nature, origin and purpose. Finally, you should use your own knowledge of the context of the source to assess its value.

Section B questions

These questions ask you to reach a judgement on an aspect of the topic studied. The questions will have the form, for example, of 'How far…', 'To what extent…' or 'How accurate is it to say…'. The questions can deal with historical concepts such as cause, consequence, change, continuity, similarity, difference and significance. You should consider the issue raised in the question, consider other relevant issues, and then conclude with an overall judgement.

The timescale of the questions could be as short as a single year or even a single event (an example from Option 2C.2 could be, 'To what extent was Russia's involvement in the First World War responsible for the fall of the Provisional Government in 1917?'). The timescale could be longer depending on the historical event or process being examined, but questions are likely to be shorter than those set for Sections A and B in Paper 1.

Use of time

This is an issue that you should discuss with your teachers and fellow students, but here are some suggestions for you.

1. Do not write solidly for 45 minutes on each question. For Section A it is essential that you have a clear understanding of the content of each source, the points being made, and the nature, origin and purpose of each source. You might decide to spend up to ten minutes reading the sources and drawing up your plan, and 35 minutes writing your answer.
2. For Section B answers you should spend a few minutes working out what the question is asking you to do, and drawing up a plan of your answer before you begin to write your response.

Preparing for your AS Level exams

Paper 2: AS Level sample answer with comments

Section A

Part A requires you to:

- identify key points in the source and explain them
- deploy your own knowledge of the context in which events took place
- make appropriate comments about the author/origin/purpose of the source.

Why is Source 12 (page 230) valuable to the historian for an enquiry into the impact of the Norman Conquest on everyday life? Explain your answer, using the source, the information given about it and your own knowledge of the historical context. (8 marks)

Average student answer

The source is from the *Anglo-Saxon Chronicle* dated 1087 and gives a poetic review of England under the rule of William the Conqueror. It has an extensive list of complaints. William is criticised for his 'avarice' and 'greediness'. He took people's money 'with injustice', suggesting taxes were high. It tells of the harsh punishments imposed in the new royal forests which included being 'blinded' for killing a deer. People could only get on if they 'follow the king's will', suggesting that his was arbitrary and cruel. It also singles out castles as being a tool of oppression. It ends by asking the Almighty God to 'grant forgiveness of his sins' suggesting that the overall impact of the conquest was negative. This must have been a widespread view as it states that both 'powerful' and 'wretched' men lamented it. It does not mention some of the major impacts, however, which included the harrying of the North, religious reforms by Lanfranc and the complete replacement of the old Anglo-Saxon nobility.

> This paragraph identifies the key points from the source and makes some inferences about the negative impact of the Norman Conquest. The candidate, however, also needs to expand upon these comments with specific own knowledge.

The provenance tells how the source was written by the monks of Peterborough monastery. As it is an unusually frank assessment, they must have been speaking truthfully. The *Anglo-Saxon Chronicle* at this time was one of the last sources being written in the English language. It was also an annual compilation of important events in England for that year. As a result it gives historians a view of what people were thinking in 1087. As William the Conqueror died in that year and his son, William Rufus, took the throne, it would encourage a reflective attitude and perhaps worry for the future as it did not seem likely that Norman rule would be ending soon.

> This paragraph focuses on the nature and origin of the source. While some own knowledge is used to place the source in its historical context, it is far too limited.

Overall the source, together with the provenance, makes it clear that people were unhappy with the impact of the Norman Conquest. The Norman regime was harsh and served only the needs of the king.

> This is a general conclusion which needs a greater level of explanation to be more effective.

Verdict

This is an average answer because:

- it identifies a range of points from the sources and makes inferences about the nature of Norman rule; greater own knowledge is needed to develop these points
- it discusses the nature of the source and places it in its historical context

- there is an overall judgement but it needs more specific illustration and explanation to add substance.

Use the feedback on this answer to rewrite it, making as many improvements as you can.

Paper 2: AS Level sample answer with comments

Section A

Part B requires you to:

- interrogate the source
- draw reasoned inferences
- deploy your own knowledge to interpret the material in its context
- make judgement about the value (weight) of the source in terms of making judgements.

How much weight do you give to the evidence of Source 17 (page 259) in an enquiry into the disorder in Normandy under Robert Curthose? Explain your answer, using the source, the information given about it and your own knowledge of the historical context. (12 marks)

Average student answer

The account by Orderic Vitalis gives a bleak picture of Normandy under the rule of Robert Curthose. Always regarded as spoilt and incompetent by his father William, Robert had nevertheless received control of the Duchy upon William the Conqueror's death in 1087. After returning from the Crusades a hero in 1100, Robert's grip over Normandy was weakened as a result of the actions of over-powerful barons such as Robert de Belleme. When Duke Robert attempted to besiege Robert de Belleme at the castle at Vignats, he found that much of his own army deserted him. There was also considerable interference from his own brother, Henry I of England, who had the aim of re-uniting England and Normandy. Henry gradually conquered the Duchy between 1104 and 1106, with a decisive battle occurring at Tinchebrai.

Henry justified his invasion by arguing that Normandy was in disorder and the Church needed protecting. The source provides extensive evidence of Duke Robert's misrule and singles him out for serious criticism. He is described as a 'figurehead' rather than an actual leader, who seemed unable to act in a positive way as a result of 'lethargy'. He is also accused of failing in his duties as Duke by not providing for the 'church of god and the helpless people'. As a result 'thieves and robbers' are unchecked. In an age when religious observance was taken very seriously, Robert is also accused of allowing the desecration of Church buildings by turning them into a 'communal storehouse'.

Orderic Vitalis was an Anglo-Norman monk based in the monastery of St Evroul. He is regarded as an accurate historian whose *Ecclesiastical History* sought to redress the anti-English attitudes put forward by the first generation of Norman writers such as William of Poitiers. This adds to its reliability and weight. Furthermore he wrote it between 1114 and 1141 and so the events described in the source would have been within living memory of many, increasing his opportunities for finding out the reality. The fact that his descriptions are vivid suggests that he had little doubt in his mind that Robert was a poor leader.

I would regard this as a valuable source about the disorder in Normandy. It is by a trusted writer and he gives a strong impression of a Duchy in considerable disorder.

> This answer provides a potted history of Robert Curthose and some of the reasons for the disorder in Normandy. Apart from the reference to the source in the first sentence, there is no discussion on the value of the source content. As a result this paragraph fails to answer the question.

> The candidate uses this paragraph to outline the key points made by the source. While the answer correctly picks out many negative comments about Robert, the candidate does not deploy specific knowledge to confirm or challenge the source content. There is also no clear focus on the question.

> This is the strongest section of the answer. The candidate explains why Orderic Vitalis can be considered a useful source. Some own knowledge is brought in to explain this viewpoint.

> This conclusion gives a judgement on the question but it is poorly explained.

Verdict

This is an average answer because:

- there is some interrogation of the source but opportunities to draw inferences are neglected
- there needs to be greater use of own knowledge
- while the strengths of the source are discussed, the weaknesses are not, meaning the answer lacks balance

- there is not a consistent focus on the question
- there is an overall judgement but it lacks substance.

Use the feedback on this answer to rewrite it, making as many improvements as you can.

Paper 2: AS Level sample answer with comments

Section A

Part A requires you to:

- identify key points in the source and explain them
- deploy your own knowledge of the context in which events took place
- make appropriate comments about the author/origin/purpose of the source.

Why is Source 12 (page 230) valuable to the historian for an enquiry into the impact of the Norman Conquest on everyday life? Explain your answer, using the source, the information given about it and your own knowledge of the historical context. (8 marks)

Strong student answer

This source is of immense value in learning about the impact of the Norman Conquest. Produced in 1087 after William the Conqueror's death, its purpose was to single out the particularly hated aspects of his regime. It is a frank and bitter assessment, showing that even two decades after the Battle of Hastings, the people of England regarded themselves as defeated. Castles are given prominence for their role in having 'wretched men oppressed'. This is not surprising. Castles had been unknown in Anglo-Saxon times and they were built by the Normans to control the population. The most famous example was the White Tower in London, built of stone to dominate England's largest city psychologically. A further impact concerns high taxes as he 'seized from his subject men many a mark'. The monks may well have had the raising of the geld tax from two to six shillings per hide in 1084 in mind. This was done to fund the war in the Maine. Forest Law is given extensive coverage in the poem, showing that this was a particularly resented impact. This is not surprising because the Forest Laws were draconian, preventing people from grazing cattle and gathering wood. Twenty villages were destroyed to make the New Forest.

The fact that the source is from the *Anglo-Saxon Chronicle* adds to its value. By 1087 the Peterborough monks were the only ones still recording history in the vernacular, with all other official documents being in Latin. As such it is the only source historians have that gives a contemporary insight into the views of the defeated English. The other principal sources are either from the heavily biased Norman accounts of William of Poitiers and William of Jumieges or the Anglo-Norman accounts. While produced by respected writers such as William of Malmesbury and Orderic Vitalis, they were writing in the mid 12th century when relations between the English and Normans were starting to improve. As a result they lack the immediacy of the *Anglo-Saxon Chronicle*. Of course when Source 12 was written the great religious foundations were under Norman control. By 1086 only three Anglo-Saxon abbots remained. However the use of the language of the defeated and its bitter tone shows a distinct lack of Norman influence. The monks who produced the annual entries were normally circumspect in tone. When they described the harrying of the North, for example, it was in one sentence. This vivid account shows that following William the Conqueror's death, they felt much freer to state their true feelings.

> This is a strong first paragraph, which begins with a clear focus on the question. The contents of the sources are then analysed, with inferences being drawn. In addition the candidate develops the points raised from the sources with specific own knowledge.

> This paragraph focuses on the nature and origin of the Anglo-Saxon Chronicle and why it is a valuable source for historians. The deployment of specific own knowledge is strong, with interesting links being drawn to some of the other main sources of this period.

Verdict

This is a strong answer because:

- it has sharp focus on the specific question
- it makes use of evidence in the source and its introduction
- it deploys appropriate own knowledge.

Paper 2: AS Level sample answer with comments

Section A

Part B requires you to:

- interrogate the source
- draw reasoned inferences
- deploy your own knowledge to interpret the material in its context
- make judgement about the value (weight) of the source in terms of making judgements.

How much weight do you give to the evidence of Source 17 (page 259) in an enquiry into the disorder in Normandy under Robert Curthose? Explain your answer, using the source, the information given about it and your own knowledge of the historical context. (12 marks)

Strong student answer

The source would carry some weight for any enquiry into the disorder in Normandy. Orderic Vitalis is considered one of the pre-eminent Anglo-Norman historians. He used techniques common to modern historians including archival research and gathering eyewitness testimony where possible. His comments on Normandy in this period are especially informed because the monastery he would later join, St Evroul, was caught up in a lot of the disorder. Although Orderic himself was not present at the time of the disorder, he had access to people who lived through it.

The source highlights the suffering of the Church and population 'dominated by godless bandits'. Chief bandit was Robert de Belleme, who brought about considerable disorder to the Sees region of Normandy in his efforts to regain his Norman inheritance following expulsion from England by Henry I. Robert failed to contain this baron, with his siege at Vignats falling apart following desertions, while at Exmes castle his forces were defeated by a surprise attack from Belleme. Other abuses of the Church occurred under Robert. Similarly, disorder was brought to the Evreux region following the death of William of Breteuil. This view of disorder in Normandy is also given backing by contemporary accounts such as the *Anglo-Saxon Chronicle*.

However, the overall weight that can be given to this source's depiction of disorder in Normandy is limited. It is significant that Orderic Vitalis focused heavily on the suffering of the Church. Orderic was trying to undermine Robert's greatest asset, which was his status as a crusader and defender of Christendom. This is because, as a support of Henry I, Orderic needed to show that the king of England had justification for deposing his brother, who was ruling his inheritance by right. While this political purpose limits the source's reliability, it does make it useful for finding out how Henry I and his supporters built up a case for the conquest of Normandy.

Clearly a short source cannot develop all the reasons for instability in Normandy. While Orderic places the blame for the disorder solely on Robert's shoulders as a result of his 'lethargy', it leaves out the significant role played by Henry I. It is also wrong to portray the disorder which Belleme wrought as signifying anarchy. His actions were instead typical of barons who were intent on securing what they regarded as their land or inheritance. While in general an excellent historian, Orderic Vitalis was far from an impartial witness in this case and cannot be relied upon to give a measured report on Duke Robert.

> A very strong opening which is sharply focused on the question. Specific own knowledge is used to explain why Orderic Vitalis is of value to historians.

> This is a well-constructed section, placing the source's negative view of Robert Curthose in its wider historical context.

> In this paragraph the candidate provides balance to the answer by considering the limitations of the source. The first sentence also highlights where the candidate thinks the balance lies in terms of source value.

> An informed paragraph, using specific own knowledge to challenge the content of the source.

Verdict

This is a strong answer because:

- it interrogates the source and comments about key points
- it makes effective comments about the strength and weakness of Orderic Vitalis as a historian
- it brings in specific own knowledge about the disorder and links this source to other evidence from the time
- it makes an overall judgement about the value of the source.

Paper 2: AS Level sample answer with comments

Section B

These questions assess your understanding of the period in some depth. They will ask you about the content you learned about in the four key themes, but may not ask about more than one theme. For these questions remember to:

- give an analytical, not a descriptive, response
- support your points with evidence
- cover the whole time period specified in the question
- come to a substantiated judgement.

How accurate is it to say that Duke William's leadership was the main reason for his success at the Battle of Hastings? (20 marks)

Average student answer

On 14 October 1066 William defeated the English King, Harold Godwinson, in battle. There are many reasons for William's victory at the Battle of Hastings including his leadership but there are many others.

William was a highly skilled warrior. Following the death of his father, William became Duke of Normandy but his duchy fell into disorder as rival barons competed for power. There were several occasions when William had to flee his castle to escape kidnap attempts. When he was 18 he fought his first battle against rebellious Norman barons. Most famously, in 1051 the town of Alençon rebelled against him. William lay siege to the castle and, after capturing it, cut off the hands and feet of the defenders. In 1054 and 1057 William defeated a double invasion by the Count of Anjou and King of France. In 1063 he took over the neighbouring province of Maine and the following year he gained control of Brittany. These experiences turned William into an experienced fighter.

William's opponent was the Anglo-Saxon King, Harold Godwinson. Harold was also a fearsome warrior. He had become Earl of Wessex after the death of his father in 1053. As the richest earldom in England, it gave Harold an income of around £5,000. He achieved military fame when he defeated the Welsh King. When Edward the Confessor died in January 1066, Harold was appointed his successor by the Witan. There were two main rivals to the throne however: William of Normandy and Harold Hardrada. The latter invaded England in September 1066, defeating Earls Morcar and Edwin at Gate Fulford. This forced Harold to march north. Taking only five days, he surprised the Viking army and defeated it at Stamford Bridge. It is said that Harold's victory was so complete that only 30 ships out of an original invasion fleet of 300 returned to Norway. This battle success, however, counted against Harold when it came to fighting against William at Hastings because it meant his troops were tired before battle and he had also lost some of his important warriors. Some people argue that Harold should have waited before engaging William. This shows that Harold's leadership was not as good at William's.

This is an example of how not to start an answer. The candidate has not made any substantial points on the question, nor is there any judgement here.

This paragraph considers William's background. The details about his youth are not relevant to this question. The information relating to his military successes is accurate and potentially relevant, but it is too narrative. The candidate only links the material to the actual question in the very last sentence. To give it more focus a better opening sentence to this paragraph would be 'William's victory at Hastings was partly based on his wide experience of military leadership.'

This paragraph contains a lot of accurate information about Harold, but only some of it is helpful in answering this question. The most useful section relates to the impact of the Battle of Stamford Bridge. This directly affected the outcome of Hastings by weakening Harold's army.

When these two leaders met on Senlac Hill on 14 October, their armies were very different. Harold occupied the top of the ridge and formed his army up behind a shield wall. Some of his men were professional soldiers but many were farmers, called up in the fyrd. William's army had foot soldiers, archers and cavalry. In terms of disposition, in the centre were Norman troops, on the left Breton and on the right men from the rest of France. They were professional and experienced. William had created this formidable army through his leadership. He had spent the months prior to Hastings collecting and then training this army. He had also gained the support of the pope by arguing that Harold firstly was not the rightful king and secondly had broken an oath of loyalty to him.

> The candidate has made two important points. The first relates to the differences between the two armies while the second concerns William's logistical and diplomatic actions prior to the battle. They should be expanded in two separate paragraphs.

There were several key events in the battle itself. William at first used his archers and then infantry to attack the shield wall but without success. At about midday some of his troops retreated and were chased by the Anglo-Saxons, before William's cavalry encircled and killed them. This made William realise that this trick could be used to weaken the shield wall. He successfully used it three times. Finally, just before it got dark, William launched one final attack. In this King Harold was either killed by an arrow or hacked down by Norman knights, or possibly both. The Bayeux Tapestry is uncertain as it seems to show all of this happening.

> This simply tells the story of the battle. It could be given a more analytical edge and greater focus on the question by identifying four distinct ways that William led his army well in the battle including his willingness to try new tactics and the way he drove his army on after a long day of fighting.

William's success at Hastings was also influenced by sheer luck. As Harold Godwinson fought Harold Hardrada at Stamford Bridge the wind changed direction and William was able to sail across the Channel. This meant that there was only 19 days between Godwinson's two battles, therefore leaving his troops exhausted. When William landed in the south of England he stayed along the coastline and started destroying the area around Hastings. This forced Harold to come down from London. William was also lucky that Harold was struck by an arrow. Harold's death caused the Anglo-Saxon army to fall apart.

> The candidate is providing some level of balance by examining alternative reasons for William's victory besides his leadership skills. Their explanation is, however, limited.

Thus I have shown that William's leadership skills were the main factor behind his victory at the Battle of Hastings. Even though there are other factors which influenced the victory it can be seen that if William hadn't been such a great leader then his victory would most probably not have occurred.

> Candidates should not use a phrase such as 'Thus I have shown' in the conclusion: a simple 'To conclude' is sufficient. This conclusion is brief and does not explain why William's leadership was so important.

Verdict

This is an average answer because:

- there is some attempt at explanation, but there are descriptive passages, including some which do not appear directly relevant
- the material included is accurate, but is lacking in depth in several places

- there is an attempt to reach an overall judgement, but it is not entirely secure.

Use the feedback on this answer to rewrite it, making as many improvements as you can.

Paper 2: AS Level sample answer with comments

Section B

These questions assess your understanding of the period in some depth. They will ask you about the content you learned about in the four key themes, but may not ask about more than one theme. For these questions remember to:

- give an analytical, not a descriptive, response
- support your points with evidence
- cover the whole time period specified in the question
- come to a substantiated judgement.

How accurate is it to say that Duke William's leadership was the main reason for his success at the Battle of Hastings? (20 marks)

Strong student answer

As England's reigning monarch, Harold enjoyed many advantages including support of the nobility, knowledge of the country and access to its rich resources and manpower. Despite this, William was able to defeat Harold at Hastings. While Harold was let down by his own poor decisions and peasant based army, William's victory ultimately rested on his own outstanding leadership. In preparing for the battle William won papal support, while he used his prior military knowledge to build up a professional army. Most importantly, his leadership came to the fore in the battle itself.

William's success at Hastings rested partly on his excellent leadership prior to battle. He secured the support of the pope by presenting his planned invasion as a crusade against a corrupt country. This was important because papal approval attracted additional troops, while the papal banner raised morale. In preparing his army, William showed excellent logistical leadership. He was able to keep his full army in camp for two months while he waited for the right conditions to cross the Channel. During this time disorder, disease or hunger did not break out. On landing William ravaged Sussex, knowing that he needed to force an early, decisive confrontation with Harold. If not he risked being bottled up on the Hastings peninsula and running out of supplies. William's leadership therefore brought about the battle he wanted, with the best army he could have hoped for.

At several key moments in the battle itself, William's leadership proved crucial. At his army's lowest point when a rumour circulated that he was dead, William rallied his troops by pushing back his helmet and showing that he was alive. Next, when the Breton troops initially retreated, he saw how the Anglo-Saxon shield wall could be eroded by the tactic of feigned flights. The shield wall was defensively strong and had to be broken if William wanted victory. Finally, towards dusk when his troops were exhausted, William motivated his army to make one last attack. It was this assault which killed Harold. William's excellent battle performance reflected that fact that he was a formidable warrior, who had fought his first battle at Val-es-Dunes in 1047, aged 18.

This is a strong opening paragraph. The candidate places the answer within the context of Harold's strengths and offers the view that William's leadership skills were mainly responsible in securing victory. The candidate also provides balance by acknowledging that other factors had a role.

This is a well developed paragraph. The crucial steps Harold took before the battle are analysed. The paragraph finishes by summarising their relevance to the battle of Hastings.

William's leadership in battle is explored in this section, with several precise examples being offered. This goes to the heart of the question and so needs to be fully developed. The final sentence attempts to explain why William was an excellent military leader and so is relevant to the rest of the paragraph. It could be expanded if time permitted.

Although William's leadership was the main reason for his victory, other factors played a role including poor decision-making by Harold. Chiefly he engaged William too quickly following the battle of Stamford Bridge and the forced march back to London. This was a mistake for two reasons. If Harold had waited he could have assembled an overwhelming army as the fyrd had been mobilised and earls Edwin and Morcar had promised reinforcements. By not waiting Harold went to battle with exhausted troops. He had also not made good the losses from Stamford Bridge, which included experienced housecarls. The effect of a lack of seasoned troops was seen when the untrained peasants repeatedly broke the shield wall in response to the feigned retreats. Harold's motivation in rushing to battle may have included a desire to protect the people of his own earldom from being ravaged. Although honourable, this appears reckless.

Having explained why leadership was the key reason for success, the candidate now moves on to look at alternative factors which played a role. This ensures that the answer is balanced. Harold's mistakes are an important area to focus on because, as the introduction set out, he was in a very strong position as king.

Harold's next set of mistakes was in the battle itself. Fighting in the Viking style, he commanded his troops on foot rather than horseback. This limited his ability to control his army in the thick of the fighting. Harold also missed an opportunity. When the Breton troops fled from the hill at around noon and a section of Harold's men pursued them, he did not order a general charge. This could have resulted in a Norman rout, as they were in general disorder at this stage. Harold's poor battle performance is surprising given his previously successful military record, which including defeating Harold Hardrada and Gruffydd of Wales.

Focusing on Harold's leadership in battle, this paragraph examines a potential missed opportunity. It could be further developed by offering some overall evaluation of Harold's battle performance, pointing out that he did pursue a sound defensive strategy and so should not be criticised too heavily.

Another important reason for William's success was the quality of the armies. Although roughly equal, numbering around 8,000 men each, the Norman army was made up of professional soldiers. Its greatest assets were the archers and cavalry. The constant attacks by the cavalry and feigned flights helped undermine the shield wall. In contrast the Anglo-Saxons had no cavalry and few archers. It was instead made up largely of untrained peasants. While it could be argued that the Anglo-Saxons were outclassed, it must be remembered that the battle was close and for most of the day the Normans were unable to break the shield wall. As a result this cannot be seen as a decisive reason.

In conclusion William's leadership was central. He created a powerful army and led it with expertise in battle. Other factors such as Harold's mistakes and the differing qualities of the two armies also had an outcome, but were not as important.

This paragraph begins with a well-constructed first sentence, which links to the question and gives the theme of the paragraph. While the importance of the Norman cavalry is then explained, the candidate does not address the role played by archers.

The conclusion is the weakest part of the answer. While it comes to a firm judgment, the candidate makes a brief case only for why leadership was important. The conclusion could also be more evaluative by explaining why the alternative factors were not as important.

Verdict

This is a strong answer because:

- the key issues relevant to the question are all explored
- there is a wide range of accurate material deployed to support the points made
- the argument throughout the answer is well-organised, coherent, logical and persuasive.

Preparing for your A Level Paper 2 exam

Advance planning

1. Draw up a timetable for your revision and try to keep to it. Spread your timetable over a number of weeks, and aim to cover four or five topics each week.
2. Spend longer on topics that you have found difficult, and revise them several times.
3. Above all, do not try to limit your revision by attempting to 'question spot'. Try to be confident about all aspects of your Paper 2 work, because this will ensure that you have a choice of questions in Section B.

Paper 2 overview

AL Paper 2	Time: 1 hour 30 minutes	
Section A	Answer 1 compulsory source question	20 marks
Section B	Answer 1 question from a choice of 2	20 marks
	Total marks =	40 marks

You should familiarise yourself with the layout of the paper by looking at the examples published by Edexcel. The questions for each section are followed by eight pages of lined paper where you should write your answer.

Section A questions

This question asks you to assess two different types of contemporary sources totalling around 400 words, and will be in the form of 'How far could the historian make use of Sources 1 and 2 together to investigate…?' Your answer should evaluate both sources, considering their nature, origin and purpose, and you should use your own knowledge of the context of the sources to consider their value to the specific investigation. Remember, too, that in assessing their value, you must consider the two sources, taken together, as a set.

Section B questions

These questions ask you to reach a judgement on an aspect of the topic studied. The questions will have the form, for example, of 'How far…', 'To what extent…' or 'How accurate is it to say…'. The questions can deal with historical concepts such as cause, consequence, change, continuity, similarity, difference and significance. You should consider the issue raised in the question, then other relevant issues, and conclude with an overall judgement.

The timescale of the questions could be as short as a single year or even a single event (an example from Option 2C.2 could be, 'To what extent was Russia's involvement in the First World War responsible for the fall of the Romanovs in 1917?'). The timescale could be longer depending on the historical event or process being examined, but questions are likely to be shorter than those set for Sections A and B in Paper 1.

Use of time

This is an issue that you should discuss with your teachers and fellow students, but here are some suggestions for you.

1. Do not write solidly for 45 minutes on each question. For Section A it is essential that you have a clear understanding of the content of each source, the points being made, and the nature, origin and purpose of each source. You might decide to spend up to ten minutes reading the sources and drawing up your plan, and 35 minutes writing your answer.
2. For Section B answers you should spend a few minutes working out what the question is asking you to do, and drawing up a plan of your answer before you begin to write your response.

Preparing for your A Level exams

Paper 2: A Level sample answer with comments

Section A

You will need to read and analyse two sources and use them in tandem to assess how useful they are in investigating an issue. For these questions remember to:

- spend time, up to ten minutes, reading and identifying the arguments and evidence present in the sources; then make a plan to ensure that your response will be rooted in these sources
- use specific references from the sources
- deploy your own knowledge to develop points made in the sources and establish appropriate context
- come to a substantiated judgement.

How far could a historian make use of Sources 15 (page 233) and 18 (page 238) together to investigate the extent to which the English Church was reformed under William the Conqueror? Explain your answer, using the source, the information given about it and your own knowledge of the historical context. (20 marks)

Average student answer

Church reform was an important issue during William the Conqueror's reign as William had ◄ won papal support for his invasion of England by portraying the English Church as corrupt and in need of reform. It was also important because the headquarters of the western Church in Rome were becoming increasingly determined to extend its control over churches and also make sure canon law, the universal law of the Church, was being obeyed. Pope Gregory VII would even go to war when the German Emperor Henry IV resisted his demands.

Led by Archbishop Lanfranc, significant change did take place. He condemned simony, pluralism, nepotism and clerical marriage. He made sure bishops were based in large cities and he gave archdeacons increased power. He also built many new cathedrals in the Romanesque style. However there were limits to Church reform. William realised the Church was a major source of power and influence. It held over a quarter of landed wealth, while archbishops, bishops and abbots were important political figures. As a result he was unenthusiastic about reform and resisted Rome increasing its control over the Church. The only reason William's stance did not result in a more serious dispute with Rome was because Gregory was too diverted by the conflict with Henry IV.

> This paragraph provides an effective overview of the reasons for Church reform. However little credit can be given for this accurate information because the sources have not been referred to and so it is not answering the question. Sources need to be the focus of the answer from the start, with specific own knowledge being used to expand on the points they raise.

> Once again the candidate has detailed some precise knowledge on Lanfranc's reforms and William's relations with the papacy but the sources are not mentioned.

The two sources highlight these two differing attitudes to Church reform. Source 15 clearly ← shows the reform process in action. Lanfranc can be considered as fully supportive of it. In this extract he outlines the movement of several bishoprics from rural to urban areas. He says that priests should not be involved in giving the death sentence. He also says that religious offices should not be bought and sold. Lanfranc is clearly trying to improve the Church in this extract. Source 18 reveals that the King is not at all supportive of the reform movement. He directly refuses Pope Gregory's request for fealty, claiming that this had never been promised. The nature of the sources adds to their usefulness. They are by the leaders of the English Church and the King of England respectively. The first deals with the internal organisation of the Church, while the second concerns its external relations with the papacy.

Historians could certainly make use of the two sources to aid their investigation into the extent of Church reform in England. The two documents are similar in that they are official statements of policy. This makes them useful for finding out what was happening. They also highlight that Lanfranc and the King had different attitudes to reform. While Lanfranc passed laws to improve the Church, William is seen as blocking the efforts by the Pope to increase its influence over England.

> The candidate finally makes use of the sources, picking out some relevant details on Church reform. This answer would have been improved if there had been full integration between the own knowledge deployed in the first two paragraphs and the source points raised in this paragraph. The candidate has also missed the significance of the comments in Source 18 about William agreeing to pay Peter's Pence. This should be used to develop the point that William the Conqueror was overall supportive of Church reform and wanted to maintain good relations with the papacy.

A conclusion which directly answers the question, although the analysis of William's attitude to Church reform is only partially correct.

Verdict

This is an average answer because:

- it does identify arguments in both sources but has not read the second source carefully enough to identify the broader range of views expressed. NB: Failure to read sources carefully and thoroughly enough is a common fault. Many candidates latch on to part of an argument and their answers consequently lack balance

- it does deploy precise own knowledge but fails to integrate it with the sources
- it does come to a sound overall conclusion.

Use the feedback on this answer to rewrite it, making as many improvements as you can.

Paper 2: A Level sample answer with comments

Section A

You will need to read and analyse two sources and use them in tandem to assess how useful they are in investigating an issue. For these questions remember to:

- spend time, up to ten minutes, reading and identifying the arguments and evidence present in the sources; then make a plan to ensure that your response will be rooted in these sources
- use specific references from the sources
- deploy your own knowledge to develop points made in the sources and establish appropriate context
- come to a substantiated judgement.

How far could a historian make use of Sources 15 (page 233) and 18 (page 238) together to investigate the extent to which the English Church was reformed under William the Conqueror? Explain your answer, using the source, the information given about it and your own knowledge of the historical context. (20 marks)

Strong student answer

The two sources provide valuable but differing perspectives into the nature of Church reform under William the Conqueror. The first, Source 15, is by Archbishop Lanfranc and is therefore of immediate interest to historians. Lanfranc was an Italian scholar who, before the conquest, was abbot of Caen in Normandy and William's friend and spiritual adviser. Following the deposition of Stigand in 1070, he became Archbishop of Canterbury and took on the task of reforming the English Church, which was seen as out of step with many of the intellectual trends coming from Rome. Source 15 is an official record of decisions taken at a Church synod in 1075. Five years into Lanfranc's tenure, it therefore provides historians with a dry, business-like assessment on how reform was progressing. The fact that it has been signed by all those present further underlines its accuracy.

A strong opening which explains the background of Source 15 and the importance of Lanfranc to the question of Church reform.

Its content is similarly useful in investigating reform. It addresses Lanfranc as the 'primate of the whole island of Britain'. This is significant because it shows that Lanfranc has established the primacy of Canterbury over York, thereby allowing him to lead and reform the English Church as a whole. Two significant reforms are recorded. First it details how the bishoprics of Sherborne, Selsey and Lichfield were being moved from 'townships to cities'. This brought England into line with the continental view that bishops should be based in large towns close to the flocks. Lanfranc placed great stress on this type of administrative reform, believing that it was the first step towards the enforcement of higher moral standards. Next Source 15 attacked the buying and selling of 'holy orders not any position in the church'. Known as simony, this was condemned under canon law, but had been widely ignored in England. It was part of Lanfranc's efforts to root out corrupt practices such as pluralism and clerical marriage. The very fact that it is a record of an ecclesiastical synod is also a major point in itself. These had been rare occurrences in Anglo-Saxon England but ten were convened by Lanfranc and used as a way to introduce reform and establish consistency in the Church.

This paragraph offers a thorough analysis of the content of the source, explaining it further using precise own knowledge.

The second source, 18, is equally valuable to historians as it provides another elite perspective on church reform, but this time stressing its limits. As a reply by William to Pope Gregory, it must be considered a formal statement of William's policy towards Rome. As such it directly addresses one of the fundamental areas of Church reform: papal–state relations. Under the reforming papacy, Rome was attempting to exert greater leadership over the western Church. Both these figures are also central to understanding Church reform. William claimed ultimate leadership of the English Church. Pope Gregory was one of the strongest advocates of expanding papal power and gave his name to the Gregorian reform movement.

> This paragraph uses some good own knowledge to place Source 18 within the context of the Gregorian reform movement.

In contrast to Source 15, which championed reform, the content of Source 18 is useful as it shows that William was determined to resist papal encroachment. He firmly but politely rejected the pope's desire that William pay homage for England, stating 'I have never desired to do fealty, nor do I desire it now.' As a result of supplying the papal banner at Hastings, Rome was attempting to claim increased control over English affairs. However it does not indicate that papal relations were as distant as in the Anglo-Saxon period. There is some measure of warmth in the letter. William also agrees to the payment of Peter's Pence, an annual payment to Rome. This reflects the fact that William was pious and had built up a reputation as a reformer while Duke of Normandy. There is nothing in this letter which Lanfranc would have objected to. While also a reformer, he, like William, was determined to maintain his full control over the English church and Lanfranc avoided attending papal synods.

> This paragraph is clearly focused on the question and shows good integration between the source and own knowledge. The candidate uses the reference to Peter's Pence in the source to develop a rounded view of William's attitude to Church reform.

In conclusion the historian can make extensive use of both sources. This is because they provide contemporary insights into the attitudes and actions of the three key individuals who were central to reforming the Church. They also reveal the nature of Church reform. This was focused on administrative modernisation and anti-corruption. It was led by Lanfranc and supported by William. It did not extend to sacrificing power to Rome.

> The candidate finishes their answer with a clear judgement, explaining how the value of both sources stems from their nature, origin and differing perspectives on Church reform.

Verdict

This is a strong answer because:

- it is rooted in the sources and identifies and illustrates their key features
- it deploys a sound range of own knowledge to support the points and provide some context
- it sustains focus and develops a clear argument

- there is a clear judgement which follows on from the arguments put forward
- while the candidate has found that both sources are valuable to the historian, it is also valid to challenge the usefulness of the sources based on their content or nature and origin.

Paper 2: A Level sample answer with comments

Section B

These questions assess your understanding of the period in some depth. They will ask you about the content you learned about in the four key themes, but may not ask about more than one theme. For these questions remember to:

- give an analytical, not a descriptive, response
- support your points with evidence
- cover the whole time period specified in the question
- come to a substantiated judgement.

How significant was English resistance to the Norman Conquest in the decade after the Battle of Hastings? (20 marks)

Average student answer

This essay will argue that English resistance was very significant in the decade after the battle of Hastings.

William faced serious resistance from the moment he landed in England. In the Battle of Hastings King Harold was able to field an army of around 8,000 men. Although the Anglo-Saxons were ultimately defeated, the battle lasted the whole day, which was unusual as most medieval battles lasted a few hours at most. The level of the resistance put up by the English can be seen from the fact that Harold was killed, along with his brothers Gyrth and Leofwine. After Hastings feelings of resistance were still strong as Archbishop Stigand took steps to crown Edgar Atheling as the new king. Although London gave in without a fight in December 1066, the South East had clearly not been quelled. Kent rose in rebellion in the summer of 1067. This shows that William faced heavy opposition in all the areas he went to in the first year of his rule.

Similarly, the rebellions against the Normans soon spread nationwide. In 1067 the Welsh Border saw Edric the Wild lead a short-lived revolt in Herefordshire. In the South West resistance was focused on Exeter in 1068. The North saw insurrection from 1069 to 1070, while in East Anglia in 1070–71, Morcar joined forces with King Sweyn of Denmark and the thegn Hereward. There were also the countless minor attacks which went unrecorded but led William to issue the murdrum law, which was a fine imposed upon a community if the murderer of a Norman was not caught. A great deal of England did offer resistance to William.

In 1070 William carried out the harrying of the North following this region's attempts to oppose him. The most inspiring resistance came, however, from Hereward the Wake. He was an Anglo-Saxon thegn who had reportedly had his land stolen by the Normans. This drove him to take up arms and he based himself on the Isle of Ely. This was an ideal location as it was protected by marshlands but it still allowed Hereward to strike out. In June 1070 he raided Peterborough. Helping him were the Danes and Earl Morcar. Initial attempts by the Normans to take Ely failed and in the spring of 1071 William himself had to direct operations. He blockaded it with his fleet and constructed a causeway across the marshland. This allowed him successfully to storm the island.

This is not a strong start to the answer. The candidate has not provided any context to the question, outlined the main points to be examined or indicated the line of argument the answer will take.

This paragraph contains some thorough knowledge but the section relating to the Battle of Hastings is not relevant. The question specifies the decade after the battle itself. The second half of the paragraph which outlines some examples of early resistance by the English is relevant but greater development is needed.

This paragraph considers the geographical spread of the rebellions. While a valid point, it reads too much like a list of uprisings as it is missing analytical comments which could add value to the names and dates outlined. It would also be useful for the candidate to focus on the quality of the paragraph's first sentence. While it gives the theme to be discussed, it is also essential to link it to the question itself by including words from the question.

There is a lot going on in this paragraph. The candidate provides a good description of the East Anglia uprising. However, the candidate does need to explain how this rebellion challenged William's power. The northern uprising, which is the major example of English resistance, is only dealt with in one sentence and this is not enough for such a key point.

In 1075 William faced further rebellion from Ralph de Gael, earl of Norfolk, Roger de Breteuil, earl of Hereford and Waltheof, earl of Northumbria. Although the first two were French, Waltheof was an Anglo-Saxon and son of Earl Siward. They aimed to depose William and divide the kingdom into three, with one of them becoming king. To help them they also had the support of the Danes. However the rebellion ended in failure. Waltheof got cold feet and confessed the plan to William. He would end up being executed. Ralph and Roger failed to secure much popular support and their forces were defeated by an Anglo-Norman army under the command of Archbishop Lanfranc and Odo, Bishop of Bayeux.

Resistance to William was not confined to England. In the decade after Hastings he had to deal with the threat from Malcom III of Scotland, who wanted to gain control of Northumbria. In 1070 Malcolm raided this region, while he also provided a safe haven for English rebels. In the summer of 1072 William invaded Scotland in revenge, receiving homage from the Scottish king in the Treaty of Abernethy. On the continent Norman power was also challenged. In 1069 Maine, which had been taken over by the Normans in 1063, revolted. As a result of the uprisings in England, William would not be able to recapture it until 1073. Earl Ralph de Gael, who had opposed William in England in 1075, continued his resistance on the continent, basing himself in the castle of Dol. He also received help from troops from Anjou, an old enemy of Normandy. William attempted to take the castle in late 1076 but was forced into retreat by an army led by the King of France. This shows that William was facing resistance on all his borders after Hastings.

In conclusion William faced serious resistance. The English were not prepared to be ruled by the Normans and spent almost a decade fighting back. Significant rebellions occurred in the North and East Anglia, while in 1075 a small group of nobles attempted to remove William the Conqueror from power. During this period, William also had to deal with aggression from Scotland and on the continent, making his job more difficult.

The 1075 revolt of the Norman earls is potentially an interesting point to focus on, as it marks the last uprising against William's authority in England. This paragraph needs more assessment, pointing out that it was a Norman rather than an English uprising, which gained little support.

A lot of excellent knowledge is offered in this section relating to events in Scotland and France. However no credit can be given because it is not relevant to the question. The answer needs to focus on English resistance only. Malcolm III of Scotland could be brought in as the support he provided to English rebels strengthened their resistance.

The candidate finishes with an effective final judgement and an explanation of this view. By this stage a further weakness of the answer has become apparent, however. It is not balanced because the counter-argument looking at the weakness of English resistance has not been considered at all.

Verdict

This is an average answer because:

- only one side of the question is explored and so the answer lacks balance
- while some sound knowledge is deployed, it is too descriptive and needs greater analysis
- not all the information provided is relevant to the question, while some key points are under-developed

- the paragraphs need to be more tightly focused on the exact question.

Use the feedback on this answer to rewrite it, making as many improvements as you can.

Paper 2: A Level sample answer with comments

Section B

These questions assess your understanding of the period in some depth. They will ask you about the content you learned about in the four key themes, but may not ask about more than one theme. For these questions remember to:

- give an analytical, not a descriptive, response
- support your points with evidence
- cover the whole time period specified in the question
- come to a substantiated judgement.

How significant was English resistance to the Norman Conquest in the decade after the Battle of Hastings? (20 marks)

Strong student answer

After Hastings William was in a precarious position, backed up by only 8,000 soldiers amidst 2.5 million hostile Anglo-Saxons. It would take William nearly a decade before he could feel secure over his new subjects. During this time he faced resistance, especially in the North, necessitating brutality and extensive castle building. However ultimately English resistance did not pose a serious threat due to Norman determination and Anglo-Saxon weakness.

> This is a strong start to the answer. The candidate places the question in its historical context, outlines the debate and offers a line of argument.

The most serious act of resistance was the northern uprising of 1069–71. This was a significant threat because the North had a tradition of political independence stemming from its long rule under the Danes. This was seen in the way the Northumbrians had risen against Tostig in 1065. Furthermore the rebellion was led by the cream of the remaining Anglo-Saxon nobility including Earls Edwin and Morcar and Edgar Atheling. This uprising was also co-ordinated with a Danish invasion. A fleet of 240 ships landed at the River Humber and seized York. In addition the King of Scotland allied himself to Edgar Atheling, opening the possibility of Scottish intervention. Finally this rebellion encouraged revolts in Dorset, Somerset, Staffordshire and Cheshire. The savage response testifies to its threat. In the harrying, William devastated Yorkshire. According to Domesday, 80 percent of the county was 'waste' 15 years later. A cowed population would not have needed such brutality.

> The strength of this paragraph lies in its analysis of the northern uprising. Instead of describing events, five distinct ways in which this uprising challenged Norman power have been set out.

The extensive resistance by the English also prompted a massive programme of castle building. Castles were a device of war, allowing William to dominate the surrounding landscape militarily and psychologically. William clearly felt they were needed and built them in their hundreds. They were located in areas of rebellion, either in the centre of towns as at Exeter or else in strategic terrain, as seen in the chain of castles built along the Welsh border to watch over the mountain passes. Most were motte and bailey, designed for quick construction in battle-field conditions. Despite the expense, William also built stone castles at Chepstow and London, underscoring the vulnerability he felt in these key locations.

> This is a well-explained paragraph. It is often forgotten by candidates that castles were tools of repression and built to quell resistance.

However the fact remains that the English resistance was not serious enough to remove William. Many uprisings did not stretch him. Exeter only held out for 18 days for example. In the northern campaign he was able successfully to relieve the garrison at York in 1069 and then later retake York from the Danes. In East Anglia, he was at first content to let his barons deal with the threat from Hereward. Many parts of England did not rise up, including strategic London and the South East, William's corridor back to Normandy. Popular resistance had also come to an end by 1071 with the failure of the Ely uprising. Although there was an uprising in 1075, this was led by Norman earls.

> The first sentence of this paragraph clearly signposts the overall argument in this answer. Having laid out the ways in which English resistance did partially challenge the Normans in the first two paragraphs, the rest of the answer will now expand upon the line of argument first put forward in the introduction.

English resistance was not as serious as it potentially could have been due to its poor leadership. This was partly because the cream of the English nobility had been slaughtered at Hastings including Godwin and his brothers. Many warriors had fled abroad, working as mercenaries in the Varangian Guard in Constantinople. Others initially preferred to make alliances with William, most notably Edwin and Morcar, in order to safeguard titles and wealth. As a result there was no central leadership, meaning the rebellions were not co-ordinated. This gave William time to isolate and destroy each rebellion individually. There were also few great leaders for people to rally behind. It is telling that the East Anglian rising was led by a minor thegn, Hereward, rather than the elite earls.

> This is a well-explained paragraph on the underlying reasons for the weak English resistance. It is analytical and provides supporting detail.

William's actions also helped prevent English resistance becoming more serious. Directly after Hastings his brutal march around the South East forced London to surrender. When faced with rebellion in the North East in 1070, William drove his army across the Pennines in winter, taking the rebels in Chester and Stafford by surprise. His 'harrying' of the North meant this region was too scared to rise again. William's deal-making skills also reduced the scale of resistance. In the northern rebellion he bribed the Danes to leave. He repeated this in East Anglia, leaving the Anglo-Saxons exposed on Ely. In 1075 William brought Edgar Atheling into his court. This removed the last rallying point of Anglo-Saxon resistance. These military and diplomatic skills ensured the rebellions remained contained.

> Building on the previous paragraph, this section continues the answer's line of argument by exploring the role played by William in undermining resistance. The analysis is correct and there is some supporting knowledge.

In conclusion English resistance did not pose a serious threat to Norman rule. By 1071 the rebellions had been crushed and William was in full control of England. While there had been dangerous moments for William, especially in the northern uprising, he possessed the brutal skills needed to subdue the population. He was also prepared to be diplomatic in order to contain rebellion. English resistance was also limited by a failure of its own leadership. Many warriors had died or left England, while others were inexperienced and could be bought.

> A strong answer to this question must consider both sides of the argument and then weigh them up in the conclusion. The candidate has done this and comes to a well-explained judgement.

Verdict

This is a strong answer because:

- it puts both sides of the case and sustains a focus on the question set
- it has a wide range of evidence which is used to support the points made
- it reaches a secure concluding judgement
- it is well organised and communication of material is clear and precise.

England and the Angevin Empire in the reign of Henry II, 1154–89

Just over 50 years after his death in 1087, William the Conqueror's grandchildren, Matilda and Stephen, plunged England into a devastating civil war, shattering the socio-political structures of the feudal system developed after the Norman conquest of 1066. When William's great grandson, Henry II, became king of England in 1154, swathes of the kingdom were effectively semi-autonomous mini-states, in some cases run by barons who were little better than warlords.

KEY TERM

Angevin
An adjective describing someone from Anjou, in France.

SOURCE

1 An 1137 account from the *Anglo-Saxon Chronicle* describing the reign of King Stephen.

> For every great man built him castles and held them against the king … they filled them with devils and wicked men … they seized those they believed to have any … gold or silver … tortured them with unspeakable tortures … They strung them up by the thumbs, or by the head, and hung coats of mail on their feet. They tied knotted cords round their heads and twisted it until it entered the brain. They put them in dungeons … many thousands they starved to death. Some they put into a crucet-house, that is, into a chest that was short and narrow, and not deep, and they that they broke all his limbs. They were continually levying an exaction from the towns, which they called Tenserie [a payment to the superior lord for protection], and when the miserable inhabitants had no more to give, then plundered they, and burnt all the towns… Then was corn dear, and flesh, and cheese, and butter, for there was none in the land.

King Henry I had only one legitimate heir, his daughter Matilda. England had never experienced a queen regnant; it was considered unnatural for women to govern. Nevertheless, Henry I had made his barons swear to accept Matilda as his heir, and they had done so, including her cousin, Stephen. However, when the time came in 1135, Stephen took the throne instead. Civil war ensued.

At the same time that Stephen and Matilda were fighting each other for the English throne, Matilda's husband, Geoffrey of Anjou, was fighting for control of Normandy, which he succeeded in taking in 1144. Meanwhile, the conflict in England dragged on.

There was no outright victory in the fight for the English throne, although Stephen nominally remained king. But, despite having two sons himself, he made Matilda's son, Henry of Anjou, his heir. It would require considerable political skill, a fearsome reputation and an indefatigable spirit to restore the kingdom after the devastation of Stephen's reign. Henry had all these qualities, and the impact he made on 12th century England remains significant. In restoring Crown authority, Henry II formed the heart of the English legal system and revived the predecessor of the modern **Exchequer**. He also laid the foundations of England's troubled relationship with Ireland.

KEY TERM

Exchequer
The government department that evolved to deal with Crown finances. The term derives from a piece of cloth, checked like a chess board, upon which complex sums could be done when auditing the accounts.

1135 – Death of King Henry I of England, Duke of Normandy; his nephew, Stephen, seizes the throne from his cousin, Matilda, Henry I's daughter	**1135**
1152 – King Louis VII of France divorces his wife, Eleanor of Aquitaine, who marries Henry of Anjou eight weeks later	**1152**
1154 – Death of King Stephen Henry of Anjou ascends the English throne as King Henry II	**1154**
1162 – Thomas Becket is made archbishop of Canterbury	**1162**
1166 – Henry II's major set of legal reforms, the Assize of Clarendon, is issued	**1166**
1170 – Henry II's eldest son, the Young King, is crowned. Henry and Thomas Becket are reconciled only for Becket to be murdered	**1170**
1173 – The Great Rebellion breaks out	**1173**
1180 – Death of Louis VII of France; his son takes the throne as Philip II, later called Philip Augustus	**1180**
1185 – Henry II sends his son John to Ireland with the intention of his becoming its High King; John fails	**1185**
1188 – Henry II's second son, Richard, turns against his father and does homage to Philip II of France	**1188**

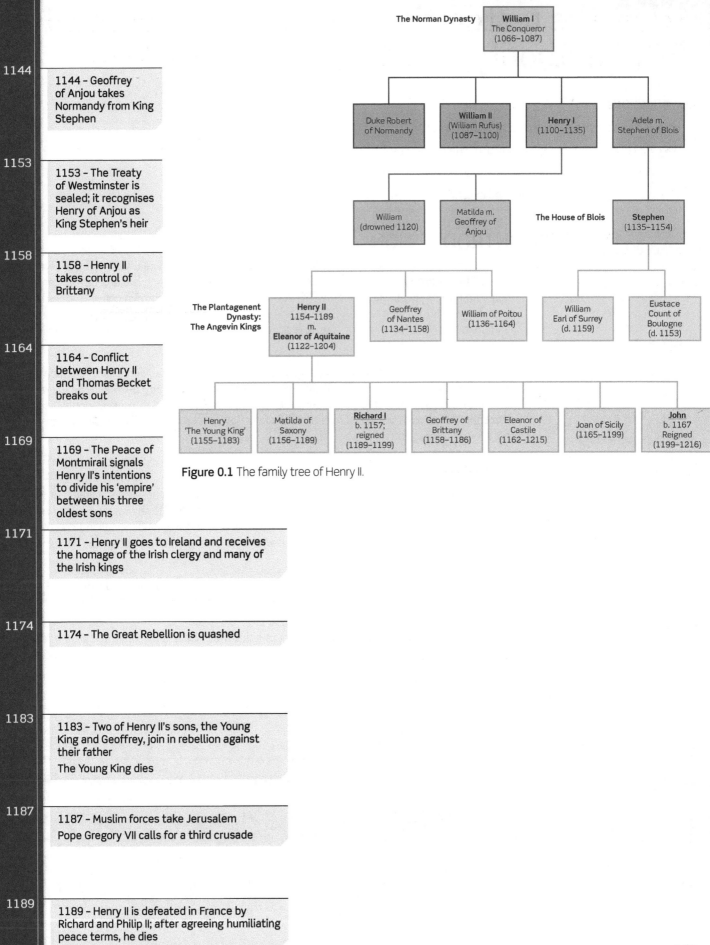

Figure 0.1 The family tree of Henry II.

1144

1144 – Geoffrey of Anjou takes Normandy from King Stephen

1153

1153 – The Treaty of Westminster is sealed; it recognises Henry of Anjou as King Stephen's heir

1158

1158 – Henry II takes control of Brittany

1164

1164 – Conflict between Henry II and Thomas Becket breaks out

1169

1169 – The Peace of Montmirail signals Henry II's intentions to divide his 'empire' between his three oldest sons

1171

1171 – Henry II goes to Ireland and receives the homage of the Irish clergy and many of the Irish kings

1174

1174 – The Great Rebellion is quashed

1183

1183 – Two of Henry II's sons, the Young King and Geoffrey, join in rebellion against their father

The Young King dies

1187

1187 – Muslim forces take Jerusalem

Pope Gregory VII calls for a third crusade

1189

1189 – Henry II is defeated in France by Richard and Philip II; after agreeing humiliating peace terms, he dies

The Norman Dynasty

William I
The Conqueror
(1066–1087)

Duke Robert of Normandy

William II
(William Rufus)
(1087–1100)

Henry I
(1100–1135)

Adela m.
Stephen of Blois

William
(drowned 1120)

Matilda m.
Geoffrey of Anjou

The House of Blois

Stephen
(1135–1154)

The Plantagenent Dynasty:
The Angevin Kings

Henry II
1154–1189
m.
Eleanor of Aquitaine
(1122–1204)

Geoffrey of Nantes
(1134–1158)

William of Poitou
(1136–1164)

William Earl of Surrey
(d. 1159)

Eustace Count of Boulogne
(d. 1153)

Henry 'The Young King'
(1155–1183)

Matilda of Saxony
(1156–1189)

Richard I
b. 1157;
reigned
(1189–1199)

Geoffrey of Brittany
(1158–1186)

Eleanor of Castile
(1162–1215)

Joan of Sicily
(1165–1199)

John
b. 1167
Reigned
(1199–1216)

2b.1 The restoration and extension of royal authority, 1154–72

KEY QUESTIONS

- What was the state of Henry II's territories in 1154?
- Why was Henry II able to gain control of the nobility by 1172?
- Why did the leaders of Wales, Scotland and Ireland submit to Henry II's authority by 1172?
- Why was Henry II able to secure and extend his French territories by 1172?

KEY TERMS

The Anarchy (1135–54)
The civil war for control of the English throne between supporters of Stephen, Henry I's nephew, and Matilda, Henry I's daughter and mother of Henry II. Neither side was able to gain decisive control and much of the country was devastated in the fighting, while barons increased their own local power in place of the weak or lacking royal authority.

Baron
Lay tenant-in-chief.

Vassal
A person who held land from a superior in the feudal system. Everyone in the feudal system was someone's vassal except the king. Vassals owed some form of service and/or financial recompense to their superiors.

Lay
An adjective used to describe people not ordained in the Church or not belonging to holy orders.

INTRODUCTION

England in 1154 was a damaged and divided kingdom, having faced nearly 20 years of civil war during **The Anarchy**. In some places royal authority was non-existent, **barons** having carved out their own realms, dispensing their own 'justice' and even minting their own coins. Hundreds of people were displaced from their lands, and had their rights and inheritances reduced by the barons and their mercenaries. Little wonder, then, that some contemporary chroniclers described England under Stephen as 'a shipwreck'.

Medieval kings were required to protect the realm, make laws and provide justice, oversee the coinage, protect the Church and provide an heir, preferably male. There needed to be the means to execute decisions and enforce the law. With no standing army, and the cost of conflict so great, mustering troops and supplies efficiently was a huge logistical problem. The feudal system enabled these things to happen.

The feudal system

The feudal system can be seen as a system of oaths and obligations based upon grants of land. In return for the lord's land and protection, the **vassal** took an oath of loyalty and promised military and other services. Ultimately all land belonged to the king and, although inheriting land and titles was well established, he had the right to take back what had been granted, especially as punishment for disloyalty or treason.

Tenants-in-chief received their lands directly from the king. They played an important role in advising him and governing the localities. The number varied, but there were 270 **lay** tenants-in-chief in 1166. Archbishops, bishops and abbots were also tenants-in-chief.

Under-tenants received land from the tenants-in-chief. Many held land from more than one lord. Again, the amounts of land, and therefore influence, they held varied. In turn, they would often grant land to tenants of their own. This is known as subinfeudation.

1154 – Henry II becomes king of England; in France he already has Normandy, Aquitaine, Anjou, Maine and Touraine

1157 – Henry takes back lands from northern England promised to Scotland before he became king

1159 – Pope Adrian IV dies, leading to papal schism

1163 – The Welsh rebel against Henry II

1154	1155	1156	1157	1158	1159	1160	1161	1162	1163

1155 – Decommissioning of illegal castles begins

1158 – Henry secures control of Brittany; the Welsh princes pay Henry homage

1160 – Henry II secures the Vexin, in Normandy, through the marriage of his son Henry to Margaret of France

The vast majority of people were peasants, working the land. At the top end were the free tenants, who paid money rent for their land. They were free to come and go as they wished. In 1166, however, approximately 45 percent of the population were **villeins**. They were tied to their lord's land and were obliged to work for him for up to three days a week, and were sometimes obliged to pay taxes known as feudal dues. Villeins were subject to the lord's justice in his own court. Of the two to two-and-a-half million people in England at the time, about nine out of ten worked the land.

The reality of the social hierarchy was more complex than the basic feudal system suggests: one man might be vassal to many lords; vassals in turn made grants to others (subinfeudation); some vassals' obligations were military, others were financial or in kind (supplying of goods and services). Thus, with land came the power of **patronage** and the ability to build up networks of vassals and tenants, allowing estates to function and providing a supply of soldiers and officials to uphold their lord's jurisdiction.

Magnates and knights

Given that tenants-in-chief played such an important role in providing the king with his military and administrative needs, establishing good relationships with them was essential and this was one reason why kings were **itinerant**. Visiting magnates enabled the king to include them in government and receive their advice. A visit from the king was also a great honour. However, the power and resources of the barons also made them a potentially threatening and destabilising influence, and so a balance had to be struck between establishing a good working rapport and firm control.

'Earl' was the only honorific title, and was bestowed by the king, but earls were not the only tenants-in-chief, nor the only men important in governing the realm. Magnates is a broader term that can be used to cover any important or influential people, including earls and archbishops, bishops and abbots.

'Knight' is a familiar medieval term that covered a wide variety of men. Some were under-tenants, supplying military service in return for land. Not all had been **enfeoffed**, however. Some were **household** knights, acting as the lord's bodyguard in return for their needs being met. Others held important official posts, such as county coroner, or acted as stewards for major barons.

KEY TERMS

Villein
A peasant who belonged to the land and was not free to leave it. Villeins were granted some land to farm themselves. However, another feature of being a villein was that they were expected to work the lord's land for two to three days a week and more at times such as harvest.

Patronage
The ability of supporters (patrons) to give lands, positions, titles and honours to others, who then become the patron's clients. Patronage enables the development of networks of clients and supporters.

Itinerant kingship
The king would travel his lands continually, taking his household with him and holding court wherever he was. There were two important reasons for this. First, to be seen: to forge relationships with tenants-in-chief and deliver justice to his people, and second, to exploit what was owed him in terms of food and services. As the king was at the heart of government, the government went with him. However, there were permanent law courts in London and the Exchequer was situated there from about 1156.

Enfeoffed
Holding land in return for service, often military, and homage. This piece of land was known as a fee or a fief and still belonged to the superior who granted it.

Household
Term covering a lord's family and servants as well as his knights and the officials who ran his estates, his chaplain and followers. A household could be extremely large and was like a family firm that oversaw all of the lord's interests and those of his family. The Royal Household was the centre of government.

1166 – Henry puts down a rebellion in Brittany; the Assize of Clarendon and Cartae Baronum

1169 – Treaty of Montmirail

1171–72 – Henry takes control of Dublin and much of Ireland

| 1164 | 1165 | 1166 | 1167 | 1168 | 1169 | 1170 | 1171 | 1172 |

1165 – Henry's expedition to bring Wales under control fails

1167 – Birth of Henry and Eleanor's last child, John

1167–69 – Henry deals with a series of uprisings and attacks in France; relations with Louis VII are bad

1170 – Murder of Thomas Becket, archbishop of Canterbury; death of Owain of Gwynedd; the Inquest of Sheriffs

1172 – Rhys of Deheubarth becomes justiciar of Wales, acknowledging Henry II as his overlord

AS Level Exam-Style Question Section A

Why is Source 1 valuable to the historian for an enquiry into why Henry II was able to enforce his control over England after he became king in 1154?

Explain your answer using the source, the information about it and your own knowledge of the historical context. (8 marks)

Tip

When it comes to historical context, think about the role and duties of a king.

SOURCE

1 Description of Henry II by Peter of Blois, in a letter to the archbishop of Palermo written in 1177. Peter of Blois was a diplomat and poet, who went to England in 1173 to serve Henry II.

Truly he does not, like other kings, linger in his palace, but travelling through the provinces he investigates the doings of all, judging powerfully those whom he has made judges of others. No one is more cunning in counsel, more fiery in speech, more secure in the midst of dangers, more cautious in fortune, more constant in adversity. Whom once he has esteemed, with difficulty he unloves them; whom once he has hated, with difficulty he receives into the grace of his familiarity. Always are in his hands bow, sword, spear and arrow, unless he be in council or in books. As often as he is able to rest from cares and anxieties, he occupies himself by reading alone, or in a crowd of clerics he labours to untangle some knot of inquiry.

ACTIVITY
KNOWLEDGE CHECK

Evaluating the feudal system

1 What are the pros and cons of the feudal system as a means of running a medieval kingdom?

2 How could the feudal system be used to prevent barons from becoming overpowerful?

WHAT WAS THE STATE OF HENRY II'S TERRITORIES IN 1154?

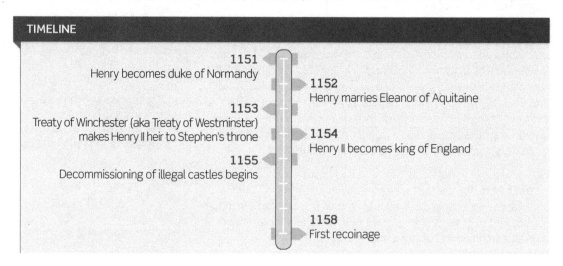

TIMELINE

1151
Henry becomes duke of Normandy

1152
Henry marries Eleanor of Aquitaine

1153
Treaty of Winchester (aka Treaty of Westminster) makes Henry II heir to Stephen's throne

1154
Henry II becomes king of England

1155
Decommissioning of illegal castles begins

1158
First recoinage

KEY TERM

Writ
An official document; a sealed, written command from the king, usually in English, to be read aloud.

Baronial power

The *Anglo-Saxon Chronicle*'s account of Stephen's reign describes an England where, in many places, the barons ignored royal authority and ran their lands like their own mini-kingdoms, issuing coinage and controlling the population through intimidation and violence. In many places the king's **writ** was unenforceable. Their power bases were usually castles, many of which were illegal, having been built without royal permission or taken from the king. However, London, East Anglia and the South East were still largely under Stephen's control.

By late summer 1153, England was weary of war and it was becoming clear that the barons' preference was for Matilda's son, Henry, to succeed Stephen, rather than Stephen's son, Eustace. Key barons such as the earls of Chester and Leicester had been lured over to Henry's side as he toured England, making individual treaties with magnates that guaranteed them their rights as landlords, sometimes over lands that they had taken. Others had always been against Stephen, believing him to be a usurper; others still calculated that their interests now lay with the grandson of Henry I, a much stronger candidate than Stephen's son, and without any issues over usurpation in his right to be king.

KEY TERM

Primogeniture
The succession of the oldest male. This did not prevent a female from inheriting, but males took precedence.

Although **primogeniture** was often followed, there were no hard-and-fast rules about successors. One important factor was the barons' support. In November 1153, the Treaty of Winchester named Henry as Stephen's heir. Stephen's other legitimate son, William, did homage to Henry for significant lands in East Anglia. The treaty was sealed at Westminster that Christmas, to general approval from England's magnates. This did not prevent Henry from taking harsh measures against illegal castles and trimming the number and size of earldoms once he was king.

Declining royal revenues

The Crown's revenues in 1154

The most pressing matter in England on Henry's accession was the restoration of royal authority. This would require the curbing of baronial power and increasing royal revenues. It is estimated that overall royal revenues had fallen by between one-half and two-thirds since 1135 due to the civil war and Stephen's loss of effective control of large areas of England.

A major source of Crown revenue, the **farm,** was a fixed sum payable every year by each county and borough, for which the sheriff was responsible and derived mainly from the king's own **demesne**. By 1154, much of the royal demesne had been lost, either because Stephen had granted it away, attempting to build baronial support, or because it had simply been taken over where he had lost effective control in an area. In other places, war had driven people from the land, which went to waste.

Losing control across large swathes of England, especially in the West, meant that Stephen had been unable to collect taxes as well. The **Exchequer** was no longer working as it should, monitoring royal revenues and calling sheriffs to account twice a year, as had been the case under Henry I.

Another issue affecting Henry II's income was that the quality of the coinage had deteriorated. The integrity of the coinage, how much silver it contained and how widely it was accepted, was vital for trade, royal revenues and the wider economy. Stephen had lost control of the coinage and, by 1154, numerous barons were minting money in his name but without authority to do so. Others were even minting their own money: the Empress Matilda's own coins were used as currency in the West of England, being issued in Bristol, Cardiff and Oxford, while in Leicester and York other barons' money was circulating. Given these issues, not only was collecting revenue problematic, but its true value was difficult for the Crown to estimate. In 1158, Henry launched a recoinage, reissuing England's money with a sufficient amount of silver. All the new coins bore an image of him, serving to reinforce his kingship, not least because it was now the only legal currency in England.

The extent of Angevin lands overseas

Henry soon established a reputation for being able to travel large distances at great speed and, given the scope of his lands on both sides of the Channel this was important. Henry II's family's power base was Anjou but, by 1154, he held Normandy (from 1150), Anjou, Maine and Touraine (from 1151) and, through marriage to Eleanor in 1152, Aquitaine.

The location of Henry's landholdings in France was important. Anjou, Maine and Touraine were strategically valuable, joining Normandy with Aquitaine so that his territories were contiguous. This made all his lands easily accessible, wherever he was in his French territories. However, the lands Henry brought together under his control were all very different in terms of languages and customs. Powerful local lords in isolated places, such as the Auvergne, did not want interference from outsiders. It was a constantly demanding task for Henry to try to maintain control over such disparate territories.

Henry's marriage to Eleanor of Aquitaine angered King Louis VII, who had secured an annulment ending his own marriage to her only eight weeks earlier. Henry, as the king's vassal, had also failed to ask permission to marry. This was a breach of feudal etiquette, as kings expected to determine the marriages of their most important vassals. Eleanor brought vast resources with her, as Aquitanian custom was favourable towards women inheriting their own lands.

Aquitaine was hard to govern. The local lords, especially in Poitou, Limoges and to the south-east in the Auvergne region, which Henry now claimed as duke of Aquitaine, were fiercely independent and their allegiance could not be taken for granted. However, it was also a wealthy region with flourishing wine, salt and pottery trades as well as major navigable rivers and trade routes. Possessing Anjou, Maine and Touraine meant that Aquitaine was connected to Normandy, another region of economic potential, and all under Henry's control. By 1154, Henry dominated the western side of France and therefore some of the most important French ports, including La Rochelle, Bordeaux and Rouen, as well as those of Bristol, Southampton and London in England. Control of such important ports gave Henry control over, and tax revenue from, the very lucrative trading on which these towns thrived.

Figure 1.1 Political map of France in the 12th century.

Key
- Louis VII's royal demesne
- Lands held by vassals of the French king
- Angevin heartlands
- Other lands also held by Henry II
- Land claimed by the dukes of Aquitaine
- The Vexin

The power of Eleanor of Aquitaine

Eleanor of Aquitaine's role is hard to evaluate. There is evidence of her involvement in courts as far apart as Normandy, Bordeaux and Bayonne but much of her influence was in Aquitaine between 1168 and 1173. This was her homeland and power base, where she was duchess in her own right. Nevertheless, she also frequently acted as co-regent for Henry in England (alongside his **justiciars**) during the early years of Henry's reign, despite frequent pregnancies, dealing with routine matters of state, overseeing the implementation of the king's orders and policies, and dispensing justice at Westminster. There are surviving writs and documents bearing her name and seal and, until 1163, she had her own chancellor and appointed her own clerk to the Exchequer.

KEY TERM

Justiciar
Appointed by the king, justiciars ran the government of England in his absence. They had discretionary powers to act upon his behalf and presided over the Exchequer, as well as overseeing the law courts.

Eleanor of Aquitaine often accompanied Henry and his court, but she also had her own household, officials and personal servants. Henry II paid for them, however, so that he could monitor and restrict the size of her household, limiting her powers of patronage and ability to administer Crown lands without his support. Nevertheless, she often travelled independently of him and there are records of her arbitrating disputes at Oxford market, at her own mill in Woodstock, Oxfordshire, and even as far away as Cornish tin mines. Unfortunately the accounts of the extent of her role are patchy, as the chroniclers, being male and frequently misogynistic clergy, paid little attention to her, even though she was queen of England. There are a few glimpses of her in other records, such as letters and charters that indicate she supported and upheld Henry II's policies, certainly in the first 10 to 15 years of his reign.

Eleanor would have expected to play an important part in running Aquitaine, especially after the birth of her last child, John, and the death of Henry's mother, the Empress Matilda, both in 1167. Matilda had remained an influence over her son, especially in France; with Eleanor of Aquitaine giving birth to eight children in 15 years, her ability to take an active role in supporting Henry II was sometimes restricted. After the birth of John, however, Eleanor established her own court in Aquitaine and oversaw much of its day-to-day government with her son Richard at her side.

SOURCE
2

Eleanor of Aquitaine riding through France. From a 12th to 13th century fresco in Chinon, France.

ACTIVITY
KNOWLEDGE CHECK

1 Complete a SWOT analysis of Henry II's position in 1154 upon becoming king of England.

   Strengths and **W**eaknesses need to refer to the actual situation Henry was facing.

   Opportunities and **T**hreats refer to *potential* developments to consider so that Henry can prepare for the threats and exploit the opportunities.

2 Based upon your SWOT analysis, draw up a five-point action plan for Henry II successfully to achieve securing the English throne in 1154.

3 Take each of the points in the action plan and explain how they might be affected by Henry's holding of lands in France.

WHY WAS HENRY II ABLE TO GAIN CONTROL OF THE NOBILITY BY 1172?

HENRY II AND THE NOBILITY 1154–72

1154
Henry of Anjou ascends the English throne under the terms of the Treaty of Winchester, sealed at Westminster in December

1157
Henry confiscates the castles of Hugh Bigod and William of Blois in East Anglia

1155
All foreign mercenaries, including those employed by the Crown, are sent home

Henry II begins a programme of decommissioning illegal castles and taking royal castles back under Crown control

Twenty-one of England's sheriffs are replaced

1162
Henry replaces half of England's sheriffs

1166
Assize of Clarendon
Cartae Baronum

1170
Inquest of Sheriffs sees up to 22 of 29 sheriffs removed and replaced with royal officials

The weakening of baronial power

By the time of Stephen's death, Henry II had already begun to establish his authority in England. The Treaty of Winchester, sealed at Westminster, confirmed his right to the throne and he had the support of the Church and England's magnates. Although he had the support of the majority of England's barons, Henry still faced potential opposition and could take nothing for granted. Stephen's son, William, had a potential claim to the throne and held considerable estates in East Anglia, and there were still overmighty subjects whose allegiance could be transferred if they decided that their best interests did not lie with the new king.

Restoring the Crown's authority was Henry's priority after the damage it had undergone during Stephen's rule. Henry spent the entire year of 1155 in England establishing his reign. His desire to expunge any encroachments on royal authority made since 1135 can be seen in numerous **charters** issued at the start of his reign.

In these charters, Henry made it very clear that any gains made by ambitious or opportunistic barons since 1135 were to be reversed, a process that would also include land or prerogatives taken by the Church. The process was not simply a land grab by the Crown. Although quite swift, it did not happen in one fell swoop and Henry treated his supporters carefully. England's magnates were important in its government and defence. However, for the feudal system to function effectively the king must be the ultimate authority.

Among the first steps taken by Henry was the expulsion of all foreign mercenaries, including several hundred under royal command. Stephen had relied upon them and they could have been useful for a king establishing his rule in a divided kingdom, so to some extent this was a bold move. Given how hated and costly they were, it was also a shrewd one. Contemporary chroniclers praised Henry, seeing this move as a sign that peace and security would be restored.

Henry's approach to controlling England's magnates was a mixture of military might, astute political decisions and increasing Crown involvement in the shires. His key strategies were:

- weakening the power bases of magnates

- bringing sheriffs under Crown control

- enforcing his feudal rights as king and overlord of England.

The methods used, and their resulting developments, can be seen as part of a long-term centralisation of power, which was also to involve legal and financial reforms.

KEY TERM

Charter
An official, sealed document from the king, usually granting rights and privileges, written in Latin.

SOURCE

From William of Newburgh, *Historia rerum Anglicarum* (The History of English Affairs) (written between 1196 and 1198) describing Henry II's first acts as king. It is thought William used written sources to add to his own eyewitness accounts in producing his *History*.

The king reflected that the royal revenues, which, in the time of his grandfather had been very ample, were greatly reduced. Through the laziness of King Stephen, royal revenues had, for the most part, passed away to numerous other masters. King Henry commanded them to be restored by those who had taken them unlawfully, and brought back to the king. Those men who had hitherto become proprietors in royal towns and villages produced for their defence the charters which they had either forced from King Stephen, or earned by their services: but these claims did not succeed, as the grants of Stephen could not stand against the claims of a lawful king. Highly indignant at first, but afterwards terrified and dispirited, they resigned everything they had usurped, and throughout each county of the kingdom, submitted to royal will.

Barons and boroughs

Medieval towns and cities (boroughs) do not sit easily in the feudal system. Land held there was rented rather than held in return for services. Towns were excellent sources of revenue for the lord: licences bought to hold markets; tolls paid when transporting goods through bottlenecks, such as bridges, town gates and harbours; fines (profits of justice). County towns were also seats of local government, where the shire courts and gaols were to be found. They were usually well fortified, with their own castles and city walls. Henry ensured that most important towns, known as royal boroughs, such as London, Lincoln, York, Winchester, Exeter, Oxford and Leicester, came under Crown rather than baronial control. Henry also made it clear that any rights granted to towns during Stephen's reign would be reversed, just as he had done with his barons.

SOURCE 4

Henry II's charters to the cities of Exeter c1154–58 and Chichester in July 1155. These are two of dozens of similar charters issued to towns all across England.

Know ye that I have granted to my citizens of Exeter all the right customs which they had in the time of King Henry my grandfather, all bad customs created since his time being abolished.

Know ye that I have granted to my citizens of Chichester who are of the merchant guild, all their liberties and free customs within the borough and without. That they may have them everywhere fully and honourably as they were wont to have them in the time of King Henry my grandfather.

Trimming the earldoms

In a bid to build his support base among the barons, Stephen had granted numerous new earldoms, complete with their privileges and royal rights, severely impacting on Crown revenue. Henry II reversed this trend by approximately halving the number of earldoms from around 22 in 1154 to around 12 by the end of his reign and creating no new ones.

Of the earls whose power grew under Stephen, Ranulf, earl of Chester, was one of the most significant. His lands stretched across the Midlands and North West. Ranulf had agreed to support Henry as king in return for considerable territorial concessions, but he died in 1153. As his heir was a child, under the feudal principle of **wardship** the earldom reverted to the Crown. When Ranulf's son came of age, Henry did not restore all his father's estates to him, keeping some and thus increasing the royal demesne. Ranulf himself had been murdered by another baron, William Peverel (a major landowner in Nottinghamshire and Derbyshire and a vassal of the earl of Chester), who then fled England. As a felon, Peverel's lands also reverted to the Crown. This was the feudal principle of **escheat**.

The destruction of illegal castles

Henry's actions against illegal or 'adulterine' castles earned him the nickname of 'Castle Breaker'. As described in the *Anglo-Saxon Chronicle*, many barons had built or seized castles, including royal ones, without permission, using them as the power bases from which to run their own 'kingdoms'.

At the end of 1154, a rapid programme of decommissioning and demolishing dozens of illegal castles was started, although some were taken into Crown control. A few barons were, however, reluctant to conform. Henry responded in early 1155 by calling a Great Council where, according to the chronicler Roger of Howden, he confronted those who still held castles which he deemed to be within his royal rights.

William le Gros, count of Aumale and earl of York since 1138, had established a virtual mini-kingdom in Yorkshire. In February 1155, Henry went north, confronting William in York and forcing him to surrender, reluctantly but without a fight. The Crown took back royal properties, as well as Scarborough Castle, which Henry then had strengthened. When Earl William died, his remaining lands reverted to the Crown.

Other notable submissions followed quickly. Roger of Hereford handed over the royal castles of Gloucester and Hereford. Hugh Mortimer, a Welsh **Marcher** baron, surrendered that July after Henry besieged three of his castles, at Wigmore, Cleobury and Bridgnorth, simultaneously. Hugh paid homage to Henry and Cleobury was destroyed, although the castles of Wigmore and Bridgnorth were returned to him. That Hugh was allowed to keep his lands shows a king confident that he had brought his vassal to heel.

KEY TERMS

Wardship
If an heir was under age when inheriting, the lands would revert back to the Crown. Once the heir was old enough, the lands and titles would be restored to the heir upon payment of a sum of money known as a 'relief'. While the Crown held the land, all the incomes it generated would go to the king.

Escheat
The reverting of lands back to the Crown either when the landholder dies without heirs or if the landholder commits a serious crime, especially treason.

KEY TERM

Marcher
Marcher lands were lands that bordered the territory of another prince or baron. The two most significant for Henry II were probably the Welsh Marches and the Norman Marches, which bordered the land of the king of France. Marcher lords were usually given greater powers and privileges than other nobles as they were defending key territories and would often have to respond quickly to incursions.

Figure 1.2 England in the time of Henry II.

Overall, Henry held on to 30 of the castles he took back from England's barons. This played a major part in restoring Crown authority. In 1154, there had been 225 baronial and 49 royal castles, meaning 80 percent of castles were in the hands of magnates. By 1214, during the reign of Henry's son, King John, the ratio was 179:93, leaving the magnates with only 66 percent. This gives a strong indication of the shift in the balance of power that occurred under Henry, as does spending an average of £760 per annum on building and maintaining royal castles. Orford alone cost £1,400 and this is dwarfed by the £6,000 later spent on Dover. Although the work done at Orford and Dover was undertaken at a time of increasing revenues for Henry, it does represent a huge outlay. However, castles were not only strongholds that could be garrisoned with troops and withstand siege warfare, they were symbols of royal power.

EXTEND YOUR KNOWLEDGE

Henry II and Hugh Bigod

Stephen had agreed with Henry, when making him his heir, that his son, William of Blois, should be granted large amounts of land in East Anglia, including large parts of Norfolk and its county town of Norwich, together with its royal castle. There was already an earl of Norfolk, however, Hugh Bigod, who had a power base in the region. When Henry II came to the throne, he recognised Hugh as earl of Norfolk, granting him his portions of its revenues, while allowing William to keep more of its land. This resulted in tension spreading throughout the county, becoming a threat to stability there, and both Hugh and William were deprived of their castles. When William died in 1159, his lands were shared between his widow, his sister and the Crown. Hugh did not get his castles at Framlingham and Bungay back until 1165, when he paid a fee of £666. Henry kept Hugh's castle at Thetford and built another at Orford, near Framlingham, to keep Hugh's influence in check.

AS Level Exam-Style Question Section A

How much weight do you give the evidence of Source 4 for an enquiry into how Henry II established his authority in England on becoming king in 1154?

Explain your answer using the source, the information about it and your own knowledge of the historical context. (12 marks)

Tip
Sources of official evidence, such as charters, are not 'neutral' documents because they simply convey the monarch's orders. They give a clear indication of the monarch's intent and, in this case, portray a particular image of Henry II that he wished to project. This is worth considering in your answer.

A Level Exam-Style Question Section A

How far could the historian make use of Sources 3 and 5 together to investigate Henry II's approach to the government of England?

Explain your answer, using all the sources, the information given about them and your own knowledge of the historical content. (20 marks)

Tip
When considering Henry II's approach to government, think about the nature of Source 4. This gives an indication of his approach as much as the content does.

Cartae Baronum, 1166

Establishing and collecting feudal dues was another key strand of Henry II's policy of restoring the balance of power in favour of the Crown. Cartae Baronum (1166) was central to this. It was a national survey of all tenants-in-chief, which required them to disclose the number of knights they were owed by their tenants. The number of knights that the tenant-in-chief owed the king – the *servitium debitum* – was dependent upon the amount of land they were granted (how many **fiefs** or **knight's fees**). However, the number of knights they actually had from their tenants was often rather more than this.

KEY TERMS

Servitium debitum
The feudal due owed by tenants-in-chief to supply the king with knights. The number of knights owed was based upon the amount of land held.

Fief or knight's fee
A fief was land held by a vassal in return for knights. Each knight's fee meant that one knight was owed. If ten knight's fees were held then ten knights were owed.

Cartae Baronum was both a method and an example of increasing Crown power. All tenants-in-chief had to give information detailing the lands and **honours** that they held directly from the Crown. The survey was immense in size and scope and required a well-organised and efficient government, since it covered earls, barons, bishops and abbots. It recorded information on:

- tenants-in-chiefs' own land holdings

- their sub-tenants and the service they owed

- which sub-tenancies had been made before 1135 and which had been made since

- how many knights the tenants-in-chief had who were not enfeoffed but who received some other form of recompense, enabling them to have more knights than they held knight's fees

- the names of all of these men.

There were two key issues for Henry here: **scutage** and oaths of allegiance.

KEY TERMS

Honour
Another term for a fee (the terms are used interchangeably): land held by a tenant-in-chief in return for loyalty and service.

Scutage
Meaning 'shield tax', it was paid by tenants-in-chief instead of providing knights for military service.

Scutage was based upon the number of knights owed the king for land granted. Henry II, however, wanted to tax the *actual* number of knights that a baron had, including those who were not enfeoffed. This increased royal revenue considerably. Henry had more lands to defend than any previous English monarch, his military commitments stretching across the Channel to Normandy and down to the South of France.

All of these knights would have sworn oaths of allegiance to their lords. In addition, although their lords would have sworn oaths of allegiance to him in turn, Henry wanted to cut out the middle man. Every knight belonging to his tenants-in-chief would be expected to swear allegiance directly to the king.

Cartae Baronum also provided updated information on the king's wealthier subjects and was used to form the basis of all future assessments when the Crown required extra income.

The Inquest of Sheriffs, 1170

Sheriffs (and their deputies, bailiffs and constables) were vital for successful local government in the 12th century. Their roles included: collecting the annual farm; presiding over the shire court; visiting the **hundred court** and checking **tithings**; reading out writs and commands from the king; collecting evidence for criminal offences serious enough to be heard by the king's judges when they visited; maintaining royal castles; and keeping the peace. Thus, the sheriff was the most important point of contact between the Crown and the localities.

Since the time of William the Conqueror, sheriffdoms had increasingly become hereditary posts. During Stephen's reign, many barons had either taken the office for themselves or ensured that one of their men held it. The result of both these trends was that sheriffs could no longer be relied upon to put the interests of the Crown first.

As early as September 1155, Henry II replaced 21 of England's sheriffs and then about half again in 1162. A major set of legal reforms in 1166, the Assize of Clarendon (see Chapter 2), considerably increased the sheriff's powers; they also had more rights at the expense of the barons. For example, sheriffs could not be prevented from entering anyone's land in pursuit of a felon. This made creating 'mini-kingdoms' all but impossible; barons could no longer protect their men by denying sheriffs access to either them or their lands. The king's men, on the king's business, could go where they pleased as and when necessary. By 1170, concerns were increasing about the sheriffs' abuse of power. As a result Henry launched another major government investigation, the Inquest of Sheriffs.

The Inquest of Sheriffs was national and wide ranging, demanding written reports of every payment made to the sheriff of each county in the previous four years. Such was its scope and detail that it went beyond the sheriffs and also wanted to know of any fines or financial demands made by almost everyone who had any official capacity. Everything was recorded – amounts, dates and reasons. After the inquest was finished, of 29 sheriffs in England 22 were dismissed. Their replacements were usually royal officials from the Exchequer.

SOURCE

From the Inquest of Sheriffs 1170. This comes from a translation of the Latin charter that set out the scope of the Inquest. It was made in response to complaints against sheriffs of their conduct since the increase in their powers under legal reforms made by Henry II in 1166, known as the Assize of Clarendon.

11. And let inquiry be made concerning fines and amercements, whether anyone has been released for reward or love from what he had been first amerced, and by whom this has been done.

13. Let inquiry be made as to those who owe homage to the lord king and have not paid it, either to him or to his son, and let their names be recorded.

15. And after they have been examined, let my sheriffs and officers be employed about the rest of my affairs and let them swear on oath to apply themselves lawfully to the inquisition to be made throughout the lands of the barons.

KEY TERMS

Hundred court
A hundred was a subdivision of England for administrative purposes. It came below counties, but above manors. It had two important officers: bailiffs, who served writs on behalf of the sheriff, and the constable, who was responsible for policing. It met every four weeks.

Tithings
Groups of free males over the age of 12, whose responsibility it was to enforce the law, raise the alarm, arrest suspects and report on any crimes the others might commit.

Like Cartae Baronum, the Inquest of Sheriffs was both a method and an example of strengthening royal power. From 1170, sheriffs were to be royal appointments and accountable to the Crown. Henry had clearly demonstrated that they were not beyond his reach and could easily be dismissed. In his biography of Henry II from 2000, W.L. Warren describes 1170 as 'a turning point in the history of the office of sheriff'. From this time sheriffs were more likely to be professional royal officials, trained in the Crown's service.

ACTIVITY
KNOWLEDGE CHECK

Henry II had a range of strategies for strengthening the Crown and bringing the nobility back under control.

1 Gather evidence showing the use of the following methods of restoring the Crown's power:

a) political

b) military

c) financial.

ACTIVITY
WRITING

Speed writing: How did Henry II restore Crown authority to England by 1170?

You have 20 minutes to answer the question: 5 to plan and 15 to write. This will require some important decisions about what is the best evidence to use and which developments are most important. Try to show how factors combined when possible. Does your conclusion fit what you are planning to include?

> **AS Level Exam-Style Question Section B**
>
> To what extent was Henry II's military prowess the most important reason enabling him to restore royal power by 1172? (20 marks)
>
> **Tip**
> *This is a multi-factor question, but you must deal with the stated factor (Henry II's military prowess) first. You should spend between one-third and one-half of your essay on the stated factor. The other factors are up to you, but two or three more should be enough. Remember, you get more marks for analysis and evaluation so including too many other factors will limit your ability to do this.*

WHY DID THE LEADERS OF WALES, SCOTLAND AND IRELAND SUBMIT TO HENRY II'S AUTHORITY BY 1172?

Anglo-Welsh relations

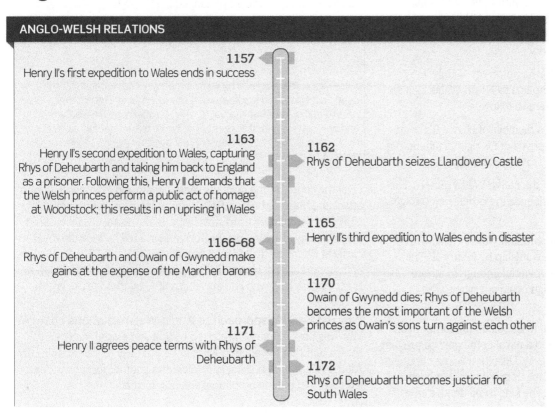

ANGLO-WELSH RELATIONS

1157 — Henry II's first expedition to Wales ends in success

1162 — Rhys of Deheubarth seizes Llandovery Castle

1163 — Henry II's second expedition to Wales, capturing Rhys of Deheubarth and taking him back to England as a prisoner. Following this, Henry II demands that the Welsh princes perform a public act of homage at Woodstock; this results in an uprising in Wales

1165 — Henry II's third expedition to Wales ends in disaster

1166–68 — Rhys of Deheubarth and Owain of Gwynedd make gains at the expense of the Marcher barons

1170 — Owain of Gwynedd dies; Rhys of Deheubarth becomes the most important of the Welsh princes as Owain's sons turn against each other

1171 — Henry II agrees peace terms with Rhys of Deheubarth

1172 — Rhys of Deheubarth becomes justiciar for South Wales

What was Wales like in 1154?

Wales was unstable and therefore a potential threat to England's western borders. Sometimes dominant English kings had sufficient power to establish some control, but it was difficult. The southern and eastern parts of Wales were occupied by the Marcher lordships of William the Conqueror, who had established earldoms such as Pembroke, Glamorgan and Brecon along the Anglo-Welsh borders. Originally intended to defend England's borders, they had greater autonomy than usual and were given to the king's most trusted followers. The northern and central parts of Wales tended to be under the control of Welsh princes and were riven with **internecine** warfare.

> ### KEY TERM
>
> **Internecine**
> An adjective describing people killing each other from, for example, the same family, tribe or people.

By the middle decades of the 12th century, two strong native Welsh leaders had emerged: Owain Gwynedd of Gwynedd and Lord Rhys ap Gruffydd of Deheubarth. They had contained or destroyed rivals among the other native Welsh princes and had made considerable territorial gains at the expense of Anglo-Norman barons.

Henry II embarked upon three expeditions to Wales: in 1157, he went to bring Owain Gwynedd to submission; in 1163, he set out against Lord Rhys ap Gruffydd; and in 1165, Henry attacked North Wales. Yet, by 1171, Henry and the Welsh princes had made a peace that lasted into the 13th century.

Henry II's first and second Welsh expeditions, 1157 and 1163

Henry I had established a measure of control over Wales but this royal authority had not survived Stephen's reign. By 1154, when Henry II came to the throne, only the ruler of Powys was prepared formally to acknowledge his authority.

Henry II met with his barons at Northampton on 17 July 1157 and secured their support for a campaign to North Wales against Owain of Gwynedd. His reasons were as follows.

- Owain's brother, Cadwaladr, was a member of Henry II's court and claimed that he had been deprived of his rightful inheritance. As his overlord, Henry had a duty to defend his rights.

- Owain was the most powerful of the native Welsh princes. His submission would be likely to influence the others, encouraging them to submit as well.

- The earldom of Chester, which bordered North Wales where Owain was stronger, was held in wardship by Henry II. The previous earl, Ranulf, had been powerful enough to ignore Stephen, so a successful campaign could strengthen the Crown's authority there.

Henry mustered a strong force of at least 30,000 (in comparison with a force of 3,000 Welshmen) and a naval contingent to prevent Owain fleeing to the island of Anglesey. Despite this, the campaign nearly ended in disaster. Henry led his troops into an ambush and the royal standard-bearer, believing the king to be dead, threw away his banner and fled, causing the rest of the army to panic. Only when Henry fought his way out was discipline restored.

Marching to Rhuddlan, Henry succeeded in bringing Owain to terms without a battle. Owain did homage in return for recognition of his lordship of Gwynedd; Cadwaladr's rights were restored; and the English king had successfully asserted his authority over North Wales. Rhys of Deheubarth followed suit in 1158, although he was not happy and, in 1162, seized Llandovery Castle while Henry was in France. Upon his return in 1163, Henry marched into Wales and captured Rhys, bringing him back to England as a prisoner.

To reinforce his authority over Wales, Henry summoned all the Welsh princes to his court at Woodstock on 1 July 1163, along with the king of Scotland, and he required them to perform public acts of homage as his vassals. Hostages were also taken from Rhys. The following year, Rhys began a massive uprising against the English. It broke out in Gwynedd, Deheubarth and Powys against the Anglo-Norman occupation of their lands. Henry's response was another campaign.

Henry's third Welsh expedition, 1165

After summoning a council at Northampton in October 1164 to request large numbers of infantry from his barons, hiring mercenaries from the continent and a mercenary fleet from Dublin, Henry set out on his third expedition to Wales. However, Owain of Gwynedd and the princes of Powys united their forces with Rhys's army to meet the threat.

Although it was the summer, the rain was torrential and the winds bitter, supplies ran low and Henry's army was bogged down. The Welsh, with their greater knowledge and experience of the area, harried and attacked the English forces, eventually forcing Henry's retreat. Furious, Henry ordered Welsh male **hostages** to be blinded and castrated while the women had their noses and ears cut off. In all, 22 Welsh hostages were mutilated and, according to Gerald of Wales, some were hanged.

> ### EXTEND YOUR KNOWLEDGE
>
> **Hostages**
> The use of hostages was common practice in the Middle Ages and its 'rules' were understood. The historian Robert Bartlett describes it as 'a cruel sanction and a key feature of power politics'. The hostages were held to make sure that the terms of the agreement were adhered to, and were often high-status individuals. For this to work as a strategy, however, hostages faced the very real possibility of mutilation or death if terms were broken.

Over the course of the next few years, Owain and Rhys continued to attack the Marcher barons. Rhys captured territory surrendered in 1157 and demolished Cardigan Castle. In the north, Owain crossed the River Clwyd, taking Basingwerk, and in 1167 he took the royal castle at Rhuddlan. In 1168, he sent envoys to Louis VII, offering help and support against Henry II. This was a clear signal of his defiance to the English king who had seen himself as overlord of the Welsh.

Why did Henry's approach to Anglo-Welsh relations change?

War was never Henry's preferred option and experience had shown him that Owain and Rhys were not easy to defeat militarily. After 1165, more pressing problems and another fortuitous death led Henry to pursue a political solution instead.

While Rhys and Owain were making gains in Wales after Henry's retreat, Henry faced rebellion and conflicts in France between

1166 and 1169. Finally, by 1171, Henry was planning an expedition to Ireland to deal with some overambitious vassals. Peaceful relations with Wales would be vital for good access to, Ireland, and put an end to further distractions there while subduing the Irish. An opportunity for a change in Anglo-Welsh relations came with the death of Owain in 1170, following which the nobles of Gwynedd and Powys turned on each other rather than remaining united against Henry.

Rhys of Deheubarth's perspective changed, too, after Owain's death and he did not wish to lose the gains he had made since 1165. In 1171, when Henry was in Pembroke preparing to set sail for Waterford, Rhys met with him and freely offered his submission. Henry accepted and agreed to recognise Rhys's rights to his lands, then released his son, whom he was holding hostage.

Henry was politically astute. His bigger concern at the time was access to Ireland, where he intended to intervene in a conflict between the Irish and some of his own vassals. The best route was through Wales. Henry's previous expeditions had already shown him how easy it would be for his forces to be ambushed by much smaller Welsh forces. In 1172, Rhys became justiciar of southern Wales, securing his own position still further, as any attack upon him would be an attack upon a royal official.

SOURCE

 6

From *Brut y Tywysogion* (*The Chronicles of the Princes*). The *Chronicles* are made from a collection of contemporary annals from abbeys across Wales. They describe events after Henry II's first expedition to Wales in 1157.

After peace had been made by all the Welsh princes with the king, Rhys, son of Gruffydd, alone prepared to wage war with him. And he confederated all South Wales and all his friends. And when the king heard of this he sent messengers to Rhys, to inform him that it would be well for him to repair to the court of the king before he brought England and Wales and France about his head; and that there was none excepting himself in opposition to the king. After having taken counsel with his good men, he went to the king's court, and there he was compelled, against his will, to make peace with the king, under the stipulation of receiving the Cantred Mawr and such other cantred [an administrative division of 100 villages] as the king be pleased to give him. And though Rhys understood that deceit, he accepted those portions and held them peaceably.

SOURCE

 7

Details of Henry's 1165 Welsh campaign from the *Annals of Roger de Howden*, a history that covers 732–1201. Nothing is known of Roger before 1174. He served Henry II in the 1170s and is also thought to have been a member of the clergy. He used official documents as well as other sources in his writing.

Henry, king of England, returned from Normandy to England, and marched with a great army into Wales, where he lost many of his nobles, barons and men. He also did justice upon the sons of Rhys, and upon the sons and daughters of his nobles, for he had the eyes of the male children put out, and cut off the noses and ears of the females.

AS Level Exam-Style Question Section A

Why is Source 6 valuable to the historian for an enquiry into Henry II's relationship with the Welsh princes Owain and Rhys?

Explain your answer using the source, the information about it and your own knowledge of the historical context. (8 marks)

Tip
Source 6 sees events from a Welsh point of view. This does not necessarily make it less valuable. In what ways could the provenance increase its value to the historian?

A Level Exam-Style Question Section A

How far can the historian make use of Sources 6 and 7 to investigate why Henry II had problems in establishing himself as overlord of Wales?

Explain your answer using the sources, the information about them and your own knowledge of the historical context. (20 marks)

Tip
Source 7 is very short. You will need to use historical context to develop its content effectively.

England, Scotland and the submission of Malcolm IV

ANGLO-SCOTTISH RELATIONS

1149
King David I of Scotland knights Henry of Anjou in Carlisle

Henry promises to honour the concessions granted to Scotland in 1139 regarding Northumberland and the north-western regions of Cumberland and Westmoreland as well as a claim to Huntingdonshire

1153
King David dies and is replaced by 12-year-old Malcolm IV

1154
Henry of Anjou becomes King Henry II of England

1157
Malcolm IV surrenders the lands promised to Scotland by Henry II in 1149

1163
Malcolm IV joins the Welsh princes in giving Henry II homage publicly at Woodstock; he has to provide hostages, including his youngest brother, David

1165
Malcolm IV dies and is succeeded by his brother, William, known as 'The Lion'; relations with Henry II deteriorate quickly

1168
William proposes an alliance with Louis VII of France

1170
William and David attend the coronation of Henry II's eldest son, Henry, as King of England

How did Anglo-Scottish relations develop?

Anglo-Scottish relations in the 12th century were complex. The border between the two countries was fluid, frequently in conflict. King David I, who had supported Henry II in his quest for the English throne, was succeeded in 1153 by his 12-year-old grandson, Malcolm IV. The Scottish nobles kept Malcolm busy with conflict and tensions requiring his attention, with an uprising in Argyll that same year. Despite his youth, Malcolm did strengthen his position in Scotland, but was not able to act against Henry II when he went back on his oath to King David.

In 1157, Henry II secured from Malcolm the surrender of the lands south of the Solway and Tweed, including Northumberland. Having invited Malcolm to England, Henry made it clear to him that he could no longer tolerate Scotland's possession of England's territories. According to William of Newburgh, the Scottish king recognised that he had no alternative but to agree with Henry's demands. He recognised that Henry had far more resources than he did and was too powerful. In return for acquiescing to Henry's demands, Malcolm was made earl of Huntingdon. Having duly paid homage, acknowledging his status as Henry's vassal, Malcolm then accompanied him on campaign to Toulouse in 1159.

In 1163, when the Welsh princes came to England to perform public homage to Henry at Woodstock, Malcolm was also summoned. He had to provide hostages, including his youngest brother, David. Other than reinforcing Henry's status as the superior king, there were some political concerns behind this. Malcolm had been making alliances with foreign nobles, with Brittany in 1160 and with Holland in 1162. It is also possible that, given Malcolm's poor health and childlessness, Henry wanted clearly to establish his relationship with Scotland before Malcolm's brother, William, a very different proposition, succeeded him.

William 'the Lion' succeeded to the Scottish throne in 1165. Within a year, relations between the two kings had deteriorated and William's proposal of an alliance with Louis VII in 1168 did not help matters. However, reconciliation between Henry and Louis in 1169 was followed by an improvement in Anglo-Scottish relations. In 1170, when Henry II decided to crown his eldest son king of England, both William and his brother David attended the coronation and were invited to Windsor where Henry knighted David.

Henry II and the submission of the Irish kings and bishops

HENRY II AND IRELAND

1155
Pope Adrian IV issues a papal bull supporting Henry II should he invade Ireland

A council at Winchester discusses the possibility but nothing comes of it

1161
The position of the kings of Munster and Leinster, who have joined forces to reform Ireland, is weakening in the face of conflict from other Irish kings, especially Rory O'Connor of Connacht

Muirchertach Mac Lochlainn's power in Munster collapses

1166
Dermot MacMurrough, king of Leinster, is forced from Dublin by Rory O'Connor

1167
Dermot MacMurrough approaches Henry II for support against Rory O'Connor; Henry agrees

1168
Richard fitz Gilbert de Clare (Strongbow) is approached by the Irish king, Dermot MacMurrough of Leinster, to join his forces against another Irish king, Rory O'Connor

1170
Anglo-Norman forces led by Strongbow arrive in Ireland and defeat Rory O'Connor

Strongbow is given Dermot MacMurrough's daughter's hand in marriage

Thomas Becket is murdered in Canterbury Cathedral on 29 December

1171
Dermot MacMurrough dies and Strongbow claims the kingdom of Leinster

He is soon pushed back to the Irish coast by Rory O'Connor; Strongbow's appeals to Rory are ignored

Henry II prepares to journey to Ireland with an army and lands in October, having come to terms with Strongbow

Numerous Irish kings and bishops make their submission to Henry; exceptions are Rory O'Connor and the kings of Meath and Ulster

1172
Henry II leaves Ireland for Normandy to reconcile with the Church

What was Ireland like in the 12th century?

Ireland in the 12th century was made up of several small kingships, none of which had been able to assert its authority over the others. Unlike other places in Europe, neither the Church in Ireland nor the kings controlled the law. Instead there were 'brehons', guardians who had the responsibility to preserve and interpret the law, which had developed from ancient Celtic practices.

Although Christianity was the main religion, the pope's actual influence was weak. The Irish had kept many ancient customs, traditions and laws, including divorce. The Church did not approve and wished to bring Ireland more firmly under its authority. However, in Ireland the Church, like the kingdoms, was divided along old tribal lines. As early as 1155, the Church made clear its support for Henry II if he should decide to invade Ireland. The English pope, Adrian IV, issued a **bull** to that effect. The matter was discussed in a council meeting held at Winchester in 1155, but taken no further.

KEY TERM

Bull
Formal proclamation made by the pope.

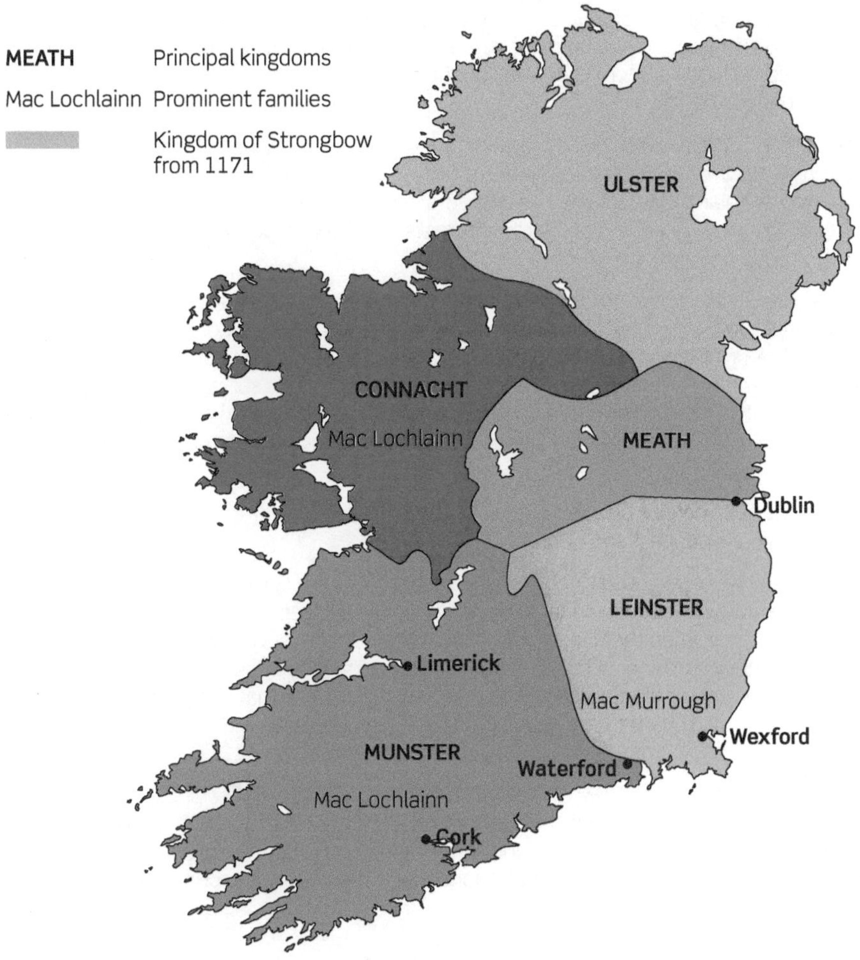
MEATH Principal kingdoms
Mac Lochlainn Prominent families
Kingdom of Strongbow from 1171
ULSTER
CONNACHT
Mac Lochlainn
MEATH
Dublin
LEINSTER
Limerick
Mac Murrough
Wexford
MUNSTER
Waterford
Mac Lochlainn
Cork

Figure 1.3 Map of Ireland showing its largest ancient kingdoms and key towns in the 12th century.

Attempts to unite and reform Ireland were under way by the middle of the 12th century, led jointly by the kings of Munster and of Leinster, Muirchertach Mac Lochlainn and Dermot MacMurrough. They were opposed by other Irish kings, the strongest of whom was Rory O'Connor, king of Connacht. By 1166, Muirchertach Mac Lochlainn was dead and Dermot MacMurrough had been driven out of Dublin by O'Connor. He went to seek help from Henry II early in 1167 and Henry allowed him to recruit soldiers from among his vassals. The most significant of these was Richard fitz Gilbert de Clare from the Welsh marchers, commonly known as 'Strongbow'. Richard was in debt and saw a chance to improve his fortunes: MacMurrough offered him his daughter's hand in marriage and the succession to his kingdom of Leinster in return for his help.

In August 1170, an Anglo-Norman force led by Strongbow landed in Ireland, recapturing Waterford and Dublin from Rory O'Connor. Although few in number, the Anglo-Normans had the advantage because of their unfamiliar military techniques. Their skirmishing archers, disciplined footmen and mounted knights soon routed the native Irish soldiers who lacked armour and some of whom were armed only with stones. It was a ferocious conflict resulting in the slaughter of hundreds of Irish.

MacMurrough drove his rivals out of Leinster but did not live long after his victory and died in May 1171. Strongbow claimed the kingdom as his successor. However, this decision angered both the Irish and the overlord for his other lands, Henry II.

EXTEND YOUR KNOWLEDGE

What were Henry II's motives for invading Ireland?

This question gives rise to some controversy. Was it early English imperialism? Did having permission from the pope – the only ever English pope – make a difference? Was Henry seeking absolution for the murder of Thomas Becket (see page 354) or was he seeking an inheritance for his youngest and favourite son, John?

Nicholas Breakspear, who became Adrian IV, was the only English pope there has been. During his short papacy, he issued a papal bull in 1155 authorising Henry II to conquer Ireland. However, this should not necessarily be interpreted as an expression of English desire to control the Irish. Adrian was committed to strengthening the Church elsewhere too, with varying degrees of success. In the event, Henry II did not respond to this bull and it was Dermot MacMurrough who sought Henry II's help in 1167. Nevertheless, Henry still had the force of the bull behind him.

Greater authority for the Church in Ireland had been a goal before Adrian IV. Archbishop Theobald also pushed the idea of invading Ireland in 1155, perhaps with the aim of securing the jurisdiction of the archbishops of Canterbury over Ireland. One of Henry II's first acts in Ireland was to organise a council of Irish bishops to promote the Church's moral and economic interests. This is perhaps not surprising given Becket's murder.

What about English imperialism? The concept of English or Irish nations was not developed at this time. In Ireland there were rival kings involved in their own power struggle and, when Rory O'Connor agreed to hold Connacht as a vassal of Henry II, it was also recognised that he would be high king of those areas not under English control. England too was in a state of flux, having not long since suffered civil war and having undergone a transformative invasion by a foreign power only 100 years before. When Henry II did go to Ireland, it was in response to problems caused by vassals he had sent to support Dermot MacMurrough, king of Leinster.

However, territorial gain as a motive cannot be ruled out, as by the time Henry went to Ireland he was also in need of territory to settle on his youngest son, John.

The other connection between the papacy and Henry II's invasion of Ireland concerns the murder of Thomas Becket, but the pope involved was Alexander III. Becket's murder in December 1170 caused outrage across Europe. The first indication that Henry was forgiven came in letters issued in 1172 concerning the need to bring Ireland into line with the rest of Christendom and in which Henry was described as a great and devoted son of the Church. It was in the spring of 1172 that the Church summoned Henry and issued a formal charter of reconciliation for the archbishop's murder.

Nevertheless, it was Henry II's invasion of Ireland that began a long, troubled and often violent history as successive English monarchs tried to complete what he had started: the conquest of Ireland. Mary Frances Cusak, writing in the 19th century, was in no doubt that Strongbow's arrival on Irish soil was 'a source of misery to Ireland'. Had Henry II not been called back to Normandy for reconciliation, David Carpenter (2003) says he had intended: 'a further campaign. The history of Ireland might have been very different if he had carried it out and completed the conquest.'

In Ireland there were no clear rules about inheritance and Strongbow's forces were challenged by Rory O'Connor of Connaught. Pushed back to the coast and besieged in Dublin, Strongbow tried to come to terms, offering submission to O'Connor in return for Leinster, but this was refused. For his part, Henry II saw Strongbow's actions as those of a disaffected vassal trying to establish a position of private power beyond his overlord's jurisdiction and control. He placed a trade embargo on Ireland and commanded the Anglo-Normans there to return or face harsh penalties. He confiscated Strongbow's lands in England and prepared for an expedition to Ireland in October 1171.

Faced with a determined enemy on one side and an angry king on the other, Strongbow sent messages to Henry that he would submit if he were allowed to keep what he had won, but as a vassal. When Henry arrived in Ireland he made his anger clear to Strongbow. It was, however, agreed that:

- Strongbow would take the lordship of Leinster

- Henry's men would garrison and control Dublin, Waterford and Wexford

- Hugh de Lacy would be given Meath as a fief from Henry and would be constable of Dublin.

Henry also intended to set up a royal administration in Dublin to oversee his vassals.

This was achieved so easily because, when Henry arrived in Waterford with his forces, numerous Irish kings and bishops offered Henry peaceful submission (although Rory O'Connor did not). For them, the stability that Henry could bring to Ireland was the overriding factor.

THINKING HISTORICALLY   Causation (6a)

Seeing things differently

Different times and different places have a different set of ideas. Beliefs about how the world works, how human societies should be governed or the best way to achieve economic prosperity can all be radically different from our own. It is important for the historian to take into account these different attitudes and be aware of the dangers of judging them against modern ideas.

Henry II, the Church and the conquest of Ireland

When Henry II invaded Ireland in 1171 he had many reasons. However, he also had the backing of the Roman Catholic Church. In 1155, Pope Adrian IV issued a papal bull that authorised Henry to conquer Ireland for the Church and allowing him to hold it as the pope's vassal. Although Henry II did not follow the bull to this extent, he did establish a council to reinforce the Church's authority and rights. The Church wanted to put a stop to ancient Irish social traditions, such as divorce. The bull said that this was to 'strive to imbue the people with good morals, and bring it to pass ... [that] the Christian religion planted and made to grow, and all things which pertain to the honour of God and to salvation'.

Answer the following questions:

1 What attitudes do you think had given rise to the idea that the Christian religion needed to be imposed where it was not being properly followed or where it did not exist?

2 What does 'imperialism' mean? What are cultural and economic imperialism?

3 Henry II has been accused of imperialism by intervening in Ireland. Do you think he would have changed his mind about intervening in Ireland if he had known the problems English intervention in Ireland would bring hundreds of years later?

4 Attitudes to religion and imperialism are very different in 21st century Britain from almost any other century before but especially from medieval ideas.

   a) Are there any other ways in which medieval attitudes differed from those current in the UK today?

   b) Why do you think they are different?

5 How important is it for historians to deal with events in the context of the beliefs and values of people in the past as well as seeing them as part of a greater pattern?

A council attended by the majority of Irish bishops soon after Henry's arrival agreed upon 'proper' marriages as defined by the Roman Catholic Church and that all **tithes** must be paid. Despite Henry II's role in the murder of the archbishop of Canterbury, Thomas Becket, in 1170, the Irish bishops had no qualms over their dealing with him. Alexander III was a political pope who recognised two important facts. First, there was a **papal schism** and the support of a powerful king such as Henry II was extremely useful for Alexander. He did not want England's king transferring his allegiance to the **antipope**, Victor IV. Secondly, under Henry's overlordship the Roman Catholic Church could become a real power in the land, just as elsewhere in western Christendom. He made his feelings very clear in describing Henry as 'our dearest son in Christ'. Furthermore, the previous (English) pope, Adrian IV, had issued Henry II with a bull instructing him to take Ireland as the Church's vassal. It was clear that Rome had had designs on Ireland for some time already.

KEY TERMS

Tithe
A tax owed to the Church equivalent to one-tenth of crops grown or income earned.

Papal schism
A split in the Roman Catholic Church occurring when more than one pope is elected.

Antipope
When two popes are elected, one is called the antipope.

SOURCE

The events of 1171 in Ireland as described in *Brut y Tywysogion*, a contemporary chronicle written and compiled by monks in Wales.

In that year, Richard, son of Gilbert Strongbow, having with him a powerful body of cavalry, sailed for Ireland. And in the first attack he took Port Lachi; and after having formed a friendship with King Dermot, and demanded his daughter in marriage, with his aid he got the possession of the city of Dublin, through immense slaughter.

And after pope Alexander had heard that the archbishop [of Canterbury] had been put to death, he sent letters to the king of France and others, commanding them on pain of excommunication, to compel the king of England to appear at the court of Rome to make restitution for the death of the archbishop. And when Henry perceived of this, he began to deny that it was through his counsel that the archbishop had been killed; and despatched messengers to the pope, declaring that he could not go to Rome because of those matters.

In the meanwhile, a great part of the year had run out. In that interval, the king became alarmed at the papal excommunication,* and left the French territories and returned to England, making it known that he would go and subdue Ireland.

*The source is unclear here. Although Alexander III banned Henry from hearing mass until he had paid penance, he never actually excommunicated him.

SOURCE

A description of the events in Ireland in 1172 from the *Annals of Roger de Howden*, a late 12th century chronicler from the North of England. Roger acted as an emissary for Henry II in Ireland in 1174.

Both archbishops as well as bishops [of Ireland] acknowledged Henry, king of England, and his heirs, as their kings and lords for ever, which they also confirmed by charter. After this the King of England sent the archbishops and bishops of Ireland to the city of Cashel, to hold a synod upon the ordinances of the Church.

At this synod it was ordained that children should be brought to the church, and there baptized in clean water... It was also ordained that tithes should be paid to churches out of all possessions: and that all laymen who could think it proper to have wives, should have them in conformity of the laws of the Church. The king of England also sent a copy of the charters to pope Alexander; who confirmed to him and his heirs the kingdom of Ireland.

A Level Exam-Style Question Section A

How far could the historian use Sources 8 and 9 together to investigate the reasons why Henry II went to Ireland in 1171?

Explain your answer using the sources, the information about them and your own knowledge of the historical context. (20 marks)

Tip

There is a lack of clarity in Source 8. Does this limit the usefulness of it as a source? Use what you know about the historical context of events to establish the validity of the rest of the evidence in Source 8.

ACTIVITY
KNOWLEDGE CHECK

1 Chart the development of Henry II's relationship with Wales on a fortune graph. Along the horizontal axis mark the years from 1154 to 1172; on the vertical axis mark a 'Success Index' from 0 to 10. A score of 10 would represent a stable, strong relationship with Henry recognised as overlord. A score of 0 would represent a full-scale war against united Welsh princes that threatens England's security.

2 Using the graph identify two key turning points in the relationship and explain their significance.

3 Compare Henry II's experiences with the Welsh and the Scottish. Why was it easier for him to deal with the Scottish as opposed to the Welsh? Write a one-sentence hypothesis and exchange it for the hypothesis of the person sitting next to you. To what extent do you agree with their hypothesis? Write two to three sentences that explain how far you agree and why.

4 Venn diagram. What caused Henry II's involvement in Ireland: politics, religion or empire building? List as many reasons as you can why Henry II became involved in Ireland and divide them into politics, religion and empire building. Some reasons will be hard to place into one category. You should put them into the appropriate overlapping areas of the Venn diagram.

WHY WAS HENRY II ABLE TO SECURE AND EXTEND HIS FRENCH TERRITORIES BY 1172?

Although in England Henry was king and overlord, in France he was a tenant-in-chief, albeit a very powerful one. On occasion Henry II appealed to Louis VII before taking action; if he approached a situation with the overlord's backing, there was no higher authority to whom his vassals could appeal. At other times, Louis VII exploited Henry's vassals' discontent with their lord, encouraging rebellion.

THE DEVELOPMENT OF THE ANGEVIN EMPIRE

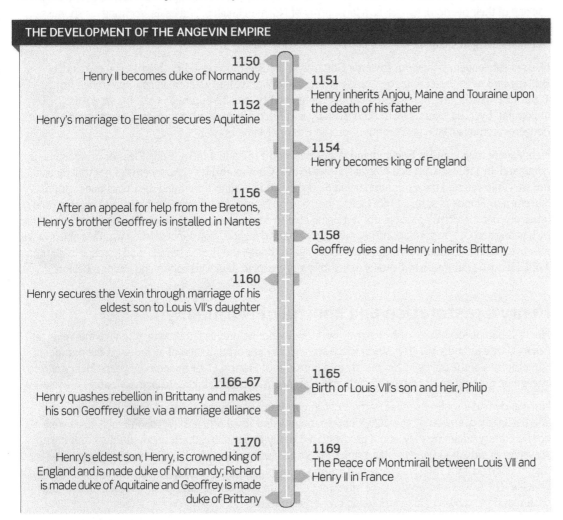

1150
Henry II becomes duke of Normandy

1151
Henry inherits Anjou, Maine and Touraine upon the death of his father

1152
Henry's marriage to Eleanor secures Aquitaine

1154
Henry becomes king of England

1156
After an appeal for help from the Bretons, Henry's brother Geoffrey is installed in Nantes

1158
Geoffrey dies and Henry inherits Brittany

1160
Henry secures the Vexin through marriage of his eldest son to Louis VII's daughter

1165
Birth of Louis VII's son and heir, Philip

1166–67
Henry quashes rebellion in Brittany and makes his son Geoffrey duke via a marriage alliance

1170
Henry's eldest son, Henry, is crowned king of England and is made duke of Normandy; Richard is made duke of Aquitaine and Geoffrey is made duke of Brittany

1169
The Peace of Montmirail between Louis VII and Henry II in France

Acquisition and control of Brittany

Brittany came into dispute in 1156 owing to rivalry between leading nobles: Hoël count of Nantes in the south and his sister Bertha and her husband, Eudo of Rennes, in the north. Hoël had seized control of Nantes, but its citizens disliked him and appealed to Henry II. Normandy and Brittany were traditional rivals and so the Bretons turning to the duke of Normandy for help seems strange. The main reason is probably that Bertha had a son, Conan, by her first marriage to Alan of Richmond, in England. Conan therefore had a claim to Brittany but, as earl of Richmond and one of Henry's vassals, he would have needed Henry's permission to attempt to make good his claim.

Although there is no surviving record that this is what Conan did, it seems likely as he had Henry's full support when he travelled to Rennes and defeated his stepfather, Eudo. Meanwhile, Henry expelled Hoël from Nantes and installed his brother, Geoffrey, as count. When Geoffrey died in 1158, Henry claimed his lands. However, Conan took control instead.

Henry could have gone straight to Brittany to confront Conan but instead went to King Louis VII. Although not keen to recognise Henry as duke of Brittany, Louis recognised the reality of both Henry's power and his claim as brother of the previous count. In Brittany, brothers were recognised as having strong claims to inherit each other's land. There were other, political factors to consider.

- Henry was hoping for a marriage alliance between his son Henry and Louis VII's baby daughter, Margaret. At this point Louis had no son and the betrothal made good political sense for him too.

- Louis' most trusted adviser Abbot Suger, suggested that, given the relative military weakness of the **Capetians**, the prudent policy was to work with powerful vassals. By invoking the feudal relationship, the king's status was recognised.

Louis VII made Henry his **seneschal**. When Henry summoned Conan to Avranches, he did so with the backing of their overlord, as well as a large army of Norman knights, and easily securing his submission. Henry had successfully dealt with one of his vassals by showing that the feudal system was to be respected. Despite being Louis's seneschal, he was now clearly in control of Conan and Brittany.

Henry's subsequent behaviour towards Conan and the Bretons caused problems. The dukes of Brittany had never been able to exercise strong control and Henry's increasing interference from 1162, such as ensuring that Church appointments and Breton inheritances went his way, was unpopular. By 1165, barons from both Brittany and Maine formed a league against him, led by Ralph Fougères from his castle at Combourg on the Breton/Maine border.

Henry spent much time in England and Wales between 1163 and 1166, leaving Eleanor of Aquitaine in command. In 1165, she ordered Norman forces to take Combourg. Her orders were neither well received nor well followed and the expedition failed. Fougères and his allies continued their resistance. Upon his return to France in spring 1166, Henry marched on Maine, destroying Combourg and crushing the rebellious barons. Blaming Conan for not being able to control his lands, he deposed him in favour of his own young son Geoffrey, whom he betrothed to Conan's daughter, Constance. Henry was thus able to take effective control of Brittany as both were under age. Although the Breton barons paid homage in autumn 1166, Henry had to return to Brittany in the following years to deal with continuing minor rebellions.

Henry's restoration and control of Normandy

Henry II had become duke of Normandy by 1150 but not before his father agreed to give the Vexin and Gisors Castle to Louis VII. The Vexin was a strategically important piece of territory on the borders of the territories of the dukes of Normandy and the kings of France. Over the coming years, Henry was to strengthen his hold on the duchy through political means, including taking back the Vexin.

Normandy had a system similar to the English earldoms and shires. It was divided into vicomtés and bailliages, overseen by the duke's chosen barons and royal officials. Royal officials' posts were not hereditary, meaning they could be dismissed easily and making them accountable to the duke. A system of writs had been in place since 1135 and Henry established an Exchequer, similar to that in England, by 1166. This gave him an organised bureaucracy enabling the enforcement of key policies. There was also a system of itinerant judges, under Henry's control, to oversee justice and ensure that the duke's rights were being properly exploited.

To strengthen his hold on Normandy further, Henry launched investigations into land tenures and taxes. Castles and lands lost under Stephen's tenure as duke were taken back and feudal dues were assessed and exploited. Exchequer accounts for 1171 show that income had almost doubled. Inquests such as those determining Henry's lands and rights in Bayeux helped to increase ducal income, as did the enforcement of feudal dues, especially scutage and wardship. There was a full-scale Cartae Baronum in Normandy in 1172.

Henry's policies in Normandy mirror those he instigated in England, pursuing lands, castles and revenues belonging to the duke, which had been lost under Stephen. The ability to collect and record data made establishing and maintaining a firm grip on his lands easier.

Relations and conflict with Louis VII of France

Anjou, Maine and Touraine, 1156

In 1156, Henry II's brother, Geoffrey, rebelled against him and it was not the first time. The issue was Anjou, Maine and Touraine, which Henry had taken as his, but which Geoffrey claimed had been given to him on their father's deathbed in 1151. In 1152, Geoffrey joined with Louis VII in his quarrel with Henry over his inheritance. Together with King Stephen's son, Eustace, Geoffrey attacked Normandy but Henry defeated them. In 1156, however, Henry used the feudal system to his advantage.

He performed homage to Louis VII in February 1156 for Anjou, Maine and Touraine before defeating Geoffrey's rebellion after besieging his strongholds of Chinon, Mirebeau and Loudon. Geoffrey, unable to appeal to Louis as overlord of France due to Henry's act of homage, accepted the lordship of Loudon and a pension of £1,500.

Henry was politically astute, knowing when to use the feudal system in France to achieve his aims. It could be argued that he was manipulating Louis VII, as both men knew who was the stronger and wealthier, as well as who was militarily more successful, and so Louis VII was bound to go along with what Henry wanted. On paper, Henry could have done as he liked in France without fearing Louis VII as his overlord, yet he frequently preferred to conform to the dictates of the feudal system. If nothing else, his actions made it clear to his own vassals that Henry II expected the proper form to be followed. At least when it suited his purpose. It is a matter of debate whether Henry II actually paid homage to Louis VII once he became king of England. However, he was also aware of how concerned Louis VII was about Angevin dominance. There is no evidence that Henry II saw his lands as an 'empire' and the term 'Angevin Empire' would not have been one that he would have recognised.

The Vexin, 1158–60

The acquisition of the Vexin by Henry II demonstrates an aptitude for wily politics and diplomacy, starting in 1158 with the betrothal of his son, Henry, to Margaret, the daughter of Louis VII by Constance of Castile. The agreement was made when Henry was three and his fiancée a baby. The Vexin was part of Margaret's **dowry** and, if she and Henry were properly married within three years, Louis would hand it over completely. Louis saw the betrothal as part of a long-term strategy. As yet he had no male heir and, were that to remain the case, his descendants might still occupy the French throne through his daughter.

KEY TERM

Dowry
A sum of money, or piece of land, that forms part of a marriage agreement.

Henry II, however, wanted the Vexin and was not prepared to wait for the children to come of age before they married. He ensured it happened as fast as possible, using the papal schism that occurred after Adrian IV's death. Henry asked for dispensation to allow the marriage to take place from one pope, Alexander III, by promising to support him rather than the antipope, Victor IV. Henry II was a powerful king, much more so than Louis VII, and Alexander III agreed.

Normandy and the Île de France: border disputes, 1167–68

Although boundaries between Henry's and Louis's French lands were more or less settled by the mid-1160s, there was renewed conflict towards the end of the decade.

When, in 1167, Henry was laying waste to the lands of a usurping baron in the Auvergne, Louis took advantage of his absence and raided the Vexin. Henry stormed back to Normandy, taking Louis's arsenal at Chaumonte by surprise and sending mercenaries swimming upriver to break in secretly while he launched a diversionary attack at its walls. Chaumonte was set alight. Louis was furious and retaliated by sacking the Norman towns in the Vexin. This set in train a series of raids and skirmishes along the border of Normandy.

Henry did not want a serious war with France. Although a good soldier, he preferred to avoid war whenever possible. More importantly, the Scots and Welsh had sent envoys to Louis promising their help against Henry II and offering hostages as a sign of their serious intent. Henry's French vassals pleaded with Louis to support them after particularly ferocious attacks, first on rebels in Aquitaine and then Brittany (not all of whom had been quashed in 1166), and went as far as offering their homage to him directly.

Henry did not wish to negotiate with Louis under these circumstances and so began a series of devastating attacks on the lands of Louis's vassals along the borders of Normandy in 1168. He set fire to more than 40 villages and destroyed the castle at Neufchâteau before ravaging the lands of the count of Perche. The aim was to demonstrate that Louis could not protect his own vassals and to impress upon the French king the necessity of coming to terms with him. By the end of 1168, Louis made approaches to his rival for a lasting peace. The talks were held in January 1169 at Montmirail.

The significance of the peace of Montmirail

The agreement reached with Louis at Montmirail allayed his fears about an overpowerful Angevin 'empire'. Henry also wanted to solve the problem of providing inheritances for his three eldest sons. These two ends were achieved by Henry II agreeing to divide his dominions.

- The eldest son, also called Henry, was to inherit England, Normandy and Anjou. He was crowned in 1170 and became known as 'The Young King'.

- The second son, Richard, was to inherit Aquitaine as the vassal of the French king.

- The third son, Geoffrey, was to have Brittany as a vassal of the 'Young King' in his capacity as duke of Normandy. The 'Young King' was then to do homage to Louis for Brittany. Until Geoffrey assumed full control himself, Henry II also recognised Louis as his overlord for the duchy.

Additional terms included a proposal that Richard should marry Louis's daughter, Alice. Louis was happy to accept the treaty. With two of his sisters being married to the counts of Blois and Champagne, Louis's heir, Philip, would have close relations running much of France which, after Montmirail, should ensure he was more powerful than Henry's sons or any other vassal.

After Montmirail, Louis VII tried to reconcile Henry II with his rebels in Brittany, Maine and Aquitaine remaining from the earlier unrest. Henry, however, forged ahead on his own, demolishing the remaining castles belonging to the rebels in Brittany. The rebels' fortifications in Aquitaine were also destroyed. He came to terms with the rebellious counts of Angoulême and La Marche, ordered a great ditch to be dug on the borders of the Vexin and built a new castle at Beauvoir in Maine. He also purchased the heavily fortified castle of Montmirail. These actions sent clear messages to both the rebels and Louis that Henry could deal with his own vassals – severely – and did not require any intervention from the overlord of France.

The peace of Montmirail was an opportunity for Henry and Louis VII to end the series of conflicts that had afflicted their relationship. Henry renewed his allegiance to Louis for his French lands and young Henry did homage to him for Brittany and Normandy, while Richard did so for Aquitaine. The threat of Philip having to face an overmighty Plantagenet vassal was allayed by dividing the 'Angevin Empire' between Henry's sons. Also, by betrothing Alice of France to Richard, the links between the Plantagenets and Capetians would be strengthened further. When he ascended the throne, Philip would head the most powerful family in France; his brothers-in-law would be dukes of Brittany, Normandy and Aquitaine. Montmirail was designed to be a lasting peace. It didn't work out that way.

EXTEND YOUR KNOWLEDGE

King Louis VII of France (1120–80)
As the second son of Louis VI (Louis the Fat), Louis VII had not grown up expecting to be king of France. He married Eleanor of Aquitaine and they had two daughters. The marriage was annulled in 1152 and Louis later married Constance of Castile, with whom he had two more daughters. After Constance's death in 1160, Louis married Adele of Champagne, with whom he had his son and heir, Philip, in 1165.

Louis's position as king of France was very weak by 1154 and was further damaged by Henry II, who took control of Brittany and the Vexin. Until the birth of Philip in 1165, Louis's main strategy as king of France was co-operation with his more powerful vassals.

Although Louis died in 1180, he had been very ill for at least a year before and Philip had been ruling France as King Philip II.

ACTIVITY
KNOWLEDGE CHECK

1 Compare Henry II's approach to his French lands with his approach to England. Draw up a chart that shows evidence and examples of Henry strengthening his control under the following headings: (a) Strengthening the feudal system; (b) Increasing revenues; (c) Military force.

2 Compare Henry's use of the feudal system in England and France to strengthen his territories.

3 Value continuum. Was it Henry II's strength or Louis VII's weakness that was more important in Henry having so much land in France under his control? Choose five key pieces of evidence to support your decision. They must reflect your answer.

ACTIVITY
SUMMARY

Henry II in England: action plan review

1 Look back to the action plan that you drew up for Henry II at the start of his reign. Review what you have learned about Henry's actions in England.

2 Which of the points in your plan are similar to what Henry actually did?

3 What methods did Henry II use that you did not have in your plan?

How did Henry II gain and maintain control of his empire by 1172?

4 According to the chronicler Gerald of Wales, Henry II dreaded war. Reviewing what you have covered so far, how accurate do you think Gerald's view of Henry II was?

WIDER READING

Ackroyd, P. *The History of England: Foundation*, Macmillan (2012)

Carpenter, D. *The Struggle For Mastery*, Penguin (2003)

Castor, H. *She-Wolves: The Women Who Ruled England Before Elizabeth*, Faber (2010)

Jones, D. *The Plantagenets: The Kings Who Made England*, Harper (2012)

Wilson, D. *The Plantagenets: The Kings That Made Britain*, Quercus (2014)

Fiction is sometimes worth reading for a flavour of the era, and the books suggested below are well researched

Penman, S. *Time and Chance*, Penguin (2002)

Penman, S. *When Christ and His Saints Slept*, Penguin (1995)

A Level Exam-Style Question Section B

'It was not military success but skilful politics that enabled Henry II to secure his lands in France by 1172.'

How far do you agree with this opinion? (20 marks)

Tip

This requires an analysis of the two key factors given in the essay title and a judgement as to their relative importance. Although this essay can be approached in two halves (military success, skilful politics) you might like to consider other ways of organising your answer. In an exam, if one reason is tackled first, and then the other, you could run out of time and there needs to be a balance between the two to achieve a good answer.

2b.2 Reforms in England, 1154–89

KEY QUESTIONS

- How did Henry II develop the central institutions of government?
- To what extent were Henry II's financial reforms successful?
- What was the impact of Henry II's legal reforms?
- How did the nature of kingship change under Henry II?

KEY TERMS

Centralisation
Describes a political set-up in which decisions are made and enforced through a central authority, often located in one central location. Power is usually concentrated in the hands of one person or a small group.

Debasement
The devaluing of a currency. When coins contained precious metals, debasement was usually achieved by reducing how much precious metal each contained.

Moneyer
Individual craftsman who minted the currency under contract from the Crown.

Plea
Something alleged in a court of law and/or pleaded by the plaintiff, the person initiating the lawsuit.

INTRODUCTION

As an itinerant king with a realm straddling the Channel, Henry II needed to develop a strong, well-organised government capable of running England in his absence, where it is estimated he spent only 37 percent of his reign. One key feature of Henry II's government was the growth in royal authority through increasing **centralisation**. A series of measures covering the law and finance contributed greatly towards this, as did restoring and regularising the offices and institutions of government.

The men Henry chose to serve him in key positions had experience in English government, which was something he lacked, and expertise in fields such as finance, justice and administration. He included men who had served Stephen. This was not a time to be partisan but practical and to take calculated risks: men who had served Stephen loyally because he was king could probably be expected to do the same for Henry.

The problems faced by Henry II on taking the English throne in 1154 extended beyond political power. King Stephen had lost control of the coinage, resulting in coins of uncertain minting and quality. Furthermore, **debasement** of the coinage was a continual problem, as pennies were clipped or made with insufficient silver. Henry II returned England to one centrally controlled currency, with a high silver content. Other measures included the reduction in the number of **moneyers**.

Perhaps the most long-lasting impact Henry II had stemmed from his legal reforms. A large part of the king's role was to hear **pleas** in his own court and ensure that his people received justice. After King Stephen's anarchic reign, the law and the legal framework needed overhauling. Furthermore, medieval England's legal system was based on a variety of courts with different and sometimes overlapping jurisdictions, giving landowners considerable power in their own localities. This included the Church, which also had its own courts and laws. Henry's legal reforms ensured that the law became increasingly standardised, systematic and structured. This contributed to strengthening the power of the king – including financially – and increasing contact between the Crown and the locality.

1154 – Henry II becomes king of England

1158 – Henry's chancellor, Thomas Becket, secures a marriage alliance with France

1162 – Thomas Becket becomes archbishop of Canterbury and resigns as chancellor, signalling the start of poor Crown–Church relations

1164 – The rift between Crown and Church deepens after Henry tries to redefine their relationship in the Constitutions of Clarendon

1166 – Henry launches Cartae Baronum, a national inquiry into tenants-in-chief

Regular visits by the king's justices to the regions are re-established

Assize of Clarendon is promulgated

| 1154 | 1155 | 1156 | 1157 | 1158 | 1159 | 1160 | 1161 | 1162 | 1163 | 1164 | 1165 | 1166 | 1167 | 1168 | 1169 | 1170 | 1171 |

1170 – Henry II launches the Inquest of Sheriffs, a massive inquiry into England's sheriffs, which results in the majority being replaced

The archbishop of Canterbury, Thomas Becket, is murdered by four of Henry II's knights, leading to Henry being internationally reviled

HOW DID HENRY II DEVELOP THE CENTRAL INSTITUTIONS OF GOVERNMENT?

The Curia Regis

The Curia Regis was the king's court. In the Middle Ages, much of its business was the law: making it, dealing with pleas and dispensing justice. However, it was also the main forum of government with important financial responsibilities, including determining the raising of revenues. When important decisions were to be made, all magnates would be summoned to the king's court for a great council, wherever he happened to be.

SOURCE

1 A contemporary depiction of the Curia Regis showing Henry II's son, King Richard I, with his barons.

1172 - Henry II establishes control over much of Ireland

1173–7 - Henry II faces the Great Rebellion as Louis VII, Eleanor of Aquitaine, his sons, the king of Scotland and several English barons all rebel against him

Henry defeats the rebellion and his position is stronger than ever as a result

1176 - The Assize of Northampton develops Henry II's legal reforms: punishments are made harsher and new possessory assizes are introduced

1178 - The popularity of Henry II's legal reforms results in the establishment of a permanent court at Westminster to deal with the backlog of cases from the regular visits of the king's justices to the shires

1180 - Philip II becomes king of France

1183 - Death of the Young King

Henry's refusal to name Richard as his new principal heir causes friction

1187 - Jerusalem falls to the Muslim warrior Saladin

The pope calls for a new crusade

1188–89 - Henry II begins raising the Saladin tithe, a new tax in England to provide funds for the crusade

Henry's son Richard joins with Philip II of France and they attack Henry's French heartland, including Anjou and Maine

1189 - Henry II dies in France, where he has been defeated by Richard and Philip II

| 1172 | 1173 | 1174 | 1175 | 1176 | 1177 | 1178 | 1179 | 1180 | 1181 | 1182 | 1183 | 1184 | 1185 | 1186 | 1187 | 1188 | 1189 |

The Curia Regis was also the embodiment of the king's power. It made a statement about his wealth and strength; it was an arena for literature, culture and other entertainments. It was also where political careers could be made and power struggles won or lost. Henry II's court was particularly large, wealthy and widely travelled. In the king's absence from England, justiciars oversaw the government.

Under Henry II the Curia Regis did not change significantly, although it certainly became more effective, especially in his absence. Analysis of those attending regularly during his reign shows that there were not many earls or magnates. The majority were the king's friends and men appointed by him to serve in various offices, such as his chancellor, constable or chamberlain. Nevertheless, Henry's choice of official was also increasingly focused on men with knowledge of particular aspects of government. This was part of a gradual trend of moving away from giving important posts to nobles simply because of their status. By the end of Henry II's reign, the *Dialogue of the Exchequer* clearly stated that the king could appoint anyone he wished into his service, regardless of how, or from whom, they held their land.

The justiciars and the chancellor

The justiciars
The role of the justiciar was essentially to act as regent in the king's absence and deal with matters for which he had not had the time when he was in the country. The post of justiciar was not part of the king's official household and he was superior to anyone who was, no matter how important they might be. When in France Henry remained in contact with England through messengers and royal writs – he had 25 ships on constant standby to ferry men and royal documents across the Channel.

Much of the role of the justiciar was focused on the law and he was the senior royal judge. He heard difficult legal cases and gave advice to other judges on points of law. During the reign of Henry II, he came to organise the growing body of the king's itinerant justices. Leading on from this role, he was expected to see that peace was maintained throughout the realm in the king's absence.

Other duties of the justiciar included responsibility for the administration of government throughout the realm, for which he had to travel the kingdom frequently. This made him an important point of contact between the crown and local barons, and he needed to develop good working relationships with them, requiring a certain measure of diplomatic skill. Given that he was also tasked with raising revenues as and when necessary, it was even more important that he maintain strong links with the king's tenants-in-chief.

For the first part of his reign, Henry appointed two justiciars, Richard de Lucy and Robert, earl of Leicester.

The chancellor
The chancellor ran chancery, the king's writing office where writs and charters were drawn up. Essentially the chancellor was the king's secretary, and therefore at the heart of government as well as the hub of England's administration. He would usually be a member of the clergy, as they were the most important pool of literate and educated men in the country and filled chancery as clerks. All petitions and pleas passed to the king also went through the chancellor and so judicial work took up a great deal of his time, more so after the legal reforms put in place by Henry II.

The position of chancellor was a very powerful one: for example, the chancellor could attend all meetings of the king's council without an invitation; he had control of the king's seal, which was required for all official documents. Overseeing the writing of official documents made him privy to a wide range of government business. From 1154 until 1162, England's chancellor was Thomas Becket, who had been an archdeacon serving in archbishop of Canterbury Theobald's household.

The roles of significant individuals

Richard de Lucy

Richard de Lucy's family was prominent in Essex, an area that had been King Stephen's stronghold and was a wealthy county close to London. To have it in loyal, capable hands was useful when Henry was establishing himself in England. Richard de Lucy had steadfastly supported Stephen until the king's death and he rewarded Henry's faith in him with the same loyalty. Although not from the nobility, after the death of Robert of Leicester in 1168 he was England's sole justiciar and could be described as the most powerful man in England after the king.

Described by John Guy as 'a self-made man' who 'lacked pedigree', Richard de Lucy was certainly expert at court politics, building alliances and becoming an invaluable asset to Henry's government. He worked extremely well with Robert of Leicester, as they divided their time and talents effectively.

Throughout Henry II's reign and until his death in 1179, Richard de Lucy, known as 'The Loyal', served the king in a wide variety of tasks. He frequently oversaw the Exchequer, where his experience as a successful sheriff of Essex proved useful, as he understood how to improve revenues from the royal demesne. He became one of Henry's regular justices from 1166 and later often attended the developing central court in Westminster.

It was Richard de Lucy who advised the monks of Canterbury that they should accept Henry's nomination for archbishop of Canterbury, Thomas Becket, in 1162. He was also instrumental in drawing up the Constitutions of Clarendon, a list of the customs of England as they had been in Henry I's day, written from the collective memories of the king's officials and counsellors. Ironically this fuelled the conflict between Henry II and Becket that resulted in the archbishop's death.

Richard de Lucy led the fight-back against rebellious English barons in 1173–74. Despite this, he was made to hand over his castle at Ongar in 1175. However, by the mid-1170s, Henry's trust in him was such that Richard de Lucy was authorising expenditure from the Treasury and issuing writs in his own name that had equal authority with the king's. The role of justiciar became an increasingly well-defined and formal office under Richard de Lucy, contributing to the stability in England by the end of Henry's reign and beyond.

Bishop Nigel

Bishop Nigel of Ely had introduced stringent procedures for managing the Exchequer in the reign of Henry I. Henry II appointed him to revive and reform the Exchequer, as it had become largely ineffectual under Stephen. Bishop Nigel instituted the twice-yearly sessions of the Exchequer court at which sheriffs were called to explain their financial dealings on the king's behalf, recording the accounts on parchments, which were rolled and stored in tubes. By enabling royal finances to be regularly monitored and checked, Bishop Nigel's innovation, known as **pipe rolls**, significantly improved the financial administration of the realm, centralising it and increasing the accountability of the sheriffs for Crown revenues. The Exchequer was also a court, dealing mainly with disputes over the collection of taxes and other revenues.

The pipe roll evidence indicates that, by the time of his death in 1169, Bishop Nigel had successfully revived the Exchequer's practices, re-establishing it as an efficient, organised government department. As an important member of Henry's government, Bishop Nigel contributed to key policies, especially those concerned with revenues such as the restoration of royal demesne, as well as acting as a justice and presiding over judicial hearings, not only in the Exchequer's court but in the king's courts too. As with Henry II's other key officials, Bishop Nigel had experience and ability in more than one field.

Thomas Becket

As chancellor, Becket served the king diligently, forging the chancellorship into a larger, more important part of the government machine. From having only 11 clerks under Stephen, when appointed Becket increased the number to 16 and soon had 52. One of the strengths of Henry II's reign was its ability to produce large numbers of writs, charters and official documents, resulting in improved records and record keeping. Although not one of the more exciting aspects of exercising power, it was important for effective government and key to Henry's legal reforms. Becket also had a permanent working space for the clerks built at the Palace of Westminster, creating for the first time a dedicated office for the clerks when they were in London.

> **KEY TERM**
>
> Pipe rolls
> Medieval accounts of royal finances kept by the Exchequer.

Becket also attended the Exchequer, where his role was to pick up and challenge any mistakes or anomalies. When funds were needed for an expedition to France in 1157, it was Becket who not only helped to revive scutage (see pages 315–316) but also imposed it as a flat 20 shillings from each of the tenants-in-chief. This was regardless of how many knights they owed payment for, thereby raising far more than was actually needed. As part of the Curia Regis, Becket sat with the tenants-in-chief hearing court cases brought for the king's justice, but he also travelled England as one of the king's itinerant judges.

Becket took on the aspects of kingship that Henry found onerous, especially those involving ceremony. He also represented the king abroad, leading a lavish embassy to France to negotiate the marriage of young Henry to the infant daughter of Louis VII in 1158 and successfully brokering a deal that resulted in their betrothal. This was an important piece of diplomacy that strengthened relations with the French king after previous attempts in 1157, led by Henry himself, had achieved very little.

In many respects, Becket was of a similar mould to Richard de Lucy: he did not have the benefit of noble birth, yet rose to high position in English politics; he was a man of many talents and wide experience who could readily be slotted into any one of a number of roles; he enjoyed a close relationship with, and the trust of, Henry II.

SOURCE

2

From Ralph of Diceto's chronicle *Ymagines Historiarum*, written between 1171 and 1202. Ralph of Diceto was a member of the clergy and became dean of St Paul's Cathedral. As he frequented Henry II's court, his histories and writings were based upon eyewitness testimony as well as documents. He studied law and admired Henry II's focus on law and order.

The king of England, seeking to benefit those least able to help themselves, found out that the sheriffs, while involved in public duties and fiscal business, were mindful of their own interests. Wherefore, becoming more and more anxious for the common weal, at certain times he entrusted the administration of justice in his realm to other loyal subjects. This he did in order that the coming of public officials throughout the shire might strike terror into the hearts of the wrongdoers, and that those who cheated him of taxes and thus affronted the king's majesty might incur the royal displeasure ... he wished to test the loyalty of his many servants. Diligently he sought out those who were lovers of justice in their various callings, and inquired among a countless host of men for one who was not corrupted by office. Thus steadfast in his purpose he again and again made changes in personnel ... For at one time the king made use of abbots, at another of the earls, at another of the tenants-in-chief, at other times of servants of his household and his most intimate counsellors to hear and judge cases.

AS Level Exam-Style Question Section A

How much weight do you give the evidence of Source 2 for an enquiry into how good Henry II's choice of government officials was?

Explain your answer using the source, the information given about it and your own knowledge of the historical context. (12 marks)

Tip
The source implies that King Henry II sometimes had to purge his government officials, especially at local level, of corruption. This does not necessarily mean that he was failing.

ACTIVITY
KNOWLEDGE CHECK

1 Henry II was an itinerant king. How did he ensure that he maintained strong control of England in his absence? Refer back to the content of the previous chapter.

2 What potential sources of discontent for the nobility can you find in Henry II's approach to governing England?

3 What can Source 2 tell us about Henry II's approach to government?

TO WHAT EXTENT WERE HENRY II'S FINANCIAL REFORMS SUCCESSFUL?

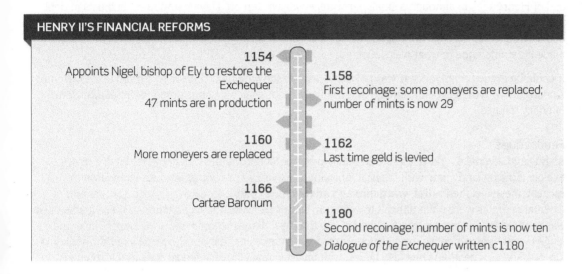

HENRY II'S FINANCIAL REFORMS

1154
Appoints Nigel, bishop of Ely to restore the Exchequer
47 mints are in production

1158
First recoinage; some moneyers are replaced; number of mints is now 29

1160
More moneyers are replaced

1162
Last time geld is levied

1166
Cartae Baronum

1180
Second recoinage; number of mints is now ten
Dialogue of the Exchequer written c1180

The revival of the Danegeld

Taxation was a key source of revenue for Henry II, but the disruption of the civil war and the consequently inaccurate records made the task of collecting taxes problematic, as they were often based upon the amount of land held. The Danegeld (also known as the geld) was an ancient tax levied at two shillings per **hide**. Under Henry I it had become an annual tax, although Stephen was not able to maintain it. Henry II revived the geld in 1156 but not only was it very unpopular, it was very inefficient too for several reasons.

- Confusion over land ownership and the devastation of the civil war led to 24 percent of expected income from the counties being written off as **waste**. The *Anglo-Saxon Chronicle* described vast tracts of England as being lain to waste, often because of people fleeing the land during the civil war.

- The geld was therefore susceptible to political conflict, especially disputes over land tenure.

- Where records did exist, they were often out of date.

- Numerous exemptions were granted, especially to favoured magnates and religious houses. In addition, towns did not pay because their landholding was based on a different measure (virgates – approximately 30 acres), not hides.

Henry II only levied the geld once more, in 1162. The failure of the revived Danegeld to have any significant impact upon royal revenues led to the development of tallage, a new form of tax, and the increased importance of researching, reviving and monitoring the collection of feudal dues.

Tallage

A new source of taxation was the tallage, used by Henry II after the geld lapsed. A tallage was basically a tax levied by a lord upon his tenants. The king levied it on royal demesne, including most towns and boroughs, which he had not done with the geld. Henry II raised tallage fairly regularly and, although it yielded slightly less than the geld had once done, it tapped the wealth of the towns and its yields were more predictable.

Scutage

Originally paid if a landholder could not meet the quota of knights required, or if a knight wished to be excused military service, scutage had become a tax. The *servitium debitum* (see page 295), established in the 11th century, was not very efficient at raising an army in appropriate numbers for Henry II's needs. There was also an increasing tendency to hire larger numbers of mercenaries, which was expensive.

KEY TERMS

Hide
A measurement of land, generally used in rural areas.

Waste
A term used in the accounts to describe land which was not generating income, for example due to failed crops, and/or which had become wasteland, for example due to depopulation.

Cartae Baronum (1166) gave Henry II a complete picture of how many knights his tenants-in-chief actually held, enabling him to extend scutage to every knight's fee from 1168. However, the 1168 and 1172 attempts to raise it fell into arrears. This was not uncommon and most of it was collected by the end of Henry's reign, although a small percentage was written off. Having important subjects in debt to the Crown was a standard method of controlling them. If the king's displeasure was incurred, debts could be called in. Overall, although in theory the barons' scutage obligations increased, in reality it made little difference to what was collected.

It could be argued that Henry II was politically astute, showing flexibility when certain taxes were not working, as with the geld and scutage. Alternatively, it could also be considered to provide evidence of policy failures.

Feudal dues

As England's feudal overlord, there were many other potential sources of income for Henry II to exploit. Holding land came with financial obligations as well as providing services. In addition to escheat, these included **relief**, **wardship** and **advowsons**. After Stephen's reign, land tenure and inheritance rights were often difficult to establish. Under Henry II, the exploitation of these feudal dues was restored by means of rigorous inquiries into the royal demesne and regular investigations of the king's feudal rights when his royal justices visited the counties to hear court cases. Henry's travelling justices (see next section) were also tasked with investigating all owing feudal dues in the counties.

Dona

Dona, or aids, were another form of financial demand stemming from the rights of the feudal lord. These were for specific occasions such as the knighting of the lord's son or the marriage of his daughter; they were also raised to fund crusades. Henry II used aids to help finance crusading activity in 1166 as well as for the Third Crusade at the end of his reign. However, aids were also demanded without any of these reasons. For example, Henry II raised an aid for his (failed) expedition to Toulouse in 1158–59, when he hoped he would make good a claim on the region he had inherited upon marrying Eleanor of Aquitaine. The Exchequer demanded a total of £2,725 from 33 cities and towns; £440 from 12 sheriffs; £3,133 from the Church; £2,341 from knights and other lords in 23 counties; and £362 from the Jews.

The restoration of royal lands

Incomes from the royal demesne

Royal demesne was land held directly by the king. The revenues he received from this land were known as the county farm. It was a permanently fixed amount and the sheriff was responsible for collecting it.

The farm

The farm was an important source of royal revenue, but had diminished under King Stephen, who had given away considerable grants of land to favourites. Much royal demesne had simply been taken, where there was no strong Crown presence or because of careless or corrupt sheriffs. This was called **purpresture**. There were also lands where the tenant-in-chief had died without an heir, especially after the civil war. Known as escheats, they should have reverted back to the king. Between 1154 and 1165, Henry instigated detailed inquiries to determine losses of demesne by purpresture and escheat, and return it to Crown control.

Pipe roll evidence shows that the farm of some counties, such as Bedfordshire and Hampshire, was not paid at all in the first year and much of what should have been collected later was written off as 'waste'. 'Waste' entries covered a multitude of reasons why sums were missing from the farm, including confusion over who held what land and records being out of date or incomplete. In this way the pipe rolls reflect the nature and scale of the task faced by Henry II in restoring royal demesne. However, in bringing barons back under Crown control, he was able to make up some of what was missing. It is generally acknowledged that Henry II halved the number of earldoms, taking the land back under royal control or in some cases reducing barons' landholdings. Land taken from Hugh Bigod in 1158, for example, saw the farms from Norfolk and Suffolk increase hugely as a result

KEY TERMS

Relief
A tax paid upon inheriting land.

Wardship
The right to look after the lands of an underage heir. All income from the land went to the Crown until the heir was old enough to inherit. As has been seen, Henry II did not always return all the land to the heir.

Advowson
The right to appoint a member of the clergy to a vacant office. The Church held its land from the king, who could collect the revenues from vacant bishoprics. For this reason, monarchs often delayed appointing new bishops.

KEY TERM

Purpresture
Land belonging to one landholder that has been encroached upon by another.

The county farm rose from an average of £5,000 per annum in the first four years of Henry II's reign to £6,000 by 1162–63. Although the amount was fixed, an extra payment known as the 'increment' was charged where it was quite clear that the farm was based on outdated information and far below what it should have been. By the end of Henry's reign, it was £6,500 per annum. Despite this success, however, its significance as a component of royal income declined from 53 percent in 1157–58 to only 38 percent by the end of the 1160s. This means that royal revenues were increasing elsewhere, as Henry II was finding other sources of income.

The forest

The forest was a specific type of royal landholding detested the realm over. Not necessarily wooded, these often vast tracts of land were taken by the king for hunting but could encompass villages and towns as well. Most of Essex was royal forest. These lands came under a separate and very harsh set of laws, which Henry II rigorously enforced: punishments for killing game such as deer or wild boar could result in a death sentence, for example. However, the main objective of the forest was to maximise revenue rather than simply to provide exclusive hunting grounds. Offences punishable by fines included:

- cutting down trees for their timber
- clearing land for planting arable crops (assart)
- encroaching on, or enclosing, forest land (purpresture).

The royal forest in Wiltshire, for example, generated £1,295 in 1175–76 from fines imposed. The king made money from the forest in other ways too. He sold rights to graze animals, cut trees or hunt certain animals (although hunting licences were usually reserved for the nobility). The forest helped to boost royal revenue, but it did nothing for Henry II's popularity with any of his subjects.

SOURCE

3 Henry II's son, King John, hunting in the royal forests, from a 14th-century manuscript in the collection of Sir Robert Bruce Cotton (1571–1631).

A Level Exam-Style Question Section A

How far could the historian make use of Sources 4 and 5 together to investigate the extent of Henry II's success in raising royal revenues in 1154–70?

Explain your answer, using both sources, the information given about them and your own knowledge of the historical context. (20 marks)

Tip

Apply what you know carefully and think broadly. Why are the amounts expected and owing for Danegeld and scutage the same in 1158–59? Break the figures down a little more and think about what you know that can help explain them. How successful do you think Henry II's attempts to improve the farm have been? What problems did he face that could explain this? Look at the amounts left owing, not just claimed income – can any conclusion be drawn from them?

SOURCE 4

This evidence is based on Henry II's pipe rolls. The originals were drawn up by the Exchequer, from which the historian Emilie Amt has collated the following statistics. The figure 'All sources' includes other revenues expected but not listed here.

Revenue claimed in pipe rolls 1155–56

Source	Totals claimed (expected income)			Left owing (outstanding debts)		
County farms	£9,221	12s.	5d.	£1,109	10s.	4d.
Danegeld	£4,561	6s.	7d.	£139	15s.	6d.
Aids	£2,356	15s.	3d.	£96	2s.	4d.
Scutage	£626	16s.	8d.	£67	16s.	8d.
Forest	£232	17s.	5d.	£38	18s.	5d.
All sources	£22,149	13s.	3d.	£2,377	8s.	9d.

Revenue claimed in pipe rolls 1158–59

Source	Totals claimed			Left owing		
County farms	£10,548	13s.	1d.	£599	17s.	4d.
Danegeld	£5	14s	0d.	£5	14s.	0d.
Aids	£8,766	1s.	2d.	£340	0s.	3d.
Scutage	£60	0s.	0d.	£60	0s.	0d.
Forest	£127	5s.	8d.	£30	16s.	8d.
All sources	£29,942	17s.	2d.	£5,474	19s.	8d.

SOURCE 5

This source comes from Florence of Worcester and concerns the Inquest of Sheriffs. Florence of Worcester was a monk and chronicler who died in 1118. However, his chronicle was maintained by others after his death. Although their identities are uncertain, it is likely they too were monks.

After celebrating the feast of Easter, the king went from thence to London, and there held a great council … making laws for his kingdom; and he dismissed nearly all the sheriffs of England; and their bailiffs, for having ill-treated the liege men of his realm … Afterwards the king caused all the liege-men of his realm, the earls, barons, knights, free tenants and even villeins, to swear, on the holy gospels, in their several counties, that they would tell the truth, namely, what and how much the sheriffs and their bailiffs levied on them, and what judicially, and what extra-judicially, and what for default. But great injury was thus done the English nation, for, after the inquisition was made, the king reinstated some of the sheriffs in their offices, and they became afterwards more oppressive than they were before.

Reform of the coinage in 1158 and 1180

The quality of the coinage before 1158

For an economy to function successfully, the currency has to be trusted and accepted. In medieval times, this hinged on the amount of silver contained in the coins, which was a specified amount checked by weighing money against a standard pound weight. The king licensed moneyers and their output was monitored by the Exchequer. By c1180, Richard Fitz Nigel had finished his compilation of the standardised procedures of the Exchequer in his *Dialogue*, which included the procedure for monitoring the quality of the currency, implying that Henry's government was taking more effective central control. Coins were to be smelted, a random selection handed over to the sheriff. Base metals liquefy at far lower temperatures than precious metals, enabling the silver content of money to be extracted and weighed. Underweight coins or poor quality output resulted in heavy fines or brutal punishments. If substandard coins could be traced back to a moneyer, he was tried and punished, otherwise the sheriff had to make good the difference. Either way, the Crown did not lose out on revenue because of poor quality currency.

The recoinages of 1158 and 1180

Henry II only had two recoinages, in 1158 and 1180. One reason for this was that he abandoned the practice of regularly changing the designs of the coins. Another reason is that there was a shortage of silver in the 12th century. The historian W.L. Warren has said that the 1158 recoinage was 'makeshift, a useful but clumsy measure which speaks of a government not as yet able to undertake central control'. However, the fact that there were only two recoinages can also be seen as a sign of stability.

The 1158 reform of the coinage was comprehensive: established moneyers were dismissed and a new penny was introduced, which weighed more. This was lucrative for royal coffers: outgoing moneyers were charged hefty fees for coins that were substandard or had other issues and new moneyers paid for their offices. There was another, smaller purge in 1160, suggesting that there were still moneyers whose coins had been substandard or who had not fulfilled their role to the Crown's satisfaction.

The 1158 recoinage was not very successful in the long term, as clipping and counterfeiting reduced the real value of the coins, despite the more rigorous monitoring of moneyers. The number of mints was cut and Henry II placed a great emphasis on punishing forgery, which became a capital offence in 1176 under the Assize of Northampton. The 1180 recoinage, which lasted until 1182, was far more successful and its coins were in circulation until the middle of the 13th century.

SOURCE

6 A Henry II short cross penny from the 1180 recoinage, minted c1180–82 in Winchester.

Mints

The 1158 recoinage also saw the beginning of the reorganisation of the mints. There were royal mints in most counties, with extra along the south and east coasts where foreign trade was centred and in Somerset and Wiltshire, which traditionally had more than one. First, in 1157, parts of the North of England that had been given to Scotland were returned and this led to establishing new, English mints in Carlisle, Durham and Newcastle. In addition, ecclesiastical mints were phased out. The total number of mints was greatly reduced over the course of Henry II's reign, from 47 in 1154 to 29 in 1158. This was in part achieved by centralising moneyers, bringing them together to work in one place, making monitoring coin quality easier. Over the next two decades this number fell to 17 and, after the recoinage of 1180–82, only ten places had royal mints: Carlisle, Exeter, Lincoln, London, Northampton, Oxford, Wilton, Winchester, Worcester and York.

Another key development was creating new, separate exchanges. Previously old or foreign coins were exchanged by moneyers, which had been quite lucrative for them. Part of the recoinage of 1180 was to reorganise the administration of mints and their profits along Norman lines. New, professional, experienced exchangers, receiving salaries from the king, were brought in and the role of moneyers was limited to the making of the coins.

AS Level Exam-Style Question Section A

Why is Source 7 valuable to the historian for an enquiry into the effectiveness of Henry II's control of the coinage?

Explain your answer using the source, the information given about it and your own knowledge of the historical context. (8 marks)

Tip

Focus on the information given about the source as well. The historical context is very important here. Think about what the Dialogue of the Exchequer *was and what it represented.*

SOURCE 7

From the *Dialogue of the Exchequer*, written c1180. It set down the processes and procedures of the Exchequer in a handbook that could be learned and applied by royal officials. The teacher and student have been discussing the testing of coins.

Student: Why should one pound lose more in the test than another, when the standards of all the moneyers ought to be the same?

Teacher: It happens because of counterfeiters and those who clip coins ... Some have maintained that this kingdom's money is not legal tender if the pound loses more than sixpence from the weight it should have ... if, after the coins have been tested twice, the moneyer is condemned and punished, the coins presented at the Exchequer are melted down into bullion by the smelter and their weight is credited to the sheriff. But all this is almost obsolete now, and no longer strictly followed, since infractions are so common in the matter of coinage. But when the quality of money returns to the proper and lawful standard, it will be necessary to restore observance of the ancient law.

EXTEND YOUR KNOWLEDGE

Royal revenue and the Jews of England

The Jews of England came under the king's protection. This was necessary because of violent anti-semitism, fuelled by unfounded rumours of blood sacrifices as well as both religious and economic factors. As usury was forbidden by the Bible, Jewish moneylenders were the main source of credit in England and this explains why it was in the king's interest to safeguard them. Henry II was the first English king to use credit on a large scale, borrowing at least £12,000 between 1155 and 1166. Under his protection, the supply of credit from Jews grew considerably and was accessed by many of his subjects.

There were other methods of extracting money from the Jews, too. When a Jewish moneylender died, outstanding debts owed him would be taken up by the Crown, so that the Exchequer could collect the repayments. There is also pipe roll evidence that Jewish moneylenders would appeal to the king to help them recover debts, in exchange for a sum of money.

Henry II also taxed England's Jews: for example, in 1159, when he called for an aid from them; in 1168, a 5,000 mark levy was recorded; when raising money for the Third Crusade at the end of his reign (and into Richard I's), there is some evidence that as much as 10,000 marks was raised. By the end of Henry II's reign, taxation of the Jewish community in England had replaced borrowing as the main source of income from them.

The importance of Richard fitz Nigel

Richard fitz Nigel's primary importance was in the development and running of the Exchequer and is best seen in the *Dialogue of the Exchequer*, his detailed description of the Exchequer's workings, completed by the end of the 1170s. Fitz Nigel was the illegitimate son of Nigel of Ely and, by 1160, he was treasurer of the Exchequer, overseeing the running of England's financial affairs. His expertise was laid out in the *Dialogue*, which was in effect a thorough and comprehensive handbook to be applied by Exchequer officials, improving and standardising procedures. It included:

- the strict auditing of accounts, both shire and of the royal household, according to clear procedure
- clearly laid down roles for Exchequer officials
- the method by which the coinage was to be tested to verify that it was of the necessary quality.

The restoration and development of the Exchequer and its procedures, plus better record keeping and monitoring of sheriffs, helped strengthen royal authority. For example, Exchequer officials could determine if the king's demesne was not being well managed; any money claimed by the sheriff for the maintenance of the king's lands had to be explained. Furthermore, after the chaos of civil war, the regenerated Exchequer uncovered instances of royal land having been encroached upon and land where the holder had died without heirs and which should revert back to the Crown.

The work of re-establishing and reforming the Exchequer might not have held the glory of military campaigning considered so important in the Middle Ages, but it was central to enabling Henry II to rule effectively and to raise revenues for armed expeditions and the defence of his territories.

SOURCE

8

The Exchequer of Ireland from a medieval Irish manuscript (1299). The Irish Exchequer was established in 1210, based upon the English model, after Henry II had begun developing an English-style government in Ireland after his 1172 invasion.

The impact of financial reforms on increasing royal income

Restoring royal authority meant restoring England's finances. Evidence from pipe rolls suggests that, before 1166, royal revenues averaged £13,300 per annum, although figures for 1155–57 show it was as low as £10,300. After 1166, the average revenue rose to £20,400 and from 1179 to the end of Henry's reign had risen to £23,300. On average, Henry's revenues were almost £22,000 per annum. The evidence therefore points to a strong financial recovery, with 1165–66 as something of a turning point.

Overall, Henry II's reign did see some significant financial reforms and developments, especially around the strengthening of the Exchequer, the reforming of the coinage, the updating of pertinent information and the increasingly rigorous pursuit of the king's rights and feudal dues. Such administrative changes enabled the strengthening of both royal authority and finances after Stephen's reign. However, the impact of these measures cannot account for rising royal revenues under Henry II.

In terms of royal income, although a great deal was done to restore the farms and royal demesne, it cannot explain the growth in income Henry II achieved. Neither do developments in taxation explain it. To answer the question of why income grew, it is necessary to focus on legal reforms too, which began in earnest in 1166.

ACTIVITY
KNOWLEDGE CHECK

1 Draw up a table with three columns headed 'Land', 'Currency' and 'Taxation/aids'. Under each, list the main steps taken by Henry II to increase Crown income.

2 Now identify evidence of the successes and failures under each heading.

3 Rank them in order of most/least successful and explain your reasoning.

> **A Level Exam-Style Question Section B**
>
> 'Henry II's financial reforms were extremely successful in strengthening royal authority in England.'
>
> How far do you agree with this statement? (20 marks)
>
> **Tip**
> *Think broadly, not just in terms of statistics and overall revenue. Break the topic down. The word 'extremely' will enable you to challenge the statement more clearly than if the suggestion was that they were simply 'successful'.*

WHAT WAS THE IMPACT OF HENRY II'S LEGAL REFORMS?

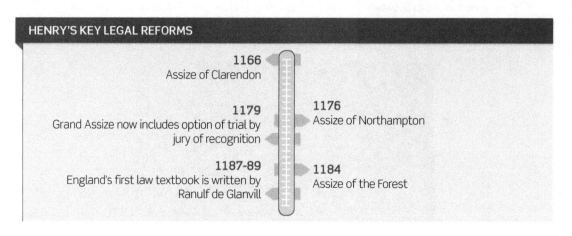

HENRY'S KEY LEGAL REFORMS

- **1166** Assize of Clarendon
- **1176** Assize of Northampton
- **1179** Grand Assize now includes option of trial by jury of recognition
- **1184** Assize of the Forest
- **1187–89** England's first law textbook is written by Ranulf de Glanvill

Medieval courts and court cases

Court	Overseen by	Jurisdiction
Manor	Lord	Managed the manor and its fields; focused on social and economic matters concerning the lord's lands and the running of his estates. Also where all males over 12 years old promised to keep the peace. Met every four to six weeks on average.
Hundred	King's agents – sheriff or his deputy, or a lord in private hundred courts	Dealt with: small debts; disorder not serious enough to be a breach of the king's peace; land disputes between common folk; minor crimes like petty theft. The sheriff checked tithings here and twice a year oversaw the frankpledge (oath binding the men of a manor to answer truthfully for one another in any investigation). Met up to once a fortnight.
County (shire)	King's agents – sheriff	Meeting every four to six weeks, it was usually overseen by the sheriff, who read out general writs and royal commands here. It arbitrated disputes and minor trials were dealt with here according to local custom. This was also where disputes between vassals of two different lords were heard.
		This was where the king's itinerant justices would come to hear Crown pleas – those involving criminal offences such as murder, rape, robbery and theft. When this occurred the county court became the king's court and had a wider jurisdiction. It also dealt with civil disputes where writs had been issued.
Forest	King's agents – royal forester; forest justices	Oversaw offences committed under the laws of the royal forest. Royal forests were patrolled regularly by the king's officials and overseen by a royal forester. There were special sessions of the forest courts overseen by the king's itinerant justices.
King's	King	The ultimate court of appeal. Enforced the king's rights; tried tenants-in-chief and serious disputes/crimes. However, many people pressed the king to hear their cases (pleas) and this was one of his key roles as he travelled the realm – to be seen to do justice.

To understand Henry II's legal reforms, it is necessary to know that legal cases divided into criminal and civil pleas. The most serious criminal pleas, such as assault or fighting, were considered really serious if they led to a breach of the peace, in which case they could only be heard by the king or his justices. These were **Crown pleas**.

Civil cases started with a **writ** rather than a criminal offence. Any case that began with a writ would be heard in the king's courts. Although some of these involved the Crown prosecuting an individual, if one private individual sued another it was known as a **common plea**.

The Assizes of Clarendon (1166) and Northampton (1176)

These reforms laid out codes and procedures that would develop a more systematic approach to law and order across the realm, as well as increasing the power of the monarch in the localities. Henry II's aim was to unify under his authority the various local jurisdictions existing in England at the time.

The **Assize** of Clarendon's main concerns were **juries of presentment** and sheriffs' powers. It introduced:

- empanelling (enrolling) of juries of presentment by sheriffs
- standard procedures and punishments for Crown pleas
- sheriffs to have full access to all lands, people and courts of landowners to pursue named suspects or investigate those staying with them or under their protection
- restrictions on sheltering strangers.

KEY TERMS

Assize
A court session. Quarterly assizes, for example, are court sessions held four times a year. However, the term 'assize' is also used to describe Henry II's different sets of new legal procedures, hence the names relating to where these were drawn up.

Juries of presentment
Twelve 'lawful men' from the county and four from the vill were required to present the names of anyone thought guilty of a crime that came under the jurisdiction of the king's justices, or was thought to have harboured criminals.

Juries of presentment and the powers of sheriffs

The first part of the Assize of Clarendon focused on juries of presentment, which were to present the names of anyone its members believed had committed a crime. The sheriff was then responsible for making enquiries and bringing them to trial. To do this, the Assize of Clarendon gave them the right to enter anyone's land in pursuit of a criminal, with powers of arrest such that no lord could claim jurisdiction over those captured.

The Assize of Clarendon also gave the sheriff considerable powers to prevent barons from interfering with the pursuit of justice and the king's business. Sheriffs were empowered to enter any land in pursuit of criminals and to require anyone's help in their capture, decreasing barons' powers locally as they could no longer protect any of their vassals accused of a crime. Given the lack of law and order, and the levels of intimidation and violence prevalent under King Stephen, these measures were important.

One other impact of the Assize of Clarendon was the Inquest of Sheriffs in 1170. Having given the sheriffs much greater authority, issues about their abuse of power resulted in this thorough investigation and the removal of 22 sheriffs from office (see pages 296–297). Even before 1170, Henry II had twice replaced large numbers of county sheriffs whose loyalty and impartiality was in doubt, but the new powers given them in 1166 seem to have led to even greater impropriety and certainly caused far greater resentment.

The development of juries of presentment does indicate greater reliance on local knowledge as a means of instigating a court case, as well as building upon the already established notion of a community 'policing' itself. Tithings already made local males over the age of 12 responsible both for pursuing criminals when a crime took place and for informing on each other if any of them had committed a crime. In one sense this is a move towards eyewitness or sworn testimony.

However, it is difficult to make too much of a more rational approach to justice evolving, given the enshrinement of trial by water as the preferred method of determining guilt under the Assize of Clarendon.

Juries of presentment did not mean trial by jury, however. Those accused of criminal offences were put to **trial by ordeal**. If they failed, they were condemned to be hanged, or mutilated and banished from the realm within 40 days. Even those who passed the ordeal – and about two-thirds did – were exiled if there was any evidence that they were of bad character. Such reliance on what might be 'hearsay' would have no place in a modern justice system.

KEY TERM

Trial by ordeal
A method of determining the guilt or innocence of someone accused of a crime. They would be subjected to painful or dangerous tests. If they passed the tests, it was felt that God had shown that they were innocent.

Despite the continued use of trial by ordeal, earlier moves towards more rational methods of determining guilt, such as sworn testimony, can also be found in Henry II's legal reforms. Given that most cases concerned land tenure, a jury's local knowledge was very useful in determining who should hold what land. Charters and writs were often presented as evidence too.

Under the Assize of Clarendon the accused were to hand over their chattels before trial to act as surety. If found guilty, their chattels were sold and the proceeds went to the king, making a valuable contribution to royal revenues and helping to explain the increase in royal revenues from profits of justice.

SOURCE 9
From *The Chronicle of Battle Abbey*, written between 1066 and 1176. It concerns Abbot Warner of Battle Abbey, who was petitioning the king about an issue over the tenement of Barnhorn, held in Sussex by Gilbert de Baillol (a vassal of Count John of Eu), which the abbey claimed had belonged to it in the days of Henry I.

This abbot managed to become a friend of the king and thus he took before him a complaint about Barnhorn. At the abbot's request the king sent a writ to John, count of Eu, ordering him to do full right to the abbot concerning the tenement, and warning that if he did not, the sheriff of Sussex would do so, in order that the king might hear no more complaint about this matter. But for long [John] did nothing and made all sorts of excuses to avoid the suit. Such proceedings wasted a great deal of time in fruitless effort but the abbot would not give up. He kept petitioning the king, both personally and through his friends, and at length got the case transferred to the royal court. But the king would now be crossing to Normandy and now returning to England on his own affairs. Therefore, although the case was over a long period of time brought before the justices who presided over his court in the king's palace, and, although the king, now by notifications, now by demands, now by commands very frequently ordered justice to be done to the abbot, never could the issue be satisfactorily settle.

Further sheriffs' powers

The power and influence of the barons in the court system was greatly undermined in other ways too. Sheriffs had the right to enter the estate of any noble to ensure that all the men of the manor had taken the frankpledge.

Concern for strangers, or men who were wandering the country without having any apparent lord, also formed part of the Assize of Clarendon. There were restrictions on lodging someone unknown for more than one night. After this, they were to be held until their lord could be found and had vouched for them.

ACTIVITY
KNOWLEDGE CHECK

1 What does Source 9 tell us about why Henry II's legal reforms were necessary?

2 In what ways did Henry II's legal reforms strengthen royal authority in the localities?

3 Which of Henry II's reforms improved access to justice and how?

The Assize of Northampton, 1176

In 1176, Henry II reinforced and developed the Assize of Clarendon with the Assize of Northampton. It was issued in January 1176, after King Henry II had put down a large rebellion in England (and France) in 1173–74. Key measures were:

- the division of England's counties into six circuits for the king's justices to visit

- a new oath of fealty required for every man, from earls to villeins

- punishments for lesser crimes were made harsher, now including the loss of a hand as well as a foot

- arson and forgery were added to the Crown pleas that justices could hear

- two new possessory legal actions were developed (*novel disseisin* and *mort d'ancestor*).

Novel disseisin and mort d'ancestor

Novel disseisin and *mort d'ancestor* were possessory assizes, meaning they dealt with issues of land possession. They addressed pleas that were very common: plaintiffs brought pleas of *novel disseisin* over being unfairly dismissed from their land; *mort d'ancestor* concerned being denied their rightful inheritance.

Novel disseisin and *mort d'ancestor* could both be brought using new standardised writs, brought in under the Assize of Northampton. They were important for two reasons.

- They were extremely popular, generating an increase in caseload leading to five members of the Curia Regis sitting (permanently as it happened) at Westminster to deal with a backlog of pleas unheard by the justices in **eyre**.

- They used **juries of recognition**. These juries testified on oath to the facts of the matter as they knew them. The justices then decided the verdict. Although initially only available for *novel disseisin* and *mort d'ancestor*, this was an important step towards trial by jury and a more rational, evidence-based system.

Given the upheaval of King Stephen's reign, it is perhaps surprising that these possessory assizes were not brought in until 1176. However, they were introduced after another period of unrest in parts of England, as several barons rebelled against Henry II in 1173–74 (the Great Rebellion, see Chapter 4).

They are also indicative of the nature of Henry II's legal reforms, in that they were brought in over the course of his reign, often in response to developing needs, rather than being a major, co-ordinated attempt at a wholesale reform of England's legal system. Both *novel disseisin* and *mort d'ancestor* were part of a wider evolution of writs throughout Henry II's reign.

KEY TERMS

Eyre
A term referring to both the circuit of counties travelled by the justices and the courts they held.

Jury of recognition
Jury used to determine the right to hold a piece of land. Using local knowledge the jurors swore to tell the truth about the facts of the case as they knew them and judgement was based upon this rather than trial by ordeal.

The development of standardised writs

Under the Normans, writs were drawn up for each individual request. Cases brought about by writs were heard in the king's courts. Under Henry II there developed throughout his reign a core of frequently requested writs, 'mass' produced in set forms for set situations. The majority concerned land tenure.

Standardisation of writs made the justice system faster and more accessible. Anyone who was free, and could afford to, could buy a writ and pursue an appeal; at a cost of 6d they were within most people's reach. Standardised writs were important for three reasons.

- They gave greater protection to free tenants: a baron could no longer simply demand that they attend his court to defend themselves against accusations. Even a lord had to obtain a writ first.

- Being so much more accessible, they increased the Crown's involvement in the localities by bringing more cases to the king's justices.

- They increased the standardisation of the procedure for, and the experience of, justice across the realm.

As a result, the county courts increasingly became the focus of justice in England. By the 1180s, no free man needed to answer in a lord's court concerning his free tenement without a royal writ being issued.

Ranulf de Glanvill

Standardised writs were also an important factor in the development of the first legal textbook, Ranulf de Glanvill's *Treatise on the Laws and Customs of the Kingdom of England*. Structured around the common writs, it explained how each was to be used. It became the reference point for **common law** and the administration of justice throughout the realm for centuries. It is still available today, one of the last translations being printed in 1997.

> **KEY TERM**
>
> **Common law**
> There are two key aspects to this term:
>
> 1 It means that legal procedures and justice are the same throughout the country.
>
> 2 Common laws derived from refining existing customs and developed through judges' decisions in courts. This process began in the Middle Ages before there was a parliament to make laws (statutes). According to the National Archive, the first Act of Parliament was passed in 1497, under Henry VII.

The court of King's Bench

Henry II's reforms generated a huge amount of work. Although the Crown pleas aspect of the eyre was unpopular, the purchases of standardised writs, especially for *novel disseisin* and *mort d'ancestor*, imply that **civil pleas** were greatly in demand. By 1178, the legal system was struggling with the increased workload: in eight counties the eyre had been unable to hear all the cases brought before it. In response more justices were appointed and England's circuits were reorganised.

However, the most effective immediate solution was the creation of a special body to hear the backlog of cases, transferring them to a tribunal in London where they would be judged by five members of Henry's Curia Regis. Established in 1178, although not yet a new, separate court, it was referred to as 'the Bench'. It came to sit permanently, leading to the development of the Court of the **King's Bench,** the most important court in the land, with seniority over all others because of its close links with the monarch, who would hear some cases himself. Again, using a writ, any plaintiff could, in theory, bring their case to the King's Bench for review.

Having five members of the Curia Regis permanently assigned to sit in London and hear cases from across England also contributed to developing the standardisation of the law. It contributed to its centralisation too, as the law was becoming centralised not simply because cases were heard by judges appointed by central government but also because there was a physical, central 'home' of England law developing in London. It also reinforced, perhaps more clearly than before, the idea that the king was the permanent, ultimate source of justice, because the King's Bench sat regardless of whether the king was in the country or not.

> **KEY TERMS**
>
> **Civil plea**
> Began with a writ and covered cases concerning rights, land tenure, feudal obligations, inheritance. Some civil pleas involved the Crown.
>
> **King's Bench**
> A new, permanent court in London that emerged as a result of the eyres of Henry II's reign being overwhelmed with work. Established in 1178, it consisted of five members of the Curia Regis, who were instructed to 'hear all the complaints of the realm and do right'.

The Assize of the Forest (1184) (also known as the Assize of Woodstock)

The rules of the forest were essentially at the king's whim. The Assize of the Forest made them part of England's acknowledged law. As with other assizes, its preamble states that it was made with the 'advice and assent' of the magnates of the realm. Given how unpopular the forest was, this can be seen as a sign of Henry II's control, in that he was able to enforce the rules without any apparent opposition.

The beginning of the first clause of the Assize of the Forest makes Henry II's intent very clear:

'First he forbids that anyone shall transgress against him in regard to his hunting rights or his forest in any respect.'

The running of the forest also reflects the effective organisation of medieval government, as there was a whole hierarchy devoted to its administration, including forest justices and regular forest eyres which, as with other eyres, investigated and reinforce the king's rights, contributing to increased Crown revenues.

The extent of changes to the system of royal justice under Henry II

Itinerant justices and general eyres

The concept of itinerant royal justices travelling the country to hear important cases was not new, but under Henry II visitations by justices in eyre became more regular and systematic and their role expanded. Until about 1166, sheriffs and local officials could hear Crown pleas in the absence of the king's justices. After that date, this practice at eyres became more regular and, by 1170, was much more frequent and could last several weeks. This raised and strengthened the profile of royal authority in the shires.

1176 saw the first true general eyre; Henry II divided up England into six groups of counties, each to be visited by his justices simultaneously. Between 1176 and 1189, there were eight general eyres, a frequency and regularity meaning the king's justices were able to take over from sheriffs and local officials. Justices were also sent for between eyres if necessary, as the Assize of Clarendon made it clear that sheriffs would send for the king's justices if a robber, thief or murderer was caught and no eyre was imminent.

Regular visits by royal justices were important because their experience was far more wide ranging than a sheriff's and as they were essentially London-based, their judgements were more likely to be impartial and less influenced by local landowners. They also contributed to the legal procedure becoming increasingly standardised. When eyres had finished, the justices regrouped in Westminster to discuss their judgements, helping to spread common practice. In addition, a number remained in London and those on eyre who came across problematic cases could refer to them for advice.

KEY TERM

General eyre
Systematic, nationwide visitation of the kings' justices within a limited time frame. However, this is a modern term. In the Middle Ages they were known as 'eyres for all pleas'.

This gave greater continuity, routine and a sense of professional cohesion. From this there developed a core group of about 20 expert judges.

The impact of Henry II on law and justice

Henry II's legal reforms brought a uniformity of procedure and punishment across England. The writing of the textbook by Glanvill remains a landmark in the history of the law and reflects the development of a standardised, common law. The greater use of juries and sworn testimony, although not replacing trial by ordeal, does indicate a more rational system developing. However, the modern trial by jury involving defence and prosecution lawyers was still a long way off.

Henry's actions to tackle law and justice in England had an impact in several different ways:

- an increasing emphasis on the categorisation and definition of royal rights
- a corresponding decline in the influence of magnates
- increasing the standardisation of laws and legal procedures
- greater access to the king's justice via the expansion and development of writs and regular eyres
- the development of a core of expert, professional judges.

Winners, losers and royal authority

The most popular aspect of Henry II's legal reforms were the standardised writs, which sped up the process of justice and made the king's courts available to all free men. By the 1180s, no free man had to attend the lord's court concerning the land he rented. Writs had to be paid for, but their popularity suggests that they were affordable. The ability of barons and local lords to circumvent the law, or break it with impunity, was curtailed. The use of knights, especially on juries of recognition, also strengthened the link between king and under-tenants. Thus, the barons were losers in Henry II's legal reforms to a large extent. Their influence even at county level was diminished as freemen turned to the king's court for justice.

Villeins still received justice at the hands of the local lord, depending to an extent upon the legal action brought and what types of case he had the right to try. Furthermore, the development of the standard writ for determining someone's status also suggests that a considerable number of people were 'accused' of being a villein, sometimes resulting in loss of free status and bringing them more fully under baronial control.

SOURCE

 A standardised writ from the reign of Henry II concerning villein status.

The king to the sheriff, greeting. R., who claims to be a free man, has complained to me that N. seeks to reduce him to villein status. Therefore I command you, if the aforesaid R. gives you security for prosecuting his claim, to transfer that plea before me or my justices on such-and-such day, and to see that he goes in peace meanwhile. And summon the aforesaid N. by good summoners to be there then, to show why he unjustly seeks to reduce him to villein status. And have there the three summoners and this writ. Witness R., etc.

 Evidence (5b)

The importance of context

Documents (texts) are like small pieces torn from a larger tapestry (context). Historians have to reconstruct the larger pattern into which documents might fit in order to use them to construct accounts of the past. The problem is that texts can have multiple contexts. Historians often debate how best to contextualise the documents that they interpret.

Source 10 is an example of a standardised writ, in this case concerning one person challenging another person's claim that the first person was their villein.

1 Summarise the key points from Source 10.

   a) What issue does it concern?

   b) What action is to be taken?

   c) What does it suggest about obtaining justice under Henry II?

   d) What conclusions can be drawn about how strong Henry II's government was?

   As well as noting the content of the document, it is also important to realise that the form of the standardised writ concerning villein status appeared in Glanvill's text, hailed as evidence of justice becoming more standardised under Henry II, for which he is called 'the founder of the common law'.

2 The timeline below provides a possible context for the writ in the wider story of Henry II's restoration of Crown authority in England. The development of standardised writs was ongoing during Henry II's reign.

   1135–54 Reign of King Stephen, during which there is a civil war. Stephen's reign is often referred to as 'the Anarchy', although contemporaries called it 'the shipwreck'

   1154 Henry II comes to the throne and begins the process of bringing the barons under the authority of the Crown by decommissioning illegal castles and taking back land that belongs to the royal demesne

   1166 Regular eyres of England are reinstated; the Assize of Clarendon

   1170 Inquest of Sheriffs

   1173 Rebellion by some barons in England as part of the Great Rebellion against Henry II, including France

   1174 Great Rebellion is put down by Henry II, in England and France

   1176 The Assize of Northampton including the introduction of possessory assizes and standardised writs for *novel disseisin* and *mort d'ancestor*, which prove very popular

   1178 Establishment of King's Bench at Westminster

   1188 Glanvill's *Treatise on the Laws and Customs of the Realm of England*

   a) How does the development of a standardised writ to determine someone's status as a villein fit in with these events?

   b) What was Henry II trying to achieve with his reforms?

   c) What is the link to possessory assizes?

The standardised writ will lead to certain conclusions when interpreted in the wider context of Henry II's aims of re-establishing law and order and restoring Crown authority after King Stephen's reign. There is, however, a contrasting interpretation if we locate it in another context, that of England's first legal 'textbook'.

The fact that it was a standardised writ means that determining someone's status was a common issue. The demand for so many writs concerning determining villein status developed as a result of Henry II's legal reforms, especially possessory assizes, hence its appearance in Glanvill's *Treatise on the Laws and Customs of the Realm of England*. Thus, it was under Henry II that strict guidelines about who was a villein were formally laid down for the first time in Glanvill's text, along with what it meant to be a villein.

Standardised writs had to be purchased in the first place and security provided by the person challenging another's claim that they were their villein. Villeins had neither legal status nor rights; they could be sold; rebellious villeins could be punished as their lord saw fit, including corporal and humiliation punishments; they could be arrested and imprisoned by the lord; Henry II's possessory assizes did not apply to them.

3 Explain how Henry II restoring the Crown's authority in England could lead to the development of so many standardised writs, including *novel disseisin*, *mort d'ancestor* and challenging claims of villein status.

Consider all the information provided together and answer the following questions:

4 How much can the development of a standardised writ challenging someone's claim that they are a villein be taken as evidence of the negative impact of Henry II's legal reforms?

5 Why is it important for historians to spend time thinking about the possible contexts for a document such as a writ before they start to use it to draw conclusions about the past?

The implications of Henry II's legal reforms for the power of the monarchy

Justices in eyre

Justices in eyre and sheriffs, with their new powers, had an important role in strengthening the power of the monarchy in the shires. By 1189, the remit of the justices in eyre encompassed: judging and punishing Crown and criminal pleas as well as civil pleas between private individuals; investigating royal rights and feudal dues, and their violation; enforcing the king's new legislation and procedures; investigating local officials, ensuring that civic duties had been fulfilled and punishing any malpractice; gathering information about outlaws; anything the Exchequer or the king wanted done, such as taking oaths of fealty or assessing taxes on towns and royal manors.

Profits of justice

Profits of justice increased royal revenues quite significantly after the Assize of Clarendon. First, the chattels of the accused went to the king. Secondly, the justices in eyre investigated everything thoroughly, including the business of the sheriff, the king's rights and ensuring that the community had been fulfilling its obligations. If it had not, **amercements** were imposed and, for this reason, the eyre was very unpopular. Records showed that being fined happened quite frequently to juries. The 1176–77 eyre, including forest fines, generated £30,300 of revenue, compared with the farm's £4,300.

KEY TERM

Amercement
A fine for breach of regulations or minor infringement of procedure. For example, a jury could be fined if proper legal procedure was not followed.

Anything that contributed to royal finances helped to increase royal authority. Perhaps the most important aspect of the profits of justice was that they represented income streams, rather than occasional payments into the Exchequer like tallage or scutage.

The king's rights

Another way in which the eyre generated income for the king, increased his authority and strengthened his grip on the localities, was by thoroughly investigating his rights and feudal dues. This aspect of the justices' work, started by Henry II, grew considerably. A document known as the **Articles of Eyre**, which was a series of questions that covered a wide range of matters, was sent to the sheriff in advance of the justices. He then empanelled a jury who, on oath, had to answer truthfully the questions asked in the articles. Using local testimony is another indication of justice becoming more rational under Henry II.

KEY TERM

Articles of Eyre
A list of questions sent in advance of the eyre, demanding answers on issues such as malpractice of the king's officials, issues concerning wardship, escheat, relief and other such royal rights.

Many aspects of visitations by justices in eyre represented oppressive and unwelcome Crown interference and were resented. Overall, Henry's legal reforms sidelined the barons' courts, fostering a more direct link between king, under-tenants and free men, giving them a greater role to play in local justice, as well as greater protection.

ACTIVITY
WRITING

Analyse Sources 11 and 12. They are both from the *Dialogue of the Exchequer*.

1 Identify words or phrases that you do not understand and research their meaning.

2 Identify words and phrases that show the writer's feelings on the treatment of criminals.

3 How might you account for the difference in the impression the author gives of those imposing justice in Source 11, compared with Source 12?

4 Write a short paragraph explaining the author's views on criminals and how they are treated.

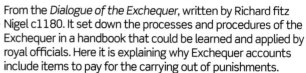

SOURCE 11

From the *Dialogue of the Exchequer*, written by Richard fitz Nigel c1180. It set down the processes and procedures of the Exchequer in a handbook that could be learned and applied by royal officials. Here it is explaining why Exchequer accounts include items to pay for the carrying out of punishments.

In some counties there are people who, by virtue of their tenancies, lay avenging hands on condemned criminals, hanging some, mutilating others, and inflicting other punishments, according to the magnitude of their crimes. On the other hand, there are counties where money is paid out by the treasury for the punishment of such culprits. Therefore, whatever the sheriff pays to the greedy and loathesome [sic] men who put such justice and judgements into effect, taking money for shedding blood, is credited to him by Exchequer custom.

SOURCE 12

In this text the *Dialogue of the Exchequer* considers why not all death sentences are carried out.

When a notorious criminal is arrested by the royal servants who keep the peace of the realm because of the great number of crimes and in order to free the land of such evil deeds, the judges sometimes agree that if such as person, having confessed to a crime, is willing to challenge his partners in crime and is able to prove their guilt in trial by combat, then he will escape the death he deserves and depart in safety, completely abjuring the realm. Some of them, on the other hand, make a deal beforehand with the judges, and although they prove the charges they do not depart in safety, but they escape being hanged or otherwise shamefully executed – as they deserve by their own confession – and instead, being punished by mutilation, they become a miserable spectacle for the people and discourage similar crimes by their terrible example.

ACTIVITY
KNOWLEDGE CHECK

1 What evidence is there for and against the idea that the legal system became more rational under Henry II?

2 Work in pairs. One person should take the point of view of a free man, the other of a baron. What were the pros and cons of Henry II's legal reforms? Think as broadly as you can. To what extent has access to justice improved? To what extent have the changes empowered you? How has your role changed?

HOW DID THE NATURE OF KINGSHIP CHANGE UNDER HENRY II?

The growing political and economic power of the king

Henry II's reforms and approach to governing England, often at the expense of the barons, contributed to the changing nature of kingship. It was not that Henry II no longer needed the feudal system, but he aimed to reinforce the king's position, bringing the barons under control rather than doing without them.

Increasingly regular eyres and the standardisation and mass production of writs meant that more cases than ever before were heard by the king's justices. Decreasing instances of barons' private gallows also suggests that they would have noticed their courts being increasingly sidelined.

Furthermore, in local government the sheriff was, by 1170, a royal appointment, loyal to the Crown rather than the local baron. The Inquest of Sheriffs represented a significant break with the past in that being a local magnate no longer qualified a person for being their county's sheriff. Not only did it replace most incumbents with loyal, royal officials it also investigated a wide range of financial dealings in detail, as Source 13 shows. This points to an increasing centralisation of government, although in terms of hierarchy under the king rather than a central location. The increase in sheriffs' powers also indicate a subordination of barons' interests to those of the Crown.

SOURCE

From the Inquest of Sheriffs in 1170. Here the scope of the inquest is being defined.

1. In the first place let inquiry be made concerning the sheriffs and their bailiffs as to what and how much they have received from each hundred and from each vill and from each man, since the lord king crossed over to Normandy, by reason of which the land and the people have been oppressed; and what they have received by a judgment of the county or hundred, and what without a judgment. And let that which they ascertain has been taken by a judgement be written down separately; and let inquiry be made concerning all exactions, both as to the cause and the evidence.

2. Likewise let inquiry be made as to what and how much land the sheriffs or their bailiffs have bought or mortgaged.

3. Likewise let inquiry be made concerning the archbishops, bishops, abbots, earls, barons, sub-tenants, knights, citizens and burgesses, and their stewards and officers as to what and how much they have received from their lands since the above date, from their several hundreds and their several vills, and from each of their men, both with judgment and without, and let them write down separately all these exactions and their causes and occasions.

The Assize of Arms, 1181

Although not a set of legal reforms, the Assize of Arms established laws regarding who was allowed to hold arms, how many and of what type. It led to a massive, intrusive, national survey into incomes, armour and weaponry. In the enforcement of the Assize of Arms, the role of the sheriff and king's justices was paramount: the sheriffs investigated the local population of all ranks and gathered the testimony; the king's justices heard the sworn testaments. The power and jurisdiction of the Crown was increased yet again.

In some ways, the Assize of Arms shows that the king needed the barons and their men, even free men, to be suitably armed for the defence of the realm. However, it can also be seen as an affront to baronial rights as the Crown determined permissible armaments and there were severe penalties for breaking the rules about this.

SOURCE 14

From the Assize of Arms, 1181. Reproduced from G.D.G. Hall, ed. and trans., *Documents Illustrating the History of Civilization in Medieval England 1066–1500*, 1969.

Let the justices cause oaths to be taken by lawful knights or other free and lawful men of the hundred or the borough as many as they shall see fit, who shall have the value of chattels which make it necessary for him to have a coat of mail, a helmet, a lance and a shield according has been said; to wit, that one by one they will name to them all from their hundreds and neighbourhoods and boroughs who have sixteen marks either in chattels or revenue, and likewise those who have ten marks. And afterwards let the justices cause those jurors* and others to be registered; who have an amount of chattels and revenues, and afterwards in their presence, in the hearing of all those persons, let them cause this assize concerning the having of arms to be read, and that they swear that they have these arms according to the aforesaid value of chattels or revenue and that they will hold them at the service of the lord king…

*Here meaning someone who has taken an oath.

The three major, national surveys undertaken during the reign of Henry II (Cartae Baronum in 1166; the Inquest of Sheriffs in 1170; and the Assize of Arms in 1181) are again indicative of a government that was highly organised and administratively capable, but so was William I's Domesday Book. The fact that there were three major surveys under Henry II, however, perhaps indicates a government becoming increasingly interested in the finer details of people's lives as a basis for its policies and especially its revenue raising.

Relations with leading barons

The reduction of the number of earldoms by half by the end of his reign, and the acquisition or demolition of illegal castles, are two key examples of Henry shifting the balance of power between Crown and barons that have already been dealt with, as has the Assize of Clarendon (1166) and the Inquest of Sheriffs (1170). The impact of Henry II's reforms on his relations with barons are more subtle and not as easy to quantify, as they primarily concern the increasing need for educated, experienced professionals with knowledge of finance and law in order to run the government of England.

Bureaucratisation and professionalism

Two key trends in the changing nature of kingship that potentially impacted upon the barons were bureaucratisation and professionalism. As the law and Exchequer developed, so did the need to have as officials men who were capable of fulfilling these administrative needs, rather than simply focusing on men with power bases across the kingdom that could be marshalled by the king in time of conflict.

Men like Richard de Lucy and Ranulf de Glanvill often came from educated rather than noble backgrounds, with specialist knowledge or professional experience. Although by no means from poor families, they do illustrate the expansion in the role of the knightly class. Hugh Bardolf is also an example, serving as an itinerant justice and then on the King's Bench from 1185. Another 'career' servant with a strong specialism was Richard fitz Nigel.

The historian Ralph Turner has concluded that such men were more interested in developing rational, procedural approaches and maintaining records than men of the traditional nobility would have been. Thus, they instituted a more bureaucratic approach to government than had been the case previously. The *Dialogue of the Exchequer* highlights this, as does Becket's employment of dozens of clerks in the Chancery, manifesting itself in the production of paperwork, which seems to have ballooned under Henry II. The mass production and popularity of standardised writs are evidence of this.

The fundamental nature of kingship did not change: the king was still itinerant; his Curia Regis remained the ultimate source of justice and legislation; his control over the currency and taxation continued; and his role leading in war and making peace was unchanged. In doing all this he needed the barons. However, birthright was no longer all that was required to play a part in government at national level, as baronial power and influence was undermined locally: nobles now faced competition from the 'lower orders'.

EXTRACT

1 This list showing the members of Henry II's court who were the most frequent witnesses to his charters is an extract from research compiled by the historian Nicholas Vincent and presented in *Henry II: New Interpretations*, published in 2007. The men named were present at Henry II's court throughout his reign, for varying lengths of time.

Name	No. of charters	Role/status
1. Thomas Becket	420	Chancellor/archbishop
2. Richard du Hommet	331	Constable
3. Manasser Biset*	276	Dapifer‡
4. Reginald, Earl of Cornwall	247	Earl
5. Geoffrey Ridel	208	Archdeacon/bishop
6. Richard de Lucy	206	Justiciar
7. Warin fitz Gerald	176	Chamberlain
8. Richard of Ilchester	172	Archdeacon/bishop
9. John of Oxford	136	Dean/bishop
10. Ranulf de Glanvill	128	Justiciar
14. Robert, Earl of Leicester	105	Earl/justiciar

*Biset was an important landowner in England. He was the son of an under-tenant.

‡A dapifer was a steward.

AS Level Exam-style Question Section A

How much weight do you give the evidence of Extract 1 for an enquiry into Henry II's relations with England's barons?

Explain your answer using the source, the information given about it and your own knowledge of the historical context. (12 marks)

Tip
Think about the evidence used by Nicholas Vincent in deriving this list.

The importance of itinerant kingship in maintaining royal power in England and the Angevin Empire

Centralisation and itinerant kingship

Perhaps the key trend in Henry II's government was the centralisation of power. There was a more direct relationship between Crown and people than before, even though only 37 percent of Henry's reign was spent in England. In many ways, the centralisation of power made itinerant kingship stronger and enabled the king to travel his territories more, building vital relationships with local lords and nobles and showing off the majesty of his court. His indefatigable energy and appetite for activity was one of the most remarked upon features of Henry's personality. Building relations with local barons remained an important part of his job description and their importance should not be underplayed. Nevertheless, it cannot be denied that the balance of power between Crown and barons changed.

An absent king with a permanent presence

Henry II established an organised, well-administered and highly visible government that did not need him to be present to function. He had competent and loyal justiciars and capable key royal servants; increasingly accountable sheriffs; a core of expert judges; a self-administering Exchequer and legal system. (After Robert Beaumont's death in 1168, there was only one justiciar, Richard de Lucy. He served until 1178, when Ranulf de Glanvill took over.)

In some ways, Henry's reforms in England built on the idea of itinerant government – travelling justices being the prime example. By ensuring that sheriffs were Crown appointees and, largely, royal officials after 1170, Henry was able to use centralisation to strengthen the Crown's presence in the localities. Again, this helped to strengthen itinerant government by tightening the Crown's control over partisan barons. The Inquest of Sheriffs was the last major reorganisation of sheriffs during Henry's reign.

THINKING HISTORICALLY Change (6a)

Separately and together

The growth of the power of the Crown under Henry II

Below are some different types of history that historians may identify:

Political history

Religious history

Economic history

Military history

Social history

International history.

These are thematic histories, where a historian focuses on a particular aspect of change. For example, an economic history of the British Empire would focus on trade and economic reasons for the expansion of the empire, whereas a political history of the empire would focus on governance of the colonies and strategic reasons for its expansion.

Work in groups.

1 Write a definition for each type of history.

2 Here are some events in the period considered in this chapter. The first two are 'political' events:

1154 Henry II becomes king of England

1155 Henry begins decommissioning illegal castles

1162 The geld is collected for the last time

1166 Assize of Clarendon

1170 The Inquest of Sheriffs

1176 The Assize of Northampton.

a) Why was decommissioning illegal castles important to Henry II maintaining the throne?

b) Think about some examples of how Henry II decommissioned illegal castles. With what other area of history does this overlap?

3 What political changes came about because of the Assize of Clarendon in 1166 and the Inquest of Sheriffs in 1170?

4 Was the decision to stop collecting the geld economic or political or both?

5 What were the social changes brought about by the Assizes of Clarendon and Northampton?

6 Did Henry II order the Inquest of Sheriffs for economic or political reasons?

Work in pairs.

7 Write a statement attacking 'thematic history'.

8 Write three statements defending 'thematic history'.

9 Explain why 'thematic history' occurs.

ACTIVITY
KNOWLEDGE CHECK

1 Using Extract 1, investigate the careers of some of the witnesses to Henry II's charters that you have not come across in this textbook. What are their backgrounds? Why might they have been so important to Henry II?

2 Refer back to Source 2 and Extract 1 as well as the text above. What conclusions can you draw about the key characteristics Henry II was looking for in his choice of official?

EXTEND YOUR KNOWLEDGE

Was Henry II anti-baron?

Henry II certainly weakened the barons' powerbase. However, his drive to extend royal power was not aimed only at them. Henry II was, for example, mindful of the development of towns and boroughs, not allowing them to develop communes (semi-autonomous towns, which largely ran their own affairs), which was the trend on the continent. Barons continued their role in advising the king, raising troops and maintained control over their villeins. Robert of Leicester and Reginald of Cornwall are two examples of very influential barons. Even Hugh Bigod, who had run up against Henry II's strengthening of royal power, was frequently to be found at court in the 1150s and 1160s. He raised a retinue for the king's campaign against Wales in 1165, at which time he was given responsibility for Norfolk and Suffolk. Justiciars and important officials often came from the ranks of England's barons, but under Henry II that was no longer either necessary or sufficient to be given the post. He also increased the use of under-tenants and knights, for example on juries, especially when it came to the investigation of Articles of Eyre. The feudal system with its oaths of allegiance, homage and obligation was still at the heart of governing the realm, especially at local level. However, barons were monitored more than they had been before, although working with barons remained an important part of Henry's developments. The Assize of Clarendon starts:

Here begins the Assize of Clarendon, made by King Henry II, with the assent of the archbishops, bishops, abbots, earls and barons of England... In the first place, the aforesaid King Henry, with the consent of all his barons, for the preservation of peace and the keeping of justice, has enacted.

Reproduced from G.D.G. Hall, ed. and trans., *Documents Illustrating the History of Civilization in Medieval England 1066-1500*, 1969.

To think of Henry II's reforms as supporting the rights of the individual, championing the lower classes or in terms of other modern concepts is erroneous. He did have an interest in justice and there was a great deal to be done given his starting point. He certainly helped tenants in his reforms, enabling them to protect themselves against their lords and ensuring that a lord had to go through official channels to bring a case against a tenant. However, barons were still important. Failure to maintain a working relationship with them led to John's grip on the crown being seriously threatened.

ACTIVITY
SUMMARY

You should use relevant source information as well as text when completing these activities.

Henry II's finances

Create a table of all the ways in which Henry II increased royal revenue by using the topics on financial and legal reforms. Use one column for each of the topic headings.

Henry II's reforms

Henry II has been described as 'a great reforming monarch'. The word 'reform' implies improvements. From each section identify key improvements/benefits of Henry II's policies for the following: monarch; barons; knights; free men; villeins. This could be done as a table or a spider diagram. Do not expect to find evidence for all points. The patterns of evidence (where there is most/least) can be useful for drawing conclusions. Then do the same with the main concerns of each group in relation to Henry II's policies.

Money, power or justice?

This could be done as a Venn diagram, a chart or a spider diagram. What were Henry II's aims in developing the government of England: enhancing his power; justice; increasing his wealth? Review all his key policies. You might want to analyse the Assize of Clarendon, for example, in its component parts.

Success and failures

List the successes and failures of Henry II's financial and legal reforms. Break down evidence such as the restoration of the royal demesne and Assize of Clarendon and use dates where possible.

WIDER READING

Carpenter, D. *The Struggle for Mastery: Britain, 1066-1284*, Oxford University Press (2003)

Danziger, D. and Gillingham, J. *1215: The Year of Magna Carta*, Hodder & Stoughton (2003) This title contains quite a lot about Henry II and his impact on the barons; of particular use is the index on the forest and Henry's judicial reforms

Jones, D. *The Plantagenets*, Collins (2003)

Episode 2 in Tony Robinson's *Crime and Punishment* series, a documentary for Channel 4, is very interesting on Henry II's legal reforms and their wider impact; it is available on DVD

The National Archive has a wide range of source material. Although these sources are in Latin, the National Archive website also provides clear 'users' guides' on the value of the sources to historians, giving another insight into medieval history

2b.3 Henry II and the English Church, 1154–74

KEY QUESTIONS

- What problems did Henry II face with the Church in England?
- What caused the conflict between Henry II and Becket, 1162–64?
- Why was a solution so hard to find?
- How successfully was the conflict between Henry II and the Church resolved, 1172–76?

INTRODUCTION

The medieval Roman Catholic Church was an international, political organisation as well as the religious institution looked to by western Europe for moral and spiritual guidance. The pope in Rome claimed spiritual authority over everyone in feudal society, including kings. Co-operation between Crown and Church was central to medieval politics and important for both. Whoever became king was deemed to have done so, in theory, by the will of God. The archbishop of Canterbury, through his central role in the coronation ceremony, anointed the man and thus turned him into the monarch. The Church, through its religious teaching, was key in legitimising a king's right to rule. In turn, kings promised in their coronation oaths to protect and uphold the Church. By the time Henry II came to the throne in 1154, there had been two crusades to the Holy Land, called by the pope but led and fought by secular princes.

Early medieval rulers also relied upon the Church for the more practical business of government, because literacy was largely the preserve of clerics and monks. Church officials were valued and could use their role to influence important decisions in many situations. The Church also controlled a lot of land, making it extremely wealthy and powerful, plus easier to gain support for its causes. The Church was therefore a good choice for younger sons of important families who would not inherit lands and titles but could nevertheless look to be influential through attaining high office in the clergy.

Determining who was a member of the clergy was not always straightforward. Approximately five percent of the male population could claim that status, however not all of these men were ordained priests. Some, in what was termed the 'minor orders', would read lessons in church or help officiate at mass. In monasteries there were lay brothers as well as the ordained monks who were, in effect, servants, but could be considered members of the clergy.

There was a growing belief among the clergy in the 11th and 12th centuries that the Church should not sully its hands with temporal concerns but should instead devote its energies to moral and spiritual matters. These ideas, known as Gregorian reform, developed in the 11th century. Its two

1135 – Death of King Henry I

1154 – Henry II becomes king of England and appoints Archbishop of Canterbury Theobald's archdeacon, Thomas Becket, as his chancellor

1159 – The death of Pope Adrian IV results in a papal schism; Alexander III becomes the pope, while Victor IV becomes the antipope

1162 – Election of Thomas Becket as archbishop of Canterbury, who then resigns as chancellor of England

| 1135 | 1140 | 1145 | 1150 | 1155 | 1160 |

1152 – Conflict between King Stephen and the Church over its refusal to conduct the coronation of his son, Eustace

1158 – Thomas Becket leads a diplomatic mission to France to secure a marriage alliance between Henry II's son Henry and Louis VII's daughter Margaret

1161 – Death of Archbishop Theobald

core beliefs were that the Church was set apart from all other orders in society and that there should be **papal primacy**. Gregorian reform also aimed at establishing higher moral standards for clergy and returning the Church to its purer, more spiritual roots. This reform could, in theory, impede the authority of secular authorities to exercise power over such matters as key Church appointments in their states, or to restrict the role played by the clergy in government.

Given what was potentially at stake, with the clergy being both subjects of the overlords from whom the Church held its lands as well as sworn to obey the pope, clashes between Crown and Church were inevitable. Such conflict was, in any case, nothing new, but the murder of an archbishop at the hands of the Crown was.

> **KEY TERM**
>
> Papal primacy
> The idea that the pope has supreme power over the Church and should exercise his power over it unhindered.

WHAT PROBLEMS DID HENRY II FACE WITH THE CHURCH IN ENGLAND?

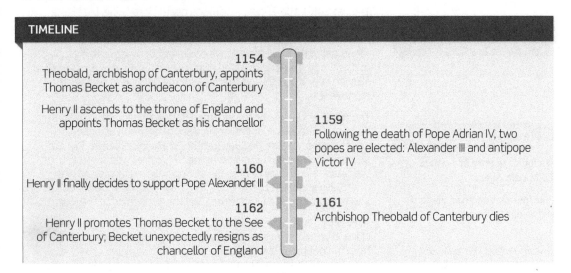

TIMELINE

1154
Theobald, archbishop of Canterbury, appoints Thomas Becket as archdeacon of Canterbury

Henry II ascends to the throne of England and appoints Thomas Becket as his chancellor

1159
Following the death of Pope Adrian IV, two popes are elected: Alexander III and antipope Victor IV

1160
Henry II finally decides to support Pope Alexander III

1161
Archbishop Theobald of Canterbury dies

1162
Henry II promotes Thomas Becket to the See of Canterbury; Becket unexpectedly resigns as chancellor of England

Papal influence

Co-operation between Crown and Church was important for both parties in the Middle Ages. Whoever became king was deemed to have done so, in theory, by the will of God. The Church, through its religious teaching and central role in the coronation ceremony, was key in legitimising a king's right to rule. Without the Church's support a king's reign could be severely weakened, if not untenable. In turn, kings promised in their coronation oath to uphold the Church.

1164 – Henry draws up the Constitutions of Clarendon. Becket summoned to trial Northampton on charges of embezzlement. Becket flees England.

1172 – In Ireland, Henry II establishes a council of clergy to reform the Irish Church and bring it under papal control

Compromise of Avranches seals Henry II's forgiveness for Becket's murder

1174 – Henry II returns to England and does penance at Canterbury

1187 – The pope calls for the Third Crusade to the Holy Land

1189 – Henry II dies, without going on crusade

| 1165 | 1170 | 1175 | 1180 | 1185 | 1190 |

1163 – Henry II is inundated with complaints about criminal clergy upon his return to England

1170 – June: Coronation of Henry II's oldest son, the Young King

1 December: Thomas Becket returns to England

29 December: Thomas Becket is murdered at Canterbury Cathedral

1173 – Thomas Becket is canonised

1176 – Final details of reconciliation of Henry II with the Church are worked out and agreed

1188 – Henry II raises the Saladin tithe, a tax to help fund the crusade

SOURCE 1

From *The Annals of Roger of Hoveden* (also known as Roger of Howden), describing the duties of the king in a section called 'The Laws of Henry the Second'. From 1174, Roger of Hoveden served Henry II in a number of important roles, often negotiating between the king and religious houses. His writing tended to side with the king. The pope mentioned is probably the seventh-century John IV.

The king, as being the **vicegerent** of the Supreme King [God] is appointed for the purpose of showing due respect to and protecting the worldly kingdom and the people of God, and, above all things, His Holy Church and of ruling and defending it from those who would injure it, and of removing from it, and crushing and utterly dispersing all evil-doers; and if he does not do so, then the name of king will not belong to him, pope John truly testifying that he loses his name of king who does not act as king.

KEY TERM

Vicegerent
Deputy ruler, usually administrative.

AS Level Exam-Style Question Section A

Why is Source 1 valuable to the historian for an enquiry into where power and authority ultimately lay in the Middle Ages?

Explain your answer, using the source, the information given about it and your own knowledge of the historical context. (8 marks)

Tip
Do not expect the source to provide you with 'the answer' concerning where power and authority lay. History is real life, albeit in the past, and things are rarely clear cut.

Throughout the 12th century, there had been increasing Church interference in Crown affairs. Henry I had been sent numerous papal letters concerning his approach to the Church, and this greater willingness of the papacy to intervene in even very minor matters continued into the reign of Henry II. It led to increasing numbers of English clergy applying to the pope for bulls of protection and privilege for their church or abbey. However, the lands and properties held by the Church were granted by the king, for which there were feudal obligations. The relationship between the English Church and the English king was therefore complicated. Did issues over the privileges and rights of Church properties concern the pope or the king?

Papal support had been important to Henry in becoming king of England. Archbishop Theobald, supported by the pope and England's bishops, had refused to crown Stephen's son, Eustace, king and thus establish him as his father's heir. In addition, the English clergy had taken an oath to punish any breach of the Treaty of Westminster (see pages 288 and 292) with **excommunication** or **interdict**. As such it was important for Henry II to maintain the support of the Church, especially in the early years of his reign. However, by 1160, papal schism had put the king in a stronger position.

Papal influence has already been seen in Henry's actions in Ireland. According to John of Salisbury, as early as 1155 Henry II wrote to Pope Adrian IV seeking his permission to invade Ireland. Although the eventual expedition did not result directly from a papal directive, Henry's approval from Pope Alexander III in 1172 was important, especially at a time when Henry's reputation was suffering owing to the murder of the archbishop of Canterbury, Thomas Becket. Politically, Henry needed to make amends with the Church to strengthen his own position.

EXTEND YOUR KNOWLEDGE

Battle Abbey – a case study in papal influence
The case of Battle Abbey, which was heard by the king, highlights the issue of how uncertain division of authority was. During the hearing, Bishop Hilary of Chichester was severely rebuked by Henry for his belief that the pope alone could grant privileges to members of the clergy. The king believed that his own, God-given prerogatives allowed him to do this and that William the Conqueror had set the precedent.

The privileges in question concerned Battle Abbey, in the Chichester diocese. There was a long-running dispute between Bishop Hilary and the abbot, Walter de Lucy (brother of Henry's justiciar, Richard de Lucy – see page 313) over whether the abbey was subject to the bishop's authority or not. The bishop believed it was and had eventually appealed to the pope, as a result of which Walter de Lucy was excommunicated. Walter de Lucy then appealed to the king.

At Henry's court hearing, the abbot produced a charter, which he claimed was from William the Conqueror, freeing Battle Abbey from the bishop of Chichester's authority. If this royal charter was accepted, then so was the idea that a king had the right to intervene in ecclesiastical affairs and grant ecclesiastical privileges to clergy. Bishop Hilary believed that this right was the pope's alone. When presenting his case before the king, Hilary stated his belief that the Church should be free of all secular control and that the pope was the ultimate source of authority for the clergy. Unsurprisingly, Henry did not agree and accused Hilary of attacking his God-given royal prerogatives. Hilary, he believed, owed loyalty to him, by his oath of fealty. According to *The Chronicle of Battle Abbey*, the king terrified the bishop into submission.

The Battle Abbey case also shows, therefore, that members of the clergy were happy to accept royal jurisdiction when it suited them. It also shows that whereas the king saw the clergy as his subjects, bound to the feudal system with oaths of fealty and gifts of land, many in the Church believed that there was a higher authority in the pope.

KEY TERMS

Excommunication
Religious punishment, administered by the Church, banishing someone from the Church and therefore the sacraments such as Holy Communion, confession and the last rites.

Interdict
Religious punishment, banning a person or place from Church services and privileges.

Church courts

Church jurisdiction and canon law

The Church had its own laws, known as canon law, and its own courts, which heard cases on issues such as heresy, blasphemy, usury, sorcery, marriage, adultery and also any crime in which a member of the clergy was accused. This right for members of the clergy to be tried in a Church court was known as 'benefit of clergy'. Approximately five percent of the male population could claim it, although not all were ordained.

The Church was one step ahead of Henry II's justiciar, Ranulf de Glanvill, in establishing its laws and legal procedure. This codification of canon law had taken an important step forward in c1140 with the publication of Gratian's *Concordia,* setting out one, authoritative source of canon law. Its underlying principle was papal superiority over even secular powers, at least in theory. Alongside this was a growing belief in the Church, especially among monks, that obedience to papal authority was paramount. This was potentially very threatening to monarchical authority.

Overlapping jurisdictions

Certain legal cases had very blurred boundaries when it came to determining whether they belonged in a Church or secular court. For example, suppose a layman was suing a member of the clergy. Should the case be heard in a Church court? Could the layman expect impartial justice in a Church court? What about cases concerning Church property? The Church received its land from the king. What about cases where members of the clergy committed crimes that came under Crown pleas, such as murder, rape or robbery? Those crimes were under the remit of royal justices. Weren't the clergy the king's subjects too?

There was also the issue that ecclesiastical courts applied much more lenient sentences to clergy than they could expect from a secular judge, usually some form of penance. Any fines applied in Church courts would go to the Church, which would have provided more incentive to establish clearly which cases belonged to whose courts.

The Church's attitude to moral offences

Church jurisdiction over the lay community

The Church ruled on issues such as marriage and it stated that the essence of marriage was freedom of consent; both bride and groom had to participate of their own, free will. There were bans on marriages where people were more closely related than sixth cousins, and there were bans on marrying in-laws or godparents. Other issues over which the Church could preside included adultery, blasphemy, heresy, bastardy and a range of moral issues. The prosecution of moral offences was very irregular, there was no standardised system. When it came to the morals of the clergy there were more problems to be tackled.

Criminous clerks

The treatment of criminous **clerks** (clergy who had been accused of committing a serious crime) was central to Henry II's dispute with Becket. The Church's attitude to the morality of its clergy was often lax, despite the development of a movement within it that saw clergy as a distinct, separate class of people who should be treated differently *but* should also act differently. Many of the clergy had privileged positions in society and yet there was plenty of evidence that this was often abused.

Extortion

One lesser example of a criminous clerk was a case of extortion brought against a dean in the archdiocese of York. He had falsely accused a woman of adultery and then taken a bribe from her husband in return for her acquittal. He was summoned before Henry II and confessed. The archbishop of York's treasurer then insisted he be handed over to the Church. In response to Richard de Lucy's angry outburst that the treasurer was overlooking the king's authority, the archbishop of York's treasurer replied that the king had none because the culprit was a priest.

> **KEY TERM**
>
> Clerk
> Another term for a member of the clergy, commonly used in the Middle Ages.

Rape and murder

Hundreds of serious crimes committed by clergy were documented, including rape, murder, robbery and violent offences. Between 1154 and 1163, when Henry was confronted with the issue, there had been over 100 murders alone committed by clerks. The majority of these offences were committed against lay people. Even accepting that the Church had its own system of laws and courts, Henry had an obligation to provide justice for *all* his subjects. The issue was whether all his subjects were receiving justice if the clergy were tried in their own courts. The evidence presented to Henry suggested not.

One significant case was that of Philip de Brois, a clergyman in Bedford. He was charged with murdering a knight and acquitted by the bishop of Lincoln's court, but the sheriff of Bedford was dissatisfied with the outcome and attempted to re-open the case in king's courts in summer 1163; Philip reacted abusively towards him. The king was informed and angrily demanded justice on two counts: homicide and disrespecting a royal officer. Although Henry wanted Philip de Brois to be tried again in a secular court, he did agree to the Church courts handling the matter again. Philip de Brois was found guilty. In trying to appease the king with a harsher punishment, the then archbishop of Canterbury, Thomas Becket, went beyond the limits of his authority by banishing Philip de Brois; this was a punishment reserved for the Crown. He made the same error when sentencing a priest from Bow, in London, to branding for having stolen a silver chalice from the Church of St Mary.

Another case for which Henry demanded trial in a secular court was that of a priest in Worcestershire accused of raping a girl and murdering her father. From Henry's point of view, any ordained member of the clergy who broke their vows to these extents no longer merited the privilege of a Church court. In the wider context of increasing Crown authority and, over the course of his reign, harsher punishments for law breakers generally, the demand that clergy who committed non-religious crimes be tried in the king's courts fits with Henry's general approach to ruling England. However, this particular aim was taking Crown rights further than his professed goal of returning them to where they had been at the end of Henry I's reign in 1135. This therefore suggests that Henry had a wider agenda when it came to the Church.

By 1164 there were other, more personal issues with the clergy directly contributing to the serious conflict between Crown and Church that emerged in 1164. However, even before then there was friction between these twin sources of power that, in reality, ultimately needed one another to ensure and enforce obedience to their authority.

Clerical interference in secular affairs

The Church's role in the realm

The Church had plenty of potential to interfere in secular affairs. High clergy often held high government office and when, for example, Henry II first established the idea of the King's Bench, two of the five justices he appointed were clerks. Bishop Nigel of Ely was tasked with re-establishing the Exchequer, and chancery relied upon clergy to function. Despite the important role these clerics played, from the point of view of the king there was another potential authority in the land that could cause conflict. One dispute in the 12th century had resulted in the archbishop of Canterbury withholding homage to King Henry I. This was not the sort of precedent to which Henry II wished to return.

There was also an increase in both the number of ecclesiastical courts and the number of cases they heard. This trend had been growing during the 12th century, stemming from Church reforms that increased the status and jurisdiction of the Church. In the 11th century, Pope Gregory VII (1073–85) had set about trying to centralise and reform its government, emphasising its divinely ordered status. He had insisted that all important Church appeals be referred to Rome and, in the 12th century, the codification of Church law was undertaken. Complete by around 1140, it defined the laws and jurisdictions of the Church and contributed to the increase in ecclesiastical courts and cases. Furthermore, the clergy increasingly looked to Rome, rather than the king, to settle disputes over Church lands and privileges.

The Church and politics

Another example of the Church's potentially limiting the king's ability to manoeuvre in secular affairs concerned the coronation of Henry's heir, also called Henry, who became known as the Young King. Henry II had benefitted from the archbishop of Canterbury's refusal to crown Stephen's son, Eustace, to ensure a smooth transition after Stephen's death. Crowning the heir while the old king was still alive, and reigning, although not an established custom in England, was not unknown and there was no particular reason for Theobald to have refused.

For Henry II, his son's coronation was important in establishing young Henry's position as heir to the throne. He had planned for contingencies, securing papal dispensation that the archbishop of York could conduct the ceremony if there were no archbishop of Canterbury. This was exactly the situation in 1162. Theobald had died in the spring of 1161 and, although he approached Thomas Becket about becoming archbishop in February 1162, the chancellor wavered over his decision for weeks. Henry therefore instructed the archbishop of York to crown the Young King, but the bishops in the archdiocese of Canterbury refused to participate, even with Henry's papal dispensation. The coronation did not go ahead.

However, Henry also intervened in Church matters. At the end of the 1150s, the Church was weakened by papal schism. Upon Adrian IV's death in 1159, two popes emerged: Alexander III and the antipope Victor IV. Henry issued a writ in December 1159 forbidding any contact with the papacy until he had made his decision whom to support. This was to be expected. By 1161, however, relations between Henry II and Theobald were deteriorating. Evidence from John, the dean of Salisbury's, letters, suggests that Theobald was disappointed that the king had used the papal schism to secure the marriage of five-year-old Prince Henry and his younger French bride, Princess Margaret, by offering to support Alexander's papacy in return. Thus, Henry II secured the Vexin, a vitally strategic piece of land on the borders of Normandy (see page 360). Furthermore, Theobald believed that the king had deliberately withheld information to which he, as archbishop of Canterbury, ought to have been privy. This reflects a general downturn in Crown–Church relations by the 1160s.

EXTEND YOUR KNOWLEDGE

Gregorian reform

A dispute between Pope Gregory VII and the Holy Roman Emperor, Henry IV, in the 11th century is generally seen as the starting point for a major reform of the Roman Catholic Church. Stemming from the issue of whether a secular ruler had the right to invest bishops and abbots, it led Gregory VII to establish a clear set of rights and regulations governing the Church and its relations with secular authorities.

Gregory saw the Church as a divine institution and therefore supreme, with authority over monarchs and states. In practical, political terms it was not possible to enforce this. However, he did set about trying to centralise the government of the Church, insisting that all important appeals and issues be referred to Rome. This movement continued into the 12th century and beyond, although many bishops did not want to come under the pope's authority to that extent, preferring the freedom to build their own power bases in their own countries.

The influence of Gregorian reform can be seen in Thomas Becket's attitude to the relationship between Church and Crown after he became archbishop of Canterbury in 1162. For example, he insisted that the clergy were a separate, special group under their own king and laws. His letters to Henry II, written in 1166, also reinforce the idea of Church superiority over lay rulers.

ACTIVITY
KNOWLEDGE CHECK

1 What does Source 1 suggest about the relationship between Crown and Church in the Middle Ages?

2 Make a bullet point list of evidence that Henry II should have been concerned about in relation to the Church impinging on his prerogatives as king of England.

3 What evidence is there that the Church needed to protect itself from Henry II?

4 To what degree was authority in England divided between the Crown on one hand and the Church on the other? Using your notes in answer to questions 1–3, select five pieces of evidence that support your decision.

WHAT CAUSED CONFLICT BETWEEN HENRY II AND BECKET 1162–64?

TIMELINE

1162
Thomas Becket becomes archbishop of Canterbury and resigns from his position as chancellor of England

1163
January Henry II arrives back in England and receives hundreds of complaints against criminous clerks

October Council of Westminster

December Pope Alexander III sends envoys to Becket asking him to reconcile with the king; Becket agrees

1164
January Council meeting at Clarendon; Constitutions of Clarendon are produced

October Becket attends king's court at Northampton to answer charges against him; he flees to France

December Henry II takes action against Becket, his family and household

Why was Becket elected as archbishop of Canterbury in 1162?

Becket had already served Henry II loyally as Chancellor, promoting the king's interests and taking on duties that Henry found burdensome, such as entertaining dignitaries or the more ceremonial aspects of kingship. With Becket in position as archbishop of Canterbury, Henry felt that he would have a much better chance of bringing the Church in England under royal authority, especially as the Church was weakened by schism.

Convincing the Church

Thomas Becket wavered for weeks after Henry asked him to be archbishop of Canterbury in February 1162. Ironically, Becket thought that it would bring his good relationship with the king to an end. There were other potential candidates who might be considered but, more practically, there were the revenues to be gained from keeping the post vacant. The king's position as feudal overlord allowed him to collect the rents and revenues from any bishop's or abbot's lands where there was not an incumbent member of the clergy and therefore decisions about new appointments were often delayed.

Perhaps the most likely alternative choice to Becket was Gilbert Foliot, bishop of Hereford and, from 1163, bishop of London. He is recorded as having opposed Becket's appointment and he was not the only one. The monks of Canterbury were not convinced that he was an appropriate choice. They were finally persuaded by Richard de Lucy, his brother Walter de Lucy, abbot of Battle Abbey, Hilary, bishop of Chichester, and some other bishops that Becket would be a useful mediator in Crown–Church relations, indicating that one was necessary. Gilbert Foliot remained unconvinced. The king had his way and Thomas Becket was ordained.

Henry II chose Thomas Becket for his archbishop of Canterbury as he expected him to remain chancellor and, combining the two posts, would help him to achieve control over the Church in England. Becket, however, resigned as chancellor, much to Henry's annoyance, and threw himself into his new role. This appears to have been the start of the breakdown in relations between Becket and the king.

Becket's transformation

Often depicted as a worldly man who enjoyed drinking and womanising with Henry II, Becket became a very religious man once archbishop of Canterbury. The reason for this is a matter of debate, but Becket's change into a pious, serious member of the clergy seems to have been sudden and complete. When his body was being prepared for burial, it was found that he wore a hair shirt, which chafed the skin and crawled with lice, and his body showed signs of scourging. Whatever lay behind his change in behaviour and the resulting apparent change in allegiance, Henry II was furious. Becket had, in his eyes, betrayed him, something he found very hard to forgive.

Henry's demands for reform

From the outset of his reign, Henry had asserted royal authority over his tenants-in-chief, ruling the kingdom with a strong government that increasingly standardised financial and legal procedures. Bringing justice, and law and order under more centralised control, with greater powers for Crown officials, was bound to cause tension. Henry wanted to impose a new, standardised system for dealing with criminous clerks in England, seeing it as an issue of his authority. He had raised the matter upon his return to England in January 1163, when he had been inundated with complaints of serious crimes committed by clergy.

It could be said that Henry II's approach to the Church was part of a wider agenda that included the Assize of Clarendon, the Inquest of Sheriffs, the Assize of Northampton and the development of common law. Although his attempt to deal with the Church came before these other initiatives, Henry's wider aims are important to understanding the context of what he wanted to achieve. However, as the boundaries of Crown rights and authority were extended and strengthened, the issue of where ultimate authority lay for the clergy was brought into greater focus.

How did Henry II see the political relationship between Church and Crown?

Henry II wished to restore England, and especially Crown authority, to what it had been in 1135. This was central to the Church reforms he presented. Although Henry I's relationship with the Church had not always been smooth, he did secure some recognition from the papacy of the 'customs' of the Norman kings who preceded him. William the Conqueror had imposed restrictions upon the clergy including the following.

- Clergy could only obey a papal summons with permission from the king.

- No-one could receive a letter from the pope unless the king had read it first, and agreed.

- No **papal legates** could visit England without the king's permission.

> **KEY TERM**
>
> Papal legate
> Someone sent by the pope to represent him at the courts of other sovereigns and rulers. Usually, but not necessarily, an ordained member of the Roman Catholic Church.

Henry I also negotiated with the papacy to keep the homage of the bishops and abbots who received land from the Crown; in other words, it tied them into the feudal system of which he was overlord.

The reforms that Henry II presented to the Church in 1163 reflected the status quo under his grandfather and was based upon these rights and powers. However, it also went further in attempting to extend the Crown's reach over clergy who had committed serious, non-religious crimes.

The Council of Westminster, October 1163

The first important clash between the king and his archbishop of Canterbury came after the Philip de Brois case in summer 1163. It also followed hot on the heels of Becket excommunicating one of the Henry's tenants-in-chief without referring the matter to the king, which was not the way that either William the Conqueror or Henry I had insisted things were done.

In October 1163, at a council meeting in Westminster, Henry demanded that all clergy accused of crimes be handed over to his officers after trial for sentencing. Becket would not agree to this. The Church alone, he said, should continue to try criminous clerks. There was some discussion among certain bishops that canon law allowed for convicted priests to be returned to secular courts for punishment at the discretion of the bishop. In a few cases this had already happened in England.

However, Becket was not prepared to relinquish his point. The guidance implied in the Bible, he claimed, was that God does not judge in the same case twice, and therefore to punish clergy more than once was against God's word. Stripping a man of his clerical status was sufficient punishment. Furthermore, he argued a point that directly undermined Henry's authority: that the clergy were separate from the rest of the population; Christ was their king and they were ruled, and punished, according to their own laws. This reflected a significant body of opinion in the 12th century Church, more generally among monks rather than clergy who were involved in the more practical world of government and secular politics.

The crunch point came when Henry asked the clergy if they were prepared to stand by the customs of England and acknowledge that he had the same prerogatives as his predecessors. Yes, replied Becket, the Church would honour and observe the customs of England *saving our order*. This phrase was a qualification meaning in effect that they would not agree to anything they believed went against the Church or canon law.

Henry stormed away from Westminster. He confiscated all the castles held by Becket directly from the Crown and removed his son, young Henry, from the archbishop's household. Although the battle lines had been drawn, the situation was in no way irretrievable. However, Henry II was a determined man, confident in his God-given prerogatives, very sure of his own rights and status and equally sure that his archbishop could be made to submit. Thomas Becket was also a very determined man, confident in his God-given prerogatives and also aware of his new rights and status. Two such personalities were bound to clash.

The aftermath of the Council of Westminster

Henry II summoned Becket to a private meeting at Northampton. The two men met in a field to discuss their differences alone, but the archbishop was adamant that any agreement had to have the qualifying statement 'saving our order' added to it. This was, essentially, a licence to disregard anything the Church did not agree with. Henry would not accept Becket's terms.

When informed of events at Westminster, Pope Alexander III, who needed Henry II's support against the antipope Victor IV, sent envoys to Becket with orders for him to be more conciliatory.

Becket eventually gave his verbal agreement to observe the 'ancient customs' of Henry I's reign, but the king wanted Becket to give his agreement before the barons and bishops of the realm because Becket's defiance at Westminster had been public. Becket agreed to do as Henry wanted at a council at Clarendon, near Salisbury, in January 1164.

> **SOURCE 2**
>
> Letter written by Gilbert Foliot, bishop of London, to Thomas Becket circa September 1166. Gilbert Foliot, an older, more experienced bishop, disliked Becket whom he regarded as an upstart.

The kingdom gave devoted and holy service to the priesthood; and the priesthood very strongly supported to god effect every command of the king … They did not oppose one another or taking opposite positions challenge one another. There was one people … The peace of Church and kingdom consisted in this: each cherished the other … and were joined in unanimous will … we were hoping … for an increase of graces with your promotion, and see, from that moment, everything was turned upside down … a man of your prudence should have ensured that the disagreements gradually arising between the kingdom and you did not grow too serious and you did not grow too serious, that a tiny spark did not flare up into so great a fire, to the ruin of many.

> **SOURCE 3**
>
> From an Icelandic saga, written in the early 14th century, using earlier Latin and French accounts. It describes the Council of Westminster in October 1163. The original saga, now lost, was written in the mid 13th century, but an account of Becket and his death appeared in another religious saga around 1200, so Becket's story was known in Iceland from at least that time.

'We have been silent awhile' [Henry] said, 'and meekly listened how you bishops are willing to dispose yourselves towards our royal rights and rule here in England. Now that we have been watching your doings we have been thinking and peacefully searching our mind, as to what kind of fault ye might happen to have found in us, that we must needs be deemed less worthy than other kings, who have been before us, to wear an untottering Crown, in virtue of such law, enactments and royal prerogatives, as each one has had and enjoyed in due succession, and no learned men before you listed to withdraw from royal honour …

But with greater truth we know, that there are with us men so wise [who] have testified to be a true interpretation of the law that evil-doers, even such as are ordained, shall be delivered unto rightful punishment by kingly power.'

> **SOURCE 4**
>
> A 14th-century depiction of Becket before Henry II.

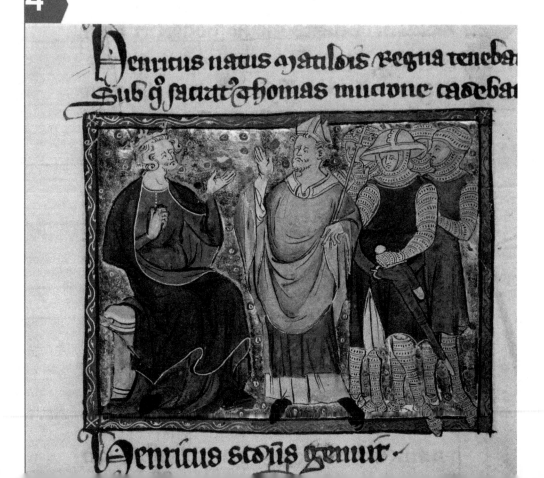

The Constitutions of Clarendon

The council convened at Clarendon in January 1164 lasted two weeks. There Becket was supposed to publicly promise to abide by England's 'ancient customs'. What he was not expecting, however, was the Constitutions of Clarendon, a written list of 16 clauses defining the relationship between secular and canon law to which the bishops were expected to put their seals. The document asserted the power of the Crown over the Church in England. Becket knew that the verbal agreement to customs that were not written down that he had agreed to was very different from what Henry now wanted.

Henry had 'moved the goalposts'. As far as he was concerned, Becket had promised to abide by the customs of England. It is true that key parts of the Constitutions did indeed reflect the practices of Henry I, which the Church had accepted and therefore were the customs of England. However, the way in which the Constitutions of Clarendon were written did more than that. The Constitutions were specific about the limitations of the clergy's authority. Those parts that were open to interpretation were the king's rights, such as when he would give permission for appeals to Rome. Any such interpretation depended on the royal will. The stakes were high and Becket was uncertain of how to proceed.

Key clauses

The key cause of contention was clause 3, which attempted to deal with the 'criminous clerks' issue. Henry II wanted clergy accused of a crime to go first to the royal court to establish their clerical status. This status was not as clear cut as it sounds because it did not just include ordained men; it could include lay brothers and other, minor orders. If they were clergy they could be tried by a Church court. Any clergy found guilty by the Church court would have their clerical status rescinded and they were then to be handed back to the secular court for punishment.

The Constitutions of Clarendon also reinforced the feudal relationship between the king and senior clergy and would have ensured the monarch's authority over the Church in certain circumstances. For example:

- Clause 4: Bishops and archbishops could not leave England without royal assent.

- Clause 7: Barons and royal officials could not be excommunicated (a sentence that was the pope's prerogative) without royal permission having been obtained first.

- Clause 8: There was to be no appeal to the pope in clerical cases without the king's permission.

- Clause 9: Any land dispute that involved clergy had first to go to a local jury who would decide whether it was held under a Church tenure. If so, then the matter would go to the Church courts. Otherwise, the dispute would stay in the king's courts.

- Clause 11: Clergy holding land from the king as tenants-in-chief were liable for the usual feudal services.

However, clauses 10 and 13 of the Constitutions of Clarendon did safeguard the Church against obstruction by the king's officials or intimidation by the nobility:

- Clause 10: Anyone from a city or the royal demesne who did not obey a Church summons for an offence could be placed under interdict and the matter referred to the king's local officials. If the officials failed to support the Church, they would be punished by the king and the accused dealt with by the bishop.

- Clause 13: Nobles who prevented the Church from doing justice to, or for, its own people were to answer to the king.

These two clauses of the 16 that made up the Constitutions of Clarendon did support the Church, although Becket complained that, overall, the Church's rights and Church privileges were very restricted.

Becket's attitude to reform

The bishops did not want to remove the qualification 'saving our order' from their agreement to abide by the customs of England as laid down by Henry. Becket stood firm alongside them, despite being locked in a room for two days of constant threats and intimidation as the king sent barons to browbeat them into submission. On the third day, Becket capitulated and agreed to Henry's demands, swearing an oath to keep the customs of the realm demanded by the king. This gave the bishops little choice but to follow suit.

However, Becket realised his mistake when he was presented with a *written* version of the Constitutions of Clarendon very soon afterwards, to which Henry insisted the bishops put their seals. Becket refused. Sealing a written agreement was more binding than making a written one, and when the terms defining Crown rights were so generous at the expense of the Church. Although Becket had made a stand, he had alienated his bishops. They refused to put their seals to the Constitutions of Clarendon, but unfortunately their verbal agreement was sufficient. They had sworn to uphold customs they disliked, following the lead of their archbishop who now refused to seal the document as the king commanded.

Becket's next move compounded his difficult situation. He accepted a chirograph from Henry. This was a document copied out three times and cut with jagged edges that could later be matched up to guard against forgeries. By accepting a copy, Becket was legally binding the Church to the Constitutions of Clarendon.

THINKING HISTORICALLY | Causation (6b)

Attitudes and actions

Individuals can only make choices based on their context. Prevalent attitudes combine with individual experience and natural temperament to frame an individual's perception of what is going on around them. Nobody can know the future or see into the minds of others.

Context

Henry II wanted to restore royal authority in England to what it had been in 1135 in all spheres, including the Church. This included the limits on the Church's powers imposed by Henry I, as well as a new clause concerning the king's right to punish clergy guilty of secular crimes.

Henry II had chosen Becket to be archbishop of Canterbury because he believed Becket would serve his interests as effectively as he had as chancellor. He intended Becket to remain as chancellor, but Becket resigned, infuriating Henry.

At the start of 1163, Henry had been presented with hundreds of complaints about the clergy committing serious crimes including murder, rape and robbery.

When Henry first put forward the guidelines that were to define Crown-Church relations at Westminster in 1163, Becket had only consented 'saving our order'. This was unacceptable to Henry II, but Becket gave in and agreed publicly at Clarendon to drop the qualification.

There was a papal schism and Pope Alexander III wanted Henry II's support against the antipope Victor IV.

At Clarendon, the bishops would not agree to drop the qualification 'saving our order' and Becket supported them. After three days of intimidation, he told the bishops to swear to uphold what became known as the Constitutions of Clarendon without any qualification.

Action

Henry II then 'moved the goalposts'. He presented Thomas Becket with a written document containing the Constitutions of Clarendon and requiring the seal of all England's bishops. There had not been any indication that the clergy would have to put their names to a written agreement. This pushed Becket too far.

Answer the following questions individually and then discuss your answers in a group.

1 Why might Henry II have believed that Thomas Becket would agree to sign a written document?

2 Why might Henry II have thought publicly at Clarendon that his demands were reasonable?

3 Why might Henry II have believed that the pope would agree to his restrictions upon the power of the Church in England?

4 Why might Becket have changed his mind and told the bishops to agree to the Constitutions of Clarendon, without qualification?

5 How far should the historian try to understand the context of the beliefs and values of people in the past when explaining why individuals make choices in history?

Gilbert Foliot, writing to Becket in 1166, admonished Becket's weak leadership at Clarendon, describing the bishops as being 'thunderstruck' and 'clinging to each other in astonishment' at the turn of events. Becket's own letters say that he opposed the Constitutions in his name only in order to divert the king's wrath from the bishops. He reinforced this by later offering his resignation to the pope on the grounds that his leadership and advice to the bishops had been poor, and that by encouraging them to accept the Constitutions of Clarendon he had done great damage to the institution he was supposed to protect. He had failed in his loyalty to the Church. Henry also saw an issue of loyalty, but in his eyes it was an act of treachery by one of his vassals.

Becket must take some of the blame for this by his actions: he had capitulated, signed and then gone back upon his word. He lacked the ecclesiastical experience of his bishops and had been weak in giving in when they had supported him, although given the high stakes and the pressures of the situation mistakes were almost bound to be made. Unfortunately the consequences were serious, and ultimately fatal.

EXTEND YOUR KNOWLEDGE

Becket and the chirograph

After the bishops and archbishops put their seals on the Constitutions of Clarendon, Henry ordered a chirograph to be made. This was a legal document, upon which the terms of an agreement were written out three times on a single piece of parchment and then cut into individual copies with deliberately jagged edges. This meant that it would always be possible to tell the actual copy presented in case of dispute by matching it to the other two. When Becket accepted his copy, it was taken as his legally binding consent to the Constitutions of Clarendon in both secular and canon law.

The historian John Guy cites Roger of Pontigny's account of this significant event as a deliberate act on Becket's part when the archbishop openly stated to the king that he intended to take it only 'as precaution and defence of the Church, so that by this evidence we may know what is done against us'.

This shows a level of political naivety that is surprising when it comes to Becket. He was an experienced member of the king's Curia and and successful political operator at court. He must have known the significance of what he was doing and of the slant that Henry II would give his actions. The king portrayed the archbishop as having accepted a legally binding agreement to the Constitutions of Clarendon, which was strong evidence in Henry's favour.

However, Henry's mother, Matilda, saw Henry's writing down of the Constitutions of Clarendon as his most important mistake, coupled with his hatred of Becket clouding his judgement. She also disagreed with some of the clauses and felt that the Church needed reassurance that the king's justices would not attack its liberties.

Later events in France, when Becket went to Pope Alexander (see below), reinforce Pontigny's account that Becket took the chirograph as irrefutable proof of Henry's intent towards the Church, which the king could not deny either. It could be seen as a shrewd move on Becket's part, making it hard for Henry to deny how significant and, to some extent, unprecedented were the demands he was making of the Church in England.

ACTIVITY
KNOWLEDGE CHECK

1. The Constitutions of Clarendon were about more than criminous clerks. Using the information in the text and the text of the Constitutions itself, which can be found online, identify the ways in which it strengthened Henry II's position according to whether they:

   a) concern issues of justice

   b) concern his position as feudal overlord

   c) concern Henry's authority over the Church in England.

2 A traditional portrayal of the relationship between Becket and Henry II is shown in the 1964 film *Becket*, which is available on DVD and can also be found online.

   a) Which character is shown more sympathetically, Becket or Henry II?

   b) What does it suggest about Becket's transformation upon becoming archbishop of Canterbury?

3 Which events leading to the failure of the Council of Clarendon can be blamed on Henry II?

4 Did Becket betray Henry II? Find evidence for and against opposing views.

Conflict between king and archbishop

The conflict between Crown and Church, Henry and Becket, continued throughout 1164 until it came to a head in Northampton that October, with a court case designed to force the archbishop's resignation. The king decided to use the forum of his own court to attack Becket as a tenant-in-chief. After days of tension, threats and intimidation, and with the outcome bound to go against him, Becket finally resorted to fleeing England.

Summer 1164

Henry initially summoned Becket to his court in September 1164 concerning the case of John fitz Gilbert, one of Becket's own vassals who was also marshal of the royal household. John fitz Gilbert had brought a grievance to the archbishop's court, where it had been dismissed. He then complained to the king who, as overlord, sent for the archbishop to appear before his court. However, Becket did not attend. His position was that John fitz Gilbert's case had been an empty, frivolous one.

The case, highlights again the problems of where the boundaries lay when it came to Crown–Church jurisdictions. Henry had summoned Becket as his vassal, but Becket had replied as the archbishop of Canterbury. This led Henry to summon him to Northampton on matters unconnected with the Church. Events there and in the aftermath do not show the king in a good light.

Northampton, October 1164

Becket was summoned to Northampton for contempt of court, but Henry then added an accusation of embezzlement from when Becket was still chancellor. Once more the king was 'moving the goalposts' in the hope of achieving his aim: bringing down the archbishop of Canterbury. By focusing on Becket's career as chancellor, he could avoid giving him the opportunity to pose as defender of the Church. This moved the battle to the firmer ground of what were clearly secular crimes belonging under the Crown's jurisdiction. Nevertheless, there were still problems in separating Church and Crown: a decision in the king's court was arrived at by the tenants-in-chief, including the bishops.

Accusations of other financial misdeeds were added to the original charge. The bishops, fearing reprisals from Henry, gave judgement against Becket, although he had forbidden them from doing so. This illustrates the problem faced by the Church being part of the feudal system and so serving two masters. Did they obey the Church or the Crown? Although the clergy had often appealed to whichever authority suited their purpose, the Constitutions of Clarendon brought the question of which master ultimately had their loyalty to a head. The Constitutions of Clarendon favoured the Crown, making the restrictions on the Church clear and, as they were written down and to be sealed by the bishops, binding. Even his mother later remarked that Henry's big mistake was having the Constitutions written down for the bishops to seal.

The personalities of Henry II and Becket dominated proceedings and the situation continued to escalate. On 12 October, Becket celebrated mass, making another public gesture by taking the large, silver archiepiscopal cross from the cross bearer to make his entrance. The bishop of London tried to take it from him, but failed. Becket did have a flair for the grand gesture, as he had shown after the Constitutions of Clarendon, and as he later proved before the pope.

The bishops revealed to Henry that the archbishop of Canterbury had broken the Constitutions of Clarendon by appealing to the pope against them on the grounds that they did not have the right to judge him. When the king sent men to ask Becket if this were so, he said that he was placing himself under the pope's protection. Becket had chosen which master to serve.

Searching for a solution

For the bishops, it was not so easy. Whatever they did, they would be going against either their king or their archbishop. Becket's resignation would have offered them a way out, but he was resolute. Eventually they concocted a political solution: if the king would lift his command that they judge Becket, they would themselves appeal to Alexander III and beg the pope to remove him from his office. Henry agreed.

There was one final act to be played out. Becket refused to hear the barons' judgement over the charges of financial irregularities against him and left the chamber carrying his cross. That night he left England for France. Louis VII was more than happy to welcome Henry's latest enemy, the archbishop of Canterbury.

The fundamental problem causing the conflict was two huge, political institutions vying for authority and jurisdiction. However, when the personalities of Henry II and Thomas Becket combined with the politics and legal theories, the arguments and counter-arguments that were put forward went round in circles, unable to lead to an answer. Neither king nor archbishop would compromise.

Becket's flight into exile

Following Becket's flight to France, where Alexander III was staying as Victor IV controlled Rome, Henry II sent a mission to the pope asking him not to shelter the archbishop of Canterbury, whom he described as a 'traitor' and 'great enemy'. Although in a weak position and needing Henry on his side of the schism, the pope prevaricated.

Becket at the papal Curia

In the meantime, Becket arrived at Alexander III's papal Curia in France. Throwing himself at the pope's feet, he offered Alexander a copy of the Constitutions of Clarendon. He then went on to read it, adding his own interpretation of the king's intentions. After this, he offered the pope his archiepiscopal ring, weeping as he did so and repenting that such a tragedy had befallen the Church in England when it was supposed to be under his care. Alexander refused to accept the ring. Contrived or not, Becket's performance was well judged and made it difficult for the pope to do anything other than offer his support. Becket remained archbishop of Canterbury and the pope had shown him an important gesture of support. Becket then set up his own court at Pontigny, in France, from where he continued his fight against Henry.

SOURCE 5

Alan of Tewkesbury's account describing the bishop of London, Gilbert Foliot, addressing Pope Alexander III in November 1164. Gilbert Foliot was leading a delegation sent by King Henry II to present the king's case in his dispute with Archbishop Becket. Alan of Tewkesbury's account was written 15 years later. He collected materials on Becket as a memorial to him.

Of late there has risen in England a dissension between the king and the priesthood on a minor and unimportant matter, which could have easily been settled if discreet moderation had been shown. But my lord of Canterbury, following his own individual opinion and not acting on our advice, has pushed the matter to extremes and not taken into account the evil of the times or the harm which might arise from such hostility. In doing so he has laid a trap both for himself and his brethren. Had we given our consent to his proposals, matters would have become worse. But because we would not be led astray by him, as indeed we ought not, he has tried to lay the blame for his rashness on the lord king, on us and indeed on the whole realm. So, in order to cast infamy on us, his brethren, he has taken to flight, although not violence has been used nor even a threat uttered against him – as it is written 'The wicked fleeth when no man pursueth'.

Henry's revenge

Henry exacted revenge upon Becket's family and household over the Christmas period of 1164. He took away all the property of the archbishop of Canterbury and his clerks; all the incomes from the lands of Becket's family or clerks were withheld; he ordered the deportation of Becket's entire family and household along with anyone who had helped Becket flee England, regardless of age or infirmity. It is estimated that as many as 400 were forced to leave. Henry also prevented all revenues owed to the pope from leaving the Exchequer. There were to be no appeals to Rome without his permission and anyone bringing letters from the pope or archbishop into England was to be arrested and either hanged or cast adrift.

Even by Henry's standards, this was an impressive display of fury against the man upon whom he had relied so much since becoming king and with whom he had established a close relationship. If it was intended to force Becket to back down, it did not work. Becket stayed in France, from where he fought his battle against Henry for the next six years.

SOURCE 6

From Pope Alexander III to Thomas Becket, archbishop of Canterbury, written after the Northampton court of 1164. The pope had already declared the sentence passed against Becket (removing his goods) invalid since Becket had nothing that did not belong to the Church.

Since the days are evil and much has to be endured for the circumstances of the times, we beseech your discretion, we advise, we counsel, we urge, that in your whole conduct respecting your cause and that of the Church, you display caution, prudence, and circumspection, doing nothing in haste or precipitately, but at the right time and gravely; so that in all possible ways, consistent with the liberty of the Church and the dignity of your office, you will labour to recover the favour and good will of his majesty the king of England. And until next Easter you should uphold the said king in that you should forbear to take action against his person or territories. For then God will give us better days, and both you and we may take proceedings with safety.

AS Level Exam-Style Question Section A

How much weight do you give the evidence of Source 5 for an enquiry into why the conflict between Henry II and Becket developed in 1164?

Explain your answer using the source, the information given about it and your own knowledge of the historical context.

Tip

Read the information about the source carefully. Whose version of events is it giving – Alan of Tewkesbury's or Gilbert Foliot's?

A Level Exam-Style Question Section B

'Becket's ambition was the main cause of the conflict between Crown and Church 1162–64.' How far do you agree with this opinion?

Explain your answer. (20 marks)

Tip

As the stated factor, you need to tackle the idea of 'Becket's ambition' in some depth. You have come across some conflicting evidence about Becket as a man and as archbishop of Canterbury. Use this to your advantage to enable you to develop a discussion.

ACTIVITY
KNOWLEDGE CHECK

1 Summarise Henry II's arguments for, and Thomas Becket's arguments against, the Constitutions of Clarendon.

2 Now look at the wider conflict causing Crown–Church relations to deteriorate in 1162–64. Identify which events support the view that Becket was to blame and which events support the view that Henry II was to blame.

3 What insights can be gained from Source 5 about the pope's concerns over the escalation of the conflict between Becket and Henry II?

4 Starting with your answers to 1 and 2, compile a list of causes of the deterioration of Crown–Church relations and divide them into:

- political
- religious
- personality.

Your list should include some of the longer-term issues from earlier in the chapter. There will be some overlap, for example with political and religious causes. Think about how you will handle this when organising your evidence.

THE FAILURE TO COMPROMISE, 1169-70

TIMELINE

1169

January Henry II and Becket meet at Montmirail but fail to settle their dispute

Easter Becket excommunicates the bishops of London and Salisbury as well as several members of the royal household

September Henry II issues decrees severing links between England and Alexander III and Becket

November Henry II and Becket meet at Montmartre, Paris

1170

June Henry the Young King is crowned by the archbishop of York

July Henry II and Becket are reconciled at Frétval

1 December Becket lands in England

29 December Becket is murdered in Canterbury Cathedral

The failure to reach a settlement

After several years of conflict, Henry II and Thomas Becket agreed to meet at Montmirail in France in January 1169. The meeting was unlikely to be successful as neither man had yet reached the point where he was willing to compromise. Although Henry II made it known at the meeting that Becket had not been sent into exile, but was free to return at any time, with no conditions attached, Becket would not be moved. He did not trust the king, but there was also the issue of pride. Henry II would take back Becket as long as it did not appear that the archbishop had won. Becket was willing to return as long as it did not appear that he had lost. However, Montmirail was significant as their first meeting in over four years.

The actual aim of the conference at Montmirail was to settle differences between Henry II and Louis VII and to settle inheritances on Henry's sons. Mediators appealed to Becket to make the first move by offering to accept the matter of England's 'customs' without any qualification. It began well enough, with Becket approaching the kings of England and France and kneeling before Henry, who told him to rise. His first words also boded well: 'On the whole matter which is between us, my lord king, I throw myself on your mercy and on your pleasure.' This was swiftly followed, however, with 'saving the honour of God'. In other words, nothing had changed. Herbert of Bosham later recorded the reaction to Becket's words (Source 7).

SOURCE

7 From Herbert of Bosham's late 12th-century biography of Thomas Becket. Herbert of Bosham was a key member of Becket's household. He is describing events at Montmirail in 1169.

Henry raged at Becket denouncing him as proud, vain and ungrateful, and turning to King Louis said, 'Observe, if you please, my lord, whatever his lordship of Canterbury disapproves, he will say is contrary to God's honour, and so he will always have the advantage of me.' King Louis remonstrated with Becket, and the mediators pleaded with him, the barons, both English and French, abused him; but Becket calmly but firmly refused to withdraw his qualification, and the assembly broke up in disorder.

The pope's reaction was also swift, sending more legates to try to bring about a resolution to the conflict.

The diplomacy of Pope Alexander III

Papal diplomacy in changing circumstances

Pope Alexander had already tried to mediate the dispute since Becket first fled into exile, sending letters and envoys, attempting to rein in the archbishop of Canterbury. Becket had been made a papal legate in 1166, with the power of excommunication, and he used this power in his quarrel with Henry.

In spring 1166, he sent a series of three letters to King Henry, progressing from moderate tones in the first to angry threats in the last. In June, he had excommunicated numerous members of Henry's government, including those he held responsible for drafting the Constitutions of Clarendon, and warned the king himself that he would be subject to **anathema** unless he made amends for what he had done to the Church. Henry's retaliation was to threaten to transfer his support to the antipope, Victor IV. Given that his position was unstable, Alexander III ordered Becket not to take any further action against the king. He also appointed two more legates to England, tasking them with reconciling the conflict.

Other attempts at papal diplomacy had taken place.

- In 1167, Pope Alexander dispatched two cardinals to mediate, but they failed.

- In 1168–69, three monks succeeded in arranging the meeting at Montmirail in January 1169, which failed.

- After Montmirail, Alexander III sent two representatives, Vivian and Gratian, to negotiate a settlement, they failed.

Developing circumstances by 1169 made compromise more likely. All the while Alexander's position was under threat from the antipope, Victor IV, who was supported by the Holy Roman Emperor, Henry's position remained the stronger. However, from 1169, relations between Alexander and the Holy Roman Emperor were improving and the balance of power between Crown and Church was changing as a result.

Another consideration for Henry was that, as bishops died, he was unable to get new ones ordained. During the course of the quarrel, this affected Bangor, Bath, Lincoln, Hereford, Ely and Chichester.

Perhaps most importantly, by 1169 Henry wanted to hold the coronation of his son, the Young King. He had already failed to do this once, when he was without an archbishop of Canterbury after Theobald's death. The coronation was part of a wider plan aimed to end hostilities with the king of France and involving settling inheritances on his three eldest sons, secured at Montmirail in January 1169. It now needed to be followed through with their investitures as an important step towards reassuring Louis.

Diplomacy frustrated, 1169

Over the winter of 1167–68, the pope had suspended Becket's right to excommunicate Henry's officials until spring 1169, hoping it would make reconciliation more likely, but it had not. When the right was reinstated, Becket used it, becoming more strident in his approach and excommunicating the bishops of London and Salisbury as well as several of the king's other officials. He gave notice that Richard de Lucy and Richard of Ilchester would be next unless they returned Church lands and made reparations. Although Gilbert Foliot managed to rally support from his fellow bishops in his appeal against his excommunication, the pope was unmoved and he had to accept the sentence. Reports from the time sent back to France also note that the remaining English bishops opposed to Becket were losing their enthusiasm for the fight against him.

Alexander III's situation had improved greatly by the summer, which caused problems for the English clergy. Until then, the majority had felt it wise to obey the king, but this strategy was no longer the immediately obvious one: their other master was growing stronger. As a result, several bishops, including Bishop Hilary of Chichester, published Becket's pronouncements against Henry II's supporters. Gilbert Foliot remained resolutely opposed to the archbishop of Canterbury; the archbishop of York, on the other hand, was wary about refusing to do as Hilary had done.

Throughout 1169, papal legates tried to bring Becket and Henry together to negotiate a settlement. Henry seemed willing at first but would not commit to anything concrete. The papacy warned Henry about any further delaying tactics, after which the king said that Becket could return as long as he abided by the Constitutions of Clarendon. When the legates tried to get Henry to give some guarantees, he again procrastinated. This was not the only way in which the king was frustrating papal diplomacy. The legates complained that he changed his answers and would not set out anything in writing. The irony is, of course, that it was putting the Constitutions of Clarendon in writing that was one of the key triggers of the original dispute.

Becket became more angry at what he perceived to be the weakness of the papacy in the face of Henry II's political games. In the autumn of 1169, he threatened several of Henry's household and then Henry himself with excommunication and England with interdict. Henry's reaction to this turn of events was his toughest yet. He issued a set of decrees that made it clear he was willing to break with both Pope Alexander and Becket.

KEY TERM

Anathema
An ecclesiastical curse or ban that often accompanied excommunication.

The Autumn Decrees of 1169
The decrees included the following points.

- Anyone carrying instructions concerning the interdict from the pope or the archbishop was a traitor and would be deported, along with their family.

- The sending of letters to, or receiving of letters from, the pope or the archbishop was banned.

- There were to be no appeals to either pope or archbishop.

- Ports were sealed and no member of the clergy was to leave England without a licence.

- All clergy abroad were ordered back to England and if they refused their lands were forfeit.

- Supporters of Becket were to have their property taken.

- Sheriffs were to take oaths from everyone over the age of 15 to observe these decrees.

'Everyone over the age of fifteen' included the bishops, who were summoned to London to promise their agreement. However, none of them responded and some even fled to monasteries. This was a clear sign that the loyalty of the English clergy could no longer be relied upon. Not only was Alexander III in a stronger position, but Henry's demands were pushing the clergy much further than they were now prepared to go.

Another diplomatic mission, 1169
Hosted and mediated by Louis VII of France, there was another meeting between Henry II and Thomas Becket in November 1169, at Montmartre. By this time, the need to settle the dispute was important for all three, as one item on the agenda was the coronation of Henry, the Young King, and his wife, Margaret of France. This was important in bringing the peace agreement decided at Montmirail to fruition.

The substance of the negotiations suggests that both sides were serious. The customs in the Constitutions of Clarendon that had originally been a cause of such contention no longer seemed to be a problem; the restoration of sequestered property was agreed; and reparations for loss of revenues was discussed, although this latter point highlights that there were still serious differences between the two sides. Becket estimated his losses were £20,000 but would accept half of that sum, while Henry only offered 1,000 silver marks, equivalent to a mere £666. Louis eventually persuaded Becket that he should not allow money to get in the way of a meaningful peace agreement. Despite what appear to have been major strides forward, there was one sticking point: the kiss of peace.

Becket insisted that Henry give him the kiss of peace. This was customary to seal a legal agreement or officially end a dispute. Henry, however, refused on the grounds that he had taken an oath that he would never give Becket the kiss of peace again. Perhaps in light of Henry's paltry offer of 1,000 silver marks in compensation, this outcome reflects that he was never serious about Montmartre after all.

Henry stalls again
Alexander III's patience with Henry seems finally to have run out. Unless Henry agreed to the terms arrived at in Montmartre, there

would be an interdict on his continental lands as well as the one that Becket had threatened England with. Furthermore, after an appropriate breathing space, the Constitutions of Clarendon were to be revoked. For his part, Alexander III would instruct Becket to behave with humility before his king.

Henry, in a wily move, bought himself some time by offering to submit the entire dispute to the pope and to abide by his decree. If nothing else, the sentences of interdict were suspended.

SOURCE 8 Thomas Becket's letter to Henry II written after their meeting at Montmirail in January 1169.

... I was ready to place myself entirely in God's mercy and yours, so that I might earn your peace and favour. But, my lord, that form of words did not please you unless I promised to observe the customs which our predecessors had observed to yours. I conceded, therefore, my lord, that I would observe them, as far as I could, saving my order, and that if I should know of anything else that I should promise more fully and more clearly, I was prepared to do it... Since it did not please you to accept those assurances ... for I remember that I am bound by oath to preserve your life, limbs and all earthly honour to do whatever I can do for you, according to God, as for my dearest lord.

SOURCE 9 From Roger of Wendover's account of events in 1169. Roger of Wendover was a monk and chronicler of St Alban's monastery between 1231 and 1235. He continued writing the history of England from 1154 that had been started at the monastery, using recent accounts of key events.

The same year were sent two legates, Vivian and Gratianus, to make peace between the king of England and the archbishop of Canterbury; but though their powers were equal, their opinions were different, and it was not likely that in the end they should be found to agree, when in the outset their feelings were so conflicting; thus Gratianus failed to find favour with the king, and Vivian with the archbishop.

The same year, Gilbert, bishop of London, crossed the sea to present himself before pope Alexander, and render an account of his causes for appeal. Passing through Normandy, where king Henry then was, he consulted with the king how they might circumvent the blessed archbishop of Canterbury and blacken his righteous cause in the sight of the holy pontiff. At length they agreed together that the king should send to Rome a solemn embassy, expressly declaring that, unless the pope would at once use severity in quelling the archbishop's pride, himself and all his barons and clergy would renounce their obedience to the pope.

A Level Exam-Style Question Section A

How far could the historian make use of Sources 8 and 9 to investigate the reasons why there was a failure to reach a compromise between Becket and Henry II in 1169?

Explain your answer, using both sources, the information given about them and your own knowledge of the historical context. (20 marks)

Tip
Think carefully about the range of information in both sources. For example, what can Source 8 tell you about Becket's personality as a factor, as well as events at Montmirail? What do you know about why Gilbert of London would be appealing to the pope?

The coronation of the Young King in June 1170

Time was running out for the coronation of the Young King. After events at Montmartre, Louis VII was losing patience with Henry and losing faith that he would be true to the agreement on the inheritance made at Montmirail. Henry decided that the archbishop of York would crown the Young King at Westminster Abbey. The ceremony took place on 14 June 1170. Becket and the pope reacted angrily to this attack on the ancient rights of the archbishops of Canterbury. Alexander III authorised Becket to:

- suspend the bishops who had taken the oath to the Constitutions of Clarendon

- excommunicate those who had taken part in the coronation of the Young King

- place an interdict on England

- use these powers as Becket saw fit in order to force the king to meet terms acceptable to the Church.

Henry II was a step ahead of them. No sooner was his son crowned than he offered, essentially, the terms agreed at Montmartre, including the peaceful return of Becket to Canterbury and the restoration of the property of the See of Canterbury. Henry II had also promised that Becket could re-crown the young Henry together with his wife, Margaret, upon his return and agreed that Becket could discipline the bishops as he saw fit. Becket accepted these terms, after a few days of talks, on 22 July 1170 at Fréteval in France. The issue of the kiss of peace did not figure on either side, although Becket would not return to England until Church property seized by Henry II had been returned. Nothing was mentioned about the Constitutions of Clarendon either.

Henry and Becket agreeing so suddenly after the Young King's coronation seems out of keeping with the intense and protracted conflict of the past six years and more. Although there was heated debate and discussion at Fréteval, the fact was that the dispute was over. It is argued that Henry II appealed to Becket's vanity and status-conscious nature through his direct attack on the rights of the archbishop of Canterbury. It would certainly be a relief for Pope Alexander that the dispute was over and with little long-term damage done to the See of Canterbury. Yet it is still difficult to understand why, suddenly, the two sides were reconciled. Perhaps for Henry, as John Guy suggests, Fréteval was 'a tactical retreat' … He would live to fight another day and had no intention of allowing the "ancestral customs" to be sidelined or rescinded.'

Becket's return to England

Becket returned to England on 1 December 1170. Accounts indicate that Becket was warmly welcomed by the people and lesser clergy of Canterbury. However, just because Henry was satisfied with the outcome of Fréteval did not mean that Becket's enemies in England were reconciled with the archbishop of Canterbury. Becket had the day before finally excommunicated the archbishop of York and the bishops of London and Salisbury. He described his return to England in a letter to Pope Alexander (Source 10).

SOURCE
10 Thomas Becket's letter to Pope Alexander III, written on 5 December 1170.

When those enemies of ours had got certain news of [Becket's return] they decided therefore to have the seaports to which they suspected we would come guarded and carefully watched by armed forces of their soldiers and henchmen, so that we should not be able to enter the country without their making a thorough examination of all our baggage and sequestrating all the letters … from your majesty … The henchmen, whom we have mentioned above, were moving in arms around the shore, directing their course as the aforementioned York and bishops of London and Salisbury instructed.

[The letter continues, describing an encounter Becket had with Henry's men concerning the fate of the archbishop of York and bishops of Salisbury and London.]

But when we arrived at our church, the king's officials immediately approached us and commanded us in his name to absolve the suspended and excommunicated bishops, since the lord of York and the bishops of Salisbury and London had informed the king that the action taken against themselves rebounded to the king's injury and the overthrow of the customs of the realm … But we replied … that no man is allowed to undermine what the **Apostolic See** has decreed. Nevertheless, they were pressing insistently and threatening that the lord king would take amazing and extraordinary action unless we agreed. We said that if the bishops of London and Salisbury would swear in our presence according to the Church's form that they would obey your mandate, we would … do whatever we could in this matter, saving the respect due to you … When this was reported back … York, seeking partners in his rebellion and agitators for the schism, responded that an oath of this kind should not be taken except by the king's will, especially by bishops, because it was contrary to the prince's dignities and the customs of the realm.

KEY TERM

Apostolic See
A term used to describe the pope, or the authority of the Roman Catholic Church.

The conflict continues

From Becket's letter it would appear that the archbishop of York and the bishops of London and Salisbury were concerned about the letters excommunicating them. However, Becket had sent these on ahead of his return. Although he was willing to reverse the sentences of the bishops, reversing the sentence of the archbishop was a different matter, as he could only be absolved by the pope.

This treatment by Becket incensed the archbishop and bishops to such an extent that they crossed the Channel to take their grievances to the king, who was holding his Christmas court at Bures, in France. Upon hearing their complaints, Henry II is said to have raged against Becket exclaiming 'who will rid me of this turbulent priest?' Whether or not these were his exact words, the outcome of his outburst is in no doubt. Becket was murdered in Canterbury Cathedral on 29 December 1170.

What is perhaps surprising about Henry's reaction to the news from England was that he had known Becket was going to excommunicate the bishops, so this cannot be sufficient to explain his anger.

Becket excommunicating his enemies. From an early 13th-century French history of the life of Thomas Becket.

Henry's reaction to Becket's return to England

There is other evidence, from William FitzStephen, that adds to the picture of events. FitzStephen knew both Becket and Henry II well: he had been one of the archbishop's clerks, but had made his loyalty to the king clear during the course of the conflict. He was also present at Canterbury when Becket was murdered. FitzStephen's account of events in 1170 describes Becket riding around Kent at the head of a strong force of knights after his return to England. It is not necessarily what Becket did that outraged the king so much as the manner in which he behaved.

Whether Becket's riding at the head of an armed guard was a gesture to emphasise his power and status, or a measure taken for his protection, the king could not ignore Becket's actions. This was not the sort of behaviour Henry II would have expected and could certainly have been enough to provoke him. Had Becket not changed? Was he intent on establishing himself as a power in the land? It might be that Becket felt he needed the protection, especially if the story of the bishops sending word to the Young King in Windsor that Becket wanted to depose him is true. When he sought to meet the Young King, he was certainly prevented from doing so and ordered back to Canterbury.

According to William FitzStephen, those of Henry's barons present at his Christmas court seem to have been of the opinion that Becket still constituted a threat to royal power. One man, unnamed by FitzStephen, advised the king that there could be no peace or stability while Becket remained and it was this, the account suggests, that provoked a tirade from the king bemoaning that the men he had promoted in his household stood idly by while he was mocked by a low-born clerk.

Whatever the exact circumstances, the words Henry spoke in anger were translated into action by Reginald FitzUrse, William de Tracy, Richard Brito and Hugh de Moreville's man, Hugh of Horsea. Becket was brutally murdered while celebrating mass on 29 December 1170, his brains hooked out and smeared across the stone floor.

The impact and significance of Becket's murder

When news of Becket's murder was delivered to King Henry he was distraught, shutting himself in his room for three days, so that family and friends were concerned for his sanity and safety. There was outrage across Christendom, with Louis VII calling for military action against Henry with the aim of deposing him.

The immediate aftermath

Many reviled Henry II for Becket's murder and there were calls for his excommunication. In the days after hearing the news, Pope Alexander broke off talks he was holding with English envoys and refused to speak to anyone English for a week. He excommunicated the knights and anyone else involved in Becket's murder, including those who had encouraged or sheltered them before or since. His dealing with Henry, however, was shrewd. Rather than excommunicating him or laying an interdict upon England, Henry was prohibited from entering a church. The pope would send envoys to judge when he was humbled enough to return.

Before long, news of miracles at Becket's tomb began spreading. Although a divisive figure while alive and one whose tenure as archbishop of Canterbury was not especially successful, in death Thomas Becket became a celebrated Christian martyr. For example, only six days after the murder, a woman called Britheva was reputedly cured of blindness by rags dipped in Becket's blood and pressed on her eyes. Canterbury Cathedral is still a place of pilgrimage to this day.

SOURCE
12 A 14th-century pilgrim's badge of Thomas Becket. These would be worn by pilgrims en route to Canterbury to visit Becket's tomb.

A Level Exam-Style Question Section B

'The personalities involved were the greatest obstacles to finding a solution to end the conflict between Thomas Becket and Henry II.'

How far do you agree with this opinion? Explain your answer. (20 marks)

Tip

Personality cannot be quantified. Instead, you will have to cite events and evidence that illustrate both Thomas Becket and Henry II. Make your selection objective and guard against seeing one as a 'goodie' and the other as a 'baddie'.

ACTIVITY
KNOWLEDGE CHECK

1 Identify all the reasons why reconciliation took so long to achieve and then ultimately failed.

2 Now divide them into political issues, religious issues and personalities.

3 Was Becket's murder inevitable? If so, why? If not, then how might the dispute have developed instead? You will need to use your knowledge and understanding of the issues, events and personalities to develop your argument.

THE SETTLEMENT BETWEEN KING AND CHURCH, 1172–76

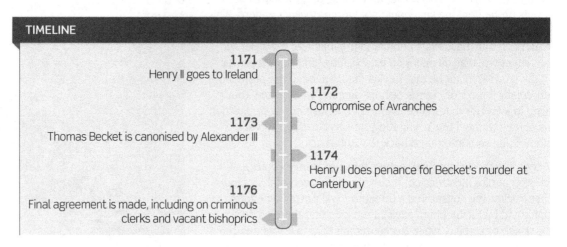

TIMELINE

1171
Henry II goes to Ireland

1172
Compromise of Avranches

1173
Thomas Becket is canonised by Alexander III

1174
Henry II does penance for Becket's murder at Canterbury

1176
Final agreement is made, including on criminous clerks and vacant bishoprics

Pope Alexander was careful not to overexploit the advantage that Henry's guilt provided and the resulting measured response made sense. With Becket's death, the pope recognised that there was an opportunity for proper reconciliation between Crown and Church. There had been a strong personal, even emotional, angle to the dispute, which was based upon the men's long-term friendship and which seemed to have developed when Becket was chancellor. This was now gone and suggests it may have been one of the main obstacles to achieving reconciliation.

The Compromise of Avranches

It was well over a year after the murder of Becket that Henry was summoned to Normandy to hear the terms for his absolution. In Ireland at the time, there is evidence of his reconciliation with the Church in warm letters sent to him by Pope Alexander, referring to him as a 'dearest son of the Church' and praising what he had achieved there. The pope was especially pleased at the bringing together of Irish clergy at a council established by Henry to deal with the immoral conduct of the people there. Furthermore, Henry's intervention in Ireland began establishing some form of potentially unifying authority there that could support the Church. Nevertheless, before obeying the summons, Henry prevaricated.

The wording of what Henry II agreed to at Avranches was carefully chosen. Henry agreed to abolish '*evil* customs' that *he* had introduced. The '*ancient* customs' mentioned were not necessarily implied by this and it meant that the agreement was sufficiently open to allow for further discussion. The king did have to agree to release the bishops from the oath they had taken to observe the Constitutions of Clarendon.

On Sunday 21 May 1172, Henry performed a public ceremony of penance at Avranches Cathedral, where he swore the following:

- to provide money for 200 knights to crusade in the Holy Land
- to restore all property to the Church of Canterbury
- not to obstruct any appeals to Rome by the clergy
- to abolish all customs prejudicial to the Church.

Crown–Church relations in England after Avranches

After Henry's very public penance and the Compromise of Avranches, Crown and Church settled into the more familiar pattern of supporting and reinforcing each other. In 1173, Henry's choice of bishops for Ely, Bath, Winchester and Norwich was approved by the Church, even though all four men had been against Becket in the quarrel. However, the vacancies at Chichester and Hereford were filled by Becket's supporters. As for the new archbishop of Canterbury, this time Henry left the election to the monks, although he is reported to have asked that they did not choose anyone like Becket.

It is also notable that when Louis VII of France called for papal support in a conflict with Henry II in 1173–74 (the Great Rebellion – see Chapter 4), the pope refused.

Saint Thomas Becket

One other event of note in 1173 was the **canonisation** of Thomas Becket. Miracles were declared to have happened at his tomb in Canterbury Cathedral and his blood was said to have healing properties. Interestingly, Henry II himself might have had cause to believe in Becket's miracles. Having left England in 1171, he did not return until 1174 to put down the Great Rebellion, which involved the king of Scotland. The first thing he did upon his return was to go to Canterbury Cathedral and allow himself to be subjected to a long and painful penance at the hands of the monks, after which he lay prostrate on the floor before Becket's tomb. The next morning, the king of Scotland was captured in a field near Alnwick, Northumberland and sent to Henry with his feet tied under his horse. Henry went on to defeat the Great Rebellion with ease.

> **KEY TERM**
>
> Canonisation
> The process of becoming a saint. There was no formal process until 1234, although usually miracles would have occurred and the deceased would have had to have died for the Christian faith.

Relations with the pope after Avranches

The issues at the heart of the Constitutions of Clarendon and the quarrel with Becket were addressed, to some extent, in 1176 when Henry and the Church reached agreement on certain points. The king conceded that a member of the clergy should not be made to appear before a secular judge unless it was either for an offence against the royal forest or for an issue that clearly concerned the man in question as a tenant of the Crown. There were, however, no clear guidelines as to what constituted a member of the clergy. Instead, the king agreed to accept the Church's definition, which was flexible. If it was settled that the accused was a member of the clergy, then punishment was to be decided and implemented by the Church alone – there were to be no double punishments. This has become known as **benefit of clergy**. Only if the accused fled before proof of his status was decided would he no longer be entitled to it, and be outlawed. So, regarding the most contentious clause of the Constitutions of Clarendon, Becket had won: no clergy were to be tried in the king's courts. Finally, Henry also stipulated that, unless the circumstances were extraordinary, he would not hold an empty bishopric for more than a year.

> **KEY TERM**
>
> Benefit of clergy
> The exemption for the clergy, including monks and nuns, from being tried in secular courts.

The extent of Henry's success

In some respects, the conflict with the Church and Becket's murder had changed very little in regard to Crown–Church relations. The king's ability to choose candidates for high ecclesiastical posts and offices remained, although he exercised it with more caution. Members of the clergy continued to serve the Crown and, in 1173, the pope approved Henry's nomination of several who had been prominently anti-Becket to key political posts.

The wording of parts of the Compromise of Avranches was vague enough to please both parties. No 'evil customs' were specified and Henry felt that there were very few – if any – as he wrote in a letter to the bishop of Exeter. It was for the king to determine which of his realm's customs were evil. As for the Church, English bishops agreed to obey Henry and the laws of the realm *saving our honour*. It is difficult to know, therefore, what had changed in practical terms.

If there are positives for Henry from the settlement with the Church, the rights of the Crown to deal with issues concerning Crown tenants were defined, even if the case concerned a member of the clergy, and the royal forest continued to be a special case.

If Henry is judged in terms of his aim of restoring (and extending) the customs of the Crown to those it had in 1135, he had not been hugely successful. He had agreed not to impede appeals to Rome, whereas Henry I had authorised control over letting clergy leave England to travel to the pope. It was agreed, however, that Henry II could ask for security if he harboured any doubts about the intent of those who went. When it came to papal legates visiting England, the example of Cardinal Vivian landing without permission, en route for Ireland and Scotland, shows that Henry was still forceful, but perhaps more judicious, in his dealings with the pope's men. Although Vivian was approached and made to swear to conform to the king's will, Henry also gave him an escort and letters of protection to ensure safe passage, as well as ordering all clergy to treat him with the full honours a cardinal deserved.

Perhaps the most significant failure concerned the benefit of clergy, which was not removed until Henry VIII's break with Rome in the 1530s. In 1176, Henry II agreed that anyone who murdered a member of the clergy should receive an extra punishment – that the guilty party and his heirs be disinherited. As for who was or was not a clerk, that issue was never addressed.

Interpretations (5c)

Good questions/Bad questions

Below are approaches attributed to three famous historians. They are generalisations for the purpose of this exercise.

Herodotus: he looks for the interesting story, the drama and the colourful characters

Leopold von Ranke: he is interested in how great men use their influence to bring about change

Karl Marx: he looks underneath the events to see what patterns there are over long periods of time and how ordinary people fit in

Work in groups.

1 Devise three criteria for what makes a good historical question.

2 Consider what you know about the conflict between Henry II and the Church, 1163-76.

   a) Each write one historical question based on that subject matter.

   b) Put these in rank order, with the best question first, based on your criteria from question 1.

3 Using a piece of A3 paper, write the names of the three historians so they form a large triangle, one name at each point.

   a) Write your questions from 2a on the piece of paper so that their positions reflect how likely the historians are to be interested in each question. For example, Becket's role in causing the dispute would be of more interest to Herodotus and von Ranke than Marx. This question would be placed on the triangle between their names. A question that might interest all three would be placed in the middle.

   b) Add some further questions. Try to think of questions that only one of these three would be interested in.

4 Take it in turns to try to answer the questions you have created in the style of one of the historians. See if other members of the group can guess which historian it was.

Answer the following questions individually using the examples created by the above activity.

5 Does one method of constructing history lead to a better reasoning than others? Explain your answer.

6 Explain why all historians who deploy rigorous methodology are, to an extent, useful sources for the study of the past.

SOURCE
13
From an anonymous account of the submission of Henry II to the papal legates at Avranches in May 1172.

Secondly, to abrogate in their entirety the obnoxious statues of Clarendon and all evil customs which had been introduced into God's churches during his reign. Moreover such evil customs as were in existence before his time were to be restricted in accordance with the mandate of the lord pope and the counsel of the ecclesiastics.

AS Level Exam-Style Question Section A

How much weight do you give the evidence of Source 12 for an enquiry into the extent of the Church's victory over Henry II in the conflict of 1164–70?

Explain your answer using the source, the information given about it and your own knowledge of the historical context. (12 marks)

Tip
Although the author is anonymous, the information given can be shown to be accurate by referring to the actual Compromise of Avranches. It might be your knowledge that is more important in determining the weight you would give the source.

A Level Exam-Style Question Section B

'Thomas Becket was victorious in death; but his victory was a triumph for his reputation, not the triumph of his cause.'

How far do you agree with this opinion? Explain your answer. (20 marks)

Tip
This is a dual focus essay that asks you to look at two statements: that Becket's reputation came out of the conflict extremely well; that Becket's cause did not triumph. Both will need discussing in order for you to answer the question fully and reach a reasoned conclusion.

ACTIVITY
KNOWLEDGE CHECK

1 To what extent does the outcome of Henry II's conflict with the Church show that he was in the wrong? Use a value continuum to illustrate your answer and explain it with three key reasons/pieces of evidence.

2 Compare your value continuum with those of two to three others who have different answers from you. Between you, come up with one value continuum answer that you can all agree to and present your findings to the class.

3 What lessons might Henry II have drawn from his conflict with the Church between 1164 and 1176? How far would they confirm that ultimate authority lay with the king in England? Explain your answer. You might like to write it as advice to his heirs on dealing with the Church.

ACTIVITY
SUMMARY

Key turning points

1 Review the chapter and highlight three key turning points that led to Becket's murder. At least one ought to be long term and at least one short term. Explain your choices.

2 It has been suggested that Thomas Becket wanted to be a martyr. What evidence is there of this in his behaviour after he became archbishop of Canterbury?

3 Winners and losers. Evaluate the outcome of the Becket dispute. Bearing in mind what each was aiming to achieve, who won? Use a value continuum to show this, with Thomas Becket as the 100 percent winner at one end and Henry II as 100 percent winner at the other. Underneath, give five specific pieces of evidence that led you to this conclusion.

4 Now that you have finished this chapter, watch the film *Becket* (starring Richard Burton and Peter O'Toole, available on DVD) and write a review of it as a historian. How historically accurate is it? Are there any scenes that you would cut or any you would add? Explain why. You could produce a script or short video of any new scenes you would like to make.

WIDER READING

Guy, J. *Thomas Becket*, Penguin (2012)

Duggan, A. *Thomas Becket*, Hodder Education (2004)

Staunton, M. (ed.) *The Lives of Thomas Becket*, Manchester University Press (2001) This contains a great deal of contemporary source material

The text of the Constitutions of Clarendon is available on the Yale University website http://avalon.law.yale.edu/medieval/constcla.asp

2b.4 Crises of the Angevin Empire, 1170-89

KEY QUESTIONS

- What rivalries existed in the Plantagenet family?
- Why did the Great Rebellion break out in 1173?
- How did the Great Rebellion impact upon royal power?
- Why did Henry II die a diminished king?

INTRODUCTION

Henry II was king of England. In France, however, he was a vassal of the French king, Louis VII. Despite this, the lands he held in France made him a more powerful figure than the king. This was a position of which Louis VII was acutely aware. In May 1152, Henry had married Eleanor of Aquitaine, whose marriage to Louis had been annulled just eight weeks previously. She had taken the duchy of Aquitaine with her to her new husband and, by the end of the 1150s, Henry had established his dominion over most of western France, as far south as the county of Quercy and as far south-east as the Auvergne. However, this was a notoriously difficult region to control, being isolated, desolate and the stronghold of very independent local lords and barons.

The birth of a long-awaited son and heir, Philip, in 1165 gave Louis added impetus for strengthening his position in France. This was not easily achieved, given his relative lack of power and resources, coupled with the fact that Louis VII was known for his piety rather than as a warrior. It was clear that Louis did not have the power to enforce his superior status over Henry.

By 1165, Henry and Eleanor had three surviving and thriving sons and three daughters. Their last child, another son, John, was born in 1167. In some respects, having so many sons might appear to be another advantage that Henry had over Louis. However, once 'the heir and the spare' are born, sons can provide problems. They all have to be provided with a suitable inheritance and resources appropriate to their status. This was exploited by Louis VII and later by his son, Philip II. In fact, perhaps Henry's greatest weakness turned out to be his sons.

A domineering and ebullient man, Henry did not relinquish control easily. His sons, as volatile and self-assured as their parents, and just as aware of their status, chafed under their father's restrictions, favouritism and unwillingness to share power. The major crises of the Angevin Empire all stemmed from a combination of family feuds and jealousies, helped along by the kings of France. Where Louis VII was ineffectual, however, his son Philip II proved to be stunningly effective. So effective was he at accumulating and concentrating power for the Crown of France that he has gone down in French history as Philip Augustus.

1151 – Henry Plantagenet does homage for Normandy and cedes the Vexin to King Louis VII

1154 – Henry Plantagenet becomes King Henry II of England

1158 – Betrothal of Henry's son, Henry (b.1155), to Margaret of France (b.1157)

1164 – Thomas Becket flees to exile in France

1167 – Birth of Henry and Eleanor's fourth son, John, known as John Lackland because of his lack of an inheritance

1170 – Murder of Thomas Becket in Canterbury Cathedral
Louis VII calls upon the pope to launch military action against Henry II

| 1151 | 1152 | 1153 | 1154 | 1155 | 1156 | 1157 | 1158 | 1159 | 1160 | 1161 | 1162 | 1163 | 1164 | 1165 | 1166 | 1167 | 1168 | 1169 | 1170 |

1152 – Louis VII's marriage to Eleanor of Aquitaine is annulled and she marries Henry Plantagenet eight weeks later

1156 – Henry takes control of Brittany

1160 – Marriage of Prince Henry to Margaret of France
The Vexin is taken by Henry II

1165 – Birth of Louis VII's son and heir, Philip

1169 – The Treaty of Montmirail sets out the inheritances for three of Henry's four sons

WHAT RIVALRIES EXISTED IN THE PLANTAGENET FAMILY?

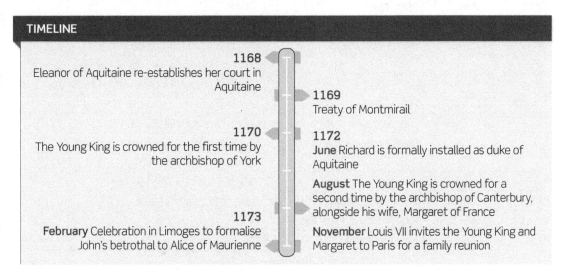

TIMELINE

1168 Eleanor of Aquitaine re-establishes her court in Aquitaine

1169 Treaty of Montmirail

1170 The Young King is crowned for the first time by the archbishop of York

1172
June Richard is formally installed as duke of Aquitaine

August The Young King is crowned for a second time by the archbishop of Canterbury, alongside his wife, Margaret of France

1173
February Celebration in Limoges to formalise John's betrothal to Alice of Maurienne

November Louis VII invites the Young King and Margaret to Paris for a family reunion

Henry's plans for his sons' inheritance

The Angevin Plantagenets

Henry **Plantagenet** and Eleanor of Aquitaine had a large, robust family; only their firstborn, William, had not survived childhood. Having so many children should have been advantageous; daughters could make good marriage alliances with strategically important rulers of other territories but having four sons was more challenging. It was vital to have a male heir and, given the unpredictable nature of 12th-century life, having a 'spare' was also important. However, all four of Henry and Eleanor's sons would need lands to govern and this would not be easy to provide; they were also well aware of their ancestry and status and had expectations accordingly.

Henry and Eleanor appear to have loved their children dearly, although that did not prevent them from having favourites. This is always dangerous in a family, but especially one where disagreements can easily turn to bloodshed. Richard was his mother's favourite, John his father's, and this was to have serious long-term consequences. Jealousies over titles and slights of status were keenly felt in Henry and Eleanor's family. Some contemporary chroniclers said that they were spawned from the devil, the 'Devil's brood'.

KEY TERM

Plantagenet
A major ruling English dynasty. It was founded by Henry II's father, Geoffrey of Anjou, who had become known as Geoffrey Plantagenet because he wore a sprig of broom in his hat. The medieval Latin name for the broom plant was *Planta genista*. The House of Plantagenet, as it became known, began with the Angevins.

1174 – The Great Rebellion ends; Henry is victorious over his wife, sons, the kings of France and Scotland and several English barons

1180 - Louis VII dies

1183 – The Young King dies, ending his rebellion

Henry refuses to name a new principal heir

Henry does homage to Philip II

1186 – Henry's third son, Geoffrey, dies in a tournament

1188-89 – Philip II and Richard are united against Henry II and begin attacking the heartlands of his French territories

1171 1172 1173 1174 1175 1176 1177 1178 1179 1180 1181 1182 1183 1184 1185 1186 1187 1188 1189 1190

1173 - First major Angevin family crisis
The Great Rebellion begins

1179 - Louis VII falls ill and is incapacitated; Philip II assumes the crown

1182 – Second Angevin family crisis begins as Henry's sons fall out

Henry, the Young King, turns against Richard and their father

1185 – John's expedition to Ireland fails

Henry's aim has been to make him its king and he has a crown made ready; it is not needed

Philip II turns Geoffrey against Henry II

1187 – The pope calls for the Third Crusade

Philip II and Henry's son Richard are united in a desire to go to the Holy Land

1189 – Henry II dies, having been defeated by Richard and Philip II

He learns of John's turning against him just before his death

Henry II and Eleanor of Aquitaine's children: their marriages and inheritances

Child	Dates	Marriage	Titles*
William	1153–56		
Henry	1155–83	Margaret of France	King of England (alongside Henry) 1170–83
			Duke of Normandy (alongside Henry) 1169–83
			Count of Anjou (alongside Henry) 1169–83
Matilda	1156–89	Henry, duke of Saxony	
Richard	1157–99	*Betrothed:* Alice of France	Duke of Aquitaine 1169–99
		Berengaria of Navarre	Count of Poitou 1172–99
			Duke of Normandy 1188‡
			King of England 1189–99
Geoffrey	1158–86	Constance of Brittany	Duke of Brittany 1169–86
Eleanor	1162–1215	King Alphonso VIII of Castile	
Joan	1165–99	King William of Sicily	
		Count Raymond VI of Toulouse	
John	1167–1216	Isabel of Gloucester	Lord of Ireland 1177–1216
		Isabel of Angoulême	King of England 1199–1216
			Duke of Normandy, count of Anjou 1199–1204
			Duke of Aquitaine 1199–1204

*Titles are given as on the date of the Treaty of Montmirail, as that was when the inheritances were decided.

‡Richard paid homage to Philip II for Normandy in 1188.

Which territory for which son?

In 1158, Henry's chancellor, Thomas Becket, negotiated a marriage alliance between the king's eldest son, also called Henry, and Louis VII's daughter, Margaret of France. The marriage had gone ahead in 1160, much to Louis's anger, when they were still small children. Margaret's dowry was the Vexin, a strategically vital piece of land on the borders of Henry's duchy of Normandy and Louis's own demesne, the Ile de France. However, the birth of Louis's son and heir, Philip, in 1165 added to his desire to strengthen his position as king of France and the loss of the Vexin became more of an issue.

Henry's third son, Geoffrey, was betrothed to Constance of Brittany, daughter of Count Conan, in 1166, and he would one day assume the position of duke.

Although nothing specific had been set aside for Richard, the second son, he was his mother's favourite and, when she had returned to Aquitaine on a permanent basis in 1168 after the birth of her last child, John, he went with her. Richard spent the next few years travelling the duchy, learning and apparently preparing to take over as its duke one day.

It was to be providing for Henry and Eleanor's last child, John, born in December 1167, that was to be problematic, right until Henry's death in 1189. Nicknamed John Lackland, because of his lack of inheritance, this was not an immediate problem when, in 1169, Henry and Louis VII signed the agreement of Montmirail, in which the inheritances of Prince Henry (the Young King), Richard and Geoffrey were settled.

The division of Angevin lands between Henry's sons

The Treaty of Montmirail, 1169

Relations between Henry II and Louis VII took a turn for the worse in 1167, leading to a spate of border attacks and skirmishes in the Norman marchers. By the end of 1168, both Louis VII and Henry II wanted to bring an end to the conflict. A peace conference was held at Montmirail in January 1169.

The meeting planned for Montmirail had a great deal depending on it. As well as discussing peace terms with Louis, Henry and Becket were to meet in an attempt to reconcile their differences. They failed. However, there was important progress as far as coming to terms with Louis VII was concerned. By dividing up his 'empire' between his three eldest sons, Henry allayed fears of an Angevin ascendancy in France. Relations between the two kings had stabilised, with any existing concerns and tensions put aside. Or so it seemed.

Henry's oldest son, young Henry, was to inherit the kingdom of England, the duchy of Normandy and Anjou. His lands in France would be held as a vassal of the king of France. Richard would be duke of Aquitaine, also as a vassal for the French Crown, and would marry Louis's daughter, Alice. Geoffrey would have Brittany as a vassal of the Young King, who would hold it as a vassal of Louis VII. Doing this acknowledged that Henry II (and Henry the Young King) had the right to Brittany, but from Louis. This strengthened the position of the French Crown in the long run and would give the heir to the French throne much more secure foundations for his reign. The outcome appeared to satisfy both Louis's concerns about Angevin dominance of France and Henry's concerns to provide his sons with appropriate inheritances.

The significance of the Treaty of Montmirail

The significance of the Treaty of Montmirail in ensuring Henry's sons their French inheritances was, according to the historian W.L. Warren, 'that he was offering Louis the prospect that his son Philip would one day be able to preside over a family consortium controlling the major part of the kingdom'. Louis VII had already made marriage alliances for Philip's half-sisters, Marie and Alix, with the counts of Blois and Champagne, respectively.

The significance of Montmirail to Henry's sons did not live up to their expectations. To secure the treaty, the coronation of Henry and Margaret as king and queen of England was necessary, as were the investiture ceremonies and acts of homage for Normandy, Aquitaine and Brittany. These duly went ahead. However, the money and power actually provided to the Young King, Richard and Geoffrey was insufficient to enable them to rule in their own rights. Although only 15, 13 and 12 years of age in 1170, their frustrations with their father soon turned into hostility and then conflict. Eleanor of Aquitaine had a hand in this too.

EXTEND YOUR KNOWLEDGE

Crowning the Young King

In keeping with the French custom, young Henry was crowned to secure his succession to the English throne as soon as practicable. On 14 June 1170, his coronation was celebrated by the archbishop of York rather than the archbishop of Canterbury because Henry's conflict with Thomas Becket was continuing. He had papal dispensation for the archbishop of York to do this dating back to before the conflict had begun.

One aim of the archbishop of York taking the cherished and sacred duty of the archbishop of Canterbury was to bring Thomas to the negotiating table and settle the dispute, with the promise of a second coronation, this time including the queen. Becket was murdered before this could happen. However, on 27 August 1172, there was a second coronation. As there was no replacement archbishop of Canterbury at this time, the ceremony was conducted in Winchester by the archbishop of Rouen, when Margaret was also crowned queen of England.

To differentiate him from his father, Henry became known as 'the Young King'. He was/is not known as Henry III because, despite his coronations, he did not share in Henry II's power.

The position of Eleanor of Aquitaine

The year after the birth of John in 1167, Eleanor returned to Aquitaine and from this time onwards she saw little of her husband. This is not surprising, given the nature of kingship and the vast territories held by Henry II. Eleanor was more than capable of acting as a justiciar in Henry's absence and there is plenty of evidence of her doing so, especially in England and Aquitaine.

Heiress of Aquitaine

Eleanor's father had been the last duke of Aquitaine and she was his heir in her own right. However, she had married Louis VII only four weeks after her father's death. This was when the duchy first united with France. When the marriage was annulled in 1152, Eleanor was determined to take her lands with her. Her new husband, Henry Plantagenet, was more than a match for Louis should he try to claim Aquitaine. This goes some way to explaining the haste with which Eleanor remarried, only eight weeks after her previous marriage was over. Although she had inherited Aquitaine from her father and according to ancient Aquitanian customs she could in theory rule the duchy herself, there was little practical chance of this. The patriarchal, restrictive influence of medieval Christianity, with its negative attitude towards women, made it highly unlikely that Eleanor could have successfully ruled in her own right. Quite apart from social constraints, there were always plenty of other barons willing to seize any opportunity to increase their territories and status. It appears that certain of them had plans to kidnap Eleanor on her way back to Aquitaine, or at least to hurry there to offer marriage. Henry beat them to it.

Estrangement from Henry

Despite the practical benefits of marriage to Henry II, it does appear to have been a love match as well, at least at first. However, over the course of the years 1168–73, Eleanor of Aquitaine and Henry II undoubtedly became estranged. One theory put forward is that Eleanor was tired of Henry's affairs and that one in particular had enraged her jealousy, that with Rosamund Clifford. Rosamund was probably more than just a fling for Henry II if the monument he had built to her when she died in 1176 is anything to go by.

When the monks of Limoges faced a rebellion in their town of La Souterraine, they appealed to Henry, not Eleanor, to deal with their vassals. This clearly showed Eleanor the reality of exercising authority in her own lands. For an ambitious, capable woman who had grown up in a region where traditionally women were generally held in high regard, this must have been galling, although unsurprising given that the request came from monks. Since returning to Aquitaine in 1168, she had established her own court there and spent a great deal of time travelling the duchy, often with Richard, rebuilding relations with local lords who had disliked Henry's attempts at imposing his will and government structures on Aquitaine. Henry could provide protection and support for Aquitaine from external threats, but it seemed to come at the expense of Eleanor's power and authority within the duchy itself.

Eleanor and Richard

By 1172, after his investiture as duke of Aquitaine, Richard was reaching an age where he would expect to exercise some real authority and power there. As Eleanor's favourite son, he would then be able to replace Henry as a male authority figure in the duchy, while she would be able to exercise greater influence through, and possibly alongside, him. However, Henry's aim in the investitures of his sons was simply to establish their inheritance. Despite the acts of homage that formed an important part of the ceremonies, Henry did not feel obliged to share control of his lands, and indeed was unwilling to do so. Unfortunately, his wife, sons and others interpreted the situation differently, expecting higher statuses to be reflected with increased power.

It is noticeable that, by 1172, Eleanor had started issuing some charters in her own name in Aquitaine, rather than jointly with Henry. Others were issued jointly in her and Richard's names. Since 1168, Richard had accompanied his mother, learning the ropes of government. However, even after his investiture in 1172, Richard, like his mother, did not have the necessary authority to govern Aquitaine, a key cause of his own rebellion against Henry. Richard, despite being invested as duke, felt that Henry II would not relinquish the control he ought to have done. Both Henry and Richard each clearly believed that they were the ultimate authority in Aquitaine. This was reinforced in February 1173 when Count Raymond of Toulouse, a region claimed by the dukes of Aquitaine, did homage for his territories first to Henry II, then to the Young King and finally to Richard. According to the Treaty of Montmirail, Richard was to hold Aquitaine directly from the French Crown, yet homage had first been paid to his father and older brother.

Given her strong will and proud heritage, it is likely that Eleanor, like her sons, resented Henry's overbearing authority and control of what she saw as rightfully hers. However, what she could achieve was limited: all of Aquitaine's revenues went to Henry and she had no military resources to call upon. In effect, the real power lay with Henry, a fact not lost on Richard.

WHY DID THE GREAT REBELLION BREAK OUT IN 1173?

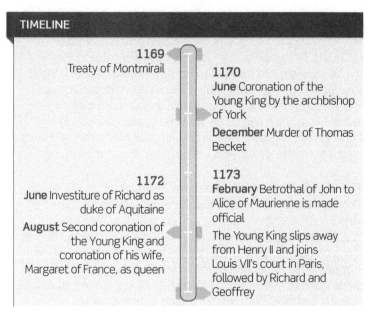

TIMELINE

1169 Treaty of Montmirail

1170
June Coronation of the Young King by the archbishop of York

December Murder of Thomas Becket

1172
June Investiture of Richard as duke of Aquitaine

August Second coronation of the Young King and coronation of his wife, Margaret of France, as queen

1173
February Betrothal of John to Alice of Maurienne is made official

The Young King slips away from Henry II and joins Louis VII's court in Paris, followed by Richard and Geoffrey

The opposition of the English barons to Henry II

The earls of Chester, Norfolk, Leicester and Derby were the leading English rebels against Henry II. Discontent had been increasing as a result of castles and lands being taken and also following Cartae Baronum and the increased powers of sheriffs under the Assize of Clarendon and the Inquest of Sheriffs, which saw an end to noble control of those important and lucrative posts.

The earl of Chester had not inherited his father's full lands. As a minor he had been made the king's ward and his estates were under Henry II's control. With his aim of trimming the barons of power and returning England to how it had been in 1135, Henry had kept some of the earl's estates for himself after the young earl came into his inheritance.

Hugh Bigod had, at times, served Henry II. However, he had also been denied control of Norwich by the king and had had his holdings in East Anglia reduced. He had also lost two of his castles and had been charged £666 to have them returned. The Young King promised him control of Norwich in return for his allegiance.

Robert of Leicester, son of Robert de Beaumont, the justiciar who had died in 1168, had more prosaic reasons for his treachery; he disliked having to pay scutage and had been amerced £333 for a breach of the peace.

William de Ferrers also had a grudge based on being denied the title of earl of Derby and had also lost what he believed to be his rightful inheritance from his mother, Margaret Peverel.

According to William of Newburgh, in 1174 'there were only a few barons in England who were not wavering in their allegiance to the king and ready to defect'.

King William of Scotland

Henry II had gained Scottish support on the road to the English throne by promising the Scottish king, David I, that he would grant him Northumberland. David died just before Henry II became king of England, being followed by a young, inexperienced heir, Malcolm IV, also known as 'Malcolm the Maiden' or 'Malcolm the Fair'. Malcolm was no match for Henry II and had been forced to give up Northumberland and to do homage to Henry, recognising him as overlord. Malcolm's brother, William I, who became king of Scotland in 1165, was a different proposition altogether. The rebellion provided him with the opportunity to redress Scotland's grievances.

Henry's failure to grant his sons a role in government

Family relations were not Henry's strong point. Two strong-willed parents, one with a violent temper, had produced sons who, now they were teenagers, unsurprisingly chafed at parental authority. However, this royal teenage rebellion was much more serious than rebellion in a normal family: rifts in the royal family could lead to civil war.

Henry II had given young Henry, Richard and Geoffrey titles, lands and expectations. Vassals had even been required to perform homage to them. Yet, whereas Henry had been duke of Normandy in his own right at 16 and king of England by 19, he did not give his sons the opportunity to run their own lands at the same age. He expected their obedience and loyalty to him not only as their father but as their overlord, even though he had conferred on them the same status as he held. Young Henry, Richard and Geoffrey had been used to getting their own way in many things and had often been indulged by their parents, but this time they were expecting far more than Henry II was prepared to give.

SOURCE

1 The Young King's coronation, where Henry II can be seen serving his son. He did this to emphasise young Henry's status, although he never shared power with him. From the *Becket Leaves*, a French poem about Thomas Becket produced c1220–40 and attributed by some to Matthew Paris (c1200–59).

Context is everything

The coronation of the Young King

Work in groups.

Take an A3 piece of paper. In the middle draw a circle about 18 cm in diameter. Within the circle is the evidence itself, outside the circle is the context. Study Source 1.

1 Think of a relevant question that the source could be helpful in answering.

2 Inside the circle, write a set of statements giving information that can be gleaned only from the source itself without any contextual knowledge.

3 Outside the circle, write down statements of contextual knowledge that relate to the source.

4 Draw annotated lines to show links between the contextual statements and the information from the source. Does the context change the meaning of the information?

Now answer the following question:

5 Explain why knowledge of context is important when gathering and using historical evidence. Give specific examples to illustrate your point.

John Lackland

Born in 1167, John was barely two years old when the Treaty of Montmirail was agreed. In the treaty Henry had provided inheritances for his three eldest sons. His youngest son, John, was often called 'Jean Sans Terre' or 'John Lackland' in reference to his lack of inherited land. With no obvious territories to settle upon John, making a useful marriage for him could prove problematic. Henry already had his eye on an alliance with Count Humbert of Maurienne. Maurienne was a small but strategically advantageous territory in the south-east of France, neighbouring Provence and encompassing areas of the Alps. In 1172, a deal was struck that John would marry Alice of Maurienne and would bring three strategically important castles to the match: Loudon, Chinon and Mirabeau, all of which were in the Young King's French lands and so their loss was a particular cause of discontent for him.

Limoges, 1173

In February 1173, Henry II and Eleanor of Aquitaine entertained Count Humbert in Limoges, along with King Sancho VI of Navarre, King Alfonso II of Aragon and Count Raymond V of Toulouse. The details of Alice of Maurienne's betrothal to John were finalised, and she came to live in Eleanor of Aquitaine's household. Count Raymond meanwhile acknowledged Eleanor of Aquitaine's claim to Toulouse. In 1158, Henry had attacked Toulouse with the intention of taking it from Raymond, but he had failed. At that time, Raymond had the backing of Louis VII, who was generally very supportive of any of Henry's rebellious vassals. However, since then Louis VII and Raymond had disagreed and the count switched his allegiance to Henry.

The change of allegiance to Henry II and acknowledgement of Eleanor's claim was sealed with an act of homage. Rather than do homage to Eleanor or Richard as his overlord for Toulouse, Raymond performed it to Henry II and the Young King. This implied that, ultimately, Toulouse was theirs, although they were the dukes of Normandy and kings of England, not Aquitaine. This gesture angered both Eleanor and Richard.

The Young King's frustrations

The Young King was handsome, charismatic and very popular, but had neither the powers nor the revenues to run the territories he had been given. In his father's absence, England was run by Richard de Lucy, and by 1170 the Exchequer and judiciary were developing into self-regulating systems of government. In short, there was nothing for the Young King to do. His father also chose the members of the Young King's household for him and would not give him the allowance he felt fitting for his station and lifestyle.

Although he loved his son, Henry II was not blind to his faults. He considered the Young King too immature to take on major responsibilities; he was a spendthrift, idle and vain, too fond of pleasure and entertainment, especially tournaments. By 1172, young Henry was increasingly frustrated at his lack of power and resources. His father-in-law, Louis VII, sympathised with him and appears to have encouraged him to demand control of one of his territories from Henry II.

During the week of festivities in Limoges to celebrate and seal Henry II's alliance with Count Humbert of Maurienne, the Young King spoke out against his father, complaining of his refusal to delegate any power, and the lack of income to meet his needs and status. He also made it known that he was furious at being expected to give up three of his castles to John, saying that Henry had no right to authorise this without his consent. Henry did not agree.

In the immediate run-up to the outbreak of the Great Rebellion in summer 1173, there had been the matter of the election of a new archbishop of Canterbury, Richard of Dover. The Young King had not been consulted about it, despite the fact that the issue had caused some controversy. Upon hearing of the appointment, he sent a letter to Rome to complain about the decision and hoping to reverse it. He did not succeed. The new archbishop of Canterbury was elected on 3 June just as the first attacks of the Great Rebellion began. It is perhaps not surprising that Henry II did not consult the Young King, since he had left his father on 5 March. However, it would also serve to underline the Young King's issue with his father.

By 1173, the Treaty of Montmirail had become worthless as far as Henry's sons were concerned. It had promised much, but delivered little. When combined with their ambitions and jealousies, and some outside help, events moved quickly from family feuding to outright rebellion.

Henry's sons' flight to Paris

Louis VII
The marriage alliance between young Henry and Margaret of France that had been agreed in 1158 now proved useful to Louis VII. Having been steamrollered into an actual marriage in 1160 so that Henry could gain control of the Vexin, Louis found himself in a position to turn the tables on him. As father of the recently crowned queen of England, he could legitimately make known his feelings that his daughter and son-in-law should be given the incomes and powers befitting their status. Perhaps more importantly, however, he could help widen Plantagenet family rifts, along with the aim of destroying Henry II's power base in France.

In November 1172, Louis VII had held a grand family reunion, which was attended by his daughter, Margaret, and son-in-law, the Young King. Already aware of growing tensions with Henry II, Louis hoped to deepen the divide. The reunion followed a meeting between father and son in Normandy, at which young Henry again demanded his inheritance – a demand that was again refused – Louis encouraged him to demand more. Concerned by this interference, Henry II demanded his eldest son's return for Christmas.

The Young King's flight to Paris
Exactly what finally triggered the Young King's decision to slip away from his father at Chinon Castle on the night of 5 March 1173 cannot be known. However, there are several things that happened immediately in the run-up to what could be described as his escape. First, young Henry had just celebrated his 18th birthday, by which age Henry II had been running Normandy for a couple of years. Already angry, this fact cannot have been lost upon the Young King. Secondly, Henry II seems to have been keeping his son very close, requiring him to travel through Aquitaine at his side as he secured key castles against the possibility of a rebellion by his own family. Count Raymond of Toulouse had warned Henry II in January of a plot by his closest family members to depose him. As a result, it appears that Henry was keeping an even tighter rein on his son than previously. Thirdly, the rumours had led Henry II to banish many of young Henry's knights from his own household. This further reinforced his son's anger and bitterness towards him, as well as leaving the young man isolated from his own supporters.

Chroniclers report that, once free from Chinon, young Henry rode straight for Louis VII's court, where he was treated as the king of England. This must have strengthened his grievances about being denied a role in government and unable to express his status as a king by being kept short of revenues and not being allowed to choose his own household.

The Young King in Paris
Louis VII welcomed young Henry to Paris and began to set him up for the coming fight. A great council of barons was summoned to Paris to pledge support to the Young King, who promised that he would not seek peace with his father without their consent. King Louis ordered that a seal be made for young Henry, so that he could make and authenticate his own charters. This would enable him to 'purchase' support through grants of land and offices. There were plenty willing to be bought. Philip of Alsace, count of Flanders, was promised Kent and £1,000 per annum, while his brother, Matthew of Boulogne, settled for the French county of Mortain.

There is a well-known tale told by William FitzStephen among others. Henry II sent a delegation of bishops to negotiate with his son and request that the Young King return to Normandy. When asked by Louis who had sent the message, the bishops said that the king of England had. Louis replied that the king of England was with him and added that the world knew that Henry II had resigned his kingdom to his son. Louis would have been quite aware of the idea of crowning the next king in advance, and that it did not necessarily mean a transfer of power. His son-in-law was, after all, known as the Young King and not Henry III. Louis was clearly being provocative. He intended to have his own son, Philip, crowned as soon as he was old enough, an event that would happen in 1179, when Philip was aged 13.

Richard and Geoffrey's flight to Paris
Once Richard and Geoffrey heard of their brother's flight to Paris they followed. Richard's expectations had, like his older brother's, been quashed. As Richard was too young to run Aquitaine independently in 1168, Eleanor had established a regency council with the intention of managing it herself in the meantime.

However, Henry still controlled the resources, both financial and military, meaning that there was very little that Richard, or his mother, could achieve in their own right. Like the Young King, Richard found Louis VII both sympathetic and supportive. With encouragement from Eleanor of Aquitaine, Richard followed his brother to Paris, where Louis knighted him upon his arrival, furthering the rift with his father.

Geoffrey, at 14, was the youngest of the rebelling brothers. An intelligent, quick-witted individual, he does not seem to have been liked if contemporary accounts are anything to go by. Deceitful, devious, ambitious and an able soldier he was to prove more than once that he was willing to betray his family. He joined with Louis as well, possibly sensing that the size of the impending rebellion would be able to defeat his father and give him Brittany. However, it is more likely that he too went to Paris with his mother's encouragement.

SOURCE 2

From Jean de Fantosme, *Chronicle of the War between the English and the Scots in 1173 and 1174*. Jean was a poet–composer who lived through the Great Rebellion. He was a cleric based in Winchester and a supporter of Henry II. The *Chronicle* is a work of literature, probably intended to be performed by minstrels to inform people of the Great Rebellion.

A king without a realm is at a loss for something to do: at such a loss was the noble and gracious Young King. When through his father's actions he could not do what he wished, he thought in his heart that he would stir up trouble for him. He departed secretly, crossed the Loire by a ford, and took neither food nor drink until he reached St. Denis, he told the whole of his story to the king of France.

King Louis of France was at St. Denis, and he held a council ... Thoughts of the old king of England oppressed him; Louis, the noble king, was nearly out of his mind with grief, when the count of Flanders looked up and said to the king of France: 'Do not be so downcast! You have many mighty barons to wreak havoc on your enemies. Let there be no vassal in your realm who is capable of bearing arms ... who does not swear his oath to you ...

Count Theobald of France rose up and said '... [King Henry] will find no safety anywhere, be it in open country or in forest, if he does not restore to the Young King his rightful inheritance.'

SOURCE 3

From the *Dialogue of the Exchequer*. Written in c1189 by Richard fitzNigel, it set down the procedures of the Exchequer in a handbook for royal officials, written in the form of a dialogue between teacher and student. The teacher is explaining to the student how great a king Henry II is.

Note, then, how miraculously the man resisted himself, in the shape of his own children. For certain stubborn little foxes suborned his own sons ... while they were young and therefore blank slates, and vulnerable to every impulse of mind; and at last they turned 'his own flesh' against their father as if against an enemy ... and those counsellors who were closest to him plotted against him, saying to his sons and to his enemies, 'Persecute him and seize him, for there is no one to rescue him.' ... So when the wife was raging without cause against her husband, the sons against their father, and the servants against their lord, would it not be accurate to say a man is fighting against himself?

A Level Exam-Style Question Section A

How far could the historian make use of Sources 2 and 3 together to investigate the extent to which Henry II was to blame for the outbreak of the Great Rebellion in 1173?

Explain your answer, using both sources, the information given about them and your own knowledge of the historical content. (20 marks)

Tip

Use your own knowledge of the historical context to evaluate the usefulness of Sources 2 and 3 by determining how much they mirror what you know. It would be very easy to criticise Source 2 as literature intended to entertain. Find out about minstrels to add another angle to your evaluation.

Eleanor of Aquitaine's opposition to the king

Whatever else the different chroniclers and sources say, there does seem to be a large body of evidence that suggests the Young King and his brothers had plenty of encouragement in developing their resentment of their father. Many had their own reasons for doing so and/or grudges against Henry II. Louis VII was true to form in supporting Henry's sons against him, while Eleanor hoped to regain her political influence.

The traditional reason given for Eleanor of Aquitaine's opposition to Henry II was his extramarital affairs, especially one with Rosamund Clifford that had begun possibly as early as 1165. Little is known about Rosamund that is not legend or rumour, although it was largely expected and accepted that kings had mistresses and fathered bastard children. Since 1168, Eleanor had been living apart from Henry II, establishing her own court in her duchy of Aquitaine and building relations with the local barons and lords there. Given Eleanor's background and political aspirations, it is unlikely that she would have planned and risked a full-scale rebellion solely because the king was having extramarital affairs.

EXTEND YOUR KNOWLEDGE

A woman scorned? Why did Eleanor of Aquitaine turn against her husband?

The traditional explanation of a wife seeking her revenge for her husband's many mistresses, especially Rosamund Clifford, relies solely on seeing Eleanor in a traditional 'female' role of 'a woman scorned'. This is far too simple, as it shows little awareness of medieval women, and Eleanor in particular, beyond the parameters laid out for them by the Church and generalised social mores.

Eleanor of Aquitaine's personality and life experience did not fit the traditional mould for a wife, who was expected to be obedient to her husband. This was made clear in a letter written to her, at Henry's request, by the archbishop of Rouen after she had rebelled (see Source 6).

Eleanor of Aquitaine was a woman who had seen the world. She had caused a scandal by insisting that she go on the Second Crusade with her then husband, Louis VII. She recruited her own vassals for the cause and, once there, helped with seeing to the wounded. Coming from Aquitaine meant that she was able to inherit and govern her own lands. However, in the kingdom of France there was the Salic law, which expressly prevented a woman from inheriting the throne. Eleanor's father had educated her to govern Aquitaine, although her inability to take to the battlefield as a woman was a limitation, despite her prowess on horseback. Marriage to Henry was therefore useful to her (and it did seem to be a love match) but, with his dominating personality and the wider attitudes to women at the time, Eleanor's influence on Aquitaine was curtailed, and this was a great source of resentment and frustration to her.

Attitudes towards women in the south-west of France, where Eleanor had grown up, were somewhat different from elsewhere in Christendom. For example, under Aquitanian law a wife's adultery was not punished by imprisonment or execution as elsewhere. Women in Aquitaine took part in public life. The founder of the abbey of Fontevraud, where Eleanor of Aquitaine, Henry II and Richard I are all buried, believed women to be the superior sex, as well as being better administrators and managers of estates than men.

Once more is understood about Eleanor of Aquitaine's personality, upbringing and expectations, the simple assertion that she rebelled against her husband because of his affairs carries less weight. In addition, it was tacitly expected and accepted that a king would have mistresses and father illegitimate children – Henry I had 20 born out of wedlock. It could even be a welcome relief for the wife from pregnancy and childbirth, which was very dangerous. That said, Eleanor's union with Henry was very fertile until John's birth in 1167, by which time Eleanor was 45. It was then that she returned to Aquitaine, living apart from Henry and establishing her own court and power base. It was not until five years later that she encouraged and joined her sons in rebellion against their father.

Richard and Geoffrey were still young enough not to be politically independent and Richard especially came under his mother's influence. He was being groomed to become duke of Aquitaine as his grandfather had been. Wanting Richard to continue from where her father left off is a key consideration in explaining Eleanor's opposition to Henry II. However, when he was in Aquitaine, Henry assumed control of affairs, as he had in the first months of 1173, holding court at Limoges.

Having established her own court there, and given the general antipathy in Aquitaine to Angevin rule, it is possible that her husband's taking control when he arrived underlined who was considered to hold ultimate power in the duchy. When combined with Henry's control of financial and military resources, this would have added to the frustration she already felt. By 1172, Eleanor had already issued some writs in Aquitaine in her own name, or hers and Richard's, which is indicative of her aspirations.

Although her exact motives are not known for certain, it was not long after the meeting at Limoges that the Young King and his brothers fled to Paris. Soon after that, Eleanor and her uncle, Raoul de Faye, encouraged the lords of southern Aquitaine to rise up against Henry II. The barons of the Poitou and Angoulême regions of Aquitaine rallied to the cause, although those from La Marche, in the east, and Limousin and Gascony, further south, did not become involved.

SOURCE 4

A verse from the troubadour Richard le Poitevin, who had visited Eleanor of Aquitaine's court on several occasions. It was composed at the time when Eleanor of Aquitaine and Raoul de Faye were encouraging the Aquitanians to rebel against Henry II.

Rejoice, O Aquitaine! Be jubilant, O Poitou!

For the sceptre of the King of the North Wind is drawing away from you.

THINKING HISTORICALLY Causation (5b)

Causation relativity

Historical events usually have many causes. Some are crucial, while others are less important. For some historical questions, it is important to understand exactly what role certain factors played in causing historical change.

Significant factors in the outbreak of the Great Rebellion in 1173

- The Angevin Empire in France made Henry II a more powerful figure than King Louis VII. Louis wanted to reverse the situation and provide his son with a strong inheritance.

- Henry II had a domineering, volatile personality.

- Since becoming king in 1154, Henry II had been making the English barons more subject to royal power through decommissioning castles and making reforms such as the Assize of Clarendon in 1166.

- Eleanor of Aquitaine had been estranged from Henry II since 1168.

- Henry II did not allow his sons the power to run the territories given them in the Treaty of Montmirail in 1169.

- Prince John's inheritance was agreed at Limoges in January 1173, including land from the Young King.

Answer the following questions:

1 How important was the settling of an inheritance on Prince John in the timing of the Great Rebellion?

2 How great was the impact of the Treaty of Montmirail upon Louis VII's position in France?

3 How important were events in England in causing the Great Rebellion to break out in 1173?

4 How significant was Eleanor of Aquitaine's role in fomenting the Great Rebellion?

5 Was it possible for Henry II to have avoided the Great Rebellion?

6 Who was more important in causing the Great Rebellion: Henry II or Louis VII?

7 What roles did each of the factors above play in causing the Great Rebellion?

The queen's capture

While her sons were in Paris, Eleanor gathered support for their cause in Aquitaine. The Poitevins were especially forthcoming, as were the counts of Angoulême and the powerful Lusignan family. She then planned to follow on to Louis VII's court but was captured en route, disguised as a man, by Henry II's men, possibly having been given away by spies in her court.

It would appear that she was an instigator of her sons' rebellion and she certainly had sympathy with their cause. The contemporary chronicler, Ralph of Diceto, found her role to be unprecedented. Looking back through history, he said, he could find tens of cases of sons turning against their father, but none of a wife turning against her husband. Only Gerald of Wales, a severe critic of Henry II, took a different line; he believed that Eleanor of Aquitaine was inspired by God to turn against Henry. Gerald saw the Great Rebellion as divine retribution for the murder of Thomas Becket (see pages 351–353).

Henry II commanded the archbishop of Rouen to write a long letter to Eleanor, admonishing her for having rebelled against her husband and, through her disobedience, upsetting the entire social and political order. She was expected to be obedient twice over, once as a wife and again as a subject. Whether she saw herself as a subject in Aquitaine is a matter for conjecture. She was certainly willing to act as if she did not.

Eleanor's part in the Great Rebellion was short lived, but this does not mean that it was not significant. She was held in captivity for the remainder of Henry II's reign. However, her capture did nothing to reconcile Richard with Henry.

Effigies of Eleanor of Aquitaine and Henry II from their tombs at Fontevraud Abbey in France.

From a letter written by the archbishop of Rouen, on Henry II's instructions, reminding Eleanor of Aquitaine of her duty as his wife and subject. It was written before her capture by Henry's men.

Pious, Queen, most illustrious Queen, we all of us deplore, and are united in our sorrow, that you, a prudent wife if ever there was one, should have parted from your husband … Still more terrible is the fact that you should have made the fruits of your union with our Lord King rise up against their father. For we know that, unless you return to your husband, you will be the cause of general ruin. Return then, O illustrious Queen, to your husband and our lord. Before events carry us to a dire conclusion, return with your sons … Bid your sons, we beg you, to be obedient and devoted to their father, who for their sakes has undergone so many difficulties, run so many dangers, undertaken so many labours.

ACTIVITY
KNOWLEDGE CHECK

1 What reasons were there for the English earl Hugh Bigod in particular to take up arms against Henry II? You may wish to look back at Chapters 1 and 2 for more detail on Hugh Bigod.

2 What reasons were there for English barons in general turning against Henry II? You may wish to look back at Chapters 1 and 2 for more detail on the English barons.

3 Using the text and the sources, assess who had the bigger role to play in causing the Great Rebellion: Henry II, Eleanor of Aquitaine, Louis VII or the Young King? Use a pie chart to show your conclusions and list the most significant evidence against each of the four alongside.

AS Level Exam-Style Question Section A

How much weight do you give Source 6 for an enquiry into the importance of Eleanor of Aquitaine's role in the Great Rebellion in 1173?

Explain your answer using the source, the information given about it and your own knowledge of the historical context. (12 marks)

Tip
Think carefully about the authorship of this source.

HOW DID THE GREAT REBELLION IMPACT UPON ROYAL POWER?

TIMELINE

1173

April Eleanor of Aquitaine is captured en route to Paris

May The Great Rebellion breaks out

July William the Lion begins raiding the North of England

September Parley at Gisors fails to resolve anything, after which rebel mercenaries land in England

October Rebel forces led by Earl Robert of Leicester are defeated; Earl Robert is captured

1176

Assize of Northampton

Justices in eyre ensure castles designated in the aftermath of the Great Rebellion are totally destroyed

Punitive forest eyre

Rebellion in Aquitaine is put down by Richard

1180

June Philip II renews the Treaty of Ivry

Death of Louis VII

1174

Easter William the Lion invades England again

May Henry goes to Anjou and Poitou

June Hugh Bigod takes Leicester

8 July Henry II arrives in England

12 July Henry II does penance at Thomas Becket's tomb

13 July William the Lion is captured

Siege of Rouen begins

11 August Henry II returns to Normandy to lift the siege of Rouen

August/September Louis VII and the Young King sue for peace

23 September Richard surrenders to Henry II

30 September Treaty of Montlouis

1177

Treaty of Ivry

Rebel barons in the Gascony region of Aquitaine are put down by Richard

Henry's victories in England and the Angevin lands

Henry's allies

Henry II did have some important allies for his cause. Richard de Lucy, Henry's surviving justiciar, remained loyal to him, as did other key parts of government such as the barons of the Exchequer. Towns, the merchant classes, London and the judiciary also supported Henry II, as did the Welsh and the Church. Only eight years before, Owain of Gwynedd had offered Louis VII Welsh support against Henry II. Since Owain's death in 1170, there had been a **rapprochement**, which held firm in the face of the rebellion. It was not only in the British Isles that Henry had allies. The key basis of support for Henry II in France was in Normandy. Otherwise, however, Henry found that, if not directly fighting for the Young King, there were other nobles willing to use the opportunity presented by their overlord having to fight elsewhere to enable them to make a few gains of their own.

When hostilities broke out in May 1173, Normandy bore the brunt of the attacks against Henry II. Although Scotland invaded England, this was contained until 1174. Before then, England sent all the resources it could muster to France in support of their king.

1173: Hostilities and parley

Hostilities broke out in May 1173, with assaults on Normandy, the ultimate aim being to capture Rouen. Philip of Flanders and Richard, the Young King and Louis VII, with Geoffrey in tow, all attacked Normandy's eastern borders, while the Bretons launched an assault from the west.

Henry II's first instinct was to trust the defences he already had in place in Normandy and secretly to cross over to England to assess the situation. Although only there a few days, his men attacked and besieged the rebel city of Leicester. Henry quickly returned to France, having organised supplies from England to help him with the battle he would be facing in Normandy.

KEY TERM

Rapprochement
Re-establishing good relations, especially in foreign policy or international affairs.

Henry fought hard through the summer of 1173 and each of the initial campaigns against him in France was a failure. Philip of Flanders withdrew from the fortress of Verneuil that he was besieging upon hearing the news that his brother, the count of Boulogne, had been killed. This was a blow to the rebels. The Young King was too inexperienced to co-ordinate their armies and so Louis VII took control. He proved to be inept and so the rebel forces lacked the cohesion necessary to focus and co-ordinate their resource effectively.

Away from Normandy there were risings in other parts of the Angevin Empire. Anjou and Maine renounced their loyalty to Henry, and that September Count William of Angoulême, Guy de Lusignan, Geoffrey de Lusignan and the Poitevin lords expelled Henry's officials from their lands in Poitou. Henry's response was to send in a large army of mercenaries who laid waste to the region between Tours and Poitiers, destroying or capturing castles and uprooting or burning crops. They were not the only ones to use a **scorched earth policy**; Henry's sons did the same. There was little open warfare during the Great Rebellion; instead, there was plundering and burning of towns and villages, and the besieging of castles.

The rebels' campaign was petering out by the end of summer 1173 and a **parley** was arranged at Gisors for September. Although Henry was prepared to offer revenues and castles, he was still unwilling to delegate any power and so Louis VII advised the rebel sons to reject the offer. The earl of Leicester was present, and was especially insistent that no deals should be done with Henry, whom he insulted and threatened. The earl of Leicester undertook to continue the rebellion in England and his castle became one of the chief centres of revolt. He also sent a force of Flemish mercenaries to East Anglia, which landed at the end of September 1173. Thus the fighting continued.

The Great Rebellion in England, 1173

By the end of August, Scotland had invaded England and devastated northern counties as far south as Yorkshire. Richard de Lucy, who had succeeded in capturing Leicester, called a truce and marched north, where he forced the Scots back over the border and dealt with Lothian in the same manner. King William agreed a truce until January. Meanwhile, on hearing that the earl of Leicester's army had landed, Richard de Lucy quickly returned south. On 17 October, with the help of local people armed with clubs and agricultural implements, Richard de Lucy and England's constable, Humphrey de Bohun, and the earls of Gloucester, Arundel and Cornwall defeated the earl of Leicester's soldiers in the marshes near Bury St Edmunds and captured the earl and his wife. After this the rebellion in the South of England faltered.

With the onset of winter, the campaigning season was put on hold. Louis did not do anything until July 1174, hoping to persuade Henry to return to England, as William the Lion had again invaded that Easter. Henry instead headed south that May and fought in Anjou and Poitou, subduing the rebels there and then dismantling and dispersing Eleanor of Aquitaine's court in Poitiers. As well as dismissing her servants, he took control of their daughter, Joanna; the Young King's wife, Margaret of France; Alice of France and Constance of Brittany, who were betrothed to Richard and Geoffrey; and John's intended, Alice of Maurienne. That done he returned to Normandy.

SOURCE

From Gerald of Wales, *On the Instruction of Princes*. Gerald of Wales, a clergyman, had a position at court and immediate knowledge of the circumstances he relates. However, he was severely critical of Henry II and his family. It is thought that this book was written c1216.

For about two years after the triumphal death of our martyr [Thomas Becket], his son Henry went over to his father-in-law, Louis, king of France, together with his two brothers, the counts of Poitou and Brittany, and revolted from his father against him, at the same time having many accomplices and favourers amongst many of the nobles, not only in England, but beyond the sea ... For since his domestics were his enemies, and that the enmity of those added to the same family is amongst the worst of plagues, this added to the weight of his grief and despair; and those soldiers whom he had selected from his bed chamber, men in whose hands he placed equally both his death and life, going over from him in a hostile spirit, and almost every night, to join his sons, were sought in vain in the morning.

KEY TERMS

Scorched earth policy
A military strategy, often in retreat, of burning and destroying anything that might be of use to the enemy.

Parley
A conference between opposing sides, especially in armed conflict. Although not a truce, it usually concerns terms from an armistice (laying down of weapons). From the French verb parler meaning 'to talk'.

AS Level Exam-Style Question Section A

Why is Source 7 valuable to the historian for an enquiry into how serious a threat the Great Rebellion of 1173–74 was to Henry II?

Explain your answer using the source, the information given about it and your own knowledge of the historical context. (8 marks)

Tip

Read sources carefully to pick up on key words and short phrases that can tell you a great deal. Remember that being part of the king's bedchamber was a great honour as it meant being in close contact with him when he had withdrawn from the public areas of court.

A Level Exam-Style Question Section B

'Henry II's sons were not the cause of the Great Rebellion. They were nothing more than puppets operated by his enemies.'

How far do you agree with this opinion? Explain your answer. (20 marks)

Tip

The wording of the question is very useful here. By saying they were 'nothing more than puppets' it is suggesting that they cannot be blamed. You should be able to challenge this part of the question.

The capture of William of Scotland

By Easter 1174, the situation in England was deteriorating. William the Lion was laying siege to Carlisle and rebellion had broken out in the North of England and the Midlands, Nottingham having fallen to the rebels. The Young King and the earl of Flanders were also preparing to invade and had sent a force of mercenaries on ahead which, led by Hugh Bigod, took Norwich on 18 June 1174.

Another Becket miracle?

It was at this point that Henry II decided to return to England. After he landed on 8 July, he went straight to Canterbury to seek forgiveness and perform penance for Thomas Becket (see page 355). This he did on 12 July. On 13 July, William the Lion was caught in a field near Alnwick and was sent south, feet tied beneath his horse, as Henry's prisoner. This event marked the beginning of the end of the rebellion in England. Henry II went to the rebel-held castles of Huntingdon and Framlingham, besieging both until each surrendered.

While Henry was in England, Louis VII launched further attacks on Henry's French territories. In summer 1174, he besieged Rouen, Normandy's capital. By August, it was clearly not working, traffic entering the city from the west via the River Seine. On 10 August, a truce was agreed but was immediately broken by Louis, who made a last-ditch attempt to take Rouen before Henry arrived. It failed. Louis VII fled Rouen and sued for peace before the end of September.

Richard fights on

Richard's headquarters were in Saintes, Aquitaine, where he had turned the cathedral into an arms depot. His father, however, possessed not only greater resources and experience but astonishing speed. He took the city gates by storm. Richard and a few followers escaped downstream to Taillebourg. Although Richard was safe, he had lost his military stores as well as 60 knights and 400 archers captured in Saintes.

Richard struggled on stubbornly until hearing that Louis VII and the Young King had sued for peace. Richard was angry but convinced his cause was lost. On 23 September, he met with his father, weeping and throwing himself at his feet, begging forgiveness. A week later peace negotiations were concluded in Montlouis.

Under the terms of the agreement at Montlouis, the Young King had to agree that John would be provided for with castles and revenues from England, Normandy and Anjou. However, Henry did agree that his eldest son could have two residences in Normandy and an allowance of £15,000 per annum. Richard was also given two residences and half the revenues of Poitou, while Geoffrey was to have half the revenues of Brittany.

The earls of Chester and Leicester were to remain imprisoned, as was King William of Scotland. Although no mention was made of Eleanor of Aquitaine, she stayed captive until Henry's death in 1189.

The Treaty of Falaise, 1174

This was the treaty agreed upon by Henry II and William I of Scotland in December 1174, after which William was released. Its key terms were as follows.

- William was to pay homage to Henry for his lands and to swear an oath of fealty to Henry II.

- The bishops and abbots of Scotland also had to recognise Henry II as their liege lord; likewise the Scottish barons, who had to do homage and swear fealty to the king of England and his heirs.

- England was given five key castles: Roxburgh, Berwick, Jedburgh, Stirling and Edinburgh.

- William was to give Henry 21 hostages, including his brother, David, thus securing William's good behaviour.

William of Scotland's hopes thus ended in humiliation and he did not rebel again in Henry II's lifetime.

KEY TERM

Constable of England
A high-ranking member of the royal household who would serve as military commander in the king's absence.

AS Level Exam-Style Question Section B

How accurate is it to say that Louis VII was the most significant factor in explaining Henry II's victory in the Great Rebellion of 1173–74?
(20 marks)

Tip

The question is inviting you to consider other factors as well as what the question gives you. However, you must start with the stated factor and should explore it thoroughly before moving on.

The short-term impact of Henry's victories on royal power

The Great Rebellion had lasted 18 months and had stretched from Scotland to Aquitaine. Henry II emerged from it stronger than before, a king at the height of his powers. He had beaten three of his four sons; two kings, several barons of northern France and four key English earls. His wife remained in his custody. The blame for the rebellion was focused on the Young King's advisers, with suggestions that there had been a 'treacherous faction' at work.

SOURCE 8

Richard being crowned in 1189. From Roger of Wendover, *Flowers of History*. Roger of Wendover was the chronicler of St Albans Monastery from 1231 to 1235 and based his account both on his own recollections and the recent writings of other chroniclers and observers.

The Great Rebellion reinforced the good relationship Henry II had forged with the Welsh (see pages 298–299). Henry returned various lands back to the Welsh princes in 1177, Ellesmere in the north and Merioneth in the south, in return for promises of fealty and homage. As for Scotland, the Treaty of Falaise made Henry II's supremacy complete. The earls of Chester and Leicester remained prisoners until January 1177, when they had their estates restored. Henry's leniency with the English rebels was criticised by members of his Curia Regis, but his magnanimity was also a sign of strength: Henry did not need to punish the rebels too harshly as his position in England was, by this time, unassailable.

The Assize of Northampton and the eyre of 1176

During the Great Rebellion, royal authority had been undermined. Once again powerful barons had challenged the Crown. In 1176, Henry promulgated the Assize of Northampton, which tightened up punishments and added that anyone who was generally known to be of 'ill repute' was to be banished from England. It allowed the king's justices to hear a wider range of cases, including arson and forgery. It also introduced standardised writs for *novel disseisin* and *mort d'ancestor*.

When Henry's justices were sent on eyre in 1176, they were commanded to collect information about who had custody of England's castles and they were also instructed to ensure that castles that had already been destroyed were utterly demolished and that any due for demolition were razed to the ground. There had also been considerable encroachment of the royal forest in England during the Great Rebellion, resulting in a punishing forest eyre, led by Alan de Neville between 1176 and 1178, that brought in £12,000.

Henry's French lands

In 1177, Henry II met with Louis VII to sign the Treaty of Ivry, a friendship treaty that included an agreement to undertake a joint crusade but, more importantly, to respect each other's rights. Any issues where there were still problems would be put to arbitration.

Impressed with his determination and leadership skills, Henry soon gave Richard more responsibility than his brothers, allowing him sufficient resources and powers to govern Aquitaine. He was given the opportunity to bring Poitou and Aquitaine firmly under control, during which time father and son often worked together. In 1176 and 1177, after a family conference and with additional resources from Henry II, Richard successfully put down rebellions in Angoulême and Gascony.

Richard's rule in Aquitaine was resented by the regional barons and can be seen as evidence of his success. Angevin authority was recognised as far south as the Pyrenees. However, the resentment was also because of Richard's ruthlessness. Henry often worked alongside Richard, supporting him as necessary. Henry was unimpressed with the Aquitanian barons'

grievances, even though, according to Roger of Howden, they included serious accusations of Richard's sexual misconduct with their wives and daughters as well as other women.

EXTEND YOUR KNOWLEDGE

How did Henry's sons develop in the aftermath of the Great Rebellion?

The Great Rebellion was not the last family rebellion with which Henry II had to deal. After 1182, each of his sons rebelled against him at one time or another and for one reason or another. To understand the family dynamic of the 1180s in a little more detail, it is useful to consider how the boys changed as they matured.

Henry's approach to governing the empire began to change after the Great Rebellion; he gradually stepped back from direct control of Aquitaine and Brittany. Although at first he controlled the other halves of the revenues of Aquitaine and Brittany, and appointed his own advisors, he gradually delegated more power to his sons.

Between 1176 and 1179, the Young King was in his French lands, Normandy and Anjou, Maine and Touraine. He did not apply himself to the task, however, and bored quickly of routine, preferring tournaments, fashion and entertainments, running up large debts and often requiring his father's intervention in both financial and political matters. In short, the Young King did not seem to have matured and he certainly had done nothing to increase his father's confidence that he could manage his inheritance.

Richard had impressed Henry considerably during the Great Rebellion and was given the task of governing Aquitaine. He received money for mercenaries and the necessary powers to make decisions, going beyond what had been agreed at Montlouis. From time to time, Henry II himself would join his son in Aquitaine, which sent a clear signal of his backing and approval.

The result was that Richard flourished. Under him the power of the duke of Aquitaine was greater than ever before. Richard forged a formidable reputation for himself, including for ruthlessness and cruelty. In 1177, he defeated the count of Angoulême and took a string of vital castles in the duchy's heartland. In 1178, he put down two robber barons, whose lawless conduct included robbing pilgrims. By 1179, Richard was, for all intents and purpose, duke of Aquitaine. Even the lordship of the Pyrenees came to recognise his authority, which had never been properly established as the barons alternated their allegiance between Aquitaine, Toulouse or the king of France as suited them.

Geoffrey was knighted in 1178, and successfully dealt with a leading Breton rebel in 1179. Brittany developed relatively peacefully in the latter half of the 1170s and began to establish English-style administration and government.

As for John, he was sent to Ireland in 1185 to establish himself with a view to becoming king. Henry II had a crown of gold and peacock feathers made. It was not needed. John's expedition was a disaster. The only Irish unity he succeeded in nurturing was that of the Irish kings against him.

SOURCE

From Roger of Wendover, *Flowers of History*, describing the events of Christmas 1173.

The army of Flemings, who had been sent over by count Philip, were allowed to return ... The troops of the Young King left England without impediment. Moreover Robert earl of Ferrars and Roger de Mowbray, whose castles of Thirsk and Stutbury were at that time besieged by the king ... asked for peace. William earl of Gloucester met the king and promised implicit obedience to his commands. Thus the glorious king having conquered all his enemies, crossed into Normandy on the 7th of July [sic]...

When King Henry landed in Normandy, on the 11th of July, he found the city of Rouen besieged; for king Louis of France and the young king Henry, with the count of Flanders, had assembled a large force in the absence of the king, and severely pressed the citizens; but when the King of France heard that the king of England was coming, he retreated, not without some detriment to his reputation, and the English soldiers seized a large quantity of his arms and munitions of war.

Louis king of France and the count of Flanders, beginning to feel the expenses which they had incurred in the cause of the young king of England, and reflecting on the loss of life and property which had fallen on their subjects, promised to abstain from invading Normandy; and they did their best to reconcile the king with his sons, who, as they well knew, had incurred their father's malediction [curse], the hatred of the clergy, and the imprecations [curses] of the whole people.

SOURCE

From the Assize of Northampton in 1176.

Item, let no one either in a borough or a vill entertain in his house from one than one night any stranger for whom he is unwilling to be responsible unless there be a reasonable excuse

Item, let the justices of the lord king cause an investigation to be made concerning dispossessions carried out contrary to the assize [refers to earlier parts of the Assize of Northampton], since the lord king's coming to England immediately following upon the peace made between him and the king, his son.

Item, let the justices receive oaths of fealty to the lord king ... from all those who wish to remain in the kingdom, namely from the earls, barons, knights and freeholders, and even villeins. And whosoever shall refuse to take the oath of fealty may be arrested as an enemy of the lord king

Item, let the justices see to it that the castles which have been destroyed are utterly demolished, and those which are due for destruction are razed to the ground

---

A Level Exam-Style Question Section A

How far could the historian make use of Sources 9 and 10 together to investigate the impact that the Great Rebellion had on Henry II's power in his own territories?

Explain your answer, using both sources, the information given about them and your own knowledge of the historical context. (20 marks)

Tip
Source 10 does more than simply tell you what the king did to enhance his power after the Great Rebellion; it also suggests something about the nature of the Great Rebellion as well.

ACTIVITY
KNOWLEDGE CHECK

How would you best characterise the impact of the Great Rebellion on Henry II's reign during 1174–80:

- a blip in Henry II's power that had very little impact

- a serious threat to Henry II's power that he dealt with ruthlessly

- an opportunity for Henry II to increase his power

- a lesson from which Henry II learned and modified his behaviour?

To make up your mind, first study the contemporary evidence. What conclusions can you draw from it? Then study the text. What factual evidence is there from Henry's actions about what impact the Great Rebellion had on him and his power? You should use the balance of evidence to support your choice. Alternatively, based upon what you have read, develop your own option.

Extension

To what extent do the sources stand up to the factual evidence? Do they completely coincide? Are they completely different? If there is a difference in some cases, can you explain why?

WHY DID HENRY II DIE A DIMINISHED KING?

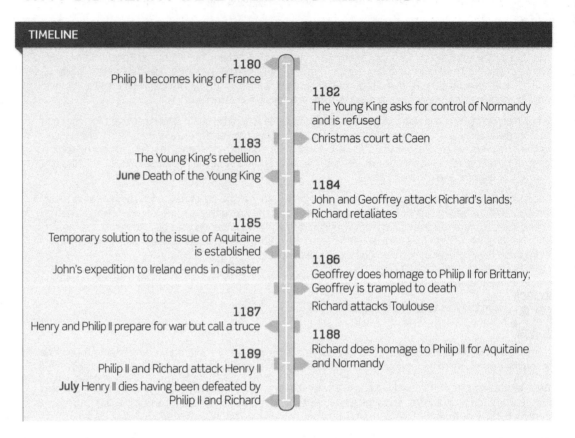

TIMELINE

1180
Philip II becomes king of France

1182
The Young King asks for control of Normandy and is refused

Christmas court at Caen

1183
The Young King's rebellion

June Death of the Young King

1184
John and Geoffrey attack Richard's lands; Richard retaliates

1185
Temporary solution to the issue of Aquitaine is established

John's expedition to Ireland ends in disaster

1186
Geoffrey does homage to Philip II for Brittany; Geoffrey is trampled to death

Richard attacks Toulouse

1187
Henry and Philip II prepare for war but call a truce

1188
Richard does homage to Philip II for Aquitaine and Normandy

1189
Philip II and Richard attack Henry II

July Henry II dies having been defeated by Philip II and Richard

The new king of France

When Louis VII suffered a stroke in 1179, his son, Philip, took the reins. On 28 June 1180, Philip met with Henry II to renew the treaty of Ivry. By the autumn of 1180, aged 15, he was king in his own right. Philip II's immediate concern was with securing his father's throne and overcoming a court power struggle for control of him. Philip even turned to Henry for help, first to reconcile with his mother and then to warn off the count of Flanders. Although young, Philip was politically astute and Henry's support enabled him to subdue his own rebellious vassals. He began to establish his court and government along Henry's lines.

In 1183, Henry and Philip met at Gisors, where Henry did homage for his French lands. If Roger of Howden is correct in saying that he had never done homage before, this perhaps indicates Henry's aim of easing tensions with France by trying to allay fears of Angevin dominance. The kings' relationship had therefore started on a positive, constructive note.

The deaths of the Young King and Geoffrey

The Young King's second rebellion

In the summer of 1182, young Henry asked his father to give him control of Normandy, but was again refused. Although the Young King's tantrum did not last, it was clear that Plantagenet family relations were still rocky. Matters came to a head when unhappy Aquitanian lords offered to recognise young Henry as their duke if he would rid them of 'the tyrant Richard'. Although Henry did not take action immediately, it was clear that he had an opportunity to extend his territory at his brother's expense.

At this point, Richard decided to strengthen his castle at Clairvaux, on the borders of Aquitaine and Anjou. The Young King saw this as a provocation and raised the question of whether Richard was preparing for war against him. Given the renewed family tensions, Henry II held a great Christmas court at Caën with the aim of solving the differences between his sons.

Henry II's plans, rather than soothing tensions, served to intensify the brothers' jealousy. He asked Richard and Geoffrey to do homage to young Henry, hoping that reinforcing his seniority would satisfy him. Richard refused, saying he was as nobly born as his brother. His father talked him round by insisting that Aquitaine's future was beyond doubt and it would belong to him and his heirs forever. However, now the Young King was upset, and refused to accept Richard's homage, citing the strengthening of Clairvaux as his reason.

The immediate dispute was quickly solved by Richard handing over Clairvaux Castle to his father. It was not a long-term solution, so old Henry called his three eldest sons together at Angers to swear a promise of perpetual peace. This was complicated by the necessity of including the rebellious Aquitanian nobles who had asked for the Young King's support against Richard in the first place. Henry II sent Geoffrey to the Limousin to arrange a truce with the discontented barons and bring them to Angers. Instead, Geoffrey joined them. As news of the quarrel between the brothers spread, other Aquitanian barons took the chance to rebel. The Young King went to fetch Geoffrey home but instead joined the rebels. Richard's grasp on Aquitaine was under threat.

The main focus of this quarrel between the Young King and Richard concerned the latter's fears over Aquitaine. Richard was peculiarly attached to the region and could never countenance relinquishing it, even for a larger prize as Henry II would later discover.

Henry II and Richard against the Young King and Geoffrey
Henry II went to meet with young Henry and Geoffrey, hoping to restore family harmony. Unfortunately, he was apparently mistaken for a raiding party and attacked. The Young King, having failed to convince his father that it was a genuine error, went to the citadel of St Martial in Limoges while Geoffrey took mercenaries to terrorise the southern region of the Limousin. Having run out of patience with young Henry and Geoffrey, Henry II joined with Richard and they besieged St Martial.

On 1 March 1183, reinforcements arrived for Henry II and Richard. As the siege dragged on the Young King, running out of money, plundered St Martial and then left in search of more to pay his mercenaries. He attacked and captured the castle at Aixe nearby, but three days later, on 26 May 1183, fell ill, and died on 11 June. This ended the rebellion, but not the family conflicts.

The ins and outs of the squabbles between Henry's sons are intricate and indicative of a complete lack of trust between brothers and between father and sons. They are also evidence of endemic family vanities, jealousies and tensions. Philip II was to prove adept at capitalising on the opportunities presented to him by the quarrelling Plantagenets, which worsened after the Young King's death.

Now that the Young King was dead, Philip II wanted the return to France of his sister's dowry, the Vexin, along with its castles. Henry II did not want to lose this important part of Normandy's defences. It was eventually agreed that Henry could keep it if he paid Margaret £2,700 per annum and granted the Vexin to whichever of his sons married Philip's sister, Alice. It was later agreed that this should be Richard.

Rivalry: Richard and John
The death of the younger Henry in June 1183 had, in theory, made Richard heir of England, Normandy and Anjou as well as Aquitaine. The crux of the next crisis was that Henry II wanted his youngest son, John, to be given Aquitaine, which Richard refused to hand over. Henry gave John permission to invade and take it by force. In June 1184, John and Geoffrey launched a series of raids into Poitou; in retaliation, Richard attacked Brittany. The situation worsening, Henry tried once again to settle the succession, even bringing Eleanor of Aquitaine out of captivity to attend all-important council meetings at which the matter was to be discussed.

It would appear that by now Richard was so suspicious of his father that, whatever Henry said, he felt sure that he was being deceived. He continued attacking Brittany in 1185. The only solution he would accept was to hand Aquitaine back to his mother, and that she, he and his father would rule it jointly. This agreement was perhaps made possible by Henry sending John to Ireland that year, having had a crown made for his coronation there as high king. By the end of the year, John's expedition had proved a disaster, there was no coronation and he returned as he had set out, with no secure inheritance. It had also become clear that Henry II still controlled the finances and resources of Aquitaine and that the real authority continued to lie with him. Neither of these developments did much to relieve Richard's fears over Aquitaine.

For the rest of Henry II's reign, Richard was plagued with doubts about his father's intentions regarding him and John. Henry II seemed reluctant to name Richard as his principal heir and this created a deep division between father and son that was ultimately exploited by Philip II. First, however, he worked on Geoffrey.

Intrigue: Philip and Geoffrey
Philip II shrewdly focused his attentions on Geoffrey next. Geoffrey realised that, between his mother's favourite, Richard, and his father's favourite, John, he had no hope of inheriting anything other than Brittany. Philip II made him a seneschal of France and their friendship secured Geoffrey a status at the French court that he had not previously experienced. In 1186, he did homage to Philip for Brittany. To Henry this was a treasonable act because the homage for Brittany was owed to the duke of Normandy. Before Philip could use Geoffrey's ambition and jealousy against his father, however, Geoffrey was accidentally trampled to death in August 1186.

Immediately there arose a conflict between King Henry and King Philip. As overlord of France, Philip claimed wardship of Geoffrey's children, a daughter and a baby son born seven months posthumously. Henry II also claimed custody of the children, who were in his keeping. Although a truce was agreed, the matter was not settled. Added to this was Philip's growing suspicion of Henry II over the proposed marriage of his sister, Alice, to Richard. It had not yet gone ahead and it was becoming increasingly clear that it was unlikely to. Richard may have already fallen in love with Berengaria of Navarre by this time; however, there were also rumours that Henry himself had seduced Alice and wanted to keep both her and, therefore, the Vexin.

AS Level Exam-Style
Question Section A

Why is Source 11 valuable to the historian for an enquiry into the importance of Philip II in explaining why Henry II had lost control over his French lands by the end of his reign?

Explain your answer using the source, the information given about it and your own knowledge of the historical context. (8 marks)

Tip

Source 11 concerns 1186, although think about the behaviour Philip II is showing in this source. Is it typical? Does it coincide with other examples?

SOURCE

11

From Gerald of Wales, *On the Instruction of Princes*, c1216. Here he is describing events surrounding Geoffrey's relationship with Philip II c1186. Gerald of Wales worked for the archbishop of Canterbury in the 1170s and for Henry II from the 1180s.

For this had been the perverse nature of king Henry, that, with all his power, he excited and perpetuated quarrels between his sons, hoping from their discord to gain peace and quietness to himself. But count Geoffrey had so attached himself to the minds of king Philip and of all the nobles of France, that, by their unanimous vote he was created seneschal of France; and he was raised to so great a power, and was admitted with such great familiarity with the king, and had so excited both the king of France and the whole of that realm generally, against his father and his brother by his persuasive words that, if he had not been prevented by death, he would have raised against them such disquietude as they had never before experienced ... King Philip was afflicted with such deep sorrow and despair at his death ... that he ordered him to be buried before the high altar in the cathedral church of Paris...

Richard's and John's ambitions and treachery

The deaths of the Young King and Geoffrey caused fears of Angevin dominance over the French king to re-surface. Henry's plan for defusing those fears had been to divide his territories between his sons. Now that he had only two sons left, the territories each controlled would be greater. Henry had wanted John to inherit Aquitaine, but Richard resolutely refused, and expected to take the Young King's lands as he was now the elder son. Henry would not name his principal heir, perhaps to hold French fears at bay until the issue of his sons' inheritance could be settled to his liking. The result, however, was to alienate Richard completely and drive him into Philip's camp.

From 1186, Philip's relationship with Henry deteriorated. The count of Toulouse had appealed to Philip as overlord against a series of devastating attacks on his territory by Richard, backed by Henry. Philip demanded that Henry take action. Henry did nothing. After a series of meetings and skirmishes in the Vexin, and the arresting of Henry's vassals in Philip's lands and vice versa, Henry was still refusing to co-operate. By early summer 1187, France was preparing for war. Philip II had a range of reasons to attack Henry II.

- Henry was holding his sister, Alice.

- Henry still had control of the Vexin.

- Henry was still holding Brittany through his grandchildren, although Philip II was the feudal overlord.

- Henry had done nothing in response to Philip's command that he stop Richard attacking Toulouse.

Both men prepared to fight, and on this occasion Richard and John lined up alongside Henry. One reason for this could be that Philip attacked Berry. Berry, a region of central France, gave access to Anjou and Aquitaine, striking into the heart of territory coveted by both Richard and John. This was not a family reunion, but self-interest on the part of Henry's remaining sons.

Philip and Henry came close to a pitched battle, each side drawing up in battle array. The arrival of a legate from Pope Urban III calling for all Christian princes to unite on crusade to the Holy Land led to a truce of two years. It was not to last, but did provide a breathing space that had another, more serious consequence: a bond of alliance between Richard and Philip. There were two strong, common causes bringing them together: first, they were both passionate about a crusade to the Holy Land; second, neither trusted Henry II's intentions and by 1189 they had joined forces against him.

The alliance of Philip and Richard against Henry

The events directly leading to Richard turning against Henry in 1189 occurred in 1188 after Philip II attacked Angevin lands at Raymond of Toulouse's request because of yet another conflict with Richard. Although not enthusiastic at first, Henry fought with Richard against Philip. In October 1189, a truce was called. However, Richard's distrust of his father was running deep by this time. Not only had the succession still not been settled, but he feared that Henry would make him give up the lands he had taken from Raymond. Richard began to negotiate directly with Philip. The two men arrived together at a peace conference with Henry II in November 1188, which shook Henry. The discussions became fraught. Richard's fears that his father would make him give up any lands that he had taken increased, so he did homage to Philip there and then for Normandy, Aquitaine, Anjou, Maine and Touraine. By spring of 1189, Richard had joined forces with Philip against his father.

Philip II was politically astute. His long-term aim was to destroy the Angevin power bloc in France and he saw the opportunities that Angevin family jealousies provided. He was in a better position than Louis had been because, by having successfully dealt with his vassals in eastern France, he had earned a reputation as a strong king.

By supporting Richard in his belief that he ought to be Henry's principal heir, Philip was able to capitalise once again on the Plantagenet's dysfunctional family dynamics. He drove a wedge between Henry and Richard and deepened the divisions between Richard and John. Richard was also politically astute. In the short term, allying himself with Philip II gave him the best chance of achieving his goal of being Henry's principal heir, just as the count of Flanders had pointed out.

SOURCE 12

From *The Annals of Roger of Hoveden* (also known as Roger of Howden). Roger of Hoveden was one of Henry II's government officials, who served him from 1174. Here he is describing immediate events in 1189 leading up to Henry II agreeing to come to terms as laid down by Philip II.

The king of France had sent him word that ...on the ... Monday, at about the third hour, applying their scaling ladders to the walls on the side of the Loire ... the city was taken by storm, and in it eighty knights and a hundred men at arms.

To their great disgrace, on the one side, the Poitevins were plotting treachery against their liege lord the king of England, and on the other side the Bretons, who had joined the king of France and had obtained from him letters patent, to the effect that he would never make peace with the king of England unless the Bretons were included in the treaty. Accordingly, the king of England, being reduced to straits [limited means or resources], made peace with Philip of France on the following terms ...

SOURCE 13

From Gerald of Wales, *On the Instruction of Princes*. Gerald, a clergyman, had a position at court and immediate knowledge of the circumstances he relates. This extract is about Alice of France.

But this sister of king Philip ... had in good faith been entrusted by her most Christian father to the guardianship of the king of England, to be united in marriage to his son, the count of Poitou; but the count absolutely refused to marry her, by reason of the infamy which shortly afterwards rose against her on account of too great a familiarity contracted with his father; for it was said that after the death of the youthful Rosamund, he had unchastely, and with too much want of faith, dishonoured this virgin ... For, as it is reported, after that a great and execrable hatred arose between himself and his sons and their mother the queen, because, always striving after unlawful machinations, he proposed to be separated by a divorce from queen Eleanor and to be married to the other; with this intention, indeed, that through his heirs begotten of her, by both his own powers and those of France, he might be able effectually to disinherit his former sons by Eleanor, who had troubled him.

> **A Level Exam-Style Question Section A**
>
> How far could the historian make use of Sources 12 and 13 to investigate Henry II's role in his own downfall by 1189?
>
> Explain your answer, using both sources, the information given about them and your own knowledge of the historical context. (20 marks)
>
> **Tip**
> *Source 13 contains some new, and perhaps surprising, information. There is no firm evidence for it. How does the new information fit in with what you know? What evidence is there that is familiar to you?*
> *Why might contemporary rumour be useful to this historian?*

Henry II's defeat in 1189

By the time Richard and Philip joined forces against him in November 1188, Henry II was growing weary of war. Since the summer, there had been open hostility, which had not gone well for Henry, who was finding the costs involved increasingly burdensome. The area of Berry, in Aquitaine, had already fallen to the French. At Whitsun 1189, arbitration between Henry and Philip took place at La Ferté-Bernard in Maine, where Philip II made the following demands on behalf of himself and Richard.

- Alice should be married to Richard.
- Richard should be given security of his inheritance.
- John should join the crusade to the Holy Land.

In return, Philip would restore all the lands he had seized from Henry since the previous summer.

For many contemporaries, the demands made of Henry II were unreasonable, and he refused them. The fight continued into the hot summer of 1189 and Henry's health deteriorated. Meanwhile, Philip and Richard were overrunning Maine, their success serving to convince many barons that theirs would be the winning side. This momentum led many to capitulate, excepting the city of Tours, to which Phillip laid siege.

In Philip II and Richard, Henry II was facing two young, energetic and ruthless men, whose momentum in the final conflict enabled them to command more resources and adherents than he seems to have been able to muster. Their military successes such as the surprise attack at La Ferté-Bernard, the attack on Le Mans (Henry II's birthplace) and the capture of Tours (a strategically important city with the river Loire running through it) compounded their momentum. The more successful they became, the stronger they became, not only because they captured more territory and resources but also because they looked like being the winning side. For medieval barons wanting to keep their lands and status, it was vital they back the winners.

SOURCE 14 French depiction of Philip II taking Le Mans. From a 14th-century manuscript currently located in the Bibliotheque Nationale, Paris.

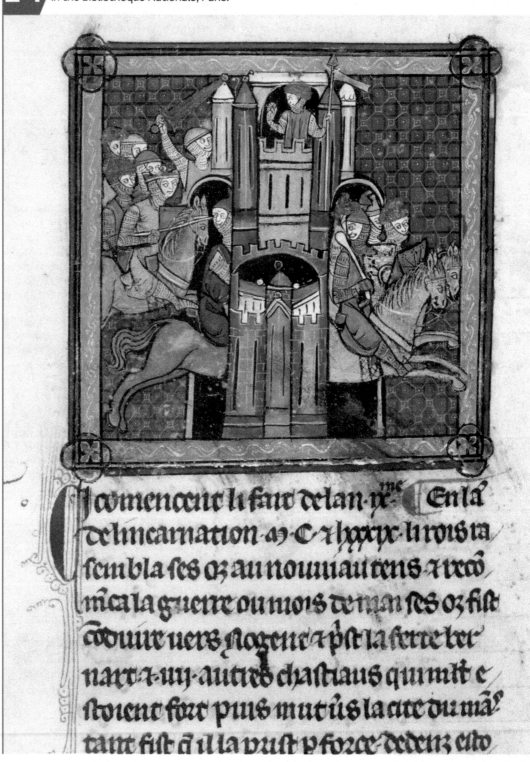

The terms of Henry's defeat

En route for the safety of Normandy, Henry suddenly confounded his supporters by heading back into Anjou. He went to Chinon, lying ill there for a fortnight as his sickness grew worse. After hearing the news of the fall of Tours, Henry met Philip and Richard to agree terms. Despite being racked with pain and having to be supported on his horse, the old king refused the offer to sit in comfort. The terms were read to him.

- Henry was to place himself wholly at the will of King Philip.

- He was to do homage to the king of France for his French possessions.

- King Philip was to receive 20,000 marks.

- Henry was to give up Alice, who was to marry Richard on his return from the Holy Land.

- Richard was to receive the fealty of Henry's barons on both sides of the Channel and thus be recognised as lawful heir to all his father's lands.

- Three major castles in Anjou or the Vexin were to be handed over.

Henry agreed, but on 6 July he died. The last news he heard was that John had joined Richard and Philip.

Henry was 56 when he died. His lifestyle had been continually strenuous, never staying in one place very long, and endlessly consumed with conflict and political struggle, with which his family relationships were inextricably bound. Nevertheless, when apparently giving the kiss of peace to seal the final agreement, he was planning to revenge himself on his oldest surviving son. His last words to Richard were 'God grant that I may not die until I have had my revenge on you.'

EXTRACT 1

From *Dungeon, Fire and Sword: The Knights Templar and the Crusades* by John J. Robinson, published in 1992. Here Robinson is describing the relationship between Philip II and Richard.

Their one common trait was their mistrust of each other, which meant they had to leave on crusade together. Neither would take his army away and leave his European lands at the mercy of the other. Whatever love or lust had brought them together in a homosexual affair years earlier was gone now.

EXTRACT 2

From *Richard I* by John Gillingham, published in 2002.

For his lies and half truths on this matter [Richard] has been much pilloried, but if he blatantly stated that he would never marry Alice, war with Philip was the likely result. It by no means follows that he was homosexual, overly squeamish or absurdly fastidious in not marrying his father's mistress. The true cause of all this trouble was Henry ... the issue of Alice was a running sore between Philip and Richard, and made a poisonous and inauspicious start to the Third Crusade.

EXTRACT 3

From *Henry II* by W. L. Warren, published in 2000.

At Whitsuntide in 1189 they [Richard and Philip II] met [Henry II] at La Ferté-Bernard in Maine ... Philip rehearsed the demands of Richard and himself: his sister Alice should be married to Richard, Richard should be given the security of his inheritance, and John should take the Cross and join the crusade.

THINKING HISTORICALLY Evidence (6a)

Arguments and facts

Extracts 1–3 all concern the nature of the relationship between Richard I and Philip II at the end of Henry II's reign, as they were making preparations for the Third Crusade. Remember that Alice was Philip's sister, who was supposed to marry Richard, but who had been kept by Henry II as his mistress.

Work in groups.

1 Why are facts important in history?

2 Read Extracts 1 and 2.

  a) How do these extracts disagree?

  b) Which one do you think is correct? Explain your answer.

3 Read Extracts 2 and 3.

  a) How do these extracts disagree?

  b) What do you think the significance of the nature of the relationship between Philip and Richard was? Why is it so important to understand what brought the two men together? Does it matter to why Henry II ended his reign as a diminished king?

4 All of these extracts concern what brought Richard and Philip together. Is what brought them together more important than the impact of their relationship?

5 If we accept Extract 1 is wrong about the basis of Richard's bond with Philip, should we discount it as being useful? Explain your answer.

ACTIVITY
KNOWLEDGE CHECK

You will be investigating why Henry II had experienced a collapse in his power in France by the time he died in 1189. This investigation should develop in the following stages.

1 Work in pairs and prepare a case for *either* Henry II *or* Philip II as being the main reason for the collapse of Henry II's power in France.

2 Work with another pair that has looked at the other figure. Between you, you must come to a consensus of who was to blame the most. To do this, you will also need to look at the 'not guilty' party and explain why some of their actions, although significant, were not as important in causing the collapse of Henry's power.

3 Present your case to the class.

4 As you listen to the evidence presented by other groups, review the case that you have made. Does what you are hearing reinforce or challenge your case?

5 After the presentations, take a class vote to decide, overall, who was more responsible for Henry's collapse in power, Philip II or Henry II?

ACTIVITY
WRITING

Look up any of the words in the box that you do not know the meaning of, and then use them to complete the following sentences to best describe the impact a change of French king had on Henry II.

> adept, chicanery, dominion, dubious, expedient, hegemony, impervious, indefatigable, momentum, rapprochement, scruple, susceptible

To a certain extent, Angevin _____ in France was dependent upon the _____ Henry II. Although Louis VII strove to undermine his _____ he was unable to sustain any challenge and had willingly welcomed offers of _____ . In the end, Louis had to make the politically _____ choice, even if he appeared weak as a result. When Philip II became king of France, he proved more _____ at politics and war than Louis and capitalised on Henry's family's divisions. Richard, already _____ about his father's intentions concerning his inheritance, had no _____ over turning against him. Henry II ultimately found himself overwhelmed by the _____ Philip and Richard carried before them.

EXTEND YOUR KNOWLEDGE

How important was the death of Louis VII for Henry's fortunes in France?

The French kings were not as strong as the Angevins at this time (certainly not under Louis VII), but they wanted to change this balance of power within France. Henry II was the greatest obstacle to this. Even though Louis was Henry's overlord, it was not possible for him to enforce this position. Louis VII therefore tended to ally with anyone causing Henry problems. Furthermore, given Henry's four ambitious and determined sons, Louis VII and Philip II did not have far to look if they wanted to undermine him.

While Henry was fit and strong, he managed to hold together his territories. As active and indomitable as he was, it appears that by his mid-fifties his health was failing. He was only 56 when he died. When he began to fail, so did his grip on his 'empire'. However, he was by then facing a new, younger, more ruthless French king in Philip II. Born in 1165, Philip was more than 30 years younger than Henry. He was cunning, ruthless, an able warrior and as prepared as Henry to break oaths and customs. Like his father, Louis, he drove a wedge between Henry and his sons. Unlike Louis, he was successful. However, Henry II must accept some of the blame for playing into Philip's hands by refusing to name Richard as his principal heir, fuelling Richard's jealousy and making it so much easier for the French king to turn him against his father.

That said, Philip had already proven himself more than capable of dealing with his own troublesome vassals, even before Henry's final conflict. Between 1181 and 1186, he fought against a feudal league of his own uncles from the Champagne region. By July 1186, he had subdued all of them, proven his military might and made treaties on his terms. Philip II was looking like the winner that his father had not been.

A Level Exam-Style Question Section B

'Henry's actions in 1183–89 made him the author of his own downfall.'

How far do you agree with this opinion? Explain your answer. (20 marks)

Tip

Start with the evidence you have and use that to make up your mind. Do this at the planning stage, before you begin writing. It might be that there is not a 50:50 split for and against the judgement and, if so, you should aim to reflect this in your answer.

ACTIVITY
SUMMARY

Draw a fortune graph of Henry II's effective control over his territories, 1170–89.

Mark the years along the horizontal axis and a score of 1–10 on the vertical axis. A score of 1 would indicate Henry II losing his titles and lands; a score of 10 would reflect Henry II being completely in control across all territories, with no uprisings or rebellions. Remember that there were often pockets of trouble and that areas to the south and east of Aquitaine were difficult to control fully. Henry II would not score a perfect 10 and *effective* control could therefore be 8–9. Reserve the lower scores for co-ordinated, planned rebellions, especially if on more than one front. Sporadic, unconnected uprisings could imply a short-term loss of control and might score 6–7. Before you begin, however, make sure that you have drawn up a 10-point scale and that you know what each score means.

Identify the point at which Henry II was at his strongest.

Write a short explanation, with reference to events, of why you believe Henry was stronger at that point than at any other time.

Identify the key turning point in Henry II's final years, 1182–89.

At what point did Henry II's fortunes take their most significant downturn?

What was Henry II's greatest mistake?

If it were possible, what one thing would you advise Henry II to do differently and why?

WIDER READING

Gillingham, J. *The Angevin Empire*, Hodder Arnold (2000) This gives an outline of the Angevin Empire under Henry II and is useful for some of the accounts of specific territories

Warren, W.L. *Henry II*, Yale University Press (2000) This goes into a great amount of detail, but the last chapters add some interesting details to Henry's final years

Weir, A. *Eleanor of Aquitaine: By Wrath of God, Queen of England*, Jonathon Cape (1999) This has several chapters that give lively insights as well as some of the rumours about Henry II's love life

Roger of Wendover, *Flowers of History* is available on Google books

Roger of Hoveden, *The Annals of Roger of Hoveden* is available online via openlibrary.org

In terms of fiction, there is a trilogy of books by Sharon Penman that are useful, in particular:

Penman, S. *The Devil's Brood*, Penguin (2009)

Also of interest is:

Weir, A. *The Captive Queen*, Cornerstone (2010)

Preparing for your AS Level Paper 2 exam

Advance planning

1. Draw up a timetable for your revision and try to keep to it. Spread your timetable over a number of weeks, and aim to cover four or five topics each week.
2. Spend longer on topics that you have found difficult, and revise them several times.
3. Above all, do not try to limit your revision by attempting to 'question spot'. Try to be confident about all aspects of your Paper 2 work, because this will ensure that you have a choice of questions in Section B.

Paper 2 overview:

AS Paper 2	Time: I hour 30 minutes	
Section A	Answer I compulsory two-part sources question	8+12 marks = 20 marks
Section B	Answer I question from a choice of 3	20 marks
	Total marks =	40 marks

You should familiarise yourself with the layout of the paper by looking at the examples published by Edexcel. The questions for each section are followed by eight pages of lined paper where you should write your answer.

Section A questions

Each of the two parts of the question will focus on one of the two contemporary sources provided. The sources together will total around 300 words. The (a) question, worth 8 marks, will be in the form of 'Why is Source 1 useful for an enquiry into…?' The (b) question, worth 12 marks, will be in the form of 'How much weight do you give the evidence of Source 2 for an enquiry into…?' In both your answers you should address the value of the content of the source, and then its nature, origin and purpose. Finally, you should use your own knowledge of the context of the source to assess its value.

Section B questions

These questions ask you to reach a judgement on an aspect of the topic studied. The questions will have the form, for example, of 'How far…', 'To what extent…' or 'How accurate is it to say…'. The questions can deal with historical concepts such as cause, consequence, change, continuity, similarity, difference and significance. You should consider the issue raised in the question, consider other relevant issues, and then conclude with an overall judgement.

The timescale of the questions could be as short as a single year or even a single event (an example from Option 2C.2 could be, 'To what extent was Russia's involvement in the First World War responsible for the fall of the Provisional Government in 1917?'). The timescale could be longer depending on the historical event or process being examined, but questions are likely to be shorter than the those set for Sections A and B in Paper 1.

Use of time

This is an issue that you should discuss with your teachers and fellow students, but here are some suggestions for you.

1. Do not write solidly for 45 minutes on each question. For Section A it is essential that you have a clear understanding of the content of each source, the points being made, and the nature, origin and purpose of each source. You might decide to spend up to ten minutes reading the sources and drawing up your plan, and 35 minutes writing your answer.
2. For Section B answers you should spend a few minutes working out what the question is asking you to do, and drawing up a plan of your answer before you begin to write your response.

Preparing for your AS Level exams

Paper 2: AS Level sample answer with comments

Section A

Part A requires you to:

- identify key points in the source and explain them
- deploy your own knowledge of the context in which events took place
- make appropriate comments about the author/origin/purpose of the source.

Why is Source 5 (page 318) valuable to the historian for an enquiry into how successful Henry II was in establishing royal authority in the shires? Explain your answer, using the source, the information given about it and your own knowledge of the historical context. (8 marks)

Average student answer

Source 5 concerns the Inquest of Sheriffs, which was a major investigation by Henry II into how his sheriffs were exercising the powers he had given them in the Assize of Clarendon in 1166. It says that 'he dismissed nearly all the sheriffs', which suggests that Henry was not very successful at restoring royal authority in the shires. The problem was very large because the source describes how 'all the liege men of his realm', even villeins, had to swear about what had been done by the sheriffs and their bailiffs as well. The Inquest of Sheriffs covered all England and shows that Henry II was facing problems everywhere.

According to the source, Henry 'reinstated some of the sheriffs in their offices' and that they were 'more oppressive than they were before' implying that the king was not concerned if his sheriffs were treating people harshly but wanted men who could keep firm control in the localities. This shows that he was more concerned with royal authority than anything else.

The source comes from a chronicle written by Florence of Worcester. However, he had died in 1118 and the actual authors of the source are anonymous. This would limit the value for historians as we cannot know how much the authors knew about the Inquest of Sheriffs or how close they were to the events being described. However, the author is very clear that because of the sheriffs' actions 'great injury was thus done the English nation' and it is likely that the monks would have been aware of the problem because it was on such an enormous scale.

The source shows that sheriffs had become very unpopular by 1170 but also that Henry II was willing to try to resolve the issue, but that he hadn't been very successful in establishing royal authority in the shires.

The conclusion is very brief and focuses on the content of the source. A conclusion that included the value of the source would improve the answer.

The opening paragraph is focused on the source and has some contextual knowledge that shows the respondent understands why Henry II launched the Inquest of Sheriffs. The wording of the question has been used when making the first inference. The point about the scale of Henry II's problem in enforcing his authority is clear. However, an introductory sentence would be helpful.

The question focus is not as strong here but it does suggest that royal power was more important to Henry II than anything else. However, there needs to be a clear link to the question.

The value of the source in terms of its provenance is clearly addressed. The response has made an inference from the source about the scale of Henry II's problems and has used it to make a specific comment about the source's value.

Verdict

This is an average answer because:

- it selects and summarises key information from the source that is linked directly to the question
- it shows a basic awareness of what the Inquest of Sheriffs was and links it to the question
- it addresses the provenance of the source and its impact on its value, but one is a basic, general point

- there needs to be an awareness of the value of the source in the conclusion and a more developed focus on the question in places; the contextual information lacks detail.

Use the feedback on this answer to rewrite it, making as many improvements as you can.

Paper 2: AS Level sample answer with comments

Section A

Part B requires you to:

- interrogate the source
- draw reasoned inferences
- deploy your own knowledge to interpret the material in its context
- make judgement about the value (weight) of the source in terms of making judgements.

How much weight would you give Source 2 (page 366) for an enquiry into the why the Great Rebellion broke out in 1173? Explain your answer, using the source, the information given about it and your own knowledge of the historical context. (12 marks)

Average student answer

Source 2 tells us about how Henry II's son, the Young King, escaped from his father and went to Louis VII, who was his father-in-law, because he had not been getting his own way about ruling England. The Young King had been crowned king of England and made duke of Normandy but Henry II had not allowed him to rule them in his own right. This frustrated the Young King. This was an important cause of the Great Rebellion. Count Theobald says that the Young King must be restored to 'his rightful inheritance'. The source describes how Louis 'held a council' and that the count of Flanders reminded him that he had 'many mighty barons to wreak havoc on your enemies'. Louis VII supported the Young King because he wanted to destroy Henry II's power in France and Source 2 shows that he had a lot of support. This would help him to fight Henry and might have made him decide to support the Great Rebellion.

Source 2 was produced for entertainment purposes and so it is not possible to give it much weight. Although the source describes the meeting of Louis VII's council, it is unlikely that the author was there as he was a poet. This could mean that he used hearsay evidence or might have made it up as his aim was to entertain people and so a good story would be more important than being accurate. For example, it is known that Louis VII was much weaker than Henry II and so it is unlikely that he was as powerful as the source suggests. However, the author was a supporter of Henry II and so he might have exaggerated Louis VII's strength to make Henry look good.

Overall the source does not hold much weight for an enquiry into why the Great Rebellion broke out, although it does point out that the Young King was frustrated and supported by Louis VII who had the help of French barons.

> The quotes from the source are not being used to make inferences but as part of describing what the source tells us. However, there is one reason for the Great Rebellion given. There is also an inference drawn at the end (but not developed) and some specific knowledge about the context of the events that has been used to develop points made by the source. So far there is nothing on the weight of the source. An introductory sentence, using the wording of the question perhaps, needs to be added.

> The response is being very critical of the source by making assumptions based on the fact that this was probably written with the aim of being performed by minstrels. This does present some important problems. However, they are expressed very simplistically.

> This answer comes in two parts: source content and then source provenance. If the respondent had integrated 'own knowledge' with this source, and identified elements of what they know about the context of events, they could have produced a more balanced evaluation.

> The response has dismissed the source and then said that it does give some clear indications of why the Great Rebellion broke out. This contradiction has come about because the response focused solely on the provenance of the source as being for entertainment purposes. Even if this is the case, the source clearly holds some weight given that it matches parts of what the respondent knows.

Verdict

This is an average answer because:

- it deals with the weight of the source separately from the content
- there are some bland, default comments on the weight of the
- source that are not specific to this question
- there is no consideration of why the source might have weight for the investigation.

Use the feedback on this answer to rewrite it, making as many improvements as you can.

Paper 2: AS Level sample answer with comments

Section A

Part A requires you to:

- identify key points in the source and explain them
- deploy your own knowledge of the context in which events took place
- make appropriate comments about the author/origin/purpose of the source.

Why is Source 5 (page 318) valuable to the historian for an enquiry into how successful Henry II was in establishing royal authority in the shires? Explain your answer, using the source, the information given about it and your own knowledge of the historical context. (8 marks)

Strong student answer

Source 5 is very valuable for historians studying how successful Henry II was in establishing royal authority in the shires. The content of this source reflects the fact that 22 of England's 29 sheriffs were replaced mainly with exchequer officials who were loyal to Henry, strengthening his control of the counties.

The Inquest of Sheriffs was a general eyre called by Henry II, requiring: 'all the liege-men of his realm … even villeins, to swear, … that they would tell the truth'. This can be taken as a sign that the increased powers given to sheriffs in 1166 had backfired, having a negative impact upon royal authority as the source says 'what and how much the sheriffs and their bailiffs levied on them, and what judicially, and what extra-judicially' indicating that the sheriffs themselves did not always obey the law that they enforced.

The fact that the Inquest was a general eyre shows that Henry II had effective authority, administration and manpower. However, it was also the result of great unhappiness amongst his subjects and, for the king to respond in this way, can be seen as a sign of how concerned he was about the situation. Nevertheless, a survey of this scale would have been impossible under King Stephen. Henry II's greater control of the shires is also suggested by the last sentence, which implies that the sheriffs in place after 1170 were not much more popular but that they enforced Henry's will vigorously.

Even though the specific author of the source is unknown, given the nature of the Inquest of Sheriffs it is likely that he would have been aware of what was happening, especially as the clergy were among Henry II's 'liege-men'. The source is very valuable because it shows how successful Henry II was at establishing royal authority because it shows both sides of the issue: the unhappiness of his English subjects and his ability to deal with it.

> The opening paragraph is focused on the source and has some contextual knowledge that shows the respondent understands why Henry II launched the Inquest of Sheriffs. The wording of the question has been used when making the first inference. The point about the scale of Henry II's problem in enforcing his authority is clear. However, an introductory sentence would be helpful.

> The way in which the content of the source fits in with what is known about the Inquest of Sheriffs, why it was called and its scope, comes together very strongly. The own knowledge is specific and is used to support and develop the inferences made.

> The value of the source has been considered in terms of the context of the Inquest of Sheriffs to address another angle.

> There is a brief consideration of the utility of the source, which is helpful because it would be easy to dismiss its value because the authors are unknown.

Verdict

This is a strong answer because:

- the question focus is very strong throughout
- it makes use of evidence in the source as well as the information provided about it

- the knowledge provided concerning the historical context is specific and used effectively to discuss the source's value.

Paper 2: AS Level sample answer with comments

Section A

Part B requires you to:

- interrogate the source
- draw reasoned inferences
- deploy your own knowledge to interpret the material in its context
- make judgement about the value (weight) of the source in terms of making judgements.

How much weight would you give Source 2 (page 366) for an enquiry into the why the Great Rebellion broke out in 1173? Explain your answer, using the source, the information given about it and your own knowledge of the historical context. (12 marks)

Strong student answer

The Great Rebellion that broke out across Henry II's territories in 1173 had the potential seriously to damage Henry II's hold on his territories. Source 2 gives very clear reasons for its outbreak. The frustration of the Young King at not being allowed to rule the possessions given him by his father, Henry II, comes across: 'When through his father's actions he could not do what he wished, he thought … he would stir up trouble for him.' Although the author was a poet–composer, this reflects events in March 1173 when the Young King escaped from Henry II one night. As this source was written for minstrels, it was to both entertain and inform, so although Fantosme might focus on key events that would entertain an audience, he would also be reporting news circulating at the time.

> Understanding that the purpose of the source is to inform as well as entertain is helpful in giving a more accurate assessment of its weight. However, the response does not ignore the entertainment value of the source either.

Even though Fantosme is a supporter of Henry II, the weight of this source is increased by the sympathetic portrayal of the Young King and Louis VII. For example, his description of the Young King: 'A king without a realm is at a loss for something to do: at such a loss was the noble and gracious Young King'. Although Fantosme might not have wanted to offend Henry II by an unflattering portrayal of his son, he did not have to be so generous to Louis VII, as well as mentioning that thoughts of Henry II 'oppressed him'. Although the actual words spoken at Louis VII's council could not have been heard by Fantosme, the king did have the support mentioned. Henry II was much stronger in France than Louis VII and so the words spoken by Flanders might be an exaggeration for dramatic purposes. However, it is also true that the scope of the Great Rebellion in France was considerable and involved barons from most parts of Henry's lands, including his own sons and his wife, Eleanor of Aquitaine.

> The information about the source has been carefully looked at and the fact that Fantosme was a supporter of Henry II means that his sympathetic portrayal of the Young King and Louis VII is surprising and therefore an indication that this source is not about providing black propaganda for Henry II. Again the content of the source has been matched to historical context rather than simply writing the source off as entertainment.

Nevertheless, the fact that this source was to be performed by minstrels does account for the stirring language used. Despite that, Theobald's words reflect the view of the Young King's supporters.

The source does have its limitations in that it only deals with the Young King and Louis VII, with no mention of Eleanor of Aquitaine or princes Richard and Geoffrey. Nor is there any mention of why the Great Rebellion began in England. However, the fairness with which Henry's opponents are dealt does make this valuable as does the fact that it reflects key events that occurred in the run-up to the Great Rebellion.

> The conclusion is concise and deals evenly with the source's pros and cons as evidence.

Verdict

This is a strong answer because:

- it examines the source in light of historical context as well as with reference to the information about it, to understand its value as well as its limitations

- specific own knowledge explains some of the points made by Fantosme rather than taking them at face value
- the overall judgement about the source reflects the discussion

Paper 2: AS Level sample answer with comments

Section B

These questions assess your understanding of the period in some depth. They will ask you about the content you learned about in the four key themes, but may not ask about more than one theme. For these questions remember to:

- give an analytical, not a descriptive, response
- support your points with evidence
- cover the whole time period specified in the question
- come to a substantiated judgement.

To what extent was King Philip II the most important factor in Henry's power in France being so diminished during the 1180s? (20 marks)

Average student answer

There are many reasons why Henry II's power was diminished in France. Philip II is one of them, perhaps the main one, but there are others as well.

Henry had lots of land in France. He got Aquitaine by marrying Eleanor of Aquitaine and he was duke of Normandy after his father. He also had Anjou, which he might have taken from his brother, and he also had Brittany. He was also king of England from 1154. This made him very powerful.

Henry had four sons and they had already rebelled against him in the Great Rebellion of 1173–74. They were unhappy at not being allowed to run their lands themselves. The oldest son, the Young King, was king of England and duke of Normandy. The second, Richard, was duke of Aquitaine. The third, Geoffrey, had Brittany and the fourth, John, had nothing. They rebelled again during the 1180s and Philip II played an important part. Philip II was the only son of Louis VII of France. He became king in 1180. At first, he turned to Henry II and Henry helped him establish himself as king. However, Philip had important long term plans. He wanted to break Angevin power in France. He used the jealousies and divisions of Henry II's family to do this.

In 1183 the Young King was again frustrated and rebelled. With Geoffrey he fought against Henry II and Richard over Aquitaine. The Young King was defeated and died. Then Richard expected to be named Henry's heir for England and Normandy, but the king wanted him to hand over Aquitaine. Richard would never do this. Henry II gave John permission to attack Aquitaine. This showed Philip II that Henry II's family was as divided as ever and he used this to his advantage. Firstly he worked on Geoffrey, who was no-one's favourite and was jealous of his brothers. He made him welcome at his court and in return Geoffrey did homage to Philip for Brittany. This was a betrayal of his family, as the duke of Brittany was supposed to do homage to the duke of Normandy. Philip II was being clever as this simple act symbolised him as being the king of France's vassal first. Although Geoffrey died soon afterwards (stamped on by a horse) Philip II did not stop using Henry's own family against him and next he turned on Richard.

> Weak introduction. The respondent should have stated how important they think Philip II was and also what other factors were important.

> 'Setting the scene' is not necessary. Respondents should show what conclusions they can draw about the question – can they handle what they have been given to focus on – rather than simply stating what they know or what they would like to cover.

> This is more relevant, but is a long list. The point is that Henry II's sons had been given territories that they expected to control. There is no need to mention the Great Rebellion as it is outside the dates set in the question. So far, it has taken a long time to get to the issue in the question and the answer is still very narrative.

> This is inaccurate in parts, and narrative. It takes a while before the stated factor is mentioned. Philip II is shown as an important factor, but it is still narrative. It is only in the second half of the paragraph that there is some analysis of what Philip II was doing, but even then unnecessary narrative details crop up. Details might be interesting but respondents must be prepared to leave them out unless they provide clear evidence on the issue they are writing about and even then there must be a clear link to the question established. Evidence needs to lead to a judgement on the question.

After Geoffrey's death, Henry would still not name his principal heir. Richard believed his father was reluctant because he wanted it to be John, and Philip II played on this. This is the best example of Philip II diminishing Henry II's lands because together he and Richard fought and defeated him in 1188–89. Philip II and Richard had developed a strong bond over going on crusade and Philip played on Richard's fears over his inheritance. Because Henry II would still not decide, Richard did homage to Philip II for Aquitaine and Normandy. This showed that Philip II recognised Richard's inheritance in France when Henry II wouldn't. This also shows him as being very important in dividing both Henry's family and his lands. He was a much better warrior than Louis and a stronger king, so when he and Richard started winning lands even in Anjou and Maine, many barons swapped allegiance. It was important to back a winner, which Henry wasn't. He gave in just before he died.

> This is more securely focused on the question. The paragraph is a bit disorganised, jumping to the end of Henry II's reign and then back to Richard and Philip joining together, and then back to the end. It would be good to see some evidence of how quickly this happened and some examples of important gains – what was it that brought Henry II to the negotiating table?

There are other important reasons why Henry died a diminished king and perhaps the most important is Henry himself. If he had not had favourites, Richard would not have worried that John was going to take his inheritance. Also, he was old and sick by 1189 and was not able to match Richard and Philip, who even attacked Tours and Le Mans, which was Henry's birthplace. Before that, Henry had not dealt with the count of Toulouse who complained that Richard attacked him. The count of Toulouse went to Philip II for support in 1187. Another problem between Henry II and Philip II was Brittany. Philip wanted control over Geoffrey's children as overlord of France, but Henry II kept them. Henry also upset Philip by taking his sister, Alice, as his mistress although she was supposed to be married to Richard. Philip II was a stronger king than Louis VII and Henry was growing weaker so making decisions that led to conflict with him was unwise.

> A clear statement of to what extent Philip II was the most important cause of Henry's defeat is implied by saying Henry II was the most important factor. There is again some generalisation as Richard's key worry was that Aquitaine would be given to John, although Henry would not make it clear which son was going to get what. There is some more specific evidence but also, although a lot is referred to, much is not developed.

Henry's sons must take some of the blame for him dying a diminished king. They were all very proud and jealous, concerned that one might be seen as more powerful or high status and they didn't trust each other either. The Young King and Richard ended up in conflict in 1182 when Richard's barons turned to the Young King for support, because they disliked Richard. They also quarrelled over who should pay homage. Richard said he was as nobly born as his brother.

So overall, Philip II was probably the main reason why Henry II died a diminished king, although Henry himself must take some of the blame. His own sons too played an important part and it was Richard that defeated him in 1189, although with Philip II so that again shows his importance.

> The conclusion does not match the statement earlier when Henry II was said to be most important factor. The conclusion is focused, although short, and the last comment is useful. The response needs to consider what it was about Philip that made him so successful. Was there one point/action/development that was especially significant?

Verdict:

This is an average answer because:

- there are narrative passages and, in places, some material that does not really link to the question
- there is a lot of accurate and relevant material but it is sometimes undeveloped
- there are some judgements made about how important Philip II was although they sometimes have insufficient supporting material
- there are other factors, Henry II and his sons, but they lack the detail to give the answer a good range and depth of coverage; the third factor is especially thin
- the conclusion does not fit with evaluations made in the main body of the answer. Planning this answer better would enable the introduction and conclusion to reinforce each other.

Use the feedback on this answer to rewrite it, making as many improvements as you can.

Paper 2: AS Level sample answer with comments

Section B

These questions assess your understanding of the period in some depth. They will ask you about the content you learned about in the four key themes, but may not ask about more than one theme. For these questions remember to:

- give an analytical, not a descriptive, response
- support your points with evidence
- cover the whole time period specified in the question
- come to a substantiated judgement.

To what extent was King Philip II the most important factor in Henry's power in France being so diminished during the 1180s? (20 marks)

Strong student answer

King Philip II was undoubtedly important in diminishing Henry II's power in France by the end of his reign. He managed to take Henry's sons from him, as well as his heartland in Anjou and Maine. He was a stronger, more ruthless king than his father had been, and a better warrior. However, he was up against an older, weaker Henry. Most of the blame, however, probably goes to Henry as he created the opportunities for Phillip to divide and weaken his territories by the way he treated his sons. Perhaps what Philip II was good at was making the most of the opportunities that Henry gave him.

> The introduction is strong. The answer has clearly been planned because the respondent knows what the answer will be in advance. The reason why Henry II was more important as a factor than Philip II is given.

Philip II's most significant role in diminishing Henry's power came at the very end of the 1180s when he was able to make an alliance with Richard by manipulating his lack of trust in Henry. Since the death of the Young King, the inheritance of Henry's sons had been unclear. Richard expected to become principal heir but Henry wanted him to give up Aquitaine, something that he was not prepared to do. By 1188 the question of Richard's inheritance was undecided. Philip II used this to his advantage. Forming a bond with Richard over the coming crusade, he encouraged his fears over what Henry was going to do, especially concerning John and Aquitaine. Richard did homage to Philip for both Normandy, which had been the Young King's, and Aquitaine, showing he was prepared to do what Henry wouldn't – recognise Richard's inheritance in France and give him what he wanted. Even before then, Philip had used Geoffrey to divide Henry's family.

> The question focus is clearly on the stated factor. A sentence linking back to the question, making a judgement, would be useful, as the paragraph ends with a comment that is neither explained nor developed.

Together, Richard and Philip were able to overrun Henry's heartlands in Anjou and Maine. They even managed to besiege and capture Tours, a key city with the river Loire running through it, and attack his birthplace of Le Mans. Philip had already proven to be a stronger, more effective king than Louis VII and, with Richard too, the barons in Henry's lands were happy to give them their allegiance. Barons needed to back winners and that was what Philip looked like. The more he won, the more resources he had, and his momentum was helpful in winning more support. This was a key reason why Philip II diminished Henry II's power.

> Specific factual examples, used as evidence because they are used to make a judgement about Philip II's momentum. Some of it is not especially developed, but it makes the point and links back to the question.

Henry II himself must take more of the blame than Philip II because it was his relationships with his sons that gave Philip II the opportunities to diminish his power. The first problem that Henry II faced in the 1180s, which exposed family divisions, did not involve Philip II. When the Young King died, Henry II's decision over his sons' inheritances resulted in his losing Richard's trust. Henry insisted that John be given Aquitaine as Richard would inherit the Young King's lands. When Richard refused, Henry encouraged John to attack his brother's lands. Philip II must have been aware of these divisions, but Henry can blame no-one but himself if Richard didn't trust him, and his distrust grew. When by the end of the 1180s Henry still would not name his principal heir, Philip played on Richard's deep seated fears.

Henry also gave Philip II reasons to attack him, especially when it came to his sister, Alice. She was supposed to have been betrothed to Richard, but it was rumoured that Henry had made her his mistress and Richard certainly wouldn't marry her. By this time Henry was older and weaker. He was giving Philip reasons to start a conflict, but the balance of power was changing and Henry did not seem to see it. When Richard and Philip II joined together against him, they were more than a match for him. Henry's age and illness were factors, but beyond his control.

Another factor is Henry's sons themselves, and especially Richard. His refusal to give up Aquitaine made settling his sons' inheritance very tricky for Henry II, especially after John blew his chances in Ireland. Richard would not agree to John becoming king of England and duke of Normandy. This put Henry in a difficult position so it could be argued that Richard's jealousy and fears were unreasonable and that there was nothing to be done. Although Henry II fought alongside Richard and supported him over his attack on Toulouse, Richard still went off with Philip and did homage for Normandy and Aquitaine. So perhaps Richard's greed especially, and John's failure to secure his inheritance of Ireland, were what caused the problems that led to Henry's power diminishing.

Overall, Henry's own mistakes and misjudgements were the most important reason why he lost so much power in France in the 1180s. Even though there were some things beyond his control, his favouritism caused problems as did the way he treated his sons. Given his track record it is likely that Richard could have rebelled even without Philip. However, Henry provided Philip II with opportunities that he was willing and able to take. It seems that Henry did not realise what he was up against in the new French king.

The answer mirrors the introduction. Henry II is probably most to blame. The reason for this is explained using specific factual evidence to illustrate and support the judgement made. A little thin on reasons Philip II had to attack Henry II, and the second paragraph is underdeveloped, but it makes relevant points.

Again, a little thin but this is the third factor. Richard's conflict with the Young King at the start of the decade would provide more evidence on how the sons caused problems themselves, being very status conscious and jealous, but the point of view that Richard was being unreasonable is developed. To provide a little extra support, it would perhaps be useful to mention why Richard did homage to Philip II when he and his father had just fought together against Philip in 1188. It would also show why Philip seized the opportunity when Richard decided to deal with him directly.

The conclusion follows on logically from the answer and matches what was set out in the introduction. There is a little speculation that is not supported or explained, but the conclusion is focused and gives a considered judgement, mentioning the relative importance of Henry II as compared with Philip II as the most important factor.

Verdict

This is a strong answer because:

- the focus is maintained throughout, as is the judgement made in the introduction, which comes from a well-planned answer
- evaluations and judgements made are generally well substantiated with specific historical knowledge that shows a strong understanding of the topic and the question
- two other possible factors are discussed and their relative importance to the factor stated in the question is clear
- knowledge has been selected and used effectively; it is not necessary to include everything you know in an answer; a key skill is deciding what to include, what to emphasise and what to leave out of an answer.

Preparing for your A Level Paper 2 exam

Advance planning

1. Draw up a timetable for your revision and try to keep to it. Spread your timetable over a number of weeks, and aim to cover four or five topics each week.
2. Spend longer on topics that you have found difficult, and revise them several times.
3. Above all, do not try to limit your revision by attempting to 'question spot'. Try to be confident about all aspects of your Paper 2 work, because this will ensure that you have a choice of questions in Section B.

Paper 2 overview

AL Paper 2	Time: 1 hour 30 minutes	
Section A	Answer 1 compulsory source question	20 marks
Section B	Answer 1 question from a choice of 2	20 marks
	Total marks =	40 marks

You should familiarise yourself with the layout of the paper by looking at the examples published by Edexcel. The questions for each section are followed by eight pages of lined paper where you should write your answer.

Section A questions

This question asks you to assess two different types of contemporary sources totalling around 400 words, and will be in the form of 'How far could the historian make use of Sources 1 and 2 together to investigate…?' Your answer should evaluate both sources, considering their nature, origin and purpose, and you should use your own knowledge of the context of the sources to consider their value to the specific investigation. Remember, too, that in assessing their value, you must consider the two sources, taken together, as a set.

Section B questions

These questions ask you to reach a judgement on an aspect of the topic studied. The questions will have the form, for example, of 'How far…', 'To what extent…' or 'How accurate is it to say…'. The questions can deal with historical concepts such as cause, consequence, change, continuity, similarity, difference and significance. You should consider the issue raised in the question, then other relevant issues, and conclude with an overall judgement.

The timescale of the questions could be as short as a single year or even a single event (an example from Option 2C.2 could be, 'To what extent was Russia's involvement in the First World War responsible for the fall of the Romanovs in 1917?'). The timescale could be longer depending on the historical event or process being examined, but questions are likely to be shorter than the those set for Sections A and B in Paper 1.

Use of time

This is an issue that you should discuss with your teachers and fellow students, but here are some suggestions for you.

1. Do not write solidly for 45 minutes on each question. For Section A it is essential that you have a clear understanding of the content of each source, the points being made, and the nature, origin and purpose of each source. You might decide to spend up to ten minutes reading the sources and drawing up your plan, and 35 minutes writing your answer.
2. For Section B answers you should spend a few minutes working out what the question is asking you to do, and drawing up a plan of your answer before you begin to write your response.

Paper 2: A Level sample answer with comments

Section A

You will need to read and analyse two sources and use them in tandem to assess how useful they are in investigating an issue. For these questions remember to:

- spend time, up to ten minutes, reading and identifying the arguments and evidence present in the sources; then make a plan to ensure that your response will be rooted in these sources
- use specific references from the sources
- deploy your own knowledge to develop points made in the sources and establish appropriate context
- come to a substantiated judgement.

How far could a historian use Sources 5 and 7 (pages 347 and 348) together to investigate whether Thomas Becket was to blame for the conflict between Crown and Church in England in 1164–70? Explain your answer, using both sources, the information given about them and your own knowledge of the historical context. (20 marks)

Average student answer

Both sources suggest that Becket was a main reason behind the conflict between the English Crown and Church during the reign of Henry II. Source 5 focuses on what caused the conflict in 1164 whereas Source 7 focuses on the meeting at Montmirail in 1169. According to Source 5, Becket acted alone 'following his own individual opinion' and made some serious mistakes as a result. Source 7 shows Becket as being very stubborn, and insisting upon a qualification to his obedience that Henry II could not accept: 'he will always have the advantage of me'. This shows Becket's stubbornness because he had been insisting on adding this phrase since the start of the conflict. As both sources come from Becket supporters, it is surprising that they both attribute blame to him.

Becket was very stubborn in his dispute with King Henry, who felt betrayed by his old chancellor and friend. When he was made archbishop of Canterbury, Becket had what some historians think was a religious conversion. He suddenly became very pious and was found to have been wearing underclothes made from hair when he was murdered. He was also reported to have preferred to eat bread and water as well as not wanting to sleep in comfortable beds.

Source 5 shows that it was Becket's stubbornness that caused the conflict to drag on: 'not acting on our advice, has pushed the matter to extremes … Had we given our consent to his proposals, matters would have become worse', while Source 7 suggests it was poor leadership by the archbishop of Canterbury. Source 5 goes on to say that Becket tried to blame everyone but himself for the conflict, painting him in a very negative light. This part of the account is from Gilbert Foliot, so it is not surprising as he did not like Becket. The source does not mention how Becket and the bishops were threatened by Henry II's men at Clarendon, thus the account given is incomplete and makes Becket seem incompetent. Source 7 hints at how Henry II could behave 'Henry raged at Becket' and this was typical of the king's behaviour as he was famous for having a furious temper.

> A focused introduction that pulls out specific and relevant quotes. The provenance of the sources has been mentioned, but not developed. A lack of understanding about the provenance of Source 5 could weaken the answer: the quotes taken from the source actually concern what Gilbert Foliot said about Thomas Becket and he did not support the archbishop. It is important to read the source, and information given, very carefully.

> Responses should avoid narrative, especially when it is not directly related to the topic. This part of the answer is not rooted in the sources as they are not used in this paragraph.

> Good linking of sources' content to provenance. The answer has picked up on Gilbert Foliot as being the source of the description of events in Source 5. The source also points out where the content of Source 7 is partial, thus emphasising how poor it makes Becket appear to be. There is a useful cross-reference with Source 5 at the end of the paragraph that includes some consideration of provenance, although it could be developed.

The image of the archbishop of Canterbury in Source 7 is someone who does not give in to bullying 'the barons, both English and French, abused him; but Becket calmly but firmly refused to withdraw his qualification'. This contradicts Source 5. However, Herbert of Bosham was a strong supporter of Becket's and so this must be remembered.

In Source 5 it says that Becket made a mountain out of a molehill: 'a minor and unimportant matter … easily been settled if discreet moderation had been shown'. The Constitutions of Clarendon were a big deal for the Church, however, as in clause 3 Henry II wanted all clergy who committed crimes to be punished twice, once in a church court and again in the king's courts. Becket did not agree as he said God does not judge in the same case twice. The Constitutions of Clarendon also put lots of other restrictions on the clergy, such as not being allowed to excommunicate someone with the king's consent and no appeals to Rome unless he agreed. This shows Henry II overstepping the mark and he must take some of the blame for the conflict. This is what Foliot is referring to when he says 'Had we given our consent to his proposals, matters would have become worse.' Henry chose Becket for archbishop of Canterbury because he thought that he would be a '"yes" man' and Becket did agree to the Constitutions of Clarendon at first until they were written down.

Alan of Tewkesbury's report in Source 5 was written fifteen years after the events and this might have affected how he remembered things, although he gives lots of detail about how proceedings went. Alan must have known a lot about Becket as he was alive at the time and collected lots of material on him. Herbert of Bosham was a key member of Becket's household and would have known of the events at Montmirail, probably making his account more accurate about what happened. It is important to remember that he supported the archbishop though.

Overall the sources together offer evidence from both those who favoured Becket and those who were against him. More research would need to be done into the events at Clarendon and Becket's role in them before determining blame, especially as neither source gives much evidence about Henry II, although Source 7 does indicate his temper. The evidence gives two different views of Becket, which would need further investigation.

> Some of the language is colloquial. There is an imbalance in source use; Source 5 is used much more. Although Source 5 is the longer of the two, there is more that could have come from Source 7. Mention of the Constitutions of Clarendon could be more specific, as could knowledge of the events at Clarendon, especially concerning how Becket agreed and then went back on his promise to Henry II. The knowledge of historical context is a bit of a 'bolt on' although it does stem from Source 5.

> Some useful points about provenance, but on their own. They are also fairly general points about provenance and could have been developed – for example, Alan of Tewkesbury was collecting a lot of materials and evidence on Thomas Becket and could be expected to have a range of sources of information, given how much the conflict and murder of Thomas Becket had shaken Christendom.

> The conclusion focuses clearly on the question again and does address the issue of how historians could use Sources 5 and 7 together, with a consideration of what needs to be further investigated.

Verdict

This is an average answer because:

- question focus is generally good (although there is an element of narrative that is not focused on the question or sources) and there is some developed consideration of Becket's role using inferences from sources that have been developed with some reference to historical context
- the sources have been understood, although the evidence in them has not been fully developed: for example, there is material implying Henry II's role in the conflict that has not been pulled out; this would require more time spent planning
- there is an imbalance in source use, with Source 5 being much more prominent; the question asks you consider sources together and, although this does happen, there needs to be a closer look at Source 7
- some of the provenance of the sources has been pulled out into a separate (penultimate) paragraph and is undeveloped; it would be better to discuss the provenance of the sources and its impact on the content and usefulness of the sources together.

Use the feedback on this answer to rewrite it, making as many improvements as you can.

Paper 2: A Level sample answer with comments

Section A

You will need to read and analyse two sources and use them in tandem to assess how useful they are in investigating an issue. For these questions remember to:

- spend time, up to ten minutes, reading and identifying the arguments and evidence present in the sources; then make a plan to ensure that your response will be rooted in these sources
- use specific references from the sources
- deploy own knowledge to develop points made in the sources and establish appropriate context
- come to a substantiated judgement.

How far could a historian use Sources 5 and 7 (pages 347 and 348) together to investigate whether Thomas Becket was to blame for the conflict between Crown and Church in England in 1164–70? Explain your answer, using both sources, the information given about them and your own knowledge of the historical context. (20 marks)

Strong student answer

In some ways both sources suggest Becket was a main reason behind the conflict between the English Crown and Church 1164–70. According to Source 5, Becket followed 'his own individual opinion' and made some serious mistakes 'he has laid trap both for himself and his brethren' as a result. Source 7 shows him as very stubborn, insisting upon a qualification to his obedience that Henry II could not accept: 'he will always have the advantage of me'. Becket had been insisting on adding this phrase since the start of the conflict. However, Source 5 presents Gilbert Foliot's account of events at Clarendon in 1164, and he was not one of Becket's supporters. Also, Source 7 begins with 'Henry raged at Becket' and goes on to give an insight into the use of intimidation against him, so both sources need to be read carefully as neither is as straightforward as it might appear. However, while Herbert of Bosham was a member of Becket's household and would have witnessed events at Montmirail, Source 5 was in fact written fifteen years after 1164, which could be a limiting factor, although Alan of Tewkesbury has collected a great deal of information on Becket. This means he could have developed a good idea of what had happened when Foliot met the pope in 1164, especially as there were lots of eyewitnesses.

The portrayals of Becket and his role in the dispute between the Crown and Church in England are very different. In Source 5 his attitude is high handed and provocative: 'pushed the matter to extremes and not taken into account the evil of the times or the harm which might arise from such hostility' and result in him laying 'a trap both for himself and his brethren' whereas the Becket in Source 7 is steadfast and rises above the fury of those around him: 'Becket calmly but firmly refused to withdraw his qualification'. This difference can be accounted for by whose points of view they are. Foliot disliked Becket, was presenting to the pope his view that the archbishop was to blame for the conflict. Herbert of Bosham, however, was a supporter of Becket, and is presenting him as a calm, confident man while those around him are raging. Henry II's fury and frustration, combined with that of both English and French barons, come across as bullying and intimidation to which Becket would not give in. It could be argued they, and not him, caused the dispute especially as Henry II's temper was legendary.

Differences in the sources can also be accounted for by the dates. By 1169, Becket was more experienced and assured as archbishop of Canterbury; the position of the papacy was strengthening and Alexander III was giving him more obvious support. The Becket of 1164 in Source 5 was a relatively inexperienced archbishop and handled an explosive situation badly.

A long introduction, but it focuses very clearly on the sources, how they relate to the investigation and issues that must be considered when evaluating them. There are some developed inferences drawn, supported with quotes from the sources, and some historical context is established. Overall, the response is showing a strong grasp of both the sources and the enquiry. There is already some discussion of limitation.

The differences in Becket's role in the conflict are sharply focused on but rooted in the sources. The comparison is developed and the material evaluated using both information about the sources and the historical context. The weight of the evidence is continually being developed, although the last point about Source 5 needs illustrating.

Historical context is used effectively to challenge Gilbert Foliot's perception of the nature of the original disagreement. However, it also offers some understanding of Henry II's point of view and wider issues that led to the dispute.

Source 5 implies that Becket caused a minor issue to become a massive one by ignoring the advice of his bishops and falling into his own trap. However, the Constitutions of Clarendon were not 'a minor and unimportant matter' as they placed restrictions on the Church greater than under Henry I, clause 3 especially. There was no precedent for Henry's demands that clergy be tried in the king's courts, although the nature of the crimes committed by some clergy (rape, murder, robbery – crimes usually dealt with only by the king's courts) suggest that something needed to be done. Furthermore, Becket gave in to Henry after several days of intimidation and agreed, verbally, to the Constitutions of Clarendon and to drop the qualification 'saving our order'. He also made the other bishops swear an oath to follow the Constitutions. Intimidation of Becket by Henry's allies can also be seen in Source 7, suggesting that he was not solely to blame.

Becket then went back on his promise when Henry II presented him with a written document of the Constitutions of Clarendon demanding that the archbishop and clergy put their seals to it. By doing this Henry II changed the goal posts. This suggests that it was not Becket to blame but Henry II although Foliot does not mention this. He focuses on Becket's poor leadership as key cause, for until Becket gave in to Henry II the clergy had supported him and so they felt very let down: 'in order to cast infamy on us, his brethren, he has taken to flight'. Once they had made a verbal agreement, as their archbishop asked them to, they felt that there was no going back and Becket's conduct confused and alienated them.

Together the two sources provide a useful basis for investigating the role of Thomas Becket in the Crown–Church conflict of 1164–70, as long as their provenance and purpose are taken into account. On one level they both appear to blame Becket for causing the dispute and for it continuing. It is possible to provide evidence to support Foliot's interpretation of Becket's high-handed attitude and poor leadership as being a key factor. The archbishop's stubbornness that comes across in Source 7 can also be proven. However, both sources have evidence of Becket operating in difficult circumstances and would suggest to historians that there was more to the conflict than at first appears. This would need further investigation. Given the historical context of events, the issues implied in the sources must exonerate Becket from some of the blame.

> Historical context has been used again to scrutinise Gilbert Foliot's accusations against Becket. Important points that he has missed are brought in to imply that Becket is not to blame. However, it also shows that Gilbert Foliot's point of view can be understood and the response also implies that he was not the only one who felt let down by Becket. This could be developed with reference to the number of English clergy who did not side with him.

> The conclusion focuses clearly on how far the sources could be used for the investigation, summarising their pros and cons as well as how they can be read on more than one level. There is also some suggestion as to what other research would be needed as a result of investigating these sources thoroughly.

Verdict

This is a strong answer because:

- it is rooted in the sources; they are used and compared throughout
- the historical context of the sources has been developed and linked to their content to provide justified evaluations of them
- own knowledge is specific and relevant and used to develop and explain the points made by the sources
- the question focus is strong and maintained, leading to a focused conclusion that considers how historians could make use of the sources.

Paper 2: A Level sample answers with comments

Section B

These questions assess your understanding of the period in some depth. They will ask you about the content you learned about in the four key themes, but may not ask about more than one theme. For these questions remember to:

- give an analytical, not a descriptive, response
- support your points with evidence
- cover the whole time period specified in the question
- come to a substantiated judgement.

'Henry II's reforms transformed the nature of kingship by centralising power.' To what extent do you agree with this statement? (20 marks)

Average student answer

Henry II's most important reforms were his legal reforms and the exchequer. The exchequer was based in London and a permanent court at Westminster came to be established. Also, the king's justices would meet back in London after their eyres and discuss their judgements so there developed a common law that was made into a book, Glanvill, which was the one source of law. The king was still itinerant though and this did not change. He also still needed the barons although he took some of their powers through his reforms. In some ways the king was the centre of government and this didn't change, so the nature of kingship didn't change that much.

> Some confusion over what Glanvill was, and a little muddled, but the introduction is focused on the question.

The Assize of Clarendon in 1166 gave the sheriffs much greater powers and they were the king's men after the Inquest of Sheriffs in 1170. Henry had actually already purged the sheriffs twice so lots of them were his men, but the Inquest of Sheriffs was the most important change. Henry II also made sure regular eyres were sent round the country and, because of writs being standardised and mass produced, more and more people used the king's courts. This meant that fewer were using the barons' courts, which angered them and led some to rebel in 1173, so in this way Henry's reforms were centralising power and changing the role of the barons, making the king more powerful. For example there was a fall in the number of private gallows. Henry still needed the barons, however, and they did keep their courts as villeins were not affected by the legal reforms as they couldn't buy or afford writs. Henry's legal reforms were so popular that the eyres couldn't cope and in 1178 he told five members of his court to stay in Westminster to hear the backlog of cases. This became the King's Bench and was a central court that shows his reforms were centralising power. However, the king was still the ultimate source of power, so that didn't change, although he didn't need to be present to hear Crown pleas as there were so many regular eyres.

> A little narrative, like a stream of consciousness in places, but the point about legal reforms centralising power is made. It also points out what did not change, implying that Henry's legal reforms did not transform kingship. The point about Henry needing the barons is undeveloped.

The exchequer was important too, although Henry didn't invent it but just revived it. It became very organised and 'The Handbook of the Exchequer' was written, laying down procedures. Sheriffs had to go to the exchequer twice a year and this shows that it was centralised. However, this didn't change the nature of kingship much but it is an example of a government department that became professional. It didn't need the king to be there either, like the legal reforms. This makes it seem as though the king wasn't important any more but this wasn't the case. The king was still the focus of government.

> Chatty, and with an error ('Handbook' instead of 'Dialogue'). The point about Henry's government becoming more professional could be developed, as could the ability of part of the government to continue in his absence.

The king was still itinerant, so that hadn't changed. He still travelled the kingdom. Henry II was famous for moving from place to place very quickly, and he wore out the members of his court, who found it difficult to keep up with him. He still needed to visit barons and have good relationships with them as they were still needed to raise armies. They also offered him advice and Henry still called great councils when he needed to, like at Clarendon in 1164. Although Henry was good at keeping the barons in their place, with castle breaking and reducing the number of earls from 24 to 12, some of them did rebel.

Some of Henry II's reforms made it easier for him to travel England and stay in France because law and order and finances could all run without him. He hired lots of professional men like Hugh Bardolf or men who weren't noble, like Richard de Lucy, because they were able to run things effectively. This meant he didn't use as many barons as before, although this wasn't necessarily because he was anti-noble but because law and finance were becoming profession with guidelines and procedures to learn such as the 'Handbook' or Glanvill. In this way kingship did change as government became more focused on departments like the courts or the exchequer. No longer did people get important posts just because of who they were.

So, in conclusion, Henry II did centralise government, especially with his legal and financial reforms. However, he was still itinerant and his reforms even helped that. He also still needed a good relationship with the barons, even though centralising power in his hands did sideline them a bit and reduced their influence on the counties in favour of his own men. Kingship was in some ways more efficient and organised than before, with parts of the government not needing them to be present. And it was more professional too. But the king was still at the heart of it.

> Both sides of the argument are covered here and, although imprecise and undeveloped, there is quite a lot of accurate evidence that does lead to some relevant judgements, even if they are not well expressed or explored. The focus is largely maintained, although it does wander slightly, such as Henry being good at keeping barons in their place.

> The conclusion is focused, if a little thin, and again moving from one point to the next quite quickly, with some wording just slotted in, like the penultimate sentence. It does address what changed and what stayed the same.

Verdict

This is an average answer because:

- there are a lot of links back to the question but many are undeveloped and there is some description or historical knowledge included that is not relevant
- there is specific factual detail that indicates good, relevant knowledge but it is not always well organised or developed and it reads more like a list of reforms Henry II made without being explored

- both sides of the question are considered, but again the fast pace moving from one thing to the next does not allow for much sustained analysis.

Use the feedback on this answer to rewrite it, making as many improvements as you can.

Paper 2: A Level sample answers with comments

Section B

These questions assess your understanding of the period in some depth. They will ask you about the content you learned about in the four key themes, but may not ask about more than one theme. For these questions remember to:

- give an analytical, not a descriptive, response
- support your points with evidence
- cover the whole time period specified in the question
- come to a substantiated judgement.

'Henry II's reforms centralised power, transforming the nature of kingship.' To what extent do you agree with this statement? (20 marks)

Strong student answer

Henry II certainly made some important developments in the nature of kingship, some of which centralised power. The two best examples of this would be his legal reforms and the exchequer, especially as each was able to run from London without the king needing to be present. There was also a change in the relationship between the barons and the king. However, these reforms also enabled kingship to remain itinerant, which it always had been, although it could be argued it was now more effective than before. So, in fact, it could be said that by centralising power, Henry II made the traditional form of kingship, which was itinerant, stronger than before.

One of the key trends in Henry II's kingship was the development of the foundations of a central court at Westminster, which also led to the development of the common law. By his legal reforms, Henry II increasingly sidelined barons' courts and put justice more in the hands of the Crown. Any case starting with a writ could be heard in the king's court and by the 1180s no free man need attend the lord's court for anything about his tenancy. By standardising writs and mass producing them, so that the he didn't need to be present for them to be issued, Henry can be said to have centralised power. It also enabled him to be more effective as an itinerant monarch. The development of the King's Bench after 1178 can be seen as the beginnings of a central court, even though the king remained the ultimate source of justice. Nevertheless, it also made it easier for the king to be absent, especially as a group of professional, expert judges developed as a result of his legal reforms.

Despite this, the barons still ran their manor and vill courts, and oversaw justice for their villeins. This shows that not all justice was centralised and that there was still a role for the barons to play, albeit diminished.

The restoration of the exchequer was another key development that can be said to have centralised power. It developed into a self-administering department of government, run according to Richard fitzNigel's 'Dialogue of the Exchequer'. From Henry II's reign it was based mainly in Westminster. Although occasionally it did travel to other cities it was basically centralised both in terms of its power and geographical location. It can be argued that Henry II simply revived the exchequer, so he wasn't changing the nature of kingship. However, it developed to the point where it could run itself and this, in turn, made it easier for the king to be itinerant.

Strong introduction, focusing on the question and suggesting an alternative point of view to the question. There is also a judgement about itinerant kingship being strengthened. What is understood by centralisation of power is made clear by examples. The nature of kingship is established as being itinerant and requiring a relationship with the barons.

The second paragraph picks out key legal developments, rather than covering them all. What has been chosen enables a judgement to be formed that reflects the introduction, that itinerant kingship could be said to have been strengthened by the reforms.

The other side of the argument, that there was a limit to how far kingship changed because of Henry's reforms, is a bit thin for the law and also for the Exchequer.

The itinerant nature of kingship did not change because of Henry II's reforms and in fact they could be said to have enhanced it. Henry II still needed to travel the realm to take the rents he was owed in kind, as goods or services. It was also still important to maintain relationships with the barons, although some of their role was sidelined by the Crown. Sheriffs, for example, became royal appointments, especially after the Inquest of Sheriffs, whereas traditionally they had been in the hands of the local barons, or even hereditary posts. The impact of this was to ensure that barons no longer controlled these important local offices as they often used them to reinforce their own power. This can be seen as centralising power but it did not change the nature of kingship greatly. Henry still needed barons for raising armies. However they could no longer expect top posts in government just because of their birth. The relationship of the Crown with the barons, however, was altered to an extent by Henry II's reforms, such as the Inquest of Sheriffs in 1170 or the Assize of Clarendon in 1166.

> A discussion of how far Henry II's reforms changed the nature of kingship is again developed and derived from well-chosen evidence. The evidence given is not described but used to support judgements.

It can be argued that Henry II's reforms diminished the importance of barons in government. It is certainly true that many of the most frequent visitors to court were not noble and that Henry increasingly relied upon men from knightly families, such as Richard de Lucy, or men who had expertise rather than high birth, such as Thomas Becket. Departments like the exchequer were more reliant on professional men than barons. There were barons who felt badly treated enough to rebel in 1173. They were angry at Henry's treatment of them, especially the taking and demolishing of illegal castles. Henry also aimed to keep them under control by trimming the number of earldoms by half by the end of his reign. They did not like having their traditional power and influence cut.

> The extent of how Henry II's relationship with the barons is developed a little further. The answer does go off topic, getting sidelined by the Great Rebellion.

It is true that under Henry II key parts of government could run without his presence. Perhaps the most important reforms concerned the law and the establishment of a central court, as well as the impact on sidelining barons' power and influence in the localities, which was added to by ensuring that all sheriffs were Crown officials. Sheriffs carried on as before but there was much more power in the hands of the Crown and so it could be said to have been more centralised. It might have changed the nature of kingship to an extent, by giving the king more direct links with the shires, but most people would have noticed little difference other than perhaps the sheriffs being fairer. The king was still itinerant and in this way Henry's reforms can be said to have reinforced traditional kingship. He still relied upon his barons although he also relied upon men from lower classes. So, overall, the statement is correct to an extent, but the most important aspects of kingship didn't change.

> The conclusion is developed and reflects the main body of the answer. It pulls out the key points for both sides of the argument and delivers a focused evaluation on the question.

Verdict

This is a strong answer because:

- the question focus is maintained and the answer sustains analysis
- there is sufficient knowledge deployed to enable the answer to make judgements on the issue in the question, and to discuss it from both sides
- the nature of kingship is established in the introduction and focuses on the king being itinerant and requiring a good relationship with the barons. This establishes the criteria to be used, which are kept to throughout
- there is discussion of points for and against the statement in the question throughout the answer.

Index

Acknowledgements

The authors and publisher would like to thank the following individuals and organisations for permission to reproduce photographs and text in this book.

Photographs

(Key: b-bottom; c-centre; l-left; r-right; t-top)

123RF.com: dbajurin 75; **akg-images Ltd:** British Library 57, 84, Yvan Travert 29; **Alamy Images:** Angelo Hornak 262, B.O'Kane 102, Greg Balfour Evans 255, History Pictures 252, Jeff Morgan 218 (Source 2), Robert Harding Picture Library Ltd/Michael Jenner 234, The Art Archive 18, 114, 117, 182, 185, 187, 196, 213, The Print Collector 104, Timewatch Images 218 (Source 3); **Bridgeman Art Library Ltd:** Bibliotheque Nationale, Paris, France/Archives Charmet 380, British Library, London, UK 352, 363, British Library, London, UK/© British Library Board. All Rights Reserved 311, 334, 342, Chapel of Santa Redegonda, Chinon, France/De Agostini Picture Library/G. Dagli Orti 291, 373, Edinburgh University Library, Scotland/With kind permission of the University of Edinburgh 91, © Museum of London, UK 353, Private Collection/Photo © O. Vaering 190, Universal History Archive/UIG 317; **Corbis:** Sylvain Sonnet 369; **Getty Images:** Ann Ronan Pictures/Print Collector 37, 50, DEA/A. DAGLI ORTI 128, Jean de Courcy 32, Photo12/UIG 53, Universal History Archive/UIG 136; **Mary Evans Picture Library:** Photo Researchers 40; **National Archives:** 321; **Pearson Education Ltd:** Gareth Dewar 108; **RMN:** Réunion des Musées Nationaux et du Grand Palais/Musée du Louvre/Stéphane Maréchalle 6; **Shutterstock.com:** ChameleonsEye 96; **The Fitzwilliam Museum, Cambridge:** 319l, 319r; **TopFoto:** Topham PicturePoint 26

Cover image: *Front:* **The Art Archive:** Archives Nationales Paris/Kharbine-Tapabor/Coll. Jean Vigne

All other images © Pearson Education

Text

Amberley Publishing for extract on p.188 from *1066 A New History of the Norman Conquest* (Rex, P. 2011) p.22; **American Philosophical Society** for extract on p.45 after *Historia Francorum qui ceperunt Iherusalem* (Hill, J. and Hill, L. 1968) p.65; **Ashgate Publishing Ltd** for extracts on p.55, 58 after © *The Chronicle of the Third Crusade* (Nicholson, H. J. 2001) pp.67–68, p.214; for extract on p.59 after © *The Conquest of Jerusalem and the Third Crusade* (Edbury, P.W. 1998) p.181; for extract on p.82 after

© *Walter the Chancellor's The Antiochene Wars* (Asbridge, T.S. and Edgington, S.B. 1999) p.143; for extracts on p.94, 103 from © *The Chronicle of Ibn al-Athir for the Crusading Period from al-Kamil fi'l-Ta'rikh, Part 2* (Richards, D. S. 2007) p.17, pp.198–99; for extract on p.105 after © *The Rare and Excellent History of Saladin or al-Nawadir al-Sultaniyya wa'l-Mahasin al-Yusufiyya by Baha' al-Din Ibn Shaddad* (Richards, D.S. 2002) p.51; for extract on p.122 after © *The Fourth Crusade: Event, Aftermath, and Perceptions* (Madden, T.F. 2008) pp.28–30; **Association of British Counties (abcounties.com)** for Figure 1.2 on p.294 adapted from a map of the historic counties of England; **Bloomsbury Academic**, an imprint of Bloomsbury Publishing Plc for extracts on p.14, 122 from © Jonathan Riley-Smith, 2014, *The Crusades: A History*, p.33, pp.185–86; **Boydell & Brewer Ltd** for extracts on p.181, 186, 193, 197, 198, 249 from *The Norman Conquest of England*, Boydell Press (Allen Brown, R. 1984) pp.22–24, p.26, p.10, p.34, p.116, p.48; for poetry on p.229 from *The Anglo-Saxon World*, 2nd edn, Boydell Press (Crossley-Holland, K. 2002) p.273; for table on p.318 from *The Accession of Henry II in England*, Boydell Press (Amt, E. 1993) pp.190–94. for extract on p.331 from *Henry II: New Interpretations*, Boydell Press (Harper-Bill, C. and Vincent, N. ed. 2007) p.290. Reprinted by permission of Boydell & Brewer Ltd; **Cambridge University Press** for extract on p.112 after *Saladin The Politics of the Holy War* (Lyons, M.C. and Jackson, D.E.P. 1982) p.352, © Faculty of Oriental Studies, University of Cambridge 1982, reproduced with permission; for extract on p.178 from *Anglo-Saxon Wills* (Whitelock, D. 2011) p.75, reproduced with permission; for extract on p.259 from *Henry I* (Green, J. 2009) p.89, reproduced with permission; for extract on p.221 from *The Laws of the Kings of England from Edmund to Henry I* (A.J. Robertson, ed. and trans., first pub. 1925, pub. 2009) pp.238–43, reproduced with permission; **Columbia University Press** for extract on p.48 after *Odo of Deuil De profectione Ludovici VII in orientem* Columbia University Press (Berry, V. 1958) pp.50–51, Copyright © 1958 Columbia University Press; for extracts on p.52, 66, 83 after *A History of Deeds Done Beyond the Sea*, Columbia University Press (Babcock, E. and Krey, A.C. 1943) pp.190–191, p.55, pp. 50–51, 45–46, 70–76, Copyright © 1943 Columbia University Press. Reprinted with permission of the publisher; **History Today Ltd** for extracts on p.230, 231 from Breaking the Bonds, *History Today*, March (Morris, M. 2013), p.40, p.41, p.42; for extract on p.232 from God and the Normans, *History Today*, October (Crouch, D. 2002), p.12. Used with permission of the publisher, History Today Ltd; **John Wiley & Sons, Inc.** for extracts on p.131, 133 from *The Latin Conquest of Constantinople*, John Wiley & Sons (Queller, D. ed. 1971), reproduced with permission of John Wiley & Sons in the format Republish in a book via Copyright Clearance Center; **Llanerch Press** for extracts on p.350, 375 from *The Flowers of History*, Vol. 2, Part 1 (J.A. Giles trans. 1994), by permission of Llanerch Press Ltd – www.llanerchpress.com; **M. Evans & Co.** for extract on p.381 from *Dungeon, Fire, and Sword: The Knights Templar in the Crusades* (Robinson, J.J. 1992), reproduced with permission of M.

Evans & Co. in the format Book via Copyright Clearance Center; **Manchester University Press** for extract on p.170 from *Anglo-Saxon Writs*, No. 96 (Harmer, F.E. 1952); for extracts on p.194, 195, 196, 198, 208, 209 from *The Normans in Europe* (Van Houts, E. 2000), p.130, p.122, p.169, p.173, p.180; **Marquette University Press** for extract on p.99 after *The Crusades: A Documentary Survey*, by James A. Brundage, Copyright © 1962. Milwaukee, WI: Marquette University Press. www.marquette.edu/mupress; **Osprey Publishing Ltd**, part of Bloomsbury Publishing Plc, for extract on p.197 from *Hastings 1066* (Gravett, C. 2000) p.73; for extract on p.204 from *Campaigns of the Norman Conquest* (Bennett, M. 2001) p.58; **Oxbow Books Ltd** for extract on p.292 from *William of Newburgh: The History of English Affairs, Book 2*, Aris & Phillips (William, P.G. and Kennedy, M.J. 2007); **Oxford University Press** for extract on p.20 from *Pope Urban II's Council of Piacenza*, (Somerville, R. 2011) p.55, © Robert Somerville 2011; for extract on p.83 from *Orderic Vitalis, The Ecclesiastical History, Volume 6, 1969–80* (trans. and ed. Chibnall, M. 1978) pp. 391–3; for extracts on p.171, 179, 185 from *Life of King Edward Who Rests at Westminster* (Barlow, F. 1962, 1992), Oxford Medieval Texts, p.12, pp.30–37, pp.74–81; for extracts on p.201, 203, from *The Ecclesiastical History of Orderic Vitalis, Vol. 2: Book IV* (Chibnall, M. trans. and ed. 1990), Oxford Medieval Texts, pp.210–215, 220–237; for extract on p.206 from *The Letters of Lanfranc Archbishop of Canterbury, No. 31* (Gibson, M. trans. and ed. 1979), Oxford Medieval Texts; for extract on p.206 from *The Letters of Lanfranc Archbishop of Canterbury, No. 33A* (Gibson, M. trans. and ed. 1979), Oxford Medieval Texts; for extract on p.233 from *The Letters of Lanfranc Archbishop of Canterbury, No. 11* (Gibson, M. trans. and ed. 1979), Oxford Medieval Texts, pp.72–79; for extract on p.238 from *The Letters of Lanfranc Archbishop of Canterbury, No. 1* (Gibson, M. trans. and ed. 1979), Oxford Medieval Texts, p.166; for extract on p.246 from *The Ecclesiastical History of Orderic Vitalis, Vol. 2* (Chibnall, M. trans. and ed. 1990), Oxford Medieval Texts, pp.356–357; for extracts on p.246, 247 from *The Ecclesiastical History of Orderic Vitalis, Vol. 3* (Chibnall, M. trans. and ed. 1990), Oxford Medieval Texts, p.989, pp.102–105, pp.110–113, pp.112–113; for extracts on p.246, 254 from *William of Malmesbury, Gesta Regum Anglorum: The History of the English Kings, Vol. 1* (Mynors, R.A.B., Thomson, R.M. and Winterbottom, M. 1998), Oxford Medieval Texts, pp.542–543, pp.552–553; for extracts on p.248, 249, 250, 253 from *The Ecclesiastical History of Orderic Vitalis, Vol. 4* (Chibnall, M. trans. and ed. 1983), Oxford Medieval Texts, p.923, p.967, pp.122–123, pp.132–133; for extracts on p.258, 256 from *The Ecclesiastical History of Orderic Vitalis, Vol. 5* (Chibnall, M. trans. and ed. 1975), Oxford Medieval Texts, pp.304–305, pp.318–319; for extracts on p.259, 260 from *The Ecclesiastical History of Orderic Vitalis, Vol. 6* (Chibnall, M. trans. and ed. 1978), Oxford Medieval Texts, p.569, pp.102–105, pp.86–87, p.603; for extract on p.298 from *England Under the Norman and Angevin Kings 1075–1255*, Oxford University Press (Bartlett, R. 2000); for extracts on p.320, 328, 366 from *The Dialogue of the Exchequer* (Amt, E. and Church, S.D. 2007); for extract on p.323 from *The Chronicle of Battle Abbey*, Oxford University Press (Searle, E. (trans.) 1980) pp.213 and 215; for extract on p.326 from *The Treatise on the Laws and Customs of the Realm of England commonly called Glanvill*, 2nd edn (Hall, G.D.G. ed. and trans. 1993); for extracts on p.342, 345, 347, 350, 351 from *The Correspondence of Thomas Becket*, (Duggan, A., trans.

2000); for extract on p.366 from *Jean de Fantosme's Chronicle of the War between the English and the Scots in 1173 and 1174*, Clarendon Press (Jordan de Fantosme (original), trans R.C. Johnston 1981) verses 2, 3. By permission of Oxford University Press; **Palgrave Macmillan** for extract on p.21 after *What Were the Crusades?* 4th edn (Riley-Smith, J. 2009) pp.32–33; for extract on p.213 from *Conquest and Colonisation* (Golding, B. 2012) p.121. Reproduced with permission of Palgrave Macmillan; **Penguin Books Ltd** for extract on p.127 after *Chronicles of the Crusades*, by Joinville and Villehardouin, translated and with an introduction by M.R.B. Shaw (Penguin Books, 1963) pp.40–41, Copyright © M.R.B. Shaw, 1963; for extract on p.131 from *God's War* by Christopher Tyerman (Penguin Books, 2006), Copyright © Christopher Tyerman, 2006. Reproduced by permission of Penguin Books Ltd; **Penguin Books Ltd and Penguin Random House LLC** for extracts on p.313, 351 from *Thomas Becket: Warrior, Priest, Rebel, Victim*, Penguin (Guy, J. 2012) p.98, Copyright © John Guy, 2012. Reproduced by permission of Penguin Books Ltd and Penguin Random House LLC; **Peters Fraser & Dunlop** for extracts on p.174, 175 from *Domesday Book: A Complete Translation* (Williams, A. and Martin, G. 2013) reprinted by permission of Peters Fraser & Dunlop (www.petersfraserdunlop.com) on behalf of Getmapping Plc; **The Random House Group Ltd and Lavinia Trevor Literary Agency** for extract on p.188 from *In Search of the Dark Ages*, by Michael Wood, published by BBC Books, reproduced by permission of The Random House Group Ltd and Lavinia Trevor Literary Agency; **The Random House Group Ltd and Pegasus Books** for extracts on p.192, 201, 202, 208, 213, 216, 222, 228, 230 from *The Norman Conquest*, published by Hutchinson (Morris, M. 2012). Reproduced by permission of The Random House Group Ltd and by permission of Pegasus Books, US edition (Morris, M. 2013); **The Random House Group Ltd and Penguin Random House LLC** for extracts on p.367, 369 from *Eleanor of Aquitaine: By Wrath of God, Queen of England*, Pimlico (Weir, A. 2000), p.208, copyright © 1999 by Alison Weir; **The Random House Group Ltd and Viking Books** for extract on p.127 from *The Fourth Crusade and the Sack of Constantinople*, Pimlico (Phillips, J. 2004) pp.103–104, with permission from The Random House Group Ltd, *The Fourth Crusade and the Sack of Constantinople* by John Phillips, copyright © 2004 by John Phillips. Used by permission of Viking Books, an imprint of Penguin Publishing Group, a division of Penguin Random House LLC; **Rowman & Littlefield Publishing Group** for Figure 1.2 on p.172, extract on p.232 from *The Norman Conquest: England after William the Conqueror*, by Thomas, Hugh M. (2008), reproduced with permission of Rowman & Littlefield Publishers in the format Republish in a book via Copyright Clearance Center; **Simon & Schuster UK Ltd** for extract on p.137 extracted from *The Crusades* by Thomas Asbridge (2010), pp. 530–531, published by Simon & Schuster UK Ltd; **Stephen James Joyce** for extract on p.7 from *Ulysses*, Random House (Joyce, J. 1961) p.34, reproduced with kind permission; **Taylor & Francis Books UK** for extract on p.31 after *The Crusades: Idea and Reality, 1095–1270* (Riley-Smith, L. and Riley-Smith, J. 1981) pp. 37, 42–53, Copyright © 1981 Edward Arnold; for extracts on p.210, 211, 212, 296, 314, 326, 329, 347, 375 from *English Historical Documents: 1042–1189, Vol. 2* (Douglas, D.C. and Greenaway, G.W. 1953), pp. 895, 897, 486, 537, 450, 484, 858, 442–43, Copyright © 1953 Routledge; for extract on p.229

from *Ruling England 1042–1217* (Huscroft, R. 2005) p.97, Copyright © 2005 Routledge. Reproduced by permission of Taylor & Francis Books; **Taylor & Francis Books UK and University of California Press** for extract on p.107 after *Arab Historians of the Crusades* (Gabrieli, F. 1957), Copyright © 1957 Routledge, reproduced by permission of Taylor & Francis Books UK and University of California Press; permission conveyed through Copyright Clearance Center, Inc; **The Orion Publishing Group Ltd** for extracts on p.185, 187, 188, 203, 209, 217, 223, 229, 230, 231, 236, 244, 245, 247, 248, 251, 253, 258, 263 from *The Anglo-Saxon Chronicle*, Phoenix (Swanton, M. 2000), Introduction and other critical apparatus © Phoenix Press 2000, with permission from The Orion Publishing Group, London; **University of Michigan Press** for extract on p.131 from *The Late Medieval Balkans: A Critical Survey from the Late Twelfth Century to the Ottoman Conquest* (Fine, J.V.A. 1994) p.61; **University of Pennsylvania Press** for extract on p.41 adapted from *The First Crusade: The Chronicle of Fulcher of Chartes and Other Source Materials* (Peters, E. 1971) p.69; for extract on p.133 from *The Fourth Crusade: The Conquest of Constantinople*, 2nd edn (Queller, D.E. and Madden, T.F. 1997) p.37; for extract on p.173 from *God's Peace and King's Peace: The Laws of Edward the Confessor* (O'Brien, B.R. 1998) p.173. Reprinted with permission of the University of Pennsylvania Press; **University of Texas Press** for extract on p.189 from *Heimskringla: The History of the Kings of Norway* University of Texas Press (Sturluson, S., trans. Hollander, L.M. 2011) p.649, Copyright © 1964; **University of Toronto Press** for extract on p.69 from *The Crusaders: A Reader* (Allen, S.J. and Amt, E. 2010), first section: trans. E. Amt from *Recueil des historiens des croisades: Lois, Vol. II, Assises de la cour des bourgeois* ed. A.A. Beugnot (Paris: Imprimerie Royale, 1843), pp.53–56: second section: trans R.P. Faulkner, *Translations and Reprints from the Original Sources of European History, series I, vol. III* (Philadelphia: University of Pennsylvania Department of History, n.d.), no. 2, pp.19–23, revised; **Yale University Press** for extract on p.25 after *The Second Crusade: Extending the Frontiers of Christendom* (Phillips, J. 2007), Copyright © 2007 Jonathan Phillips; for Figure on p.285, extracts on p.297, 348, 354, 356, 361, 362, 381 from *Henry II* (Warren, W.L. 2000), Copyright © 2000 W.L. Warren; for extracts on p.381 from *Richard I* (Gillingham, J. 2002), Copyright © 1999 by John Gillingham.

Every effort has been made to contact copyright holders of material reproduced in this book. Any omissions will be rectified in subsequent printings if notice is given to the publishers.